CELTIC HAGIOGRAPHY AND SAINTS' CULTS

Celtic Hagiography and Saints' Cults

Edited by

JANE CARTWRIGHT

UNIVERSITY OF WALES PRESS
CARDIFF
2003

© The contributors, 2003

Reprinted 2022

All rights reserved. No part of this book may be reproduced, stored in a retrieval system, or transmitted, in any form or by any means, electronic, mechanical, photocopying, recording or otherwise, without clearance from the University of Wales Press, University Registry, King Edward VII Avenue, Cathays Park, Cardiff, CF10 3NS.
www.uwp.co.uk

British Library Cataloguing-in-Publication Data.
A catalogue record for this book is available from the British Library.

ISBN: 978–1–83772–022–4 paperback

Cover picture: St Meubred holding his head, stained glass window, St Neot parish church, Cornwall, by kind permission of St Neot PCC. Photograph: J. Mattingly.
Cover design by Olwen Fowler
Typeset by Megaron
Printed by CPI Antony Rowe, Melksham, United Kingdom

Contents

><

Acknowledgements	vii
Contributors	ix
Illustrations	xiii
Tables	xiv
Abbreviations	xv

Introduction   1
    JANE CARTWRIGHT

1. St David and St Davids: some observations on the cult, site and buildings   10
    J. WYN EVANS

2. Welsh hagiography and the nationalist impulse   26
    ELISSA R. HENKEN

3. Twelfth-century Welsh hagiography: the *Gogynfeirdd* poems to saints   45
    NERYS ANN JONES and MORFYDD E. OWEN

4. The harlot and the hostess: a preliminary study of the Middle Welsh Lives of Mary Magdalene and her sister Martha   77
    JANE CARTWRIGHT

The early chronology for St Patrick (*c*.351– *c*. 428): some new ideas and possibilities   102
    JOHN T. KOCH

6. Reading Muirchú's Tara-event within its background as a biblical 'trial of divinities'   123
    THOMAS O'LOUGHLIN

7.	Miracles and wonders in the composition of the Lives of the early Irish saints DOROTHY ANN BRAY	136
8.	The Northern Lectionary: a source for the *Codex Salmanticensis?* T. M. CHARLES-EDWARDS	148
9.	Fasting, flesh and the body in the St Brendan dossier JONATHAN M. WOODING	161
10.	The process and significance of rewriting Breton hagiography BERNARD MERDRIGNAC	177
11.	Saints behaving badly: sanctity and transgression in Breton popular culture MARY-ANN CONSTANTINE	198
12.	Magpie hagiography in twelfth-century Scotland: the case of *Libellus de nativitate Sancti Cuthberti* THOMAS OWEN CLANCY	216
13.	Saints, stones and shrines: the cults of Sts Moluag and Gerardine in Pictland PENELOPE DRANSART	232
14.	Pre-Reformation saints' cults in Cornwall – with particular reference to the St Neot windows JOANNA MATTINGLY	249
15.	Alba Longa in the Celtic regions? Swine, saints and Celtic hagiography KAREN JANKULAK	271

Works Cited 285
Index 319

Acknowledgements

The inspiration for this collection of essays was a conference on Celtic Hagiography and Saints' Cults held at the University of Wales, Lampeter, 8–10 September 2000. Twelve of the fifteen chapters in this volume stem from papers delivered orally at the conference. The aim, however, was not to publish conference proceedings and the chapters that are included here appear in substantially revised form. In order to ensure that the collection provided case studies from a representative sample of the Celtic regions, three other contributions (on the saints of Scotland, Ireland and Cornwall) were invited. I would like to thank everyone who took part in the conference, particularly those who delivered papers, contributed to the discussions, chaired sessions and helped make the conference a success. I am indebted to my colleagues at the Department of Welsh, University of Wales, Lampeter, for their support: David Thorne kindly organized financial support for the conference, Linda Jones provided valuable administrative assistance, Eleri Davies and Carol Thomas helped with registration and Karen Jankulak assisted in many ways, including translating Bernard Merdrignac's article from French into English. David Selwyn, Carol Dery and Caroline Pilcher of the Founders' Library kindly organized an exhibition of medieval manuscripts and early printed books to accompany the theme of the conference. I am also indebted to all of the staff at the University of Wales Press who have been involved in the production of this volume, particularly Ruth Dennis-Jones who suggested a number of improvements. I would like to thank the reader appointed by the press for valuable assistance and advice. Especial thanks are also due to my partner, John Hughes, for advice and support at all stages of the project. As editor of the collection my greatest debt is, of course, to the contributors without whom this volume would not have been possible.

Jane Cartwright

Contributors

>-<

DOROTHY ANN BRAY is an Associate Professor of English at McGill University, Montreal, Canada. She obtained her doctorate in Celtic Studies from the University of Edinburgh, and has published several articles on the folklore and composition of early Irish saints' Lives.

JANE CARTWRIGHT is Lecturer in Welsh at the University of Wales, Lampeter, and a member of the Centre for the Study of Religion in Celtic Societies. She has published various articles on Welsh hagiography, virginity and the history of the Welsh nunneries. Her book, Y *Forwyn Fair, Santesau a Lleianod: Agweddau ar Wyryfdod a Diweirdeb yng Nghymru'r Oesoedd Canol*, was published by the University of Wales Press in 1999.

T. M. CHARLES-EDWARDS is Jesus Professor of Celtic at the University of Oxford and a Fellow of Jesus College, Oxford. His most recent book, *Early Christian Ireland*, was published by Cambridge University Press in 2000.

THOMAS OWEN CLANCY lectures in Celtic at the University of Glasgow. He is the author, with Gilbert Márkus, of *Iona: The Earliest Poetry of a Celtic Monastery* (Edinburgh: Edinburgh University Press, 1995), editor of *The Triumph Tree: Scotland's Earliest Poetry AD 550–1350* (Edinburgh: Canongate, 1998), and editor with Dauvit Broun of *Spes Scotorum, Hope of Scots: St Columba, Iona and Scotland* (Edinburgh: T. & T. Clark, 1999). He has written various articles on the early church and hagiography in Scotland.

MARY-ANN CONSTANTINE is currently leading a research project on the Welsh poet and antiquarian Iolo Morganwg at the University of Wales Centre for Advanced Welsh and Celtic Studies in Aberystwyth. She has also held various research fellowships in the Department of Welsh at

Aberystwyth, and lectured on various aspects of the literature of the Celtic countries. She has published mainly on Breton folk-song: *Breton Ballads* (Aberystwyth: CMCS Publications, 1996) won the Katharine Briggs Award for Folklore. A book on fragments in traditional song (coauthored with Gerald Porter) is to be published in 2003.

PENELOPE DRANSART is Senior Lecturer and Chair of the Department of Archaeology, as well as being a member of the Centre for the Study of Religion in Celtic Societies at the University of Wales, Lampeter. Recent publications include a book on pastoralists and the llamas and alpacas they herd, *Earth, Water, Fleece and Fabric* (Reading: Harwood Academic Publishers, 2002), and articles on the material culture of religion, 'Two shrine fragments from Kinneddar Moray', in M. Redknap et al. (eds), *Pattern and Purpose in Insular Art* (Oxford: Oxbow Books, 2001) and 'Concepts of spiritual nourishment in the Andes and Europe: rosaries in cross-cultural contexts', in the *Journal of the Royal Anthropological Institute* (2002).

J. WYN EVANS, formerly Head of the Theology and Religious Studies Department at Trinity College, Carmarthen, has been Dean of St Davids Cathedral since 1994. He has written and lectured extensively on the early and high medieval Church in Wales.

ELISSA R. HENKEN, the author of *Traditions of the Welsh Saints* (Cambridge: D. S. Brewer, 1987), *The Welsh Saints: A Study of Patterned Lives* (Cambridge: D. S. Brewer, 1991) and *National Redeemer: Owain Glyndŵr in Welsh Tradition* (Cardiff: University of Wales Press, 1996), is a Professor at the University of Georgia where she teaches folklore and Celtic literature. Researching in Wales and the United States, she publishes on folklore ranging from medieval to contemporary, from Gerald of Wales to health education.

KAREN JANKULAK is a part-time Lecturer in the Department of Welsh, University of Wales, Lampeter, as well as the Director of the University's MA in Arthurian Studies. Her book, *The Medieval Cult of St Petroc*, was published by Boydell and Brewer in 2000.

NERYS ANN JONES is an Honorary Research Fellow at the University of Edinburgh where she teaches medieval Welsh literature and language. Her main research interest is the work of the twelfth- and thirteenth-century Poets of the Welsh Princes.

JOHN T. KOCH taught Celtic Studies in the United States, at Harvard and Boston College, for twelve years. In 1998, he was appointed Senior Research Fellow and leader of the research project Celtic Languages and Cultural Identity at the University of Wales Centre for Advanced Welsh and Celtic Studies in Aberystwyth. His publications include *The Gododdin of Aneirin: Text and Context in Dark-Age North Britain* (Cardiff: University of Wales Press, 1997) and (with John Carey) *The Celtic Heroic Age: Literary Sources for Ancient Celtic Europe and Early Ireland and Wales* (Malden: Celtic Studies Publications, 3rd edn 2000).

JOANNA MATTINGLY studied History at King's and Goldsmiths' Colleges, University of London. Her work changed direction on moving to Cornwall more than sixteen years ago and she now works as a freelance researcher and museum adviser. She is currently involved in a series of major exhibitions at Truro Cathedral to celebrate 125 years of Truro diocese.

BERNARD MERDRIGNAC is Professor of Medieval History at the University of Rennes 2, Brittany, France, and vice-president of the Centre international de recherches sur le monachisme celtique. He has published widely in the field of Breton hagiography. His book *Les Vies de saints bretons durant le haut moyen âge* was published by Éditions Ouest-France in 1993 and he is also co-author (with André Chédeville) of *Les Sciences annexes en histoire du moyen âge* (Rennes: Presses Universitaires de Rennes, 1998).

THOMAS O'LOUGHLIN is Senior Lecturer in Historical Theology at the University of Wales, Lampeter, and Director of Lampeter's Centre for the Study of Religion in Celtic Societies. His main area of research is the history of Latin theology in the early Middle Ages. In 1999 he published *Teachers and Code-Breakers: The Latin Genesis Tradition, 430–800* (Steenbrugis: Turnhout), followed in 2000 by *Celtic Theology: Humanity, World and God in Early Irish Writings* (Dublin: Four Courts Press), and is currently working on the Eusebian gospel apparatus.

MORFYDD E. OWEN is an Honorary Departmental Fellow in the Department of Welsh at the University of Wales, Aberystwyth, was a pupil of Kathleen Hughes and has published on medieval Welsh prose, poetry and law.

JONATHAN M. WOODING is Lecturer in the Department of Theology and Religious Studies, University of Wales, Lampeter. His recent books include: *Communication and Commerce along the Western Sealanes AD 400–800* (Oxford: BAR, 1996) and (ed.), *The Otherworld Voyage in Early Irish Literature – An Anthology of Criticism* (Dublin: Four Courts Press, 2000).

Illustrations
(between pp. 160 and 161)

><

1.1 Plan of the Cathedral Close of St Davids in 1720.
1.2 Map showing early Christian sites and monuments in the St David's area.
1.3 St David's shrine.
13.1 Painting of St Moluag bringing Christianity to the Garioch, in the parish church of Chapel of Garioch, Aberdeenshire.
13.2 Class I stone from Clatt.
13.3 The Battle stone at the parish church of Mortlach, Moray.
13.4 A carved stone cross from Clova.
13.5 Conjectural reconstruction of a shrine panel from Kinneddar.
14.1 Wives' window, St Neot: St Mabyn (Mabena), pietà, Christ, St Meubred (Meberede).
14.2 Sisters' window, St Neot: St Petroc (Patric), St Clair (Clere), St Manac (Manc), All Saints.
14.3 Young men's window, St Neot: Life of St Neot.
14.4 Two panels from Callaway window, St Neot, showing St Lallu? and St German.
14.5 Panel from Borlase window, St Neot, showing St Neot.
14.6 St Cleer holy well c.1500, as restored.
14.7 St Petroc's reliquary, Bodmin, c.1177.
14.8 Easter sepulchre or St Meubred's tomb at Cardinham.
14.9 Easter sepulchre or St Neot's tomb at St Neot.
14.10 Shrine of St Endelienta at St Endellion, now recycled as an altar.
14.11 Shrine of St Issey at St Issey, recycled as a reredos.

List of Tables

4.1	Manuscripts containing the Welsh Lives of female saints	79
4.2	Manuscripts containing the Middle Welsh Lives of Mary Magdalene and Martha	82
6.1	Daniel 3:1–24 and Muirchú's Tara-event: verbal parallels	127–8
8.1	*Codex Salmanticensis*, Lives 11–45	150–1
9.1	References to food, eating and fasting in *Nauigatio Sancti Brendani Abbatis*	171–3
12.1	*Libellus de Nativitate Sancti Cuthberti*: structure and suggested sources	220
14.1	Calendar of feast-days possibly associated with local cultsites depicted in north-aisle windows at St Neot	263

Abbreviations

AB	*Analecta Bollandiana*
Arch. Camb.	*Archaeologia Cambrensis*
AU	*Annals of Ulster, to AD 1131*, S. Mac Airt and G. Mac Niocaill (eds.), Dublin, 1981
B.A.R.	British Archaeological Reports
BBCS	*Bulletin of the Board of Celtic Studies*
BL	British Library
BNE	*Bethada náem nÉrenn: Lives of Irish Saints*, Charles Plummer (ed. and trans.), 2 vols, Oxford, 1922; rpt. 1968
BSAF	*Bulletin de la société archéologique du Finistère*
Ce. R.A.A.	Centre Régional Archéologique d'Alet
CGH	*Corpus Genealogiarum Hiberniae*, M. A. O'Brien (ed.), 5 vols, Dublin, 1985
CGSH	*Corpus Genealogiarum Sanctorum Hiberniae*, P. Ó Riain (ed.), Dublin, 1985
CRBC	Centre de Recherche Bretonne et Celtique
CMCS	*Cambridge Medieval Celtic Studies* (vols 1–25) continued as *Cambrian Medieval Celtic Studies* (vols 26–)
CRO	Cornwall Record Office
CSEL	*Corpus Scriptorium Ecclesiasticorum Latinorum*, Vienna, 1866–
DEB	*De Excidio Britanniae of Gildas*, T. Winterbottom (ed.), Chichester, 1978.
DIL	Royal Irish Academy, *Dictionary of the Irish Language*, Dublin, compact edition, 1983
EC	*Etudes Celtiques*
ECMW	*The Early Christian Monuments of Wales*, V. E. Nash-Williams, Cardiff, 1950
EETS	Early English Texts Society
EWGT	*Early Welsh Genealogical Tracts*, P. C. Bartrum (ed.), Cardiff, 1966
IMD	*Immram Maíle Dúin*
JRIC	*Journal of the Royal Institution of Cornwall*

JRSAI	*Journal of the Royal Society of Antiquaries Ireland*
JWEH	*Journal of Welsh Ecclesiastical History*
LBS	*Lives of the British Saints*, S. Baring-Gould and J. Fisher, 4 vols, London, 1907–13
NLW	National Library of Wales
NLWJ	*National Library of Wales Journal*
NSB	*Navigatio Sancti Brendani*, C. Selmer (ed.), Notre Dame Publications in Medieval Studies 16, South Bend IA, 1959; rpr. Dublin, 1989
OED	*Oxford English Dictionary*, Oxford, 1989
OPS	*Origines Parochiales Scotiae. The Antiquities Ecclesiastical and Territorial of the Parishes of Scotland*, C. Innes (ed.), vol. 2 (1), Edinburgh, 1854
PRIA	*Proceedings of the Royal Irish Academy*
Proc. Soc. Antiq. Scotl.	*Proceedings of the Society of Antiquaries Scotland*
RC	*Revue Celtique*
RCAHMS	The Royal Commission on the Ancient and Historical Monuments of Scotland
RIC	Royal Institute of Cornwall
SC	*Studia Celtica*
VB	*Vita Brendani*
VSBG	*Vitae Sanctorum Britanniae et Genealogiae*, A. W. Wade-Evans (ed. and trans.), Cardiff, 1944
WHR	*Welsh History Review*
ZCP	*Zeitschrift für celtische Philologie*

NOTE ON REFERENCES

All works, apart from those listed above and also unpublished manuscript sources, are referred to in the notes by the author and short-title system; full bibliographical details are given in the list of Works Cited (p. 285–318).

Introduction

JANE CARTWRIGHT

This volume comprises a collection of fifteen articles on various aspects of the cult of saints in Wales, Ireland, Brittany, Scotland and Cornwall. As well as discussing some of the most prominent figures in the pantheon of Celtic saints (for example, David, Patrick, Brigit and Brendan), the individual studies collected here also shed light on the veneration of local saints and highlight the importance of vernacular hagiography and the cults of universal saints in the Celtic-speaking regions. The period covered in the book as a whole is a broad one spanning the centuries from the mid-fourth century to the early twentieth century. The primary focus, however, is on the medieval period and the hagiographical texts and traditions which surround a selection of the Celtic saints. The main sources employed here are the Lives of saints, the prose and poetic narratives which were composed to glorify the saints, celebrate their feast-days, record their biographies and miracles and assert the rights of their particular churches or the dioceses they represented. In addition to examining examples of Latin *vitae* and vernacular hagiographies, the essays also consider evidence from a wide range of different sources, including historical documentation, legendaries, native poetry, songs, shrines, relics, holy wells and church dedications, as well as archaeological and visual evidence. The study is not intended to be exhaustive, and merely aims to make available some of the fruits of recent research in the field and to provide a representative sample of case studies from all of the Celtic regions.

A considerable amount of extremely valuable research has been undertaken recently on the saints of the individual Celtic regions.[1] However, few academic collections bring together case studies from all of the Celtic areas and most which have the word 'Celtic' in their titles focus primarily on one or two of the Celtic regions.[2] The present volume aims to build on the studies already undertaken and to give the opportunity for comparison between the different Celtic regions, as well as to highlight any points of contact, common cultural inheritance and cultural diversity. The same saints (or at least saints with similar names and traditions) are frequently venerated in more than one of the Celtic-speaking regions of Europe.[3] It is well known, for example, that Irish saints are said to have settled in Wales and Scotland, and Welsh saints' names occur in place-names and church dedications in Cornwall and Brittany. Cults and narratives travel, and this may be indicative of increased intercommunication between the different Celtic regions during the medieval period. The earliest Life of a Welsh saint, St Samson, was written in Brittany at Landévennec.[4] According to the late eleventhcentury Life of St David, Patrick left Wales in order to make way for St David. Some of the earliest extant sources for David are of Breton and Irish origin.[5] Furthermore, St Non, David's mother, appears to have been even more popular in Brittany than she was in Wales in the Middle Ages. Although there is no Welsh *buchedd* (Life) which focuses specifically on Non, there is a medieval Breton miracle-play which gives a voice to the saint and focuses on her experiences.[6] A sixteenth-century tomb at Dirinon also purports once to have been her resting place.[7] Nerys Ann Jones and Morfydd E. Owen refer to the 'common inheritance of hagiographical material of Wales and Brittany' and suggest that the twelfth century may have seen a 'renaissance in Welsh–Breton connections'. Thomas O. Clancy, in his study of the twelfth-century 'Irish Life of St Cuthbert', demonstrates that, although the Life is not Irish in origin, its Scottish-based author drew on the testimony of leading Irish churchmen, and he proposes that the text is a unique witness to a large range of informal contacts between Ireland and Scotland during this period. Karen Jankulak uncovers fifteen examples of a particular hagiographical motif: the majority are found in the Lives of saints from Ireland, Scotland, Wales, Somerset, Cornwall and Brittany. Jankulak argues that although the motif appears to originate in classical legend, its geographical distribution in the medieval Lives of saints is no accident, and that this appears to suggest points of contact between the different Celtic regions and highlights the frequency with which hagiographical elements were borrowed.

As Mary-Ann Constantine points out, in hagiography saints who may be considered as 'outsiders' are often adopted or adapted to the particular culture in question, and this is not confined to the Celtic regions. Vernacular translations of the Lives of universal saints, such as the Middle Welsh Lives of Mary Magdalene and Martha, testify to their popularity, particularly in the late medieval period. Visual representations of universal saints sit comfortably alongside depictions of lesser-known, local saints, all of whom were considered to be powerful intercessors who could assist the faithful in their quest for physical and spiritual healing. Mattingly notes that there is sometimes a local dimension to the cults of the universal saints of Christendom, as appears to be the case with the saints depicted in the north-aisle windows at St Neot parish church in Cornwall. Cults appear to have been enhanced by the acquisition of saints' relics. For example, St German, bishop of Auxerre, who is depicted in stained glass at St Neot, was venerated elsewhere in Cornwall including, of course, at St Germans which possessed some of the saint's corporeal relics. St Neot himself, whose narrative Life is depicted visually in late-medieval stained glass, was appropriated by the Anglo-Saxons. His relics were translated to Eynesbury in Huntingdonshire in the late tenth century. As might be expected, hagiographical borrowings are not restricted to the Celtic areas. St Brendan, the subject of Jonathan Wooding's article, may well have been popular in Ireland, Scotland, Brittany and Wales, but he also had an Anglo-Norman Life. Hagiography, as Bernard Merdrignac reminds us, means 'sacred writings', and it is not surprising that the single most influential source employed by hagiographers in their attempts to produce sacred writings is Holy Scripture, as demonstrated in this collection by Thomas O'Loughlin.

Thus, the majority of articles in this volume are concerned with the literary texts which accrued to saintly characters; the circumstances which led to their production; the sources upon which hagiographers drew; and their function within both secular and ecclesiastical politics. Other issues addressed include the relationship between written and oral hagiographies as well as the relationship between hagiography, pilgrimage and cult sites. Some of the articles shed light on the early Christian period, particularly in Ireland; however, it should be emphasized that the aim of this compendium is not to generalize about monastic practice and ecclesiastic structure in all of the Celtic regions in the early medieval period.[8] Neither is it intended to claim that there was any specific form of spirituality which was unique to the Celtic regions. The concept of the 'Celtic Church' has been justifiably challenged by Kathleen Hughes and largely demolished by Wendy Davies.[9] Romantic notions of a specific form of 'Celtic Christianity' which is eco-friendly, Trinitarian and concerned with 'presence, poetry and pilgrimage' still linger.[10] However, the tide is beginning to turn: few scholars now consider the saints to have been 'passionate wanderers' visiting almost all of the religious sites which bear their names. Ian Bradley, whose book *The Celtic Way* (1993) described Celtic Christianity as 'a gentle, mystical, affirmative and holistic faith, firmly biblical and strongly influenced by Desert Fathers, while assimilating many pagan beliefs and practices',[11] has also provided one of the best critiques (to date) of the concept of 'Celtic Christianity'. In *Celtic Christianity: Making Myths and Chasing Dreams* (1999) he notes: 'it is tempting to suggest that Celtic Christianity is less an actual phenomenon defined in historical and geographical terms than an artificial construct created out of wishful thinking, romantic nostalgia and the projection of all kinds of dreams about what should and might have been.'[12] So, let us turn to the individual studies which comprise this volume and provide a preview of the research topics presented in each of the essays.

J. Wyn Evans traces the history and development of the cult of St David, focusing primarily on the cathedral site and its environs. In the first detailed article on the cathedral and relics at St Davids since the relics were radiocarbon dated in 1996, Evans provides a perceptive study of the evolving layout of the cathedral buildings and points out that certain architectural features, such as the slope of the nave floor, may in fact have more to do with the geology and topography of the site than they do with the shrine and cult of St David. He highlights the connection between St Davids and other saints, such as Justinian, Andrew and Patrick, and proposes that the original cult site of St David may have been located elsewhere. The cathedral at St Davids became a major pilgrimage site and attracted hordes of pilgrims and numerous eminent visitors throughout the Middle Ages – little wonder since two pilgrimages to St Davids were considered to be the equivalent of one pilgrimage to Rome.

St David's pre-eminence amongst Welsh saints is also emphasized in Elissa R. Henken's article. Henken examines the ways in which hagiographies have been used as political tools by both the Church and the State. The Latin Life of St David, composed in the late eleventh century by Rhigyfarch (son of the bishop of St Davids), played a significant role both in the struggle for an independent Welsh Church and in the attempt to establish the supremacy of St Davids over the other Welsh dioceses. The saints, who were perceived as guardians of the land and defenders of the people, could be used to empower the medieval dioceses, assert rights and privileges and verify a church's claim to specific tracts of land. Whilst most of the Welsh saints remained local heroes, others such as Beuno in the north and David in the south became important on a national level. Indeed, as Henken demonstrates, St David – 'the ever-adapting icon of Welshness' – came to epitomize national character (even Nonconformity) and was continuously adapted to the ever-changing socio-political context.

A detailed knowledge of secular and ecclesiastical politics in twelfth-century Wales also informs Nerys Ann Jones and Morfydd E. Owen's study of the *Gogynfeirdd* poems to saints. Welsh poetry is an extremely valuable source for any study of the Welsh saints, and the three twelfth-century poems by Llywelyn Fardd, Cynddelw Brydydd Mawr and Gwynfardd Brycheiniog which praise Cadfan, Tysilio and David respectively are the earliest hagiographical texts extant in Middle Welsh. Jones and Owen unravel the complex set of circumstances which led to the commissioning of the individual poems and shed new light on the dates of their composition, the sources upon which the poets drew, their intended audiences and their function within both secular and ecclesiastical Welsh politics.

Vernacular prose hagiography forms the basis of my own study in chapter four. Rather than focus on the native saints, the essay examines Middle Welsh *bucheddau* which relate the legends of two of the universal saints of Christendom – Mary Magdalene and Martha. The article traces the development of the medieval cults of the composite Magdalene and her sister Martha, both of whom are credited with evangelizing Provence, and examines the Welsh *bucheddau* in the context of the extant Welsh manuscripts. It is proposed that these saints had a particular relevance within the lay household and that the Welsh Lives of the female saints may have been intended primarily for a lay audience rather than for an audience of religious sisters or clerics (as previous readings have suggested).

The collection then turns to Ireland and two articles follow which focus on Ireland's premier saint, the Briton, Patrick. While John Koch discusses the St Patrick of history and evaluates the early source-material, including the autobiographical writings, Thomas O'Loughlin focuses on one particular episode in the seventh-century *Vita Patricii* written by Muirchú. Koch, building on the work of scholars such as Esposito, Dumville, Binchy and Charles Thomas, proposes a number of new possibilities relating to Patrick's identity and discusses the significance of the obits of St Patrick, favouring the *c*.430 date. O'Loughlin's detailed analysis of the scene which describes Ireland's first Easter Vigil at Tara highlights the range of scriptural sources used by Muirchú in his particular portrayal of the 'trial of divinities'. A paradigm for the trial is found in 1 Kings 18:17–40; the city of Tara may be compared to Babylon; and King Loégaire appears to be modelled mainly on Nebuchadnezzar and Herod. O'Loughlin demonstrates that not only is Patrick's triumph over paganism modelled on the clash of the two religions depicted in the Book of Daniel, but that verbal echoes may also be found embedded in Muirchú's text.

The same event is one of the many miracle stories considered by Dorothy Ann Bray in her article on Irish hagiography. Rather than view the miracle-working Irish saints as 'holy magicians' or 'heirs of the druids', Bray focuses on the role that miracles played in the composition of early Irish hagiography. She reminds us that we should view hagiographical texts as works of literature and suggests that folkloric elements are integral to the composition of the *vitae* in that they are 'consciously employed in the art and aesthetics of the text'. Certain types of miracle recur over and over again, and there is a recognizable 'canon' of miracles ascribed to the saints. The professional hagiographer, Bray proposes, 'was expected to know his miracle stories and know how to apply them appropriately'.

T. M. Charles-Edwards focuses on five *vitae* found in the *Codex Salmanticensis*, the most important extant collection of Irish saints' Lives. Sts Daig, Mochta, Éogan and Mac Nisse were all patrons of northern churches and the Second Life of Mo Lua appears to have been produced for his northern church at Druim Snechta rather than his principal church at Clonfertmulloe. These short Lives are also all arranged in order of feast-days covering the period from 4 August to 3 September. Charles-Edwards proposes that the source for this group of *vitae* was a Northern Lectionary which may have abbreviated Lives originally written in the eighth or ninth century. Thus, via the application of a succinct textual archaeology, Charles-Edwards exposes a new source for this important Irish compendium.

Jonathan Wooding concentrates on one of Ireland's more renowned saints who, as we have seen, has a substantial hagiographical dossier – St Brendan, best known for his seven-year sea voyage. Wooding warns against accepting voyage tales as evidence of actual journeys made by the saints. Instead, he reads the *Nauigatio* of St Brendan as an allegory of the monastic life, in which the journey made by Brendan and his monks represents the sacred year with its emphasis on the cyclical performance of the monastic liturgy. References to food, fasting and feasting abound, and the author of the *Nauigatio*, who appears to be familiar with contemporary monastic practice, appears to be commenting on the rule and observances of strict eremitical communities such as the Céli Dé.

Brittany, a region with an abundance of hagiographical sources both medieval and modern, is represented in the collection by two articles: one which looks at a wide range of Breton *vitae* from the Carolingian to the

Romance periods, and another which focuses primarily on Breton ballads composed in the nineteenth and early twentieth centuries. Both Bernard Merdrignac and Mary-Ann Constantine emphasize the fluidity of hagiographical texts and traditions which are continuously evolving and adapting to the needs of new audiences and differing contexts. Hagiography, Merdrignac argues, needed to be meaningful to its time. As a result, these religious texts were constantly revised, copied, abbreviated, or completely rewritten. For example, while several versions of the Lives of St Guénolé were composed by the same author (Wrdisten), the Lives of St Malo were rewritten over a period of several centuries by a variety of different authors. Merdrignac examines the differing attitudes of hagiographers towards their texts; the types of rewriting discernible in the work of Breton hagiographers and the motivations which might have governed these revisions. Constantine, on the other hand, contrasts the *vita*, which tends to provide a complete narrative of the saint's life, with the 'unofficial' hagiographies found in folk narrative. Orally transmitted Breton ballads often preserve only fragmentary traditions which are frequently unorthodox or ambiguous and may be interpreted in a variety of different ways. In songs and ritual traditions, often associated with healing, the saints are occasionally abused or mistreated: for example, the wooden statue of St Servatus is ritually smashed to pieces in order to assure a fruitful harvest, and the wives of fishermen at Léon ritually 'drown' their saints in an attempt to ensure that their husbands will not be killed at sea. The saints themselves are occasionally portrayed as misbehaving or acting in a violent manner towards sinners. Constantine argues that the combined processes of oral transmission and popular interpretation, closely akin to the generation of apocrypha, are a dynamic, and occasionally subversive, force creating new and potentially unsettling narratives from orthodox models.

Along with Bernard Merdrignac, Thomas O. Clancy discusses the process of rewriting or recycling hagiographical texts. He provides a detailed analysis of the evolution of one particular text, the *Libellus de nativitate Sancti Cuthberti*. Although it is often referred to as 'the Irish Life of St Cuthbert', Clancy favours the view that it was produced at the Cistercian abbey of Melrose in Scotland. The *Libellus*, which appears to be a composite of different sources, provides us with a valuable insight into one twelfth-century hagiographer's methodology: what Clancy terms 'magpie hagiography'. Among his sources are hagiographical traditions associated with St Adomnán of Iona and St Moluag of Lismore. St Moluag also features in Penelope Dransart's article on the cult of saints in Pictland. Dransart, however, focuses on Moluag's associations with north-eastern Scotland, in particular, Mortlach, Clatt and Clover, and she also considers evidence for the cult of St Gerardine at Kinneddar. She examines the relationship between material culture, cult continuity, place-names and hagiography (both oral and written), and suggests that the presence of antiquities acts as a legitimating authority for the perpetuation and creation of hagiographical traditions.

Material culture is also the subject of Joanna Mattingly's article on pre-Reformation saints' cults in Cornwall. Mattingly argues that the visual representations of saints preserved in late-medieval stained glass at St Neot parish church reflect the religious interests and preferences of the entire parish. Whilst the social elite, in this case, opted for saints of international importance, the middle classes and poorer members of the parish chose to commemorate local saints (such as Neot, Mabyn, Meubred and Manc). The principle which appears to unify the saints depicted in the north-aisle windows is that all of these saints (including some of the universal saints) had local cults and their tombs and corporeal relics were venerated at other locations within the parish. Mattingly argues that the windows may have acted as pointers to other pilgrimage sites in the area. She also helps dispel the myth that east Cornwall was completely anglicized on the eve of the Reformation, even though Cornish had not been spoken in this area for at least two hundred years.

Finally, Karen Jankulak draws together evidence from all of the Celtic regions in her examination of one particular hagiographical motif. In her article on pigs as agents of divination in the process of selecting suitable sites for the foundation of saints' churches, Jankulak analyses the geographical distribution of the motif. She considers its relationship to classical legend and also suggests that there was a complex interaction between hagiographical tradition and secular Celtic literature.

Notes

[1] A selection includes: Henken, *Traditions*; Henken, *Welsh Saints*; Sharpe, *Medieval Irish Saints' Lives*; Carey, Herbert and Ó Riain (eds), *Studies in Irish Hagiography*; Chédeville and Guillotel, *La Bretagne des saints*; Merdrignac, *Les Vies de saints*; Macquarrie, *Saints of Scotland*; Orme, *Saints of Cornwall.*

[2] Their authors often make this clear in the subtitle, and my aim here is not to criticize these works: K. Hughes, *Celtic Britain* (Wales and Scotland); O. Davies, *Celtic Christianity* (Wales); O'Loughlin, *Celtic Theology* (Ireland); O. Davies (trans.) with collaboration of O'Loughlin, *Celtic Spirituality* (Ireland and Wales). Ford (ed.), *Celtic Folklore and Christianity* covers a number of the Celtic regions.

[3] Problems of identification and whether or not to equate saints with similar

names in the Celtic regions were issues addressed by Oliver J. Padel at the conference on Celtic Hagiography and Saints' Cults held at the University of Wales, Lampeter, 8–10 September 2000 (Padel, 'How many saints in Celtic countries (particularly Cornwall)?'). See also his forthcoming article, 'Local saints and place-names'.

[4] See Bernard Merdrignac's article, below.

[5] Bowen, *Saint David of History*; Dumville, *Saint David of Wales*.

[6] Le Berre, Tanguy and Castel (eds), *Buez santez Nonn;* J. Cartwright, 'St Non: rape, sanctity and motherhood in Welsh and Breton hagiography', St David's Day Lecture, University of Wales, Lampeter, March 2002.

[7] William Worcestre *c.*1480 also claims that she was buried at Altarnun in Cornwall: Worcestre, *Itineraries*, p. 62.

[8] Valuable studies of the individual regions include Edwards and Lane (eds), *The Early Church in Wales* and T. M. Charles-Edwards, *Early Christian Ireland.*

[9] K. Hughes, 'The Celtic Church'; W. Davies, 'The myth of the Celtic Church'.

[10] Bradley, *Celtic Way*, p. 119.

[11] Ibid., the quotation appears on the book's cover. I have borrowed the term 'passionate wanderers' from E. Rees, *Celtic Saints: Passionate Wanderers*.

[12] Bradley, *Celtic Christianity*, p. vii. Another well-balanced critique is provided by Meek, *The Quest*.

1

St David and St Davids: some observations on the cult, site and buildings

><

J. WYN EVANS

With the approach of old age, the poet, Iolo Goch (*c*.1325–*c*.1400), began to consider the health of his immortal soul. The remedy that came to his mind was pilgrimage to Jerusalem, scene of Christ's Crucifixion. Age, distance and decrepitude – 'his two black sad feet stuck in fetters' – prevented him from realizing that ambition; nor, for the same reasons, could he go to Rome.[1] Instead, he wished to go on pilgrimage to Menevia (St Davids) and not only on grounds of accessibility, but also because of the spiritual attractions of 'maenol Ddewi Mynyw' (the manor of David of Menevia) in Glyn Rhosyn (Vallis Rosina). These included a number of miracles performed by St David (Dewi Sant): that no devil would tread in his land; and the guarantee of a safe journey to heaven for the souls of those who were buried in David's cemetery. Were he actually to have made the journey to St Davids, and it is not clear that he ever did, he would have been made aware of the widespread distribution of a cult in the landscape which included events, personalities and miracles associated with David; and the nearer he got to his journey's end, the more specific would those associations have been.

Iolo's reference in his poem to David, to the thurible pouring out incense, invites comparison with that other major medieval (and contemporary) pilgrimage centre, Santiago de Compostela, with its huge censer swinging on the eve of the feast of St James.[2] Indeed Ieuan ap Rhydderch, writing in the century after Iolo, in his poem in praise of David, made the comparison explicit when he sang: 'Sens a mwg ail Sain Siâm yw'[3] (The incense and the smoke – a second Santiago it is). Moreover, Ieuan praises not only the incense but the music, bells, choir, vestments, lights and organ as well as the relics and images. He also compares the temple of David in Jerusalem to the temple of David in Menevia and he, like Iolo, states that three journeys to Mynyw are the equivalent of one visit to Christ's grave; and going to Mynyw twice is as good as going to Rome once. Further, both Iolo and Ieuan set their descriptions of the building within the context of the *Vita Davidis*, rehearsing incidents and recounting miracles in poetry just as Giraldus and Rhigyfarch had done in prose.[4] They did so for the same purpose: to tie together the cathedral building and the landscape to the enhancement of the cult by emphasizing the spiritual benefits associated with David, his cult, the building that housed it and the landscape around it.

On the other hand, notwithstanding the long association between David and the present St Davids, an association taken for granted by both Iolo and Ieuan ap Rhydderch, it is possible to suggest other explanations for the link between the cult of David and the present St Davids and its environs, as well as asking whether the site and topography of the present cathedral building express the needs of the cult of David. For example, did those medieval pilgrims, who were making their way down to Menevia from north Wales, raise questions in their own minds as to the relationship between Mynyw and Hen Fynyw; and between Mynyw and 'Mynyw yn y deheu' (Mynyw in the south);[5] or the relationship between David and Llanddewibrefi? And when they got to Menevia, were they asking themselves whether some of the details they heard raised questions about the cult of David in the immediate vicinity of the cathedral? Had it been, for example, originally located in Vallis Rosina rather than Tygwyn (SM 735275) and the Whitesands Bay area? Why did Rhigyfarch, in the *vita*, and both Iolo Goch and Ieuan ap Rhydderch put such emphasis on the departure of Patrick in order to make way for David? Why was Justinian associated with David as his confessor? Was there a cult of Justinian in existence before or alongside that of David? And, in the unlikely event that they had been asking these questions, did they, as modern commentators have done, go on to ask whether the placenames and the landscape around Menevia had been influenced to accommodate a change of cult to that of David and had been presented to reflect various elements of the cult of David (Figures 1.1 and 1.2)?[6] And did those pilgrims who came from England, when they heard the relevant readings from the *vita*, believe that David had founded Glastonbury, Bath, Crowland, Repton and Leominster?[7]

It is clear that both Iolo Goch and Ieuan ap Rhydderch took it for granted that the cult had always been focused on and at St Davids. They were, after all, experiencing it at its height. William Worcestre, writing in the same century as Ieuan ap Rhydderch, offers us a collection of eleven miracles associated with David and his shrine at Menevia.[8] Some of these can be dated to the turn of the fourteenth and fifteenth centuries and attest to a renewed interest in the cult of David at around that time, thanks, perhaps, to two archbishops of Canterbury, one of whom (Chichele) had been bishop of St Davids. The popularity of the cult and the wealth it brought extended not only to the building, whose expensive fittings were described by Iolo and Ieuan, but also to the chapels around the cathedral. Browne Willis, drawing on a lost Elizabethan manuscript, certainly thought that these sites were pilgrim chapels and that they produced a substantial income for the Chapter.[9]

Indeed, it was only in 1538, less than a century after the time of Ieuan ap Rhydderch, that the cult was brought to an abrupt end, at a time when it appears to have been still successful in attracting both pilgrims and offerings. Bishop Barlow, in a letter to Cromwell, quoted the traditional Latin verse, 'Roma semel quantum, bis dat Menevia tantum' (Once to Rome gives the same value as twice to St Davids), but in a pejorative sense, before he gave the *coup de grâce* to the shrine.[10] The attitudes which Barlow condemned, and which caused him to bring the cult to an end, were precisely those which had made it attractive to so many, for example, Iolo Goch and Ieuan ap Rhydderch, the anonymous lady to whom Dafydd ap Gwilym sang,[11] and Edudful[12] and Mallt[13] who made the pilgrimage to St Davids in the hope of receiving spiritual benefit. Nor was David's shrine the only attraction in the cathedral: the famous image *Mair o Fynyw* (Mary of Mynyw) was located in the Lady chapel.[14]

It is also clear when we look at the work of the Welsh poets mentioned above that they depended in large measure for their information on the Latin *vita* compiled by Rhigyfarch in the late eleventh century. The *vita*, written around four hundred years after the death of David,[15] may be seen as an *apologia* for the antiquity, practices and validity of the Welsh church in the face of Norman aggression. It can also be seen as an expression of a cult already well developed and widely distributed in south-west and mid-Wales, and making claims to churches in England too.[16]

Rhigyfarch need not, however, have worried about Norman intentions and attitudes to St David, since Bernard, the first Norman to occupy the see of Menevia (from 1115 to 1147), began to exhibit great enthusiasm for the patron saint and his cult. Hindsight suggests that he had a fourpronged campaign in mind which directly involved David, his cult and the church which was associated with him. First of all, he sought to establish a diocesan parochial and pastoral system according to the best contemporary practice. Secondly, he sought to defend his diocese from the depredations of Norman lords, his fellow bishops of Hereford and Llandaf and monastic houses on the lookout for endowments. Thirdly, he reformed the clergy of Menevia to create a chapter of secular canons, again on the lines of contemporary practice elsewhere. Fourthly, he attempted to create or recover the metropolitan status of a Menevia independent of Canterbury; the attempt probably arose as much from the belief that David himself had been an archbishop as from Bernard's attempt to raise his church to metropolitan status.[17] In any case, the cult's significance for the way Bernard approached his episcopate is revealed at the outset of his occupancy, when he did not remove the cathedral from the spot where it stands today. He could have transferred it to somewhere both more convenient for the administration to the diocese and more accessible for the cult. Instead, he took steps to enhance and reinforce it at St Davids, presumably because of the existing associations with David. And, therefore, he constructed a new church which, according to *Annales Cambriae*, was 'dedicated' in 1131, no doubt to furnish a fitting setting – a 'shrine' in itself – for the saint's relics and an appropriate centre for his cult. It is no coincidence that it is Bernard who is credited with securing two important concessions from Pope Calixtus II: the canonization of David and the privilege which stated that two pilgrimages to St Davids were equal to one to Rome.[18]

There was, however, one drawback to the success of this four-pronged campaign. Bernard seems to have been unable to secure or even discover the whereabouts of the bones of David. William of Malmesbury tells us of Bernard's failure, after many attempts, to find the saint's body.[19] It is also worth noting that Giraldus Cambrensis does not specifically mention any shrine or corporeal relics at St Davids. Although Bernard failed to locate the body of David, it does not seem to have derailed his efforts to enhance the cult. Indeed, his success can be measured, not only in the attitudes which so attracted Ieuan ap Rhydderch and disgusted Barlow, but also in the building and the sacred landscape at St Davids (Figure 1.2).[20]

Notwithstanding the apparent failure of Bernard to secure the corporeal relics, it seems clear that there were other relics associated with David extant at around this time. In his *Journey through Wales*, Giraldus Cambrensis, writing at the turn of the thirteenth century, speaks of Bangu, the bell of David, kept not at Menevia but at Glasgwm in Elfael.[21] Composed only thirty or so years after the death of Bernard, Gwynfardd Brycheiniog's long poem in praise of David speaks of other relics of the saint, beside Bangu.[22] There was the altar covered in skins upon which no one could look, kept at Llangyfelach; it has been identified with the one which had been given to David by the patriarch of Jerusalem.²³ There was also the golden pastoral staff, which may have been kept at Llanddewibrefi.²⁴

The wide distribution of the relics, as well as of the churches 'owned' by David which Gwynfardd lists, reveals a cult which is both well developed and widely disseminated throughout a large part of south Wales; indeed, their location may be part of a campaign to secure the allegiance of churches, such as Llangyfelach, which were clearly dedicated to saints other than David.²⁵ Further, it would be easy to see the dominance of the cult of David in south-west Wales as the result of the active patronage of the dynasty of Deheubarth, in gratitude perhaps for the *nawdd* (protection) extended to Rhys ap Tewdwr before 1081; a growth still in progress in the 1170s with the construction and dedication of the new *llogawd* (?church/?monastery) of Llan (ddewi) y Crwys.²⁶ Further, one implication of the term 'owned' is that, in some cases, the success of the cult of David came about at the expense of the cults, communities and major churches of other saints. It may also be significant that Gwynfardd lists neither Llandeilo Fawr nor Llanbadarn Fawr as being 'owned' by David. By Gwynfardd's time, both of these churches were well within the diocese of St Davids, following, on the one hand, the failure of Urban's claim to all Teilo churches and, on the other, the continuing link between the descendants of Sulien and the diocese of Menevia.²⁷ One must, therefore, avoid making too easy assumptions as to the relevance of the list of churches which David owned to any attempt to trace the expansion of the cult, rather than to the establishment of diocesan boundaries.

It might have been expected that Gwynfardd would have begun his poem with praise of the *clas* at Mynyw; would have listed the relics kept there; would have recited a list of David's miracles; and would have lauded the site and the building which housed the shrine and cult of David. It is true that Mynyw heads the list of churches 'owned' by David, and lines 210 to 245 describe events in his life relating to Mynyw, but the chief emphasis of the poem lies with Llanddewibrefi, its priests and its *clas*,²⁸ the boundaries of its area of *nawdd* (refuge) (ll. 140–8) and its five altars.²⁹ Further, as was noted above, the relics which Gwynfardd lists and praises as expressions of David's *virtus* and *braint* are dispersed away from Mynyw: Bangu at Glasgwm; the altar at Llangyfelach; and the golden *bagl* (staff), possibly at Llanddewibrefi itself.

There is, however, one church in the list whose very name raises the question of the original associations of the cult of David, and that is Hen Fynyw, Old Menevia.³⁰ Early references to David, such as those in *Armes Prydein* and Asser's *Life of Alfred*, do not associate David specifically with Mynyw – or with anywhere else for that matter.³¹ The legal tractate

'The seven bishop-houses of Dyfed' does not associate David with Mynyw either.[32] However, the description of the landing of Gruffudd ap Cynan (and/or William the Conqueror)[33] at Porth Clais in 1081 tells us that his reception party consisted not only of Rhys ap Tewdwr, the bishop and the teachers, but also of two *clasau:* 'holl clas er argluyd Dewi ac un eglwys Fynyw' (the whole community/people of the lord David and that of the church of Menevia).[34] The presence of the two bodies suggests that Menevia's inclusion within the cult of David may have been of recent origin; or it may mean that the retinue of the bishop as *esgob dewi*, David's successor, was distinguished from the clerics of Mynyw. Alternatively, it could mean that there was more than one church on site, each with its own community, as at St Andrews in Scotland.[35] There may also have been a distinction between Sulien's *familia* as archbishop and that of the church of Menevia. Whatever the true relationship between Menevia and Old Menevia, as late as the fourteenth century, the Welsh Life of David was still referring to Mynyw as 'Mynyw yn y deheu' (Menevia in the south).[36]

In any event, in the decade after this meeting, at which a compact was sworn in church on the relics (and the phrase *y greiryeu* 'his relics' presumably means those of David), the site was once again devastated by the Vikings. This was part of a sequence of raids, which included that of 1080, which saw the death of Abraham and the return of Sulien. In 1091, indeed, Menevia was destroyed by the 'Gentiles of the Isles' which may be the same raid that is mentioned in the Life of St Caradog, when, in the aftermath of a raid by Viking pirates from the Orkneys, the site was abandoned and left almost without inhabitant for seven years and a certain priest 'hardly reached the tomb of the confessor St David on the seventh day because of the thorns and briars'.[37] Two years previously, in 1089, the shrine of David itself had been despoiled, although there is no evidence as to whether it was the Vikings who did this.[38] It may be the case that the cult and relics of the saint were moved from one site to the other, as were those of St Cuthbert as they moved from Lindisfarne via Chester le Street to Durham.[39] This, too, might account for the continuing distinction between Mynyw and Hen Fynyw.

It is, therefore, possible to argue that the association of the cult of David with Menevia is secondary rather than primary. Indeed, the original saint culted at Menevia could well have been either Patrick or Justinian, both of whom have dedications near St Davids cathedral. Given the position of the peninsula as a nodal point on the western searoutes between Ireland, Wales, Cornwall and the Continent, it is likely that Christianity and the emerging monastic movement were well established by the early medieval period.⁴⁰ There are also present in Pembrokeshire Group I early Christian monuments, but no such monument is known to exist from the site or immediate vicinity of the present cathedral to which we shall now turn.

St Davids cathedral is a building with a topography all of its own (Figures 1.1 and 1.2), set in an unlikely location and on a site which has its own problems and peculiarities. It is a site long associated with David, who was said to have been born on the cliffs near the present cathedral; baptized at Porth Clais by Elfyw; and educated at Old Menevia, before returning to Vallis Rosina to found a monastery. His monasticism was austere in the extreme, as observed by Rhigyfarch in the *vita*.⁴¹

Rather than begin with the *vita*, however, a more useful way to proceed is to examine the end of the medieval cult of David. As noted above, there was until 1 March 1538 within the present cathedral a shrine of St David which also contained the relics of St Justinian.⁴² This is Bishop Barlow's description of what happened on and following that fateful St David's Day:

> Forthermore, when I admonished the canons of Sainte Davids accordinge to the kynges injunctions in no wyse to set forth fayned reliques for to allure people to supersticion, nether to advaunce the vayne observacion of unnecessary holy dayes abrogated by the kynges supreme authoritye, on sainte Davids daye the people wilfully solemnysinge the feest, certen reliques were set forth which I caused to be sequestred and taken awaye, detaynynge them in my custody until I may be advertised of your lordships pleasour. The parcels of the reliques are these: two heedes of sylver plate enclosinge two rotten skulles stuffed with putrified clowtes; Item, two arme bones, and a worme eaten boke covered with sylver plate.⁴³

As a result of this intervention, the shrine was slighted and several centuries of pilgrimage came to an end.⁴⁴

The fate of the contents of the shrine is unknown. Fred Cowley has traced them as far as Smithfield, and the likelihood is that they were destroyed there.⁴⁵ But suffice it to say that the bones discovered in 1866, walled up an in a sort of ashlar box in a niche in Holy Trinity chapel (inside St Davids), were carbon dated in 1996 and the C_{14} dates range between the late twelfth, thirteenth and fourteenth centuries.⁴⁶

Now, it is assumed that the shrine which Barlow slighted was the one erected in 1275 (Figure 1.3) by Bishop Richard of Carew, as the C text (and the C text alone) of *Annales Cambriae* tells us: 'Inceptum fuit feretrum Beati David in ecclesia Menevensis' (The shrine of the Blessed David in the church of Menevia was begun).⁴⁷ This, however, is not the first mention of a shrine at Menevia in the *Annales*. As noted above, under the year 1088 *(recte* 1089), both B and C texts tell us that 'archa (scrinium in C) Sancti David ab (de C) ecclesia (sua C) furata est, et (iuxta civitatem ex toto spoliatur C) auro argentoque quibus tegebatur spoliata est' (the box/shrine of St David was stolen from his church and despoiled of its gold and silver near the city).[48] It does not tell us what was in the box, nor does it mention bones or any other sort of relic. That did not prevent the assumption from being made that the relics themselves, whatever they might have been, were not lost, destroyed or taken away, but that they survived to be enshrined both in the cathedral 'dedicated' in 1131 by Bishop Bernard and in the greater church begun by Bishop Peter de Leia upon the demolition of the church of Menevia in 1181/2.[49] The church of 1181 is the core of the present cathedral and very substantial portions remain within the present walls.[50]

Thus, and notwithstanding the despoliation and abandonment noted above, the assumption has been made consistently that:
(a) there is continuity on the site of the present St Davids cathedral from the sixth century up to the present;
(b) the site of the monastery founded by David in the sixth century can be identified with Vallis Rosina (and this name and Menevia describe quite precisely the marshy and overgrown Alun valley in which the present cathedral stands);
(c) since the *vita* tells us that the saint was buried in his own monastery, the grave was at St Davids;
(d) after his death, the site developed as a centre of pilgrimage to his grave;
(e) the bones enshrined in the 1275 shrine were his and extracted from his tomb;
(f) the shrine of 1275 was the latest in a series extending back to the one despoiled in 1089;
(g) the configuration of the church building of 1181 reflected and expressed a long-established cult, which had received a boost in the early twelfth century when Pope Calixtus II had both canonized David and given a privilege to St Davids which included the provision that two journeys to Menevia were equal to one to Rome;[51]
(h) the previous church dedicated by Bishop Bernard in 1131 was also geared to the development of cult and pilgrimage, and that there was a shrine there too;
(i) the 1131 church was built as part of the campaign that Bernard waged to raise the profile of his diocese in his attempt to gain metropolitan status, the claim being founded on the assumption that David had been an archbishop.

It is also worth noting at this point, that it has been suggested that the base of the wall immediately behind the present high altar is the only surviving portion of Bernard's church 'consecrated' in 1131. This is the wall which contains a niche connecting Holy Trinity chapel and the presbytery. It lies below the sill of the triple lancet, but although the eastern reveal in Holy Trinity chapel is complete, that on the west side, behind the high altar, is severely truncated by the band of linear decoration below the lancets; indeed, the opening on the west side of the wall has been reduced to a small oblong opening. This is edged by purple Caerbwdi stone, adjacent to which are fragments of both yellow oolitic limestone and red brick. It is clear that it had been repaired, presumably in the Victorian period, before it was freshly pointed in 1991–2.

There are also clear traces of blocking each side of the opening, suggesting that, at one time, the opening was much wider, even perhaps a window belonging to a scheme of fenestration earlier than the triple lancets. It might be the case that the niche belonged to the church of 1131, but the surviving detail on the eastern reveal in Holy Trinity chapel suggests that it belongs to the church of 1181.[52] It is also clear that the construction of the triple lancet and the band of decoration below it not only truncated the height of the western side of the niche, but may well have rendered it obsolete.

The niche opens between Holy Trinity chapel and the presbytery below the triple-lancet windows. It was not known to be there before Gilbert Scott's restoration. He unblocked it, and discovered bones which were then buried under the floor of Holy Trinity chapel. At that period, the niche was considered to be of greater interest than the bones. It contains five crosses: four around one central pierced cross; the hole in the latter communicates between the presbytery and Holy Trinity chapel.[53] It was interpreted as a pilgrims' niche, that is, that pilgrims could come into the area behind the high altar, and look in or kneel in order to see what was happening in the sanctuary. They might also have been able to put their arms through the hollow-armed central cross and touch what was on the other side, that is, the assumption was that the shrine of David was in the present sanctuary where the high altar is now. According to this scheme, the shrine lay at right angles to the wall and the twelfth-century high altar was attached to the front of it. Such an arrangement, however, seems unlikely in a British context.[54]

Further, in order to make circulation easier for the pilgrims – and clearly it was assumed that they were coming in sufficient numbers to justify the expense of extending the cathedral forty feet to the east – a covered processional way, or ambulatory, was constructed in order to aid circulation around the building in an orderly liturgical fashion. And it is also assumed that they had some way of getting into the open courtyard thus created to the outside of the previous eastern external wall of the cathedral. Once within the space, and it is not entirely clear how it was defined to the north or to the south, it is assumed that they continued to do what they are supposed to have done prior to the construction of the ambulatory – gone up to the niche and knelt and/or looked in to the presbytery through the pierced central cross.

It is also assumed that the doorway in the west face of the north transept, which now gives access to the Song School, known as the 'pilgrims' door', was the access into the cathedral for pilgrims arriving either from Porth Clais or from Whitesands Bay and coming into the precinct over Llech Lafar, the bridge over the river Alun.[55] Alternatively, they would have come along *y feidr dywyll* (the dark road), across *pont y penyd* (the bridge of penance), over the Alun upstream of Llech Lafar. They would then have moved up the north-choir aisle through the ambulatory and antechapel, down the south aisles and out through the south door.

That particular circulation route, however, makes better sense in relation to the shrine constructed in 1275 (Figure 1.3).[56] It is assumed that its construction followed a decision to reorder the presbytery by placing the shrine on the north side to make access to both sides of it easier than when it was, putatively, behind the high altar. We should also note that the shrine was referred to as a *feretrum* (portable shrine) and this suggestion of portability is given substance a few decades later in the Black Book of St Davids, where it is stated that the burgesses and the tenants of the Welsh Hundred were bound in time of war to follow the shrine of the blessed David and the relics on either side, provided that they could come home the same night.[57] So what survives in the cathedral now is the stone base of the shrine rather than the shrine itself. It is not clear, however, whether it is in its original position, or it was moved to the north to make way for the tomb of Edmund Tudor. The earl's tomb was brought into the presbytery of the cathedral at the dissolution of the Greyfriars in Carmarthen, when it was removed from its equivalent position in front of the high altar in that church.

There is thus a clear need to interrogate the 1181 building in terms of the physical requirements of the cult of St David. The first element to question is the slope of the floor. It rises three feet in the nave; four and a half feet between nave and quire; and fourteen feet overall from the west door to the Lady chapel.[58] Now it has been suggested that this was planned and that the slope had the same function as at Santiago de Compostela, namely that of allowing the floor to be swilled down after several thousand pilgrims had passed through it; and that the east end is higher because the shrine was at that end.

That seems to me to be an *ex post facto* justification for the slope. There are other, more prosaic reasons for the peculiarities of the building. It has been suggested that the present nave, transepts and presbytery walls were laid out around the church of 1131 to keep that earlier church going for as long as possible.[59] The nave was laid out in relation to that earlier church, that is to the west of it. In any case, the site in general slopes, for the floor of the valley is about one hundred feet below Cross Square in the modern city. The earlier church was thus on the higher and comparatively drier part of the site. The rise in the middle of the building is an attempt by the architect to cope with the change of level down to the river – and we now know that he built the nave on the riverbed, and the foundations had to be covered with dumped mud to stop the outward shift of the north-nave wall.[60] The slope in the nave floor occurred because the anonymous architect could not level the ground without major engineering works and without exposing the numerous springs in the hillside, so he constructed each pier in the nave longer than its eastern neighbour, thus ensuring that the crowns of the arches and the capitals were horizontal. He also left a substantial platform, or dais, upon which rest the western piers of the easternmost bay of the nave arcade. Thus, the slope and the lift are to do with the geology and topography of the site and not with the cult.

As far as the 'pilgrims' door' is concerned, it may well have developed this function later, but it was not constructed as such in the twelfth century. The clue to what is going on here has to do with the alignment of the present chapel of St Thomas Becket which opens out of the northeast corner of the transept. It lies considerably to the north of east. The second clue comes from one of that sad series of visions concerning Giraldus Cambrensis, which convinced him (if no one else) that he was destined to be bishop of St Davids.[61] A chaplain at Menevia had a vision of the chapter meeting in the old church of St Andrew, their normal meeting place, and seeing a fiery lion going around that old church and then into the greater church. Given the conservative nature of cathedrals, that the north transept is dedicated to St Andrew and that the medieval chapter house (now the library) lies above the present St Thomas's chapel, the alignment of the present St Thomas's chapel (1220) might well preserve the fossilized alignment of the old church of St Andrew. The doorway itself is clearly earlier than the double window above, because the top of the doorway is both depressed and made up of far rougher masonry than the side orders. It has been truncated by the construction of the double window which is also asymmetrical to it. Further, the doorway is aligned on the centre of the chapel. The presence of several churches on the same site, as at Meifod or Clonmacnoise, is common on early medieval ecclesiastical sites in the Celtic west. Thus, the north transept may have been constructed across the 'old church of St Andrew' and the alignment of St Thomas's chapel may well preserve its orientation. The doorway may also preserve the location of the doorway into that 'old church'.

The presence of an earlier building may also help to explain the existence of the ambulatory. It might have been built to connect an already existing church or chapel on the site of the present Lady chapel with the main building. The thirteenth-century Lady chapel is not precisely aligned with the main building which, as was noted above, was laid out in the twelfth century. The chapel, although on the same orientation, lies to the south and east of the ambulatory. It is thus possible that it may represent the fossilized footprint of an earlier building which was not part of the twelfth-century configuration. Given that the holy well, although not now visible above ground, is located immediately outside the chapel and symmetrical to the centre of its east wall, this putative precursor might have been a well-chapel on the pattern of the now destroyed Capel y Pistyll at Porth Clais.[62]

Thus it is possible both to explain the shape, topography and disposition of the present cathedral building in terms other than the requirements of the shrine and cult of David as well as to suggest the possibility of the transfer of the cult from elsewhere at some unknown date.

Notes

[1] Johnston (ed.), *Gwaith Iolo Goch*, p. 131, ll. 1–26; Johnston (ed. and trans.), *Iolo Goch Poems*, p. 118, ll. 1–26.

[2] Bentley, *The Way of St James*, p. 135

[3] H. Lewis, Roberts and Williams (eds), *Cywyddau Iolo*, p. 245, l. 10.

[4] Gerald of Wales, *Opera*, vol. 3, pp. 377–404; J. W. James (ed.), *Rhigyfarch's Life;* Wade-Evans, (ed.), *Life of St David.*

[5] D. S. Evans (ed.), *Welsh Life*, p. 54.

[6] Heather James's paper 'The cult of St David in the Middle Ages' is an invaluable assessment of the surviving archaeological and documentary evidence relating to the cult of David in the area of the St Davids peninsula within the context of the cult at its stage of fullest development, and she rightly suggests that 'the persistence, the preservation and the development of earlier sites in the high Middle Ages in the St David's area must have been partly created by, and in response to, the demands of pilgrims' (p. 6). She follows J. W. James in suggesting that Giraldus may have been involved in this process.

[7] Wade-Evans (ed.), *Life of St David*, pp. 80–3; J. W. James, (ed.), *Rhigyfarch's Life*, p.8.

[8] I owe this information and what follows to the kindness of Michael J. Curley of the University of Puget Sound who sent me his manuscript draft of an edition of the miracles of St David in advance of publication. See also Worcestre, *Itineraries*.

[9] B. Willis, *St David's*, p. 545. Attention has been drawn to the various chapels and wells in the St Davids landscape and their links to pilgrimage by many commentators, among them, in chronological order: B. Willis, *St David's*, pp. 3–73; Yardley, *Menevia Sacra*, pp. 1–11; Fenton, *Pembrokeshire*, pp. 23–74; W. B. Jones and Freeman, *St David's*, pp. 11–47; H. Evans, *Tŵr y Felin Guide*, pp. 24–66, Middleton, *Streets of St Davids*, pp. 36–7; N. Rees, *Dewisland, passim*. Folklore also survives about the various names and associations, some of which, however, can be seen to derive from the early modern written sources.

[10] T. Wright (ed.), *Three Chapters of Letters*, p. 208.

[11] Parry (ed.), *Gwaith Dafydd ap Gwilym*, p. 269.

[12] Edudful ferch Gadwgan to whom Lewys Glyn Cothi (c. 1420–89) sang after her return from pilgrimage to Mynyw, Johnston (ed.), *Gwaith Lewys Glyn Cothi*, p. 371.

[13] Mallt ferch Hywel Selau, the subject of an elegy by Tudur Penllyn (c. 1420–85), T. Roberts (ed.), *Gwaith Tudur Penllyn*, p. 33.

[14] Foster Evans (ed.), *Gwaith Hywel Swrdwal*, p. 86, l. 63. See also G. H. Jones, *Celtic Britain*, p. 370; W. B. Jones and Freeman, *St David's*, p. 121; Yardley, *Menevia Sacra*, p. 56.

[15] D. S. Evans (ed.), *Welsh Life*, p. xii for the date of 588; and J. ab I. Williams (ed.), *Annales Cambriae*, p. 6, for the date of 601.

[16] J. W. James (ed.), *Rhigyfarch's Life*, p. 8. A century later, one church in this list, namely Glastonbury, was claiming that it was in possession of the body of David, Cowley, 'A note', pp. 47–8.

[17] I discuss Bernard and his episcopate in my forthcoming 'From Bernard to Bec' in *Pembrokeshire County History*, vol. 2. See also Gerald of Wales, *Opera*, vol. 3, pp. 153–4, for Giraldus' view of Bernard and his reform of the chapter; and for an overview of Bernard's episcopate see J. C. Davies (ed.), *Episcopal Acts*, vol. 1, pp. 238–70.

[18] Bevan, *St David's*, p. 62; Haddan and Stubbs, *Councils*, vol. 1, p. 316, are typical of a former generation of scholars who believed that David had been canonized by Pope Calixtus II.

[19] Cowley's excellent 'A note' (see n. 16 above), sums up the documentary evidence in this matter.

[20] See below the discussion of the cathedral building and my 'From Bernard to Bec'.

[21] Gerald of Wales, *The Journey through Wales*, p. 79.

[22] Owen (ed.), 'Canu i Ddewi', pp. 435–78, ll. 56–7. See also Nerys Ann Jones and Morfydd E. Owen, below, for a detailed discussion of this poem. Since it offers significant clues as to the development of the cult of David, I intend examining it more closely elsewhere. The date of the poem is related to the identification of 'Rhys Mawr Môn Wledig, reodig teg' (Great Rhys, lord of Anglesey, of the splendid gift) (l. 153) as the Lord Rhys ap Gruffudd (d.1197) at a time when he could be hailed as a political force in Wales outside his own power base of Deheubarth.

[23] J. W. James (ed.), *Rhigyfarch's Life*, p. 21; Wade-Evans (ed.), *Life of St David*, pp. 82–3; Owen (ed.), 'Canu i Ddewi', p. 452, l. 182.

[24] Ibid., p. 450, ll. 55–6; p. 452, l. 182; p. 453, ll. 186 and 187. One of the carved stones at Llanddewibrefi is still known as *bagl Dewi* (David's staff); this may preserve a folk memory of the former presence of the real relic there, ibid., p. 473.

[25] Llangyfelach was clearly the mother church of Gower, with an enormous parish extending up to and at one time including Betws (Ammanford) in Carmarthenshire, a *clas* place-name and, according to Giraldus Cambrensis, *Speculum Duorum*, pp. 262–3, virtually the second episcopal church of the bishop of St Davids. There is, however, another factor to take into account, for this is an example of a major church also being claimed for a major saint other than David, i.e. Teilo, as *Liber Landavensis* reveals. Indeed, one wonders whether the deposition of the altar there was also recent and a means of asserting the ownership of Llangyfelach by David and the bishop of Menevia, as part of the process of establishing the boundaries of the diocese, rather than of disseminating the cult of its patron saint.

[26] There is a marginal note in a later hand in the C text of the *Annales Cambriae* (London, BL MS Cotton Domitian Aiii, *sub anno* 1082) stating that Rhys ap Tewdwr gave the whole of the cantref of Pebydiog to St Davids; J. ab I. Williams (ed.), *Annales Cambriae*, p. 28.

[27] It was in 1163, only a few years before Gwynfardd composed the poem to David, that both Henry ab Arthen (ab Sulien) and his cousin Cedifor ap Daniel (ab Sulien) died, the latter as archdeacon of Cardigan. It may be significant that it was at many of the mother churches which characterized the pre-Norman polity of the Welsh Church that the archdeacons of the new order were based, e.g. at Symeon at Clynnog Fawr, D. S. Evans (ed.), *Historia Gruffudd*, p. 107, T. Jones (ed.), *Brut Pen 20 Trans.*, p. 58, reading Clynnog for Cyfeiliog; or Daniel (ab Sulien) (very possibly at Meifod) in Powys, ibid., p. 50; and Lifris son of Bishop Herwald at Llancarfan, J. G. Evans and Rhys (eds), *The Text*, pp. 274–5.

[28] Owen (ed.), 'Canu i Ddewi', pp. 442–3, ll. 63–80; T. Jones (ed.), *Brut Pen 20 Trans.*, p. 30, speaks of the priests of Llanddewibrefi in 1109 where there was a *buddugoliaeth* (privilege), and a *nawdd* (refuge) of David. See also the discussion on the poem provided by Nerys Ann Jones and Morfydd E. Owen, below.

[29] The version of the incident of 1109 noted in n. 22 in T. Jones (ed.), *Brenhinedd y Saesson*, p. 108, speaks of the violation of several churches at Llanddewibrefi. The *allorau* in Gwynfardd's poem, may thus be a synecdoche standing for 'churches'. Cf. the charters appended to the Life of Cadog, *VSBG*, p. 127, chapter 55: 'abbot of the altar of St Cadog'.

[30] Owen (ed.), 'Canu i Ddewi', p. 443.

[31] Indeed, it could be argued that the depredations of Hyfaidd, king of Dyfed, were against a *monasterium* outside his kingdom. I. Williams (ed.), *Armes Prydein o Lyfr Taliesin*, p. 5; W. H. Stevenson (ed.), *Asser's Life of Alfred*, pp. 67–8.

[32] T. M. Charles-Edwards, 'The seven bishop-houses', pp. 247–63.

[33] N. A. Jones, 'The Mynydd Carn prophecy', p. 78.

[34] D. S. Evans (ed.), *Historia Gruffud*, pp. 13–14. Bishop Nicholas Robinson had spotted the distinction between the two bodies, when he translated this line as 'ac chorus universus Sancti davidis, clerique omnes ecclesiae Menevensis' (and the whole body of St David and the clerics of the church of Menevia). See R. Williams (ed.), 'The Life of Griffith ap Cynan', p. 45.

[35] Barrow, *The Kingdom of the Scots*, pp. 213–30 *passim*. The St Andrews example reminds us of the capacity for survival and adaptation of pre-Norman ecclesiastical communities and the separate buildings used by them.

[36] D. S. Evans (ed.), *Welsh Life*, p. 9. The very full note on pp. 55 and 56 is a valuable survey of the evidence.

[37] *LBS*, vol. 2, pp. 75–8; Horstmann (ed.), *Nova Legenda Anglie*, vol. 1, pp. 167–73; Wade-Evans (ed.), *Life of St David*, p. 114. Caradog was ordained to the priesthood at Menevia and set up a community on the Pembrokeshire Barry Island. He died in 1124 and was buried in St Davids Cathedral – in the predecessor of the present building.

[38] T. Jones (ed), *Brut Pen 20 Trans.*, p. 18; J. ab I. Williams (ed.), *Annales Cambriae, sub anno* 1088, p. 28.

[39] Bonner, Rollason and Stancliffe (eds), *St Cuthbert*, pp. 367–467. It has to be pointed out that in the pre-Norman Welsh church it seems that it was not the corporeal relics that were venerated, rather the equipment that the saint had used, such as his bell, altar staff and book.

[40] C. Thomas, *Mute Stones*, pp. 51–112.

[41] J. W. James (ed.), *Rhigyfarch's Life*, pp. 12–14.

[42] To whom there is dedicated not only the small chapel on the cliffs at Porth Stinan, but also the remains of a chapel on Ramsey Island and a church at Llanstinan between Mathri and Fishguard.

[43] T. Wright (ed.), *Three Chapters of Letters*, p. 184.

[44] For details of the destruction of the shrine see my 'The Reformation and St Davids Cathedral'.

[45] Personal communication.

[46] Raw data in the possession of the author. There will be full publication following the symposium on St David held at the University of Wales, Lampeter, and St Davids in June 2002.

[47] J. ab I. Williams (ed), *Annales Cambriae, sub anno* 1274, p. 104.

[48] Ibid., *sub anno* 1088, p. 29

[49] Ibid., p. 39.

[50] See the plan and elevation of the cathedral by Taylor Scott in *The Builder* 63; Lovegrove, 'St David's Cathedral', pp. 360–82; and my own acquaintance with the building.

[51] I have never come across such a privilege, or evidence that Pope Calixtus II canonized David. The document quoted by Haddan and Stubbs, *Councils*, vol. 1, p. 316, specifies nothing of the sort. On the other hand, Baring-Gould and Fisher, *LBS*, vol. 2, p. 315, quoting the Peterborough Chronicle, clearly imply that it was Pope Calixtus II who made the concession of two journeys to St Davids. The same authors state that the Latin couplet is reported to have been discovered by Archbishop Pecham when he came to St Davids in 1284. But, writing in the twelfth century, William of Malmesbury, *Gesta*, p. 778 states clearly that Pope Calixtus himself encouraged English pilgrims to go to St Davids twice and guaranteed them the privilege of the same blessing as going to Rome once.

[52] To my knowledge no detailed description, drawing or photograph exists of the western opening behind the high altar. For much of the past three centuries it was obscured first of all by wooden panelling, and then by textile hangings. There is one intriguing point revealed by the recent digitized resurvey of the cathedral: the tomb of Edmund Tudor, relocated in the presbytery of the cathedral from the dissolved house of the Greyfriars at Carmarthen, is aligned with the niche and not with the central lancet.

[53] Lovegrove, 'St David's Cathedral', p. 377.

[54] Nilson, *Cathedral Shrines*, pp. 62–91.

[55] H. Evans, *Tŵr y Felin Guide*, p. 91 states: 'This was the actual doorway by which pilgrims came to the Shrine of St David.'

[56] At which Edward I came to say his prayers with Queen Eleanor in 1284 and made an offering and perhaps obtained the arm of St David that was in his possession at his death. The whole question as to the original position of the 1275 shrine is complicated by the fact that, as it now stands, it has clearly been subject to insensitive reconstruction. Further, it formed part of the blocking of the presbytery arches following the unroofing of the quire aisles by Parliamentary soldiers in 1648.

[57] Willis-Bund, *An Extent*, p. 37.
[58] See the plan and elevation of the cathedral by Taylor Scott, 'Plan and elevation'.
[59] Lovegrove, 'St David's Cathedral', p. 363, suggests that only the choir of Bernard's church 'was preserved for use while the newer building was in progress'.
[60] A recent borehole in connection with the cloisters scheme revealed that near the north door of the nave there were thirty feet of gravel and water beneath the building.
[61] Gerald of Wales, *Opera*, vol. 1, pp. 162–3.
[62] For the well outside the east end of the cathedral which was blocked by Sir Gilbert Scott in 1866 see Wade-Evans (ed.), *Life of St David*, pp. 67, 100. For the wellchapel at Porth Clais, the spot traditionally pointed out as that of David's baptism, see ibid., p. 77.

2
Welsh hagiography and the nationalist impulse

><

ELISSA R. HENKEN

. . . ac a blannawd [Beuno] vessen yn ystlys bed y dat, a honno a dyfawd yno yn derwen diruawr y huchet ae frasset. Ac ar vric y prenn hwnnw ef a wrthtyfawd keing hyt y llawr, ac or llawr dracheuen yn ogyuuch a bric y prenn, a thrigyaw elin yr geing ar y llawr. Ac velle y mae yn wastat. Ac od a Seis yrwng yr elin honno a bon y prenn, yn diannot y byd marw. Ac os Kymro a a yno, ny henuyd gwaeth.[1]

([St Beuno] planted an acorn in the side of his father's grave. And that grew there into an oak enormous in height and girth. And on the top of that tree a branch counter-grew to the ground, and from the ground back as high as the top of the tree. And the bend of the branch stayed on the ground. And thus it is still. And if an Englishman goes between that bend and the trunk of the tree, he will die without delay. And if a Welshman goes there, he will be none the worse.)

This former famous Welsh rugby player dies and approaches the golden gates of heaven. He was very worried because he had been a rather dirty player. But the angel lets him right in. 'Oh! Thank you, St Peter,' the Welshman remarks. 'St Peter?' replies the angel; 'he's on holiday. I'm on duty today.' 'Well, who are you?' And the angel answers: 'St David.'[2]

Here are a fourteenth-century saint's Life and a twentieth-century joke – two different genres separated by six centuries – but in each the saint takes care of his own, the Welsh.

The Welsh saints, those fifth- and sixth-century men and women whose lives as hermits, ascetic clerics, missionaries, or founders of religious centres, caused them to be termed *sant*, that is *sanctus* or saint, were generally local heroes whose cults did not extend far beyond their own immediate territories. Many of them have remained thus, surviving even the Protestant Reformation and Methodist revival, so that in their own territories their names are remembered and people can point to a stone or a field and relate its association with the saint. But some expanded their influence from local to regional and even national levels, playing a role in the politics of both Church and State.

The traditions that grew up around the Welsh saints have been recorded in a variety of forms, ranging from prose *vitae* and medieval verse to antiquarians' reports and modern field collections. According to traditions recorded in these various places, the saints took on all the attributes of kingship and were perceived as guardians of the land, of their own particular territories. Like other rulers, they bear responsibility for the total welfare of the land and people, for ensuring fertility, justice, peace and security. Lines written to Llawddog (Lleuddad) clearly state the connection between the saint and the fruitfulness of the land:

> Y wlad, ei choed, a'i hadyd,
> Llawddog oll a'u llwyddo i gyd.
> Llawddog a roddo llwyddiant
> ar ei blwyf a'i wŷr a'i blant,
> ar bob og ac ar bob iau
> ac ar erydr gororau,
> ar bob rhych ac ar bob bryn,
> ar bob grwn, ar bob gronyn.
> Llawddog yw un allwydd gwâr,
> allwydd yw i'r holl ddaear;
> Llawddog, bûm well o'i addef,
> Lle'dd awn oll, yw allwydd nef.[3]

(The land, its trees, and its seed-corn,/ may Llawddog make all succeed./ May Llawddog grant success/ to his people, his men and his children,/ on every harrow and every yoke,/ and on the ploughs of the lands,/ on every furrow and every hill,/ on every ridge and every seed./ Llawddog is a single key of cultivation [civilization],/ he is a key to all the earth;/ Llawddog, I was better from confessing him,/ wherever we all go, is the key to heaven.)

Reclaiming land from swamp and sea and providing good weather for the crops, the saints ensure a fruitful land and, in times of famine, provide new supplies, as when Illtud instantly transports three barns full of grain, or when Brigit creates a new type of fish, the *brwyniad* or sparling, out of rushes.[4] Using techniques from the wondrous to the mundane, saints make fountains flow with milk or wine, and they arrange with the local king for fishing rights.[5] The saints defend the law, using their crosiers and bells to take oaths and test for perjury, to obtain sanctuary rights, winning them from kings who have been forced to recognize the saint's superiority, and generally to provide a good, stable land for the local inhabitants. In *Vita Sancti Cadoci*, King Maelgwn tells his son that he will be able to recognize the saint's territory because there the animals graze freely and the people are open and trusting.[6]

In times of danger, the people could turn to the saint for protection. According to his *vita*, Gwynllyw brought a whole army of Anglo-Norman invaders to their knees and sent them chastened home.[7] In the twelfth century, the poet Llywelyn Fardd related the security of Cadfan's church and lands at Tywyn:

> Ni chollir o'i thir nac o'i thewdor – annedd
>   Troedfedd er dyhedd, dihawdd hepgor.
> Ni llefais neb drais dros ei hysgor,
> Ni chymwyll neb dwyll dyllu ei dôr.[8]

(Not a foot of its lands nor of its stout dwelling is lost because of war. Not easy to be without it. No one dares violence over its defences. No one, by deceit, even considers piercing its door.)

But Cadfan is not only a defender of his territory; he also defends the defenders. One line names him 'Cadfan, cedwyr nodded' (Cadfan, protection of warriors) and another states, 'Cedwis gŵr arwr arwymp drefred' (He protected the warrior, hero of a fair territory). The poet asserts that the purpose of his poem is to praise Cadfan: 'Molawd a ddyrllydd cedwidydd cad' (The guardian of the army merits praise).[9] In the same period, Cynddelw refers to Tysilio as:

> Post Powys, perging cedernyd,
> Pobl argledr, arglwyd diergryd.[10]

(Pillar of Powys, lord of defence,/ defender of the people, fearless lord.)

It is this identity, defender of the people, which predominates as the definition of 'the people' expands.

The saints are not just defenders of their territories; they are also identified with the land itself, and the traditions relate how a saint finds his proper territory. With Beuno, the search for the correct spot almost forms the theme of the saint's Life. He starts out near the Severn, but one day as he is out walking and examining his crops, he hears from the other side of the river an Englishman urging on his hunting dogs in his own language, calling 'Kergia, Kergia' (Charge, Charge). Beuno immediately returns to his disciples, tells them to gather their things, and says that they must leave the place because 'Kenedyl y gwr angkyuyeith a gigleu vi y lef tu draw yr auon yn annoc y gwn a oresgynnant y lle hwnn ac a vyd eidunt'[11] (the race of the foreigner whose voice he heard will overrun the place and they will possess it). Given the ongoing struggles of the Welsh language in the twentieth and twenty-first centuries, his recognizing through language the danger of alien intrusion seems particularly prescient. In any case, this begins a series of moves. In each place he is granted land by either a grateful or a chastened (that is, terrified) king, but there is also always some problem, such as the king's sons' improper demand for food. In one spot, he has already started building when he learns that the land is actually the patrimony of an infant and that the king had no right to give it away. The king is duly cursed and Beuno is given other lands.[12] And eventually, having crossed the whole of north Wales, he does settle at Clynnog Fawr on the north-west coast.

Not all saints have to search so hard; often the site for settlement is indicated by an animal, such as the horse which carried Tatheus until it reached the proper site and stopped with its feet fixed to the ground and bound by a golden fetter, or the dove that carried off the shavings whittled from Carannog's crosier until the saint finally followed the bird, understanding he was meant to build in the new spot.[13] Bearing a traditional mark of the Celtic otherworld, the animals are often white. Brynach and Dyfrig are each shown where to build by a white sow with her litter, Cadog by a white boar, and Gwynllyw by a white ox with a black spot on its forehead.[14] Sometimes the directions come precisely through an angelic voice, or the building materials mysteriously move at night from the wrong site to the approved one, a motif especially common in nineteenth- and twentieth-century legendry.[15]

These stories are not just aetiologies, telling how a certain church ended up in a particular spot. Because of the divine nature of the grant they also become important political statements in the assertion of a church's rights. And politics was very important in the composition of the saints' Lives.

Although traditions about the Welsh saints had long existed, they were not compiled into *vitae* until the end of the eleventh century when necessitated by changing religious and political circumstances and Anglo-

Norman influence. During the centuries of contact and conflict with the Anglo-Saxons, the Welsh Church had remained essentially undisturbed, but the Normans threatened great upheaval. The old system of the *clasau* – the Welsh monastic communities and traditional centres of learning, such as St Davids and Llanbadarn – was to be redefined and replaced by newly created dioceses and Latin monastic orders, given precise territorial boundaries, standardized into the continental pattern of ecclesiastical government, and the whole brought under Canterbury and Rome.[16] Due to this restructuring in the twelfth century, both Welsh and Anglo-Norman clerics turned to *vitae* to establish their place in the hierarchy. Welsh clerics composed *vitae* defending the honour and rights of their own saints and supporting claims of the Welsh Church against the imposition of Canterbury's authority. Anglo-Norman clerics, interested in the traditions of their newly acquired territories, used what they had learned about the local saints and composed *vitae* to assert their churches' ecclesiastical rights. Churches established their rights through the rights of their patron saints, using the *vitae* as evidence that their particular saint had been granted land and privileges by kings and had proved worthier than other saints. Through manipulation of the traditions, the clerics competed with the supporters of other saints, vying for recognition by secular authorities and by the pope of their superiority over other churches in Wales.

The most striking example of this political use of the *vitae* is provided by the *Liber Landavensis*, written around 1130, through which the Norman-created diocese of Llandaf, under the direction of Bishop Urban, sought to establish itself as the archiepiscopal seat of Wales. It claimed to itself Sts Dyfrig, Teilo and Oudoceus and presented their *vitae* along with supporting documents – most particularly land grants, each with a history of how the saint had acquired a particular set of privileges and each representing economic and political as well as ecclesiastical power. Oudoceus, an extreme example of the manipulation of tradition, is largely, or possibly even entirely, an invention of Llandaf but he, too, through his *vita*, provides verification and documentation of the church's claims. In general in the *vitae*, no matter where they were compiled, conflict between the saint and secular ruler, whatever the point of contention, ends in the saint being granted sanctuary rights and exemption from royal exaction or taxation. A church's political needs, however, can sometimes make the saint do odd things, such as when the scribe at the Norman-run Llantwit Major reports that the local saint, Illtud, helped protect the Anglo-Normans from an attack by the Welsh, making Illtud a truly confused Welsh saint.[17]

The saints, protectors of the land and supporters of land claims, are by nature intercessors, and they may be called on to intercede at either the personal or the national level in whatever way the supplicant needs – whether healing loved ones or confounding enemies, whether Dwynwen intervening on Dafydd ap Gwilym's behalf[18] or Gildas arranging for the return of Gwenhwyfar to Arthur after she has been kidnapped by King Melwas.[19] In the fifteenth century, poets called on the saints for intercession at various levels: for themselves individually, as Ieuan Llwyd Brydydd did when going to seek relief for an eye injury at St Doged's well;[20] for others, as Dafydd Nanmor did when he called on St Mwrog to protect Henry Tudor (which, given Henry's role as a potential redeemer-hero, was also asking for help for the nation);[21] or directly for the nation as a whole, as Lewys Glyn Cothi did when he ended a *cywydd* in which he had named a great many saints with the wish:

> Bid i'r saint bob dri a saith
> reoli Cymry eilweith;
> bid gobaith Cymry weithion
> yn y saint or ynys hon.[22]

(May these saints, each three and seven,/ rule Wales again;/ may the hope of Wales now rest/ in the saints of this island.)

People sometimes used *loricae* or religious charms to invoke one or more saints for protection. One particularly intriguing *lorica* dates back to at least the sixteenth century; it calls on two Welsh saints, Beuno and Curig, on one Irish saint, Patrick, on Jesus and on 'Owain, chief banner of a host'.

> Pan godwy'r boreu yn gynta,
> Yn nawdh Beino yn benna;
> Yn nawdd Kerrig, nawdd Patrig,
> Yn nawdd Gwr gwyn Bendigedig;
> Yn nawdd Owain ben lluman llu,
> Ag yn nessa yn Nawdd Iesu.[23]

(When I rise first in the morning,/ under the protection of Beuno chiefly;/ under the protection of Curig, protection of Patrick,/ under the protection of the holy blessed man;/ under the protection of Owain, chief banner of a host,/ and then [next] under the protection of Jesus.)

Whoever Owain might be (and elsewhere I argue that he may be the national redeemer-hero Owain Glyndŵr),[24] he is certainly a secular not a religious figure, and that in itself suggests the overlapping of roles of secular and religious heroes.

One saint stands out above all others as the protector and hope of the nation – David, or Dewi, patron saint of Wales. David's traditions follow the same patterns as those for the other saints, but he is given preeminence. Like the other Welsh saints, David is assigned his special territory by divine intervention, though the link between David and Vallis Rosina/Glyn Rhosyn or Mynyw, the eventual St Davids in south-west Wales,[25] is made especially strong through a set of traditions centring on the saint's birth, which is announced thirty years in advance.[26] First, David's father Sant is sent hunting by an angel and told to take his three finds, a stag, a salmon and a swarm of bees – the land, water and air representatives of the whole of nature – to 'the Monastery of the Deposit' (*Depositi Monasterium*) to be held for David. In the Welsh Life, making the point even clearer, the angel goes on to say, 'Dyro dylyet y tir y gadw y vab ny anet etwo'[27] (Give the right of the land to be kept for the boy who is not yet born). Next, Patrick, who is considering settling in Glyn Rhosyn, is sent away by an angel who tells him that he must leave it for a boy who will be born in thirty years. Then a preacher, sometimes named as Gildas, is unable to preach in the presence of Non while she is pregnant with David and finally realizes that he must leave Britain to the child and go to another island. And last, a king learns from prophecies that a boy will be born whose power will extend over the whole realm and, therefore, watches the prophesied birthplace in order to slay the infant.[28] These last two motifs, the preacher relinquishing the island to the boy and the prophecy of the boy's power extending over the whole realm, show David's power extending well beyond Mynyw, as does one more incident. The only time David comes into conflict with a secular power is when, upon arriving at Hoddnant where he intends to settle, he lights a fire. The smoke of that fire encircles the whole island and much of Ireland throughout the day. Boia, the local prince, realizes that the authority of the man who lit the fire will extend throughout the same area as the smoke, and so he sets out to destroy David.[29] David's action, recognizably the practice of taking possession of the land by lighting a fire, that is, establishing a hearth, makes as clear a statement to the audience as to Boia.[30]

That all of these traditions linking David and the land served well the political needs of St Davids, as it competed with Llandaf and other houses for primacy in Wales, does not make the traditional associations any less genuine. After all, David was, like the other saints, responsible for peace and prosperity in his lands. The twelfth-century poet Gwynfardd Brycheiniog says of David:

> Mab Sant syw gormant, gormes haint – ni ad
> Na lledrad yn rhad, rhwyd ysgeraint,
> Ysid rhad yn ei wlad a mad a maint
> Yng nghyfoeth Dewi difefl geraint,
> A rhydid heb ofud, heb ofyn amgen,
> Heb ofal cynnen cylch ei bennaint.[31]

(Wise, excellent son of Sant, does not permit oppression by pestilence nor theft unpunished, snare of enemies. There is grace in his territory, good fortune and plenitude. In the realm of David of irreproachable kinsmen, a freedom without grief, without asking anything different, without the worry of conflict around the heads of the valleys.)

However, David's territory had grown beyond Mynyw, and he was perceived as a defender of the land even before eleventh-century Norman incursions on his territory. We have very little early information on David – just a few odd references to him in Irish, Breton and English sources: the ninth-century *Martyrology of Tallaght* and *Martyrology of Oengus the Culdee* give David's feast-day, and the ninth- or tenth-century *Catalogue of the Saints of Ireland* lists him as one of the 'holy men of Britain'; the Breton *Life of St Paul of Léon* (*c*.884) names him as a fellow student of Paul, Samson and Gildas; Asser's *Life of King Alfred the Great* (*c*.893) mentions him as a powerful saint. The first clear Welsh statement we have about him shows him already established as a defender of the Welsh nation by the time the tenth-century vaticinatory poem *Armes Prydein* was written. Whether one accepts Ifor Williams's view that the poet was probably a south Wales monk, possibly from St Davids itself, who around 930 used the poem to protest against the expansion of Wessex and King Æthelstan's power and to reject the diplomatic peace created by his own king, Hywel Dda, or, along with David Dumville, one locates the poem later, *c*.935 x *c*.980, and sees it as taking inspiration from specific attempts by anti-English coalitions, the poet uses the national mythology of prophesied redeemers and places David squarely in their midst.[32] The poet calls on the Welsh and all their prophesied allies from Ireland, Scotland, Cornwall and Brittany along with the Scandinavians of Dublin to rise against the English and drive them from the land. He calls on the redeemer-heroes Cynan and Cadwaladr to come for this one final, chaotic, bloody battle in which they will rid themselves of the English forever. He also calls on David. Not only do the Welsh commend themselves to God and David; they look to David as an active saviour, in such lines as 'trwy eiryawl Dewi a seint Prydeyn/ . . . ffohawr allmyn' (Through the intercession of David and the saints of Britain/ the foreigners will be put to flight)³³ and the declaration that '[Kymry] a lluman glan Dewi a drychafant' ([The Welsh] will raise on high the holy standard of David).³⁴ Moreover, the poet prays 'poet tywyssawc Dewi yr kynifwyr' (May David be the leader of our warriors).³⁵ Although the poet's south Wales connection undoubtedly influenced his choice of saints, the certainty with which he calls on David to perform this national task suggests that even in this period David had already become identified with the entire land. In *Armes Prydein*, with seeming metonymy, the poet says men will demand of the Saxons, 'Neu vreint an seint pyr y saghyssant./ neu reitheu Dewi pyr y torrassant' (Why have they trampled upon the privileges of our saints?/ Why have they destroyed the rights of David?).³⁶

The protection of David's rights and thus those of St Davids and, by extension, Welsh national rights became a major concern of the late eleventh and twelfth centuries. Rhigyfarch's composition of the first known *vita* for David apparently served a political function in addition to its religious one. Rhigyfarch may have written it in 1081, as Nora Chadwick suggests, in part to support the policy of Sulien (Rhigyfarch's father and bishop of St Davids) in encouraging a pact between the Welsh princes, or possibly to show to William the Conqueror at the time of his pilgrimage to St Davids, urging William to recognize the position of St Davids and protect the Welsh Church from encroachment by Canterbury. Another possibility, suggested by A. W. Wade-Evans and J. W. James, is that Rhigyfarch wrote it *c*. 1090–5 to protest against interference by an already encroached Canterbury. The *vita* may also have been written in response to a first, now lost, text of Lifris' *vita* for Cadog, David's main rival in south Wales.³⁷ Whichever of these possibilities may be correct, the *vita* documents St Davids as a place of power and influence in Wales, as was due its saint.

Whenever and however its composition was inspired, the *vita* became an effective part of the struggle both for an independent Welsh Church and for the primacy of St Davids. In addition to relating David's wondrous deeds, his demonstrations of piety and learning, it establishes him as chief saint of the island and twice shows his elevation to archbishop. The first time is when David, Teilo, and Padarn go on pilgrimage to Jerusalem, where the patriarch consecrates David as archbishop.³⁸ The second time is when the clergy decide to hold a synod to determine who will be chief among them; whoever preaches most clearly and audibly will be their leader and be made archbishop.³⁹ The Synod was attended by a great many. The Latin texts state that there were 118 bishops; the Welsh text is more expansive as well as anachronistic:

A'r escyb, a'r athrawon, a'r offeireit, a'r brenhined, a'r tywyssogyonn, a'r ieirll, a'r barwneit, a'r goreugwyr, a'r ysgwiereit, a'r kreuydwyr yn llwyr, a phawb heb allu rif arnadunt a ymgynnullassant y sened Vreui.⁴⁰

(And the bishops, and the clerics, and the priests, and the kings, and the princes, and the earls, and the barons, and the noblemen, and the squires, and the entire clergy, and everybody, innumerable, assembled for the Synod of Brefi.)

With such witnesses, there can be no doubt of the authority of actions taken there. The candidates take turns preaching but none can make himself heard. The assembly then realizes that David is not present and sends for him, but he refuses to attend. They send again, and again he refuses. Finally Dyfrig and Deiniol go to invite him and fast until he agrees to attend. As David preaches, the ground rises under him, forming the hill on which now stands the church of Llanddewibrefi, and he can be heard clearly by all, even at great distances. David is made archbishop and his monastery becomes the metropolitan see of the whole country. This scene, in which the land itself proclaims David's right to it, is the one episode informants were always able to tell me during my fieldwork in Wales, no matter how little else they knew about David or any other saint. The legend still has a special resonance, which also ensures that it is taught in the schools and is the most common scene in children's St David's Day pageants.

This twofold declaration of David's archiepiscopacy is certainly an important statement in asserting the claims of the Welsh Church, but it also reflects the competition among the churches within Wales. For example, while David's *vita* omits all mention of St Cadog, Cadog's *vita* explains why *he* did not prevail at the synod. It reports that Cadog was on pilgrimage to Jerusalem at the time of the synod, that David protested that the absent Cadog would be more worthy than he, and that only at the insistence of an angel did Cadog forgive David for holding the synod without him.⁴¹ Hywel Emanuel has argued that the Synod was not originally part of Cadog's *vita* but was added in a later recension in response to David's *vita* by a cleric anxious to uphold the honour of his saint.⁴²

In the same episode, David's *vita* manages also to deal with two other rivals. The two saints sent to fetch him are Dyfrig, representative of the Norman-created diocese of Llandaf, and Deiniol, representative of the most important northern house, Bangor. The pilgrimage to Jerusalem, during which David alone is advanced to the archiepiscopate, similarly established the subordinate roles of his two companions and potential rivals – Teilo and Padarn – each with his own important centre – Llandeilo Fawr and Llanbadarn Fawr.

The churches were fighting for an independent Welsh Church and for primacy over each other, and the *vitae* were part of their weaponry. Llandaf emphasized its claim to Dyfrig and his successor Teilo. St Davids responded by asserting that Dyfrig had passed the archiepiscopal mantle to David and thus to his establishment, St Davids. In a letter presumably sent to Rome *c*. 1125–30 and recorded by Gerald of Wales, St Davids claimed that it had been a metropolitan see since the beginnings of Christianity in Britain, and that David had held the archbishopric since his consecration by St Dyfrig and proclamation by the synod.[43] Geoffrey of Monmouth joined the discussion in his *Historia Regum Britanniae*, *c*.1136, when he reported Dyfrig's resignation as archbishop and the consecration of King Arthur's uncle, David, in his place.[44] Although Geoffrey located the archiepiscopacy in Caerleon, his own addition to the tradition, he did not totally undermine the importance of Mynyw where, he stated, David died 'inside his own abbey, which he loved more than all the other monasteries of his diocese'.[45] Geoffrey's authority revalidated St David's claim on the archiepiscopacy.

A twelfth-century triad listing the Three Tribal Thrones of the Island of Britain as Wales, Cornwall and the North, that is, Scotland (note that in this case London is not at the hierarchical head of a unified Britain), asserts that Arthur was sovereign in each of the three places, and that in Wales, in what Rachel Bromwich argues is a reflection of the archiepiscopal struggle, the throne was in Mynyw, that is St Davids, and David was Chief Bishop.[46] It is worth noting the alignment of David with Arthur, the foremost national redeemer-hero in the twelfth century. Connected by their professional activities and by that favoured Celtic kinship bond of nephew and uncle (though which is which keeps changing), the secular hero and religious hero valorize each other.

St Davids became central to the fight for an independent Welsh church. In the 1130s and 1140s, at a time when Rome was beginning to look favourably on each nation having an archbishop, Bernard, the first Norman bishop of St Davids, petitioned the pope for archiepiscopal status, using the argument that the Welsh were indeed a *natio*, with their own language, law and customs.[47] The pope rejected the plea on the grounds that Bernard had already sworn allegiance to the archbishop of Canterbury, which ended the matter for Bernard personally but did not end the fight for St Davids. The struggle was continued most notably by Gerald of Wales, who at the end of the twelfth century wrote his own

Life of David and made three trips to Rome to plead his case. Nor was this a matter simply of ecclesiastical concern. A Welsh Church independent of Canterbury was important to an autonomous Wales. On his third journey to Rome, Gerald carried letters of support from Llywelyn Fawr and some of the other Welsh princes who were striving to forge the separate principalities of Wales into one political entity.

Latin *vitae* of the Welsh saints were composed both in strongly Welsh houses and in more Normanized ones, but Welsh translations exist for only two Welsh saints.[48] Whether through serendipity or design, the two in question were the two most clearly recognized as reflecting Welsh identity and whose houses were recognized as continuations of old Welsh *clasau* – David at St Davids and Beuno at Clynnog Fawr. Both translations, *Buchedd Dewi* and *Buchedd Beuno*, were written into a manuscript dated 1346 by an anchorite at Llanddewibrefi. We can only guess at the complexities involved in audience response to Latin texts (alien in both language and genre) about Welsh saints already known in Welsh tradition, but the demand for *Welsh* texts, whether or not they were ever composed for Welsh saints other than David and Beuno, suggests something of fourteenth-century concerns. These Welsh texts were written at a time of deep despair and suffering for the Welsh, after the fall of Llywelyn II and the loss of independence and before even the temporary hope offered by the redeemer-heroes Owain Lawgoch and Owain Glyndŵr. As Glanmor Williams points out, the Welsh Lives are 'as much a part of a patriotic protest against the rapidly growing exploitation of the Welsh Church by the English State in the fourteenth century as Rhigyfarch's Latin text was against the Norman incursions in the eleventh century'.[49]

The fact that it is David and Beuno whose Lives are translated also indicates that, by the fourteenth century, David had become the primary saint in the south and Beuno in the north. Their reputations had grown beyond their own immediate territories, though maintaining a north/south divide. We know, for example, that while David's cult was more widespread than the cult of any other Welsh saint in the Middle Ages – he had over fifty churches dedicated to him and more than thirty wells – none of the dedications were in the north.[50] Related evidence is found in the previously mentioned *lorica*, which calls on Owain and a number of saints, including Beuno. The fact that the *lorica* was collected in the Bala area, in north Wales, may explain not only Beuno's presence but also David's absence from a list of such powerful figures. Perhaps David's reputation continued to grow because the principal contact and thus the principal conflict with the Anglo-Normans took place in south

Wales. Conflicts with Llandaf over territorial rights pulled St Davids and thus David directly into the centre of the fray, while Clynnog Fawr and St Beuno receded in the quieter edges of the north. Whereas St Davids was in conflict with the Anglo-Normans over both ecclesiastical and secular issues, Clynnog's conflicts were primarily secular. Clynnog was never meant to be a metropolitan see; it did not have to compete with Bangor for dominance in the north in the way that St Davids had to compete with Llandaf in the south. So, while Clynnog was less troubled by the need for fine political manoeuvring and could make strong nationalist statements – such as the claim that the oak tree would kill intruding Englishmen and the reference to the offensive language of the approaching hunter – St Davids was the one always drawing attention. David's ultimate position as the patron saint of Wales is all the more striking in that, for most of the medieval period, the northern kingdom of Gwynedd dominated the land.

The power of David's traditions gave St Davids its primacy and then the fight for the archiepiscopal status of St Davids in turn stressed and validated David's importance. By the fourteenth century there can have been no doubt of David's primacy in Wales. We can see the importance accorded him even in the medieval mathematics of pilgrimages: two journeys to St Davids equalled one to Rome, and three journeys equalled one to Jerusalem. By the late Middle Ages, the identification of David with Wales, first suggested in the vaticinatory *Armes Prydein*, was complete. It was reflected in the Sequence in the Proper of the mass for St David, where he was termed 'pugil britannorum dux et doctor walicorum'[51] (champion of the Britons, the leader and teacher of the Welsh) and it was reflected in lines of poetry such as 'awn j, n, [*sic*] gweddi, bawb at ddewi/ pen rhaith wyllys, yr holl ynys'[52] (Let us take our prayer, all to David,/ chief of our delight, of the whole island), or where Wales is referred to simply as 'tir Dewi'[53] (David's land). Like the other Welsh saints, he continued as an intercessor, and the poets called on him for help, but he also became a prophet in fifteenth- and sixteenth-century *cywyddau brud*, poems prophesying the fate of the nation. For example, after lines referring to Taliesin and Myrddin as prophets, the poet Dafydd Llwyd o Fathafarn says:

> Didwyll y mae'n dywedyd
> Proffwydoliaeth maith i'n mysg
> O waith Ddewi, ddoeth wiwddysg.[54]

(Sincerely he speaks/ a great prophecy in our midst/ of the work of David, of wise, splendid learning.)

Dafydd Llwyd also clearly acknowledges David's success as an intercessor for the nation:

> A'th weddïaw dithau Ddewi,
> . . . a wnaeth rydd-did inni.[55]

(And your praying, David, / . . . has made us free.)

David is not only called on by others; he himself can call on the appropriate secular heroes to aid the nation. As a religious hero as well as a representative of the nation, he forged an unbreakable link between State and Church. Owain Glyndŵr, who led the fight for Welsh independence at the beginning of the fifteenth century, recognized this link when he developed his threefold plan for the new state: establishment of a Welsh parliament, Welsh universities and an independent Welsh Church, with an archbishop at St Davids.

The religious and the secular are repeatedly brought together through David. For example, the 500th anniversary celebrations of Owain Glyndŵr, which for various reasons occurred in 1915 rather than in 1900, marking the end rather than the beginning of his war, all centred on St David's Day. One St David's Day pamphlet prepared for schoolchildren is dedicated to Glyndŵr. After establishing who St David was, it discusses what it means to be a patriotic Welshman and asserts the importance of Glyndŵr. The integration of secular and ecclesiastical patriotism, which was already evident when the saints' *vitae* were used to fight for a Welsh Church and against alien intrusion and also when Glyndŵr made an independent Welsh Church one of the cornerstones of his threefold plan, is fully accomplished when the pamphlet explains why it is important to celebrate St David's Day in the schools:

> Am y byddwn ni, fechgyn a genethod, yn fuan yn ddynion ac yn ferched, a rhaid i ni garu a gwasanaethu ein gwlad a throsglwyddo i eraill y traddodiadau a'r sefydliadau Cymreig sydd wedi dod i lawr hyd atom ni.
>
> (Because we, boys and girls, will soon be men and women, and will need to love and serve our land and transmit to others the Welsh traditions and institutions which have come down to us.)[56]

So strong was the link that David himself could be deemed both a secular and a religious icon, as changing circumstances required. David's feast-day on 1 March, combining religious and secular customs (church sermons and wearing of the leek), was celebrated with fervour at the end of the Middle Ages. Henry VII even provided funds for its celebration by the Welsh at court. With the Protestant Reformation, however, David and the other saints did not just fall from grace; they were pushed, at least until the Welsh Reformers, reassessing the pre-Anglo-Norman British Church, decided that it had been in essence a Protestant church free of the corruptions of Rome. They saw their Protestantism not as the acceptance of radical new ideas but as a return to a purer, more honourable past. The saints were further rehabilitated by the nineteenth-century Nonconformists who recognized and approved of their asceticism. This was especially true for David who, according to tradition, from the time of his conception partook (or allowed his mother to partake) of nothing but bread and water, and sometimes cress. As Glanmor Williams put it, the Nonconformists 'have often felt able to depict David as a simple, God-fearing Welshman, scornful of the pomp of the Establishment, and true to what they like to think of as the natural Welshness, fervour, and austerity expressed in Welsh Nonconformity'.[57] The saint epitomizes the national character.

In the mean time, the celebration of St David's Day, Gŵyl Dewi Sant, had become more secular in focus and had been taken up most particularly by the antiquarian and social organizations created by Welshmen, first in London and then in other English cities heavily populated by the Welsh, in societies such as the Honourable Society of Cymmrodorion and the Society of the Gwyneddigion. With cravings for anything that spoke of home and gave them identity in an alien land, the expatriates banded together to study and honour everything Welsh. St David's Day became a way to celebrate and proclaim their Welshness and, refined and refocused by distance, St David came to symbolize not just the nation but the essence of Welshness. These societies, inspired by romantic nationalism and reflecting the exile's yearning for the homeland, through their publishing efforts and through personal contacts, exported their scholarly findings and their sense of Welsh identity back to Wales and helped fuel the rise of Welsh nationalism in the nineteenth century. In the same period, when Welsh émigrés to the United States formed immigrant aid societies, they most often named them the Saint David Society. That is the name still most commonly used by Welsh Americans congregating to cherish their Welshness, and St David's Day, marked with the other common symbols of Wales – leeks, daffodils, dragons and harps – is the social highpoint of their year.

In Wales today, people gather on 1 March to honour their patron saint. Whether in the antiquarian society or local choir or rugby club, they schedule their major annual dinner or lecture for that time, and the speeches touch on some aspect of Wales – on its history or literature or music – as well as comment on the current state of Welshness. In a day more of national consciousness than religious devotion, people wear their national symbols – leeks or daffodils or green and white ribbons – or eat them in the form of *cawl* or leek soup, and even the Methodist chapels hold services to honour this overtly Catholic saint. The day is not a call to arms, but it is nationalistic in reaffirming the cultural and historical ties that bind the people in one nation, and a nation quite distinct from neighbouring England. The calls to action come on other days – 11 December, commemorating the fall in 1282 of Llywelyn y Llyw Olaf, the last English-recognized independent Welsh prince, or 16 September, celebrating Owain Glyndŵr's uprising against the English throne in 1400. The people who gather to hear those speeches are the activists, rabble-rousers according to some, but even the most timid can celebrate St David's Day and invoke his name. One can celebrate St David's Day and still vote against devolution. St David's Day reminds people of their Welshness without forcing anyone to define it, and in that way is a more genuinely national day than the nationalist days for Llywelyn and Glyndŵr.

Nonetheless, David owes the celebration of his feast-day at least in part to the same nationalistic fervour as that invoked by Llywelyn and Owain Glyndŵr. The same nationalist scholars who recalled Llywelyn and Glyndŵr from their historical neglect to put them into service as national icons also gave new impetus to David. At the turn of the twentieth century they instituted school lessons about him (in some cases, the first the children had heard of him) and made a point of celebrating his feast-day.

However, while the nationalists may have focused new attention on David, their actions do not account entirely for his current role. After all, despite nationalists encouraging people to replace the English celebration of St Valentine's Day with a celebration of St Dwynwen, patron of love who has the power to make a couple either love each other truly or be cured of their love, interest in her had only at the end of the twentieth century begun to spread beyond her own locale in Anglesey.

David has brought with him a strong traditional identity that provides ballast to the other heroes of Welsh nationalism. Llywelyn reminds the Welsh that they were once independent; Owain Glyndŵr reminds them that they can fight to regain that independence; David reminds them that they are Welsh. And without that sense of identity, there is no nation.

David has provided a safe repository for nationalist aspirations. The traditions about him have been strong enough and varied enough to be interpreted in whatever way people have required to fit their times and to support their own preferred sense of identity – a leader in ridding the land of Saxons, a pioneer of the Roman church whose own *llan* could claim precedence and vie with Canterbury, a representative of native spiritual independence from the period before the influences of the Roman Church, an ascetic following his own path, but always one who will help his people, whether individually or collectively. Presenting his own preferred image of David – as the ideal Welsh nationalist – Gwynfor Evans, retired Member of Parliament and for thirty-six years president of Plaid Cymru the Party of Wales, wrote: 'It is impossible to think of a more worthy patron saint for Wales than David. He is one of us, a Welshspeaking Welshman who worked amongst us and who suffered for us.'[58] The point here is that David suggests *living* one's Welshness, not just demonstrating it on special occasions. A favourite line that people remind each other of, especially on 1 March, is David's final admonition to his congregation:

> vrodyr a chwioryd, bydwch lawen a chedwch ych ffyd a'ch cret, a gwnewch y petheu bychein a glywyssawch ac a welsawch gennyf i.[59]

> (brothers and sisters, be joyful and hold fast to your faith and belief, and do the little things you heard and saw from me.)

'Do the little things'. As befits a hero who links the secular and religious worlds, there is almost no distinguishing whether people are thinking of this in terms of religious or of nationalist causes. One can demonstrate one's Welshness by following the saint's banner, by speaking his language, or by tending his bit of land.

These interpretations, however, belong to the past. As Wales changes its self-identity, can David change to meet the new needs, and if so, what new form will he take? Will 'Do the little things' be read as the perfect indictment of a powerless nation – a nation under siege, just holding tight – or will it be read as David's message of empowerment, his equivalent of 'Think globally, act locally' sent across the centuries? How will David, the ever-adapting icon of Welshness, next appear? Or will he?

Notes

[1] *VSBG*, p. 17.
[2] Gwyndaf, 'Welsh folk narrative', p. 93.
[3] Johnston (ed.), *Gwaith Lewys Glyn Cothi*, p. 29,11. 51–62.
[4] *VSBG*, pp. 226–8; H. L. Jones (ed.), *Gwaith Iorwerth Fynglwyd*, p. 94,11. 51–6.

[5] See Henken, *Welsh Saints*, pp. 74–9.
[6] *VSBG*, pp. 74–6.
[7] Ibid., p. 190.
[8] McKenna (ed.), 'Canu Cadfan', p. 18,11. 71–4.
[9] Ibid., p. 17,11. 8,10; p. 19,1. 93.
[10] N. A. Jones and Parry Owen (eds), *Gwaith Cynddelw*, vol. 1, p. 33,11. 193–4.
[11] *VSBG*, p. 17.
[12] Ibid., pp. 17–20.
[13] Ibid., pp. 148, 276–8; see also Henken, *Welsh Saints*, p. 88.
[14] Ibid., pp. 8, 44, 176; W. J. Rees (ed.), *Liber Landavensis*, p. 77; Henken, *Welsh Saints*, pp. 88–9. On this motif see also Karen Jankulak's article, below.
[15] Henken, *Welsh Saints*, pp. 107–8.
[16] G. Williams, *The Welsh Church*, pp. 14–21.
[17] *VSBG*, p. 232.
[18] Parry (ed.), *Gwaith Dafydd ap Gwilym*, pp. 256–8.
[19] H. Williams (ed.), *Gildas*, pp. 409–11; Henken, *Traditions*, pp. 137, 302.
[20] *LBS*, vol. 4, pp. 394–5.
[21] T. Roberts and I. Williams (eds), *Poetical Works*, pp. 48–9.
[22] Johnston (ed.), *Gwaith Lewys Glyn Cothi*, p. 26,11. 67–70.
[23] Burdett-Jones, 'Gweddi anarferol'; Henken, *National Redeemer*, p. 143.
[24] Henken, *National Redeemer*, p. 143.
[25] Vallis Rosina, translated in the Welsh Life as Glyn Rhosyn and said in both Latin and Welsh Lives to be more commonly called Hoddnant, is the name Rhigyfarch used for Mynyw.
[26] J. W. James (ed.), *Rhigyfarch's Life*, pp. 1–3; *VSBG*, pp. 1–3; D. S. Evans (ed.), *Welsh Life*, pp. 1–2; Henken, *Traditions*, pp. 32–4.
[27] D. S. Evans (ed.), *Welsh Life*, p. 1.
[28] Gildas is named as the preacher in the Welsh Life (ibid., pp. 2–3) and in the Latin Vespasian A.xiv (*VSBG*, pp. 4–5), but not in the Latin Cotton Nero E.i (J. W. James (ed.), *Rhigyfarch's Life*). The prophecies to the king appear in the Latin Lives but not in the Welsh one (J. W. James (ed.), p. 5; Wade-Evans (ed.), *Life of St David* pp. 5–6). See D. S. Evans (ed.), *Welsh Life*, pp. xlvi-llll for a detailed statement of the differences between the texts.
[29] J. W. James (ed.), *Rhigyfarch's Life*, p. 9; D. S. Evans (ed.), *Welsh Life*, pp. 4–6; Henken, *Traditions*, pp. 47–51.
[30] In Welsh law, the right to occupy land previously owned by one's father is known as *dadanudd* (uncovering the fire). In Wales and other Celtic lands, a customary practice recognized well into the nineteenth century (though for how long before then is unknown) was that squatters could claim wasteland by building a house in one night *(tŷ unnos)* and having smoke rising from the chimney by dawn. Jenkins, *Law of Hywel Dda*, p. 101; A. Rees and B. Rees, *Celtic Heritage*, p. 157; Sayce, 'The one-night house'.
[31] Owen (ed.), 'Canu i Ddewi', p. 449,11. 11–16.
[32] I. Williams (ed.) and Bromwich (trans.), *Armes Prydein*, pp. xii-xx; Dumville, 'Brittany and "Armes Prydein Vawr"'.
[33] I. Williams (ed.) and Bromwich (trans.), *Armes Prydein*, p. 8,11. 105–6.
[34] Ibid., p. 10,1. 129.
[35] Ibid., p. 14,1. 196.
[36] Ibid., p. 10,11. 139–40.
[37] Chadwick, Hughes, Brooke and Jackson (eds), *Studies in the Early British Church*, pp. 175–6; Wade-Evans (ed.), *Life of St David*, p. x; J. W. James (ed.),

Rhigyfarch's Life, p. xi; see D. S. Evans (ed.), *Welsh Life of St David*, pp. xxiii-xxv for a discussion of these views. See also the discussion on the political background in the article by Nerys Ann Jones and Morfydd E. Owen, below.

[38] J. W. James (ed.), *Rhigyfarch's Life*, p. 20. While the Latin *vitae* use the symbolic authority of Jerusalem, the Welsh *buchedd*, written two and a half centuries later, places David's consecration in Rome (D. S. Evans (ed.), *Welsh Life*, p. 9), the seat of actual authority and, significantly, the place to which various emissaries, such as Giraldus Cambrensis, went to plead their cases for St Davids.

[39] J. W. James (ed.), *Rhigyfarch's Life*, p. 21.

[40] D. S. Evans (ed.), *Welsh Life*, p. 8.

[41] *VSBG*, p. 54.

[42] Emanuel, 'An analysis', pp. 221–2.

[43] Gerald of Wales, *De Invectionibus*, p. 143 (II:10).

[44] Geoffrey of Monmouth, *History*, p. 230 (ix:15).

[45] Ibid., p. 262 (xi:3).

[46] Bromwich (ed.), *Trioedd*, pp. cxi-cxii, 1–3.

[47] J. Davies, *History of Wales*, p. 122.

[48] Translations into Welsh appear in later periods both for the Welsh saint Gwenfrewy and for saints who belong to the broader Catholic tradition, such as Katherine of Alexandria, Margaret of Antioch, Martha, Mary of Egypt, Martin, the Virgin Mary and Anna. These are discussed in Cartwright, *Y Forwyn Fair*.

[49] G. Williams, *Religion*, p. 116.

[50] The figures long-cited were fifty-three churches and and thirty-two wells (E. G. Bowen, *Dewi Sant*, p. 89; *Settlements*, p. 51), but the latest study, done by Graham Jones as part of the Trans-national Database and Atlas of Saints' Cults, shows twentyseven parish churches, thirty-seven or thirty-eight chapels, and thirty-one wells. The key data from the database appear in G. Jones, *Saints*.

[51] Harris, *Saint David*, p. 35, from Hereford Chapter Library MS. P.3.iv.

[52] L. T. H. James and Evans (eds), *Hen Gwndidau*, p. 23,11. 18 a, b.

[53] For example, W. L. Richards (ed.), *Gwaith Dafydd Llwyd*, p. 31,1. 68.

[54] Ibid., p. 50,11. 16–18.

[55] Ibid., p. 48,11. 89–90.

[56] Welsh Department, Board of Education, *Dydd Gŵyl Dewi Sant*.

[57] G. Williams, *Religion*, pp. 124–5.

[58] G. Evans, *Land of My Fathers*, p. 96.

[59] D. S. Evans (ed.), *Welsh Life*, p. 13. This particular instruction given in the Welsh Life has a slightly different import from that in the Latin ones: 'Fratres mei, perseuerate in his que a me didicistis et uidistis' (My brothers, persevere in those things which you have learned from me and seen in me), J. W. James (ed.), *Rhigyfarch's Life*, p. 26; *VSBG*, p. 167).

3
*Twelfth-century Welsh hagiography:
the* Gogynfeirdd *poems to saints*[1]

⊁⊰

NERYS ANN JONES and MORFYDD E. OWEN

Introduction

The earliest recorded Lives of the Welsh saints, with one exception, that of the early *Vita Samsonis*[2] (written in and mainly concerning Brittany), were composed in Latin in the late eleventh and early twelfth centuries. *Vita Davidis* (Dewi) was written by the cleric Rhigyfarch sometime after 1081[3] and Lifris' *Vita Cadoci* (Cadog) belongs to the same period.[4] The Lives of *Dubricius* (Dyfrig), *Oudoceus* (Euddogwy) and *Teliavus* (Teilo) were incorporated into the *Liber Landavensis* in the twelfth century,[5] and the important collection of Lives included in British Library, MS Cotton Vespasian A xiv, which was based on an earlier collection, was copied *c.* 1200.[6] All hagiographical material in the vernacular dates from a later period[7] with the exception of three twelfth-century poems:[8] 'Canu Cadfan' by Llywelyn Fardd, 'Canu Tysilio' by Cynddelw Brydydd Mawr and 'Canu Dewi' by Gwynfardd Brycheiniog.[9] These are of particular interest, not only because of the scarcity and fragmentary nature of the documentary evidence for the Welsh saints and their cults before the Edwardian Conquest of Wales in 1283, but also because, unlike the contemporary Latin *vitae*, two, if not three of them, were composed by laymen heavily involved in the secular politics of the day.[10]

The poems form a small portion of the corpus of 12,700 lines or so of verse attributed to the professional court poets (known in Welsh as *Gogynfeirdd*) who served the ruling classes of the independent areas of Wales during the period between 1100 and 1282.[11] A high proportion of the corpus is panegyric verse, but a small body of love and penitential poetry and a few anomalous poems suggest that the poets also had roles other than that of political propagandist, and had patrons other than the political leaders of their day. Within the body of verse labelled panegyric there is variety in form and in tone reflecting the various functions of the praise poet. Some poems have obviously been designed to impress a highstatus gathering at a state occasion, others are short informal poems composed for a domestic audience.

The poems to saints clearly belong to the first of these categories. Indeed, in length, intricacy and learning, they are equal to the most dignified elegies and eulogies composed for the most powerful rulers of the period. All three are highly ornate, lengthy compositions in *awdl* metre, the product of many hours of intensive labour by master craftsmen. Their elaborate opening invocations and closing prayers are another indication of their formality. The exact nature of the gatherings for which they were intended, however, can only be surmised. It appears that each one was commissioned for a specific occasion and that each contains a specific political agenda.[12] One of the many features that they have in common is the way their contents continually vacillate between events of the sixth and twelfth centuries, a consideration which leads to considerable (deliberate) ambiguity. For as well as exalting the mediatory powers of a saint by making use of hagiographical material,[13] they also focus upon a particular twelfth-century church and community associated with his cult, uniting them with the political unit in which they are situated. Llywelyn Fardd in his ode to Cadfan focuses on Tywyn, the mother church of Meirionnydd; Cynddelw in his ode to Tysilio, premier saint of Powys, focuses upon Meifod, burial ground of the rulers of that region, and Gwynfardd Brycheiniog in his ode to St David (Dewi) focuses on Llanddewibrefi and associates his cult with Deheubarth. All three sites are archaeologically important with a history going back to the early Middle Ages and, in the case of Llanddewibrefi, to Roman times.[14] They were also important institutions in twelfth-century Wales, being major *clas* churches enjoying the patronage of the rulers of the territories with which they were associated.[15]

In this chapter we shall look at the poems as evidence for hagiography; secondly we shall consider their function within the internal politics of twelfth-century Wales; and thirdly we shall consider their significance in the wider world of ecclesiastical politics.

Evidence for hagiography

(i) *Canu Cadfan*[16]

If we regard hagiography as primarily concerned with telling the story of the saint's life, Llywelyn Fardd's poem to Cadfan gives little specific information regarding the saint and his story. His parentage is noted:[17]

> Cedwis Duw urddas, yn ŵr ac yn was,
> I fab Eneas, eurwas fyged.
> Cedwir nen, fab Gwen, a fad weled,
> Cadwent nerthnawd nerth a'm canherthed.

(God safeguarded a special status, as man and boy,/ for the son of Aeneas, honour [fitting for] a noble youth./ The chieftain, the son of Gwen, fortunate to behold, is safeguarded,/ may [the one] of mighty strength [in the] battle-field safeguard me!)

and he is said to have come from Brittany to found a church at Tywyn:[18]

> Lluniwys i Ddëws ddewis edrydd–iddaw
> Pan ddoeth o Lydaw ar lydw bedydd.

(He made a choice dwelling for God/ when he came from Brittany to a community of the baptized (*or* as one of a host of believers)).

His name is coupled with that of Lleuddad as one of the founding saints of Enlli.[19]

Cadfan is described as being of mighty strength in battle and a protector of soldiers. There is play on the *cad* (battle, army) element in his name.[20] At least two of his relics are mentioned, his crosier and gospel book, as well as his altar, and there are elusive references to his miracles.[21]

The evidence of the poem confirms what other information survives in Wales regarding Cadfan and his career. Two other early Welsh sources recognize him as one of a group of Breton saints who came to Wales and established themselves in the territory to the north of the river Ystwyth. In the Life of Padarn, Cadfan is said to have come with three other leaders, Tydecho (Titechon), Cynllo (Ketinlau) and Padarn, from Letavia.[22] In the Welsh text known as *Bonedd y Saint* (The Lineage of the Saints) dated by Wade-Evans to the twelfth century,[23] Cadfan's name is found in the section of the text (numbers 19–25) which lists saints who had come from Brittany, all of whom are associated with north Wales.[24] In his sixteenth-century Life, Lleuddad is named as the successor of Cadfan in Enlli.[25] Variants of the name Cadfan are given in the Legendary of St Malo and Treger.

In the Welsh genealogy, as in the poem, Cadfan is claimed as the son of Aeneas and Gwen Teirbron.[26] Gwen can be identified with the *Alba tribus mammis* who was the mother of St Guénolé, the heroine of a story which involved a triple birth motif, suggesting that Welsh tradition was drawing on a source similar to that used in the Life of Guénolé or was drawing on that text.[27] Gwen, according to Welsh tradition, was the daughter of Emyr Llydaw who is also regarded as the grandfather of Padarn, Tydecho and Maelrhys.[28] Emyr in later Welsh tradition is presented as the father of Hywel ab Emyr Llydaw as in the Welsh redactions of Geoffrey of Monmouth's *Historia;* Hywel ab Emyr Llydaw corresponds to the character known as Boudocus in the Latin text.[29] The name Emyr is not known from Breton sources. John Lloyd-Jones has shown that it is itself a developed form of a common noun *ymer* or *emyr* derived from Latin *imperium* or *imperator* and was probably merely a title, Emyr Llydaw meaning an Emperor or King of Brittany.[30] Such a title would imply royal or noble origins for this family of saints. Evidence for the cult of Cadfan in Brittany is, however, sparse. Loth lists *Catvan* in his *Les Noms des saints bretons* as the patron of Chapelle de Saint Caduan in Braspartz.[31] This identification is, however, doubtful since the Breton pronunciation of the name suggests that the form is not cognate with Cadfan. Bernard Tanguy regards the Welsh name as the homonym of Breton Cavan found possibly in the name of Saint Cavan in Plougomené (Finistère) and perhaps in Langavan in Saint Melour-des-Ondes (Ile et Vilaine).[32]

To sum up: despite his alleged Breton connection, evidence about Cadfan seems to stem entirely from Britain apart from possible Breton place-name evidence. The evidence of the Welsh poem concurs with what little we know of Cadfan from Welsh sources, adding little fresh detail. The poem, the saints' Lives and the genealogies indicate that a pool of historical material about Welsh saints was available in the twelfth century. This material, which included traditions associating the saint with Brittany and the use of names such as Gwen Teirbron, suggests that the Welsh were familiar with story themes used by Breton hagiographers. There is no surviving *vita* for Cadfan, but the poem, taken together with the other evidence, suggests that there might well have been. What the form of that *vita* was it is impossible to say.

(ii) Canu Tysilio[33]
The facts about Tysilio to be culled from the Welsh poem are limited and cryptic as befits the poet's style. Tysilio's parentage is given:[34]

>Tysiliaw terwyn gwyrysedd . . .
>Mab Garddun arddunig fawredd . . .
>Mab Brochfael bron hael hawl ornedd . . .

(Tysilio of furious battle prowess . . . son of Garddun honourable in his greatness . . . son of Brochfael, the generous-hearted, a terror in [pressing] his claim . . .)

He is later referred to as a descendant of Cadell and as a grandson of Cyngen.[35] The details of Tysilio's lineage conform with that found in the Welsh genealogies where he is represented as being of good British stock, the son of a king of Powys, Brochfael Ysgithrog, and the brother of Cynan Garwyn, ancestors of the twelfth-century rulers of Powys. These rulers were the patrons of Cynddelw, the poet who sang the poem.[36] There are references to Tysilio's relationship with one Gwyddfarch commemorated with Tysilio as one of the saints of Meifod in Powys.[37] Gwyddfarch, Tysilio's fellow saint, was given a vision of Rome at Meifod:[38]

> A weles ni welir hyd Frawd,
> Caer Rufain ryfedd olygawd.

(What he saw will not be seen until Judgement Day,/ the City of Rome, a wondrous sight.)

Tysilio is said to have been pursued by a wily woman:[39]

> Mad gorau maddau marthöedd,
> Ac er Duw diofryd gwragedd—
> Gwraig enwawg, anwar ei throsedd,
> A'i treiddwys, bu trwy enwiredd.

(Well did he put aside the wonders of the world,/ and for the sake of God gave up women—/ a famous woman, uncouth in her arrogance,/ came to him, it was with evil intent!)

He is depicted as the principal saint of Powys and as the defender of its people against the Northumbrians at *Gwaith Gogwy*, the Battle of Maserfelth.[40] The orbit of his power extended into Gwynedd in the west and Buellt in the south. His churches are listed:[41]

> Llan llugyrn, llogawd offeren,
> Llan tra llŷr, tra lliant wyrddlen,
> Llan dra llanw, dra llys Dinorben,
> Llan Llydaw, gan llydwedd wohen,

> Llan Bengwern, bennaf daearen,
> Llan Bowys, baradwys burwen,
> Llan Gamarch, llaw barch i berchen.

(A church of lanterns, a place for mass,/ a church beyond the sea, beyond the green mantle of the sea,/ a church beyond the tide, beyond the court of Dinorben,/ a church of Llydaw, the desire of many,/ the church of Pengwern, the chief sod of earth,/ the church of Powys, a holy, pure paradise,/ the church of Camarch, a rule of honour for its owner.)

He is presented as *periglawr* (confessional priest) of the people of Powys and Gwynedd[42] and is especially associated with Anglesey, where he offered penance, and Eifionydd, where he died.[43]

Information preserved about Tysilio from other Welsh sources is very limited. Apart from his genealogy and dedications, a gnomic dialogue poem attributed to him, and oral folklore,[44] the poem by Cynddelw is our only source of information about Tysilio. The name Tysilio is a hypocoristic form of Sulio which derives from Sulien. Scholars for almost a century have considered that the material of a lost Life of Tysilio or Sulien or Sulio, earlier Suliaw, has been preserved in Brittany in the Lives of St Suliau or Sulien, a composite version of which was included by Albert Le Grand in *Les Vies des saints*.[45] Albert Le Grand had drawn the material for his Life from the legendaries of the collegiate church of Le Folgoet and the cathedral church of Léon and from the Life of the saint used at his church at St Suliac. All these sources are now lost but a copy of the Breviary of Léon made in the eighteenth century is preserved in a Paris manuscript.[46] Two short Lives of Sulien were printed in the *Acta Sanctorum* of the Bollandists, taken from sources which Duine assigned to the diocese of St Malo.[47] The chief facts about Suliau to be culled from the Breton Lives are as follows:

> Suliau was the oldest of the three sons of Brocmail; he took to the religious life as a young man and went to Guimarcus at Meibot. He then spent seven years on Enes Suliau in Menai. When he returned to Meibot, Guimarchus had a vision of Rome. On Guimarchus' death Suliau became head of Meibot. Suliau's brother, Iago, who had inherited the kingdom died. Iago's wife, Haearnmed, tried to seduce Suliau who, as a result of this, fled to Enes Suliau and to Builth and finally to Brittany where he died in 606.

Most of these traditions concur with references in the Welsh poem, as Ann Parry Owen has shown.[48] What is lacking are the references to

Tysilio's early career as a warrior, which in a Welsh context would have a propaganda value for the Powysian dynasty, and his death in Wales, which would have local religious connotations.

Various views have been expressed regarding the relationship of the Breton and Welsh versions of the saint. Because he supposed that the feast-days of the saints differed in the two countries – Tysilio's feast being on 8 November in Wales,[49] Suliau's on 1 October in St Malo and on 29 July in Cornouaille and Domnonée[50] – Doble held the view that the two were different and that the Tysilio material was borrowed not long before the fifteenth century in order to produce *vitae* for the patron saints of St Suliac and Sizun.[51] Lobineau, however, states that, according to the Breviary of St Malo, the anniversary of Suliau's death was celebrated on 8 November and his birth on 1 October, whereas, in the Breviary of Léon, his birth was assigned to 29 July.[52] Nora Chadwick and L. Fleuriot both recognized Suliau as a saint from Powys who came to Brittany as part of the second great migration from Britain.[53] The Breton redactors of the Life of Suliau were certainly using a written document. Kerdanet, in his edition of Albert Le Grand's work in 1837, seems to have known of such documents, since he referred to a *légendaire galloise* containing a Life of Sulien which ended in a different manner, with Tysilio returning to Britain to head the Welsh saints in their struggle with St Augustine at St Augustine's Oak.[54] The locating of the story of Suliau in Wales in the Breton versions of the Life that survive suggests that the underlying source was a Welsh one. The forms of the personal and place names found in the Life, for instance *Suliau*, *Haiarnmed* and *Meibot*, can only be Welsh.[55] They are probably from a written source which belonged to the early Middle Welsh or very late Old Welsh period, that is to a time sometime in the twelfth century. This implies that manuscripts of an early Life of Tysilio must have been circulating in Brittany. What is certain is that the redactor of the Lives of Suliau and the Welsh poet Cynddelw were drawing on the same font of information. Both the Tysilio and Cadfan poems pose the question of the nature of the Breton element in Welsh hagiography in the twelfth century.

(iii) Canu Dewi[56]

St David (Dewi) died in 589. He had been the leader of an ascetic community within the Welsh Church and had strong Irish connections.[57] His principal centre was at Mynyw (Menevia) or St Davids; although judging from the number of early dedications to him, his cult was widespread throughout south Wales, in Dyfed in the west and in Gwent, Brecknock and Archenfield in the east as well as in Cornwall, Brittany and Anglo-Saxon England.[58] The development of the territorial power of St David between the sixth and twelfth centuries was the nearest parallel in Wales to the development of the power of Armagh in Ireland.[59] From at least the tenth century there is evidence to show that clerics and lay politicians were claiming superiority for St David over the other saints of south Wales.[60] It is his banner which the Welsh princes were encouraged to raise in their fight against an English king by the propagandist poet of the Welsh poem *Armes Prydein Fawr*.[61] A major manifestation of propaganda for St David's cult, perhaps in the face of Norman opposition to native practices, was the composition sometime before 1097 of the Latin *vita* of St David by Rhigyfarch during the years following a visit of William I to St Davids.[62] The vigour of the cult of St David, as we have seen, is further attested in the eleventh and twelfth centuries by the fame of St Davids as a centre of pilgrimage: William the Conqueror was among its visitors in 1081;[63] Henry II in 1171.[64] It has been argued that the sung liturgical office of St David, which preserves many hagiographical details found in his Lives, dates from the 1170s. This text also emphasizes the importance of the cult of St David at that time.[65] St David was reputed to have been canonized during the papacy of Pope Calixtus II, 1119–24.[66] During the twelfth century, firstly during the years 1140–8 (under the Norman Bishop Bernard), secondly during the years 1176–88 (under the canons of the cathedral) and then between 1198 and 1203 (under Giraldus Cambrensis), an effort was made to achieve freedom for the bishopric of St Davids from the control of Canterbury.[67] During this period the cause of David was espoused by princes from all over Wales.[68]

There is, therefore, no lack of written evidence for the great body of material about St David which was circulating in Wales during the period of the *Gogynfeirdd*. No fewer than five Latin versions of his Life are extant.[69] The earliest, mentioned above, was composed by Rhigyfarch sometime before 1097. Another was composed by Giraldus Cambrensis at the end of the twelfth century.[70] All the Lives contain hagiographical versions of the same theme, varying in the anecdotes which they preserve. Most of the hagiographical information in Gwynfardd's poem to St David, such as the story of the saint's conflict with the chieftain Boia,[71] is either paralleled in the extant Lives or mentioned in the liturgy of the saint. Some of it, however, like the story of St David's oxen, has been preserved in oral tradition alone.[72]

As in the Lives of most Celtic saints, St David's parentage is emphasized in the poem.[73] He is of faultless stock, *difefyl geraint*, the son of Sant, whom the genealogies make the son of Ceredig, the son of Cunedda Wledig, and therefore of the royal line of Ceredigion.[74] Epithets used in the poem refer to his asceticism: he is *diofredog*, that is he had vowed to abstain from worldly things.[75] Traditional claims are made regarding the far-reaching extent of his power and his Irish connections are emphasized, including the fact that Patrick had been forced to flee to Ireland thirty years before his birth.[76] Most of the information, however, consists of allusive and elusive references to anecdotes about St David. A few of these anecdotes reflect onomastic tales.[77] Others record the traditions of the associations of the saint with particular churches and their relics. One *caniad* or section of the poem is concerned solely with a list of churches claimed as belonging to St David:[78]

> Dewi mawr Mynyw, syw sywedydd,
> A Dewi Brefi ger *y* bröydd;
> A Dewi biau balch Langyfelach,
> Lle mae morach a mawr grefydd.
> A Dewi biau bangeibr ysydd
> Meidrym le a'i mynwent i luosydd;
> A Bangor esgor a bangeibr Henllan
> Ysydd i'r clodfan, i'r clyd ei wŷdd;
> A Maenawrdeifi, ddiorfynydd,
> Ac Abergwili biau gwylwlydd,
> A Henfynyw deg o du glennydd—Aeron,
> Hyfaes ei meillion, hyfes goedydd,
> Llanarth, Llanadnau, llanau llywydd,
> Llangadawg, lle breiniawg, rhannawg rhiydd,
> Nis arfaidd rhyfel Llanfaes, lle uchel,
> Na'r llan yn Llywel gan neb lluydd.
> Garthbryngi, bryn Dewi digywilydd,
> A Thrallwng Cynfyn cer y dolydd,
> A Llanddewi y Crwys, llogawd newydd,
> A Glasgwm a'i eglwys ger glas fynydd,
> Gwyddelfod aruchel, nawdd ni echwydd,
> Craig Furuna deg yma, teg ei mynydd,
> Ac Ystrad Nynnid a'i ryddid rhydd.
> Rhoddes Duw Dofydd, defnydd—o'i foli,
> Dewi ar Frefi, fryn llewenydd . . .

(Great David of Menevia, a wise master,/ and David of Brefi beside the water-meadows,/ and to David belongs lovely Llangyfelach,/ where there is joy and great devotion;/ and to David belongs the great church which is/ in the place [called] Meidrum with its graveyard for hosts;/ and Bangor's refuge and Henllan's great church/ which belongs to the greatly praised one [and] the one of the sheltering trees,/ and lowland Maenordeifi, / and Abergwili to which a gentle one belongs,/ and fair Henfynyw near the banks of the Aeron,/ with its clover-filled meadow and acorn-laden trees,/ Llanarth, Llanadnau, the churches of the leader,/ Llangadog, a privileged place which partakes of glory,/ war does not venture to Llanfaes, a lofty site,/ nor to the *Ilan* in Llywel with any hosting./ Garthbrengi, the hill of David, a place without shame/ and Trallwng Cynfyn near the meadows,/ and Llanddewi y Crwys, a new monastery,/ and Glasgwm with its church by the verdant mountain,/ a lofty clearing full of groves, where sanctuary never fails,/ fair Cregrina here, its mountain is fair,/ and Ystrad Nynnid whose freedom is available./ The Lord God established (and this is cause for praise)/ David on Brefi, a hill of joy . . .)

This *caniad* suggests that the poet had access to local information regarding churches of the cult of St David. Some of the churches mentioned by him here are found among the twelve churches founded by the saint as listed in *Vita Davidis*.[79] Most of them were situated on lands later claimed in the fifteenth-century Black Book of St Davids as belonging to the bishop of St Davids.[80] All are known to have been dedicated to St David. The poet gives details of the physical characteristics of the churches and their sites,[81] and in the case of Glasgwm, for example, he alludes to the importance of the church as the home of St David's famous bell Bangu.[82]

The churches which are most prominent in the poem, however, are Mynyw (Menevia, modern St Davids) and Brefi (modern Llanddewibrefi). Mynyw is given priority at the beginning of the list of churches. Its seniority is recognized, being the burial place of the saint.[83] The poet more particularly speaks of Mynyw as a place of pilgrimage by princes and as the site of a visit made by himself.[84] It is, however, the second church on the list, namely Brefi, which is the main focus of Gwynfardd's attention. The name of Brefi reverberates throughout the poem.[85] The poet has come to Brefi and there sings the praise of St David and Brefi.[86] He describes its church and community.[87] References to the Synod of Llanddewibrefi are used to give structure to the poem. The first *caniad*, for instance, concludes with an allusion to the hill rising up beneath the feet of St David at the synod and to St David conferring *breint* (privilege) on Llanddewibrefi.[88] The poem ends with a grand peroration listing the saints who came to Brefi to acknowledge the superiority of St David.[89] Of the three poems, 'Canu Dewi' is thus richest in its hagiography, echoing themes found in other twelfth-century sources.

The significance of the poems in relation to secular politics

Although many of the incidents recorded in these poems occur in such hagiographical material as remains, the slant given to the material is characteristic of the poetry of the *Gogynfeirdd*. The main vehicle used by the poets to promote their patrons, both secular and ecclesiastic, was encomium. In these poems, their skills as panegyric poets, honed over many centuries, are applied to the saints. They are praised for their godliness and wisdom, for their generosity and hospitality, but above all for their protective powers. In the opening section of 'Canu Cadfan', for example, forms of the verb *cadw* (to protect) occur at the beginning of several lines as Llywelyn Fardd plays with the idea of the protective function of the saint.[90] In 'Canu Tysilio' a whole *caniad* is devoted to the saint's role as protector of the men of Powys at the battle of Maes Cogwy.[91] In 'Canu Dewi' likewise, praise of the saint's ability to protect his followers is reiterated time and time again.[92]

The main emphasis in all three poems, however, is the protection which the saints afford to specific churches and communities, Tywyn, Meifod and Llanddewibrefi, the second focus of the poets' praise. The priority given to a specific *clas* church is particularly evident in 'Canu Dewi'. An ideal picture is presented of these establishments with their whitewashed walls and welcoming candles, their holy relics and altars, their devout priests, the warm welcome afforded to travellers and poets and the fine feasts, but the main quality praised by all three poets is the safety of their lands, buildings and inhabitants. Tywyn, for instance, is described as a place[93]

> Myn na llefeis trais trasglwy fyned,
> Myn na llefais dyn ddwyn eisiwed—o'r llan
> Ger glan glas dylan, o'i dylyed,
> Men na llefesir dir o'i daered,
> Men y llafasaf oes ddarymred.

(Where violent intent does not dare go,/ where no man dares take the needy from the church—/ by the shore of the blue sea, on account of its legal right,/ where no oppression is dared, on account of its right to tribute,/ where I will dare wander about [all my] life.)

There are frequent references to the *braint* (legal privilege) and *nawdd* (protection, sanctuary) which is afforded to anyone who comes within the precincts of their jurisdiction. Both *braint* and *nawdd* are native legal concepts developed in a church context from the field of secular law where *braint* means the right of enjoying full legal status or privilege.[94] In the case of a church, it is a privilege generally associated with royal grant or protection. The early poetry illustrates how a church's *braint* was conditional on the power of a secular ruler,[95] but the most explicit source for understanding the implications of the *braint* of a church is the document known as *Braint Teilo*, found in the Book of Llandaf, which specifies the *braint* of Teilo's church at Llandaf.[96] *Braint Teilo* claimed for Teilo's church immunity from secular interference, an immunity upheld by the sanctity of native law. The *Braint* claimed the same competence for the Llandaf law court as for the law court of the secular lord. This privilege was conferred by the local lord, in the case of Teilo, by the king of Morgannwg. The Cadfan poem speaks of the *braint* of Tywyn probably conferred by the ruler of Meirionnydd, the Tysilio poem of the *braint* of Meifod conferred by the ruler of Powys, the Dewi poem of the *braint* of Llanddewibrefi conferred by the lord of Deheubarth.[97] All three poems stress the *braint* of their communities.

One of the rights which formed part of the *braint* or privilege of the church was the right to give *nawdd*.[98] *Nawdd*, an ancient concept of the secular law-texts, and cognate with Irish *snádud*, was originally connected with the right of individuals to afford protection within specific temporal and geographical limits. By the thirteenth century, this right *eo nomine* is only recorded for the king and his court and for churches and saints' relics where the term is equated with the Latin *refugium*. This right was equated in territorial terms with a specific territory or *noddfa*, sanctuary place or field. Giraldus Cambrensis, using a topos common in hagiography, emphasized the importance of these sanctuaries, 'which extended as far from the church as cattle could travel grazing during the day and where criminals could flee from the wrath of the local lord'.[99] We have a definite historical record of the importance of the sanctuary offered by Llanddewibrefi, since in 1109 the chronicle records the fact that the partisans of a local nobleman, Cadwgan, and his son Ithel fled to the sanctuary of the church of Llanddewibrefi.[100] Gwynfardd speaks of fleeing to the *nawdd* of St David,[101] and in a series of lines, offers what may be a definition of the geographical extent of the *noddfa* of Llanddewibrefi, from Carawn to Tywi, from the Llyndu to Twrch:[102]

> Diogel ei nawdd i'r neb a'i cyrcho . . .
> O Garawn gan iawn, gan ehöeg,
> Hyd ar Dywi, afon firain a theg,
> O'r Llyndu, lle'd fu llid gyhydreg,
> Hyd ar Dwrch, terfyn tir â charreg.

(His sanctuary is secure for those who seek it . . ./ from Caron with its fair rule, with its purple hue,/ as far as Tywi, a fine fair river,/ from Llyn Du, broader was the roused tumult,/ as far as Twrch, where the land is bounded by a stone.)

All three poems, to a greater or lesser degree, seek to reinforce the traditional legal rights of those centres and were probably first performed in the presence of a territorial lord and his followers as well as the members of the religious community.[103] However, the nature of the gathering and the circumstances which led to the commissioning of the poet are not the same in the case of each poem, as is revealed by a close study of the texts.

(i) Canu Cadfan

Apart from Cadfan and Lleuddad, the only other individual praised by name in Llywelyn Fardd's poem is Morfran, abbot of Tywyn. He is also praised in the Welsh chronicle, *Brut y Tywysogyon*, in an entry for the year 1147.[104] During that year a dispute arose between Cadwaladr ap Gruffudd ap Cynan, lord of Meirionnydd, and his nephews, Hywel and Cynan, sons of his brother Owain Gwynedd. The brothers mustered their armies and made for Meirionnydd, Hywel approaching from his lands in Ceredigion to the south, and Cynan from the north. Having failed to gain the support of the men of Meirionnydd the two brothers decided to attack Cadwaladr's stronghold, Castell Cynfael, an earthwork castle near Tywyn. The castle's steward was Morfran, abbot of Tywyn, who, according to the chronicle, 'refused to tender his homage to them though he was tempted at times with harsh threats, at other times with innumerable gifts that were being offered to him, for he preferred to die worthily than to lead his life deceitfully'.[105] The castle was attacked and taken. Cadwaladr was forced to withdraw from Meirionnydd and Cynan ruled in his place. The chronicle reports that Morfran managed to escape unharmed, but nothing is said of what became of him during the reign of Cynan.

References to a 'great plan to claim [Meirionnydd]' and to the bringing of arms 'from the south' suggests that the overthrow of Cadwaladr might have been the impetus for the poem, as Catrin T. Beynon Davies proposed.[106] After many years of serving a lord whose wholehearted support is indicated by the fact that he named his eldest son Cadfan,[107] Morfran was faced with a new master, one whom he had opposed with men and arms. It is likely that it was not only the abbot's position which was at stake, but the whole future of the community at Tywyn. A crisis of this nature called for a measure of diplomacy. What better way of gaining Cynan's favour than to commission Llywelyn Fardd, a court poet of Gwynedd, to compose a poem of praise to Cadfan, his church at Tywyn and his land of Meirionnydd, to be sung in the presence of the new lord?

As well as reminding his audience of the authority of the saint and the special privileges granted to his church, the poet presents an ideal picture of peaceful coexistence in Meirionnydd, the land of Cadfan:[108]

> Uchelwlad Cadfan myn yd gydfyddbreswyl
> Uchel Efengyl ufyl ofydd,
> A'r fagl ferth werthfawr wyrthau newydd
> A ludd i'r gelyn ladd ei gilydd;
> A'i harglwydd gwladlwydd, gwlad lewenydd,
> A wna ei noddfa yn dda ddiwenydd . . .
> A'i habad roddiad rhad rhy ddyrydd;
> Atan rhy ddyran o'i lan luosydd,
> Rhy ddylif cynnif can fodd Dofydd . . .

(The exalted land of Cadfan where there continually coexists/ the exalted Gospel [Book] of the humble ruler,/ and the precious, fair crosier [performing] new miracles/ which restrains the enemy from killing his opponent;/ and its lord who brings prosperity to his land, joy of [his] people,/ who makes its refuge sound [and] blessed . . . and its abbot, a generous giver, who bestows grace (*or* blessing);/ to us he distributes numerous gifts from his church . . ./ he arranges battle (*or* conquest) which is pleasing to God . . .)

Cynan is not named in this passage or elsewhere in the poem, but traditional epithets like *arglwydd gwladlwydd* and *gwledig gwlad Ednyfed*[109] could apply to a twelfth-century lord of Meirionnydd as well as to its patron saint. Ambiguity of this kind pervades the poem and, in the work of one who was undoubtedly a master of his craft, it must surely be deliberate. The poet's intention was that his audience should identify both territorial lord and abbot with Cadfan and his companion Lleuddad. Thus he could praise them both without causing offence to either and also emphasize the need for cooperation between them, as in the following passage:[110]

> Dau ŵr a folaf fal y'm ceinad—Dofydd
> Dau deg, dau ddedwydd, dau rydd roddiad,
> Dau ddoeth yng nghyfoeth, yng nghyfaenad,
> Dau gu, dau gyfiaith, dau wynieithad,
> Dau a wna gwyrthau er goleuad—rhagddudd,
> Dau ddiludd eu budd er bodd eirchad,
> Dau gefnderw oeddynt ni ferwynt frad:
> Cadfan i gadw llan, ef a Lleuddad.

(I praise two men as the Lord permits me,/ two fair [men], two blessed [men], two generous givers,/ two wise [men] in authority, in harmony,/ two beloved [men], two fellow-countrymen, two holy men,/ two who perform miracles in order to [spread] light before them,/ two whose gifts, to the satisfaction of suppliants, are unhindered,/ they were two cousins who did not plot treachery:/ [may] Cadfan protect [the] church, [both] he and Lleuddad!)

(ii) Canu Tysilio
It has been shown that the poem in praise of Cadfan was closely connected with Meirionnydd politics in the twelfth century. One would, therefore, expect the poem to Tysilio to be associated in a similar way with the politics of twelfth-century Powys, especially since its author, Cynddelw, was so closely involved not only with the cause of its ruler, Madog ap Maredudd, and his successors, but also with the welfare of its warriors and noblemen.[111] It is true that the poem's main focus is the church of Meifod, burial place of Madog and his forefathers, and that allusions are made to the saint's descent from the royal line of Powys and to his role as defender of the people of Powys in the battle of Maes Cogwy, but Tysilio is also depicted as 'confessional priest of the people of Gwynedd'[112] and as chieftain of the lands of Anglesey:[113]

        Tud wledig, elwig elfydden,
        Tir gẃraidd gorwyf rhag unben,
        Tirion Môn, meillion ym morben . . .

(Chieftain of a country, a land beneath [his] protection,/ a valiant land, proud before a chieftain,/ the meadowland of Anglesey with clover on its shore . . .)

Reference is made to Penmynydd in Anglesey as his place of retreat and to Eifionydd as the place of his death.[114] These allusions to Tysilio's Gwynedd connections suggest that the poem is not a simple appeal for support to Madog ap Maredudd by the community of Meifod, and this is confirmed by the poem's first reference to the church as a place 'beyond Gwynedd':[115]

        Caraf-i lan a'r llên gan gadredd
        Ger y mae Gwyddfarch uch Gwynedd.

(I love a church and the clerics of might/ near the place where Gwyddfarch is beyond Gwynedd.)

This places 'Canu Tysilio', not in the court of the prince of Powys sometime during the reign of Madog, as suggested by its most recent editor,[116] but in Gwynedd, probably in the last decade of the reign of Owain Gwynedd who died in 1170. After the death of Madog ap Maredudd in 1160 and the division of Powys, which followed the killing of his heir, Llywelyn, soon afterwards, Cynddelw sought patronage at the royal court of Gwynedd. During this time, southern Powys was threatened by a power struggle between Madog's son, Owain Fychan, who held the *cantrefi* of Mechain and Cynllaith and was supported by Owain Gwynedd and his allies, and Madog's nephew, Owain Cyfeiliog, who held Cyfeiliog and Caereinion and was supported by the English Crown. This conflict was not resolved until 1167 when Owain Gwynedd took Cyfeiliog and Caereinion ensuring that Owain Fychan would rule unopposed for the following three years.[117]

Meifod in the south-eastern corner of Mechain, formerly at the heart of the united Powys, was, between 1160 and 1167, on the border between the lands of the two Owains. Amidst the poet's descriptions of its wealth and beauty, its privileges and its hospitality, there are indications that its future was perceived to be under threat. The poem's fourth *caniad* opens defiantly with an account of Tysilio's feats at the Battle of Maes Cogwy, but closes quietly with a heartfelt prayer for God to stand by us now, just as Tysilio had stood by the people of Powys in his time:[118] 'Sefis ef, sefid Duw gennyn!' (He stood [by them], let God stand by us [now]!).

The poem, therefore, appears to have been composed as a response to a political crisis. It can be interpreted as an appeal by the community of Meifod to Owain Gwynedd to intervene in southern Powys in order to resolve the stalemate between the two cousins and to ensure peace. The first part of the final *caniad*, which opens with a characteristically ambiguous reference to the poet's patron as *Prydain ddragon*, can be read as praise of Owain whose generosity is compared with that of Tysilio. It goes on to give assurances concerning the support and welcome which such a 'brave Brython' would receive at Meifod:[119]

> Ym Meifod y maent arwyddon
> Arwraidd i wraidd Frython,
> Ei mawrwledd, ei medd, ei maon,
> Ei threthau i'w thraethadurion,
> Ei deugrair, gywair gyweithon,
> A gyfyd yn gyfoethogion:
> Ei Hynaf henyw o'i thirion,
> Handid rhydd rhwng ei dwy afon;
> Ei Sygynnab glew, gloyw roddion,
> A folaf, a folant feirddon.

(In Meifod there are heroic portents/ for a brave Brython,/ its great feast, its mead, its people,/ its payments to its singers,/ its two relics, upright friends,/ who rise up as men of property:/ its Elder comes from its land,/ it is free between two rivers;/ its valorous Prior, bright his works,/ whom I praise, whom poets praise.)

(iii) Canu Dewi
Unravelling the problem of the historical significance of 'Canu Dewi' is a more complicated issue. There are at least three clues by which this poem may be dated. The first is the reference to Rhys ap Gruffudd, lord of Deheubarth, as *Mon wledic* (lord of Anglesey).[120] A claim for supremacy over Anglesey was, by the twelfth century, tantamount to claiming supremacy over the whole of Wales. There were three dominating figures in Welsh politics during the twelfth century who might have made this claim: Madog ap Maredudd, prince of Powys, who died in 1160, Owain Gwynedd who died in 1170 and Rhys himself who died in 1197. It is unlikely that any poet would venture to refer to Rhys as *Mon wledic* before the death of Owain Gwynedd in 1170.[121] The poet further refers to a specific visit by Rhys to the south, possibly to St Davids, to avenge the theft of cattle.[122]

The two other clues are found in the list of saints called to the synod of Llanddewibrefi in the final *caniad* of the poem. Among them are the saints of *Angaw* (Anjou), Brittany and Maelienydd. Mention of Anjou would have had no meaning in the sixth century and must have had a twelfth-century significance. The first Angevin king was Henry II, who succeeded to the throne in 1154. In one of the versions of Chrétien de Troyes's *Erec*, line 6589, the Angevin Empire is regarded as having extended from Anjou to Wales, and in *Perceval*, line 4114, it is St Davi whom Arthur invokes: 'par mon seignor saint Davi/ Que l'an aore et prie en Gales' (by my lord St David whom they worship and pray to in Wales).[123] The interest of the Angevins in the cult of St David is attested by the visits paid to St Davids by Henry II in 1171 as well as by the political ramifications of the struggle of St Davids to achieve metropolitan status.[124] Rhys ap Gruffudd preserved a peaceful relationship with Henry II from 1172 until the king's death in 1189.[125] By including the saints of Anjou in the list of saints subjugated to St David at Llanddewibrefi, the superiority and antiquity of the cult is emphasized. The reference to the saints of Brittany in the same list, although it may reflect the age-old link between Wales and Brittany, may additionally reflect the Angevin connection, since Henry was regent of Brittany from 1166 to 1181.[126]

The third clue is found in the reference to the saints of Maelienydd, a sub-kingdom in east mid-Wales. This claim that the saints of Maelienydd were subordinate to St David may reflect the struggle between the bishoprics of St Asaph and St Davids for control of the churches of Ceri, which was considered part of Maelienydd. The struggle was resolved by the secession of the churches to St Davids in 1176.[127] The reference may, however, reflect the special relationship between Rhys ap Gruffudd and Cadwallon ap Madog ab Idnerth, lord of Maelienydd, in the 1170s.[128]

These references taken together suggest a date in the 1170s for the poem. The poet probably created it to be recited on a set occasion at Llanddewibrefi when a bishop (see below) and the Lord Rhys were present.[129] What other motivation lies behind it? In so far as the tradition of the synod of Llanddewibrefi was being generally used as a weapon by twelfth-century clergy in Wales in their attempts to win metropolitan status for St Davids, the poem can be regarded as a propagandist document which uses the Welsh language and, in so doing, asserts the Welshness of St David's cause:[130]

> I foli Dewi da Gymräeg—eofn,
> O fodd bryd a bron, o brydest chweg,
> O brydest ddyllest ddull ychwaneg
> I Frefi a Dewi, doeth Gymraeg.

(To praise David [in] good confident Welsh/ with desire of mind and heart, in fair song,/ in song arranged [in] excellent form,/ to Brefi and David [in] wise Welsh.)

It has been suggested that the poem belongs to the 1170s. In 1176, David Fitzgerald, bishop of St Davids, died and the see became vacant. One of the names put forward by the canons of the cathedral as bishop was that of Giraldus Cambrensis, incumbent of a church dedicated to St David, archdeacon of Brecon, son of a first cousin of Rhys ap Gruffudd.[131] Giraldus, who wrote a Life of St David, probably at a later date,[132] was anxious to achieve metropolitan status for the diocese. The ecclesiastical politics of 1176 might be what lies in the background of 'Canu Dewi'. If, however, the poem was produced during an interregnum in the bishopric, it is difficult to explain the reference in line 268 to a bishop officiating at Llanddewibrefi,[133] unless one faction in the church had already accepted Giraldus Cambrensis as bishop of St Davids; this, however, is unlikely. It is perhaps more likely to have been produced in 1175 when David Fitzgerald was still alive and Giraldus Cambrensis newly appointed archdeacon of Brecon. What is certain is that our poem in a subtle way, with its constant reference to the synod of Llanddewibrefi, was advocating a metropolitan status for St Davids. Such a policy had both a national and international ecclesiastical significance, since its ultimate aim was for the Welsh church to be independent of Canterbury. Perhaps, however, the immediate message of the poem is not ecclesiastical.

This poem, like the other two, probably contains an element of secular politics. There are several tantalizing references. As mentioned above, Rhys ap Gruffudd's association with Anglesey is emphasized. Three sections speak of possible hostile threats in the future which St David will help them to withstand. Fear is expressed of a hostile force, probably from Ireland, and the situation compared with that of the great alliance of the battle of *Cad Dybrunawg*, probably a form of the name of the battle of Brunanburh referred to in *Armes Prydein*, the earliest poem to show the political force of the cult of St David.[134]

> Ban ddêl gofyn arnam-ni rhy byddwn ofnawg
> Rhag gormes cedyrn Cad Ddybrunawg;
> Ar Dduw a Dewi, dau niferawg,
> Yd alwn bresen breswyl fodawg . . .
>
> Pan ddêl rhyfel a rhwysg Ffichti
> Ros elfydd, pob celfydd geilw Dewi . . .
>
> O'r daw llynges drom, drwm ei geiriau,
> I geisiaw cymraw, cymryd preiddiau
> Rhwng Mynyw a'r môr, mawr a droau
> A fydd ar eu llu-hwy lliw dydd golau,
> Collant a'r llygaid a'r eneidiau;
> Ni welant na lliant nac eu llongau,
> A chyngor a wnânt â chenhadau
> I hebrwng iddaw ebrwydd drethau.
> Trydy pla Wyddyl (aflwydd diau!)
> Trydy budd Mynyw, mynawg biau.

(Whenever pressure may come to us, we shall be fearful/ in the face of the oppression of the mighty of Brunanburh,/ God and David, two who possess hosts/ shall we invoke constantly and continuously on earth . . . Whenever war and the onslaught of the [Irish] Picts may come/ to the land of Rhos, every man of art will invoke David . . . If a heavy fleet comes with terrifying greetings,/ to seek to cause terror by seizing plunder/ between Menevia and the sea, awful consequences/ will come to their crew at daytime./ They will lose both [their] eyes and lives;/ they will see neither the sea nor their ships,/

and they will seek to make peace through messengers/ by sending to him swift tributes./ The Irish, one of three plagues (a certain failure),/ will be one of the three benefits of Mynyw, a highborn one holds it.)

In his ambiguous time-warp fashion the poet mentions other associations between St David and Ireland, the relationship between Patrick and the saint and the hostility of the Irish chieftain Boia.[135] The use of the indefinite subjunctive *(dêl)* in the lines quoted above most probably means that these reflect the clichés of vaticination. The lines, however, could refer to fears of a real attack. Was the feared future attack the Irish plague referred to in lines 226–7?

If an Irish attack is feared – Viking raids had more or less come to an end by the mid-twelfth century – what kind of scenario can we imagine lying behind the poem? We have argued that the poem should be dated after the death of Owain Gwynedd, when it might have been feasible for Rhys to assert his power in Anglesey. After the death of Owain Gwynedd and his son Hywel, another son, Maelgwn, fled to Ireland for refuge.[136] Might the feared attack have been one of retribution towards Rhys ap Gruffudd for interfering in the affairs of Gwynedd? A more plausible explanation might be found by associating it with Anglo-Norman politics in south Wales. The emphasis throughout the poem is primarily on St David's association with Deheubarth:[137]

> A'r Dehau ef biau a Phebidiawg . . .
> Ac i foli Dewi dothwyf i'r Dehau . . .

(And he it is who possesses the South and Pebidiog . . . And it is to praise David that I have come to the South . . .)

Pebidiog, originally belonging to St Davids,[138] became a marcher lordship, granted by Henry I to Bernard, bishop of St Davids, though there seems, according to Giraldus Cambrensis, to have been a dispute between the bishop and Meilyr Fitzhenry regarding the holding of the lordship.[139] The assertion of the right of St Davids to Pebidiog, quoted above, might reflect this uncertainty. The early part of Rhys ap Gruffudd's career was almost totally occupied with reasserting Welsh power in south Wales. As a consequence of this Welsh resurgence, Norman lords such as Richard FitzGilbert of Clare, earl of Pembroke (Strongbow), the Geraldines and Robert Fitzstephen, associated with Cilgerran, had lost much power and, with the blessing of Henry II, responded to the invitation given them by Diarmait to help him regain the kingdom of Leinster.[140] In 1170,

Strongbow, by his marriage with Aífe, daughter of Diarmait, was recognized as heir to the kingdom of Leinster. The success of the Cambro-Norman expedition in Ireland made Henry II so nervous that he went to Ireland in 1171, visiting St Davids on his way and presenting the cathedral with two capes of brocaded silk for the use of the cantors, to reassert his overlordship over its members.[141] It is possibly this visit which is reflected in the lines describing how Gwynfardd went to St Davids, perhaps as a member of the retinue of the Lord Rhys to meet Henry:[142]

> Ac i Fynyw ethwyf, eithaf Dyfed,
> A theÿrnedd ethynt a theÿrnged,

(And it is to Menevia that I have been, at the extreme point of Dyfed,/ And princes have taken tribute [there]).[143]

Returning in 1172, when he heard mass at St Davids cathedral on Easter Monday,[144] Henry made Rhys ap Gruffudd Justiciar of South Wales. It might be this background which made Gwynfardd so conscious of Ireland and of attacks from there by either the Irish or the Cambro-Normans.[145]

But what is the purpose of the poem? Why was it sung? The overwhelming emphasis on Llanddewi suggests that its primary purpose was to celebrate some event at Llanddewibrefi – perhaps the rededication of the church after a time of rebuilding.[146] The mention of the *clas*, perhaps a community still organized on a kin basis[147] and priests,[148] suggests that it was the local clerics who commissioned the poem. Llanddewibrefi was, however, such an important cult centre that any celebratory event held there would attract both clergy and laity from the whole of the diocese of St Davids and account for the presence of the bishop and the Lord Rhys. This would have given the poet an opportunity to refer to the current problems of the diocese and possible threats of hostile attacks from Ireland, and to exalt the cause of the primacy of the cult of St David.

Significance in ecclesiastical politics

An attempt has been made to place the poems in their Welsh hagiographical and political context. The native context does not entirely explain why these poems to saints were composed in the twelfth century. In order to do that it is necessary to consider the poems against a wider background. The overt emphasis on the cults of the Welsh saints found in the poems is also attested to by genealogies and twelfth-century *vitae*.

Were there any external factors which stimulated this movement? The organizing genius of the Normans who conquered England and invaded Wales, setting up their marcher lordships and penetrating the Welsh heartland, required written documentation of all sorts. In England, suspicion of the traditions of the native saints inspired the activities of the Fleming Goscelin, chaplain to the monks of Wilton, as well as those of Saxons of the Chapter of Canterbury, such as Eadmer and Osbern, who collected and recorded the Lives of Anglo-Saxon saints.[149] In Wales, Rhigyfarch's Life of St David was written following the visit of William I to St Davids. Other Anglo-Norman kings such as Henry II, who visited St Davids, showed an interest in the Celtic saints.[150] In Welsh vernacular terms, the official court-poetry was the best kind of documentation available. As Professor R. R. Davies has pointed out, the poets who formed one of the mandarin classes of medieval Celtic society, offered services comparable to those of the emergent civil service and judiciary of the English.[151]

So we have a general interest in saints' cults. The Anglo-Saxons who recorded the acts of their own saints were on the defensive; the impact of the ideas of continental churchmen made the Anglo-Saxons want to defend their own native traditions. The Welsh Church also felt the impact of these foreign churchmen.[152] In 1092, the Breton Hervé, William Rufus's chaplain and the namesake of a Breton saint,[153] was made bishop of Bangor;[154] in 1107, Urban of the bishopric of Worcester, perhaps the greatest of all the manipulators of Welsh hagiographical traditions for the benefit of his see, was made bishop of Llandaf;[155] and in 1115,[156] Bernard, chaplain to the wife of Henry I, was made bishop of St Davids.[157] These foreign bishops 'defined and demarcated' afresh the Welsh dioceses, exploiting the traditions of their sees, collecting the relics of their saints, while strengthening at the same time their control over the local Church.[158] As Professor R. R. Davies has pointed out, 'the most visible expression of the transformation of the local church in Wales in these centuries was the building and rebuilding of the parish churches'.[159] This building and rebuilding would strengthen the awareness of the local saint's cult, even if the power of the *clas* was weakened. By the mid-twelfth century there was yet another threat to the power of the Welsh *clas* churches in the shape of the continental monastic orders, notably the Cistercians. Madog ap Maredudd was the last of the princes of Powys to be buried at Tysilio's church at Meifod in 1160;[160] his distinguished successor, Owain Cyfeiliog, became the patron of the abbey of Strata Marcella, which was founded in 1170, and was buried there.[161] The native princes of Cadfan's Meirionnydd became patrons of Cymer abbey, founded in 1199.¹⁶² A few miles upstream from Llanddewibrefi is the site of the Cistercian abbey of Strata Florida. It was founded in 1164 by Robert Fitzstephen,¹⁶³ and by early in the 1170s it had become the home of the text which lay behind the Welsh *Brut y Tywysogyon*, the major Welsh chronicle, which has a distinct Deheubarth basis.¹⁶⁴ In the face of impending changes, it was natural that the *clasau* should commission poems asserting their rights and singing the praises of their patron saints.

The intrusion by churchmen from without opens another question, namely the Breton element in twelfth-century Welsh hagiography. The twelfth century saw a renaissance in Welsh–Breton connections. The greatest manifestation of this is the work of Geoffrey of Monmouth, himself possibly a second- or third-generation Breton, whose *Historia Regum Britanniae* has a strong Breton element.¹⁶⁵ The Breton Hervé was appointed to the bishopric of Bangor in 1092, albeit that he subsequently had a very chequered career. Bretons such as the Fitzalans of Oswestry were prominent among the marcher lords whose lands bordered on those of Madog ap Maredudd.¹⁶⁶ Could it have been associates of the Fitzalans who were responsible for conveying a Life of Tysilio to Brittany? Professional interpreters took the Matter of Britain to France.¹⁶⁷ There was probably a renewed consciousness of the relationship between Brittany and Wales, as Giraldus Cambrensis illustrated when he demonstrated the relationship between Welsh, Breton and Cornish.¹⁶⁸ In this atmosphere, it would clearly be useful propaganda for native Welsh churchmen to claim a Breton connection for the saints of some of the major *clas* churches. On the other hand, those who took the *Matière de Bretagne* to the Continent to enrich that literature would not be against pirating the occasional Welsh Life, such as that of Tysilio, to enrich the narrative repertoire of their own saints.

To sum up: this study has tried to draw attention to a number of themes. Firstly, the poems to saints testify to a general interest in traditions associated with saints in twelfth-century Wales. In the cases of Cadfan and Tysilio no independent *vitae* have survived, although the story of the latter's life preserved in Brittany as part of the the Lives of Suliau must, on the linguistic evidence, derive from a Welsh source. There are multiple versions of *Vita Davidis* which illustrate both the interest taken in his cult and its importance in the twelfth century. Secondly, the poems testify to a consciousness of the common inheritance of hagiographical material of Wales and Brittany. This is illustrated by the use of story themes common to both countries, such as the triple birth motif reflected in the name of Gwen Teirbron, *Alba tribus mammis*, the genealogical references to saints from Brittany found in 'Canu Cadfan' and the survival of the Tysilio story (fragmentarily attested to in 'Canu Tysilio') in a Breton source. The cult of St David is also richly attested to in Breton tradition as shown by the late medieval Breton play *Buez santez Nonn*. Thirdly, the communities of major *clas* churches, such as Tywyn, Meifod and Llanddewibrefi, were using hagiographical material in the poetic vernacular to assert their rights on a provincial level, associating their patron saints with the politics of Meirionnydd, Powys and Deheubarth. 'Canu Dewi' offers yet another dimension, demonstrating the significance of the saint in both the national and international arenas of the twelfth century. Just as the tenth-century poet of *Armes Prydein* called on a unity of forces in the name of St David, the *Gogynfeirdd* poets were invoking the native saints as a force to be used as a weapon in secular political manoeuvring. Finally, the overt interest in the cults of the native saints, shown in these poems, is both a reflection of and a reaction against the general ecclesiastical movements of the twelfth century, namely the Anglo-Norman interest in saints' cults and the introduction into Wales of new ecclesiastical Orders, such as the Cistercians, who dimmed and finally extinguished the light of the old *clas* churches.

Notes

[1] In this chapter Morfydd E. Owen was responsible for the discussion of 'Canu Dewi', the sections on hagiography of all three poems and on the significance of the poems in ecclesiastical politics. Nerys Ann Jones contributed the sections on the status of the poems and on the political significance of 'Canu Tysilio' and 'Canu Cadfan', suggestions and extracted the bibliography from the footnotes. We are grateful to Huw Pryce for helpful information.

[2] Fawtier (ed.), *La Vie de saint Samson*; Flobert (ed.), *La Vie ancienne*; Kenney, *Sources*, pp. 173–5.

[3] J. W. James (ed.), *Rhigyfarch's Life* and the literature cited at n. 77.

[4] See Emanuel, 'An analysis'; Brooke, 'St Peter of Gloucester'.

[5] See, for instance, W. Davies, *The Llandaff Charters*.

[6] Hughes, 'British Museum MS Cotton Vespasian A xiv'.

[7] J. E. C. Williams, 'Bucheddau'r saint'; D. J. Jones, 'Cerddi'r saint'.

[8] Although these three poems are the only poems to saints which survive from the period of the *Gogynfeirdd*, the twelfth-century Life of Gwynllyw refers to a poem written to that saint in the British tongue by a 'Britannus quidam uersificator' (a certain British versifier), *VSBG*, p. 182. The mass of later *cywydd* material is apolitical in a secular sense, cf. D. J. Jones, 'Cerddi'r saint'.

[9] These poems are preserved in either or both of the principal manuscript collections of *Gogynfeirdd* poetry, the Hendregadredd Manuscript, written in the early

fourteenth century at the Cistercian abbey of Strata Florida, and the Red Book of Hergest, written for a lay patron from the Tawe valley by a lay scribe about 1400. See Huws, *Medieval Welsh Manuscripts*, pp. 75–7, 79–83, 193–226; G. Charles-Edwards, 'Scribes'. For the Cadfan poem see McKenna (ed.), 'Canu Cadfan'; McKenna, 'The hagiographic poetics'; for Tysilio, see Parry Owen (ed.), 'Canu Tysilio Sant'; Parry Owen, 'Canu Cynddelw Brydydd Mawr i Dysilio Sant'; for Dewi, see Owen (ed.), 'Canu i Ddewi'; Owen, 'Prolegomena'. See also H. Lewis (ed.), *Hen Gerddi Crefyddol*, pp. 32–40, 43–52, 84–9; C. T. B. Davies, 'Cerddi'r tai crefydd', pp. 10–15, 260–77, and Owen, 'Trois poèmes'.

[10] There is a slight possibility that Gwynfardd Brycheiniog might have been a cleric. His name may mean something like 'holy' or 'blessed poet', see further Owen in Bramley et al. (eds.), *Gwaith Llywelyn Fardd I*, pp. 417–18.

[11] On the *Gogynfeirdd* see, for instance, J. E. C. Williams, *Poets of the Welsh Princes*.

[12] In this they are similar to some of the Latin Lives (see, for example, W. Davies, 'Property rights') and *Braint Teilo* which reached its final form at a time of crisis for the diocese of Llandaf (see W. Davies, '*Braint Teilo*').

[13] For the mediatory powers of Welsh saints see W. Davies, *Wales in the Early Middle Ages*, p. 173.

[14] Tywyn, Llanddewibrefi and Meifod all have early-medieval inscribed stones, see *ECMW*, pp. 98–9, 172–3, 178–9. For the Roman site at Llanio farm, Llanddewibrefi, and its tentative identification with the *Bremia* of the Ravenna Cosmographer see J. L. Davies, 'The Roman period', pp. 302–6. Meifod was once spuriously considered to be a Roman site as was nearby Mathrafal, associated with the kings of Powys from the end of the twelfth century, but recent archaeological work has failed to find evidence of Roman remains in the latter, see Arnold and Hugget, 'Mathrafal, Powys' and 'Excavations at Mathrafal'.

[15] See J. W. Evans, 'The survival of the *clas*'. The identification of saints with specific political units is old in Wales; cf. for instance, the old kingdom of Gwynllwg, whose name derives from that of Gwynllyw, and the kingdom of Brycheiniog whose name derives from Brychan. Examples from Ireland are better known, although without the same kind of lexical connection between the names of the saints and the kingdoms; see, for instance, the association of Uí Néill territories with Patrick or Columba (n. 59 below).

[16] The extracts which follow are based on McKenna's edition, in Bramley et al. (eds), *Gwaith Llywelyn Fardd I*, poem 1. The translations are our own.

[17] Ibid., p. 17, ll. 11–14.

[18] Ibid., p. 17, ll. 37–8. At least two interpretations of the line are possible depending on the interpretation of *ar* which can mean among other things 'to' in introducing a place or person approached (see *Geiriadur Prifysgol Cymru*, s. v. *ar*[1] §7) or 'as one of' when followed by an ordinal (§3) or 'in' (§5), then translating 'in a host of believers'.

[19] McKenna (ed.), 'Canu Cadfan', pp. 19–20, ll. 121–2, 137–40, and see B. F. Roberts, 'Enlli'r Oesoedd Canol', pp. 27–9.

[20] McKenna (ed.), 'Canu Cadfan', p. 17, ll. 8 and 14.

[21] See, for example, ibid., p. 18, ll. 50–2. For the importance of gospel books as relics see Gerald of Wales, *The Journey through Wales*, p. 253; Henken, *Traditions*, p. 175. For the importance of crosiers see I. Williams, *Beginnings*, pp. 184–5. For the importance of relics in other Celtic lands see J. Smith, 'Oral and written'.

[22] *VSBG*, p. 254.

[23] Ibid., p. xvii.

[24] *EWGT*, pp. 57–8, and cf. Miller, *The Saints of Gwynedd*, pp. 90–4.

[25] See *LBS*, vol. 3, pp. 370 ff., where Baring-Gould and Fisher recognize two saints bearing the name Lleuddad: Lleuddad ab Alan from Armorica and the Welsh Lleuddad ap Dingad.

[26] *EWGT*, pp. 57–8.

[27] Duine, *Sources hagiographiques*, pp. 40–8; Balcou and Le Gallou, *Histoire littéraire*, vol. 1, pp. 40, 95, 166; Merdrignac, *Recherches sur l'hagiographie*, vol. 1, pp. 187, 192; Bromwich (ed.), *Trioedd*, pp. 346–7, *s.n.* Emyr Llydaw and for Gwen see Kerlouégan, 'Les Vies de saints bretons', p. 208.

[28] *EWGT*, pp. 57–8.

[29] Bromwich (ed.), *Trioedd*, pp. 346–7; H. Lewis (ed.), *Brut Dingestow*, p. 268.

[30] See Lloyd-Jones, 'emyr, ymer, ymher'.

[31] Loth, *Les Noms des saints*, p. 20.

[32] Information provided by B. Tanguy, but see also Loth, *Les Noms des saints*, p. 20.

[33] The extracts which follow are based on Parry Owen's edition of the poem in N. A. Jones and Parry Owen (eds), *Gwaith Cynddelw*, vol. 1, poem 3. The translations are our own.

[34] Ibid., p. 29, ll. 13–19.

[35] Ibid., p. 29, l. 37 and p. 32, l. 142.

[36] *EWGT*, p. 59. For Cynddelw see N. A. Jones and Parry Owen (eds), *Gwaith Cynddelw*, vol. 1, pp. xxv-xliii.

[37] Ibid., p. 30, l. 46 and also the note. For dedications in general see Wade-Evans, 'Parochiale Wallicum'.

[38] Parry Owen (ed.), 'Canu Tysilio Sant', p. 32, ll. 162–3.

[39] Ibid., p. 29, ll. 27–30.

[40] Ibid., p. 31, ll. 111–34, and on the battle see Rowland (ed. and trans.), *Saga Poetry*, pp. 124–5.

[41] Parry Owen (ed), 'Canu Tysilio Sant', p. 32, ll. 148–54.

[42] Ibid., p. 32, l. 173 and p. 34, l. 232.

[43] Ibid., p. 29, l. 20 and p. 33, ll. 195–6.

[44] Jackson, 'Colloquy'; Henken, *Traditions*, pp. 269–73.

[45] Le Grand, *Les Vies des saints*, pp. 481–7, translated in Doble, *Saint Suliau*, pp. 7–14.

[46] Quoted as Paris, MS Bibliothèque national de France 22321, in *LBS*, vol. 4, p. 296. See also Doble, *Saint Suliau*, pp. 35–6, for the text.

[47] Duine, *Sources hagiographiques*, p. 347; Bollandus et al. (eds), *Acta Sanctorum*, vol. 49, October 1, p. 197.

[48] N. A. Jones and Parry Owen (eds) *Gwaith Cynddelw*, vol. 1, pp. 15–16.

[49] See Aberystwyth, NLW, MS Llanstephan 117, fol. 38^v (p. 76).

[50] *VSBG*, p. 305, and cf. Le Grand, *Les Vies des saints*, p. 484 and Merdrignac, 'La Quadrature du cercle', p. 37.

[51] Doble, *Saint Suliau*, p. 26.

[52] Lobineau, *Les Vies des saints*, p. 111. See also Bollandus et al. (eds), *Acta Sanctorum*, vol. 49, October 1, pp. 196–8.

[53] Chadwick, *Early Brittany*, p. 209; Fleuriot, *Les Origines*, p. 215.

[54] Le Grand, *Les Vies des saints*, p. 606, n. 2; p. 607, n. 1.

[55] For Old Welsh orthography see M. Lewis, 'Astudiaeth o orgraff Hen Gymraeg'; Jackson, *Language and History*, pp. 67–75. The -*au* in *Suliau* must be Welsh (ibid. pp., 287–90). For the first element in *Haiarnmed* cf. Mod.W. *haearn*, OC *hoern*, Breton *hoiarn* (see Graves, *Old Cornish*, p. 533; Jackson, *Language and History*, pp. 359–60; *idem*, *Historical Philology of Breton*, p. 230; Koch, 'When was Welsh literature . . .?', p. 44). The diphthong *ei* in *Meibot* also must be Welsh (Jackson, *Language and History*, pp. 581–2, 595–7).

⁵⁶ The extracts which follow are based on Owen's edition of the poem in Bramley et al. (eds), *Gwaith Llywelyn Fardd I*, poem 26. The translations are our own.

⁵⁷ Kenney, *Sources*, pp. 239–40, 376.

⁵⁸ Bowen, *Settlements*, p. 59; Chadwick, 'Intellectual life', pp. 133–4; an Irien, 'Saints du Cornwall', pp. 167–8, and for a recent splendid summary of the importance of the cult of David (Divi) in Brittany see Le Berre, Tanguy and Castel (eds), *Buez santez Nonn*; Dumville, *Saint David of Wales*, p. 3, points out that the earliest record of St David as *aquaticus* (waterman) comes from a Breton source.

⁵⁹ See for instance, Doherty, 'The cult of St Patrick', and for the association of Patrick and Columba with various dynasties see T. M. Charles-Edwards, *Early Christian Ireland*, pp. 15–36, 238–4, 441–68.

⁶⁰ T. M. Charles-Edwards, 'The seven bishop-houses'.

⁶¹ I. Williams (ed.), *Armes Prydein*, pp. xvii–xx, 5, l. 129 and p. 4, ll. 105–6, 'trwy eiriawl Dewi a seint Prydeyn./ hyt ffrwt Ailego ffohawr all[myn]' (Through the intercession of Dewi and the saints of Britain the [foreigners] will be put to flight as far as the river Ailego), cited in W. Davies, *Wales in the Early Middle Ages*, p. 173.

⁶² N. K. Chadwick suggested that the Life was composed for William the Conqueror's visit to St Davids: see Chadwick, 'Intellectual life', pp. 175–6, a date which Kirby supported in 'A note', p. 297; J. W. James (ed.), *Rhigyfarch's Life*, pp. xi–xiii, suggests a date in the 1090s; D. S. Evans (ed.), *Welsh Life*, p. xxxi, suggests a date between 1081 and 1085.

⁶³ See particularly A. G. Williams, 'Norman lordship'.

⁶⁴ T. Jones (ed.), *Brut (Red Book)*, pp. 16–17. On the importance of the cathedral site at St Davids see J. Wyn Evans's article, above.

⁶⁵ O. T. Edwards, *Matins*, p. 127.

⁶⁶ See J. C. Davies (ed.), *Episcopal Acts*, vol. 1, p. 136, n. 887.

⁶⁷ Ibid., pp. 190–232, and for a recent summary see Pryce, 'Yr eglwys', p. 146.

⁶⁸ St David was, for instance, recognized as the premier seat of Wales by the prince of Gwynedd, Owain Gwynedd: see J. C. Davies (ed.), *Episcopal Acts*, vol. 1, p. 207.

⁶⁹ An abridged version of the Latin Lives was later translated into Welsh, possibly at Llanddewibrefi in the fourteenth century. See J. W. James, 'The Welsh versions'; J. E. C. Williams, 'Buchedd Dewi'; D. S. Evans (ed.), *Buchedd Dewi; idem,* (ed.), *Welsh Life*.

⁷⁰ 1176 is the date proposed by J. W. James in *Rhigyfarch's Life*, p. xxxii, but contrast the date 1194–9 proposed by Richter, 'The Life of St David by Giraldus Cambrensis', p. 386. For that version of the Life see Bartlett, 'Rewriting saints' Lives'.

⁷¹ Owen (ed.), 'Canu i Ddewi', p. 454, ll. 230–7. Boia attempted to drive David from his settlement in Hoddnant in Mynyw with the help of his wife who sent, in traditional hagiographical fashion, her naked maids to confound him. Cf. D. S. Evans (ed.), *Welsh Life*, p. 5; *VSBG*, p. 156; J. W. James (ed.), *Rhigyfarch's Life*, p. 10; Plummer (ed.), *Vitae*, vol. 1, p. clxvi, n. 2; and Vendryes, 'Saint David et le roi Boia'.

⁷² Owen (ed.), 'Canu i Ddewi', p. 450, ll. 51–8. For the anecdote concerning David's oxen preserved until recently in oral folklore in the neighbourhood of Llanddewibrefi, see Rhŷs, *Celtic Folklore*, pp. 578–81; Henken, *Traditions*, pp. 66–8.

⁷³ Noble lineages were a characteristic of Celtic saints, see R. R. Davies, *Conquest*, p. 176; *CGSH*, pp. xiii–xiv. For St David's genealogy, see *VSBG*, p. 320.

⁷⁴ Owen (ed.), 'Canu i Ddewi', p. 449, ll. 11–18; for a recent discussion of the genealogy see Dumville, *Saint David of Wales*.

⁷⁵ Owen (ed.), 'Canu i Ddewi', p. 449, l. 45. The *diofredawc* was the man who had sworn to abstain from the things of this world. See Pryce, *Native Law*, p. 259, s.n. *diofredog*. The asceticism of St David and his community was famed, cf. O. T.

Edwards, *Matins*, p. 127; D. S. Evans (ed.), *Welsh Life*, p. 2; Gerald of Wales, *The Journey through Wales*, p. 163.

[76] Owen (ed.), 'Canu i Ddewi', p. 449, ll. 33–4. Kenney, *Sources*, pp. 239–40, 376. See Hennessy (ed.), *Chronicon Scotorum*, p. 62; D. S. Evans (ed.), *Welsh Life*, pp. xi–xii; *VSBG* p. 162: 'Verum pene tercia pars uel quarta Hibernie seruit Dauid aquilento' (But almost a third part or fourth of Ireland is subject to David the Waterman). For the association with St Patrick see *VSBG*, pp. 150–1; D. S. Evans (ed.), *Welsh Life*, pp. 1–2, 22–7 and cf. Le Berre, Tanguy and Castel (eds), *Buez santez Nonn*, pp. 117–18. For sites associated with Patrick in the area of St Davids see H. James, 'The cult of St David' (1933), p. 106 *et passim*.

[77] Owen (ed.), 'Canu i Ddewi', p. 454, ll. 238–41 refer to the Llech Lafar recorded by Gerald of Wales as being associated with an onomastic legend and the visit of Henry II to St Davids (see Gerald of Wales, *The Journey through Wales*, p. 168; *Expugnatio Hibernica*, pp. 105–7). Lines 258–9 referring to the track of St David's horse ('ac ôl ei farch') have perhaps a hidden reference to an onomastic tale associated with the various farms and a hamlet called Olmarch in the Llanddewibrefi area, see notes on the lines in the edition.

[78] Owen (ed.), 'Canu i Ddewi', pp. 450–1, ll. 85–109.

[79] *VSBG*, p. 154; D. S. Evans (ed.), *Welsh Life*, p. 4.

[80] For Bangor see Willis-Bund, *An Extent*, pp. 214–17; for Abergwili see ibid., pp. 240–51, for Llannarth see ibid., pp. 248–9.

[81] Owen (ed.), 'Canu i Ddewi', pp. 453–4, ll. 206–42.

[82] Ibid., p. 450, ll. 56–7, and Gerald of Wales, *The Journey through Wales*, p. 79: 'In the church at Glasgwm, in Elfael there is a handbell which has most miraculous powers. It is supposed to have belonged to St David and is called "Bangu".'

[83] Owen (ed.), 'Canu i Ddewi', p. 450, l. 85. In the Lives of the saints there is a reference to an angel proclaiming that no one buried in Glyn Rhosyn, the site of St Davids cathedral, would go to hell (see, for instance, D. S. Evans (ed.), *Welsh Life*, p. 4). For the general belief that burial in a saint's graveyard would ensure the mediation of the saint on Judgement Day see D. S. Evans, *Medieval Religious Literature*, p. 31.

[84] Owen (ed.), 'Canu i Ddewi', p. 453, ll. 206–11. Other references to Mynyw, however, are with one exception restricted to one *caniad* (pp. 453–4, ll. 212–45). The story of Boia (p. 454, l. 230), mentioned above, is localized in Mynyw; other references include a description of St David's settlement there, and a cryptic reference to marauders (p. 453, ll. 226–9).

[85] Ibid., p. 449, l. 30; p. 450, l. 86; p. 451, ll. 131 and 134; p. 452, ll. 139 and 162; p. 454, l. 269; p. 455, l. 286. It is interesting that Brefi, which derives from the name for the old Roman settlement, Bremia, is what is used; later this became part of the name of the parish and village, Llanddewibrefi, see Rivet and Smith, *Place-names*, pp. 276–7; Jackson, 'Romano-British names', pp. 68–82 and see Bowen, 'The cult of Dewi Sant'; *ECMW*, pp. 98–100; Gruffydd and Owen, 'The earliest mention of St David?'; *idem*, 'The earliest mention of St David? An Addendum'; Jackson, 'The Idnert inscription'; Bowen, *Saint David of History*, pp. 6–9. For recent datings and innovative, though still debatable, views on the Idnert stone, see C. Thomas, 'The Llanddewi-brefi "Idnert" stone'.

[86] Owen (ed.), 'Canu i Ddewi', pp. 451–2, ll. 132–9.

[87] Ibid., p. 450, ll. 63–80.

[88] Ibid., p. 449, ll. 27–30.

[89] Ibid., pp. 454–55, ll. 272–91.

[90] McKenna (ed.), 'Canu Cadfan', p. 17, ll. 9–14, and for the protective powers of the saints see W. Davies, *Wales in the Early Middle Ages*, pp. 174–6.

[91] Parry Owen (ed.), 'Canu Tysilio Sant', p. 31, ll. 111–34. See above n. 40.

[92] Owen (ed.), 'Canu i Ddewi', p. 449, ll. 11–18; p. 450, ll. 59–62; p. 453, ll. 200–1; p. 454, ll. 254–5.

[93] McKenna (ed.), 'Canu Cadfan', p. 17, ll. 18–22.

[94] Pryce, *Native Law*, pp. 235–9; Jenkins and Owen (eds), *The Welsh Law of Women*, pp. 49–50 and T. M. Charles-Edwards, Owen and Russell (eds), *The Welsh King and his Court*, p. 562, *s.n. braint*.

[95] See, for instance, 'Canu Heledd' where it is mentioned that the churches of Baschurch lost their *braint* after the defeat of Cynddylan and Elfan of Powys by the English (I. Williams (ed.), *Canu Llywarch Hen*, p. 39, stanza 49; Rowland (ed. and trans.), *Saga Poetry*, p. 435, stanza 49); and the tenth-century poem, *Armes Prydein*, which asks why the enemies of the Welsh trampled on the *braint* of their saints (I. Williams (ed.), *Armes Prydein*, p. 5, l. 139).

[96] W. Davies, '*Braint Teilo*'.

[97] McKenna (ed.), 'Canu Cadfan', p. 17, l. 42; Parry Owen (ed.), 'Canu Tysilio Sant', p. 30, l. 51; Owen (ed.). 'Canu i Ddewi', p. 449, ll. 20, 27, 30, 31; p. 451, l. 134; p. 453, l. 192; p. 454, l. 269.

[98] Pryce, *Native Law*, pp. 165–74.

[99] Gerald of Wales, *The Journey through Wales*, p. 254.

[100] T. Jones, (ed.), *Brut (Red Book)*, p. 60; Pryce, *Native Law*, p. 173.

[101] Owen (ed.), 'Canu i Ddewi', p. 457, l. 76.

[102] Ibid., p. 452, ll. 140, 144–8. For references to the saint's *nawdd* in 'Canu Tysilio', see Parry Owen (ed.), 'Canu Tysilio Sant', p. 30, l. 56, where the compound *balchnawdd* is used.

[103] This view is reinforced by references in the poems themselves, e.g. ibid., pp. 33–4, ll. 211–42; McKenna (ed.), 'Canu Cadfan', pp. 20, ll. 155–78; Owen (ed.), 'Canu i Ddewi', p. 450, ll. 65–72; p. 452, ll. 148–54.

[104] T. Jones (ed.), *Brut (Red Book)*, pp. 126–7; Lloyd, *History of Wales*, vol. 2, p. 490.

[105] T. Jones (ed.), *Brut (Red Book)*, pp. 126–7. For Gerald of Wales's comments on the lay abbots of Llanbadarn see *The Journey through Wales*, pp. 180–1.

[106] McKenna (ed.), 'Canu Cadfan', p. 19, ll. 135–6; see C. T. B. Davies, 'Cerddi'r tai crefydd', p. 256, and cf. the note on the line in Bramley et al. (eds), *Gwaith Llywelyn Fardd I*, p. 136. For another possible identification of Meirionnydd as the land of Cadfan, see the reference to Maredudd ap Cynan's grave in Llywarch Brydydd y Moch's elegy concerning him: 'Gwelyddyn tëyrn ... uwch bro Gadfan' (E. Jones (ed.), *Gwaith Llywarch ap Llywelyn*, p. 124, ll. 33 and 36). This reference, however, does not, as suggested in J. B. Smith, 'Cymer Abbey', p. 110 and n. 53, indicate that Maredudd was buried in the church of Tywyn. On the contrary, the phrase 'uwch bro Gadfan' (above/beyond the land of Cadfan) suggests burial, either in the Cistercian abbey of Cymer of which Maredudd was a benefactor, if *bro Gadfan* is interpreted as the lands held by Cadfan's church at Tywyn, or alongside his brother, Gruffudd, at the abbey of Aberconwy, if *bro Gadfan* is to be taken as the whole of Meirionnydd. The allusion to *tud Cynfan* (the land/people of Cynfan) protecting the grave, in l. 33, is uncertain, but Cynfan may be identified with Cynfan ap Hefan, a forefather of Ednywain ap Bradwen of Meirionnydd, see Bartrum, 'Pedigrees', p. 110 (no. 25.1).

[107] *EWGT*, p. 98.

[108] McKenna (ed.), 'Canu Cadfan', p. 18, ll. 49–60.

[109] Ibid., p. 18, l. 53 'a lord who makes his land prosper'; ibid., p. 17, l. 30 'ruler of the land of Ednyfed', referring perhaps to Ednyfed Meirionnydd who appears in the genealogies, see *EWGT*, p. 108.

[110] McKenna (ed.), 'Canu Cadfan', p. 19, ll. 115–22. The poem's portrayal of the saints as joint protectors of Tywyn is not confirmed in any other medieval source and

may well be of the poet's invention. Their portrayal as blood-relatives runs counter to the evidence of the genealogies (see ibid., p. 31, n. to l. 122), but would have aided in the identification of Cadfan and Lleuddad with Cynan and Morfran, who may well have been cousins.

[111] See T. M. Charles-Edwards and Jones, 'Breintiau Gwŷr Powys'.

[112] Parry Owen (ed), 'Canu Tysilio Sant', p. 32, l. 173.

[113] Ibid., p. 32, ll. 136–8.

[114] Ibid., p. 29, l. 20; p. 33, ll. 196–7.

[115] Ibid., pp. 29–30, ll. 45–6.

[116] Ibid., pp. 15–18. The reference to the three saints of Meifod in l. 54 suggests that the poem must have been composed after 1155, when the church was consecrated to Mary (see T. Jones (ed.), *Brut (Red Book)*, pp. 132–4), and her name probably added to those of Tysilio and Gwyddfarch.

[117] Ibid., pp. 140–9; Lloyd, *History of Wales*, vol. 2, pp. 508–21; T. M. Charles-Edwards and Jones, 'Breintiau Gwŷr Powys', pp. 199–20; N. A. Jones and Parry Owen (eds), *Gwaith Cynddelw*, vol. 1, pp. 13–15.

[118] Parry Owen (ed.), 'Canu Tysilio Sant', p. 31, l. 134.

[119] Ibid., pp. 33–4, ll. 219–28. This interpretation is confirmed by the reference in ll. 225–6 to the 'Hynaf' (Elder), probably the abbot of Meifod, as a native of Powys. What is known of the ecclesiastical history of Gwynedd during Owain's reign suggests that he was strongly in favour of the native church. See Lloyd, *History of Wales*, vol. 2, pp. 521–2; J. C. Davies (ed.), *Episcopal Acts*, vol. 1, p. 102; vol. 2, pp. 417–34; R. R. Davies, *Conquest*, p. 189 and Pryce, 'Owain Gwynedd', pp. 9–11.

[120] Owen (ed.), 'Canu i Ddewi', p. 452, l. 153.

[121] Rhys ap Gruffudd's interest in Anglesey in the 1170s is also suggested by Seisyll Bryffwrch and Gwynfardd Brycheiniog in their praise poems to Rhys: see Owen in Bramley et al. (eds)., *Gwaith Llywelyn Fardd I*, pp. 403–4 (n. to l. 29) and p. 434 (n. to l. 50), and J. B. Smith, 'Treftadaeth Deheubarth', p. 35 and n. 71, p. 49 and cf. p. 48, n. 56, and Gerald of Wales, *The Journey through Wales*, p. 186.

[122] Owen (ed.), 'Canu i Ddewi', p. 452, ll. 148–9: 'A lord of Deheubarth came to David/ to avenge like a faithful one the theft of his cattle.'

[123] Quoted in Tyndale, 'Names', pp. 268 and 182. For Henry II see Warren, *Henry II*.

[124] D. S. Evans (ed.), *Welsh Life*, pp. xxiv, xxx; T. Jones (ed.), *Brut (Red Book)*, pp. 154–7 and Lloyd, *History of Wales*, vol. 2, p. 542. An episode referring to the visit of Henry II to the Llech Lafar in St Davids in 1172 and the place of the stone in vaticinatory tradition is narrated by Gerald of Wales (see *The Journey through Wales*, p. 168; *Expugnatio Hibernica*, pp. 105–7 and n. 77 above). See the reference to the 'dear Llech Lafar', p. 454, l. 239, in Owen (ed.), 'Canu i Ddewi' – the stone and its traditions were clearly a subject of topical wonder in the 1170s.

[125] For this traditional view see R. R. Davies, *Conquest*, pp. 53–4; Pryce, 'Gerald's Journey'; but, for a different standpoint, see Gillingham, 'Henry II'.

[126] Poole, *From Domesday Book*, pp. 324–5; Everard, *Brittany and the Angevins 1158–1203*, especially pp. 35–6, where the similarities between the political situations of Wales and Brittany in the Angevin empire are discussed.

[127] Gerald of Wales, *The Journey through Wales*, pp. 10–11; Lloyd, *History of Wales*, vol. 2, pp. 558–9.

[128] Remfry, 'Cadwallon ap Madog', pp. 15–16.

[129] Owen (ed.) 'Canu i Ddewi', p. 452, l. 153; p. 454, l. 268.

[130] Ibid., pp. 451–2, ll. 136–9.

[131] Lloyd, *History of Wales*, vol. 2, pp. 559–60. For the appointment of Gerald as archdeacon see J. C. Davies (ed.), *Episcopal Acts*, vol. 1, p. 278; Yardley, *Menevia Sacra*, p. 42.

[132] See n. 70 above.

[133] See the note on the line in Bramley et al. (eds), *Gwaith Llywelyn Fardd I*, p. 476.

[134] Owen (ed.), 'Canu i Ddewi', p. 450, ll. 59–62; p. 452, ll. 176–7; p. 453, ll. 218–27. This argument depends on whether the interpretation of the name *Cad Dybrunawg* offered by Owen in the note on l. 60 of the edition of the poem, also suggested tentatively by Lloyd-Jones, *Geirfa*, p. 88, *s.n. cat* is acceptable. On the battle of Brunanburh, see I. Williams (ed.), *Armes Prydein*, pp. xxi–xxiv and cf. l. 129 of the poem where the 'pure banner of David' is raised to strengthen the Welsh in their campaign against the English. We have retained the version of the name used by I. Williams. For *Cad Dybrunawg* see further Breeze, 'The battle of Brunanburgh'. For the use of saints' relics as banners in battle see, for instance, Ní Mhaonaigh, '*Nósa Ua Maine*', pp. 377–8.

[135] Owen (ed.) 'Canu i Ddewi', p. 449, ll. 35, 37–8; p. 454, ll. 230–41.

[136] Lloyd, *History of Wales*, vol. 2, pp. 550–1 and see S. Duffy, 'The 1169 invasion', pp. 105–6.

[137] Owen (ed.), 'Canu i Ddewi', p. 449, l. 34; p. 454, l. 270.

[138] The *cantref* in which St Davids was situated. See Richards, *Welsh Administrative*, p. 170.

[139] Flanagan, *Irish Society*, p. 148.

[140] Meilyr Fitzhenry and the other Norman lords, according to 'The song of Dermot and the earl', ll. 2443 and 3443–55, invoked St David in their war cries, see Crouch, *William Marshal*, p. 96; Strickland, *War and Chivalry*, p. 65 and n. 45; and Tyndale, 'Names', p. 183.

[141] Ibid., pp. 112–36; T. Jones (ed.) *Brut (Red Book)*, pp. 16–17. For recent work on the Normans and Celts see R. R. Davies, *Domination and Conquest*; idem, '"Keeping the natives in order"'; idem, *The First English Empire*; and Gillingham, 'Henry II'.

[142] Gerald of Wales speaks of a visit of the Lord Rhys to St Davids, though not in the company of Henry II. See Gerald of Wales, *The Description of Wales*, p. 243.

[143] Owen (ed.), 'Canu i Ddewi', p. 453, ll. 206–7.

[144] Lloyd, *History of Wales*, vol. 2, pp. 542–3.

[145] See Seán Duffy's sensitive treatment of Cambro-Hibernian relations in 'The 1169 invasion', notably pp. 107–13.

[146] For instance, the present tower of the church was erected late in the twelfth century (see Dyfed Archaeological Trust Record 5135); this might be the kind of rebuilding which warranted a celebration of the anniversary of the synod of Llanddewibrefi.

[147] Owen (ed.), 'Canu i Ddewi', p. 451, l. 116, which mentions *llwyth Daniel* (the tribe of Daniel), could possibly refer to some local kin associated with the church or to its hereditary clergy, see note on the line in the edition.

[148] Ibid., p. 450, ll. 65,71.

[149] Farmer, *The Oxford Dictionary of Saints*, pp. xv–xvi; see also the ideas expressed in Campbell, 'Some twelfth-century views', and Bartlett, 'Irish, Scottish and Welsh saints', especially pp. 78–86.

[150] See especially Jankulak, *St Petroc, passim*.

[151] See R. R. Davies, *The First English Empire*, p. 131.

[152] For the best overall picture of the history of the Church during this period see R. R. Davies, *Conquest*, chapter 7, and for Deheubarth at the time of the Lord Rhys, see Pryce, 'Yr eglwys'.

[153] See B. Tanguy, *Saint Hervé*.

[154] Lloyd, *History of Wales*, vol. 2, p. 448; Griffith, *Ysbryd Dealltwrus*, p. 43; D. S. Evans (ed.), *Historia Gruffud*, p. 28; C. P. Lewis, 'Gruffudd ap Cynan'.

[155] Lloyd, *History of Wales*, vol. 2, pp. 449–551; W. Davies, *The Llandaff Charters*; Crouch, 'Urban'.

[156] Lloyd, *History of Wales*, vol. 2, p. 449; J. C. Davies (ed.), *Episcopal Acts*, vol. 2, p. 415.

[157] Lloyd, *History of Wales*, vol. 2, p. 453; J. C. Davies (ed.), *Episcopal Acts*, vol. 1, pp. 133–4.

[158] R. R. Davies, *Conquest*, pp. 182 and 184. Consciousness of the status of the diocesan cathedrals is shown in McKenna (ed.), 'Canu Cadfan', p. 18, l. 80, a possible reference to or play on the name of Bangor in Arfon, and in the references to *eglwys Dewi* (p. 17, l. 32) and to *Llanddewi* (p. 20, l. 158), possibly St Davids.

[159] There is evidence for rebuilding at Llanddewibrefi in the twelfth century (see n. 146 above and Owen (ed.), 'Canu i Ddewi', p. 438 and n. 37) as well as at Tywyn, and for the rededication of Meifod in 1156 see R. R. Davies, *Conquest*, p. 188.

[160] T. Jones (ed.), *Brut (Red Book)*, pp. 140–1.

[161] See G. C. G. Thomas, *The Charters of the Abbey of Ystrad Marchell*, pp. 11–12, 81; J. C. Davies, 'The Strata Marcella charters', and T. Jones (ed.), *Brut (Red Book)*, p. 147.

[162] Williams-Jones, 'Llywelyn's charter'; Gresham, 'The Cymer Abbey charter'; J. B. Smith, 'Cymer abbey'.

[163] Lloyd, *History of Wales*, vol. 2, p. 597; D. H. Williams, *The Welsh Cistercians*, pp. 3–4.

[164] R. R. Davies, *Conquest*, p. 197; T. Jones (ed.), *Brut (Red Book)*, p. 12; and K. Hughes, *The Welsh Latin Chronicles*, pp. 1–30.

[165] See, for instance, B. F. Roberts, 'Geoffrey', p. 989.

[166] Lloyd, *History of Wales*, vol. 2, p. 493.

[167] See Bullock-Davies, *Professional Interpreters*, for a discussion of the society which produced these interpreters.

[168] Gerald of Wales, *The Journey through Wales*, p. 231.

4

The harlot and the hostess:
a preliminary study of the Middle Welsh Lives of Mary Magdalene and her sister Martha

><

JANE CARTWRIGHT

As opposed to focusing on the Lives of native 'Celtic' saints, this chapter attempts to highlight the importance of medieval vernacular hagiography which relates the legends of internationally popular saints in the Celtic languages. The Celtic language which has been selected for this study is Welsh and the principal aim of the discussion is to shed light on two Lives which have previously received very little attention, namely *Buchedd Mair Fadlen* and *Buchedd Martha*, the Middle Welsh Lives of Mary Magdalene and her sister Martha. Before discussing these particular *bucheddau* in detail, it would be useful to consider their context within the Welsh manuscripts.

Middle Welsh Lives of female saints

Sometime before the mid-fourteenth century the Lives of Katherine of Alexandria, Margaret of Antioch, Mary of Egypt, Mary Magdalene and Martha were translated into Middle Welsh and were subsequently copied in a number of Welsh manuscripts. These Lives are grouped together as a distinct corpus in several articles which provide an overview of Welsh religious prose and Welsh hagiography, and it has frequently been suggested that they were written for an audience of religious women. J. E. Caerwyn Williams, Glanmor Williams and D. Simon Evans all link the Welsh Lives with the Middle English Katherine Group and texts such as *Ancrene Wisse*, thus suggesting that they are indicative of a renewed 'interest in the virgin life and the education of devout women'.[1] Unfortunately very little is known of the education of religious women in medieval Wales and one needs to take care when drawing direct comparisons between the Welsh evidence and the situation in England. *Ancrene Wisse* was produced originally for three female anchorites who had chosen to withdraw from their communities and spend the rest of their days in chaste and devotional contemplation. However, the same does not appear to be true of the audience for the Welsh Lives, nor do the Welsh manuscripts in question contain guides for recluses or texts, such as *Hali Meiðhad*, which place particular emphasis on the virgin life.[2] While in medieval England there were at least 150 nunneries, in medieval Wales there were only three longstanding religious houses for women and these appear to have been poorly endowed and to have had relatively few inmates.[3] In England, examples are extant of Lives of virgin martyrs composed by women as well as for women, and manuscripts containing predominantly female saints' Lives are known to have belonged to communities of religious women.[4] In Wales, on the other hand, no records have yet come to light regarding libraries or manuscripts kept in the nunneries and there is nothing in the manuscripts that specifically suggests that these Lives were produced for an audience of religious sisters. The purpose here is not to discount the relevance of the Lives of female saints within a religious milieu, be that the parish church, the monastery or indeed the convent, but merely to suggest that, within the specific context of medieval Wales and the extant Welsh manuscripts, these Lives were probably read or heard and appreciated by far more laywomen than consecrated virgins. Katherine Lewis has shown that, although the female saints were considered as appropriate role models for young virgins, married women seeking to elevate both their social and spiritual stature also adopted them as exemplars.[5] Although this group of female saints' Lives had a particular relevance for women, the primary roles the saints played as powerful intercessors ensured that they enjoyed a wide popularity amongst men, women and children, and the medieval miscellanies which contain these *bucheddau* would have been used by lay families for the combined purposes of entertainment, education and spiritual edification.

The Middle Welsh Lives of Katherine, Margaret, Mary of Egypt, Mary Magdalene and Martha do not always appear together as a complete series, nor do they always occur in the same manuscripts or in the same order, as shown in Table 4.1.[6] The Welsh Life of Gwenfrewy (St Winifred), a virgin martyr from Holywell, has also been included in this table. Although Gwenfrewy is a native saint, her Welsh *buchedd* is largely an adaptation of Robert of Shrewsbury's twelfth-century Latin Life.[7] The Lives in question usually form part of a compendium of predominantly religious texts which are occasionally accompanied by secular legends

Table 4.1. Manuscripts containing the Welsh Lives of female saints

Manuscript	Date and scribe (if known)	Lives of female saints
Aberystwyth, NLW, MS Peniarth 14	SAEC XIII[2]	Mary of Egypt
Aberystwyth, NLW, MS Peniarth 14	SAEC XIV[1]	Margaret
Aberystwyth, NLW, MS Peniarth 5 (+ Peniarth 4 = the White Book of Rhydderch)	SAEC XIV med.	Katherine, Margaret, Mary Magdalene, Martha, Mary of Egypt
Aberystwyth, NLW, MS Peniarth 15	SAEC XIV XV	Margaret, Katherine
Aberystwyth, NLW, MS Llanstephan 27 (the Red Book of Talgarth)	SAEC XIV XV Hywel Fychan	Katherine, Mary Magdalene, Martha
Cardiff, Central Library, MS Cardiff 3.242 (Hafod 16) detached portion of Llanstephan 27	SAEC XIV XV Hywel Fychan	Mary of Egypt
London, BL, MS Cotton Titus D. xxii	SAEC XV[1]	Katherine, Margaret
Aberystwyth, NLW, MS 5267B	1438	Katherine
Aberystwyth, NLW, MS Llanstephan 28	>1456 Gutun Owain	Margaret, Katherine
Aberystwyth, NLW, MS Peniarth 27iii	SAEC XV[2] Gutun Owain	Katherine
Aberystwyth, NLW, MS Peniarth 27ii	SAEC XV XVI	Mary Magdalene, Gwenfrewy
Cardiff, Central Library, MS Cardiff 2.629 (Hafod 19)	1535–6 Ieuan ap William ap Dafydd	Margaret, Katherine, Mary Magdalene
Aberystwyth, NLW, MS Llanstephan 117	1548 Ieuan ap William ap Dafydd	Margaret, Katherine, Mary Magdalene
Aberystwyth, NLW, MS Llanstephan 34	SAEC XVI[2] Roger Morris Thomas Evans	Katherine, Gwenfrewy, Mary Magdalene, Martha, Mary of Egypt, Margaret
Aberystwyth, NLW, MS 6209E	SAEC XVII David Parry	Katherine, Mary Magdalene, Martha
Aberystwyth, NLW, MS 552B	SAEC XVII	Margaret, Katherine
Aberystwyth, NLW, MS Peniarth 225	1594–1610	Mary Magdalene, Margaret, Gwenfrewy
Cardiff, Central Library, MS Cardiff 2.633 (Hafod 23)	1604 John Jones of Gellilyfdy	Mary Magdalene, Martha, Mary of Egypt, Katherine, Margaret
Aberystwyth, NLW, MS Peniarth 217 (Llyfr Siôn ap William ap Siôn o Fucheddau Apostolion a Seintiau)	1611 John Jones of Gellilyfdy	Mary Magdalene, Martha, Mary of Egypt, Katherine
Aberystwyth, NLW, MS Llanstephan 187	1634 John Jones of Gellilyfdy	Katherine
Aberystwyth, NLW, MS Llanstephan 104	SAEC XVIII[1] Moses Williams Thomas Evans	Katherine, Gwenfrewy, Mary Magdalene, Martha, Mary of Egypt, Margaret
Aberystwyth, NLW, MS Cwrtmawr 1155	1810–80 Robert Williams of Rhydycroesau	Katherine, Margaret, Mary Magdalene, Martha

and medical, scientific or genealogical material. Other religious texts which occur in these compendia include Middle Welsh translations of the Lives of St Thomas the Apostle, John the Evangelist, Martin, David, St Patrick's Purgatory, the Creed of Athanasius, the Miracles of the Blessed Virgin Mary and the Invention of the Cross by St Helen.

Peniarth 14 is the earliest extant manuscript to contain any of the Lives of this group of female saints. The portion that belongs to the second half of the thirteenth century contains the Welsh Life of Mary of Egypt, which here is not a text in its own right, since it forms part of a larger text *Gwyrthyeu e Wynvydedic Veir* (The Miracles of the Blessed Virgin Mary).[8] The Life of Margaret occurs in the portion of Peniarth 14 that belongs to the first half of the fourteenth century. The Lives of all the female saints mentioned above occur in Peniarth 5, Llanstephan 34, Llanstephan 104 and Cardiff 2.633 (formerly Hafod 23); whereas in Llanstephan 27, otherwise known as the Red Book of Talgarth, the Lives of Mary Magdalene and Martha are accompanied only by the Life of Katherine. Mary of Egypt, however, occurs in a detached portion of the Red Book of Talgarth, now known as Cardiff 3.242 (formerly Hafod 16). Thus, the earliest extant manuscript which contains all of these Lives is Peniarth 5. Originally, the manuscripts Peniarth 5 and Peniarth 4 formed one volume known as *Llyfr Gwyn Rhydderch* (the White Book of Rhydderch) which, as Daniel Huws has shown, appears to have been compiled *c.*1350 for Rhydderch ab Ieuan Llwyd of Parcrhydderch, Llangeitho, who belonged to a long line of important Welsh literary patrons.[9] Although the White Book appears to have been commissioned by Rhydderch himself, or on his behalf, it contains texts that had been translated into Welsh for his forebears in the third quarter of the thirteenth century. A colophon in the White Book notes that Brother Gruffudd Bola translated the Creed of Athanasius from Latin into Welsh for Efa ferch Maredudd ab Owain, since she desired to read the text in her native tongue.[10] Another religious text which appears in the White Book is a vernacular translation of the Assumption of the Virgin Mary, commissioned by Efa's brother, Gruffudd ap Maredudd ab Owain, from the translator Madog ap Selyf. Unfortunately, no indication is given as to who commissioned the translations of the Lives of women saints which would, no doubt, have been appreciated by both brother and sister. It is conceivable that they were produced in the thirteenth century for the same family or, alternatively, at a later date nearer the time that the White Book was compiled for Maredudd ab Owain's great-great-grandson, Rhydderch. Of course, one does not necessarily need to assume that all of these Lives were translated at the same time or for the same family.

The second oldest extant manuscript that contains the Lives of Mary Magdalene and Martha, the Red Book of Talgarth, also appears to have been owned by a lay family who were keen on sponsoring Welsh literature. This is a compendium of religious prose and poetry which does not contain the secular legends found in the White Book of Rhydderch. Brynley F. Roberts suggests that the Red Book of Talgarth was produced for Rhys ap Tomas who is mentioned in the manuscript.[11] His more renowned brother, Hopcyn ap Tomas, commissioned the same scribe (and others) to produce an important companion volume (the Red Book of Hergest) which, like the White Book of Rhydderch, included the corpus of tales known as the Mabinogion.[12]

Most of the Welsh Lives of the universally popular saints have been edited at some time or another. The Life of Margaret has been edited by William J. Rees and Melville Richards;[13] the Life of Katherine by William J. Rees, Idris Bell and J. E. Caerwyn Williams, and a new edition, based on all the extant manuscripts, is currently being compiled by Catherine E. Byfield;[14] editions of the Life of Mary of Egypt have been made available by Lewis Haydn Angell, Gwenan Jones, Melville Richards and Ingo Mittendorf;[15] the Life of Martha, however, has never been edited, and only one version of the Welsh Life of Mary Magdalene, based on a relatively late manuscript, has been published. In 1929, Gwenallt published an edition of *Buchedd Mair Fadlen*, based on Peniarth 225, which can be dated to the late sixteenth or early seventeenth century.[16] Although this includes some of the variants from other manuscripts, it does not refer to all of the most significant variants and it does not discuss the relationship between the different manuscripts. Idris Foster may have had the intention of publishing an edition of the Life of Martha, since there are unpublished notes on the Life among his papers at the National Library of Wales.[17] On the whole, the Life of Martha appears to have been completely ignored, and this is one of the reasons why I have chosen to focus on this particular Life and that of her sister Mary Magdalene.[18]

In all, *Buchedd Mair Fadlen* is extant in twelve handwritten manuscripts dating from the mid-fourteenth century to the nineteenth, and *Buchedd Martha* is extant in eight of the same manuscripts (see Table 4.2). The Life of Mary Magdalene always precedes the Life of Martha and, although the Life of Mary Magdalene occurs on its own, the Life of Martha never occurs in any of the Welsh manuscripts without the Life of Mary Magdalene. Both Lives are incomplete in the earliest extant manuscript – Peniarth 5. Folio 26 (recto and verso) contains the first section of the Life of Mary Magdalene, and a blank folio – which presumably replaces missing leaves – follows this. Folio 28 then follows

Table 4.2. *Manuscripts containing the Middle Welsh Lives of Mary Magdalene and Martha*

Buchedd Mair Fadlen	Date and scribe (if known)	Buchedd Martha
Peniarth 5, fol.xxvi^r–xxvi^v (+ Peniarth 4 = the White Book of Rhydderch)	SAEC XIV med.	Peniarth 5, fol. xxviii^r (+ Peniarth 4 = the White Book of Rhydderch)
Llanstephan 27, fol. 132^r-135^v the Red Book of Talgarth	SAEC XIV XV Hywel Fychan	Llanstephan 27, fol. 136^r-137^r the Red Book of Talgarth
Peniarth 27ii, pp. 51–9	SAEC XV XVI	
Cardiff 2.629 (Hafod 19), fols. 68^r-72^r	1535–6 Ieuan ap William ap Dafydd	
Llanstephan 117, pp. 177–80	1548 Ieuan ap William ap Dafydd	
Llanstephan 34, pp. 365–78	SAEC XVI^2 Roger Morris	Llanstephan 34, pp. 378–82
NLW 6209E, pp. 605–10	SAEC XVII	NLW 6209E, pp. 610–12
Peniarth 225, pp. 252–9	1594–1610	
Cardiff 2.633 (Hafod 23), pp. 331–46	1604 John Jones of Gellilyfdy	Cardiff 2.633 (Hafod 23), pp. 346–52
Peniarth 217, pp. 449–76 (Llyfr Siôn ap William ap Siôn o Fucheddau Apostolion a Seintiau)	1611 John Jones of Gellilyfdy	Peniarth 217, pp. 479–89 (Llyfr Siôn ap William ap Siôn o Fucheddau Apostolion a Seintiau)
Llanstephan 104, pp. 395–409	SAEC XVIII^1 Moses Williams	Llanstephan 104, pp. 410–15
Cwrtmawr 1155ii, pp. 73–6	1810–80 Robert Williams of Rhydycroesau	Cwrtmawr 1155ii, p. 76

with the end of the Life of Martha. The sorry state of Peniarth 5, in this section of the manuscript, has given rise to some confusion and may possibly explain why the Life of Martha has been ignored. In a footnote to his edition of the Peniarth 225 version of *Buchedd Mair Fadlen*, Gwenallt states that the ending of the Life of Mary Magdalene is 'different in Peniarth 5', but in fact what he is referring to is not the end of the Life of Mary Magdalene but the end of that of Martha.[19] J. Gwenogvryn Evans does not provide titles for the Lives of Mary Magdalene and Martha in his description of the contents of the White Book, and he also appears to assume that the surviving texts comprise the beginning and end of the same Life.[20] This, in turn, led Ingo Mittendorf, in his study of Mary of Egypt, to state that in Peniarth 5 the Life of Mary of Egypt was separated from the other miracles of the Blessed Virgin Mary; that it followed the Lives of Katherine and Margaret but was separated from them 'by another short text'.[21] This unidentified 'text' is, of course, the incomplete Lives of Mary Magdalene and Martha. There is good reason why the Life of Mary of Egypt should have been associated with the Lives of Mary Magdalene and her sister Martha, since the legends of Mary of Egypt and Mary Magdalene have a great deal in common. Both women are reputed to be reformed harlots who spend many years in the wilderness and attain sanctity through a strict ascetic regime of self-deprivation and penance. Both are nourished by celestial beings and avoid human contact until their final encounter with a priest. They both make preparations for their death, receive their last communion and expire. It is generally recognized that the episode relating Mary Magdalene's sojourn in the desert was added to the Life of Mary Magdalene as a result of her association with Mary of Egypt.[22] Misrahi demonstrates that the annexed episode was widespread by the eleventh century.[23] As early as the eighth century, Anglo-Saxon martyrologies refer to the Magdalene's eremitical life,[24] and there is evidence to suggest that she may have become associated with Mary of Egypt in at least one of the Celtic regions from the early ninth century. Pádraig Ó Riain states that the entry for Mary Magdalene in the Martyrology of Tallaght (28 March rather than 22 July) was 'at the expense of Mary of Egypt', since Mary of Egypt's feast-day appears as 28 March in other martyrologies.[25] In the majority of the Welsh calendars Mary Magdalene's feast-day is entered consistently for 22 July, but in Peniarth 187 a feast for the Magdalene appears on 1 April, that is the day preceding Mary of Egypt's feast in the Roman Martyrology (2 April).[26] Before looking in detail at the content of the Welsh *bucheddau* and the relationship between the different Welsh manuscripts, it would perhaps be beneficial to provide a brief history of the development of the legends of Mary Magdalene and Martha.

The development of the legends of Mary Magdalene and Martha and the notion of the composite Magdalene

Unlike most of the other female saints whose Lives were translated into Welsh in the Middle Ages, Mary Magdalene and Martha are biblical characters, not virgin martyrs. Their Lives do not follow the usual hagiographical pattern of the martyred female saint who stoically refuses to marry a pagan suitor and then has to suffer an appalling array of tortures, culminating in decapitation, in order to preserve her virginity and defend her Christian faith.[27] The medieval legends which accrued to Mary Magdalene and Martha and claimed that they evangelized Provence bear little relation to their characters in the Gospels. The medieval Mary Magdalene is a particularly interesting character in that she is a conflation of various women mentioned in the New Testament. Today, Roman Catholicism and Protestantism agree with the early eastern Church in distinguishing between Mary Magdalene, Mary of Bethany and the penitent in Luke 7:36–50. However, throughout the Middle Ages, the western Church, on the whole, regarded these women as one.[28] Thus it was believed that Mary Magdalene, from whom Christ drove out seven devils and who later witnessed the risen Christ, was the same person as Mary of Bethany, sister of Martha and Lazarus, who anointed Christ's feet and dried them with her hair (John 12:1–8). This led to her association with the unnamed sinner in Luke's Gospel who washed Christ's feet with her tears, wiped them with her hair and anointed them with ointment in the house of Simon the Pharisee. To confuse the issue further, Mark 14:3–9 and Matthew 26:6–13 also recount an episode involving an anointing, when an unnamed woman pours precious ointment on Christ's head in the house of Simon the Leper at Bethany. To a lesser extent, Mary Magdalene became associated with the woman of Samaria who was not legally married, although she had had five 'husbands' (John 4:18), and the woman taken in adultery (John 8:3): on both occasions Christ refuses to condemn publicly these women's sexual misdemeanours. The seven devils driven out of Mary Magdalene have been equated with the Seven Deadly Sins and it has frequently been assumed that the penitent's sin in Luke's Gospel was of a sexual nature. Thus, it was Mary Magdalene's conflation with women who had committed sexual crimes that led to her association with prostitution and the idea that she was a reformed harlot. In addition, Susan Haskins points out that Mary's surname, *Magdalini* in Greek, may have contributed to her promiscuous reputation, since it links her with el Mejdel, a village on the north-west bank of Galilee which was 'destroyed in AD 75 because of its infamy and the licentious behaviour of its inhabitants'.[29] By the thirteenth century, Mary Magdalene had become firmly associated with prostitution and the reforming of prostitutes, since the Order of the Penitents of Mary Magdalene was founded *c.*1225 by Rudolf of Worms.[30] These religious houses for reformed prostitutes became extremely popular in Germany, France and Italy, although there is no evidence to suggest that the order ever existed in Wales. The notion of the composite Magdalene, although prevalent before the sixth century, was sanctioned by Gregory the Great (*c.*540–604) in his homilies. In the west, this theory of unity remained relatively unchallenged until the sixteenth century when Jacques Lefèvre d'Etaples wrote a treatise on Mary Magdalene which refuted ecclesiastical tradition and suggested that there were in fact three separate women called Mary. He was apparently excommunicated as a result.[31]

The first coherent narrative relating the pre-Ascension life of Mary Magdalene appears in a tenth-century sermon attributed to Odo of Cluny. Shortly after this, a Latin *vita* appeared which gave an account of Mary Magdalene and Martha's voyage to Marseilles, and focused on Mary Magdalene's career in Gaul and her death and burial at Aix-en-Provence. While in the east, the most widely accepted legend claimed that Mary Magdalene died at Ephesus where she had fled with John and the Virgin Mary following the Ascension, in the west it was the Provençal legend that became popular. To the *vita apostolica*, set in Provence, were added further episodes including the Magdalene's sojourn in the wilderness and the story of the prince of Marseilles. The legend was to take on many different forms before evolving into the standard medieval narrative best represented by Jacobus de Voragine's thirteenth-century *Legenda Aurea*.[32] The Life of Mary Magdalene, described by Victor Saxer as 'a medieval best-seller', was included in a number of important hagiographical collections. Saxer identifies over 200 Latin versions of the legend and about the same number of vernacular translations.[33] The Lives of both Mary Magdalene and Martha occur in the *Legenda Aurea*,[34] the South English Legendary,[35] Nicholas Bozon's Anglo-Norman legendary,[36] Jehan de Vignay's *Legende Dorée*, various French and Spanish collections,[37] the Middle English *Gilte Legende*[38] and Caxton's *Golden Legend*.[39] In addition, Mary Magdalene's Life is also found in the Northern Homily Collection,[40] the Auchinleck Manuscript,[41] John Mirk's *Festial*,[42] Osbern of Bokenham's *Legendys of Hooly Wummen*[43] and *Speculum Sacerdotale*.[44] There are also two French verse Lives and various German prose and verse versions of the Life of Mary Magdalene, some of which appear to stem from the French poems.[45] Texts produced in the Celtic regions include the fourteenth-century vernacular verse Lives of Mary Magdalene and Martha in the Scottish Legendary and an incomplete Irish homily on Mary Magdalene.[46] The lengthy prologue which precedes the Life of Mary Magdalene in the Scottish Legendary is unique to this text and refers to St David (Dewi), alongside Mary Magdalene and Mary of Egypt, in a list of sinners.

Buchedd Mair Fadlen *and* Buchedd Martha

The Middle Welsh Lives of Mary Magdalene and Martha do not correspond exactly to any of the versions listed above. Although the Welsh texts mirror certain sections of the *Legenda Aurea* almost word for word, they omit other key episodes, some of which are essential to the structure of the *vitae:* it is probable, therefore, that the Welsh *bucheddau* are translations of incomplete texts rather than direct adaptations of the *Legenda Aurea. Buchedd Mair Fadlen* does not conform to the criteria set out by David Mycoff for identifying *Legenda Aurea* influence on vernacular texts:[47] for example, it omits the lengthy etymologies of Mary's name, the mention of the pseudo-Ambrose's view on the identity of the woman who blessed the Virgin's womb and the *post mortem* translation and miracles. Since numerous texts mirror the wording of the *Legenda Aurea*, it is difficult to decipher the exact relationship between the Welsh *bucheddau* and Jacobus de Voragine's work. However, the *bucheddau* are more likely to be translations of an intermediary (or intermediaries) affiliated to the *Legenda Aurea*, than to be direct adaptations of its versions.

All of the medieval versions of the Welsh texts, *Buchedd Mair Fadlen* and *Buchedd Martha*, have a great deal in common, although they also possess a significant number of variants. The two oldest extant manuscripts, Peniarth 5 and Llanstephan 27, appear to stem from the same common original, although a substantial part of both Lives is missing in Peniarth 5. However, on occasions their phraseology differs and this is reflected in later copies of the texts. Interestingly, although the sixteenthcentury Llanstephan 34 version of *Buchedd Martha* closely follows variants in Peniarth 5, the Llanstephan 34 version of *Buchedd Mair Fadlen* does not follow either Peniarth 5 or Llanstephan 27 exactly. This seems to suggest that Llanstephan 34 drew on more than one source. Since the Life of Martha is incomplete in Peniarth 5, it is tempting to suggest that the sixteenth-century Llanstephan 34 may preserve a complete copy of the original Welsh *Buchedd Martha* that may once have existed in the mid-fourteenth-century Peniarth 5.[48] NLW 6209E is a copy of Llanstephan 27 and Cwrtmawr 1155ii is a copy of Peniarth 5, since they contain the same incomplete texts. Robert Williams of Rhydycroesau notes the start of each new page in his source and this corresponds to the layout of the texts in Peniarth 5. The most notable difference between the Welsh versions of *Buchedd Mair Fadlen* is that Peniarth 27, Llanstephan 34, Peniarth 217 and Llanstephan 104 all contain an extra section of text relating details of Mary Magdalene's pre-Ascension life, noting her special relationship with Christ and identifying her as the sinner who anointed Christ's feet in the house of Simon. Here it is suggested that Mary Magdalene was due to marry John the Evangelist, but John decided to follow Christ and, as a result, Mary Magdalene threw herself into a life of sexual promiscuity and carnal pleasure:

> Lauer o lyfreü y syd yn dyuedüd pan dylysseü Ieüan Evangylur briodi Mair Vagdalen ryerchi or Iessü ido ga[n]lyn ef a chadu i foruyndaud ac fely y gunaeth. Am hynny sorri a unaeth + Mair Vagdalen ac ymrodi i bechodaü ac yn fuya i odineb.[49]

(There are many books which say that when John the Evangelist should have married Mary Magdalene Jesus asked him to follow Him and retain his virginity, and so he did. Because of that + Mary Magdalene sulked and gave herself to [a life of] sin – and above all lust/adultery.)

Peniarth 27 does not specifically mention *godineb* (lust or adultery); instead it claims that Mary Magdalene devoted herself to the Seven Deadly Sins.[50] Whereas in the *Legenda Aurea* Jacobus de Voragine emphatically denies the relationship between Mary Magdalene and John the Evangelist, declaring that 'these tales are to be considered false and frivolous', the Welsh *buchedd* makes no comment on the accuracy of this information. The additional section in the Welsh account is a summary of certain details found at the beginning and end of Jacobus de Voragine's legend. Indeed, this part of *Buchedd Mair Fadlen* has more in common with John Mirk's *Festial* than it does with the *Legenda Aurea*, for Mirk's verse homily contains a similar concise account of the pre-Ascension life combined with details of the Magdalene's failed relationship with John.[51] As in Mirk's *Festial*, this section is positioned at the beginning of the Life in Peniarth 27, but in all the other Welsh versions the additional material is appended to the Welsh Life. It appears that this additional section of text did not form part of the oldest extant versions preserved in Peniarth 5 and Llanstephan 27 for, although Peniarth 5 is incomplete, its beginning is intact and the post-Ascension Life of Mary Magdalene follows hard on the heels of *Buchedd Margred* (the Welsh Life of Margaret of Antioch). The additional section, then, may have been added to the Welsh Life possibly at the end of the fifteenth century at the time that Peniarth 27 was compiled. The Lives in Peniarth 217 and Llanstephan 104, which also contain the additional section, are copies of Llanstephan 34.

With the exception of Peniarth 27, the Welsh *Buchedd Mair Fadlen* begins with the tale of how Mary Magdalene, Maximinus, Cedonius

(Acedemus), Lazarus, Martha and Maximista (Maximilia), Martha's handmaid, were put to sea with a number of other Christians in an old boat without oars, sails or ropes and how they miraculously arrived at the port of Marseilles *(Marsli)*. The same event is narrated at the beginning of the Life of Martha – only *Buchedd Martha* does not mention Cedonius or Martha's handmaid, who is usually claimed to be the author of the text. Having arrived in Marseilles, they discover that no one is willing to offer them accommodation. This is achieved only when Mary Magdalene succeeds in terrifying the prince of Marseilles and his wife by appearing to them in their dreams. Her face aflame with rage, Mary Magdalene accuses the prince and his *cymar wennwynic* (venomous wife) of allowing the saints to starve to death. A peculiarity of the Welsh Life is that Mary not only complains that the saints have been left to die of hunger and thirst, but also that they are naked. Eventually the married couple offer hospitality to Mary and her companions and agree to be converted to Christianity if Mary Magdalene grants them a son. The princess immediately becomes pregnant, and the prince decides to set out to visit Peter in Rome. His wife insists that she must accompany him on the pilgrimage, ignoring his protestations that the journey is far too dangerous for a pregnant woman:

> 'Ot ey di minneu a af y gyt a thi,' heb y wreic. 'Nac ef argluydes,' heb ynteu. 'Kanys beichiauc uyt ti a llawer y maent o berigleu yn y mor. Namyn tric di gartref y synnyau ar yn kyuoeth an da a minneu a af ragof.' A hitheu dan wylau a dyguydaud y draet ef ac adoluyn y gadel y uynet gyt ac ef. A hynny a gafas.[52]

> ('If you go I'm coming with you,' said his wife. 'No, Lady,' he said. 'For you are pregnant and there are many perils at sea. You stay at home and look after our wealth and possessions and I'll go on my way.' And she fell at his feet weeping and begged him to let her go with him. And she was granted that.)

The Welsh text perhaps depicts the woman in a slightly more favourable light than the *Legenda Aurea*, since she is politely addressed as *Arglwyddes* (Lady). The *buchedd* also refrains from using this episode as a misogynistic device to generalize about womankind. The *Legenda Aurea*, on the other hand, notes that 'she insisted, doing as women do. She threw herself at his feet, weeping the while, and in the end won him over'.[53] At the opposite end of the spectrum, Nicholas Bozon's Anglo-Norman Life portrays the woman in a very favourable light, and suggests that God performed a miracle indicating that she should indeed accompany her husband.[54]

Cardiff MS 2.629 breaks off after the prince's protestations, omitting the pilgrimage, and continues, in a rather disjointed manner, with subsequent events at Aix and Marseilles. In all of the other versions the woman dies in childbirth at sea. Rather than allow the mariners to throw his wife's body to the sea monsters, the prince persuades them to leave her body and the distraught, hungry infant on a small hill-like island *(brynn bychan ual ynys)*. On his return from Rome he passes the same place and sees a small boy playing with pebbles on the beach. Mary Magdalene, having cared for the child for two years, then revives the woman, who immediately showers the Magdalene with praise and thanks her for assisting at the birth and feeding the child with her own breasts: 'Ti a doethost attaf urth uyng gouit a mi yn esgor ac a wassaneytheist y mi dy uronneu di yn ufud'[55] (You came to me when I was troubled and in labour and obediently you served me with your breasts).

It transpires that not only has Mary Magdalene cared for the couple's household during their absence and wet-nursed their child, but she has also accompanied the woman on a spiritual pilgrimage and visited all the same sites as the prince. On their return to Marseilles they are baptized by Maximinus. Lazarus is declared bishop of Marseilles and Maximinus becomes bishop of Aix-en-Provence. Mary Magdalene then retires to the wilderness for thirty years, where every day at the seven canonical hours she is attended by angels who lift her up into the sky. One day a priest who lives twelve miles from Mary Magdalene's abode witnesses the event. The *Legenda Aurea* notes only that his cell is a few miles from Mary Magdalene's cave and it also specifically states that her eremitic retreat is in an empty wilderness devoid of trees and streams.[56] Whilst the majority of the Welsh versions refer to her as living in a cave (*ogof*) in the wilderness (*yn y diffeith*), Cardiff 2.629 has her retire to a wooded wilderness (*y diffeith goed*) and the priest comes across her as he performs penance in the woods (*yn y koed*).[57] Given that in medieval Welsh literature encounters with otherworldly beings and saintly figures frequently take place in woodland, it is not surprising that remote woodland would have been deemed a more relevant setting for a Welsh audience than the desert or a cave at Sainte Baume.[58] None of the Welsh versions mention Sainte Baume in the *massif* of Provence.[59] The Magdalene asks the priest to contact Maximinus and inform him that she is about to die and that he should meet her in church on the feast of the Lord's passion. Maximinus meets her, as arranged, and having taken her last communion, Mary lies down in front of the altar and passes away. Maximinus anoints the body with precious balm and requests that when he dies he is to be buried near Mary Magdalene. Both Peniarth 27 and

Cardiff 2.629, like the *Legenda Aurea*, add that for seven days following her burial a sweet smell pervaded the church. *Buchedd Mair Fadlen* ends here. It does not recount the translation of her relics to Vézelay or describe miracles performed after the saint's death. Although Jacobus de Voragine's legend was composed before Vézelay's claim to the Magdalene's relics was discredited, the Welsh Life was, no doubt, compiled after the 'discovery' of an alternative set of relics at the church of St Maximin in 1279.

Buchedd Martha is an extremely short Life which recounts only the perilous journey to Marseilles in the boat with no oars or sail, the description of the saint's death and burial at Tarascon and the miracle involving Bishop Fronto's white gloves. Although *Buchedd Martha* has a great deal in common with the *Legenda Aurea*, it omits some of the most interesting episodes in the *vita*, such as Martha's encounter with the dragon of Tarascon, born of a creature capable of shooting burning excrement for up to an acre at its enemies. In the vast majority of the Latin and vernacular versions of Martha's Life the saint subdues the dragon, sprinkles holy water on the fiend and ties him up in her girdle. The inhabitants of Tarascon then promptly stone him to death:

> The dragon had come from Galatia in Asia, begotten of Leviathan, an extremely ferocious water-serpent, and Onachus, an animal bred in the region of Galatia, which shoots its dung like darts at pursuers within the space of an acre: whatever this touches is burned up as by fire. The people asked Martha for help, and she went after the dragon. She found him in the forest in the act of devouring a man, sprinkled him with blessed water, and had a cross held up in front of him. The brute was subdued at once and stood still like a sheep while Martha tied him up with her girdle, and the people killed him then and there with stones and lances. The inhabitants called the dragon *Tarasconus*, and in memory of this event the place is still called Tarascon.[60]

Since this is the highlight of the Life of Martha, its absence from the Welsh version is surprising. It is unlikely that the Welsh translator or copyist would voluntarily censor the episode. Margaret's feisty wrestling match with the devil disguised as a dragon plays a central role in the Welsh Life of Margaret of Antioch:

> Ac yna y kymerth y vorvynn santes y kythreul gyr guallt y penn ac y trevis vrth y dayar ac y dodes y throet ar y war ef ac y dyvat vrthav: 'Peit bellach a dyvedut am vy morwyndaut i.'[61]

(And then the saintly virgin took hold of the devil by the hair of his head and threw him to the ground, put her foot on the nape of his neck and said: 'Don't you mention my virginity again!')

It could also be argued that *Buchedd Catrin*, the Welsh Life of Katherine, is more violent than the vast majority of Latin and vernacular versions of Katherine's Life, since the Welsh *buchedd* contains an additional scene of violence in which Porphyrius (*Porffir*) retaliates and slays 4,000 of Maxentius' men and injures a further 4,000 before he is put to death.[62] The only explanation for the concise nature of *Buchedd Martha* is that the Welsh text is a translation of an incomplete Life. It also omits the account of how a young boy, eager to hear Martha preaching on the other side of the river, jumps into the water and attempts to swim across. He is drowned en route, but later resurrected by Martha.

In the Welsh *buchedd*, following their arrival in Marseilles, Martha and her companions travel to Aix where they convert large numbers of people to Christianity. In Llanstephan 34, Martha is described as 'doeth oed a chymen a rhadlaun a charedic gan baub' (she was wise, eloquent and full of grace and was loved by everyone).[63] Her chastity is emphasized at the beginning of the *buchedd* where it is stated that she never married or had a relationship with a man. No sooner have the companions begun on their mission to preach and convert than Martha learns that she is to die within a year and begins to suffer from a terrible fever. A week before she passes away the ghost of her sister Mary Magdalene appears to her and she realizes that her time is nigh. She requests that the lanterns around her be lit, but at midnight a strong gust of wind extinguishes the lights and she is surrounded by evil spirits carrying written lists of her sins. She prays to Christ for forgiveness and a man appears and relights the lanterns. In the *Legenda Aurea* it is Mary Magdalene who relights the lanterns. Christ offers her comfort saying that since she acted as his host and welcomed him into her house, so shall he welcome her into his. Martha's role as Christ's hostess (*llettywreic*) is continuously stressed throughout the *buchedd*. She is taken out of the house, read a section from Luke's Gospel and passes away. At the same time, far away in Perigueux (*Pentagores*), Bishop Fronto, who is celebrating mass, falls asleep and dreams that he is called to bury Martha in Tarascon. Since all of the Welsh versions omit Martha's adventures with the dragon *Tarasconen* who gave his name to Tarascon, the location of Martha's funeral is not explained in the Welsh text. The *buchedd* jumps rather confusingly from one location to another. A deacon in his own church later wakes the bishop, and Fronto, annoyed that the deacon has interrupted his dream, tells him to hurry to Tarascon because he has left his gold ring and pair of white gloves at Martha's funeral. True enough, when the deacon arrives at Tarascon he finds the objects that Fronto had lost in his dream. One of the white gloves is retained by the sacristan at Tarascon as proof of the miracle. The *buchedd* ends by stressing Martha's intercessory powers: 'A phoet truy eiryol y santes honno y delom ninneu i uuched dragywydaul'[64] (And through intercession with that saint may we attain everlasting life).

Other sources: medieval Welsh poetry, church dedications, holy wells and visual representations

While Mary Magdalene has an important role in the Welsh Life of Martha, Martha is a minor character in the Life of Mary Magdalene. Since *Buchedd Martha* omits many of the miracles that depict Martha as an active heroine performing miracles in her own right (for example slaying the dragon, preaching by the river and resurrecting the drowned boy), Martha does not develop into a fully autonomous heroine in the Welsh *buchedd*. This *buchedd* is a mere shadow of *Buchedd Mair Fadlen* and, as we have seen, it never occurs in the Welsh manuscripts unless it is preceded by the latter (see Table 4.2). As one might expect, Mary Magdalene's pre-eminence is obvious in other sources, such as medieval Welsh poetry, church dedications, holy wells and the visual arts. Martha seems to have been introduced into Wales only because of her association with her more prominent and flamboyant sister. Mary Magdalene's feast-day on 22 July is mentioned in nearly all of the Welsh calendars, but it is noticeable that Martha's feast on 29 July is not included.[65] Mary Magdalene's feast-day appears to have been widely celebrated in Wales and, as one might expect, its celebration was not confined to towns and villages where the local church was dedicated to her. At Llan-non in Ceredigion, a village traditionally associated with St Non, a fair was held annually in the fourteenth century in honour of Mary Magdalene, and the festivities lasted for three days.[66]

Although there appear to be no Welsh churches dedicated to Martha, there are thirteen churches dedicated to Mary Magdalene. Of these, Kenfig, Goldcliff and Cerrigydrudion appear to be medieval foundations and there was once a medieval town chapel in her honour at Pembroke. There was also a chapel dedicated to Mary Magdalene at the priory church at Usk and a sixteenth-century, free-metre Welsh poem, written in the form of a dialogue between Mary Magdalene and a pilgrim sinner, addresses the Magdalene as *Mair Fadlen o Frynbuga* (Mary Magdalene of Usk).

G. Hartwell Jones assumed that the pilgrim was specifically addressing a statue of Mary Magdalene at Usk which is certainly plausible, but it is equally possible that prayer is the medium of conversation between saint and sinner and that the sinner visualizes Mary mentally. Mary Magdalene *priod Ifan* (John's wife) offers the pilgrim advice on spiritual matters and steers his thoughts away from financial concerns.[67] The chapel at Llanfair Nant-y-gof is recorded as being dedicated to Mary Magdalene *c.*1600 in a document listing churches that had been appropriated to the Knight Hospitallers of Slebech in the twelfth and thirteenth centuries. It is possible, therefore, that the holy well at Llanfair Nant-y-gof was dedicated to the Magdalene rather than the Virgin Mary.[68] In addition, there were holy wells associated with Mary Magdalene at St Clears, Cerrigydrudion and Harlech (close to the castle walls).[69] Bleddfa and Wiston, previously dedicated to the Virgin Mary, were rededicated to Mary Magdalene in the early twentieth century, and the medieval foundations at Kenfig and Cerrigydrudion appear to have had earlier dedications to Cynfig and Ieuan Gwas Padrig respectively.[70]

St Ieuan Gwas Padrig appears once to have been depicted in medieval stained glass at the church in Cerrigydrudion, although the glass is no longer extant. Edward Lhuyd refers to the tradition, recorded in the parish register in 1503, that Ieuan Gwas Padrig founded the church in 440 and that the saint himself decided to dedicate his church to Mary Magdalene.[71] The sixteenth-century Welsh Life of Ieuan Gwas Padrig has an angel instruct him to build a church on the spot where he sees a roebuck.[72] This, of course, occurs at Cerrigydrudion, and the church is dedicated to Mary Magdalene and Ieuan.[73] Ieuan is also associated with Mary Magdalene and Cerrigydrudion in a poem by Gutun Ceiriog. The *cywydd* recounts the same events as the Middle Welsh Life, referring to the journey to Marseilles and the conversion of the populace in Provence. It also relates the miraculous events concerning the prince of Marseilles's pilgrimage to Rome and how Mary Magdalene reared his son for two years and resurrected his wife who had died in childbirth. Mary Magdalene's lengthy withdrawal from society is given short shrift in the *cywydd*, since her eremitic experiences are briefly summed up in one couplet which rather baldly states that she spent thirty years *mewn rhyw ogof* (in some cave). This again suggests that the traditions associated with Sainte Baume were not considered to be particularly relevant to a Welsh audience. One could also argue that, to Gutun Ceiriog, her withdrawal from society was not as pertinent as her role as sinner and penitent. The main emphasis in the poem is on Mary's role as repentant sinner weeping salty tears at Christ's feet:

> Pan weles Mair yr Iesu
> Ofn y farn arni a fu.
> Du law hallt a wylai hon
> Oi golwg uwch y galon.
> Wylo ar ei draed alwyn
> A wnâi'r Fair wen er ei fwyn.
> Golchi traed Crist yn ddistaw
> A'r dagrau'n llynnau 'mhob llaw.[74]

(When Mary saw Jesus/ she was afraid of Judgement Day./ She cried black, salty rain/ from her eyes above the heart./ Holy Mary cried a gallon [of tears] on his feet/ for his sake./ She quietly washed Christ's feet,/ and the tears were [like] lakes in each hand.)

Since she herself was forgiven of her sins, she made an appropriate intercessor on behalf of all common sinners and was perhaps a more accessible role model than many of the virgin martyrs. Mary Magdalene, *castissima meretrix* (the most chaste prostitute), unlike many of the other Christian saints revered in the medieval period, was not perfect and was not without fault. Her medieval Life demonstrated that if Christ could forgive a reformed harlot, then there was hope for all repentant sinners regardless of the magnitude of their sins. Gutun Ceiriog notes that Mary Magdalene was afraid of Judgement Day. One might expect that a saint need have no fear of Judgement Day, yet Mary Magdalene's humility and humanity ensure that, faced with the Day of Judgement, she encounters the same fears and anxieties as any other Christian. In a similar vein, Martha is depicted as being terrified on her deathbed. In *Buchedd Martha*, at midnight a gust of wind extinguishes the lights that surround Martha's bed. Ill and afraid in the dark, surrounded by evil spirits holding written lists of her sins, she calls out to Christ who comes and comforts her:

> Ac yna yd ymdanges Iessu Grist idi ac y dywaut urthi. 'Dabre,' heb ef 'uy llettywreic attaf. A thi a uydy gyt a mi yn y nef, kanys titheu amllettyeist inneu y gyt a thitheu gynt. Ar neb a alwo arnaf i yth enu di mi ae guarandauaf ef yrot ti.'[75]

(And then Jesus Christ appeared to her and said to her: 'Come to me my hostess. And you will be with me in heaven, for previously you offered me accommodation with you. And I will listen to whoever calls upon me in your name because of you.')

Fear of dying, the terrifying prospect of Judgement Day and the uncertainty of its outcome must all have seemed relevant anxieties to a medieval audience who would, no doubt, have been able to identify easily with Martha in this scene. *Buchedd Martha* is also particularly relevant within a domestic setting, since Martha is rewarded for the generosity and hospitality that she showed towards Christ in her home at Bethany. Thus, *Buchedd Martha* stresses the importance of being a good host (ess) and emphasizes that Christ rewards generosity and hospitality in the Christian household.

Similarly, in *Buchedd Mair Fadlen* the prince of Marseilles and his household are rewarded for the hospitality they extend to the saints: they eventually offer food, clothing and accommodation to Mary Magdalene and her companions and are rewarded accordingly. Indeed, the episode relating the prince of Marseilles's conversion and Mary Magdalene's relationship with his family is central to *Buchedd Mair Fadlen*. As early as the third century, Origen identified Martha and her sister Mary Magdalene as representatives of the active and contemplative forms of the religious life. Yet in *Buchedd Mair Fadlen*, before Mary Magdalene retires to the wilderness to lead a contemplative existence, she leads a full and active life performing many miracles. The most important miraclestory in the *buchedd* centres on the lay family, rewarded for their conversion and adherence to the Christian faith. The kind of miracles Mary Magdalene performs – wet-nursing, assisting during childbirth, healing and even looking after the prince of Marseilles's household and financial affairs during his absence – made her a particularly relevant saint within a lay household.

Furthermore, Mary Magdalene appears to have been considered an appropriate role model with which to compare married noblewomen in medieval Wales, and her role as myrrophore (ointment bearer) led to her specific association with healing. She is depicted carrying a jar of precious ointment on a fourteenth-century wall painting on the north wall of the chancel at Llantwit Major and she also appears on the panels of the canopy of honour in the church at Gyffin.[76] A leper hospital near the bottom of Heywood Hill in Tenby was founded *c.1236* by Gilbert Mareschal and this appears to have been dedicated to Mary Magdalene.[77] In medieval Welsh poetry she is frequently referred to as *meddyges Iesu* (Christ's physician). In a *cywydd* to Hywel of Moelyrch who had injured his knee, Guto'r Glyn compares Hywel's wife with Mary Magdalene *meddyges Iesu* and requests that Elen heal her husband successfully with her precious ointment.[78] On another occasion he compares Siân, the wife of Sir Siôn Bwrch, with Mary Magdalene and claims that Siân's generous hospitality does wonders for the poet's physical ailments.[79]

There appear to be no surviving medieval artistic representations of Martha in Wales. Images at Gresford of a female saint carrying a bunch of keys are more likely to be of St Sitha than Martha. Sitha is depicted on the font at Gresford and also in the east window of St Katherine's chapel, alongside St Apollonia (patron saint of toothache).[80] Martha may have become associated with St Sitha in the late medieval period, since Sitha, a domestic servant renowned for her piety, also became associated with domesticity and house husbandry.[81] Martha is rarely invoked in Welsh poetry. However, she is mentioned in a poem by Lewys Glyn Cothi written in order to wish Elliw ferch Henri a safe passage on return from her pilgrimage to Santiago de Compostela. Martha's perilous journey in a boat without oars or a sail seems to have made her an appropriate candidate for the task of ensuring that no storm arises during Elliw's journey across the sea.[82]

Thus, from considering the context and transfer of the Welsh Lives of Mary Magdalene and Martha, and the use made of these two female saints within the secular poetic tradition, a tentative picture can begin to be sketched of their popularity and audience within medieval Wales. Martha appears always to have remained a minor character. Contingent conditions of textual transfer to Wales resulted in an atrophied Life which, in its extant form, may have further reduced its interest to a Welsh audience. Mary Magdalene, on the other hand, was relatively popular in late medieval Wales. The Middle Welsh *Buchedd Mair Fadlen* and *Buchedd Martha*, as we have seen, are not direct translations of the versions in the *Legenda Aurea*, but probably stem from related texts. Four slightly different medieval versions of *Buchedd Mair Fadlen* exist, while *Buchedd Martha* is found in only two medieval manuscripts and one of these is a fragmentary Life. Both the White Book of Rhydderch and the Red Book of Talgarth, which appear to be household manuscripts, give an important indication of the literary interests and spiritual requirements of the Welsh gentry in the fourteenth and fifteenth centuries. The majority of the religious texts in these anthologies relate to the liturgical year in some manner and could have provided the laity (as well as the clergy)[83] with appropriate readings throughout the year, for example on saints' feast-days. Texts such as *Buchedd Mair Fadlen*, with its particular emphasis on penitence, would also have provided the lay family with suitable reading material for penitential preparation prior to confession. The Fourth Lateran Council of 1215 stipulated that everyone should attend confession and receive communion at least once a year.[84] The Dominicans, who emphasized the importance to layfolk of confession and penitential practice, made Mary Magdalene the patron of their order in 1297 and, no doubt, the Welsh Dominicans helped to diffuse her cult. Much of the legendary material in the White Book of

Rhydderch (including *Pedeir Keinc y Mabinogi*) has moral overtones and focuses on the importance of the family and appropriate social behaviour within both the kin group and the wider community. *Ystorya Boum o Hamtwn* (Bevis of Hampton), which is also included in the White Book, has been described as a pious romance 'about the founding of a family, in which marriage plays an important role'.[85] The Welsh Lives of Mary Magdalene and Martha, as we have seen, also focus on the Christian household and the importance of offering hospitality to others, while promising salvation and increased childbearing capabilities to those who welcome the saints into their household. One can easily imagine that these *bucheddau* were considered to be suitable reading material for the whole family: not only Rhydderch ab Ieuan Llwyd, who appears to have commissioned the White Book, but also his wives, Margred ferch Gruffudd Gryg and Mawd ferch Sir William Clement, as well as his ten children.[86] Even in the sixteenth century, Lives of the saints such as *Buchedd Mair Fadlen* and *Buchedd Martha* were considered to be both entertaining and edifying. A colophon in Llanstephan 117 names the scribe and hints at his motivation for copying such a collection of texts:

> Ieuan ap William ap dd: ap ejnws a jysgrivenodd y llyvyr hwn i gyd ari gost i hvn i gael o bobl y ddifyrwch o hono a lles yw heneidiav o hwn.[87]

(Ieuan ap William ap D[afydd?] wrote this book, all at his own expense, so that people would get entertainment from it and that it might benefit their souls.)

The aim of this study has been to shed new light on the Middle Welsh Lives of Mary Magdalene and Martha and to highlight the importance and relevance of these religious texts within a lay context. One does not necessarily have to accept that these hagiographical texts were indicative of a renewed interest in the virgin life, or that they were read and enjoyed exclusively by young virgins and clerics (as previous readings have suggested). They may well have been read, or heard, copied and adapted for use by more than one kind of audience, but their context in the earliest extant manuscripts suggests a bias towards the pious family. They appear to have had a particular relevance for the lay household and may be read as containing relevant messages for the good Christian family as well as for all common sinners. The texts themselves would have been highly valued within the household and considered almost as holy relics. To read or hear a reading of these *bucheddau* was to experience contact with the saints, and these particular biblical sisters, both the reformed harlot and the faithful hostess, who had experienced close personal relationships with Christ, were believed to be particularly powerful intercessors. It is hoped that this preliminary study of two Middle Welsh Lives of universal saints will encourage further research on the vernacular hagiography of the Celtic regions and the devotion this illustrates to universal (as well as native) saints.

Notes

[1] J. E. C. Williams, 'Buchedd Catrin', p. 249; G. Williams, *Welsh Church*, p. 103; D. S. Evans, *Medieval Religious Literature*, p. 76.

[2] Millett and Wogan-Browne (eds), *Medieval English Prose for Women*. Millett, 'The audience', pp. 127–56, argues that although *Ancrene Wisse* was produced originally for three sisters, it was modified for a larger number of recluses and also used by a wider audience.

[3] In 'The desire to corrupt' and *Y Forwyn Fair*, pp. 169–72, I attempt to explain why there may have been so few nunneries in medieval Wales. On the Welsh nunneries see also D. H. Williams, 'Cistercian nunneries'; *idem*, 'Usk nunnery' and Fulton, 'Poems to nuns'.

[4] Burgess and Wogan-Browne (ed. and trans.), *Virgin Lives;* Wogan-Browne, 'Clerc'; L. Smith and Taylor (eds), *Women, the Book*.

[5] K. J. Lewis, 'Model girls?', pp. 25–46.

[6] I have used Daniel Huws's dating of the Welsh manuscripts as far as possible, and where this is not available, I've referred either to the dates given in the later manuscripts or to J. G. Evans's *Report*. See Huws, *Medieval Welsh Manuscripts*, pp. 57–64. The Lives in Table 4.1 are listed in the order in which they occur in the manuscripts.

[7] On the Welsh Life of Gwenfrewy see L. E. Jones, 'Golygiad newydd'; on the different manuscript versions see especially pp. 20–31, 248–60.

[8] Angell, *'Gwyrthyeu';* Mittendorf, 'Mary of Egypt'.

[9] On the White Book of Rhydderch see Huws, *Medieval Welsh Manuscripts*, pp. 227–45.

[10] J. E. C. Williams, 'Rhyddiaith', pp. 331–6. For a valuable discussion on women's literacy in medieval Wales see Lloyd-Morgan, 'More written about'.

[11] B. F. Roberts, 'Hopcyn ap Thomas', p. 224.

[12] G. Charles-Edwards, 'Scribes'; C. James, 'Llwyr wybodau'.

[13] W. J. Rees (ed. and trans.), *Cambro-British*, pp. 219–31; M. Richards, 'Buchedd Fargred'.

[14] W. J. Rees (ed. and trans.), *Cambro-British*, pp. 211–18; Bell (ed.), *Vita*, pp. 31–9; J. E. C. Williams, 'Buchedd Catrin'; Byfield, 'A new edition'.

[15] Angell, *'Gwyrthyeu;* G. Jones, 'Gwyrthyeu'; M. Richards, 'Buchedd Mair o'r Aifft'; Mittendorf, 'Mary of Egypt'.

[16] D. J. Jones, 'Buchedd'.

[17] Aberystwyth, NLW, Idris Foster's papers, Box 20.

[18] I am currently working on editions of the two Lives.

[19] D. J. Jones, 'Buchedd', p. 330, n. 1.

[20] J. G. Evans, *Report*, vol. 1, part ii, p. 310.

[21] Mittendorf, 'Mary of Egypt', p. 208.

[22] Duchesne, 'La Légende', vol. 1, p. 358; Mycoff, *Critical Edition*, p. 14.
[23] Misrahi, 'A *vita*', pp. 336–7.
[24] Herzfeld (ed.), *Old English*.
[25] Ó Riain, *Anglo-Saxon Ireland*, p. 19.
[26] Aberystwyth, NLW MS Peniarth 187, fol. 4^V, refers to 'Dychweliad Mair Fadlen' (Mary Magdalene's return). This calendar is, however, fairly late, *c.1596*.
[27] Examples of this pattern can be seen in the Lives of Katherine, Margaret and Gwenfrewy. On the fragmentary evidence for other Welsh virgin martyrs (e.g. Maches, Tudful and Dunod) see Cartwright, 'Dead virgins'.
[28] Mycoff, *The Life*, pp. 1–2. For a detailed discussion on the theories of unity and plurality see Haskins, *Mary*, pp. 1–29.
[29] Haskins, *Mary*, p. 13.
[30] Ibid., pp. 171–3; Saxer, *Le Culte*, pp. 217–24.
[31] Hufstader, 'Lefèvre'.
[32] For a more detailed discussion on the development of the legend see Mycoff, *Critical Edition*, pp. 7–24.
[33] Saxer, *Le Culte*.
[34] de Voragine, *Legenda Aurea*, pp. 407–17, 444–7; de Voragine, *Golden Legend*, vol. 1, pp. 374–83; vol. 2, pp. 23–6 (for English translations).
[35] Horstmann (ed.), *Early South English Legendary*, pp. 462–80; d'Evelyn and Mill (eds), *South English Legendary*, vol. 1, pp. 302–15, 348–55.
[36] Bozon, *Three Saints' Lives*, pp. 3–25, 45–59.
[37] On the French and Spanish manuscripts see J. R. Smith (ed.), *The Lives*, pp. xviii–xxvii.
[38] Zupita (ed.), 'Das leben'.
[39] Mycoff, *Critical Edition*, pp. 117–44.
[40] Horstmann (ed.), *Altenglische*, pp. 81–92.
[41] Horstmann (ed.), *Sammlung Altenglishe*, pp. 163–70.
[42] Mirk, *Festial*, pp. 203–8.
[43] Bokenham, *Legendys*, pp. 136–72.
[44] Weatherly (ed.), *Speculum*, pp. 170–4.
[45] Meyer, *Légendes;* Eggert (ed.), *German Version*, pp. 152, 212–13. The Middle Low German version, which omits the pre-Ascension material and Magdalene's sojourn in the desert, appears to be an adaptation of a thirteenth-century verse Life by a Norman clerk called Guillaume.
[46] Trinity College Dublin, MS H. ii. 15a, p. 95; Metcalfe (ed.), *Legends*, vol. 1, pp. 256–95. On associations between Mary Magdalene and the Breton ballad *Mari Kelenn* see Constantine, 'Breton Mary'.
[47] Mycoff, *Critical Edition*, pp. 25–7.
[48] The orthography in Llanstephan 34 has been revised considerably.
[49] Llanstephan 34, pp. 376–7. A cross appears in the manuscript before Mary's name. All translations from Middle Welsh are my own.
[50] Peniarth 27ii, p. 52.
[51] Mirk, *Festial*, p. 203.
[52] Llanstephan 27, fol. 132^v. I have added punctuation.
[53] de Voragine, *Golden Legend*, vol. 1, p. 378.
[54] 'Meis pur rien ne volt demorer./ Dieu le voleit sanz nule fayle;/ Ceo mustra bien par mervayle' (But she was not at all inclined to remain behind. God wished it so without doubt; He showed it plainly by a miracle), Bozon, *Three Saints' Lives*, p. 13.
[55] Llanstephan 27, fol. 134^r.
[56] de Voragine, *Golden Legend*, vol. 1, p. 380. In the Anglo-Norman Life, the priest's

dwelling is twelve furlongs from Mary Magdalene's abode. See Bozon, *Three Saints' Lives*, p. 18.

[57] Cardiff 2.629, fols 69ʳ–70ʳ. Prior to the event she has not seen the face of any man for thirty years.

[58] In *Pedeir Keinc y Mabinogi* Pwyll encounters Hafgan, king of the otherworld, in a clearing in woodland (I. Williams (ed.), *Pedeir Keinc*, p. 1), and in the Latin Life of Melangell, Brochfael Ysgithrog comes across St Melangell while he is out hunting in the woods. She has led a solitary existence for fifteen years during which time she has not seen the face of any man (Pryce, 'Historia', pp. 39–40). On the relationship between the forest and the otherworld in medieval Welsh literature see also P. L. Williams, '"Ar ganghennau'r gynghanedd"'.

[59] The cave at Sainte Baume, reputed to be the site of Mary Magdalene's hermitage, appears to have been associated with the Virgin Mary until *c*.1170. See Haskins, *Mary*, p. 117.

[60] de Voragine, *Golden Legend*, vol. 2, p. 24.

[61] M. Richards, 'Buchedd Fargred', p. 331.

[62] J. E. C. Williams, 'Buchedd Catrin', p. 267. The Middle Welsh Life of Katherine most closely resembles the fifteenth-century English verse Life found in Cambridge, University Library, MS Ff.2.38 and Oxford, Bodleian Library, MS Rawlinson Poetry 34, which also makes Porphyrius slay 4,000 of Maxentius' men. In *Buchedd Catrin* 50,000 spectators are killed by fragments of the spiked wheels as opposed to 40,000 in the standard Life. For a detailed discussion of the Welsh Life of Katherine and her cult in Wales (which includes a survey of previous work in the field) see Cartwright, 'Buchedd Catrin'.

[63] Llanstephan 34, p. 379. The relevant fragment of text is missing in the incomplete version in Peniarth 5 and the phrase is absent in Llanstephan 27.

[64] Llanstephan 27, fol. 137ʳ. Cf. Cardiff MS 2.633, p. 352: 'A phoyd drwy nerth y vendigedig Vair, ag eiriol y vendigedig santes honno a rrad yr Ysbryd Glan y delom ninneu i vuchedd dragywydd heb dranc, heb orffen, amen' (And through the strength of blessed Mary, the intercession of that blessed saint [i.e. Martha] and the grace of the Holy Spirit may we attain everlasting life forever, without end, Amen).

[65] Cartwright, Y *Forwyn Fair*, p. 183.

[66] S. Thomas, 'Land occupation', p. 127.

[67] Parry-Williams (ed.), *Canu Rhydd*, pp. 289–91; G. H. Jones, *Celtic Britain*, pp. 318–19.

[68] NLW, Slebech Park Papers and Documents, 247A; Trier, 'Holy wells'. I am grateful to Julie Trier for sending me information on the dedications at Llanfair Nanty-gof prior to the submission of her thesis.

[69] Wiliam Middleton refers to a well dedicated to Mary Magdalene in a sixteenth-century poem which criticizes idolatry and worship of holy wells, although he does not mention the well's location. See I. Williams, 'Protestaniaeth', p. 243, l. 4. On poetic references to holy wells in Wales see Daniel, 'Y Ffynhonnau'.

[70] G. Jones, *Saints*. I am grateful to Graham Jones for sharing his work on dedications with me prior to the publication of this volume.

[71] Lhuyd, *Parochialia*, pp. 116–17.

[72] For a similar motif involving pigs see Karen Jankulak's article in the present volume.

[73] *LBS*, vol. 4, p. 426.

[74] D. J. Jones, 'Buchedd', p. 328, ll. 7–14.

[75] Llanstephan 27, fol. 136ʳ.

[76] Gray, *Images*, Plate 58b (for image at Llantwit Major). Madeleine Gray suggests

that the fragmentary figure of another female saint, also on the north wall of the chancel at Llantwit Major, is a painting of the Virgin Mary whose 'presence here may indicate the location of a temporary Easter sepulchre'. She also proposes that the head of a female saint in the north window of the chancel at Treuddyn may possibly depict Mary Magdalene, since it is similar in style to the depiction of Mary Magdalene at Grappenhall (Cheshire) (ibid., p. 23). However, stylistic similarities do not necessarily indicate that this is the same saint, for similar cartoons are known to have been used to depict different saints.

[77] Cule, 'Early hospitals', p. 110.

[78] I. Williams and J. L. Williams (eds), *Gwaith Guto'r Glyn*, p. 119, ll. 25–9.

[79] Ibid., p. 123, ll. 19–22; p. 125, ll. 61–4. Mary Magdalene is referred to as 'meddyges Duw i hunan' (the physician of God himself) in the anonymous free-metre poem mentioned above. See Parry-Williams (ed.), *Canu Rhydd*, p. 289, l. 10.

[80] Gray, *Images*, Plate 25.

[81] St Petronilla is also depicted holding keys. Both Petronilla and Sitha appear on a screen at North Elham and in this instance both saints are named. See Tasker, *Encyclopaedia*, pp. 157, 160–1.

[82] Johnston (ed.), *Gwaith Lewys Glyn Cothi*, p. 189, ll. 53–6.

[83] Huws, *Medieval Welsh Manuscripts*, p. 245, suggests that the quires which contain the Lives of the female saints in Peniarth 5 were composed as part of a separate programme and that they were 'written presumably for use by a cleric'.

[84] Haskins, *Mary*, p. 133. On the Dominicans at St Maximin see ibid., p. 129.

[85] McSparran and Robinson (eds), *Cambridge*, p. xi. Cambridge, University Library, Ff.2.38, a Middle English household manuscript, has a great deal in common with the White Book of Rhydderch including the arrangement of its contents which proceeds from religious material to moral tales and secular romances. It also shares a number of texts with the White Book including Bevis of Hampton, an unusual fifteenth-century verse Life of St Katherine which, as we have seen (n. 62) is similar to the earlier Middle Welsh prose Life. Its copy of the Life of Mary Magdalene is from Mirk's *Festial*.

[86] According to his genealogy in Dwnn, *Heraldic Visitations*, vol. 1, pp. 45, 85, Rhydderch married twice and had ten children, but the same text (vol. 1, p. 131), suggests that he had a third wife called Annes, and that she was the mother of the poet Ieuan ap Rhydderch. See also H. Lewis, Roberts and Williams (eds), *Cywyddau Iolo*, pp. xxiv–xxv. Lloyd-Morgan notes that the White Book may have been produced for Rhydderch's wife (Lloyd-Morgan, 'More written about', p. 158).

[87] J. G. Evans, *Report*, vol. 2, p. 568. The manuscript is now badly stained: only fragments of red ink are legible.

5
The early chronology for St Patrick (c.351–c.428): some new ideas and possibilities

JOHN T. KOCH

Introduction: 'ego Patricius peccator'

Patrick is perhaps the most historical of Celtic saints, having not merely left us writings (as have Gildas and Adomnán, for example), but writings that are richly autobiographical. Nonetheless, the Patrick of cult and hagiography is hard for us to set aside with would-be objectivity. One of the great advances in critical methodology for the study of St Patrick in the later twentieth century has been recognizing the need to separate the evidence of hagiography and that for the early cult of Patrick, on the one hand, from that of the primary sources, essentially Patrick's own writings, on the other. A particularly important milestone articulating this necessity was D. A. Binchy's well-known article 'Patrick and his biographers ancient and modern'.[1] Henceforth, evidence of the Patrician cult and *vitae* were to be used, if at all, only with the greatest wariness, when approaching Patricius Bannaventensis himself and his times.[2] That this is the essential method for the study of the historical Patrick hardly needs to be justified again now. But this process of critical disengagement of primary sources from hagiography remains incomplete. In the first place, the hagiographers were clearly not unaware of Patrick's *Confessio* and *Epistola ad milites Corotici*, in fact, very much to the contrary; Muirchú's *Vita* for example relies very heavily on the *Confessio* and *Epistola* (which we can refer to collectively as the *opuscula*). Therefore, scholars can easily fall into the trap of using Patrick's writings consciously or unconsciously to confirm, validate and refine the composite Patrick known largely from the cult and hagiography. A further factor is that Muirchú and his successors did not simply apply layers of their own purposeful inventions to the doctrines derived from the *opuscula*; they made use of other written sources and old traditions, many of which have apparently not survived independently. In other words, we cannot ignore the possibility of pre-hagiographical historical evidence now surviving only embedded in the hagiography. For example, the tradition of Patrick's Brittonic oath *mo de broth* (Old Welsh *muin duiu braut* 'by the God of Judgement' or 'by the judgement of God') was probably not invented by the hagiographers and seems likely to go back to Patrick himself,[3] who we know from the *Confessio* to have been a Brittonic-speaking Briton.[4] Furthermore, other elements seem to derive from a dossier of Palladius, such as the connections with Auxerre and Bishop Amator.[5] Though such details can be excluded as not having any *direct* connection to the historical Patrick, they may well, depending on their ultimate sources, reflect otherwise lost written records of the fifth-century Irish Church.

Our clear-sighted appreciation of the Patrick of history is further clouded by two less obvious factors. First, the Patrick legend is not confined to the Middle Ages, nor to the Celtic countries, nor even to the Church. In the United States, for example, St Patrick is, like Santa Claus and the Easter Bunny, the secularized and commercialized persona that now overshadows the associated Christian feast. Many of us, even if we now regard ourselves as non-believers, cannot remember a time before we had heard of St Patrick, and thus our deepest thoughts and feelings about him lie beyond the effective reach of introspection.

Second, Patrick's first and most effective hagiographer was Patricius Bannaventensis himself. Immersed in the popular culture, we come at the subject of Patrick predisposed to think of him positively and as an important figure. Turning as specialists to the *opuscula*, many of us find in them an exceptional and moving quality. We (as practitioners of secular professions in the twenty-first century) probably do not believe in the 'silly' miracles in the *vitae*, but most modern readers do find themselves believing in the author of the *opuscula*, his trials, his mission, the quality of his character, and that he actually experienced his vividly described voices and visions. The *Confessio* and *Epistola ad milites Corotici* succeed brilliantly in getting and keeping the reader on the author's side. By contrast, whether it is in spite of the virtuosity of his rhetoric, or partly because of it, Gildas repels the modern reader. The author of *De excidio Britanniae* does not conform to modern notions of saintly spirit, and his bitter vituperations run dangerously close to inspiring sympathy for those he condemns. But we tend to accept Patrick's pleading against now-silent opponents. For example, the

Confessio's repeated protestations against accusations of financial selfaggrandizement have rarely suggested to modern writers the possibility that there might be some substance to the charges. Similary, when in the *Epistola* Patrick says that Coroticus and his men should be called 'ciues daemoniorum' (fellow citizens of demons) and not 'ciues Romanorum sanctorum' (fellow citizens of the holy Romans), we tend to ignore the broader historical context, that the warfare in which the relevant episode took place was primarily a matter of the Roman Christian world defending itself against peoples who were most often pagans, barbarians and aggressors, all well enough illustrated by Patrick's own life story. Having justifiably left aside the evidence of hagiography, the cult, the non-contemporary annals, legends and folklore, we are left with a Patrick who speaks to us from a fifth-century Ireland that is essentially a prehistoric vacuum or an ahistorical Age of Saints. We need not worry, for example, over the extremely negative moral valence that the hagiographers have placed on Lóegaire mac Néill and the Tara kingship; Patrick himself names neither. Patrick's struggle, his associates and his opponents (with the likely exception of Coroticus) mean to us only what Patrick wishes them to mean to us.

I am not saying that Patricius Bannaventensis was not the good and honest man that he clearly thought he was and so many of his readers still do. What I am saying is that if this is our initial reaction as investigators into the primary Patrician evidence, then this attitude is a serious impediment. To allow such an attitude to lie under the surface will contaminate our work on the historical Patrick. In fact, to conclude *a priori* that the Patrick who wrote the *opuscula* – whenever he lived and whatever he actually did – has already proved himself to be a saintly man effectively inhibits us from finding any known context for him. Situated in a real context, Patrick's own *acta* could not possibly be so one-sidedly pure, the attacks against him (if their authors and reasons were known) could not possibly be so groundless, and his opponents could not possibly be so two-dimensionally wicked and misguided. The Patrick known only from the *opuscula* is too saintly to have accomplished much of lasting significance in the nasty and chaotic circumstances along Rome's disintegrating north-western frontier.

We have, of course, no agreed dates for Patrick's career. This again is largely Patrick's own doing. He names no datable contemporaries and gives no certain reference to identifiable major events. His perspective is, throughout, ahistorical. Gildas, in contrast, places his *De excidio Britanniae* within a historical construct: first there were the *Britanni*; the *Romani* came, and *Britannia* became *Romania;* then, after a series of calamities and withdrawals, the Romans left permanently, Britannia was Britannia once more, the *superbus tyrannus* invited the *Saxones* to defend against the *Picti* and *Scotti*, the *Saxones* revolted, the *Britanni* appealed to 'Agitius ter consul' (Aëtius, consul for the third time), and so on. But Patrick writes as if the Roman Empire had always existed and always would exist with Britain as part of it. Distinct *Britanni* or *Galli* do not exist as peoples; rather they are the *Romani* of the *Britanniae* and the *Galliae*, the provinces of Britain and Gaul. It is a migration period with no motion: no new peoples arrive on the stage in the course of his life story, the *Picti, Scoti* or *Hiberionaci*, and pagan *Franci* seem always to have been where they appear in Patrick's account. The *aduentus Saxonum* is not recounted; in fact, the English are never mentioned. Christianity is static in Patrick's account. The Britons – even the three generations of Patrick's family that he mentions – appear always to have been Christians and, likewise, the Romans of Britain and Gaul in general. The faith is spreading only in Ireland and, there, only in connection with Patrick's immediate activities.

In 1988, I wrote a paper arguing for the early Patrician chronology of Mario Esposito,[6] that is, born about 350,[7] died about 430. As I argued then, not only did Esposito's theory remain compelling on its own historical basis, but this early chronology also better suited the linguistic evidence that the author of the *opuscula* was writing during the period that corresponds to the earliest stratum of Latin and Brittonic loanwords into Irish. This point is illustrated by the evidence of the three borrowings of the early type to be linked to the career of Patricius Bannaventensis: *Cothraige* < *Patricius, Coirthech* < *Corotīcus*, and *mo de broth/muin duiu braut.*[8]

In the balance of the present chapter, I shall add some evidence for this theory and explore possible identifications for Patrick. The identifications have not entered the discussion, partly because they do not fit the standard Patrician chronologies, but I think also because they would imply a Patrick incompatible with the widespread belief that he was indeed a saint and (most importantly) with what we think a saint should and should not do. In any event, the obstacle is not, as I see it, the facts as stated in the *opuscula.*

The three Patricii: St Patrick, Patricius fisci patronus, *and* off[icina] Patrici[i]

In my earlier article, I trawled for men documented in careers in and around Britain, who were named Patricius and who flourished in the fourth and fifth centuries.[9] I found two. The first had a connection to a Romano-British regime and, for the second, there is direct physical evidence from northern Ireland. They are, respectively, the financial advocate of 'Emperor' Magnus Maximus in 385[10] and the man named on an ingot (reading 'EX.OFF.|PATRICI', that is, from the *officina* of Patricius) deposited, no earlier than *c*.420, in a large hoard of late-Roman silver at Ballinrees, near Coleraine, co. Derry.[11] A total of five possibilities follow:

(1) Patricius Bannaventensis ≠ P. fisci patronus ≠ P. officinator
(2) P. Bannaventensis ≠ P. fisci patronus = P. officinator
(3) P. Bannaventensis = P. fisci patronus ≠ P. officinator
(4) P. Bannaventensis = P. officinator ≠ P. fisci patronus
(5) P. Bannaventensis = P. fisci patronus = P. officinator

It will not be possible to prove or disprove any of these alternatives beyond doubt. I shall, therefore, try to set out the relevant points and suggest to what extent each identification is possible or likely.

Taking the Ballinrees ingot first, that the moneyer and Maximus' financial officer are one and the same is relatively likely in view of their names, dates, professions, shared Insular connections and the fact that of the 731 coins identified at Ballinrees, 52 were issued by Maximus.[12] Whether or not the *fisci patronus* had also served as a *monetarius* (minter), he no doubt was well informed of the activities of the Imperial mint at Trier, and the *officinator* had some such specialist background.

How likely is it, then, that the Patricius of the ingot is St Patrick? First, let us keep in mind the striking coincidence that the name Patricius, rare or perhaps non-existent in the remains of Roman Britain *per se*, appears twice in the meagre contemporary records of fifth-century Ulster. There is no agreed interpretation for the hoard. Booty captured from Roman Britain has been suggested.[13] An alternative view takes the silver as payment to returning Irish veterans of Roman forces.[14] The latest coins at Ballinrees were issued by Constantine III (407–411),[15] the usurper from Britain, and the Western Emperor Honorius, including a near mintcondition *siliqua* of 419–23.[16] The most likely date of deposition thus belongs to the decade 420 x 430, the final decade of Patricius Bannaventensis' career according to the present theory. Such a chronology would thus explain why the hoard was never reclaimed, if St Patrick were the owner and died shortly after deposition. Ballinrees also contained an ingot stamped CVRMISSI, and the discovery of a second ingot stamped CVRMISSI, this time from Kent, supports an immediate south British source for the Ballinrees material as a whole.[17] The author of the *opuscula* tells us that he sold his rank (*nobilitas*) for his ministry (*Ep.* §10), presumably converting land or office for something portable. He says that he repeatedly gave gifts to Irish kings and salaries to their sons as travelling companions (*Conf.* §52), that he incurred expenses in his travels throughout Ireland (*Conf* §51), that he was still spending at the time of writing the *Confessio* and would continue to spend to the limit (§53), that he gave 'up to the price of fifteen men' to the brehons (ibid.),[18] and he discusses the ransoming of Christian captives with thousands of coins (*Ep.* §14). Since Patrick also tells that he repeatedly refused jewellery and any form of donation from his Irish converts, we must assume that his expenditures were made in the form of portable funds supplied to him from Britain and/or Gaul.

The general consensus is that the Ballinrees ingot was not produced at an Imperial workshop, but at a private *officina* owned by a man named Patricius.[19] As Britain produced silver throughout the Roman Period[20] and the late-Roman inscribed ingots found in Britain and Ireland are typologically distinct from the continental examples, it is likely that the Ballinrees ingot was made in Britain. As mentioned, the other inscribed ingot from the hoard reads CVRMISSI. This has been suggested to be an abbreviation of the unattested formula *curator missionum* ('keeper of discharge' – whatever that would mean), and therefore some sort of official stamp.[21] However, the *comparandum* from Kent which reads 'ex-off | cvrmissi' renders this reading unlikely, since the first two words are separated by space and a punct and the second line is not divided at all;[22] one can see from the other inscribed ingots brought together in Painter's article that it is most usual for abbreviated words to be separated. Therefore, we more probably have *Curmissus*, a Romano-Celtic name belonging to a British moneyer whose cultural background was similar to Patrick's.

In the discussion following a reading of my earlier paper in Massachusetts in 1988, John Carey and Paul Meyvaert made the interesting suggestion that St Patrick and Patricius *fisci patronus* might have been the same person. That might have been the lucrative post that Patricius Bannaventensis sold to finance his Irish mission. Since then, I have given some preliminary consideration to the three-way equation. The figure from Trier fits the author of the *opuscula* in several details. First, taken in the context of the *opuscula* alone and assuming the conventional mid to late fifth-century Patrick, the references to *Franci, Romani Gallorum Christianorum* and *tot milia solidorum* (many thousands of *solidi*) *Ep.* §14) are curious. Otherwise, Patrick speaks from only his personal experience or quotes scripture. Why, then, would he make an exception with this odd piece of hearsay from north-east Gaul, if that is all it is? Furthermore, Patrick does not introduce this information as though it were common knowledge. Rather, it reads as though Patrick is lecturing his British readers concerning a practice of which he has special knowledge, though they were unaware of it. The feeling comes through in the translations of Hood,[23] Hanson and Blanc,[24] Conneely[25] and Howlett,[26] like that of de Paor, which follows:

> This is the custom of the Christian Roman Gauls: they send worthy holy men to the Franks and other heathens with as many thousand *solidi* as are needed for the redemption of baptized captives. You [Coroticus], on the other hand, kill them and sell them to a foreign people that does not know God; you betray the members of Christ as if into a brothel.[27]

This passage is especially odd if we suppose that Patrick was writing about 470 x 490 and then (while discussing the threat to British and Irish Christians from pagan barbarians) never thought to mention the Anglo-Saxons, but the Franks of Gaul instead. However, if the *opuscula* were written by the former *fisci patronus* of Trier, that Patricius had probably died before the Saxons revolted in south-east Britain. He would, on the other hand, have had abundant first-hand experience of hostile pagan Franks, huge quantities of Roman coins and whatever official financial steps were taken for safeguarding the Christian population of Roman Gaul.

There is little wasted motion in Patrick's brief writings. The passage above dangles a subtle but unmistakable offer to resolve the matter with a coin ransom to be delivered by a clerical ambassador. Such a strategy would have been closely consistent with Patrick's acknowledged methods of dealing with hostile potentates in Ireland. If the author of *Epistola* owned the Ballinrees hoard with its 1701 *siliquae*, the sly offer was made in good faith. But for a Patrick with a 462 or 493 obit, who lived in the coinless mid or late fifth century, the anecdote would be an empty curiosity, with no practical edge.

In the 380s, free Frankish tribes, still pagan, were settled east of the lower and middle Rhine, not far from Trier. Archaeological remains also reveal that Franks, using pagan burial practices, settled in large numbers within Roman territory in the provinces of Germania I and II and Belgica I and II, including the neighbourhood of Trier.[28] Magnus Maximus (whom Patricius *fisci patronus* served) had repeated major confrontations with pagan Franks. In seizing power in Gaul in 383, he killed the Emperor Gratian's *comes domesticorum* Mallobaudes, who also held the title *rex Francorum*. Shortly thereafter, another pagan Frank named Bauto became *magister militum* of the young rival emperor of the west, Valentinian II. In about

383/4, Bauto stirred Trans-Rhenine barbarians to attack Maximus' northern frontier.[29] Bauto died a year later to be succeeded as *magister militum* by another pagan Frank Arbogastes.[30] Quoting the lost Chronicle of 'Sulpicius Alexander', Gregory of Tours (*Historia Francorum* ii.9) tells us that when Maximus fell in 388, three pagan Frankish warleaders crossed the Rhine at Cologne, terrorizing the Gallo-Roman populace. A response was then organized at Trier under the generals Quntinus and Nanninus, whom Maximus had appointed to defend Gaul in his absence. Their forces met disaster east of the Rhine. The frontier was not restored until the following year when Arbogastes, then based at Trier, was able to bring his fellow tribesmen to terms with an exchange of hostages. In the meantime, the same Arbogastes had pursued and killed Maximus' son and heir Victor.[31] Otherwise, the triumphant Theodosius is reported to have shown clemency to the former followers of Maximus, some receiving further promotion.[32] It is, therefore, unlikely that Patricius of Trier was killed in 388/9. More probably, he lived and worked on under the cloud of his connection with the defunct regime. In short, if St Patrick had been the attested Patricius *fisci patronus*,[33] his mention of *Franci, Romani Gallorum Christianorum* and *tot milia solidorum* would come from the core of his personal experience, like most of what he says.

This identification would also help to resolve the contradictory cases as to whether Patrick had ever been in Gaul. The continental sojourn of hagiography leads to the false expectation that the author of the *opuscula* would be knowledgeable concerning fifth-century theological issues. On the other hand, it is difficult to see him as altogether lacking experience of Gaul and Gallo-Latin. Mohrmann concluded that the *opuscula*'s Latin (though limited and awkward) had been affected by living continental speech, closely comparable to that found in popular texts of the first quarter of the fifth century.

> Everything in Patrick's Latin points to a beginning and to isolation. There is uncertainty in his Latin usages; there is clearly a lack of Latin tradition. Therefore he has to fall back upon his own limited knowledge of Latin and upon his Bible. There are no traces in his vocabulary, nor in the general structure of his Latin, such as to make it probable, or even plausible, that he found in Ireland an already developed 'Irish' Christian Latin, going back to continental tradition. But in that case the undeniable continental elements in his Latin can only be explained by personal contact with continental Latin.[34]

Patricius *fisci patronus* is mentioned only in the near contemporary Chronicle of Sulpicius Severus (ii.51). There he is found playing a role in the condemnation of the Priscillianists by Maximus at Trier in 385. The Spanish Bishop Priscillian and his followers were widely regarded as heretics by leaders of the church in Gaul and Italy, including St Martin and St Ambrose, both of whom visited Trier during the protracted affair. However, most church leaders came to disapprove strongly of the outcome, in which secular authorities had judged bishops on religious issues and meted out death sentences.[35] It was also believed that the defendants had been tortured. Initially, the accusations were made by fellow bishops, and the charge was heresy. But before the Priscillianists were condemned, the clerical prosecutors withdrew, perhaps sensing the ethical dilemma and tide of opinion. Maximus appointed Patricius in their place. The charge became adultery and black magic (*maleficium*). The choice of a *fisci patronus* to try a heretic/sorcerer has been explained by Sulpicius Severus' remark that Maximus 'wanted to confiscate the property of heretics' (in the letter *Gallus*); the charge is echoed by Theodosius' panegyrist Pacatus.[36] And Sulpicius' Chronicle tells that the defendant Tiberianus had his property seized. Thus, Maximus may have relied on Patricius because the case had turned into a revenue source at a time when the prefecture of the Gauls faced imminent war from the rivals Valentinian II and Theodosius.[37] Priscillian himself and six of his closest associates were beheaded. Two further followers, Instantius and Tiberianus were exiled 'in Sylinancim insulam quae ultra Britannias sita est' (to the Isle of Scilly beyond Britain).[38] This is the first extant reference to Scilly. It is significant as a reminder of the British base of Maximus' regime and demonstrates the likelihood that the prosecutor Patricius knew western Britain and its maritime approaches. A further detail reflecting the ascendancy of a Romano-British Christian elite at Trier at this time is the fact that the city's bishop when the trial began was named *Britto* (the Briton).[39] It was most probably Britto from whom Maximus received baptism on taking power in 383.[40]

Patricius Bannaventensis leaves no doubt that he was a wealthy man. As mentioned above, Patrick's *Confessio* tells us repeatedly that he spread the faith in Ireland by making payments to men in power and accepting no offerings from converts. For a missionary with resources, this practice was an effective manipulation of a small-scale society's gift economy, or of what we might call in the early Irish context *céilsine* (clientship).[41] Patrick's behaviour subverted the pattern by refusing all return gifts, thus placing his exchange partners in a position of permanent obligation vis-à-vis himself and his successors. It was likewise the essential function of the Roman *patronus* (in the term's earlier sense) to acquire and protect a following of *clientes*, using personal wealth to buy the obligations of the weak. Thus, St

Patrick's unusual, but effective approach to his mission may have continued the pragmatic generosity he had learned in the earlier building of networks of political influence. All of this highlights a peculiarity shared by these two Patricii: both pursued controversial strategies to forward Christian agendas, directly applying overt financial power in secular settings.

Though a secular officer, Patricius of Trier could not have prosecuted Priscillian had he not been a devout and self-proclaimed orthodox Catholic, zealous in his faith. Such an attitude was indeed the essence of the state policy of Maximus' regime.[42] The central issue of orthodoxy was then the full divinity of Christ, as opposed to the Arian view, whereby Jesus as a creation of God the Father was subordinate or at least secondary. This is one theological dispute of which the author of the *opuscula* was apparently aware. *Conf.* §4 is a credal statement that Patrick terms 'mensura fidei Trinitatis'. Its Nicene orthodoxy is clearcut: 'et huius filium Iesum Christum, quem cum Patre scilicet semper fuisse testamur, ante originem saeculi spiritaliter apud Patrem, inenarrabiliter genitum ante omne principium' (and His Son Jesus Christ, Whom with the Father, to be sure, we bear witness always to have existed before the origin of the age, spiritually begotten with the Father in a way that cannot be narrated, before all beginning).[43] By the present chronology, Patrick's fervent Christianity had been known in Britain since he returned from captivity some ten to twelve years before the trial of Priscillian. As the grandson of a priest, the son of a deacon, a deacon himself by this time (*Conf.* §27) and a declared Nicene, Patricius Bannaventensis would have been a suitable representative for the fanatical Maximus.

A great deal has been written on Patrick's 'Rule of Faith'.[44] A consensus has emerged that its closest extant antecedent is the Rule of Faith from the *Commentary on the Apocalypse* of the late third-century martyr, Victorinus of Petavium. In fact, it might be said that Victorinus is the only presently agreed patristic source recognizable in the *opuscula*.[45] Patricks's *mensura fidei* also shows distinctive similarities to the 'creed' of Auxentius, Bishop of Milan 355–74;[46] Auxentius was an Arian, but there was nothing Arian about his creed or its basis from Victorinus. Rather, it probably reflects the wording known at Milan and the Imperial court there in the 360s. It is likely, therefore, that something along the lines of the statements of Victorinus and Auxentius had been current at the court at Trier in the 380s. Hanson has concluded that Victorinus' 'Rule of Faith ... was certainly the basis for the Rule of Faith of the ancient British church'.[47] But Patrick's *mensura* is easily explained without any such sweeping conclusion if we suppose that he is the Patricius who defended Nicene orthodoxy on behalf of the Gallic Emperor in 385.

It is apparent from the *opuscula* that Patrick's mission was under some cloud of suspicion. Much of the *Confessio* answers charges whose substance we must infer. Charles Thomas's formulation of these strikes a balance between intuition and caution.

General
1 That when, years beforehand, it was agreed that the Church in Britain should establish this new See in Ireland, Patrick arranged to be appointed as its first Bishop for his own purposes, viz. to enrich himself, taking advantage of his local knowledge of the Irish and their language and manners.
2 That Patrick expected to finance the mission in some way not authorised by the Church; because, even though asked, he refused to accept the normal endowments being offered at the time.

Specific
3 That he improperly received valuable gifts (*ornamenta*) from rich Irish converts, notably rich Irish women converts.
4 That he took money from converts when he baptised them.
5 That he took rewards from converted and baptised Irishmen as an inducement subsequently to ordain them.
6 That by all such grossly improper conduct over a number of years he brought the Church into disrepute, and his associates and himself in danger, among hostile and pagan Irish elements.[48]

If we limit ourselves to the *opuscula*, we shall know next to nothing about the years between Patrick's return to Britain in young adulthood and his Irish mission in later life. In this vacuum, his deep anxiety over these points strikes us as either an irrational paranoia or as an offstage calumny perpetrated by unjust critics. However, if Patrick had been a moneyer, if his name was to be seen stamped on silver bars, and especially if the proceedings of Trier 385 lurk in his missing years, then the suspicions and Patrick's defensiveness about them were inevitable. As mentioned, the suppression of the Priscillianists had involved a controversial policy of confiscation. It is also likely that Patricius of Trier emerged from the trial a rich (that is an even richer) man. And of course, all of Maximus' officers were tainted by a regime which had come to be viewed after its overthrow, in certain influential quarters, as illegitimate. That this was so even for some in Britain is shown by Gildas' treatment of Maximus as emphatically illegitimate.[49]

The chief obstacle to St Patrick = Patricius *fisci patronus* is that a man with Patrick's limited Latin education would have been an unlikely choice for Maximus' advocate. While this point should be considered, other factors outweigh it. First, Patrick probably apologized excessively for his Latin as a rhetorical device.[50] Though Patrick repeatedly says that he was despised by many due to the consequences of his interrupted education, he never says that he failed to advance for these reasons. Rather, he rose – despite any lack of polish – to the high station commensurate with the class to which he was born. Thus, his father had been a deacon *(Conf.* §1), and he became one (§27). Patrick tells that his father had been a *decorio (Ep.* §10), and then he immediately says that he sold his own *nobilitas*, implying that he had inherited the rank himself. It is clear from the Theodosian Code (12.i.43–170)[51] that the office of *decurio* was hereditary. In both instances in the *opuscula*, the only reason why Patrick tells the reader of his father's offices is to prove his own hereditary qualifications. The Theodosian Code also shows that it was very common for a *decurio* to belong to the powerful hereditary guild of advocates and that members of both groups were likely to have inherited wealth *(advocati* or *patroni;* 12.i.46,[52] 12.i.61[53] *(patroni)*, 12.i.87,[54] 12.i.98,[55] 12.i. 116,[56] *Novellae Theodosii* 10.i,[57] *Novellae Valentiniani* 2.ii,[58] 32.i[59]). The fact that Patrick apologizes because, unlike others, he had not finished training in 'iura et sacras litteras' (law and sacred letters) *(Conf.* §9) is at least a hint that he had entered both professions, despite the inadequate preparation for which he feels he must apologize.

Second, Patricius probably did not argue against the Priscillianists by himself. The Theodosian Code (11.xxx.41) places the *aduocatus fisci* (otherwise called *patronus fisci)* in a position of oversight: 'The fiscal representatives who preside over cases involving the privy purse or the sacred imperial treasury shall undertake the trials in the presence of the fiscal advocate.'[60]

Third, that Maximus had appointed a *fisci patronus* to prosecute heretics shows that the prime consideration was not skill in legal rhetoric, but rather trustworthiness and efficacy in financial matters. These concerns might have favoured the special promotion of a younger supporter from the Romano-British aristocracy. Again, from the Theodosian Code (10.x.2):

> if several men have obtained from Us the office of defender of the fisc, that one shall be preferred to all others who is recognized as superior in integrity, more powerful in learning, and more capable than the others in his proved trustworthiness, even if he has obtained from Our Clemency this special grant of imperial favor after the others.[61]

Fourth, in 385, the Britons in Maximus' following had been on the Continent since summer 383. If St Patrick was among them, his colloquial Latin and practical grasp of Roman law probably had keener edges in 385 (at age 32–4) than when he composed the *opuscula* in old age after intervening decades in Britain and Ireland.

To summarize this section, we can make three circumstantial cases: (1) that Patricius *fisci patronus* = Patricius *officinator;* (2) that Patricius *officinator* = St Patrick; (3) that Patricius *fisci patronus* = St Patrick. If Esposito's chronology for St Patrick is accepted, no major historical obstacles to (2) and (3) remain. Nonetheless, I present these cases as possibilities rather than proved. I do not think these possibilities can be ruled out because Patrick himself and his hagiographers present him as a very good man and because all the histories take the side of Maximus' rivals and present Maximus' regime as wicked and overreaching.

Palladius, the computus of Patricius, and the 493 obit

The Irish annals give two eras for Patrick's death – one set of entries clustering between 457 and 462 and often calling him *Senex Patricius* or *Sen Phátraicc* and another between 487 and 496 in which he is often called *archiepiscopus et apostolus* and the like.[62] I shall use as shorthand '461' and '493' for the two groups. Neither comes close to Esposito's chonology, according to which Patrick died *c.*430. In the light of current understanding regarding the earliest possible contemporary Irish annals,[63] both obits are no doubt retrospective insertions made in periods significantly later than the events described and therefore cannot be used with any confidence to establish a Patrician chronology.[64] Nonetheless, the '461' and '493' obits probably did not come out of thin air, and thus some burden rests on the argument for Esposito's chronology to explain how dates late by roughly 35 and 65 years arose.

In essence, my proposal is that the various omissions, duplications and confusions comprising the 'two Patricks' problem are recurring reflections of the central historical conundrum of the origin of the Irish church, namely that Rome said that the first bishop in Ireland was a man from Gaul named Palladius, whereas Irish Christians knew that their first bishop was a Briton named Patrick. If we suppose that Palladius actually preceded Patrick, then the confusion over the 'two Patricks' is purely an Irish confusion: fifth-century Rome, though generally uninformed about Ireland and its Church, knew better than the Irish.

The earlier obit usually appears to be secondary, implying prior knowledge on the part of the annalist of the later obit. There are fewer of the late obits and they are shorter. Furthermore, the *Senex Patricius* label implies prior knowledge of another *Patricius*; there is no comparable distinction in the late obits. The early obits of the Annals of Ulster (457 and 461) say 'quies Senis Patricii, ut alii libri dicunt' (the death of Old Patrick, as other books say) and 'hic alii quietem Patricii dicunt' (here others tell of Patrick's death).[65] The '461' obit is consistent with the Patrician hagiographical scheme of the late seventh-century Muirchú and Tírechán and later sources; so there is no mystery as to what 'alii libri' these could be. Nor are we at a loss as to the ultimate textual inspiration for this 'Armagh' chronology for a Patrician mission of *c*.432-*c*.461. The entry for 431 in Prosper's Chronicle – 'ad Scottos in Christo credentes ordinatus a papa Caelestino Palladius primus episcopus mittitur' (to the Gaels who believed in Christ Palladius is sent as first bishop by Pope Celestine)[66] – would have either directly or at one or more removes provided the chronological anchor in one of the following ways: (1) Patrick's hagiographers had to assimilate the *acta* of the first two bishops as one historical composite, or (2) they had to pre-empt Palladius by showing Patrick to be as early or nearly as early. The solution found in *notae supplementaria* of Tírechán[67] is reminiscent of the Irish vernacular modes of reconciling traditions of the conceptions and parentage of heroes, as, for example, in the multiple birth in *Compert Con Culainn*.[68] Thus, consistent with Prosper, we are told that a 'Paladius', also named Patricius, was sent to Ireland by Pope Celestine. This first Patricius' only act was to be martyred. Then straight away Celestine and the angel Victor sent the second Patricius. For the purposes of heroic biography, the two missions, like the three conceptions producing one surviving child in *Compert Con Culainn*, remain functionally one.

If we begin the question of the assimilation of Palladius to Patrick with Tírechán §56, that puts us in the range *c*.670 x 805 and in the literary domain of Armagh's propaganda. However, Ó Cróinín, arguing from computistic evidence, would open the question in north Munster *c*.633.[69] Two key texts are involved. Cummian, in his letter to Ségéne of Iona, makes a survey of Easter cycles differing from the Insular reckoning. The first he describes is attributed to 'sanctus Patricius papa noster'. We also have a seventh-century Irish text containing the prologue of a *computus* ascribed to a Patricius. Details of the *computus* given in both texts concern a nineteen-year Paschal cycle of the Alexandrian type, also regarded (though incorrectly) as the 'Nicene' cycle, which is an important point here. Therefore, along with the name Patricius, the nature of the cycle confirms that these two texts refer to the same *computus*. According to Ó Cróinín, Patricius Bannaventensis could have known only the 84-year (Pseudo-)Anatolian cycle, used by the Britons and the Gaels of the North into the eighth century.[70] The '84' was itself a fossil of the fourth-century church of Roman Britain.[71] On the other hand, as Ó Cróinín explains, a bishop trained, as Palladius was, at Auxerre and/or Rome in the late fourth or earlier fifth century would also have known of the Alexandrian cycle, which was used, for example, by St Ambrose of Milan, who defended and explained it at length in a letter of 386.[72] Therefore, Ó Cróinín argues, the Patricius of the nineteen-year *computus* must in fact be Palladius. The fact that the 'Patrician' *computus* was known amongst the north Munster clerics (unconnected to the Patrician *paruchia*) and that it has left no trace in the archive of fifth-century Patrician records preserved at Armagh render Ó Cróinín's 'Palladian' explanation a definite possibility. He reaches the following historical conclusions, extrapolated from the later conventionial Patrician chronology.

[*ante* 431] The 84-year Easter cycle of Columbanus' time and beyond 'may well have continued a usage already established in the fledgling Irish Christian communities of pre-Palladian times, for those first converts were certainly under British influence'.

[*post* 431] Palladius alias Patricius, author of the nineteen-year computus 'was not able to overcome the already firmly implanted British Easter'.

[*c*.461 x *c*.493] The mission of Patrick the Briton, author of the *Confessio* and *Epistola;* hence the *computus* of Palladius alias Patricius is 'the oldest Irish Christian text'.

[*ante c*.632] 'Palladius's table . . . passed into the southern sphere of influence, only to see its true origins obscured by the inexorable advance of the Patrician legend.'[73]

Several implications fall out from this framework. First, the fledgling, bishop-free, pre-Palladian Irish Christian community appears to have been tenacious, even well organized. On the other hand, the Palladian mission – despite its papal authority and apostolic priority – was limited and ineffective. Even with Patrick's relatively late start and the severe obstacles, as described by the British Patrick himself, the renown of the name Patricius was earlier and more widely circulated than we had known. Thus, already *ante c*.633 – some forty years before Tírechán and fifty or sixty before Muirchú – the legend had spread beyond Ulaid and Armagh to eclipse the reputation of the actual first bishop of the Irish on his own southern turf. Are we to think in terms of a lost *vita* (pre-dating Cogitosus' *Vita Brigitae* of *c*.650 x *c*.685)[74] or of an oral legend having this impact? In either event, the legend was both irresistible and national, or well-nigh national, by *c*.600. Confronting it, the successors of the true first bishop lost confidence in their founder (and Rome) and replaced his name with that of the British latecomer. Even so, and while sandwiched between the 84-year pre-Palladian Christians and 84-year Patrician and post-Patrician British missionaries, the Palladian camp somehow preserved the nineteen-year *computus* under its pseudonymous attribution.

There are implausibilities in the foregoing that can be avoided by assuming an early Patrick. With a pre-Palladian Patrick, Palladius and his co-workers would have encountered Christians who regarded themselves correctly to be converts of an earlier bishop named Patricius. According to *Confessio* §14, there were 'many thousand' such converts. If the fledgling pre-Palladian church, as envisioned by Ó Cróinín, and the Patrician church were thus one and the same, we might expect them, like the Romano-Britons, to use the 84-year (Pseudo-)Anatolian cycle. Thus, the Palladian nineteen-year cycle would represent a localized post-Patrician superstratum rather than a strangely persistent substratum. If the Palladian mission had been pragmatic, they would necessarily have adapted to the existing Patrician cult and organization. And to promote the newfangled Roman observance of the Alexandrian *computus*, the Palladian party might have attributed their table to a pseudo-Patricius sooner rather than later, responding to the fifth-century Patrician fact, rather than to the advance wave of the late seventh-century Patrician legend. In this way, the 'Patricius' of Cummian's letter would be, like most pseudonyms,[75] an invocation of a more famous predecessor, not a successor. And the *computus* of Patricius, post-dating the *opuscula*, would not be 'the oldest Irish Christian text', but the first in the line of Irish texts posthumously attributed to Patrick.

Is this Palladian theory necessary at all? Dumville advances the discussion,[76] reminding us of our ignorance of practices in fourth- and fifth-century Britain. The more serious alternative to Ó Cróinín's explanation would hinge upon whether Patrick the Briton ever visited Gaul.[77] If he journeyed to Gaul during Maximus' reign between 383 and 388 (as would have been likely for any aristocratic Romano-British male in young maturity at the time), he might have learned of the Alexandrian Easter, which was observed by some western churches in 384 and 387.[78] If St Patrick was Patricius *fisci patronus*, he probably met Ambrose of Milan at Trier in 384 x 386, when Ambrose came as Valentinian II's emissary to Maximus.[79] Ambrose espoused the Alexandrian cycle, presenting it as sanctioned by the Nicene Council of 325, the font of orthodoxy.[80] Maximus was ever anxious to appear the pious protector of Nicene Catholics in northern Italy (against their Arian rivals) and was solicitous of their influential bishop.[81] There can be little doubt but that Trier (and its well-placed Romano-Britons) heeded Ambrose's detailed directives set out in favour of the Alexandrian date for Easter at 25 April 387 (as opposed to the traditional Roman computation at 21 March that year).[82] Therefore, it is possible that Patrick brought a nineteen-year 'Nicene' *computus* to Ireland as early as 390 x 400, as part of his slender portfolio of essential Christian texts. It then could easily have been overwhelmed and marginalized by subsequent missionary activity from Britain after contacts with Gaul had broken down. In short, Ó Cróinín's theory of Palladius as the source of the *computus* of Patricius is possible but unnecessary. In either event, I see no way in which this piece of evidence favours post-Palladian mid or later fifth-century dates for the mission of Patricius Bannaventensis.

Notes

[1] *Studia Hibernica* 2 (1962), pp. 7–173.

[2] I use 'Patricius Bannaventensis' to mean the man who wrote the *Confessio* and *Epistola ad milites Corotici*, to avoid ambiguity in connection with any of the proposals to the effect that more than one historical figure has contributed to the formation of the 'St Patrick' of medieval literature and tradition as, for example, in O'Rahilly's *The Two Patricks*. The surname Bannaventensis is based on *Bannauenta*, the probable and widely adopted restoration of Patrick's name for his home, 'qui fuit uico Bannauem Taberniae' (which was *Bannauem Taberniae*) (*Confessio* §1).

[3] The oath occurs in Muirchú, see Bieler (ed. and trans.), *Patrician Texts*, pp. 106–7, 208. The Old Welsh version is in *Sanas Cormaic*, see Bromwich (ed.), *The Beginnings of Welsh Poetry*, pp. 14–15; Stokes (ed.), *Three Irish Glossaries*, p. 28. For the author's earlier discussion see '*Cothairche*, Esposito's theory', pp. 180–1.

[4] This conclusion is inescapable in light of *Confessio* §9: 'nam sermo et loquelo nostra translata est in linguam alienam' (for our speech and words have been translated into a foreign language).

[5] *Amator* or *Amatorex* occurs in Muirchú's *Vita*, Pref. §9; Alsiodorum = Auxerre in §6.

[6] Esposito, 'The Patrician problem'.

[7] I would prefer the date 351–3, so that Patrick's abduction at age sixteen 'together with many thousands of his countrymen' (*Conf.* §1) occurs during the *barbarica conspiratio* of 367–8/9, rather than during the relative peace in the years before or after. On the date of the 'Great Raid' see Blockley, '"Barbarian conspiracy"'; Tomlin, '"Barbarian conspiracy"'.

[8] For my interpretation of the derivation of these three forms, see '*Cothairche*, Esposito's theory', pp. 180–7, 197–202. For an alternative explanation see Harvey, 'Significance of *Cothraige*', pp. 1–9. See now also, Ó Riain, 'When and why was *Cothraige* . . .?'. As I argued earlier, I still think that to have the name *Cothraige* come to be used for Patrick in Irish sources and also strongly resemble an early loan of Latin *Patricius* into Irish can hardly be coincidental. And, as far as the historical linguistic point goes, there are also the other two early loanwords *(Coirthech* and *mo de broth)* directly linked to Patrick in the hagiographical texts. These would have to be 'explained away' separately to remove Patrick's career from the horizon of firststratum borrowings.

9 There is no example of Patricius as *nomen, cognomen* or *praenomen* in the *Epigraphic Indexes* of Goodburn and Waugh, *Roman Inscriptions of Britain* 1. In the *Prosopography of the Later Roman Empire*, we find seven Patricii in the period AD 260–395 (A. H. M. Jones, Martindale and Morris (eds), *Prosopography* I, p. 673) and seventeen in the period AD 395–527 (Martindale, *Prosopography* II, pp. 837–43). Of these, none are known to be British, and only one has a Romano-British connection: i.e. the Patricius who in 385 acted as the *Fisci Patronus* (advocate of the Imperial purse), as described in the *Theodosian Code* 10.xv, Pharr (trans.), pp. 281, 573. According to Russell (Review of *Britain 400–600*, p. 266): 'Both [Sims-Williams ('Dating the transition') and Koch] examine the evidence for the name *Patricius* in the later Roman Empire and in Britain . . . Sims-Williams on the basis of much the same evidence [as Koch's] concludes *"Patricius* was a common Latin name, the *Wayne* and *Kevin* of its age" (['Dating the transition'] p. 269 *[sic,* correctly p. 229]) and could therefore have been in use in Ireland long before Patrick came to Ireland.' This way of putting it obscures rather than discloses the essential detail that Harvey ('Significance of *Cothraige',* p. 3), Sims-Williams, Russell and I have between us come up with precisely *no* example of a Romano-British Patricius other than St Patrick himself and the two possibly British Patricii mentioned here. One might also ask in the face of Sims-Williams's and Russell's remarks how many Latin names, even common Latin names, were in continuous use in Ireland since 'long before Patrick came to Ireland'.

10 This Patricius is mentioned in Sulpicius Severus' *Chronicle,* ii.51.

11 On this hoard, see Mattingly, Pearce and Kendrick, 'Coleraine hoard'; Edwards, *Archaeology of Early Medieval Ireland,* p. 4; Raftery, *Pagan Celtic Ireland,* p. 216.

12 Mattingly, Pearce and Kendrick, 'Coleraine hoard', p. 40

13 Edwards, *Archaeology of Early Medieval Ireland,* p. 4.

14 Mytum, *Origins,* p. 27.

15 See Raftery, *Pagan Celtic Ireland,* p. 216.

16 Edwards, *Archaeology of Early Medieval Ireland,* p. 4.

17 Painter, 'Roman silver hoard', pp. 1–15; Raftery, *Pagan Celtic Ireland,* p. 216.

18 On the general subject of Patrick's finances see Thompson, *Who Was Saint Patrick?,* pp. 95–102.

19 Mattingly, Pearce and Kendrick, 'Coleraine hoard', pp. 43ff.; Painter, 'A late-Roman silver ingot', p. 85.

20 Frere, *Britannia,* pp. 321–4.

21 Mattingly, Pearce and Kendrick, 'Coleraine hoard'; Raftery, *Pagan Celtic Ireland,* p. 216.

22 Painter, 'A late-Roman silver ingot', Plate xxii.

23 Hood (ed. and trans.), *St Patrick: His Writings,* p. 57.

24 Hanson and Blanc (eds), *Saint Patrick, Confession,* pp. 145–7.

25 Conneely, *St Patrick's Letters,* p. 79.

26 Howlett (ed. and trans.), *Book of Letters,* p. 33.

27 de Paor, *Saint Patrick's World,* p. 111.

28 Périn and Feffer, *Les Francs,* pp. 61–72.

29 B. H. Williams, *Ambrose of Milan,* pp. 198–9.

30 Wightman, *Gallia Belgica,* p. 215; Périn and Feffer, *Les Francs,* p. 56.

31 Matthews, *Western Aristocracies,* p. 225.

32 B. H. Williams, *Ambrose of Milan,* p. 229.

33 The usual term of service for the *aduocatus fisci* or *patronus fisci* was two years, after which he would often become a *comes* in the imperial consistory, that is one of the emperor's inner circle of advisers (Pharr (trans.), *Theodosian Code,* p. 573).

34 Mohrmann, *Latin of Saint Patrick,* pp. 51–2.

[35] Stancliffe, *St Martin*, pp. 278–96.
[36] Galletier (ed.), *Panegyricus* 29, pp. 95–6; cf. Stancliffe, *St Martin*, pp. 281–2.
[37] Chadwick, *Priscillian of Ávila*, pp. 111–69.
[38] Sulpicius Severus, *Chronicle* ii, 51.
[39] Cf. Fleuriot, *Les Origines*, pp. 136–7.
[40] Matthews, *Western Aristocracies*, p. 165; B. H. Williams, *Ambrose of Milan*, p. 197.
[41] On the institution of 'gift-exchange' in pre-currency economies see Mauss, *The Gift;* M. J. Rowlands, 'Kinship'.
[42] Ruling while the Western Empire was shaken by the Arian-Nicene conflict, the opposed regime at Trier attempted to use the condemnation of the Priscillianists to consolidate church support by acting as defender of the Nicene faith (B. H. Williams, *Ambrose of Milan*, pp. 197–8; cf. also Wightman, *Gallia Belgica*, p. 216 and n. 53; McLynn, *Ambrose of Milan*, p. 161). Maximus displayed ostentatious orthodoxy when he wrote to Valentinian II in Milan in 386, complaining of the persecution of Nicene churches in Valentinian's territory, from which follows a very thinly veiled threat of invasion on this justification. In his letter to Pope Siricius of about the same period, Maximus cites his punishment of Priscillian as evidence of his ardent orthodoxy (Matthews, *Western Aristocracies*, p. 181; B. H. Williams, *Ambrose of Milan*, p. 216). Sulpicius Severus *(Dialogus* ii.6 in *CSEL*, vol. 1, pp. 187–8) tells how Maximus' empress was such a devoted Christian that she would dismiss her servants to wait personally on St Martin with slavish humility.
[43] Howlett (ed. and trans.), *Book of Letters*, p. 55. I am not competent to judge how meaningful the credal statement of *Conf.* §4 would have been unless Patrick had thought that Arianism (that is, the separate substance of the Father and Son) was still a 'live' theological issue.
[44] See Oulton, *Credal Statements;* Bieler, 'The "Creeds"'; *idem* (ed.), 'Libri epistolarum', pp. 97–107 (with further bibliography); Hanson, 'The rule of faith'; *idem, Search for the Christian Doctrine of God*, pp. 76–7.
[45] Hanson, 'The rule of faith', pp. 25–36, has forcefully rejected any influence from Augustine's *Confessiones* (contrast Conneely, *St Patrick's Letters*).
[46] For instance, Hanson, 'The rule of faith'.
[47] Ibid.; *idem, Search for the Christian Doctrine of God*, p. 76, n. 79.
[48] C. Thomas, *Christianity in Roman Britain*, p. 340.
[49] DEB §§13–14; cf. T. M. Charles-Edwards, 'Bede, the Irish and the Britons', p. 47.
[50] Though I cannot confirm David Howlett's ideas on the complex patterning of Patrick's writings, Howlett has demonstrated convincingly that Patrick's thinking in Latin was complex, well-structured and elegant.
[51] Pharr (trans.), *Theodosian Code*, pp. 348–66.
[52] Ibid., p. 348.
[53] Ibid., p. 351.
[54] Ibid., p. 355.
[55] Ibid., p. 356.
[56] Ibid., p. 359.
[57] Ibid., p. 496.
[58] Ibid., p. 517.
[59] Ibid., pp. 543–4.
[60] Ibid., p. 328.
[61] Ibid., p. 281.
[62] For collections of both see Dumville, *Saint Patrick*, pp. 29–33.
[63] See Ó Cróinín, 'Early Irish annals', pp. 74–86; Smyth, 'Earliest Irish annals', pp. 1–48.

64 Cf. Binchy, 'Patrick and his biographers', 71–3.
65 *AU*, pp. 44–7.
66 Mommsen (ed.), *Chronica Minora*, i.473.
67 Bieler (ed. and trans.), *Patrician Texts*, pp. 164–7, §56.
68 Van Hamel (ed.), *Compert Con Culainn*.
69 Ó Cróinín, 'New light on Palladius', pp. 276–83.
70 Wales (some of it, at least) did not come into conformity with the Roman Easter until 768. However, it would be wrong to think of a monolithic Brittonic Church marching in step on this, or any, point of doctrine. Bede (HE v.15) says that some of the Britons accepted the Roman cycle in Adomnán's time *c*.686–703. Bede would have been most aware of North Britons.
71 C. W. Jones (ed.), *Bedae Opera*, pp. 78–93; Ó Cróinín, 'New light on Palladius', pp. 276–83.
72 With reference to the celebration of Easter the following year. See McLynn, *Ambrose of Milan*, pp. 280–1; cf. C. W. Jones (ed.), *Bedae Opera*, pp. 35–7.
73 Ó Cróinín, 'New light on Palladius', pp. 281–3.
74 The exact date of Cogitosus' *Vita Brigitae* is not certain and must be inferred, hingeing largely on the key reference to him by Muirchú, as that later writer's *pater*. Cogitosus was a propagandist for Kildare's archiepiscopal primacy and thus shows an active disinterest in Patrick and Armagh. It is often assumed that Cogitosus' *Vita* is the earliest 'Life of Brigit' (e.g. Richter, *Medieval Ireland*, p. 78; Ó Cróinín, *Early Medieval Ireland*, p. 158; cf. Hughes, *Early Christian Ireland*, p. 227). However, the anonymous *Vita I Brigitae* (Connolly, 'Vita prima') is of disputed date. Whatever the precise date of the extant *Vita I*, it and the ninth-century mostly Irish *Bethu Brigte* ((ed.) Ó hAodha) may derive independently from a seventh-century pre-Cogitosus 'Primitive Life' (Esposito, 'Earliest Latin Life of St Brigid'; *idem*., 'Notes on Latin Learning and Literature'; K. R. McCone 'Brigit in the seventh century'; Sharpe, *'Vitae S. Brigitae'*, pp. 81–106). The *Vita I* and *Bethu Brigte* both mention Patrick and present their own heroine as subordinate to Patrick. Even if these two do reflect a 'Primitive Life of Brigit' as old as the mid-seventh century, there is no guarantee that their deference to Armagh's primacy is not the result of later editors, and no one is currently claiming that there was any 'Life of Brigit' earlier than a generation later than Cummian's Letter of *c*.633.
75 We don't have far to look for a *comparandum*. The Insular 84-year cycle was attributed to the third-century Syrian bishop Anatolius, but is often claimed to be a sixth-century Irish forgery. Columbanus knew and believed the attribution *c*.600; *Epistula I*, Walker (ed.), *Columbani Opera*, pp. 2–3.
76 Dumville, *Saint Patrick*, pp. 85–8.
77 A view for which Ó Cróinín ('New light on Palladius', p. 278 n. 7) 'hold[s] no brief'. The reference to *fratres* and *sancti Domini mei* in *Galliae* (*Conf.* §43) is not decisive in determining whether or not Patrick had visited Gaul.
78 Ó Cróinín, 'New light on Palladius', pp. 279–80; cf. C. W. Jones (ed.), *Bedae Opera*, pp. 35–6.
79 H. Chadwick, *Priscillian of Ávila*, pp. 133–8; Stancliffe, *St Martin and his Hagiographer*, p. 283. Victricius of Rouen formally received relics from Ambrose of Milan (Paulinus of Nola, *Letter* xviii.4 to Victricius *c*.399 in *CSEL*, vol. 29; Thurston and Attwater, *Butler's Lives of the Saints*, vol. 3, p. 276). It is thus alternatively possible that Patrick had received Ambrose's Alexandrian *computus* second-hand via Victricius. Patrick, in his dream, beheld 'Victoricius cum epistolis innumerabilibus' (Victoricius with innumerable letters) (*Conf.* §23), which raises the possibility that he had received texts from the Gaulish bishop with the similar name Victricius, known to have visited in the 390s.

[80] Walsh and Ó Cróinín, *Cummian's Letter*, p. 190.

[81] Some modern writers have not, I think, adequately weighed the possible impact of shifting politics on our witnesses in attempts to gauge the degree of friction between Maximus and churchmen like Ambrose and Martin. Texts written after Maximus' fall in 388 and the labelling of his rule as a usurpation probably retrospectively exaggerated the dissent of 385. Cf., e.g., Stancliffe, *St Martin*, p. 283. Similarly, Maximus had, in the first place, intervened in the Priscillianist affair aiming to please orthodox churchmen. The resonating disapproval, no doubt, grew to a consensus only in the aftermath and at least partly as a result of Maximus' fall from power.

[82] McLynn, *Ambrose of Milan*, pp. 280–2.

6

Reading Muirchú's Tara-event within its background as a biblical 'trial of divinities'

><

THOMAS O'LOUGHLIN

Introduction

One of the best-known scenes in Insular hagiography is that from Muirchú's *Vita Patricii*[1] which depicts Patrick as celebrant at Ireland's first Easter Vigil shortly after his arrival on Irish soil.[2] The events are presented as the great clash of two religions at the capital of the Irish, 'Temoria . . . caput . . . scottorum' (Tara . . . capital . . . of the Irish),[3] where in the course of a few hours the whole issue of the religion of the Irish was decided. Patrick is presented as going straight to the top of Irish society, virtually directly from his landing site, and then through a sequence of feats of power showing that society, its 'emperor',[4] kings, satraps, leaders, princes and other nobles[5] which is the true religion. The Christian victory is soon complete, the Irish people move from one Age of the Creation to another (from the unnamed Ages of the 'preparation for the gospel' to the Age of the Christ), and the remainder of Patrick's work is then just a mopping-up operation.[6] The Easter Vigil incident is central to the whole *Vita*, and since it is consciously presented as taking place in a central location, it has received much attention from scholars. It is usually studied as part of an attempt to understand the background to the *Vita* within the context of the bolstering of Uí Néill power, for Patrick can be seen as their family patron, in the later seventh century.

However, reading Muirchú as a witness to the political concerns of his time does not exhaust the significance of the text, and the *Vita* has also been read as throwing light on the nature of pre-Christian Irish religion. This strategy – whose principal support has been the practice of translating *magus* in the *Vita* as 'druid'[7] – has been even less successful for the description of the non-Christians. The *Vita*'s depiction of Irish non-Christians is clearly the work of someone who had Patrick as his hero and created an image of Patrick's opponents formed from a Christian view of paganism rather than based upon some real memory of the native religion. Both approaches to the interpretation of the Tara incident (on the one hand the political reading, on the other the quest for pagan religion) have been recognized recently by Edel Bhreathnach as leading to an impasse. She assumes that most of her readers view the *Vita* primarily as a deliberate buttress to Uí Néill expansion and their claims to the kingship of Tara, and her examination of Muirchú led her to this conclusion:

> Muirchú's *Life of Patrick* represents Lóegaire, like Conaire Mór in *Togail Bruidne Da Derga*, as a king doomed as his *gessa* are transgressed. He could not triumph over Patrick. Muirchú consistently portrays Lóegaire in an unfavourable light, and his depiction of the king of Tara does not reflect that of a propagandist on behalf of the Uí Néill but rather of an ecclesiastic championing Patrick and, in particular, Christianity.[8]

If that is the case, then can an explicitly Christian reading of the incident throw light on Muirchú's intentions and world? This chapter is an attempt to explore this possibility by locating the sources Muirchú draws upon in formulating his Tara scene.

I have recently argued that Muirchú deliberately constructed his image of the conversion of Ireland by Patrick through building up a dramatic picture of that event imagined as a baptism located within the liturgy of the Easter Vigil.[9] As such, it is a drama to be read against the already well-known liturgical drama of Christ fulfilling his promise to come and bring deliverance from Adam's sin, to bring light, fire and life, and to bring the beginnings of a new existence through baptism. In short, I argue that Muirchú knows that whatever happened in the actual conversion of Ireland some centuries earlier, the effect of that conversion was, in theological terms, the same as the effect of baptism. Moreover, since the effect of baptism on the whole community of Christians was most clearly expressed in the Easter liturgy, then that liturgy provided the ideal paradigm within which his audience could accurately imagine what had happened, and be thereby edified. Here I should like to take that argument further by noting the range of scriptural sources that Muirchú used, and how the event fits into a well-defined category of miracle story found in the Christian scriptures which I shall call a 'trial of divinities'.

Sources

Towards the beginning of the *Vita*, Patrick is identified by Muirchú as being like Moses, Jonah and John the Baptist.[10] While this could be no more than a random selection of biblical figures with which to draw attention to his sanctity, these named figures are also those who have much in common with Patrick at Tara. All were considered prophets who were to bring about the coming of Christ, and all had to bear witness before the rulers or in the capital cities of their respective regions: Moses before Pharaoh;[11] Jonah in Nineveh;[12] and John the Baptist before King Herod.[13] However, while this theme of prophecy seems central to Muirchú's vision of Patrick, when he wants to describe the actual encounter between the holy man and the wicked foreign king he needs an example where the saint not only emerges victorious, but where the contrast of the simple Patrick facing a powerful enemy is even more sharply drawn, and for this he turns to the story of Nebuchadnezzar, king of Babylon, as found in Dan. 3:1–23 and 91–7. This text, often referred to as *Nabuchodonosor rex*, as the phrase is used repeatedly in the text, was known not only as a wondrous story, but was the scriptural location for two of the most used canticles of the Christian liturgy.[14] The story had the character of a clash of divinities (those who worship idols versus those who worship the true God) whereby the righteous not only triumph but also gain, through the demonstration of divine power, the submission of the opposing king. The text, apart from its direct appeal to Muirchú as fitting his purpose, may also have been part of the Easter Vigil sequence of readings and so had a direct relevance to the scene in which he imagined the Tara-event.[15]

At this point an excursus is called for in order to note that the *Vita* contains evidence about how Muirchú read this whole passage. The story of the trial of divinities forms a distinct unit within the text of Daniel and, in Hebrew, the text runs continuously for thirty verses. In the Septuagint this story became the context in which the canticles, which go by the name of the Song of the Three Young Men, found a home, and the text presents the young men as singing these while in the furnace, so in the Septuagint the whole enlarged story contains ninety-seven verses.[16] Jerome recognized this textual discrepancy, and with his usual suspicion of text not found in Hebrew – based on his equation of *Hebraeica* with *ueritas* – he, most unusually, flags the intrusive texts with this warning: 'quae sequuntur in hebraeis uoluminibus non repperi' (I have not found the following verses in the Hebrew scrolls), and he marked the beginning of each additional verse with a special sign in the margin.[17] No doubt the reason Jerome did not excise them is that he was aware that they were already canonized through liturgical use. From Muirchú's quotations from the whole passage, for example verse 9 and then verse 50,[18] we can conclude that either he did not know of Jerome's hesitations or, knowing of those hesitations, he ignored them; for he treats the whole passage of ninety-seven verses as a single story.

The story in Daniel is of a trial of forms of worship that takes place in Babylon, presented as the greatest city, the capital of the whole earth. It is no mean place where the truth of Israel's God will be demonstrated, but rather right at the heart of things in the presence of the great king, Nebuchadnezzar. Muirchú flags this significance by making an explicit connection between Lóegaire and Tara and the Book of Daniel: Tara, we are told, is 'this people's Babylon' and Lóegaire summoned them in the same way that Nebuchadnezzar had summoned his retinue.[19] The conceit implied in Muirchú's allusion is that the events of Dan. 3 are far better known than those of Patrick and that, if they are recalled, we will possess a model with which to understand that Easter night in Brega.

The Daniel story is a simple one: the king orders a great golden idol to be set up for the whole nation to worship in a great public liturgy. All do so except Shadrach, Meshach and Abednego, and this break with the law is reported to the king who sends for them, commanding them to worship. They have no answer to make and so are cast into the fiery furnace. However, to the king's astonishment they remain unharmed. The king reprieves them, recognizes the power of their god and utters a blessing of the god of Shadrach, Meshach and Abednego (Dan. 3:28), and the three young men are promoted to hold power within the empire.

While it should be clear that the Daniel story is Muirchú's inspiration, the extent of his reliance upon it can be seen more clearly when we note the verbal parallels, as shown in Table 6.1.

Muirchú has used a number of stories from the scriptures concerning kings (Pharaoh, Nebuchadnezzar and Herod) to provide the scenery. The palace in the city of Tara is like that of Babylon, but the overall theme of the event is that of a clash of two cults, as presented in Daniel.

A trial of divinities

While the notion that the true religion can be tested in a trial – what I refer to as a trial of divinities[21] – receives little attention, it is one that exercised a major influence on Muirchú, for we can see the two fires of Easter night within a larger pattern. The paradigm for such trials can be found in 3 Reg. (1 Kgs.) 18:17–40, that is, the great clash between Elijah and the prophets Baal and Asherah at Mount Carmel.[22] The story makes its point about which divinity has real power by showing whose priest/prophet has the greatest power. Thus the story was ideal for hagiography. Elijah's strength, and so the strength of his god, is seen by the way all the odds are stacked against him. In front of 'the whole people of Israel',[23] Elijah, the lone remaining prophet of the Lord,[24] takes on the intercessory power of 450 prophets of Baal and 400 prophets of Asherah. What is at issue is which god the people should follow. Both Elijah and the prophets of Baal are to be given a bull for sacrifice and the test is to see which divinity will miraculously set fire to it when his name is invoked. The prophets of Baal prepared the bull on top of a wood pyre and prayed and danced[25] from morning until noon, but nothing happened. They then continued until evening while cutting themselves with swords and razors in a frenzy of self-mutilation, all the while being taunted by Elijah that perhaps their god is having a day off or has fallen asleep. This is a key point: the story makes the divinities and cult of the opposition look both weird and silly. Then comes Elijah's turn and he further stacks the odds against himself: he puts a trench around his altar and covers the whole offering with water so that it runs off the wood and fills the trench. Then he invokes his god with a simple prayer and, at once, the Lord's fire comes and burns the whole offering, water and all. The people recognize the true god, and fall down in worship. Meanwhile, Elijah makes sure that not one of the prophets of Baal escapes, and kills them all at the Brook of Kishon.

This story, read *historialiter*, provided a pattern for miracle stories in authors before Muirchú, such as Gregory the Great,[26] but Muirchú makes far more extensive use of it.

The first dispute is interwoven into the account of the meeting on Easter night. When the Irish leave Tara for Patrick's camp, they come with the desire that there should be a test between the leaders of the old and new religions before the king: this will decide whether the king should follow Patrick's cult or whether his own cult should rule over Patrick's.[27] Patrick is then presented as making the comparison of forces: while the king has many chariots and horses – a direct allusion to Josh. 11:4 and recalling the many occasions when Israel faced an enemy superior in such troops – he has but his trust in God to protect him and so recites a Psalms text[28] to invoke divine help.[29] Then the dispute begins,[30] and at once the differing strengths are revealed. Ercc, who recognizes Patrick's power by rising, is given life and now is buried with the saints,[31] but Lochru, who challenges Patrick and blasphemes against Christianity, is killed after Patrick prays.[32] This provokes a further test when, in fury,

Table 6.1. Daniel 3:1–24 and Muirchú's Tara-event: verbal parallels

Daniel 3:1–24	Muirchú
3:1 *Nabuchodonosor rex*	I, 10, 1 Lóegaire *rex... magnus ferox gentilisque... imperator barbarorum* lights a fire in his festival of idolatry (*idolatriae sollempnitatem* [I, 15, 1]),
fecit statuam auream...	as will Patrick,
in campo Duram prouinciae Babylonis	*in campo Brega* [I, 13, 2]
3:2 *itaque Nabuchodonosor rex misit ad congregandos...*	*uocatis ad Loigaireum uelut quondam ad Nabucodonossor regem...* [1,15,2]

The rulers gather all the important people in their kingdoms for a great act of worshipping the statue (Dan.) and 'idolatry' (Muirchú).

3:3 *tunc congregati sunt satrapae magistratus et iudices duces et tyranni et optimates qui erant in potestatibus constituti et uniuersi principes regionum*	I, 15, 2 *congregatis etiam regibus, satrapis ducibus, principibus et optimatibus populi* *insuper et magis, incantatoribus* [2 Chr. 33:6], *auruspicibus et omnis artis omnisque doni inuentoribus doctoribusue*
The king's command is made known: all must worship at the correct moment or be cast into the furnace:	The king issues an edict: all must follow the king in his fire-lighting liturgy at the right moment or face death:
3:4 *et praeco clamabat ualenter uobis dicitur populis tribubus et linguis*	
3:5 *in hora qua audieritis sonitum tubae... cadentes adorate statuam auream quam constituit Nabuchodonosor rex*	*Erat quoque quidam mos apud illos per edictum omnibus intimatus ut*

3:6	
si quis autem non prostratus adorauerit eadem hora mittetur in fornacem ignis ardentis	quicumque in cunctis regionibus siue procul siue iuxta in illa nocte incendisset ignem antequam in domu regia, id est in palatio Temoriae, sucenderetur periret anima eius de populo suo [I, 15, 3]
Then, the young men break the law and follow the liturgy and law of Israel's God.	Then, Patrick breaks the law and follows the liturgy and law of the Israel's God.
The breach is reported to the king by the religious leaders (*uiri chaldaei* [3:8]).	The king and all with him see the breach and the religious leaders are asked to advise: *Accidit ergo a Temoria uideretur uissoque eo conspexerunt omnes et mirati sunt; conuocatisque senioribus... regi dixit eis rex*... [I, 15, 5]

The religious experts report on the meaning of the breach, greeting the king:

3:8	
Rex, in aeternum uiue!	*Rex, in aeternum uiue!* [I,15, 5] and receives from his advisers an oracle.
	Muirchú then introduces an element based on Herod in Matt. 2 [I, 16, 1], and Pharaoh in Exod. 14 [I, 16, 2–4].
The king summons the young men [3:13].	The king travels to Patrick.[20]
after the audience, the king in anger orders punishments [3:19–21].	after the meeting, the king in anger orders punishments [I,18,1].
The young men remain unharmed and escape [3:24–6].	Patrick cannot be harmed and escapes [I, 18, 2–8].
The king blesses the true God [3:28–9].	In Muirchú the king has been given warnings that should have alerted him to the truth of Parick's religion [I, 15, 5]; he suffered a disaster during the night, but escaped [I, 18, 8]; and final recognition only comes at the end of further trials on Easter day [I, 21, 1].

the Irish attack Patrick but are actually defeated in their own confusion.[33] While the queen recognizes the truth as a result of this trial, the king's own acknowledgement is only a result of fear and insincerity.[34] This means that there will be need for a further trial of divinities.

This trial takes place on the following day at the king's feast at Tara. Patrick, who enters in the miraculous manner fitting to Easter day by coming among them as Christ did on the first Easter day,[35] initiates this trial and the meeting's purpose is stated with direct reference to the notion of a trial: 'ut contenderet et uerbum faceret de fide sancta in Temoria coram omnibus nationionibus' (He went there so that he might proclaim the word and demonstrate the holy faith in Tara in the presence of all nations).[36] Again, one of the company rises, Dubthach, and receives the reward of faith,[37] but the rest wish to test Patrick,[38] and the first to do so is Lucet Máel who had taken part in the previous night's trial.[39] Patrick recognizes, through divine help, the kinds of trial[40] to which they are submitting him,[41] and so is spared. While these trials lead to amazement,[42] they are not conclusive.

The result is that they agree to trials on a larger scale. The first is the suggestion from the *magus* Lucet Máel that each cover the plain with snow.[43] In this episode and the next wonder, which involves bringing darkness over the land, the conflict is presented as not just idolatry versus Christianity, but as demons versus God: the *magus* is said to invoke the demons who are the celestial enemies of God's will,[44] while Patrick, being the obedient servant of God, wishes to do nothing against the divine will.[45] But if the demons can show their power through Lucet Máel by bringing first deep snow and then frightening darkness, their power is limited for, when challenged by Patrick to remove them, they can only do so at a precise hour the following day. Patrick's god, however, knows no limitations – note the number of times Muirchú uses the phrase *Deus aeternus* (the eternal God)[46] – and with a simple prayer he can remove snow and darkness.[47] While these trials have produced a clearer demonstration of Patrick's power than those in the banquet hall, the *magi* are not yet prepared to back down.

The trial becomes more acute when the king, now presented not as a partisan of the *magi* but as the judge wishing to know which religion is more powerful, challenges them to a trial by water. Each side is to cast its books into the water, and whichever set of books remains unharmed, its god will be adored.[48] Patrick agrees, but the *magi* back down and suggest that Patrick has special power with water. So if the *magi* will not agree to a test involving water, then surely they should agree to a trial which relates to the opposite element to water – fire. Yet again, the *magi* back down for they also suspect that Patrick has special power with fire.[49] The reader is expected to appreciate that the *magi* now really know Patrick is the one with power, and that their refusal to accept this is a result of evil obstinacy. This trial is then brought to a head by Patrick with the suggestion of a test with many echoes of 3 Reg. 18. A house is to be built half of green timber and half of dried timber – this is the equivalent of Elijah's dry and wet wooden pyres. A *magus* shall go into the green side wearing Patrick's chasuble, a companion of Patrick shall go into the dry section and shall wear the magical coat *(cum ueste magica)*.[50] Then, once enclosed, both parts shall be set on fire.[51] The cross-dressing is a notable feature here which adds precision to the trial: it allows Muirchú to present a proof *per conuersionem* (by conversation) of what has happened. This was the trial par excellence, as Muirchú tells us from the start that this particular test is taking place *in conspectu Altissimi* (in the sight of the Most High).[52] So the fire is set, but the dry wood does not burn, while within an hour the house of green wood has burnt down with the *magus* inside. Lest their be any doubt that this is the work of God, and that Patrick's prayer is effective, within the burnt part Patrick's chasuble is undamaged, while within the unburnt part only the garment of the *magus* is destroyed, yet without damaging its wearer. The contrast between results is the contrast of the two gods, their religions and officers, and it is this contrast that Muirchú emphasizes through his use of *autem* (however) and *e contrario* (on the contrary).[53] The cult of the *magus* has ended in death, that of Patrick in happiness: his companion Benineus is described as *felix* (happy). At this point the whole series of tests, all forming the one great trial at the moment of Ireland's conversion, comes to an end, but lest the reader has forgotten where it all began on the previous night, Muirchú now draws attention by name to the three young men in the fiery furnace, and quotes a verse from their song. Benineus being untouched by fire is 'secundum quod de tribus pueris dictum est: "non tetigit eum ignis omnino, neque contristauit[54] nec quicquam molestiae intulit" ' (as was said about the three boys: 'No fire touched them at all, nor caused them pain or distress').[55]

The trial is now over, and it is time for the king's decision. Although he is furious with Patrick, the king's hand is held back by God's will, and Patrick takes the offensive: unless the king believes, he will die since, quoting Ps. 7:17, the anger of God has come down upon his head. Faced with this the king opts for the new faith with an elegant phrase modelled on the Vulgate translation of 1 Cor. 7:9: 'melius est credere me quam mori' (it is better for me to believe rather than to die).[56]

Significance

So why has this notion of a trial of divinities to portray the central episode of his *Vita* been so attractive to Muirchú? The key to this question may lie in the very opening image of his picture of the Tara event. The story of Patrick's mission is that of the encounter of Christianity with paganism and idolatry: Patrick travels to the 'caput omnis gentilitatis et idolatriae' (capital of all 'paganism' and idolatry).[57] It is the clash of the Lord with Satan in the form of the dragon, and so Muirchú refers to Ps. 73:14 – Patrick's action will be the breaking of the dragon's head. He will kill it in the way that Jael killed Sisera in Judg. 4:21–2 by hammering a wedge into its head. Moreover, the notion of a trial brings out for Muirchú the fact that Patrick joined faith to brave work.[58]

When we read the event at Tara through the focus of the trial of divinities we see some other features of the *Vita* in clearer relief. Firstly, Muirchú does not view Patrick primarily as a thaumaturge, nor powerful holy man – despite all the miracle stories he recalls – but rather as a prophet and liturgical intercessor. He is consciously paralleled with the prophets who went into great cities (Jonah) and before kings (for instance John the Baptist) to preach. He represents a divinity whose power is displayed in answer to simple prayer, and what makes Patrick's prayer effective is his faith combined with courage. This makes him the apostle of Luke 12:8–12 who acknowledges Christ and avoids blasphemy before men, and whom the Spirit assists when he is brought to witness before rulers.[59]

Secondly, Muirchú has formulated a sophisticated model for the relationship of Christianity to the former religion through the use of Old Testament images of the relationship of the God of Israel to that of 'the gods of the nations' around them. Each has his experts, each an elaborate cult, each has books, prophecies and an awareness of the dependence of humanity on a higher being. Because of these common elements both can enter into a trial together with the hope that the best/the true will win. While this myth requires Muirchú to invent the non-Christian Irish religious past in terms of the biblical 'nations', it allows him potentially to absorb fully whatever he actually finds in that past in terms of *praeparatio euangelii*. So, through this device, the whole history of Ireland, as he knows it, can be fitted into the providential scheme of waiting for Christianity. We should not underestimate what the *Vita* can tell us about attitudes in the late seventh century to both Scripture and the view of the people of their own history perceived as providence.

Thirdly, Muirchú sees the king as having a religious function within paganism in that it is his cult that is challenged, the *magi* report to him and, finally, he must decide once the trial of divinities is over. He models Lóegaire mainly on Nebuchadnezzar and Herod. The first has a mixed biblical reputation while the latter is always seen as wicked. However, he gives no further religious role to the king once the decision for Christianity has been made for his 'empire' – he is, after all, *imperator barbarorum*. So while the succession is in the hands of providence,[60] the king is not presented as having any continuing sacral function. This should, perhaps, receive more attention in studies of kingship as a contrast to the ordination of Áedán as king, as described in the contemporary *Vita Columbae*,[61] especially since we know of contacts between Adomnán and Muirchú.[62]

Conclusion: hagiography as performance

Contemporary writers on religious texts regarding holiness frequently point out that they should be seen as texts for 'performance' which 'map out a route for an experience [and] cannot be fully appreciated at a distance'.[63] Muirchú's task was to praise Patrick and explain the origin of his people as Christians. He does this by assuming that his readers have some notion of the power of the Christian God and an understanding of the dynamics of the Easter Vigil. The text invites its reader to perform its story within the context of those known realities. For Muirchú, Christianity demands a decision to reject idolatry and former ways, and the destruction of the dragon, Satan; and, as such, the *Vita* informs its readers about their basic religious identity. It thus provides us with a window through which to observe one perception of Christian faith in the later seventh century.

Notes

[1] I am using the edition of Bieler, *Patrician Texts*, pp. 61–123; for an English translation, and for an *apparatus biblicus*, I am using my own translation as found in O. Davies (trans.) with collaboration of O'Loughlin, *Celtic Spirituality*, pp. 91–117. All translations, unless noted otherwise, are my own; I am using the Vulgate of Weber, and shall consistently follow its numeration.

[2] *Vita* I, 14–18 (I shall cite the text by book, section and sentence number, as this will allow the reference to be located in either Bieler's edition or in a translation).

[3] *Vita* I,10, 1.

[4] *Vita* I, 10, 1.

[5] *Vita* I, 15, 2.

⁶ That the culture in which Muirchú lived had the notion of a succession of Ages – as understood by Christian writers in general – can be seen from its presence in annals that roughly date from that period. In the *Vita* the notion of preparation can be seen in the fact that Muirchú has the pagan *magi* predict that one day their religion will be replaced by another, more complete, religion *(Vita* I, 10).

⁷ See Bieler's translation, *Patrician Texts*. The word *magus* can be found in Latin as early as Cicero *(De diuinatione* 1, 23, 46) where it is said to be a Persian name for a wise man or teacher; in the Vulgate it is used nineteen times: on eight occasions it has the generic meaning of magician (Lev. 19:31; 20:6; 1 Sam. 28:3 and 9; 2 Chr. 33:6 – a phrase which finds an echo in Muirchú at I, 10, 2 and I, 15, 2; Acts 8:9; 13:6 and 8); while on eleven occasions it is used in a more restricted sense of a wise man/religious figure belonging to the east, especially Babylonia (Dan. 1:20; 2:2; 2:10; 2:27; 4:4; 5:7; 5:11; 5:15; Matt. 2:1; 2:7; 2:16) and it is this more restricted meaning, from Daniel and the Matthaean infancy narrative, which most accurately fits Muirchú's usage.

⁸ Bhreathnach, 'Temoria: caput Scotorum?', p. 73.

⁹ O'Loughlin, *Celtic Theology*, pp. 87–108.

¹⁰ *Vita* I, 2.

¹¹ See Exod. 5:1.

¹² See Jonah 3:3 and Matt. 12:41.

¹³ See Mark 6:17.

¹⁴ Namely, the Prayer of Azariah (Dan. 3:24–45) and the *Canticum Trium Puerorum* (the name used by Muirchú), often referred to as the *Benedicite* (Dan. 3:52–90). Verses 46–51 form a linking passage between these two canticles.

¹⁵ This possibility is explored in my *Celtic Theology*, pp. 98–106, but there has not been sufficient work on the Vigil readings to make a definite judgement possible. The fact that we find this passage among the Vigil readings as found in later missals, combined with its use by Muirchú in this Vigil context, makes the idea of its presence in the Easter liturgy in Ireland in the late seventh century antecedently probable.

¹⁶ For an account of this process of addition cf. Moore, *Daniel*, pp. 39–76 (and see the general background, pp. 1–38).

¹⁷ At the end of the additional material Jerome placed this note: 'Hucusque non habetur in Hebraeo et quae posuimus de Theodotionis editione translata sunt' (The material up to this point is not found in Hebrew, and that which we have given is translated from Theodotion's edition).

¹⁸ *Vita* I, 15, 5 and 20, 13.

¹⁹ *Vita* I, 15, 2.

²⁰ That the king goes to Patrick is not a case of Muirchú presenting the king as less than Patrick, and so going to him; rather, it is a consequence of wishing the king to bring out his chariots on the night of the Pasch (the Passover), so that the king's army can be vanquished as was Pharaoh's on the night of the first Pasch; moreover, Herod, who is echoed in several places here, did not have the infant brought to him, but announced that he wanted to go to where the infant was (Matt. 2:8).

²¹ In some biblical commentaries it is referred to as 'the contest of the gods' (cf. for example, Walsh and Begg, '1 and 2 Kings', p. 171), but this is inappropriate as what is central to the story is not one god contesting with another, but their respective priests seeking to show which has power.

²² In the Vulgate (18:19) they are described as *prophetae lucorum* (the prophets of the groves). However, since most modern translations identify these 'groves' as the name of a specific god, Asherah, that will be the identification given here.

²³ 3 Reg. 18:20.

²⁴ 3 Reg. 18:22.

[25] A cultic dance is the best interpretation of *transiliebant* (18:26), cf. Walsh and Begg, '1 and 2 Kings', p. 171.
[26] See Cusack, *Second Dialogue of Gregory the Great*, pp. 49–50.
[27] *Vita* I, 16, 3.
[28] Ps. 19:8.
[29] *Vita* I, 17, 2.
[30] *Vita* I, 17, 4.
[31] *Vita* I, 17, 3; for the significance of his relics now being venerated in Slane cf. my 'Tombs of the saints'.
[32] *Vita* I,17, 4.
[33] *Vita* I, 18, 1–4.
[34] *Vita* 1,18, 5–6.
[35] *Vita* I, 19, 2; Muirchú makes an explicit reference to John 20:19.
[36] *Vita* I, 19, 2.
[37] *Vita* I, 19, 4.
[38] *Vita* I, 19, 5.
[39] *Vita* I, 20, 1.
[40] *Vita* I, 20, 2.
[41] This can be seen in *Vita* I, 19, 5 where Patrick has the same degree of future knowledge as Christ before his Passion, for Muirchú alludes to John 18:4.
[42] *Vita* I, 20, 2.
[43] *Vita* I, 20, 3.
[44] *Vita* I, 20, 6.
[45] *Vita* I, 20, 3.
[46] The significance of this phrase needs further exploration.
[47] *Vita* I, 20, 3–7.
[48] *Vita* I, 20, 8.
[49] *Vita* I, 20, 8–9.
[50] There is a deliberate ambiguity here: *magica* as the adjective of *magus*, and *magica* as an adjective with the usual meaning of 'magical.'
[51] *Vita I*, 20, 10–11.
[52] *Vita* I, 20, 10 quoting Sir. 39:6.
[53] *Vita* I, 20, 11–13.
[54] Reading with MSS B and C *in apparatu textus*, in agreement with the Vulgate, rather than *contristatus est* as found in the edition.
[55] *Vita* I, 20, 13 quoting Dan. 3:50.
[56] *Vita* I, 20, 14–15; the Vulgate of 1 Cor. 7:9 is 'melius est enim nubere quam uri' (it is better for me to marry rather than to burn).
[57] For convenience, I render *gentilitas* here as 'paganism'; however, *gentilitas* is a carefully chosen word referring to Muirchú's notion of 'the nations' in contrast with the chosen 'holy nation' (see 1 Pet. 2:9).
[58] *Vita* I, 13, 2–3.
[59] This is echoed in *Vita* I,17, 5.
[60] *Vita* I, 21, 2.
[61] *Vita Columbae* III, 5; the most significant study of the religious aspects of the royal ordination is Enright, *Iona*, who does on a few occasions make comparisons and contrasts (pp. 58, 67 n. 254 and 73); and for a review of Enright's position see Sharpe (trans.), *Adomnán*, pp. 355–7.
[62] These links have been explored in my *Celtic Theology*, pp. 87–9 and in Enright, *Iona*, pp. 58 and 73.
[63] Sheldrake, *Spirituality and History*, p. 177.

7

Miracles and wonders in the composition of the Lives of the early Irish saints

⋈

DOROTHY ANN BRAY

Perhaps the most striking element of Irish hagiography, or one of its more prominent peculiarities, is the quantity of miracles and marvels attributed to the early Irish saints. The earliest *vitae*, the seventh-century Lives of Sts Brigit, Patrick and Columba, all portray their subjects as workers of miracles, as well as ecclesiastical founders, agents of God and pillars of moral virtue. But their acts of miracle-working stand out, warranting their appellation as the 'three thaumaturges' by Colgan.[1] Studies by Bieler, Heist, Stancliffe, McCone, Nagy and Picard, among others, have made scholars aware of the debt which the early Irish hagiographers owed both to their continental predecessors (especially Sulpicius Severus and his Life of St Martin) and to secular Irish tradition in the composition of the saints' *vitae* and the types of miracle stories they included. In comparing the early Lives of Brigit, Patrick and Columba to *vitae* of the Merovingian period, Jean-Michel Picard has noted that '[t]he motifs found in fifty continental Lives, scattered over two centuries, are nearly all to be found in the Lives of [these] three Irish saints'.[2] In the later Lives of the Irish saints, to be found mostly in the great collections of Irish hagiography, miracles proliferate, wonders increase and marvels become more and more fantastic. Considering this phenomenon, Irish hagiography can almost be termed thaumatology, an observation also touched upon by Picard in his examination of the marvellous in the Irish Lives.

Plummer, in the introduction to his *Vitae Sanctorum Hiberniae*, saw in many of the miracles (those which have no biblical or apocryphal antecedent) the influence of pagan beliefs, the saint as the inheritor of the druid or as a superior kind of medicine man: 'The saint is regarded as a more powerful druid, the forces underlying his religion are conceived as magical rather than spiritual and moral, and the objects and ceremonies associated with his creed and worship are only a very superior kind of "medicine".'[3] C. Grant Loomis has called the saints' thaumaturgical acts 'white magic',[4] thereby making the saints 'holy magicians' under their hagiographers' pens. Bieler, indeed, has remarked that 'hagiographical production declined after the eighth century . . . Lives of this period, which have left their traces in later texts, emphasize the miraculous power of the saint out of all proportion and show little interest in his piety or ascetic habits'.[5]

The exaggerated miracle-working of these 'holy magicians' thus apparently, to modern eyes at least, undermines the saint's position as an agent of God and a spiritual leader, and the possibility that the miracle stories might have a moral or spiritual lesson to offer is frequently overlooked or dismissed. Indeed, the miracles and miracle stories in the Irish Lives have received, in the past, very poor press. Although all students of hagiography agree with Delehaye that the primary purpose of a *vita* is to glorify the saint and increase veneration of his cult, Plummer considered it unfortunate that the Irish hagiographers chose to honour their saints by heaping miracle stories on them: 'The real interest of the writer', he says, 'is in the thaumaturgy', not in the saints' virtues.[6] Therefore, one cannot look for spiritual edification in these Lives.[7] Heist ventured:

> At worst . . . the miraculous elements of saints' legends, like the more prosaic – and hence, to a modern reader, more disarming – elements, may be the inventions of individual hagiographers. These gentlemen, however, do not as a class seem to have been gifted with remarkably inventive imaginations, nor to have been particularly eager to use them when they could find ready-made miracles that would serve them in the Lives of other saints than the ones whose legends they happened to be working up at the moment.[8]

Most recently, Ó Cróinín has reiterated the same sentiments as Plummer, that the Lives are 'less than edifying, being little more than a catalogue of miracles and wonders, some of them amusing, most of them ridiculous' or else 'dreary litanies of misplaced reverence and devotion'.[9] Many scholars now prefer either to accept the miracles as part of the conventions of hagiography or to look for the elements of secular Irish tradition influencing the composition of the Lives. They may then concentrate on whatever historical information can be gleaned from the Lives about contemporary religious practices and beliefs or about the political development of the Church.

Picard, however, tackles the very concept of the marvellous in the Lives of the sixth and seventh century, identifying the set terms used to express marvel and wonder (for example, *mirabile dictu, mirum dictu*); the marvellous comprises not only 'material prodigies' but also 'marvel at moral virtues and the interior marvels of grace'.[10] The majority of thaumaturgical miracles, he says, relate to marvels that serve to 'comfort human misery and restore man's dignity', including exorcisms, resuscitations, release of prisoners and cures, or 'evangelical miracles', those which confirm the saint's sanctity. Other marvels include dealings with the Devil, appearance of angels, visions, fantastic voyages and what he terms folklore-type miracles, mostly dealing with animals. In his survey of the marvellous, Picard points out that the Lives of Brigit and Columba do not contain a large number of evangelical miracles, in comparison to the continental Lives, while in the Lives of Patrick such miracles are more akin to folk tales. This, he feels, raises questions regarding the spiritual value of the Patrician Lives,[11] but such questions are not addressed. Picard notes the change in the character of saints' Lives from the sixth to the seventh century, when the aim at spiritual edification through a representation of the virtuous character of the holy man gave way to a trend toward ever more extraordinary miracles for the purpose of propaganda for the saint's community,[12] a trend which Bieler had also observed. Picard, however, identifies this tendency as early as the seventh century, where he observes:

> The traditional section on the perfect character of the saint becomes more and more formal and conventional: the imitation of Jesus and the saints becomes a competition in extraordinary miracles. The aim of the *vita* is no longer edification, but simply propaganda of one community through its patron saint.[13]

Clare Stancliffe, in her article on miracle stories, looks instead at the miracle stories in the seventh-century Lives of Brigit, Patrick and Columba in the context of contemporary European religious culture and hagiography; she focuses on the patterns of miracles and on how Irish hagiographers both borrowed and diverged from their continental counterparts to produce a distinctively Irish type of hagiography.[14] Stancliffe picks up on the observation made by Picard that all the miracles in the seventh-century Lives of these three Irish saints can be found in the saints' Lives of the Merovingian period; as well, she engages some of his typology of the miracles. Stancliffe discusses the high proportion of what she terms 'folk-lore type' miracles, nature miracles and 'vertical' miracles (in which the saint is in direct contact with the divine; these include angelic visitations, visions and prophecies)[15] and the relatively low proportion of miracles of healing, exorcisms or demonic encounters. On the first, she argues that the Irish hagiographers were not interested in writing up healing miracles; the lack of the latter two she attributes to the fact that the Devil did not figure greatly in the Christian tradition brought to Ireland.[16] Her statistical analysis yields some very valuable observations on the composition of these Lives; however, her point of view is that of a historian, and the Lives are ultimately treated as historical documents rather than works of literature.

Nevertheless, it is clear from this and other studies that miracles make up the major portion of the *vita* of an Irish saint and are integral to the composition of Irish hagiography, regardless of their inventiveness or lack thereof, regardless too of their supposedly unedifying yet propagandistic purpose. Joseph Nagy, in his book *Conversing with Angels and Ancients* (1997), provides one of the best demonstrations so far for dealing with this particular and peculiar genre of writing, by treating Irish hagiography not only as literature but as meaningful literature in medieval Irish culture, wherein Christian and pagan, oral and literary, intertwine rather than oppose one another. Furthermore, the elements of folklore in such literature, from whatever source, are integral to the composition of these works in that they are consciously employed in connection with the art and aesthetics of the text. While one seldom hears mention of the aesthetics of hagiography, what I would like to explore here is a possible approach to the compositional principles of Irish hagiography as displayed in the structure, configuration and use of miracle stories for, however spiritually unedifying or unoriginal and repetitive these miracles may appear, they must surely have meaning in these works, otherwise why are the Lives not just simple catalogues of ascetic acts and pious virtues? The use of narrative, anecdotes, or folk tales in the Lives continued in the practice of hagiographical composition, along with the litany of virtues (and virtuous deeds) and while the recounting of miracle after miracle may appear dreary and repetitive to a modern reader, the use of miracle stories could still allow for a spiritual or other meaningful element to be gleaned from the composition.

Bieler employed the term 'aretalogy' to describe the literary genre of hagiography, and it is perhaps worth airing his idea once again; in Bieler's view, the Christian hero, the saint, was one whose heroic virtue was manifested in supernatural power or 'white magic'. With respect to saints' Lives, he wrote:

> The term *virtutes*, Greek *aretaí*, was given by the ancients to the extraordinary and memorable deeds, often miraculous, of gods and heroes, and was taken over by those who wrote about their Christian counterparts . . . Aretalogy opened the door to the influx of all sorts of secular stories *in toto* or of selected motifs of pagan or generally superstitious character.[17]

Aretalogy, then, as an account of the miraculous deeds of the saint, allows in its etymology the association of miracle-working or magic with saintly virtues.

However, to scholars like Benedicta Ward, the use of the term 'white magic' is contrary to the medieval conception of miracles. Magic in the Middle Ages meant 'supernatural dealings with demons' and was 'condemned and set against miracles . . . Magic and miracles were two extremes, at least in theory, of dealing with the supernatural'.[18] Ward traces the medieval idea of miracles to St Augustine of Hippo who proposed only one miracle – creation, the work of God. The miraculous moved in all of nature and the everyday life of man, as signs of God's creative power; but every once in a while, an unusual manifestation of God's power occurred, an event provoking wonder and reverence in humankind.[19] Miracles were signs of God at work in the universe, signs of hope for redemption:

> Miracles were understood in the setting of a world that was seen as an extension of man and not apart from him, his desires, and his needs. Over against this unified creation was a world within a world, the 'mystic heaven' of God and the saints and miracles were one kind of connection between the two.[20]

In early hagiography, according to Ward, miracles followed a conventional pattern for proving the sanctity of a saint, a pattern established in the Gospel record of the life of Christ and in the wonders and prophecies performed by other biblical persons in both the Old and New Testaments. Miraculous events 'showed the incursion of the supernatural into the daily life of a saint, thereby authenticating his sanctity with signs, recognized and established, of true Christian holiness'.[21] This pattern of sanctity, based on the life of Christ, was an important means of distinguishing Christian miracles from pagan magic, and thereby establishing the holy man (and woman) as a Christian saint, yet Lives of saints, certainly after the sixth century, give evidence of other influences.

While Ward is careful to separate miracles and magic in the theological view, in popular belief it appeared they were not so clearly delineated. Magic, from antiquity to the Middle Ages, pervaded the popular imagination throughout Europe, but even the general populace distinguished between *maleficium* (black magic) and the miraculous. Witchcraft invoked the spectre of idolatry and disobedience, turning away from God and upsetting the balance of nature. The rewards of *maleficium* carried a high price. The performance of a miracle, on the other hand, while it might look very like magic, arose from the power of God and the rewards of faith, reinforced by the miracle, were greater by far. Valerie Flint, in her study of magic in the Middle Ages, writes:

> Miracles of particular kinds, fashioned and placed with care, became (and in part in conscious contrast to their different employment in the times of heroic enthusiasms) an ideal means of reordering, instead of eliminating, the revered and sought after magical powers of *malefici*, and of improving upon, rather than denying, the rewards these last had to offer.[22]

Miracles, according to Michael Goodich, were a means of restoring God's natural order, of reversing injustices, of punishing the wicked and rewarding the good, of returning peoples and societies to good health and a peaceful – and continued   existence.[23] Régis Boyer has also identified this theme at the core of hagiographical composition and the use of miracles, that

> [t]here is a divine order; our natural, normal human order does not correspond to it but should tend to regain it. The miracle is supposed to make the link, there is nothing incongruous in it, it bears witness to the divine order because it restores a superior state of things.[24]

Miracles form one of the nine steps which, according to Boyer, are present in a typical hagiographical scheme of composition: the others being origins of the saint, birth, childhood, education, piety, martyrdom, *inventio* and *translatio*. Although not all of these steps may be present in any one *vita*, nevertheless most of them are and they contribute to the creation of the saintly heroic type, the idealized figure of Christian virtue.[25] And miracles, it is generally and widely agreed, were intended to remind people of God's power; they held a lesson in active piety. That, in the popular imagination, was the difference between the miraculous and the magical. That the saints could perform miracles – and could outperform non-Christian magicians, druids or otherwise (as St Patrick does so decidedly in his legends)[26] – put them firmly on the side of the superior power. Magic and miracles in fact went hand in hand, and magic and miracles, following Bieler's idea of aretalogy, are part and parcel of saintly heroic virtues.

Even Boyer, however, admits that the miracles appear banal after reading several *vitae;* hagiographical composition demands certain categories of miracles, interchangeable from one Life to another.[27] But, given that the saints are types, rather than individualized personalities (as are heroes of tradition), then it is not surprising that the saints are made to conform to that type, partly through the performing of certain types of miracles.[28] While Goodich, Ward and Flint are dealing mostly with hagiography of a later period, from the twelfth century onward, their studies, like Boyer's, build on the hagiographical past; the genre is conventional enough to ensure that the basic themes and ideas continued with little or no change for centuries – as did, I must point out, the conventions of heroic saga, although no one remarks about the lack of invention or originality in a secular heroic type. But in truth there are not as many heroic sagas as there are saints' Lives; traditional heroes are not usually idealized figures of Christian moral virtue; and heroic sagas seldom, if ever, have an overtly didactic purpose. The idea also that there is a 'canon' of miracles ascribed to the saints, and to the Irish saints in particular, has been suggested through studies of the motifs in the Lives.[29] While studies of heroic biographical patterning in lives of heroes do establish a kind of 'canon' of heroic deeds, they are seldom seen as so rigidly formulaic as the miracles of the saints. But the fact that such a canon of miracles can be identified suggests that the image of virtue created in the saint was dependent on certain types of miracles, such as resuscitation of the dead, provision of food, conversing with angels and prophecy (acts which are not normally part of the heroic profile of secular heroes).

Here I would like to distinguish between the reporting of miracles and miracle stories in the Lives; hagiographers would, from time to time, simply list miracles, without elaborating on the circumstances, the motivations or the outcome. The hagiographer of the *Vita Prima* of St Brigit filled his text with anecdotes of Brigit's miracle-working, but some are little more than bald statements; chapters 113–16, 118–19, and 127–8 merely relate the saint's miracles with very little contextual framing.[30] Chapter 128, for example, says simply: 'Another day saint Brigit by God's power shifted one river from its own place to another and one can see its original course to the present day.' There is no explanation as to why she performs this miracle, for what cause or for whose benefit, but only that she was able to rearrange the landscape (no mean feat, to be sure, and worthy of a saga hero) by the power of God. This is the kind of dreary reportage which can seem so spiritually unedifying, tediously written and often pointless. However, if we accept that miracles are part of the saint's *virtutes*, the listing of miracles in this way continues to showcase the saint's sanctity, regardless of the *vita's* literary qualities. Such brief items could also be expanded into larger tales, for use in sermons or homilies. For this very episode does receive greater narrative treatment in Cogitosus' Life of St Brigit[31] where the moral of the story and the virtue of St Brigit is abundantly clear. The king of her country ordered a road to be built, and each *tuath* was given a section to construct. The most difficult section, through a river, was forced upon Brigit's *tuath* by a stronger group. Through Brigit's power, the river changed its course so that it went through the section of the oppressive *tuath*. It is possible that a reader coming across the brief mention in the *Vita Prima* might be reminded of this extended narrative. Daniel Melia and Edgar Slotkin, indeed, suggest that these brief notations in the *Vita Prima* act as a kind of 'motif index' for the hagiographer,[32] thereby providing a 'metonymic' device for producing the exempla of the saint's virtues.[33] One could draw an analogy here with the 'tale lists' of the professional storytellers, the repertoire of tales which every *fili* was expected to know and be able to recite. The professional hagiographer, it seems, was expected to know his miracle stories and to be able to apply them appropriately.

And even the bare report of a miracle was surely more appealing to the popular imagination than the conventional listing of the saint's virtues, as in the formulaic catalogue concluding the *vita* of St Bairre: 'Quid plura? omnes virtutes perfectorum virorum in se hauriebat; id est, humilitatem, obedienciam, paciencium, spem, fidem, caritatem, et cetera' (What more? all the virtues of perfect men he drew to himself; that is to say, humility, obedience, patience, hope, faith, charity, and so on).[34] Or in the concluding part of the *vita* of St Fintan:

> Caritatem iam, et humilitatem, ac mansuetudinem in aliis, et asperitatem in se ipso, pacienciam, abstinenciam, grauiaque ieiunia, vigilias nocturnas, fleccionesque genuum, et dilectionem circa omnes Christianos beatissimi senis Fintani nemo in carne hic modo in terra poterit narrare.[35]

> (No one alive on earth could possibly relate the charity and humility, mildness in other things, austerity in himself, patience, abstinence, severe

fasts, nightly vigils, genuflections, and great care concerning all Christians of the most blessed abbot Fintan.)

In the vernacular Lives, the catalogue of St Bairre's virtues exhibits similar formulaic phrasing, which is, indeed, repeated almost exactly in the Irish Life of St Berach; Bairre, for example, is 'a lion in strength and power . . . a serpent in sagacity and prudence concerning all righteousness. He was a dove in meekness and simplicity';[36] while Berach is similarly a 'lion for might and power; a dove for gentleness and simplicity, a serpent for prudence and ingenuity'.[37] Such catalogues, however, act as summaries of the miracles and events recorded in the main text of the *vitae*, a reiteration of the virtues signified by the miracles performed by the saint. These catalogues are certainly far less entertaining than, say, the story of St Cóemgen, whose asceticism was so great that he did crossvigil for six weeks, during which time a blackbird came and built a nest in his open hand. Cóemgen retained his cross-vigil until the blackbird's eggs had hatched and the nestlings grew big enough to fly away.[38] Although briefly told, the anecdote illustrates in far more concrete terms the saint's virtue in ascetic practices, as well as his kindness to God's creatures, than a mere statement that he was great in his asceticism. Previous to this anecdote, the hagiographer has Cóemgen drive a monster from a lake through prayer and recitation of psalms.[39] His ascetic practices here amplify his sanctity, illustrated through his miracle-working which, clearly, derives from his devotion to God.

Two miracle stories, chosen at random from the Life of St Berach, offer examples of more developed narratives in the miracle story; each provides a setting, a plot or motive for the miracle and an outcome to the credit of the saint.[40] In the first, the miracle is a miracle of punishment for disobedience to the saint: an army coming to raid people under Berach's protection ignores his command to stop; Berach strikes his bell against them (an act of cursing) and they are swallowed up by a bog, which becomes a lake in which their remains can still be seen (perhaps explaining a topographical feature). This miracle is followed by repentance and conversion of the survivors and a blessing from Berach, thus demonstrating his power to reward as well as punish. In the second story, there is also a punishment miracle, a resuscitation miracle, an outcome of repentance and conversion, and an explanatory note on native vegetation (Berach's rushes). In these miracles, Berach reveals his virtues of justice and compassion; he punishes the killers of his monk, but spares their souls when they repent. He restores the head of the decapitated monk, calling him back to life, as he restored God's grace to the bandits, recalling them to the hope of heavenly life. He thus behaves in all ways as expected of a saint, a man of Christian virtue.

Another kind of miracle story, of the 'folklore type' described by Picard, can be seen in the story of St Brigit and the fox in *Vita Prima*.[41] The story presents a legal context for the miracle of Brigit's ability to tame wild animals:[42] a man is arrested for killing the king's tame fox; Brigit appeals on his behalf and a wild fox presents itself as a replacement. Brigit's political power is here demonstrated, as well as her virtues of 'compassion and pity', which motivate her plea and are amplified through the miracle. The fact that the wild fox runs off immediately after the man's release is a humorous and ironic touch, strongly reminiscent of a beast fable; the moral might be: a fox is always true to its nature, regardless of a king's desire. The more ostensible lesson might be: a king should never deny justice to a saint for it may redound on him in the most adverse manner. This tale might be compared to another animal anecdote in the Life of St Ciarán of Saigir which also illustrates a saint's ability to tame wild animals.[43] However, it is more of a monastic beast fable; the fox, the wolf and the badger are sent to Ciarán as monks, and the point of the story may be a lesson in proper monkish behaviour. The fox gives in to its nature, steals Ciarán's shoes and runs away from the monastery. The badger obeys Ciarán and fetches back the delinquent who is enjoined to repent. Thus, a monk should control his nature, should not give in to the temptation to sin and, in obedience to his abbot, should do proper penance for wrongdoing.

Apart from a beast fable, miracle stories such as these recall another literary form which, I have found, is seldom spoken of in relation to hagiography, despite its biblical usage – the parable. According to M. H. Abrams, '[a] parable is a very short narrative about human beings presented so as to stress the tacit analogy, or parallel, with a general thesis or lesson that the narrator is trying to bring home to his audience'.[44] Abrams includes his definition of parable under the main heading of 'Allegory'; the OED describes a parable as 'a comparison, a similitude, an allegory' and 'a fictitious narrative (usually of something that might naturally occur), by which moral or spiritual relations are typically set forth'. I am not trying to propose that the miracle stories in the Lives of the saints are really parables of their virtues, since a miracle by definition is something which does not occur naturally. I would, however, like to suggest an analogy with the form and the idea of the parable through which to approach the miracle stories of the saints, especially where there is a developed or developing narrative surrounding the miraculous event, that is, a setting, a plot or motive for the miracle, and an outcome to the credit of the saint (this could be a moral example in repentance, a conversion or perhaps a donation to the saint). Hagiography might not have enhanced the art of storytelling in early Ireland, but its conventions and constraints did not entirely stifle it either.

What I wish to suggest is that the listing of miracles is equivalent to the catalogue of the saint's virtues; it provides a potential basis for summaries of narratives of miracles and wonders in the Lives of the saints. The miracles actualize the saint's virtues, which the hagiographer wishes to present, and they account for the existence of a recognizable canon of miracles in the corpus of Irish hagiography. The more anecdotal type of miracle – the actual miracle story, as I referred to it – offers up the saint's virtues in a rather more engaging manner than a formulaic catalogue would do, while the listing of miracles, dreary as it is to the modern reader, may well have evoked for the medieval hagiographer and homilist a larger narrative or offered the opportunity for some (limited) invention. Picard also remarks on the Irish taste for fantasy and for the marvellous, a legacy of a strong and rich oral tradition largely untrammelled in the seventh century by Roman rationalization.[45] I hesitate to suggest that such taste lingered in the later Lives of the Irish saints, since classical literature and patristic thought were also embraced by the Irish ecclesiastical literati, yet it is true to say that the Lives of the eighth century and onwards contain a high degree of the fantastic and the miraculous. I would suggest instead that this is a development in the genre, wherein miracles and wonders convey the spiritual and moral aims of the hagiographers. That they are not edifying to us is not, to my mind, the same as saying that they are not edifying at all; they simply do not speak to us in the same way.

Notes

[1] See Kenney, *Sources*, pp. 39–41, on Colgan's work.
[2] Picard, 'The marvellous', p. 99.
[3] Plummer (ed.), *Vitae*, vol. 1, p. xciii.
[4] Loomis, *White Magic*.
[5] Bieler, 'The Celtic hagiographer', p. 259.
[6] Plummer (ed.), *Vitae*, vol. 1, pp. xcii-xciii.
[7] Ibid., p. xcv.
[8] Heist, 'Myth and folklore', p. 182.
[9] Ó Cróinín, *Early Medieval Ireland*, pp. 210–11.
[10] Picard, 'The marvellous', p. 92.
[11] Ibid., p. 93.
[12] Ibid., p. 99.

[13] Ibid., p. 99.
[14] Stancliffe, 'The miracle stories'.
[15] Stancliffe borrows the term 'vertical miracles' from a study by J. L. Derouet, who classified miracles according to function: 'vertical' to describe the saint's relationship with the divine, and 'horizontal' or 'practical' to describe a miracle which affected human existence, for example healing. See Stancliffe, ibid., pp. 94–5.
[16] Ibid., pp. 99, 101–5.
[17] Bieler, 'Hagiography and romance', p. 13. See also *idem*, 'The Celtic hagiographer', pp. 243–4.
[18] Ward, *Miracles*, p. 13.
[19] Ibid., pp. 3–4.
[20] Ibid., p. 216.
[21] Ibid., p. 168.
[22] Flint, *The Rise of Magic*, p. 80.
[23] Goodich, *Violence and Miracle*, p. 149.
[24] Boyer, 'The typology of medieval hagiography', p. 35.
[25] Ibid., pp. 31–3.
[26] Hood (ed. and trans.), *St Patrick*, Muirchú 20, p. 70; Stokes (ed.), *Tripartite Life*, vol. 2, pp. 55–9. Cf. Thomas O'Loughlin's chapter, above, which discusses this scene in detail and translates *magus* as 'wise man or teacher'.
[27] Boyer, 'The typology of medieval hagiography', p. 32.
[28] See also Heist, 'Myth and folklore', pp. 181–3.
[29] See, for example, Bray, A *List of Motifs*.
[30] Connolly, 'Vita prima', pp. 46–8.
[31] Connolly and Picard (trans.), 'Cogitosus', pp. 23–4.
[32] Personal communication. My sincere thanks go to Daniel Melia and Edgar Slotkin for their suggestion.
[33] This was suggested to me by Eve Sweetser, personal communication, based on her considerable work in the field of rhetoric and narrative.
[34] Ó Riain, *Beatha Bharra*, pp. 160–1.
[35] Plummer (ed.), *Vitae*, vol. 1, p. 74 (Fintan xxii).
[36] Ó Riain, *Beatha Bharra*, p. 85.
[37] *BNE*, vol. 2, p. 42 (Berach xxx).
[38] Ibid., pp. 123–4 (Cóemgen I.x).
[39] Ibid., pp. 122–3 (Cóemgen I.viii).
[40] Ibid., pp. 40 and 41 (Berach xxvii, xxix).
[41] Connolly, 'Vita prima', pp. 47–8.
[42] This ability is demonstrated throughout this *vita*, as in ch. 124, ibid., p. 47, where she calls wild ducks to her.
[43] *BNE*, vol. 2, p. 100 (Ciarán of Saigir I.iv); also Plummer (ed.), *Vitae*, vol. 1, p. 219 (Ciarán v-vi).
[44] Abrams, *A Glossary*, p. 6.
[45] Picard, 'The marvellous', p. 100.

8
The Northern Lectionary: a source for the Codex Salmanticensis?[1]

><

T. M. CHARLES-EDWARDS

William Heist, the editor of the *Codex Salmanticensis*, rightly observed that this, the most important collection of Irish saints' Lives, was a compilation from several sources.[2] Some are still discernible in the arrangement of the collection. The best known of these sources is the one which yielded the so-called O'Donohue Lives, named after one of those who contributed texts for the compilation, Diarmaid Ó Dúnchadha.[3] The creation of the Salmanticensis collection (which, following Sharpe, I shall call **S** for short) was a matter of collaboration, with more than one contributor.[4]

The O'Donohue group has been further illuminated, since Heist's edition, by the work of Richard Sharpe. He has argued, convincingly to my mind, that the O'Donohue Lives are early, probably not later than the eighth or early ninth century. A further characteristic is that, with two exceptions, all the O'Donohue Lives concern monasteries within a 25-mile radius of the summit of Slieve Bloom, in the very centre of Ireland, on the borders of Munster, Mide and Leinster. The two exceptions are the Life of Ailbe, the premier saint of Munster, which comes first, and the Life of Munnu of Taghmon in Co. Wexford.[5] The unifying principle of the O'Donohue group is thus largely geographical; and one can perhaps make the further suggestion that, since the first Life in the collection is that of St Ailbe of Emly, while the other outlier is the First Life of Munnu, the compiler himself came from a monastery with both Munster and Leinster connections, as well as a patron saint, represented in the collection. Possible candidates include Clonfertmulloe, which lay just inside the Leinster kingdom of Loígsi, but whose founder was from Munster, and Terryglas, situated in Munster, but whose founder was from Leinster.[6]

Table 8.1 (pp. 150–1) offers a possible analysis of some constituent sections of the manuscript; it leaves aside the first ten Lives and those of Cuanna and Mochuille towards the end.[7] The symbols used in the column headed 'Sharpe's Source' are those employed by Richard Sharpe: *Φ* stands for the source of the O'Donohue Lives, *Θ* for a common source employed by both **S** and the collections in the Oxford MSS, Rawlinson B 485 and 505; **D** is the 'Dublin Collection', the main source used by Plummer for his *Vitae Sanctorum Hiberniae*. The provinces are those of the pre-Viking period, when Osraige was still part of Munster.

The unifying principle of the group with which I am concerned is only in part geographical. Instead, the Lives in the group are ordered in a sequence which follows the festal calendar (see Table 8.1, section D): these are Lives of saints whose feast-days belong to August and September and, within each month, they occur in an order dictated by the date of the feast. The implication is that these Lives derive from a lectionary, a collection of Lives arranged according to the sequence of the saints' feast-days. By contrast, one has only to plot the feast-days of those saints whose Lives were included in the O'Donohue group (A in Table 8.1) to see that this source was not a lectionary or part of a lectionary. In the section of **S** immediately after the O'Donohue group (B in Table 8.1), there is another set of Lives, from Máedóc of Ferns to Senán of Scattery Island, which are likewise not derived from a lectionary. Things begin to change with the Second Life of St Brendan of Clonfert (C in Table 8.1).[9] It begins a series of eleven Lives of saints whose feast-days belong to March, April, May and June. Moreover, the divisions between the months are generally respected: thus we have three Lives for May, three for March and April, and then five Lives for June. However, these Lives are not arranged, within their respective months, in the order of the respective feast-days. To take those for June as an example, the sequence is 17 – 7 – 3 – 9 – 9. In fact, with what are effectively two exceptions, the Lives are in reverse order of feast-day. We may treat the Lives of Columba and Baíthéne as a single item for these purposes, since it was well known that they both died on 9 June. Leaving those two and the Life of Mochutu aside, all the others are in two reverse sequences, one sequence from May back to March and a separate June sequence. This strengthens the case for seeing the ultimate source of these Lives as a lectionary, but the path of transmission was evidently more complex than it was for our group, the Lives for August and September (D in Table 8.1).

The group with which I am concerned comes next after the June Lives. It probably begins with the Second Life of Mo Lua of Clonfertmulloe, although there is a problem about this Life to which I shall return later.

Table 8.1: Codex Salmanticensis, *Lives 11–45*

Saint	Feast-day	Primary church	Province	Sharpe's source[8]
A. O'Donohue group (Slieve Bloom group)				
Ailbe	12 Sept.	Emly	Munster	Φ
Mo Lua I	4 Aug.	Clonfertmulloe	Leinster	Φ
Fintan	17 Feb.	Clonenagh	Leinster	Φ
Fínán	7 April	Kinnitty	Munster	Φ
Rúadán	15 April	Lorrha	Munster	Φ
Áed mac Bricc	10 Nov.	Rahugh	Mide	Φ
Cainnech	11 Oct.	Aghaboe	Munster	Φ
Munnu	21 Oct.	Taghmon	Leinster	Φ
Colmán	26 Sept.	Lynally	Mide	Φ
Columba	13 Dec.	Terryglas	Munster	Φ?
B. Máedóc to Senán (southern Irish group: Leinster and Munster)				
Máedóc	31 Jan.	Ferns	Leinster	Θ
Munnu II	21 Oct.	Taghmon	Leinster	Θ
Abbán	27 Oct.	Mag nArnaide + Killabban	Leinster	D
Crónán	28 April	Roscrea	Munster	D
[Laurence of Dublin]				
Flannán	18 Dec.	Killaloe	Munster	?
[Catherine]				
Senán	8 March	Scattery Isl.	Munster	?
C. March to June (generally in reverse order of feast-day)				
i. May back to March				
Brendan II	16 May	Clonfert	Connaught	?
Comgall	10 May	Bangor	Ulster	Θ
Mochutu	14 May	Lismore	Munster	D
Laisrén	18 Apr.	Old Leighlin	Leinster	?
Mac Caírthinn	24 March	Clogher	Airgialla	?
Ciarán	5 March	Seirkieran	Munster	Θ
ii. June				
Moling	17 June	St Mullin's	Leinster	Θ
Colmán	7 June	Dromore	Ulster	Θ
Cóemgen	3 June	Glendalough	Leinster	Θ

Saint	Feast-day	Primary church	Province	Sharpe's source
Columba	9 June	Iona	Britain	Θ
Baíthéne	9 June	Iona	Britain	Θ
D. The Northern Legendary				
Mo Lua II	4 Aug.	Clonfertmulloe Drumsnat	Leinster Airgíalla	Θ
Daig	18 Aug.	Inishkeen	Ulster	?
Mochta	19 Aug.	Louth	Ulster	?
Éogan	23 Aug.	Ardstraw	Airgíalla	?
Mac Nisse	3 Sept.	Connor	Ulster	?

Including the Life of Mo Lua, we have a sequence of five Lives, whose feast-days belong to August and early September. The compilation in S thus jumps from June to August, omitting July. Moreover, unlike the previous Lives, these are in the order of the feast-days (Table 8.1). Although both my group and the previous group for March to June consist of short Lives, suitable for public recitation on a feast-day, there are two reasons for keeping the August and September Lives separate from the rest: the gap created by the absence of any Life between 17 June and 4 August and, more importantly, the difference in arrangement, in order of feast-day as opposed to the previous Lives, which were largely in reverse order of feast-day. A third reason may also be added why these Lives should be distinguished from those earlier in S: in my group, the Lives for August and early September, the saints were all patrons of northern churches, from Louth northwards to Connor in the north-east and to Ardstraw in the north-west.

There is one apparent exception, which is problematic for another reason, namely the Second Life of Mo Lua. The primary church of Mo Lua was, as we have seen, Clonfertmulloe on the south side of Slieve Bloom, in the kingdom of Loígsi but very close to the border with Osraige in Munster. The First Life of this saint belongs to the O'Donohue group and sees him primarily as the patron of Clonfertmulloe. The Second Life, however, although Heist entitled it (quite reasonably from his point of view) as the Second Life of St Mo Lua of Clonfertmulloe, was not written for his primary church. It appears from its incipit and its contents that it was a version of the First Life whose intended readership and audience was the community of Mo Lua's northern church at Druim Snechta (Drumsnat, Co. Monaghan) in the early-medieval kingdom of Fernmag: the contents of the first half of the

Second Life correspond closely to the First, but the incipit reads 'Incipit vita Molua Droma Snecta'.[10] Druim Snechta is famous among Celtic scholars because of the renowned, but lost, literary manuscript, Cín Dromma Snechta. There is little chance that the Life was originally composed at Druim Snechta, for two reasons: firstly, it gives no more space to that monastery than does the First Life, nor does it play down the reasons why Mo Lua left Druim Snechta.[11] Secondly, the account of the foundation of Clonfertmulloe in both Lives omits a crucial fact about Druim Snechta. When Mo Lua had left his first foundation, he went to his king, the ruler of the Uí Fhidgente in what is now Co. Limerick. This king encouraged him to found his monastery *in peregrinatione*, away from his own people; the situation of Clonfertmulloe exactly fitted the king's advice.[12] There is a double complication behind this remark. Firstly, Mo Lua belonged, like the famous female saint, Íte of Killeedy, to a client-people called the Corcu Óche, subjects of the Uí Fhidgente.[13] Both Lives pass over the ambiguity in the notion of 'Mo Lua's people', affecting to regard that as the Uí Fhidgente. Secondly, the Laud genealogies show that there was a branch of the Corcu Óche in Fernmag, namely the very kingdom in the north in which Druim Snechta lay.[14] The king's advice could, therefore, have demonstrated the superiority of Clonfertmulloe over Druim Snechta, namely of the monastery founded far from the saint's own people as against the monastery founded among a detached portion of that people. I suspect that this contrast is one theme lying behind this story. Yet, as it appears in both Lives, no reference is made to the Corcu Óche of Fernmag. This would be especially odd if the Druim Snechta Life had been composed at that house, but it is much less odd if it is merely a version, produced for Druim Snechta, of the First Life, which was itself a product of Clonfertmulloe.

A further complication affecting the Second Life of Mo Lua is that there is another copy of it in Bodleian Library, Rawlinson MS B 485 and its daughter MS, Rawlinson B 505. For this reason Sharpe has assigned the Second Life to a source, no longer existing as such, which he calls Θ.[15] Θ is posited on the basis that there is a group of Lives common to **S** and the Oxford MSS, closely akin but not copied one from the other. The rest of my Northern Lectionary is, however, made up of Lives not found anywhere else. Hence one may reasonably ask whether the Second Life of Mo Lua should properly be assigned to Θ rather than to the Northern Lectionary. As can be seen from Table 8.1, many of the preceding Lives in **S** have been attributed to Θ by Sharpe. Yet, if we are dealing with collections of short Lives made for the purposes of being read out on the feast-day, there is no reason why a particular Life should not appear in two such collections. For this reason, evidence associating the Second Life of Mo Lua with Θ is not conclusive evidence against associating it with the Northern Lectionary. On the other hand, if the text of the Life in the Northern Lectionary is derived from Θ, the Northern Lectionary must be a relatively late compilation.

There are, therefore, two characteristics that appear to unite this small group of five Lives for August and September: they derive from a lectionary, and they all concern monasteries in northern Ireland (in the early-medieval sense in which the north began on the boundary between Brega, roughly Co. Meath, and Conailli Muirthemne, roughly Co. Louth).[16] Again, this characteristic distinguishes our group of Lives from those that precede it in **S**: those for June include two Leinster saints, Moling of Tech Moling and Kevin of Glendalough, an Ulster saint, St Colmán of Dromore, and the first two abbots of Iona, namely short Lives of Columba and Baíthéne. Our group is thus characterized by two things: being derived from a lectionary in such a fashion that the sequence of feast-days remains undisturbed and being concerned with the patron saints of northern churches. Hence the phrase in my title, 'the Northern Lectionary'.

A possible objection to this characterization of the hypothetical source as a 'Northern Lectionary' is that it is merely fortuitous that the saints whose Lives are preserved for this period of about a month were associated with northern churches. In the collections edited by Heist and by Plummer there is only one saint whose feast belongs to the period 4 August–3 September and, if one looks in the martyrologies for the saints of August and early September, few would perhaps have been regarded as of the first rank by a medieval Irishman. On the other hand, in the gap between the saints of June (Table 8.1, C. ii) and the feast of Mo Lua on 4 August there are major saints: Declán of Ardmore (24 July), whose Life is preserved only in D,[17] and Nessán of Mungret, patron of a major house for whom there is no extant Life;[18] on 4 September there is the feast of Ultán of Ard Breccáin; and there are other significant secondranking saints in this period, such as Senán of Láthrach Briúin (2 September) or Colmán of Inishboffin (8 August). What is, perhaps, more persuasive is that the Second Life of Mo Lua, who was of the first rank, was, as we have seen, associated with Druim Snechta rather than with Clonfertmulloe.

From now on I shall assume that this group within **S** was derived from a single source, and that, directly or indirectly, the source was a lectionary embracing saints of northern Irish churches.[19] For the historian, this group is not nearly so important as the O'Donohue group studied by Richard Sharpe, but it does have its moments of interest. Yet, before we come to the contents, we need to consider an aspect of dating, namely the date of the Northern Lectionary as opposed to the dates of the individual Lives.

We may begin with the compilers of S, working, according to Heist and Sharpe, in the fourteenth century, but according to recent articles by the late William O'Sullivan and by Pádraig Ó Riain, rather earlier, *c.*1300.[20] The plan of **S** is broadly as stated by Heist: the collection began with the grandest Lives of the grandest saints, probably with Patrick and Brigit (although only part of the Life of St Brigit now survives).[21] It continued with other saints of the top rank, such as Cíarán of Clonmacnois, declining to a collection of reasonably extensive Lives of reasonably important saints; this is where the O'Donohue group belongs. The third main category was of short Lives, in some cases of major saints – such as the brief Life of Columba – but generally of saints of rather more local significance. The compilers thus worked with two hierarchies in mind: a hierarchy of texts and a hierarchy of saints. The shorter texts, even of the grander saints, came later in the collection. We can thus place our group as one element in this third and lowliest category. The date of **S** is, therefore, the *terminus ante quem* for the Northern Lectionary, but it is extremely difficult to make any progress beyond this point. This is for a simple reason: our saints belong to August and September, so that what we have is only one fragment of the Northern Lectionary as I presume it to have existed at one time. One way of dating a collection is to identify the latest Life that it contains: that gives a *terminus post quem* for the whole collection. Yet, if all we have is a small fragment, we cannot follow this procedure: the latest Life is all too likely to belong to the lost portion of the Lectionary. We may have to give up any hope of dating the Lectionary as opposed to the Lives themselves.

As for the dating of the individual Lives, this depends on details of the contents. These two aspects of the collection may thus be discussed together. I shall leave aside the Second Life of Mo Lua, since its relationship to the First Life has already been discussed. It is clear that its textual ancestry goes back to the eighth century, but quite unclear when it was abbreviated to make it suitable for inclusion in a lectionary. This matter of abbreviation is important here, since what the contents may give us is an indication of the dates of the original unabbreviated Lives, not of the shorter texts we have.

The first Life to be considered is, therefore, that of Daig of Inishkeen, now just on the Co. Monaghan side of the border with Co. Louth, but in the early-medieval kingdom of Conailli Muirthemne. Like the other Lives in the group, apart from the Second Life of Mo Lua, this is the only extant

Life of the saint. As we shall see, it is important for the Life that the site of Inishkeen is only four miles north-north-west from Louth, the monastery of St Mochta, whose Life follows that of Daig in our group.[22] It is also important that the kingdom of Conailli Muirthemne was, because of its strategic position, an object of special concern to the leading kings among the Uí Néill and the Ulaid (Ulstermen). Until 735 it appears to have been regarded as part of the province of Ulster, but in that year Áed Allán, who had just fought his way to the kingship of Tara, won a major battle at Fochart, just to the north of Dundalk.[23] In this battle the king of the Ulaid was killed. After 735, Cenél nÉogain, Áed Allán's branch of the Uí Néill, had a firm ambition to control Conailli Muirthemne. From the same date there was an enduring alliance between Cenél nÉogain and the church of Armagh.[24] Since Cenél nÉogain were initially based far to the north in Inishowen, control of Conailli Muirthemne offered them a springboard for military activity in the eastern midlands and against Leinster. However, since Conailli Muirthemne was such a prize for Cenél nÉogain, it was also the object of military ambition on the part of Cland Cholmáin, principal rivals of Cenél nÉogain among the southern Uí Néill. These influences on the history of Conailli Muirthemne may be illustrated by three annal entries:

> *AU 756.4:* A hosting of the Leinstermen was summoned by Domnall [of the Cland Cholmáin, the ruling kindred of Mide, and currently king of Tara] against Niall [Niall Frossach of Cenél nÉogain, the next king of Tara], so that they were in Mag Muirthemne [the territory of the Conailli Muirthemne].
> *AU 819.2:* The death of Áed son of Niall [Áed Oirdnide of Cenél nÉogain; currently king of Tara] by Áth dá Ferta in Mag Conaille [equivalent to Mag Muirthemne; he had just been campaigning against the Leinstermen].
> *AU 879.1:* Áed son of Niall [Áed Findliath of Cenél nÉogain], king of Tara, fell asleep on 20 November, a Friday, at Druim Inasclaind [the church of Dromiskin] in the land of the Conailli.

As will be seen the connections of Cenél nÉogain with Conailli Muirthemne survived the foundation, in 841, of a Viking *longphort* on its southern boundary at Lind Duachaill, the modern Annagassan. On the other hand, the region does not seem to have had quite so central an importance after the ninth century.

The Life of Daig of Inishkeen is, for its length, full of interesting detail and relatively well arranged. The main division is between events occurring before the foundation of Inishkeen and events occurring subsequently. Although the foundation of the monastery is central to the form of the Life, Daig is not made to spend much time there. He is a great traveller as well as a great craftsman. Before the foundation of Inishkeen the Life is concerned with the other great saints with whom Daig was connected. He is reared and educated under Mo Laisse of Devenish; his career is prophesied by Mochta of Louth; he learns monastic discipline under Comgall of Bangor; and he subjects himself and his monastery (not yet founded) to Ciarán of Clonmacnois.[25] Different aspects of his monastic formation are thus associated with different saints. After the foundation of Inishkeen, Daig goes on a journey which includes a considerable stay in Connaught, a province closely associated with Clonmacnois.[26] This establishes links with lesser churches, notably with communities of nuns – Daig was a great patron of nuns, something for which he received a rebuke from a successor of Ciarán of Clonmacnois.[27]

Two possible indications of date are contained in the Life. The first emerges out of Daig's role as a great craftsman, a goldsmith and a scribe (he both writes the gospel book and constructs the ornamented bookcase). Mochta's prophecy, which is in any case crucial since it contains the vital statement that Inishkeen will not be subject to its close neighbour, Louth, but to the distant Clonmacnois, includes a remark that Daig will make a reliquary for Mochta's remains.[28] The practice of enshrining the remains of saints in such reliquaries, constructed by a goldsmith such as Daig, did not become common in Ireland before the second half of the eighth century; among the annalistic references to shrines and enshrining, one, *AU* 818.5, has an especial importance since it concerns the shrine of Mochta, perhaps the very one alleged in the Life to have been made by Daig.[29]

Another clue to the date of the Life is contained in the very first section, a precise statement of the saint's parentage, in which he is ascribed to the people known as the Ciannacht Breg. These were a vassalpeople subject to the branch of the Uí Néill known as Síl nÁeda Sláne, rulers of Brega, namely the province lying between Conailli Muirthemne and the Liffey. In the genealogies of the saints, however, Daig is made into a descendant of Éogan mac Néill, the eponymous ancestor of Cenél nÉogain.[30] This claim would give Cenél nÉogain legal rights in the church of Inishkeen as the kindred of the patron saint or *érlam*.[31] It is perhaps reasonable, therefore, to associate the pedigree given to Daig in the genealogies with Cenél nÉogain power over Conailli Muirthemne. Since the latter remained a distinct kingdom with a royal dynasty that retained its genealogical links with the Ulaid, the easiest way for Cenél nÉogain to exercise direct influence would have been through gaining power over churches.[32] The Life, however, as we have seen, associates Daig with

Brega in the lands of the southern Uí Néill, a position which implicitly rejects Cenél nÉogain claims. It is unlikely that the Life belongs to a period before Cenél nÉogain gained power in the region, namely before 735, since the detail about Mochta's reliquary suggests a rather later date. It is more likely that we have two contemporary but conflicting claims about Daig's ancestry. That the Life was sympathetic to the southern Uí Néill is also indicated by the stress it places on Inishkeen's subjection to Clonmacnois, since the latter, itself situated in Mide, was closely associated with the neighbouring Cland Cholmáin.[33] So far as they go, therefore, these indications would fit a ninth-century date, although a somewhat later period is not excluded.[34]

The Life of Mochta of Louth is much less detailed and offers correspondingly less evidence for dating.[35] What is striking is how little space is allotted to St Patrick. Our earliest sources for St Mochta see him as a disciple of St Patrick.[36] The Annals of Ulster even preserve what purports to be the beginning of a letter by him: 'Mauchteus, a sinner, priest, disciple of St Patrick, sends greetings in the Lord.'[37] He is similarly described by Adomnán in the Life of Columba.[38] We know that the monastery of Louth had links with Armagh at a later date: the Heir of Patrick, for whom the Book of Armagh was written, came from Louth, and some scholars would ascribe a considerable role to Louth in the textual transmission of writings about St Patrick. It is similarly interesting that the attitude to *magi* (druids), betrayed by the Life is not the uncompromisingly confrontational line of the Patrician tradition, but the gentler one associated with St Brigit. These are somewhat intangible indications; they suggest to me, not so much a date, as a standpoint that, like that of the Life of Daig, was not supportive of the allied claims of Armagh and Cenél nÉogain.

The most interesting detail in the Life of Éogan of Ardstraw is an encounter between the saint and Lugaid mac Sétnai, ancestor of that branch of Cenél Conaill which produced the O'Donnells.[39] Lugaid's son Fiachna killed one of Éogan's monks in the entrance to the oratory at Ardstraw, and thus within the most sacred ground. This deed was done with the consent of Lugaid, his father, and it evoked the following response from the saint:[40]

> From your seed no one will ever reign, no one will be without the disgrace of some bodily deformity. Nine days from now Fiachna, your son, will die; and his seed will never, at any one time, exceed the number five.

Once the son had died, the father did penance and promised a perpetual rent from himself and his descendants of one scruple of silver every three years. Éogan then said to him, to comfort him for his offspring's loss of the kingship:[41] 'Your descendants will be royal counsellors and judges; and no one's kingship among your people will endure unless with their counsel.' And the Life adds: 'All these things were accomplished and are being accomplished.'

This is an interesting variant on a common Irish hagiographical theme. What makes it especially intriguing, however, is that it was fulfilled only in the short term. In the seventh and eighth centuries, the ancestors of the O'Donnells were indeed excluded from the kingship, but this ended in the late ninth century. A king from among Lugaid's descendants is attested in the obit of Éicnechán son of Dálach in 906;[42] this rise to power was already indicated by the title given to the latter's father, Dálach mac Muirchertaig, in his obit in 870, *dux generis Conaill*.[43] The original unabbreviated Life may have been composed in the eighth or the first half of the ninth century.

The *Codex Salmanticensis* was intended to be a national collection of saints' Lives.[44] Among its sources, however, were other collections made on a more regional basis. The Northern Lectionary, I suggest, was one such regional source. The original Lives on which it drew were of different authorship and date, perhaps as early as the eighth century in the case of the Life of Éogan of Ardstraw, slightly later for the Life of Daig of Inishkeen. Although all these Lives come from the area which, by the ninth century, was seen as belonging to the association or community of St Patrick, none of them is strongly Patrician, and two may be quietly subversive of Patrician or Cenél nÉogain claims. Not merely, then, is the collection regional, but the Lives themselves possibly defend local churches from the threat of the greatest church and the most powerful dynasty of the area. There is no indication to show when the original Lives were abbreviated and incorporated into what I have ventured to call the Northern Lectionary; but they remain, even in their shortened form, an interesting group.

Notes

[1] I am grateful to Richard Sharpe for reading a draft of this paper. He is not be held responsible for any errors I may have made.

[2] Heist (ed.), *Vitae*, pp. xlvi-xlix.

[3] Heist, 'Dermot O'Donohue'; Sharpe, *Medieval Irish Saints' Lives*, pp. 297–339.

[4] For different suggestions about the date of the MS and also the place of origin, and the compilation of the collection see, apart from Heist and Sharpe, Ó Riain, 'Codex Salmanticensis', and O'Sullivan, 'A Waterford origin'.

⁵ Herbert, 'Literary sea-voyages', discusses particular aspects of the Life of Ailbe, which she regards as an eighth-century text. Herbert, 'The *Vita Columbae*', discusses the Life of Cainnech.

⁶ *Vita I S. Lugidi*, cc. 30, 34, 35, Heist (ed.), *Vitae*, pp. 137, 138; *CGH*, vol. 1, pp. 55–6.

⁷ For the complete contents of the MS see Heist (ed.), *Vitae*, pp. xvi–xviii, and Sharpe, *Medieval Irish Saints' Lives*, pp. 231–4. The latter gives the contents in relation to the quiring.

⁸ This is the nearest identifiable source used by **S**, not the ultimate source.

⁹ This is the Life otherwise important because it is not conflated with the *Nauigatio*.

¹⁰ 'Incipit vita Molua Droma Snecta', Heist (ed.), *Vitae*, p. 382. For its situation in Fernmag (roughly Monaghan Town to Clones and not to be confused with the latemedieval Farney) see *Vita II S. Lugidi*, c. 11, Heist (ed.), *Vitae*, p. 384. The grid reference of the modern Church of Ireland church is H 607 309.

¹¹ *Vita II S. Lugidi*, cc. 13–14, Heist (ed.), *Vitae*, pp. 384–5.

¹² *Vita I S. Lugidi*, c. 30, Heist (ed.), *Vitae*, p. 137; *Vita II S. Lugidi*, c. 14, Heist (ed.), *Vitae*, p. 385. I have discussed this passage briefly in *Early Christian Ireland*, p. 257.

¹³ The relationship between the client-people, Corcu Óche, and the Uí Fhidgente, a branch of the Éoganachta, is indicated by the beginning of the First Life (c. 1): 'Sanctus Lugidus de genere Corchode [=Corco [Ó]che] Nepotum Fithgente oriundus fuit' (Heist (ed.), *Vitae*, p. 131). This detail is omitted in the Second Life. Íte, similarly, was claimed by the new overlord, as shown by comparing Meyer (ed.), 'Laud genealogies', p. 309, with *AU* 552.1 and the Life of Íte, c. 33, Plummer (ed.), *Vitae*, vol. 2, pp. 128–9 (the Uí Chonaill Gabra were the western branch of the Uí Fhidgente).

¹⁴ Meyer (ed.), 'Laud genealogies', 307.26; 308.11.

¹⁵ Sharpe, *Medieval Irish Saints' Lives*, pp. 337–8, 395.

¹⁶ It may be argued that it is more closely relevant to the Northern Lectionary that all belong to the province of Armagh as constituted in the twelfth century; yet it corresponds more closely to the ninth-century 'community (*samad*) of Patrick' *(AU* 851.5) than to the later archiepiscopal province.

¹⁷ Plummer (ed.), *Vitae*, vol. 2, pp. 32–59.

¹⁸ See Plummer, Catalogue, No. 289, in his *Miscellanea Hagiographica Hibernica*, p. 252, for possible (but doubtful) evidence in the works of Archbishop Ussher that there still survived, in the seventeenth century, a Life of Nessán of Mungret.

¹⁹ Sharpe, *Medieval Irish Saints' Lives*, p. 240, conjectures that three of these Lives, those of Mochta, Éogan of Ardstraw and Mac Nisse of Connor, were obtained through John Mac Tighearnán, who came from Airgíalla. It is not clear why he does not include the Life of Daig.

²⁰ O'Sullivan, 'A Waterford origin'; Ó Riain, 'Codex Salmanticensis'.

²¹ Sharpe, *Medieval Irish Saints' Lives*, p. 240.

²² Inis Caín Dega / Inishkeen, H 932 070 (the Round Tower); Lugmad / Louth, H 95 01.

²³ AU 735.2.

²⁴ As shown by the former's co-sponsorship of *Cáin Phátraic*, which began in 734 (*AU* 734.3); cf. Herbert, *Iona, Kells, and Derry*, p. 63.

²⁵ *Vita S. Dagaei*, cc. 1–7, Heist (ed.), *Vitae*, pp. 389–91.

²⁶ *Vita S. Dagaei*, cc. 18–20, Heist (ed.), *Vitae*, p. 393.

²⁷ *Vita S. Dagaei*, c. 16, Heist (ed.), *Vitae*, p. 392.

²⁸ *Vita S. Dagaei*, c. 3, Heist (ed.), *Vitae*, p. 389.

²⁹ Annalistic references cluster in the early ninth century: *AU* 798.2; 800.6; 801.1;

809.3 (+809.7); 811.1; 818.4, 5; 819.8; 829.3; 831.1, 5; 832.5; Hennessy (ed.), *Chronicon Scotorum*, p. 818. Cf. Doherty, 'The use of relics', pp. 89–104.

[30] *CGSH* §§ 19, 82.

[31] T. M. Charles-Edwards, '*Érlam*'.

[32] For kings of Conailli Muirthemne after 735 see *AU 752.7*, 824.8; on their genealogies see Thornton, 'Early medieval Louth'.

[33] For example, *AU 762.6* shows the *familia* of Clonmacnois supporting one possible candidate for the succession.

[34] Linguistic evidence is sparse: the name of the abbot of Clonmacnois in c. 16 is given as Oenu, which suggests a date of original composition no later than the twelfth century; the Latinized forms *Lassirianus* (alongside *Lassrianus*), *Comgello* (contrast the *Comgalli* of the Life of Mac Nisse, c. 12), *Cathbotum* (by late Old Irish Cathbad), all suggest a fairly early date within the Old Irish period, but Latinized forms often preserve early spellings which would not be employed in purely vernacular forms.

[35] Two purely vernacular forms of names preserve final *-o* in the genitive: Ailello (c. 10) and Edo (< Áedo; c. 16).

[36] Sharpe, 'Saint Mauchteus'.

[37] *AU 535.1*.

[38] Adomnán, *Vita S. Columbae*, Second Preface.

[39] *CGH*, vol. 1, p. 163 (144 d 37).

[40] *Vita S. Eogani Episcopi Ardsratensis*, c. 15, Heist (ed.), *Vitae*, p. 403.

[41] Ibid.

[42] *AU* 906.2; Hennessy (ed.), *Chronicon Scotorum*, p. 905.

[43] *AU* 870.3; Hennessy (ed.), *Chronicon Scotorum*, p. 870.

[44] Heist (ed.), *Vitae*, p. xxxviii.

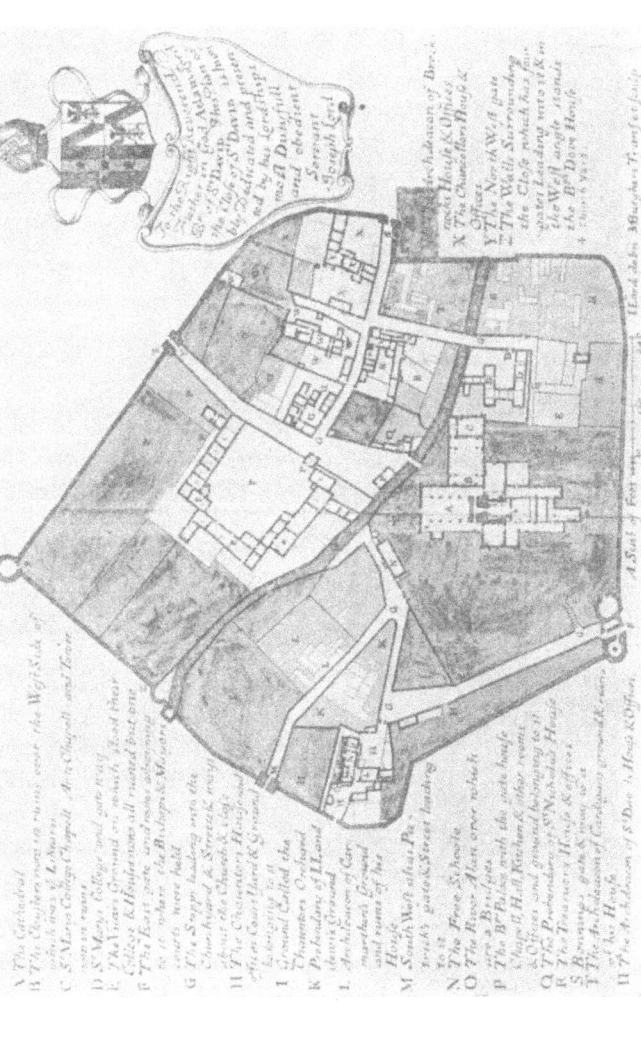

Figure 1.1 A plan by Joseph Lord of the Cathedral Close of St Davids in 1720 in E. Yardley, Menevia Sacra, F. Green (ed.), London, 1927. Courtesy of the Dean and Chapter of St Davids Cathedral.

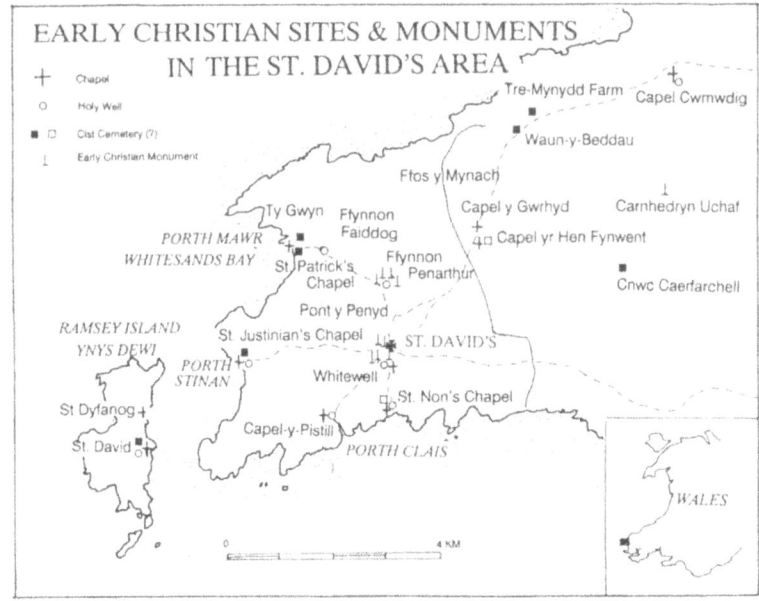

Figure 1.2 A map from H. James, 'The cult of St David in the Middle Ages' in M. Carver (ed.), *In Search of Cult: Archaeological Investigations in Honour of Philip Rahtz,* Woodbridge, 1993, pp. 105–12, Figure 14.1, p. 107.

Figure 1.3 An illustration of St David's shrine from P. A. Robson, *The Cathedral Church of Saint David's: A Short History and Description of the Fabric and Episcopal Buildings,* Bell's Cathedral Series, London, 1901, p. 51. Photograph: J. Valentine.

Figure 13.1 Painting by Amanda Potts of St Moluag bringing Christianity to the Garioch, in the parish church of Chapel of Garioch, Aberdeenshire. Photograph: P. Dransart.

Figure 13.2 Class I stone from Clatt, now at Knockespoch House, Aberdeenshire.
Drawing: P. Dransart.

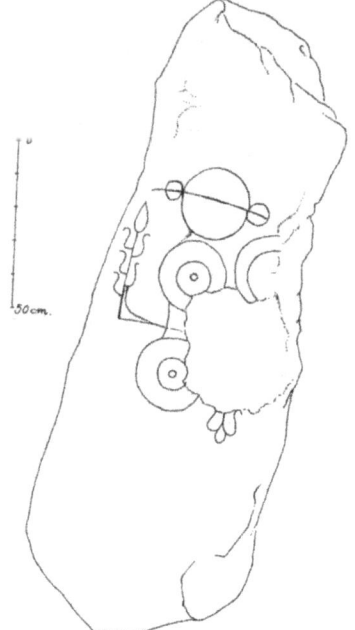

Figure 13.3 Parish church of Mortlach, Moray, with the Battle stone in the foreground. Photograph: P. Dransart.

Figure 13.4 One of four carved stone crosses, now lost, from Clova. Photograph: © Crown copyright, RCAHMS.

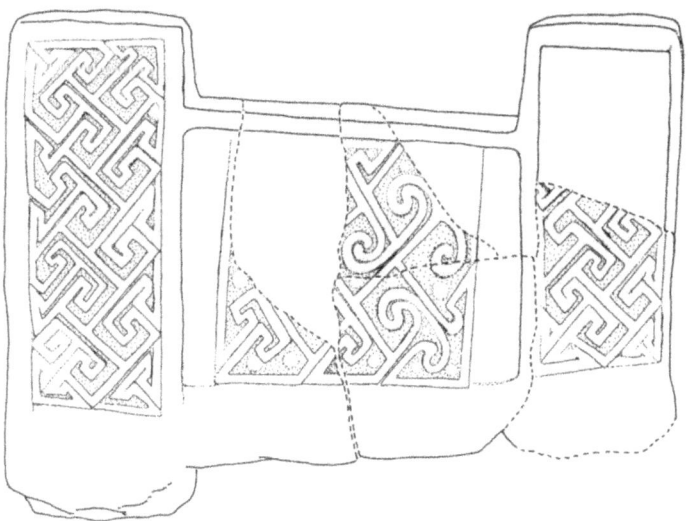

Figure 13.5 Conjectural reconstruction by P. Dransart of a shrine panel from Kinneddar, Elgin Museum 1939.6.

Figure 14.1 Wives' window, St Neot: St Mabyn (Mabena), pietà, Christ, St Meubred (Meberede). Photograph: © RIC [Eneog47d].

Figure 14.2 Sisters' window, St Neot: St Petroc (Patric), St Clair (Clere), St Manac (Manc), All Saints. Photograph: © RIC [Eneog47c].

Figure 14.3 Young men's window, St Neot: Life of St Neot. Photograph: © RIC [Eneog47b].

Figure 14.4 *T*wo panels from Callaway window, St Neot, showing St Lallu? and St German. Photograph: © RIC [Eneo471p].

Figure 14.5 Single panel from Borlase window, St Neot, showing St Neot. Photograph: © RIC [Enoe47ip].

Figure 14.6 *St* Cleer holy well c.1500 as restored. Photograph: ©RIC [Eclew008].

Figure 14.7 St Petroc's reliquary, Bodmin, c.1177. Photograph: © RIC [EBODpc02].

Figure 14.8 Easter sepulchre or St Meubred's tomb at Cardinham. Photograph: © RIC [Ecari004].

Figure 14.9 Easter sepulchre or St Neot's tomb at St Neot. Photograph: J. Mattingly.

Figure 14.10 Shrine of St Endelienta at St Endellion, late fifteenth century, now recycled as an altar. Photograph: © RIC [Eendi009].

Figure 14.11 Shrine of St Issey at St Issey, late fifteenth century, recycled as a reredos. One panel of the original appears to be missing. Photograph: © RIC [Eissi010].

9

Fasting, flesh and the body in the St Brendan dossier

JONATHAN M. WOODING

The hagiography and cult of St Brendan present unusual challenges of interpretation, both in terms of their complicated documentary record, and in terms of the conceptions of monastic theology which this very popular saint was, over time, brought to represent. This complexity is especially seen in the development of the theme of flesh as an image of bodily mortality in the *Vita Brendani*, and in the more detailed discussion of fasting and flesh in the voyage tale *Nauigatio sancti Brendani abbatis*. These texts, most famous for their imaginative depiction of monastic voyages of self-exile (*peregrinatio*), present unusually dramatic depictions of scenes of the monastic life of the eighth century.[1] These scenes, typically for monastic *vitae*, exemplify aspects of monastic leadership and authority. The theme of mortality through association with flesh is found in the *Vita Brendani*. The subsequent development of it in the *Nauigatio* is exceptional both in detail and theological focus and is arguably a particular comment on contemporary debates concerning monastic practice as followed by groups such as the Céli Dé. A study of this element in both *Vita* and *Nauigatio* has the potential to shed light upon the context of composition of the *Nauigatio*, as well as upon developments in the hagiographical genre.

The Vita *and* Nauigatio Brendani

The *Vita* and *Nauigatio* are only approximately dated. The *Vita Brendani/Betha Brénnain* which survives in various Latin and Irish versions is now a thoroughly corrupt text: the subsequent widespread transmission of the *Nauigatio*, and its frequent conflation with the *Vita* in the process, have resulted in the failure of any clean copy of the *Vita Brendani* to be preserved in the earliest collections.[2] The *Vita* would, nonetheless, appear to antedate the *Nauigatio*[3] For the *Nauigatio*, David Dumville has suggested a date prior to 786 on the basis of the political claims contained in its opening genealogy. Giovanni Orlandi suggests a date coincident with early Viking raiding. The present writer would date the text on the basis of its probable references to the Irish discovery and abandonment of the Faroe Islands (*c*.730-*c*.795).[4]

These finer dating questions notwithstanding, it would appear that, around the beginning of the ninth century, the *Nauigatio* author was inspired by the voyage episodes in *Vita Brendani* and other *vitae* – such as the *vitae* of Sts Ailbe and Columba – to write a stand-alone narrative of a saint's voyage to the promised land, with Brendan as its protagonist.[5] The resulting voyage-tale (*Nauigatio*) of St Brendan is neither a biographical narrative, nor a *miracula* of any conventional type; it appears to be more or less *sui generis* in structure.[6] We do not know whether the *Nauigatio* author chose Brendan as the protagonist of his story on account of the author's own cult affiliations, or simply because Brendan was, already, the saint with the most developed voyage narrative.

The unprecedented style and structure of the *Nauigatio* account for its often eccentric and uncritical reception. A credulous belief that voyage tales are evidence of actual travels of saints has, in the past, been a feature of studies in Celtic hagiography; even in a more critical age, the seven-year voyage which forms the central narrative thread of the *Nauigatio* is all too often accepted as representing some sort of reality of a voyage by the saint.[7] Such credulity blinds readers to the fact that, if the tale has a continuous thread running through it, it is as much the cyclical performance of the monastic liturgy as the more obvious voyage element;[8] the tale might almost be described as a liturgical narrative, if such a genre might be defined.[9] The continuous scenes of the monastic life which the *Nauigatio* presents, with meals and fasts at the centre, are not the simple *mise-en-scène* of a monastic setting, but an essential element of the narrative.

The feasts of the liturgical calendar provide nodal points in a tale which seeks to build a narrative upon the cyclical passage of 'monastic time', which is itself based on the sacred year of the liturgy.[10] Constant references to food and eating, among other details of daily existence for the monks, represent the dramatic fleshing-out of some of the other days of the monastic year. If anything, the *Nauigatio*'s constant emphasis on food and its consumption (or non-consumption, in the case of fasts) brings to mind the taxonomic treatment of diet and fasting in monastic rules and penitentials, as well as the calendrical organization of some of these texts.[11] There are over forty references to eating of food, or abstinence from it, in the *Nauigatio* (see Table 9.1, p. 171). Almost every location in which the monks find themselves in the *Nauigatio* is the occasion for a regulated fast, a gift of food, a welcoming meal or a liturgical feast. Only one of the locations visited in the tale and only two out of twenty-eight chapters[12] of the published text are without a reference to food or fasting. Even a text such as Rhigyfarch's *Vita Davidis*, for example, in describing the extremely ascetic community of David, refers to food and fasting in only thirteen out of sixty-eight chapters.[13] Notwithstanding that food and its production are major activities in the monastic existence, the *Nauigatio*'s references seem exceptional in number for any hagiographical tale.

An author may (as Evelyn Waugh famously admitted of his first edition of *Brideshead Revisited*) for circumstantial reasons be simply preoccupied with food and, while writing to the accompaniment of a rumbling stomach, 'throw in' references to eating. This is unlikely to be the case with the *Nauigatio* author. Allowing that his hagiographical models were mostly short voyage-tales, which were used to present parables of monastic practice, we should commence with the working hypothesis that the *Nauigatio*, like these individual episodes, has a distinct intent to exemplify some questions or other of monastic practice.

Mortality and purity as a narrative element

Brendan's voyage in the *Vita* is in the tradition of the voyages of other ocean *peregrini* in early *vitae* which, above all, seem to emphasize a tension between monastic *stabilitas* of life and the desire to enter a more eremitic life. In Adomnán's *Vita Columbae*, Cormac Ua Liatháin and Báetán Ua Nia Taloirc make voyages of *peregrinatio* into the ocean to seek a *herimum/desertum in oceano*. This is the search for a 'place of higher *peregrinatio*': typically, a place in which one would have one's retreat, die and be resurrected.[14] They are not successful and find themselves fated to return. In *Vita Albei*, Ailbe visits an ocean paradise, from which he returns carrying a token in the form of a fruiting branch. Despite the call of this retreat, Ailbe returns to lead the monks who have been lamenting his departure. The nature of the paradise itself is not developed.[15]

Brendan's voyage in the *Vita Brendani* differs from these other voyages in being the only one to carry the reader to the destination. To build upon and prolong the basic 'out and back' story, to make a longer voyage-episode, the author of the *Vita* employed retarding elements which are also found in the stories in Adomnán.[16] Cormac fails once because he has brought along a disobedient monk. Brendan takes along three brethren who travel without the permission of their abbot (§5). These represent impurities in the body of the chosen, obedient community. They need to be disposed of before the climactic scene of entry into the *Terra secreta*. Another potential retarding impurity is provided by the inherent mortality of the boat of hide. This motif is unique to the *Vita Brendani* (though images of hide and mortality are used in Cormac's third voyage, into the sea of beasts, in *Vita Columbae*).[17] The retarding factor appears, initially at least, to stem from the immortal nature of the land itself. This immortal quality is implicit in the *Vita Albei* episode; it is fully developed in the *Terra secreta* of the *Vita Brendani*. Though there is no evidence that the author of *Vita Brendani* knew *Vita Albei*, or vice versa,[18] there was evidently a shared conception of this otherworld which was further elaborated in *Vita Brendani*. When Brendan initially fails to find the promised land, St Íte tells him:

> Mortuorum pellibus animalium uectus, promissam non adipisceris terram. Inuenies autem, facta de tabulis naue.
>
> (As a passenger in the hides of dead animals you will not attain the land promised to you. You will attain it, however, in a boat made of planks.)[19]

The Oxoniensis recension further explains that:

> Terram enim a Domino tibi ostensam non inuenies in pellibus mortuorum animalium; quia terra sancta est ualde, in qua sanguis humanus non est effusus.
>
> (You will not find the land shown to you by God in the hide of dead animals, as it is a very sacred land, in which blood of men has not been spilt.)[20]

The monks travelling in their boat are immortal souls wearing a garb of mortality.[21]

The mortality of the boat, symbolic of the imperfection of the body of the community, is presented as a simple retarding factor in the voyage to an 'unfallen' place. It may have been this mortality element of Brendan's story which made him an especially apposite subject for the *Nauigatio*, in its more enumerative allegory of the monastic life. If so, however, the paradise of the *Nauigatio* has become a different type of land from the one in the *Vita*. The promised land in the *Nauigatio*, as O'Loughlin has demonstrated, is certainly the New Jerusalem, which it is not, explicitly at least, in the *Vita*.[22]

In the *Nauigatio*, the hide boat is not presented as the cause of the seven-year delay in entering the promised land, nor are the three latecomers. The ostensible reason for delay is given by the youth whom the monks encounter in *Terra repromissionis*: 'you could not find it immediately because God wished to show you his wonders on the wide ocean' (§28). This is, of course, not really a reason at all. The steward on the Island of Sheep speaks of seven years of 'trials' *(periclitationes)* on the ocean, before they may be admitted to the promised land (§15), but there is no sense of a cumulative grace accruing from this programme of trials. Whatever the *Nauigatio* represents in terms of structure, it is not a simple parable of improvement or divestment.

The *Nauigatio* is distinctly more concerned with individual degrees of bodily purity than is *Vita Brendani*. Brendan is described from the outset as a man of 'abstinence' (§1). When the monks are sent to gather flesh from a beast, it is noted that: 'from the time of his ordination to the priesthood [he] tasted nothing in which the spirit of life drew support from the flesh' (§16).[23] Brendan, in abstaining from flesh, presents a differing profile, however, from his monks. Throughout the *Nauigatio* we are, further, confronted by figures who maintain various degrees of abstention from different foodstuffs. The emphasis in these scenes is on maintaining a diet under spiritual direction; on the occasion when Brendan lets each of his monks take what he feels he needs from a well, it proves perilous, as each monk takes an excess and falls into a slumber (§14).

Problems of excess of zeal in ascetic practice, especially disobedience in terms of excessive fasting, were a strong theme in early Irish monastic literature. The correspondence of Gildas with Finnian demonstrates that this was a central concern to sixth-century clergy; Columbanus' reference to this correspondence in the seventh shows the continuous concern with the issues both of unregulated pursuit of fasting and of *peregrinatio*.[24] Parables in the *vitae* focus on the issue of fasting, just as the voyage-episodes in the *vitae* focus on the issue of *peregrinatio*.[25]

The increasing number of monastic rules and penitentials in the later seventh and eighth centuries bears witness to a desire to provide, as well as simply exemplary stories in hagiography, a more detailed framework for monastic life. Over the course of some centuries of patristic and later discourse, eating had come to be seen increasingly as requiring regulation on account of its potential to pollute the pure body.[26] Augustine had placed strong emphasis on the regulation of quantity. Eating was to 'repair' the wastage of the body and excess was to be avoided. Food itself he did not see as necessarily a pollutant, though already in Augustine's time extremes of fasting by monks and hermits posed more complex theological questions. In the view of Jerome, and in the monastic vision sketched for the west by John Cassian, the extreme abstinence of the desert fathers and their 'precursor' Paul, the 'first hermit' – who appears in the *Nauigatio* – was seen as a form of heroic extreme. This extreme example needed to be factored into debates regarding abstinence and its effects on monastic discipline. The Irish, Meens has argued, were less reluctant than other early medieval theologians to use the examples of Leviticus and Deuteronomy in making more elaborate taxonomies of food.[27] This, in turn, emphasized the imagery of purity and pollution in meat (cf. the 'spotless lamb' of the *Nauigatio*'s Easter celebration: Lev. 1:10; Deut. 17:1). If the eating of flesh conveyed pollution in terms of its state of decay, or, itself being dead, conveyed a vicarious mortality to the recipient, the regulation of such consumption might become linked to a desire for bodily purity which might, in turn, address the causes of bodily sin. This theme of flesh as pollution is developed in Ireland in the seventh-century *Paenitentiale Cummeani* and in the *Canones Hibernenses;* it attained perhaps its most severe interpretation in the *Canones Adomnani*.[28]

It makes sense to see the extraordinary structure of the *Nauigatio* as relating to the programmatic structure of such penitential monastic rules.[29] The *Vita Brendani*, though concerned with the problem of mortality as a polluting factor, was not especially concerned with food and eating. Even the latest of the Irish versions of the Life, which includes a larger range of incidents than any of the Latin Lives, has only a few scenes of eating or fasting (the conflated *Nauigatio* itself aside).[30] In the *Nauigatio*, however, we are presented with a series of images of different types of regulated eating and abstinence: the killing and eating of flesh across the days of Easter; the regulated diet, though varying in quantity, consumed by the monks of St Ailbe; the unvarying abstinence of Paul the Hermit.

The context of the Nauigatio

The Island of Sheep/Paradise of Birds archipelago in the *Nauigatio* appears to relate, if obliquely, to accounts of contemporary, or near-contemporary, anchoretic settlements on islands to the north-west of

Ireland.[31] While these are not our concern here, they more generally indicate an interest on the part of the *Nauigatio* author in contemporary monastic activity, not simply in the deeds of saints from the 'golden age' of the *vitae*.

The enumerative element in the *Nauigatio* has been held by Dorothy Bray to suggest that it may have been written as a comment on the eremitical ideas of the Céli Dé, with whom the *Nauigatio* shares an overt interest in the finer points of monastic food consumption as well as their temporal context.[32] This is not unlikely in view of the *Nauigatio* author's interest in contemporary events. Brendan's principal church was at least in contact with Tallaght and its discipline, and this might suggest a plausible link between Brendan's cult and the discourse of Céli Dé-type eremiticism.[33]

Bray sees Brendan, in his general abstinence from flesh while allowing it to his monks, as manifesting the basic profile of a Céle Dé. When we turn to the subject of fasting, we note, along with Dorothy Bray, more than a few similarities of the *Nauigatio* to the programmes enumerated in *Tecosc Maíle Ruain* (the teaching of Máelruain of Tallaght, d.791), and in the rule of the Céli Dé. The Céli Dé, under the rule of Máelruain, abstained from meat, except where compelled to do otherwise.[34] Forty-day fasts, which are followed by Brendan and his monks, are also stipulated in the rules of the Céli Dé – though forty days can scarcely be described as an eccentric period for fasting.[35] The Céli Dé made seven-year penances which might provide a model for the seven-year voyage of the *Nauigatio*,[36] though Brendan's voyage itself seems to contradict Máelruain's teaching on *peregrinatio*, which was explicitly to stay at home.[37]

Indeed, while some of the correspondences between the rule of the Céli Dé and the *Nauigatio* seem striking, there are some notable differences between the *Nauigatio*'s regime and that of Máelruain. Let us consider some of the references to consumption of flesh. Brendan, like the Céli Dé, eats only a vegetarian diet. His monks eat meat, and this does not prevent them being admitted into the *Terra repromissionis*. Brendan's monks eat flesh at Easter. This was permitted to the monks of Tallaght, but only in the absence of other foodstuffs.[38] In the *Nauigatio*, as O'Loughlin observes, in eating flesh Brendan's monks are, conversely, altering their diet to *celebrate* fully the Resurrection of Christ.[39] Iasconius, the giant fish, does overturn their pot when they attempt to cook flesh on his back at Easter; far from seeing this as a rebuke, Brendan later observes that this simply shows that Christ can reduce *all* living things (§21). Fish and flesh are thus no different; the differentiations made by zealous fasting are irrelevant in the eyes of Christ. This brings to mind the words of the apostle Paul: 'nothing is unclean in itself but it is unclean to any who thinks it is unclean' (Rom. 14:20). In the scene of the fight between the two beasts (§16), the brethren flout the Levitican definition of purity by eating carrion, because the Lord has fed them by his intervention (cf. Ps. 74:14). In the same way as Paul's comments stand as a rebuke to the dietary taxonomy of Leviticus and Deuteronomy, the *Nauigatio* author appears to rebuke the sort of authoritarian programmes espoused by the Céli Dé. The message appears to be that everyone may have a different programme: 'One man feels he may eat anything, while the weak man eats only vegetables. Let not him who eats despise him who abstains; and let not him who abstains despise him who eats' (Rom. 14:3).

A very obvious signifier to the *Nauigatio* author's direct interest in the Pauline conception of 'stewardship' is seen in the episode in which Brendan asks the steward of the Island of Sheep why the sheep of the island are so huge that their forms blot out the grass. The steward replies: 'Nemo colligit lac de ouibus in hac insula, nec hiemps distringit illas, sed in pascuis semper commorantur die noctuque' (No one milks the sheep in this island, nor are they strained by winter. They stay in the pastures always, day and night).[40] The steward is not sustained by the produce of the sheep. Like the apostle Paul he may be entitled to take reward on account of his labours, but explicitly refuses to take them: 'Who tends a flock without getting some of the milk? . . . Nevertheless we have not made use of this right' (1 Cor. 9:7–12). The gigantic size of his flock is the consequence of his inaction. The *Nauigatio* author is here directing us to the Pauline discussions of perfect stewardship in 1 Corinthians and Romans.[41]

Fasting, work and stewardship

That not all monks are given to pursue the same regime is reflected in the very varied consumption of food by the different monks. Barrind, at the opening of the tale, visits the monastery of *Insula deliciosa*: an ideal monastery.[42] The monks here, living close to paradise, '[n]ihil aliud cibi nisi poma et nuces atque radices et cetera genera herbarum' (are given nothing to eat except fruit, nuts, roots and other greens).[43] Mernóc and Barrind, when they visit the promised land from *Insula deliciosa*, do not need to eat or drink at all. When Brendan's monks arrive in the same land, they eat fruit from the trees and drink from the wells (§28). There is no clear message here concerning appropriate measures of food. Each has his own requirements.

The fasts and meals in the *Nauigatio* are not obviously part of any sort of progressive programme in which the monks are ritually cleansing their bodies for entry into the promised land. Unlike in the Anglo-Norman version of the tale by Benedeit, their fasting is not explicitly directed at gaining any particular end, such as being revealed the location of the promised land.[44] Like the monks of St Ailbe whom they encounter, they eat more at feasts than on other days. Their fasts are fasts; their other food consumption does not constantly strive to *resemble* fasting. In this they differ from the Céli Dé: the emphasis in the rules of the Céli Dé is on progression across the seven-year penance. The monks in the *Nauigatio* are, conversely, following a cyclical pattern. Brendan explicitly does not fast to an extreme, he only joins his monks in the same fast. Feeding to them, as to St Augustine, is to repair the daily 'wastage of the body' and, in the Christian feasts, to commemorate the life of Christ.[45] Their fasts do not involve any obvious subtraction of elements from their diet.[46] Paul the Hermit is provided as an example of someone who *has* come to make such subtractions – but it should be noted that he, like his literary model, is *not* a monk.[47] Brendan is therefore not a Máelruain-figure, in some way vicariously purifying his lesser brethren along their path to the promised land through living his own, more pure, life.

The work of monks

Perhaps the oddest feature of the *Nauigatio*'s treatment of eating and fasting is that the monks of St Brendan's crew contradict a basic tenet of monastic existence in accepting food as the gift of God. Never in the voyage do they appear to eat food which they have cultivated themselves. They are delivered to places where food grows, or is washed up; food is brought to them by the steward and by the monks of Ailbe.

When Brendan meets Paul the Hermit, the question of their living off charity is the subject of comment. Paul explains:

> Et tu dicis in corde tuo non esse te dignum monachicum portare habitum cum sis maior quam monachus. Monachus uero labore manuum suarum utitur et uestitur, deus autem de suis secretis per septem annos pascit te cum tua familia et induit.
>
> (In your heart you feel that you are not worthy to be a monk. But you are greater than a monk. A monk uses the labour of his hands to clothe himself, but God from his own secret supply feeds and clothes you and your company.)[48]

Again this appears to be a Pauline argument concerned with faith as against works. Brendan and his monks are chosen to follow a path laid out for them. *Peregrinatio* is the correct path if followed under authority: Brendan and his monks always submit to the authority of their spiritual directors, such as Enda, the steward, and, when they ship their oars and drift, the Lord himself (§6).

The visit to Paul is at a key moment in the narrative: it is the last of the irregular encounters in the cyclical, seven-year pattern of voyages. Though Paul is represented here as a disciple of Patrick, the episode is modelled upon Antony's encounter with Paul of Thebes, even down to detail of the caves in which the hermits live and the wells outside the caves.

The reference to Paul may also emphasize the tension between Paul, who pursued the eremitic life and died in the desert, and the responsibility of abbots, such as Brendan, to lead their flock.[49] This was Paul's dying message to Antony:

> His Antonius auditis flens et gemens, ne se desereret atque ut comitem talis itineris acciperet, precabatur. Et ille, Non debes, inquit, quarere quae tua sunt, sed quae aliena. Expedit quidem tibi, sarcina carnis abjecta, Agnum sequi: sed et ceteris expedit fratribus, ut tuo adhuc instituantur exemplo

> (Antony with tears and groans began to pray that he [Paul] would not desert him, but would take him for a companion on that journey. His friend replied: 'You ought not to seek your own, but another man's good. It is expedient for you to lay aside the burden of the flesh and to follow the Lamb; but it is expedient for the rest of the brethren to be trained by your example.')[50]

Brendan's meeting with the 'first hermit' serves to emphasize the difference of his destiny from Paul's. He is fated to be a leader; it is given him to lead his men to the promised land. Paul can die in the desert, but Brendan cannot.[51] In this, Paul seems to develop the role of the elderly anchorite in the *Vita* who lives and will die in the promised land.[52] In the *Nauigatio* the narrative role of the elderly hermit remains necessary, but the promised land itself, only in the latter text explicitly the New Jerusalem, appears to require a different type of steward.

Conclusion

The *Nauigatio* takes us on a tour through a seascape of monks and hermits, all living slightly different lives and disciplines. Brendan's monks are neither the best of these, nor the worst; monks whom they encounter living a more extreme discipline are evidently *not* given to have the type of revelation which is given to Brendan's monks. These monks observe discipline and degrees of abstinence toward food and drink, but also celebrate the feasts to experience the joy of them. The resemblance of the *Nauigatio* to the rules of the Céli Dé is more or less a conscious statement by the *Nauigatio* author. He is providing a critique, perhaps either as an insider or as someone who is close to, or has left, a similar eremitical monastic community.

The message of the *vitae* voyages is against excess, instead emphasizing the will of God. The *Nauigatio* develops this model in terms of a cyclical year. Far from being incidental detail of the hagiographical foreground, the unusual representation of the consumption of food and drink is crucial to the structure and progression of the narrative.[53] The monks await their entry into the promised land not through progressive preparation but by celebrating the historic events of the life of Christ in the liturgy. The 'last things' are events in time, but the sacred year of the liturgy is cyclical – as symbolized by the fish which bite their own tails in *Nauigatio* §§10 and 21. In the liturgy it is granted that the monks may celebrate year-to-year and increase their faith and knowledge, but only by learning again from what they already have learnt before, not by moving forward.[54] Through this cyclical foreground the reader is taken to the final events in time: an ultimate revelation of the last things in the tradition of apocalyptic visions. The message of the tale is that we must be content with the cycle unless otherwise advised.[55]

Table 9.1. *References to food, eating and fasting in* Nauigatio Sancti Brendani Abbatis

Location	Event
Insula deliciosa (§1)	Monks eat only fruit, nuts, roots and other greens.
Terra repromissionis (§1)	Barrind and Mernóc are one year without food or drink.
Insula deliciosa (§1)	Barrind and Mernóc are two further weeks without food.
Clonfert (§3)	Brendan and his brethren fast for 40 days, 3 days at a time.
Aran (§3)	No reference to food.
Corca Dhuibhne (§4)	40-days' provisions for boat.
Corca Dhuibhne (§5)	3 latecomers threaten to starve to death if they are not taken.

Ocean (§6)	Provisions consumed, always taken at evening time.
Rocky island (§6)	The brethren are tempted to take water without permission.
Rocky island (§6)	The brethren are miraculously fed bread and fish for 3 days and nights.
Rocky island (§7)	Exorcized brother receives Eucharist.
Rocky island (§8)	A youth brings the brethren bread and water to last them until Easter.
Island of Sheep (§9)	The brethren kill a sheep for Easter.
Island of Sheep (§9)	The steward brings the brethren bread on Good Friday.
Near Island of Sheep (§9)	The brethren cook raw meat on the back of Iasconius, who flees.
Paradise of Birds (§11)	The steward brings the brethren food to last until Pentecost.
Paradise of Birds (§11)	The brethren are told to take dry bread and water from the spring.
Ocean (§12)	Eat every second or third day for three months.
Monastery of St Ailbe (§12)	Tempted to take water without permission.
Monastery of St Ailbe (§12)	The monks of St Ailbe are fed roots and bread, which appear miraculously every day (double portions on Sunday and feast-days). The monks eat in shifts if there is insufficient room at the table.
Monastery of St Ailbe (§13)	After Epiphany the brethren leave, having received provisions.
Ocean (§14)	Sail until Lent. Food runs out.
Island of Soporific Well (§14)	The brethren eat plants and roots 'which the Lord has prepared' and drink from well. The brethren fall into a deep sleep according to the measure they have consumed.
Island of Soporific Well (§14)	The brethren eat only what they need for every third day until Maundy.
Ocean (§14)	After 3 days the brethren drift for 20 more days eating every third day.
Island of Sheep (§15)	The brethren take 'supper' and then are provided by the steward 'with loaves and drink and flesh and other good things'.
Island of Sheep (§15)	The steward brings them food on Paradise of Birds (Easter Sunday) and again, as they

	leave, comes in a boat with food (Pentecost).
Ocean (§16)	After 40 days the brethren encounter a beast. It is killed by another beast. They cut it up and preserve it. The brethren must gather plants and roots for Brendan as he does not eat meat.
Island of Three Choirs (§17)	The brethren are fed with fruits which each last one brother for 12 days.
Ocean (§18)	The brethren fast for 3 days.
Ocean (§18)	Grapes are dropped by a bird – each lasts one man for 12 days.
Ocean (§18)	The brethren fast for 3 more days.
Island of Grapes (§18)	The brethren eat grapes for 40 more days.
Island of Grapes (§18)	The brethren take grapes to last them until Christmas.
Ocean (§21)	The brethren are afraid of fish, Brendan reminds them that they were not afraid to light a fire and cook meat on Iasconius.
Ocean (§23)	The brethren take food after the encounter with the pillar.
Ocean (§25)	Judas is tormented except at feasts.
Island of Paul the Hermit (§26)	Paul tells St Brendan he has lived on fish for 30 years, then water for 60.
Island of Paul the Hermit (§26)	The brethren get water.
Ocean (§27)	The brethren live only on water every third day.
Island of Sheep (§28)	The steward gives the brethren food (Holy Saturday).
Island of Sheep (§28)	The brethren fill vessels to sustain them for 40 days until destination.
Terra repromissionis (§28)	The brethren eat fruit and water of the *Terra repromissionis* for 40 days.

Notes

[1] Bourgealt, 'The monastic archetype', pp. 109–21.

[2] In general: Burgess and Strijbosch, *The Legend of St Brendan*, pp. 4–12; Plummer, 'Some new light', pp. 124–41; Ó Caoimh, 'St Brendan sources', pp. 17–24; Wooding, 'St Brendan, Clonfert and the ocean'; Sharpe, *Medieval Irish Saints' Lives, passim*.

[3] The question of the priority of relationship is a vexed one, which I will note only in passing here. The arguments that *VB* is earlier than *NSB*, or vice versa, depend upon a number of assumptions. The older, 'nativist' assumption was that *NSB* was naturally a bowdlerization of a native genre and therefore based on *Immram Maíle Dúin*. That *IMD* knows both *VB* and *NSB* is shown by the figures it gives for Máel Dúin's companions; it

is also likely in terms of the structural evidence that *IMD* is in fact later than, and based on, *NSB*. *VB* and not *NSB* is the Brendan story known to the compiler of the Litany of the Pilgrim Saints (*c*.800–900 AD). Finally, it seems less likely that *NSB* would have been so radically rewritten by compilers of a *later VB* than that *NSB* is a more thematic, topical, expansion of *VB*. This question requires further consideration.

⁴ Cf. Dumville, 'Two approaches', pp. 89ff. Orlandi, *Navigatio S. Brendani: I Introduzione*, pp. 72–3; Wooding, 'The Latin version', pp. 14–25.

⁵ Mac Mathúna, 'The structure and transmission', pp. 313–57; Plummer, 'Some new light'; Herbert, 'Literary sea-voyages', pp. 182–9.

⁶ Wooding (ed.), *The Otherworld Voyage*, especially ix–xvi – the Irish *immrama* ('rowings-about/voyages') would appear to derive from imitation of the *Nauigatio* itself. On the *Nauigatio* and *Vita Brendani* see also Burgess and Strijbosch, *The Legend of St Brendan*. All references to the *Nauigatio* are to the edition by Selmer, using the chapter numbers of his edition (these are also used in the most recent translations). All translations are based on those by O'Meara (trans.), *The Voyage of St Brendan*.

⁷ Wooding, 'Monastic voyaging', pp. 226–45; Severin, *The Brendan Voyage*.

⁸ The tale includes an entire office complete with antiphons, an Easter mass and numerous other details of monastic liturgy. See Curran, *The Antiphonary of Bangor*, pp. 169–77; O'Loughlin, 'The monastic liturgy'.

⁹ O'Loughlin, *Journeys on the Edge*, pp. 91–8; O'Loughlin, *Celtic Theology*, pp. 178–80.

¹⁰ On the origins of the monastic conception of time in the liturgy in general see Bradshaw, *The Search for the Origins*, pp. 171–91 and references. The pattern of growth through performance of liturgy across the monastic year is best outlined in Casel, *The Mystery of Christian Worship*, pp. 63–5 and p. 67. See also O'Loughlin, *Celtic Theology*, pp. 178–81.

¹¹ This enumerative tendency, also evident in native law texts such as *Críth Gablach*, is regarded more generally as an Irish contribution to the development of detailed penitentials and 'tariffed penance': see Dunn, 'Gregory the Great', pp. 248–9.

¹² Excluding §29 in Selmer's edition, which Orlandi has identified as a later addition.

¹³ Wade-Evans (ed.), *Life of St David*. Even the 'rule' depicted in §§21–31, pp. 13–15, refers to food and its production in only four out of the eleven chapters.

¹⁴ T. M. Charles-Edwards, 'The social background', pp. 43–59; Adomnán, *Vita Sancti Columbae* I.6; I.20, pp. 30–1; 46–7.

¹⁵ *Vita Albei* §54, Heist (ed.), *Vitae*, pp. 130–1.

¹⁶ Though we cannot rule out the possibility that the narratives concerning Cormac (perhaps in a similar way to the visions included in Bede's *Historia*) are themselves paraphrases of longer narratives already existing.

¹⁷ Adomnán, *Vita Sancti Columbae* II.42, pp. 168–9.

¹⁸ It is most likely, however, that the author of the *Nauigatio* was using *Vita Albei*. See Wooding, 'St Brendan, Clonfert and the ocean'.

¹⁹ *Vita Brendani* (Salmanticensis Vita Altera) §10, Heist (ed.), *Vitae*, p. 32.

²⁰ *Vita Brendani* (Oxoniensis) §71, Plummer (ed.), *Vitae*, vol. 1, p. 136. Cf. also *Betha Brénnain Clúana Ferta* XCII, *BNE*, p. 64.

²¹ Wooding, 'St Brendan's boat', pp. 77–92.

²² O'Loughlin, 'Distant islands', pp. 1–20.

²³ Bray, 'Allegory in the *Navigatio*', p. 7.

²⁴ For summary see most recently Dumville, *Saint David of Wales*, pp. 11–15. Also Sharpe, 'Gildas as a Father of the Church', pp. 93–205.

²⁵ Cf. *Vita Samsonsis* I §10–11, Flobert (ed.), *La Vie ancienne*, pp. 162–5. For

examples of parables of *peregrinatio* see below.

[26] See, in general, Grimm, *From Feasting to Fasting*, especially pp. 157–90.

[27] Meens, 'The uses of Old Testament', pp. 73–5; Meens, 'Pollution', pp. 3–19.

[28] Bieler (ed.), *The Irish Penitentials*, pp. 108–35 (*Cummeani*); pp. 160–75 (*Hibernenses*); pp. 176–81 (*Adomnani*).

[29] See most recently J. Stevenson, 'The monastic rules of Columbanus', pp. 203–16.

[30] A doe provides milk to the youthful Brendan (§5); the Devil tempts the brethren with thirst (§30, a variant on the water temptation scene in the *Nauigatio);* the story of the giant cat (§46, see n. 40 below); the cursing of a stream because fishermen will not provide fish (§49); the story of Dobarchú and the salmon (§50). See *Betha Brénnain*, Plummer (ed.), *Vitae*, pp. 44–95.

[31] Wooding, 'Monastic voyaging', pp. 226–45.

[32] Bray, 'Allegory in the *Navigatio*', p. 7.

[33] In general see Etchingham, *Church Organisation*, pp. 248–61. In *Tecosc Maíle Ruain*, the interpretation of the requirements of bodily purity is presented in terms of the relations of Máelruain with his disciples – including with the heads of other major houses; it is notable that these include, amongst others, the *erenagh* of Clonfert, Muirchertach mac Olchobair. *Tecosc Maíle Ruain* §38, E. Gwynn (ed.), *The Rule of Tallaght*, pp. 22–3.

[34] *Tecosc Maíle Ruain* §§23, 40, ibid., pp. 15–16, 24–5; *Riagail na Céle nDé* §7, ibid., pp. 66–7.

[35] *Tecosc Maíle Ruain* §§46, 52, ibid., pp. 28–9, 32–3.

[36] *Tecosc Maíle Ruain* §52, ibid., p. 54; *Riagail na Céle nDé* §13, ibid., pp. 32–3; 66–9. The numbers three and seven themselves are common in theological programmes. See MacQueen, *Numerology*, pp. 18–25.

[37] *Tecosc Maíle Ruain* §12, E. Gwynn (ed.), *The Rule of Tallaght*, pp. 8–11; cf. O'Dwyer, *Célí Dé*, p. 191.

[38] *Riagail na Céle nDé* §§8,15,40, E. Gwynn (ed.), *The Rule of Tallaght*, pp. 6,10, 24.

[39] O'Loughlin, *Celtic Theology*, p. 178; *Riagail na Céle nDé* §6, E. Gwynn (ed.), *The Rule of Tallaght*, p. 66, allows for relaxation of the fasts at Easter, but not the regular consumption of meat.

[40] *NSB*, §9, pp. 19–20.

[41] As an example of how the *Nauigatio* may subtly develop scenes from the *Vita*, this steward, alone with his giant sheep, seems to be a reflex of the *Vita's* episode of the saint meeting with the giant cat. In this episode the cat has grown gigantic from eating the fish which have increasingly been left uneaten as one by one the original twelve brethren die. Only one monk remains with the cat by the time Brendan visits. The parallel is in general with the sheep of *NSB* and may also be a reference to recent events in monastic history, namely the story, reported by Dicuil, in which colonies of anchorites had deserted the islands to the north-west (i.e. the Faroes), leaving behind 'countless sheep'. The *Nauigatio* author does appear to show knowledge of these in his description of the Sheep/Birds archipelago. The death scene of the cat is probably taken up separately, to become the fight between two sea monsters at *Nauigatio* §16. See Wooding, 'Monastic voyaging', pp. 237–9; Wooding, 'Les Saints et le bétail'.

[42] The description is based on that of Nitria in the *Historia monachorum* of Rufinus.

[43] *NSB*, §1, p. 5.

[44] 'E enz el nun al Saint Espirit | Juine faimes que la nus guit, | E junum le quarenteine | Sur les treis jurs la semaine' (In the name of the Holy Spirit, let us fast so he may guide us there; let us fast for a period of forty days, on three days in every week), Short and Merrillees (eds), *The Anglo-Norman Voyage*, ll. 131–4.

[45] Cf. *NSB* §1, p. 9.

⁴⁶ Cf. *Riagail na Céle nDé* §47, E. Gwynn (ed.), *The Rule of Tallaght*, pp. 76–7.

⁴⁷ His reason for going on the ocean is even cast in terms of a genuine penance for the crime of disturbing a saint's grave, cf. K. Meyer (ed.), *Cáin Adámnáin* §45, pp. 30–1.

⁴⁸ *NSB* §26, p. 73. Cf. Jerome, *Vita Pauli*: 'Vae mihi peccatori, qui falsum monachi nomen fero' ([Antony to Paul]: Woe to me a sinner, who does not warrant the name monk), Hurter (ed.), '*Sancti Hieronymi*', p. 40.

⁴⁹ This scene was also a favourite subject for high crosses: Ó Carragáin, 'The meeting of Saint Paul and Saint Antony', pp. 1–58.

⁵⁰ Jerome, *Vita Pauli* §12, Hurter (ed.), '*Sancti Hieronymi*', p. 40.

⁵¹ It is interesting to note in this connection that, whereas Mernóc and Ailbe both set out for the promised land without their brethren – and the brethren lament this in both instances *(Vita Albei* §54, Heist (ed.), *Vitae*, pp. 130–1; *Nauigatio* §1) – Brendan is the only monastic leader who is given to lead his brethren there.

⁵² Mac Mathúna, 'The structure and transmission', pp. 331–4.

⁵³ See Herbert, 'Hagiography', pp. 85–6; Wooding, 'St Brendan's boat', p. 92.

⁵⁴ Casel, *The Mystery*, pp. 63–5.

⁵⁵ I would like especially to thank Tom O'Loughlin, Karen Jankulak, Ian Bradley, Dan Tipp, Glyn Burgess and Morgyn Wagner for much helpful discussion.

10
The process and significance of rewriting in Breton hagiography

>⊲

BERNARD MERDRIGNAC

Introduction

In terms of its etymology, hagiography is Holy Scripture: 'Following upon St Jerome, Cassiodorus, Isidore, or a similar compiler of a glossary used the word *hagiographia* to speak of sacred writings.'[2] This was also true of the authors of the *vitae* of medieval Breton saints. Wrdisten, the abbot of Landévennec who drew up the *vita* of St Guénolé *c*.874, speaks therefore of the *lectiones* of 'each doctor following the teachings of holy Catholic Scriptures' *(quocumque agiographorum sectatore catholicorum doctore,* 1, 20).[3] Almost at the same period, it seems,[4] the author of the *vita* of St Magloire, introducing the narrative of a miracle performed during the lifetime of his hero claims to know it 'by a revelation of the Holy Spirit' *(Spiritu Sancto revelante,* IV, 9).[5] Here is, thus, a hagiographer who considers himself, all modesty cast aside, as an 'inspired author'.[6]

Indeed, the authors of these *vitae* seek to actualize and update the sacred history by showing that divine virtue operated constantly, here and now *(hic et nunc* as the pedant might say!), by means of the saints. Hagiography is an edificatory literature in the proper sense of the term. This is why, although the Bible was held as the authority in perpetuity, *vitae* were ceaselessly recast and rewritten throughout the whole of the Middle Ages.[7] This 'fluidity' in the transmission of hagiographical texts is, without a doubt, worthy of further scrutiny. However, the recent assessment of work in France on medieval Latin hagiography in the last thirty years, undertaken by François Dolbeau, underlined the pioneering nature of the research on this subject in the area of Celtic hagiography.[8] As a result of philological enquiries, it is possible to scrutinize within a historical perspective the process of 'rewriting' certain *vitae* of Breton saints of the eighth to twelfth centuries.

Before proceeding, it seems to me indispensable to borrow from François Kerlouégan a double definition of 'rewriting'. In the prosaic sense, 'rewriting is writing or drafting anew a text in order to modify it – as opposed to recopying – to improve its style, or adapt it to other texts, or to certain readers'. According to linguists, rewriting is defined as a process of hypertextuality which relates 'a text B (hypertext) to an earlier text A (hypotext) upon which it grafts itself in a way which is not restricted to commentary'. Clearly, this involves a simple or direct transformation: one says the same thing in a different fashion. To cite the example given by François Kerlouégan: Joyce's *Ulysses* transfers the action of the *Odyssey* to twentieth-century Dublin.[9] To return to the corpus of Breton *vitae*, these attempt in a similar fashion to transpose the biblical message into the historico-legendary setting of Brittany's origins.

I will attempt, therefore, in this chapter to set out, first, the fundamental significance of the differing attitude of exegetes and hagiographers with respect to the source text. Then I will describe the various types of rewriting shown in the work of the Breton hagiographers. Finally, I will attempt to examine some of the motivations which might have governed these literary revisions.

Attitude to the source text

Naturally, considering the practical conditions of medieval editing, the convenient distinction between rewriting and recopying is hardly applicable to the production of manuscripts of this period. Moreover, the idea that the Latin Bible transmitted the Word of God, fixed once and for all, is purely a theoretical view. Throughout the entire high Middle Ages, various versions of the Holy Scriptures were circulating. Until the ninth century the Vulgate vied with the *Vetus Latina* and the *Itala* and, even in the thirteenth century, the biblical text was far from being standardized. Nevertheless, the wish to return to an original text in order to arrive at the revealed truth underlies all medieval exegesis. This is why, in his *Admonitio generalis* of 789, Charlemagne enjoined that 'we should carefully correct the catholic books'. Later, in his *Epistola generalis* (786–801?), he rejoiced in having 'with the universal help of God, rigorously corrected all the books of the Old and New Testament, which had been corrupted by the incapacity of their editors'.[10] Among other attempts to produce a better Bible, the work of revision inspired by Alcuin (d.804) exercised great influence because of the subsequent pre-eminence of the scriptorium of Saint-Martin-de-Tours. Thus a Gospel Book of Landévennec dating from the second half of the ninth century gives for the Gospel of St Matthew a text emanating from the Bible and revised by Alcuin at the request of Charlemagne 'that a single and correct version be adopted in the *regum Francorum*'.[11]

In contrast to the approach of medieval exegetes, hagiographers did not hesitate to create 'new from the old' *(post vetera nova cudere)* as wrote Wrmonoc, the monk of Landévennec of whom the bishop of Léon, Hinworet, requested, in 884, a version of the *vita* of Paul Aurélien intended for the students of the episcopal school.[12] The author claimed to 'adorn' the noble deeds of his hero by describing them 'with more clarity than before in older works' *(Praef.)*[13] which he nevertheless did not refuse to reproduce. However, in the same spirit, less than a century and a half later, a monk of Fleury-sur-Loire named Vital deemed it proper to recast entirely the work of his predecessor, 'so muddled by Breton verbosity *(Britannica garrulitate)* that it became troublesome to its readers' *(Praef.)*. This led Vital to assert the connections between the Bible, which constituted the norm, and hagiography, which acted in an exemplary capacity: 'In sacris etenim Scripturis normam inuenimus iure uiuendi; in exemplis uere praecedentium Patrum formam assumimus bene operandi' (in Holy Scripture, we find a rule for the judicious life; in the examples of the Fathers who have gone before us, we find, in addition, the manner of properly carrying it out).[14]

These musings of an eleventh-century hagiographer show the value of attempting to understand to what extent our perception of the 'manner of thought' of a medieval *literatus* is gained by investigation into recensions derived or recast from these *vitae*. Because of its confessional origins, which have assigned to it the task, since the eighteenth century, of establishing the historicity of a saint and of scientifically separating verifiable from legendary developments, hagiographical criticism has privileged the single earliest redaction of a text to the detriment of consideration of later versions. At the beginning of the twentieth century, the Bollandist Hippolyte Delehaye denounced the 'plague of revisions' and deplored that it was often difficult to discern 'if one had evidence of separate witnesses or if the same account was repeated in different terms'. From his point of view, in the case of many of the hagiographical texts, although 'the comparison of a long list of manuscripts and a minute examination of variants' would never be entirely pointless, 'these activities are often without appreciable results for the only end that mattered, the reconstitution of the primordial text'[15] (the notorious 'archetype'!).

In contrast, from the moment the historical personality of the saint is no longer the essential preoccupation of research, the study of the variations of a hagiographical text, of its alterations and its departures,[16] takes on its entire significance in a context of historical anthropology. This allows one to discern the evolution of these 'models' of sainthood in which successive generations located their conception of human perfection, and to envisage the history of a cult and of sainthood over a long period of time.[17] In the short term, if increased attention is paid to the conditions of work of the hagiographers, the question of the literary status of the genre in the Middle Ages cannot be bypassed, in Brittany anymore than elsewhere. This has, in fact, important implications, as much literary as historical.[18] What is the dividing line between copying and rewriting a text? On what criteria does one decide whether one must consider a text to be a simple copy cobbled together from variants of a *vita* or to be a distinct version, rewritten with particular intent? For this reason, the concepts of 'editorial metamorphosis' of a text, and of 'metamorphosis' of the text 'by rewriting' elaborated by Guy Philippart, show themselves to be especially pertinent in this regard, even if there is not a sharp distinction between the one and the other. According to Philippart, as successive copies are made the text undergoes metamorphoses, 'accidental or intentional, originating in the practices of medieval edition. It undergoes others, more substantial, once it is submitted to a rewriting on the part of a *literatus*.' Between these two states, there is a spectrum of intermediary situations:

> simple retouchings first, tending to normalize a text with respect to its grammar, or tending to embellish it with respect to its style, or tending to distort its original sense; interpolations; *abbreviatio*; the creation of a 'new' œuvre by assembling borrowed pieces of diverse sources; plagiarism by mere modification of the proper names; versification, etc.[19]

The Breton hagiographical corpus clearly illustrates each one of these situations. The very notion of rewriting is familiar to Breton hagiographers, for whom the reference to an older source had the status of cliché intended to give authority to their own redaction. This commonplace is found in many *vitae* of the Carolingian period and later. It appears already at the very beginning of the first *vita* of St Samson which, whatever the specific date one might assign to its composition (from the seventh to the ninth century), is the foremost of Breton hagiographical productions. The author claims to borrow, among others, from the *Acta* of St Samson, 'which were brought overseas by the aforesaid holy deacon named Henoc [the cousin of the saint], written in a delicately refined style' (*Prol.*, 2).[20] Joseph-Claude Poulin, while being seriously critical of the historical value of the first *vita* of St Samson, does not reject the possibility of the existence of these 'more elegant' *Gesta (emendatoribus gestis*, I, 1) an echo of which it seems possible to discern throughout the *vita*.[21] We have already noted above that in 884, in the prologue to the *vita* of St Paul Aurélien, Wrmonoc proposed, on the contrary, to correct the stylistic deficiencies which according to him disfigured the 'ancient writings' *(veterum chartis)* which the hagiographer 'embellished'. The approach is the opposite of that of the author of the first *vita* of St Samson, but it stems from the same hagiographical commonplace. It is evident that Wrmonoc is referring to and plagiarizing the *vita* of St Guénolé, composed a decade earlier by his abbot Wrdisten, whom he presents explicitly as 'his master who achieved an admirable work of writing' (*Prol.*).[22] He himself had recourse to an identical phrase – the *veterum . . . cartis* [*sic*] (writings of the ancients) – to describe the 'brief Life, woven by a pious fervour, of the eminent father of the monks, Guénolé; which he proposed to revise and to attempt to adapt upon blank pages' *(Praef.)*.[23]

This dialectic between the 'ancient' and the 'new' is not limited to the scriptorium of Landévennec in the Carolingian period. In fact, we have recently brought to light indications of contacts between hagiographical scriptoria of the ninth century (Landévennec, Alet, but also Redon and Léhon).[24] We find this cliché in the preface which the deacon of Alet, Bili, decided to place at the head of his collation of the *vita* of St Malo (*c*.870). The hagiographer claims to follow an earlier source which the bishop of Alet, Ratvili, asked him to revise: 'we have wished to write this book according to the example given by one of our predecessors, not in honour of the learned, but indeed for ourselves' (*Praef.*).[25]

The recourse on the part of hagiographers to this commonplace raises, admittedly, for the historian the question of the actual existence of such sources, perhaps near-contemporary with the events they purport to describe. But is this not more likely a stylistic device meant to confer authority (in the etymological sense of the term – *auctor*: 'someone who authorizes') on the writings of these Carolingian authors? It would, nevertheless, be hypercritical to abandon on principle the theory of the disappearance of versions earlier than those which are known to us. In this regard, Jean-Christophe Cassard judiciously compares the remarks of Bili, in the prologue of his *vita* of St Malo to a notice of St Cado contained in the *Cartulary of Quimperlé*. Bili wrote in the middle of the ninth century:

Seeing that the Acts and the Lives of several saints were falling into oblivion because of the negligence of those whose duty it was to conserve them, we set ourselves the task of correcting the Life of St Malo and we take care to keep it safe so that it should not be neglected by the ignorant and subsequently be lost nor that it should not come to pass, as has sometimes happened, that one misbelieves it in the future. *(Praef.)*[26]

Two centuries later, charter CI of the *Cartulary of Quimperlé* lends itself to a study of an example which strengthens the reasonableness of the deacon of Alet's remarks. The charter laments the disappearance of the older *vita* of St Cado, relating that such a *vita* was borrowed (probably in the ninth century)[27] 'by a priest named Tudhuarn who, leaving the country, took it beyond the Vilaine and died in a strange land without ever having returned it'.[28] In support of this possibility of the presence of older texts behind Carolingian or central medieval *vitae*, Jean-Christophe Cassard, moreover, noted that these contain toponyms or anthroponyms transcribed in an orthography conforming to sixth- or seventh-century linguistic contexts, which later authors could not have restored. Therefore, these 'might have depended on documents of an earlier period which they adapted to the contemporary taste, but all the while retaining various linguistic features belonging to an original period'.[29]

Types of writings

Having argued for the possible existence of older sources invoked by certain medieval authors, the historian must consider another question: this concerns the various ways in which a text might be recast by Breton hagiographers. Rather than draw varied examples from texts of different eras, I will draw on the example of the Life of St Lunaire,[30] all the more significant as its prologue, exceptionally, does not invoke the cliché of an older source. However, this hagiographical dossier shows almost all the emendations so far mentioned: stylistic revisions, abbreviations, plagiarisms and interpolations.

St Lunaire is, above all, known in Brittany by his cult and toponyms. After the Viking invasions of the tenth century, his relics ended up being honoured in the Cluniac priory dedicated to him in the enclosure of the castle of Beaumont-sur-Oise (Val-d'Oise). The cult of St Lunaire (Léonor, Liénoire) in Normandy explains the fact that the only complete version of his *vita* is found in a fourteenth-century manuscript legendary emanating from the library of the Cistercian abbey of Notre-Dame de Bonport (Eure). An incomplete copy (lacking the first few paragraphs) is found in a thirteenth-century manuscript (Paris, Bibl. Sainte-Geneviève, 1289), probably from the diocese of Saint-Malo.[31] The insertion of *repons* (responses) in this latter manuscript by a more recent hand shows that it had by then been adapted to liturgical purposes. Variations, for the most part minor, between the two versions make it difficult to judge whether they represent two different recensions or, rather, one phrased in slightly different terms.[32] Moreover, the narrative describing the manner in which the saint and his companions develop the land which they have colonized since their arrival (chs 8–10) follows a different scheme in each manuscript. But this inversion cannot be due to an error in the foliation as, in the Breton manuscript, several transitional sentences which do not occur (and with good reason) in that of Notre-Dame de Bonport bestow on the original binding a logical appeal. The text, therefore, has been deliberately manipulated at this point. In summary, these two texts seem to emanate from different manuscript traditions of one version of the *vita* of St Lunaire.

The posited original version might have dated from the eleventh century, judging from what we know of it from these two intermediaries, but it seems to have undergone various layers of redaction.[33] Subjected to a deeper philological investigation, its Latin text seems to have juxtaposed Celticisms and Gallicisms. In addition to these lexical items, other indications support the notion of a composite text. For example, the account of the clearing by the saint and his companions of the site upon which they installed themselves tells how they celebrated the minor hours where they laboured: in the morning they went to the obedience[34] to work, and during their work, they sang the hours appointed by the Rule, that is, prime, second, terce and sexte.[35] The celebration of the minor hours on the spot is provided for by the Rule of St Benedict (50, 1–3) for monks who cannot reach the oratory by the appointed time. However, with the mention of the *secunda hora* as following prime, the text departs from usual Benedictine tradition. On the contrary, in Celtic monastic practice, no doubt in order to provide a time of sleep after matins, the celebration of prime was delayed until the second hour.[36] One is reasonably led to suppose that the author of the *vita* found in the Bonport Legendary tried to abide by his source, which he was attempting to rewrite, and which referred to one or other older rule which referred to *secunda*. But at the same time he felt constrained to align himself with the Benedictine Rule by reintegrating prime to its place in the enumeration of the minor hours.[37]

The existence of a *vita* of St Lunaire pre-dating the rewriting in the eleventh century, the only one at present available in its entirety, is supported by the analysis of the fragments of this *vita* found in various documents: an abbreviation transcribed at the beginning of the seventeenth century by André du Chesne (1584–1640) from a manuscript of Arras (now lost); the lessons devoted to the saint in a Saint-Malo breviary of the beginning of the sixteenth century (destroyed in the Second World War); and, above all, in several folios from a tenth-century copy preserved in a composite legendary (Orléans 347 (291))[38] which belonged to the abbey of Saint-Benoît-sur-Loire, which had strong links with Brittany. The existence of these fragments was made known in 1982 by the Bollandist Jacques van der Straeten, but he was convinced by a brief examination of the manuscript that they belonged to the version of Notre-Dame de Bonport.[39] However, the mere fact that these fragments were recopied as early as the tenth century calls into renewed question all that he has written on the late character of this *vita*. On the other hand, a close examination of the text which they furnish allows one to realize that one is certainly in the presence of a version which is different from that of the eleventh century, and that, moreover, this former text could not have been the source of the latter version.[40] Finally, by chance, the Saint-Benoît-sur-Loire version also contains the episode of the clearing of the obedience and of the celebration of the minor hours by Lunaire and his brethren. But here these are enumerated in accordance with the Benedictine Rule: 'prime, terce, sexte', with no question of *secunda*. It is inconceivable that the author of the Notre-Dame de Bonport version took the initiative to insert the reference to the *secunda*, which would have been obsolete since the Carolingian period, as the Saint-Benoît text confirms. One must, therefore, conclude that a source common to both was treated differently by the two hagiographers. One corrected the text without hesitation by substituting prime for *secunda*; the other respected his model more, although he rationalized it by inserting prime. As the Rule of St Benedict was spread in Brittany after 818, this date supplies a *terminus post quem* for the earliest version of the *vita* of St Lunaire.

The example of the *vita* of St Lunaire illustrates some of the problems raised by the process of rewriting by medieval hagiographers. A very old early version, to which no later hagiographer refers, but of which we find traces in the manuscript of Saint-Benoît-sur-Loire (and perhaps also in the abbreviated version of Arras and in the lessons of the Saint-Malo Breviary), was continuously revised and corrected in order to suit fluctuating historical circumstances.

The motives for revision

This tendency to rationalize and update hagiographical texts is the principal interest of the study of rewriting of *vitae* for the historian of ideas, who must take account of the motives for rewriting. The philologist has much to gain from the analysis 'of the formal procedures employed to amplify or to abbreviate a work'. However, in the Middle Ages such rewriting is not merely a literary gesture: it responds to precise aims: 'to glorify God, to honour the saints, to augment the style of students, to transmit dearly held ideas, to preserve the possessions of the community, to adapt the text for the public.'[41] The cleric charged with rewriting a *vita* was bound by stylistic, pedagogic and ideological considerations which cannot be divorced from the political, theological and economic context in which he worked. In order to illustrate this remark made by François Kerlouégan, I will differentiate the example of a single author creating several versions of one text[42] from the example of several authors who judged it necessary to recast a text.

The Lives of St Guénolé

The *scriptorium* of Landévennec, especially productive in the second half of the ninth century, lends itself to a fruitful study of the former example inasmuch as the abbot Wrdisten composed at least three versions of the *vita* of St Guénolé during one or two decades. It is useful as well to recall that there is also a brief version of the *vita* which has at times been attributed to Wrdisten, but which many researchers consider to have been his source, and which some attribute to Clement, a monk whose 'premature death' was lamented by the abbot of Landévennec and from whom we have at least one alphabetical hymn to St Guénolé.[43] By contrast, Joseph-Claude Poulin advances compelling arguments to see this version as a later abbreviation (tenth to twelfth century), composed in the north of France or in England.[44] I shall not here comment on this debate which, although it may concern the process of rewriting, risks taking this investigation too far from its subject matter. In the context of the present investigation, it seems to me preferable to concentrate on the motivations which governed the composition by Wrdisten of his various versions of the *vita*. In fact, the rewriting of older *vitae* (if one believes their authors) constitutes a convincing indication of the state of 'Carolingian renaissance' in ninth-century Brittany.[45] It is significant that Wrdisten judged it fitting to insert in the *Vita major Winwaloei* a diploma promulgated in 818 by Emperor Louis the Pious, which introduced the 'Rule of Father Benedict' to Landévennec (and probably to other monastic establishments in the region) in order to 'bring them into harmony with the universal Church confided [to him] by divine disposition' (II, 14).[46] From that time onwards, the efforts of the Breton monks to express themselves in grammatically correct Latin echoes that of the memorandum (probably dictated by Alcuin) *De littera colendis* promulgated by Charlemagne since 796, as a result of the council of Frankfurt. This document praised the monks for having contributed 'by their pious prayers' to the success of the Carolingian policy, but deplored that the intentions 'which a pious devotion dictated internally to them' should be tainted by the 'uncultivated language' of their writings. In this context, the stylistic efforts of the Breton hagiographers of the ninth century speak, above all, of spiritual motivations. Nevertheless, no doubt they also reflect the desire to defend and to illustrate their own traditions, in the face of a potential calling into question of these by the French Church, by presenting them in irreproachable form.[47] Apart from the texts which have recourse to *sermo humilis* (the commonplace sentence, of elementary structure subject–verb–complement), there are those which resemble the narrative sentence of Livy or of the Ciceronian *copia dicendi* (prose of oration). That is, some hagiographers had recourse to *sermo rhetoricus*, the baroque sentence which is marked by complex disjunctions and by an obscure vocabulary approaching that of the *Hisperica Famina*.[48]

Unlike his disciple, Wrmonoc, who pushed the bombastic style to the extreme in his *Vita Pauli Aureliani*, the abbot Wrdisten composed, 'at the unanimous request of his brethren', a *Vita major* of the patron of his monastery, St Guénolé, whose style can be located between the simple sentence and the artistic sentence. This *vita*, written in Latin prose bordering on poetry, with several pieces of verse inserted here and there, constitutes the most 'ancient complete example of a *vita* marked by the prosimetric style' which had become reasonably popular in the Carolingian era.[49] The work is divided into two books: the first describes the early life of the saint; the second his life after the foundation of Landévennec. Wrdisten alternates narrative chapters with long homilies embellished with references to Holy Scripture, the writings of the Church Fathers and of classical authors. These borrowings offer a view of the rich library which the hagiographers of Landévennec had at their disposal.[50] Although the argument has not convinced all its detractors, it seems to me that the presence of doxologies at the end of several chapters (I, 15; I, 18; II, 8; II, 26)[51] preserves traces of the original lessons read at the office which might have come from the source which the abbot of Landévennec claimed to be rewriting.

The third book of this *vita* is a recapitulation in hexameters of the two preceding books. The first twelve strophes (of thirteen), each one of eight hexameters (except for chapter 6 which is made up of 9 lines), faithfully follows the prose narrative. Fifteen irregular strophes (from 6 to 44 lines) follow, in which Wrdisten heaps up literary reminiscences.[52] 'Selfrewriting', in which an author rewrites (in prose or verse) a 'hypotext' he himself has previously written (in verse or prose), belongs to a literary genre known as *opus geminatum* or *geminus stylus*. Let us borrow from François Kerlouégan a few examples of this process which consists of creating two parallel versions of one text, the one in prose, the other in verse: in the second half of the fifth century Sedulius composed a *Paschale Carmen* which he then rewrote in prose under the title *Pascale opus*; Bede (*c*.673–735) composed a *Vita Cuthberti* in verse which he then developed in prose; Raban Maur (847–56) composed his *De Laudibus Crucis* first in verse and then in prose. The initiative of the abbot of Landévennec, then, is located in an enduring literary convention.[53] However, it bears repeating that the medieval hagiographer did not write for his mere aesthetic pleasure. The prose is accessible to a larger public than the verse, which is addressed to educated readers. The prose *Vita major* of St Guénolé was intended for public reading to the monastic community of Landévennec, hence the long sermons interspersed within it. The versified third book was reserved for solitary meditation.[54] The desire to adapt a hagiographical text for the listeners or readers to whom it was directed is confirmed by the example of the hagiographical dossier of St Willibrord composed by Alcuin. In order to celebrate the apostle of Frisia the cultural adviser of Charlemagne had composed a trilogy which took into account the audience for each piece of the dossier: a Life in prose for the use of the monks; and a poem for meditation by the *scolastici*, to which was added a sermon destined for the populace.

The parallel between the work of the promoter of the Carolingian renaissance and that of the abbot of Landévennec is strengthened if one considers the *Omelia* for the feast of St Guénolé which the latter composed immediately after the *Vita major*. The incipit 'Omelia die natali sancti Guingualoei ad lectiones pertinens nocturnas et habita ad populum' (The homily of the feast-day of Guénolé suited to readings for nocturnes and deliveres to the populace) clearly expresses the text's double function: it furnishes, on the one hand, the twelve readings for the office of nocturnes of the feast of St Guénolé; on the other hand, it forms the matter of a sermon intended to be read to the assembled populace on that occasion. The author in fact specifies (lect. 12) that the feast of 3 March, the anniversary of the death of Guénolé, has been transferred (probably at the end of the eighth or beginning of the ninth century) by his predecessors to 28 April, the anniversary of the translation of the saint's relics. Thus the feast will not be in danger of falling during Lent and can therefore be celebrated 'publicly by the populace'. The author explicitly refers (*Prol.*; lect. 2) to the first book of 'the *vita* which [he] recently composed' and he borrows textually from this *vita* the 'catalogue of virtues' of his hero. He retains, while abbreviating, the narrative thread of his model and prunes the edificatory passages addressed to the community. He thus rewrites (*rescribimus*) 'a more concise text', accessible to a less intelligent or more preoccupied audience:

> We write this either as a reply to those who were not directly able to have access to, or were not able to understand, our creation in previous writings, or, directed at those who, occupied by other things and without sufficient leisure, wished to obtain a summary of the miracles of the saint. (*Prol.*)[55]

The fact that the group of *vitae* composed by Wrdisten to the glory of St Guénolé is achieved in the context of rewriting associated with the Carolingian renaissance is supported by the examination of the *vita* which he dedicated to John, bishop of Arezzo (872–90).[56] The prelate, known from several imperial and pontifical documents, was an influential member of the entourage of Emperor Charles the Bald. This *literatus*, popularizer of Greek texts and enthusiast for theology was also a fervent collector of relics.[57] It is not, therefore, surprising that Wrdisten sent relics of St Guénolé to the bishop showing the gratitude for the reception which he gave to the monk Peter of Landévennec, 'our brother and also your loyal supporter'.[58] These precious relics were accompanied by their 'operating instructions': a new *vita* of the saint consisting of an assemblage of the two previous texts. The prologue is followed by six chapters reprising the 'notice' contained in chapters 9–14 of Book II of the *Vita major*. The diploma of Louis the Pious, designed to create a favourable impression upon an intimate of the imperial court, figures in its proper place. Wrdisten follows this with a literal transcription of the *Omelia* (chs 7–19). One can agree with Joseph-Claude Poulin that, 'no doubt wearied by his lengthy efforts to depict all the nuances of St Guénolé, or pressed by circumstances, Wrdisten probably availed himself of an easier solution by inserting two pieces of previous works into an offering to a benefactor and long-time friend'.[59] Nevertheless, the selection of the texts making up this patchwork are not without significance: these, it seems to me, argue strongly that the diploma of Louis the Pious ordering the Breton monks to conform to the Benedictine Rule did not significantly mark a rupture with existing traditions.[60] In summary, the abbot of Landévennec can be situated in the course of the Benedictine reform pronounced by Benedict of Aniane in the preface of his *Concordia Regularum* (818–20): 'the blessed Benedict took his rule from all the others and in some fashion has assembled into one sheaf a number of sheaves.'[61]

The three vitae *of St Tudual*

Two of the three *vitae* of St Tudual which are known to us are themselves the work of one author, whose purpose can be located within the context of the Gregorian reform, which affected Brittany at an earlier date than has often been argued. Moreover, this dossier enables us to examine the question of the connections, at times ambiguous, between rewriting and forgery. These *vitae* are located within a rich hagiographical production which flourished in the diocese of Tréguier in the eleventh and twelfth centuries (and which embraces also the *vitae* of Sts Cunual and Maudez, if not that of St Efflam).[62] Hubert Guillotel has noted the basis of this production in the religious reorganization of Brittany after the year 1000: the intention was to justify, with reference to its antiquity, the establishment of the diocese of Tréguier, although it is not attested until 990 at the earliest.

The authority of the great historian of Brittany, Arthur de La Borderie, imposed at the end of the nineteenth century a chronological classification of these *vitae* of St Tudual which for a long time was not disputed to any great extent. According to him, a *Vita Ia* of St Tudual composed by his disciple, Louénan, must have existed. Louis Duchesne and François Duine, however, argued that, in any case, this text cannot have pre-dated the ninth century. Again according to Arthur de La Borderie, a *Vita IIa* must have been rewritten at the beginning of the eleventh century, before being amplified several decades later by a *Vita IIIa* which can be dated with respect to the episcopacy of Martin (*c*.1050), as it relates that he benefited from a posthumous miracle of St Tudual. However, with good reason, Louis Duchesne did not consider the episode in question as a *terminus a quo*, and proposed to extend to the twelfth century the date of redaction of this *Vita longior*. The detailed examination of the hagiographical dossier of St Tudual by Hubert Guillotel has rendered the propositions of Arthur de La Borderie entirely obsolete.[63] Nevertheless, Guillotel confirms that, as Arthur de La Borderie had indeed perceived, the long version *(Vita IIIa)* is merely a padded version of the medium-length version *(Vita IIa)*, 'with modifications and additions here and there', intended essentially to lend authority to changing political and religious circumstances over the course of the eleventh century.

Above all, Hubert Guillotel focused on the personality of Martin, bishop of Tréguier, in the middle of the eleventh century. He was probably chaplain to Geoffrey Martel, count of Anjou, a circumstance which might explain the intervention of the saintly bishop Aubin of Angers on the side of St Tudual in the latter's three *vitae*. In addition, as a reforming papacy attempted to reserve to itself the creation of new dioceses, it may have seemed necessary for the diocese of Tréguier to prove its antiquity. The most convenient way of doing this was to identify the seat of the diocese (whose creation would fall foul of the new regulations about to be imposed) with a *civitas* of late antiquity; this would act as 'proof of antiquity'. In 1056, at the council of Châlon-sur-Saône presided over by the legate Hildebrand (the future Gregory VII), Martin took the epithet *episcopus Auximorum* (bishop of the Osismes). But since this title had already been claimed, with better arguments, by the bishop of the neighbouring diocese of Léon, Martin probably judged it a better idea to rely on early sources in which the Hiémois (*pagus Osismensis*), homonym of the Armorican *civitas Osismorum*, adjoined the *pagus Lexvinus*, that is to say the region of Lisieux (or Lieuvin). Therefore, he was moved to insert in the *Vita IIa* (ch. 5) an episode in which King Childebert raised Tudual to the episcopal seat of *Lexobie* (erroneously identified with the Gallo-Roman site of Yaudet which is near Tréguier). In order to give authority to his hagiographical assemblage, Martin went so far as to explain that, following a pilgrimage to Rome, Tudual was elected pope under the name Léon Britigène, 'as the Roman catalogue states' (ch. 6). Again according to Hubert Guillotel, in order to accommodate these innovations, Martin bolstered them with reference to a so-called older source which he described as a '*vita* written in the barbarous language of the *Scoti*' (ch. 1; cf. also ch. 13), that is to say probably in a debased Latin.[64] Thus he was led to forge the text of the *Vita Ia* which 'mechanically propelled Tudual into the northern *pagi* of Brittany according to the names which were given to these *pagi* in the middle of the eleventh century'.[65]

This convincing argument provokes two complementary series of remarks. On the one hand, if one believes the longer *Vita IIIa*, the forgery attributed to 'St Louénan, his disciple', was in the form of a 'charter' *(volumen)* containing 'the names of donors and witnesses' (ch. 6). This implies that the text of the *Vita Ia* which has come down to us was, as François Duine argued, 'merely a notice which preceded a cartulary or some land-registry'.[66] Two charters which Martin had drawn up as chaplain to the count and countess of Anjou have survived;[67] thus, he had the skills neccessary to carry out this operation.

On the other hand, inasmuch as the forgery which he created was composed, according to Martin, 'in the barbarous language of the *Scoti*', the hagiographer naturally tried to make *Scotia* the native land of

Tudual. This blunder by the Angevin cleric no doubt provoked the redaction of the longer version, the *Vita IIIa*, probably at the end of the eleventh century or beginning of the twelfth century. If the *Vita IIIa* does not deny the substance of the *Vita IIa* which it is revising and padding, it nevertheless explicitly describes its purpose as 'the extirpation of the error of those who, misled by the Breton error of describing as Irish (*Scotigenas*) those who come from across the sea, attempted to make this great saint a native of *Scotia*' (*Praef.*). This ethnic attribution was clearly defamatory in eleventh-century Trégor, as shown in the tale of a posthumous miracle occurring later in the same *vita*. The drowning of a noble adolescent who was at Tréguier for Pentecost provoked a veritable riot. The body was taken to the church and placed before the altar: 'The barbarous mob abused with insults the patron saint whom it had come to celebrate, and scorned him as an Irishman and abetter of murder.' The insults roused the saint, and his relics soon resuscitated the young man (ch. 32). The author of the longer version (the *Vita IIIa*), who thus integrated into his tale the prejudices of the Trégorois against the Irish, merely strove to remove any misapprehension concerning his origin in the service of the greater glory of the holy patron saint of Tréguier.

The hagiographical dossier of St Malo

Having attempted to illuminate some of the motivations which might bring a single author to compose several versions of the same *vita*, I would like to consider the case of the *vitae* of St Malo, which were rewritten over several centuries by successive authors.

There are, in fact, at least five versions of the *vita* of St Malo composed by different authors from the ninth to twelfth centuries. Three of these Lives were compiled during the ninth century by almost contemporary hagiographers, who nevertheless had different objectives. One of these served as the source of two redactions of the Romance period. Is it possible to assess the significance of these successive versions of the *vita*? Scholars agree in dating the *vita* dedicated by Bili to Bishop Ratvili to c.870. According to Ferdinand Lot, there is compelling evidence to show that a long anonymous *vita* of the saint was the source that Bili claimed to be rewriting; this longer anonymous *vita* itself was then rewritten and a brief anonymous *vita* was produced.[68] However, in reconsidering the hagiographical dossier of St Malo, Joseph-Claude Poulin judiciously inverted Lot's scheme, showing, following François Duine, that the *Vita longior* was merely a later amplification of the brief anonymous *vita*.[69] On the other hand, Poulin is less justified in seeing in the brief anonymous *vita* the *Vita primigena* used by Bili as a source. To my mind it is preferable to consider that this source, already much deteriorated during the lifetime of Bili, was subsequently lost. This hypothesis allows us to take into account the variations imposed between one version and another in the narration of the navigation of St Malo following that of St Brendan. The episode is much more developed in the version redacted by Bili than in the anonymous versions, a fact which led Joseph-Claude Poulin to assume that Bili, who merely invokes 'tales of men worthy of belief, from generation to generation' in his *vita*, here deviated from his source to apply himself directly to the traditions referring to St Brendan. In his account of the search for the Island of Imma by Malo, Brendan and their 905 companions (I, 15–24; 95 according to the anonymous versions), Bili transposed, in the manner of Insular *immrama*, the monastic theme of *peregrinatio* into an account of maritime wandering. The paschal and eucharistic symbolism with which the hagiographer invested the marvellous motifs which he set in his work attempted to magnify the monastic priesthood. Of course, this priesthood cannot be devoted to the ministry, but is granted to consecrate unusual virtues. For this reason, according to Bili, Malo ended his search and landed on an unknown island during the Easter Vigil (I, 19–31); here the eucharistic metaphors are implicit in the text. In contrast, the anonymous versions deliberately eliminate this episode, which provides the entire spiritual significance to the narration of the voyage. Inasmuch as, in contrast to Bili, these hagiographers immediately (ch. 7) stressed the object of the expedition (the famous Island of Imma which they identified explicitly with the terrestrial Paradise), the search could not, according to them, result in anything other than failure. Everything unfolded as if the authors had decided that their hero would not attain Paradise and was not tempted to rest in contemplation and idleness.[70] Rather than seeing, in these differences of rewriting, the traces of a rivalry between episcopal clergy represented by Bili and the monastic ideals which, as Poulin argued, underlie the brief anonymous *vita*, I believe that the point is to be found elsewhere. Bili rewrote his model by transposing motifs of the *immrama* into the perspective of the *peregrinatio*; the anonymous author censored the central passage of the journey of St Malo because the literary genre of the *immram* to which this episode belonged seemed to him to belong to a tale of profane adventures, pointless in a hagiographical narrative.

In support of this interpretation, it is useful to consider the rewriting of the Romance period, the authors of which only knew (or merely drew upon) the anonymous version. Sigebert de Gembloux (d.1112), ordered by the abbot Thietmar to correct the 'barbarisms and solecisms' of the anonymous, prudently distanced himself from his model in referring to the *vita* of St Brendan: 'If anyone wishes to read it, may he learn from the opinion of those knowledgeable that which is to be believed' (ch. 6). Another version from the beginning of the twelfth century, sometimes attributed – without decisive arguments – to the archbishop of Dol, Baudri of Bourgueil (d. 1130),[71] is even more explicit in suppressing almost 'everything which seems not conducive to the examination of the monastic state', that is to say almost the entire tale of the voyage: 'If anyone wishes to know about them, he can find them in the book of the peregrination of St Brendan' (ch. 6). The marvellous adventures of the voyage of St Malo, at the same time as vernacular versions of the *Nauigatio sancti Brendani*, placed such voyages securely within the realm of profane literature, and no longer suited to the genre of hagiography.

In conclusion, it would be reductive to consider the 'fluidity' of the rewriting of these *vitae* as a mere consequence of the habits of work in medieval scriptoria. It seems to me that rewriting is inherent in the very nature of the hagiographical text. The cliché of the older source (whether real or fictional) used by Breton hagiographers in order to confer authority on their productions did not prevent them from priding themselves on making 'new from the old'. As Pádraig Ó Riain has perceptively remarked, regarding Wrmonoc's formula (*post vetera nova cudere*), the events in which the saint was embroiled, supposing they really occurred, had long ago lost their historical and contingent significance. Nevertheless, they retained a potential exemplary value. This is why the rewriting of a *vita* does not merely result from new stylistic trends to which older material was adapted. The tone and narrative structure of a text were profoundly recast in the service of practicality.[72] This edificatory literature which, above all, has as its point the realization of sacred history needed to be meaningful to its time. This is why, as I hope to have shown, the analysis of a composite text such as the *vita* of St Lunaire allows successive strata of redaction to come into view, strata intended to be adapted to various historical circumstances. This is why the various versions of the *vita* of St Guénolé have as their purpose the demonstration that the patron saint of Landévennec did not deviate from the criteria of sainthood of the Carolingian reform. In the same way, two centuries later, the bishop of Tréguier attempted to overcome the relatively vague origins of his diocese by presenting the career of St Tudual, its presumed founder, in terms of the ecclesiastical reform of the eleventh century. Finally, the reading of successive versions of the *vita* of St Malo, written over the course of several centuries, allows us to see how the motif of the maritime journey lost its spiritual significance to such an extent that it ended by being expunged by hagiographers of the Romance era as a tale of profane adventure.

In summary, the study of the processes of rewriting furnishes the historian with a tool with which one can better examine the evolution of models of sainthood presented to the faithful. I have not examined here the example of St Samson whose *vita* is the foremost of its genre in Breton hagiography and which itself merits an examination which would surpass the limits of this chapter. His *Vita Ia* (possibly seventh to eighth century) calls him a 'bishop' and describes his miraculous episcopal consecration, but is not at all concerned with the status of Dol, and attributes essentially monastic virtues to its hero. While not necessarily agreeing in all matters with the conclusions which Joseph-Claude Poulin reached from this state of affairs, it must be remembered, as he noted, that here Samson 'is no more than the character of an abbot of Dol who involved himself in politics'.[73] The *Vita IIa*, redacted at Dol *c*.850, is a monument of literary history of the middle of the ninth century and, on the contrary, stresses the episcopal character of the sanctity of its hero.[74] Its Benedictine redactor was concerned to affirm the metropolitan status of Dol (II, 24) which was proclaimed at the synod of 'Coetleu' in 848–9. Finally, *c*.1129, the archbishop of Dol, Baudri de Bourgueil, rewrote the *Vita IIa*, no doubt at the consecration of the new abbey of the Dolois enclave of Saint-Samson-sur-Risle where he most often resided. This is why he insisted on the status of Pental (Saint-Samson-sur-Risle) which he presented as the 'second seat of Dol (II, 9). Since the metropolitan quarrel between Tours and Dol was underway, Baudri, who had obtained the *pallium* only as a personal entitlement, was concerned to establish that the archiepiscopate had been conferred 'not only on St Samson but also on his successors' (II, 24). In such a context, it should be noted that Samson does not embody here the type of the saint-bishop. Baudri, who was also the author of a *vita* of Robert d'Arbrissel, presented his hero as a wandering preacher of the eleventh century who practised eremetical habits. The prologue of this version of the *vita*, which invoked the wornout cliché of the use of an older source within a larger theme of the conflict between 'ancients' and 'moderns', familiar to scholars of the renaissance of the twelfth century, underlines how much one would be mistaken in separating form from substance in the matter of Breton hagiography:

> Inasmuch as no one would be surprised that I, of the same generation as the moderns, have presumptuously taken it upon myself to correct an ancient source, and from this ancient material I have composed, as it were, a new history ... It is by preserving the pristine authenticity of the subject material that we give lustre to the simplicity of the purpose. Indeed, the

material, whatever it is, is of less striking value when it is not elevated by someone trained in the mastery of his art.[75]

Notes

[1] It is my pleasure to thank Karen Jankulak for translating my text into English and for suggesting some improvements. Also many thanks to Claude Fustec and Jane Cartwright for their help.
[2] Leclercq, 'L'Ecriture sainte', p. 105.
[3] See De Smedt (ed.), 'Vita S. Winwaloei', p. 209.
[4] Poulin, 'Les Dossiers de S. Magloire de Dol', p. 191: 'peu après 850' (a little after 850); *contra* Guillotel, in Chédeville and Guillotel, *La Bretagne*, p. 290: 'un texte de composition tardive' (a text of late composition).
[5] For an edition of the Life of St. Magloire see Bollandus et al. (eds), *Acta Sanctorum*, October, vol. 10, pp. 782–91.
[6] Cf. Dolbeau, 'Les Hagiographes', p. 49 and n. 3.
[7] Bouet and Kerlouégan, 'La Réécriture', pp. 160–1.
[8] Dolbeau, 'Les Travaux français', pp. 63–4.
[9] Bouet and Kerlouégan, 'La Réécriture', pp. 153–5.
[10] Riché, 'Instruments de travail', p. 151; cf. Light, 'Versions et révisions', pp. 56–65.
[11] Guillotel, 'Les Vicomtes de Léon', p. 38.
[12] Cf. Ó Riain, 'The saints', p. 270.
[13] For an edition of Wrmonoc's *Vita S. Pauli Aureliani* see Cuissard, 'Vie' (p. 417 for the preface).
[14] Bollandus et al. (eds), *Acta Sanctorum*, 12 March, vol. 2, pp. 111–20, *Praef.* Cf. Richter, *The Oral Tradition*, p. 75, n. 20.
[15] Delehaye, *L'Œuvre*, pp. 73–4.
[16] Heinzelmann, 'Manuscrits hagiographiques', p. 15.
[17] See the synthesis (with bibliography) by Vauchez, 'Le Saint', pp. 345–80.
[18] Van 'T Spijker, 'Province ecclésiastique de Tours', pp. 248–58. Cf. Philippart, 'Pour une histoire générale'.
[19] Philippart, 'Le Manuscrit hagiographique latin', pp. 33–5.
[20] Flobert (ed.), *La Vie ancienne*, p. 142.
[21] Poulin, 'Le Dossier de saint Samson de Dol', pp. 719 and 726.
[22] Cuissard (ed.), 'Vie', pp. 417–18.
[23] De Smedt (ed.), 'Vita S. Winwaloei', p.172.
[24] Cf., among others, Guillotel, 'Recherches sur l'activité'.
[25] Lot (ed.), 'Vita Sancti Machutis', p. 341.
[26] Ibid., p. 350.
[27] The mention of the river Vilaine as a border allows one to date the event 'some time before the creation of the Breton kingdom': B. Tanguy, 'De la Vie', p. 167.
[28] Maître and de Berthou (eds), *Cartulaire*, p. 255; cf. B. Tanguy, 'De la Vie', pp. 166–7.
[29] Cassard, 'La Mise en texte', pp. 367–8.
[30] Carrée and Merdrignac (eds), *La Vie latine*.
[31] I would like to thank Hubert Guillotel for kindly agreeing to examine and to collate this manuscript.
[32] Cf. Delehaye, *L'Œuvre*, p. 70.
[33] Rather than the date of ninth to tenth centuries which I proposed in Carrée and Merdrignac (eds), *La Vie latine*, p. 26.

[34] I take this opportunity to emend the translation 'ils entraient en obedience' proposed in Carrée and Merdrignac (eds), *La Vie latine*, p. 142, as Hamon rightly pointed out, *Vies*, p. 52. *obedientia* here must be taken in the sense of 'domain belonging to a religious house, whose regulation has been confided to a monk'.

[35] '... mane facto introibant in obedientiam et cum labore decantabant eorum hore canonice constitutas, hee sunt prima, secunda, tercia, sexta' (chapter 9).

[36] Cf., among others, the *Vita Columbani* by Jonas of Bobbio, or the Antiphonary of Bangor. This practice is found in rules influenced by the Hiberno-Frankish monastic movement such as those of Donat and Walbert (seventh century).

[37] Carrée and Merdrignac (eds), *La Vie latine*, pp. 16–17; Hamon, *Vies*, p. 89.

[38] It would be useful to study this document according to the principles set out by Poulin, '*Liber*'.

[39] Van der Straeten, *Les Manuscrits*, pp. 73–4.

[40] Cf. Carrée and Merdrignac (eds), *La Vie latine*, pp. 14–18. See now, Poulin, 'Les dossiers des saints Lunaire et Paul Aurélien', pp. 198–200.

[41] Bouet and Kerlouégan, 'La Réécriture', pp. 161–3.

[42] Dolbeau, 'Les Hagiographes', p. 65.

[43] Cf. Simon, *L'Abbaye de Landévennec*, pp. 27–9; see also Norberg, *Introduction*, p. 126.

[44] Poulin, 'Le Dossier de saint Guénolé', pp. 201–3. See also Brett, 'L'Hagiographie'.

[45] Cf. Riché, 'Les Hagiographes bretons', pp. 651–9; Kerlouégan, 'Les Citations d'auteurs latins profanes'; *idem*, 'Les Citations d'auteurs latins chrétiens'.

[46] De Smedt (ed.), 'Vita S. Winwaloei', p. 227.

[47] Cassard, 'La Mise en texte', pp. 382–5.

[48] See Kerlouégan, 'La *Vita Pauli*', pp. 183–9; *idem*, 'Landévennec'; *idem*, 'Approche stylistique'.

[49] Poulin, 'Le Dossier de saint Guénolé', p. 190.

[50] See Kerlouégan, 'Les Citations d'auteurs latins profanes'; *idem*, 'Les Citations d'auteurs latins chrétiens'.

[51] De Smedt (ed.), 'Vita S. Winwaloei', pp. 197–8, 204–5, 224 and 245.

[52] Poulin, 'Le Dossier de saint Guénolé', pp. 189–92; Simon (ed.), *Landévennec*, pp. 28–9.

[53] Bouet and Kerlouégan, 'La Réécriture', p. 159; Poulin, 'Le Dossier de saint Guénolé', p. 190, n. 48, adds the example of the hagiographical dossier of St Eloi.

[54] Cf. Kerlouégan, 'Approche stylistique', pp. 215–16; Dolbeau, 'Les Hagiographes', pp. 63–4.

[55] See Poulin, 'Le Dossier de saint Guénolé', p. 192–4.

[56] This *vita* has been edited by Fawtier, 'Une Rédaction'. Denis Brillet completed a thesis dealing with this version of the *vita* ('La Vie de saint Guénolé envoyée à Jean d'Arezzo [BHL 8960]') under the supervision of Marie-France Auzéry, in October 2000 at the University of Paris VIII; Chiara Garavaglia, a student at the University of Milan, has compiled an edition and translation into Italian.

[57] Fawtier, 'Une Rédaction', p. 29; Philippart, 'Jean, évêque d'Arezzo', pp. 345–6.

[58] See Poulin, 'Le Dossier de saint Guénolé', p. 197, n. 64; Merdrignac, '"Grégoire"', pp. 265–9.

[59] Poulin, 'Le Dossier de saint Guénolé', p. 197.

[60] Ibid., pp. 194–9; Merdrignac, 'Saint Guénolé', pp. 29–32. I no longer subscribe to some of the conclusions presented in this article, now somewhat superseded, especially as concerns the hypothesis of an early dating for the existence of Guénolé.

[61] For an edition see Bonnerue (ed.), *Benedicti Anianensis*. Cf. Hamon, *Vies*, p. 95.

[62] Bourgès, 'De la Vita de saint Cunual'.

[63] Guillotel, 'Le Dossier hagiographique'. This study supersedes the hypotheses which I advanced in Merdrignac, *Recherches*, vol. 1, pp. 58–61; de La Borderie, 'Saint Tudval'; Duchesne, 'Les Trois vies'; Duine, *Memento*, p. 62.

[64] For an edition of the *Vita* by Martin see de La Borderie, 'Saint Tudval', pp. 86–93.

[65] Fleuriot, *Les Origines*, p. 284, thought that the original text 'could only have been Breton'. Previously I have followed him on this point (Merdrignac, *Recherches*, vol. 1, p. 37), but I am today far less certain (see below).

[66] Duine, *Memento*, no. 15, p. 62.

[67] Guillotel, 'Le Dossier', pp. 215–16.

[68] Lot, *Mélanges*, p. 156.

[69] Poulin, 'Les Dossiers de S. Magloire', p. 166.

[70] See Raison du Cleuziou, 'La Navigation'; Merdrignac, 'La Désacralisation' pp. 13–43; Mac Mathúna, 'Contribution', pp. 41–55.

[71] Armelle Le Huërou who undertook, under my supervision, a thesis on the hagiographical *œuvre* of Baudri of Bourgueil (see below, n. 75), informs me of her scepticism, stemming from her research, as regards this attribution. I would like to thank her most sincerely.

[72] Ó Riain, 'The saints', p. 270; *idem*, 'Towards a methodology', p. 158. See also Merdrignac, '*Ut vulgo refertur*', pp. 105–7.

[73] Poulin, 'Hagiographie et politique', pp. 13–14.

[74] For an edition of the *Vita IIa* see F. B. Plaine (ed.), 'Vita antiqua'.

[75] I have borrowed this translation of the Life of St Samson from Armelle Le Huërou whose excellent thesis, 'Baudri de Bourgeuil, La Vie de saint Samson (commentaire, édition, et traduction du MS BN lat. 5350)', defended, under my supervision, in June 2000 at the University of Rennes 2-Haute Bretagne, is at the moment unpublished. See also Le Huërou, *La Réécriture*.

11
Saints behaving badly: sanctity and transgression in Breton popular culture[1]

>◁

MARY-ANN CONSTANTINE

Bad behaviour requires norms, of course, from which to deviate. And few things are more normative than the *vita:* the patterned life, a model in both intent and construction. Of course, the 'perfect' *vita* is a kind of Platonic ideal – all texts are marked by the particularities of place and time, and even the strictest generic mould allows considerable individuality in matters of style. But because this is such a highly patterned form, much of our response to any particular text depends on a sense of how it conforms to or surprises generic expectations. Most importantly, the *vita* is a story, a sequential narrative, from before birth to after death, with clearly marked stages along the way. In its literary form, the Life tends towards fullness of that story, towards the whole pattern: even episodes taken separately are invisibly, but firmly, contextualized by the rest.[2]

But in oral tradition you do not always get the whole story. Part of what I want to suggest in this discussion is that the generic 'misbehaviour' inherent in folk narrative, especially song, is also conducive to other kinds of misbehaviour, in the form of unorthodox interpretations of notions of divinity and sanctity. By generic misbehaviour I mean the constant flux of the transmission process, which always allows narratives the possibility of development and change in directions beyond the control of any kind of institution, however deep its reach into the psyche of a society. They are the same forces that lie behind the generation of much medieval apocrypha, the often brilliantly imaginative and sympathetic attempts to explain the gaps and paradoxes of the authorized Word.[3]

Songs about saints, the primary focus of this study, exist in relation both to the world of verbal or textual narrative, and to the world of practice, of gesture and iconography. The former sphere tends to be concerned with the story of the saint, with the events of a life; the latter is more interested in function, in what that saint is 'good for'. The song tradition, itself heterogeneous, reflects most aspects of popular interest in saints, but I shall be focusing here on a few songs which seem to occupy an interesting territory between these two worlds; how these narrative and functional aspects of devotion relate to each other is also part of a larger question about the interaction between 'official' and 'popular' conceptions of religion.

The material discussed here comes from nineteenth-century and early twentieth-century Brittany, from a folk tradition thick with saints; they are everywhere, in songs, stories and drama, in popular art, in gesture and ritual. Their relationship with 'official' hagiography is constant and complex, ideas and influences moving in both directions through numerous channels. They can be found in oral tales and legends, in the painstakingly copied mystery plays, and in the good book kept on every hearth: *Buhez ar Sent*, 'The Lives of the Saints', one of the prime areas for direct literate influence on the oral tradition.[4] Churches, chapels, wells and calvaries provide a permanent visual reminder of local saints and their stories in statues and paintings. Saints appear frequently in the song tradition, though less often as protagonists than in their role as protectors or intercessors. Songs which have them as leading characters usually, though not necessarily, take the form of the Life, recounting the saint's adventures and concluding with a firm reminder of his or her final resting place and cult centre:[5]

Korf St Efflam a oe kavet	St Efflam's body was found
gant paper peleh oa skrivet	with a paper, on which was written
he holl buhes karantezus	his whole life of charity and his
hag he burzudou estonus.	extraordinary miracles.

En plestin a oa digasset	The saint was taken to Plestin,
ar sant gant enor a respet	with respect. There, devout and
enan tud santel ha div (ot)	pious people you should go with
it da (gas) dezhan ho peden	your prayers.

That 'whole life' on paper is a useful reminder of the especially close relationship between written and oral sources in the field of hagiography. A well-studied instance of this is the ballad of St Enori, a princess who sacrifices her breast to save her father from a serpent and, as a calumniated wife, gives birth inside a barrel at sea to a child who will become St Budoc. 'Gwerz Santes Enori' has a close textual analogue in the fourteenth-century Latin Life of St Budoc, and a more mysterious relationship with a scattering of other texts in French, English, Welsh, Scots Gaelic and Scots, all reflections of an earlier story about a woman with a golden breast. It is an excellent example of the traditional 'full' ballad narrative, thoroughly integrating archaic and medieval elements into the oral style, related to, but not merely derivative of, a written source.[6] Rather different in style, but equally part of the oral tradition, are the songs which derive from and stick closely to the style and structure of the pious broadsheet ballad; their heavily gallicized Breton and penchant for ornate vocabulary makes them similar in tone to the *kantikou* (hymns) composed by the clergy for the saint's-day processions, the *pardons*.[7]

Models of piety and good living are plentiful, and by the beginning of the nineteenth century Brittany was firmly anchored in French if not European imagination as *the* religious province, a bastion of Catholic fervour and obedience. Yet, although Brittany was consistently portrayed by nineteenth-century writers and historians as deeply pious, and had experienced a resurgence of enthusiasm for its 'native' saints after about 1840, it is surprising to find that there was almost no specific interest in the practical manifestations of popular devotion to local saints before the late 1880s. Recent work by Alain Tanguy gives us access to and context for the notebooks of one of the pioneers in this field, Anatole Le Braz, who in the early 1890s collected material for his *Les Saints bretons d'après la tradition populaire en Cornouaille* (1893–7) and the widely read *Au pays des pardons* (1894).[8] These writings, and above all the now transcribed notebooks, reveal a considerably less orthodox approach to faith than that purveyed by official and semi-official literature.

Although modern folklore cannot be relied on (as nineteenth-century collectors and many since have wished it) as a faithful window on to the medieval past and beyond, the tradition of honouring a local saint – or deity – clearly has very deep roots. I do not think it is too bold to suggest that, looked at from a Welsh perspective, the kind of material discussed here could be used to make the imaginative leap towards a sense of what practical devotion might have meant to the people who did not get into history, who did not write the *vitae*, and whose conception of sanctity must have been a potent mixture of 'top-down' information interpreted in the traditional light of specific and immediate needs. In Wales these voices, inevitably ill-represented in the medieval literature, have been largely silent since the Reformation – and yet, as the fascinating account by Tristan Gray Hulse suggests, the relationship between communities and their local saints has perhaps been more vibrant, and more enduring, than hitherto recognized.⁹ The folk literature of Brittany may have a useful comparative role to play. It should be stressed, however, that the Celticity of the saints in question is not an issue here. Many, in fact, are 'outsiders' who have gone native, a process which is in itself highly typical of the way Brittany has adopted and adapted saints to her own ends.

Violence directed against saints

In practical popular devotion, the working relationship between believer and saint balances their respective debts and duties in a precarious harmony; either side can be perceived to transgress, to disturb that balance. One of the most intriguing aspects of this, well documented in many Catholic countries, is the physical coercion of saints who are seen to have failed their people. Rough handling can also occur as a preemptive measure: in some cases, an apparently abusive element is built into the ritual of devotion itself. In Brittany, this may take the form of a formalized gesture (such as whipping the statue of St Idunet with broom branches before making a request, 'because he is hard of hearing')[10] or it may involve a prolonged and emotional involvement, as in the vivid description given by Le Braz of an elderly pilgrim's visit to St Yves, in which the saint is cajoled, persuaded and finally threatened to force him into deciding between two accounts in a bitter village feud – a judgement, as it turns out, of life and death.[11] As early as 1610, according to Alain Croix, the wives of Léon fishermen would ritually 'drown' their saints to ensure a safe return for their menfolk.[12]

In some instances the violence is not directed personally at the saint, but is expressed through rite, with, as it were, the saint's cooperation. An especially bizarre example, noted by Le Braz in 1892, was the *pardon* at St-Gildas-en-Carnoët, involving the construction of a huge multi-level cage into which anyone suffering from toothache (or who had been bitten by a dog) placed a live hen or cock as an offering to Gildas. After the mass, the priest would pull out one of the birds and climb to the top of the church tower, throwing it into the crowd who tore it to pieces alive, all trying for the head.[13]

Perhaps the best-documented Breton example of ritualized violence is the *pardon* at Saint-Servais, in the hilly wooded area of Duault, on the border between Bro Gerne and Bro Wened: it is described in detail by Le Braz and has been studied in a recent article by the historian Michel Nassiet.[14] St Servatus, bishop of Tongres in the Low Countries, died in 384: it is not at all clear how his cult ended up in deepest Brittany, although there are records of Bretons participating in a pilgrimage to 'Saint-Servais en Allemagne' (St Servais in Germany) in about 1495. The church of Saint-Servais in Duault is first mentioned in 1547, and the incidents for which it gains a certain notoriety are recorded from the late seventeenth through to the mid-nineteenth century.

After the church service, the banner and the wooden statue of the saint were brought out to waiting rival groups of the strongest men from Kerne and Gwened; behind them other pilgrims waved not the usual pilgrim staff but the *penn baz*, or heavy stick, which they clashed together asking for a good harvest. Then the strong men would move in and try to get possession of the banner and the statue. The former was usually torn to shreds and the latter smashed to splinters, but whichever side got the main part was assured of a good harvest: women were urged to collect up the splinters in their aprons. Interestingly, Nassiet shows that people did, in fact, interpret their success with crops from year to year according to the results of the fight, and correlates periods of extreme violence with preceding summers of failed crops: many people were seriously wounded and some were even killed during this event.

It was not popular with the authorities, secular or ecclesiastical, and continual attempts were made to suppress it. In 1777, when the vicargeneral banned the procession, the Vannetais group smashed down the sacristy door and forced the priest to perform the ceremony; when the bishop of Quimper banned the *pardon* altogether, people simply went ahead without clergy. Nineteenth-century sources show the authorities gradually regaining control: the *pardon* remained banned for many years, but began again in the 1830s and the last serious violence took place in 1855. By Le Braz's day, the traditional *pardon* is already a generation away, and his description of it is filtered through the reminiscences of his elderly informant.

The violence expressed through (if not always contained by) these ritual practices reveals the perpetual anxiety that underlies the relationship of believer to saint, the need for protection or relief from harm.[15] That anxiety is also revealed in depictions of saints as powerful and even frightening beings whose actions are far from straightforwardly benevolent.

Saints behaving badly

It should be stressed here that overtly negative portrayals of saints are not common in the Breton folk tradition. Most answer obligingly when called upon in need, especially if the promise of offerings is rich enough. There is the occasional principled refusal, such as that given by St Huinél to a boatful of drowning supplicants whose past behaviour, he feels, allows him no grounds for intervention:[16]

Penaus vo d'ein hou sekourein	How can I save you
Pe ne hues groeit meit m'ofansein?	When all you have done is offend me?
Epad en overen vitin	During morning mass
Oeh bann davarn é ivet guin.	You were in the tavern, drinking wine.

But there are nevertheless enough cases of saints themselves behaving badly to raise certain questions. While many of them derive from what might be called 'official' or 'orthodox' models of misbehaviour, others do seem to reflect a more creative (and potentially subversive) understanding of the nature of saints and their power.

Bad behaviour has its didactic uses, after all. Many saints are famously tetchy, and react to insults, real or perceived, in ways that 'appear to our [modern] concepts of saintly behaviour as very violent and often cruel'.[17] In the *vitae* (and particularly in the Irish and Welsh examples), a saint's high-handed response is often a show of strength – an expression of the power of Christianity over pagan wickedness or a more local reinforcement of specific Church claims to land.

Another literary and educational model common throughout Europe is that of the sinner-saint, who offers many patterns of redemption from instant black-and-white conversions to the slow and painful learning process of the penitent. Among the latter is the aimiably obtuse St Servais, whose original seven-year penance – wearing a leaden robe – is increased threefold when, rather than submitting to God's will, he grumbles about his lot:[18]

Més Serués d'er spered santel e és bet respondet:
'Honèh zo er goal benigen, achiment ne des chet.'
'Serués, Serués, me mignon kér, chetu manket d'id te
Ret e vo d'id té hi dougein seih vlé aral arré.'

(But Servais replied to the Holy Ghost:/ 'This is a tough penance, it has no end!'/ 'Servais, Servais, my dear friend, you have failed:/ You will have to wear it for another seven years.')

Such narratives are relatively controlled: the saint's misdeeds are inscribed in a wider moral framework, and the action tends to be in the third person, distanced and descriptive. Like the didactic stories of the medieval exempla (and sometimes no doubt derived from them) they are standard reflections of the Christian ideology that so thoroughly permeates much of the folklore of Europe.[19] Yet such narratives are far from unproblematic as instruments of instruction: medieval writers, like modern film censors, were anxiously aware that audiences can swallow the bait without the hook, that vivid misdeeds might be remembered when piety is forgotten. And like the exempla, songs about sinners can cut loose from the necessary context. This brings us to the idea of generic misbehaviour, of what happens to moral stories when, through the normal processes of oral transmission – partly random and partly psychological – the narrative centre of gravity shifts.

The shift in focus is especially relevant in narratives where the *end* is the key to understanding the sanctity of the protagonist. For example, in certain versions of the much-discussed ballad of 'Yannik Skolan', Skolan, the sinner, slaughterer of cattle, rapist, arsonist and killer of newborn babes is referred to from the outset as bishop of Léon; and sometimes as *Sant* Skolan.[20] The initial effect is disturbing, as though the taboo-breaking behaviour of the protagonist is in itself an aspect of his sanctity. This is perhaps possible, especially considering that the song itself is often considered one of those talismanic pieces that imparts a blessing to the singer, and even the listener. But it is also made clear that Skolan achieves his blessedness by long penance, and the focus of the song in most versions is on the powerful moment when, after pleading, his mother releases him from her curse. The fact that there are many versions of this song also means that the full narrative context is likely to have been available to singers and listeners, even in incomplete renditions.

But the absence of a strong ending can leave the sanctity of the main character weirdly implicated in his actions, as in the following song, which the collector considered a 'fragment'. It is, by the standard narrative pattern of sin, penance and forgiveness, seriously lopsided; by modern standards the effects of its 'incompletion' are aesthetically intriguing. Bubry is a village in the northern Vannetais, where this text was collected in 1910, from Perrine Daniel, whose large stock of songs included a number of unusual pieces about saints.[21]

[. . .]	[Listen all, listen to a song]
Zavèt ziar ur stireden lostec	Made about a comet
seitec vlé-so n'é bet gùélet	no one had seen for seventeen years
Seitec vlé-so n'é bet gùélet	No one had seen it for seventeen years
quend er blé-man 'n noz nendelec	until this year, on Christmas Eve

Quend er blé-man 'n nos nendelec	Until this year, on Christmas Eve
Sant Yañn Bubri 'n es hi gùélet.	when Sant Yañn Bubry saw it.
Sant Yann Bubri 'n es hi gùélet	Sant Yann Bubry saw it
barh é Bubri, barh ér véred.	in Bubry, in the graveyard.
Barh é Bubri, barh ér véred	In Bubry, in the graveyard,
ha gueti é oé bet spontet.	and he was frightened by it;
Sant Yañn Bubri en es [ean] groeit	Sant Yann Bubry has done
pèh n'es groeit biscoah' dén erbet	what no man alive ever did,
Pèh n'es groeit biscoah' dén erbet	What no man alive ever did:
é dad, é vam en es lahet.	he killed his father and his mother.
É dad, é vam en es lahet	He killed his father and mother
hag é dér hoér en es violet.	And raped his three sisters.
Nag é dér hoér en es violet,	He raped his three sisters:
beb a vap bihan en doé bet.	Each had a little child.
Beb a vap bihan en doé bet	Each had a little child
hag an zri émant bet lahet	and all three of them were killed.
Hag an zri émant bet lahet,	All three of them were killed
an zri émant bed interét	and all three were buried;
An zri émant bed interét	All three of them were buried
didan d'hornic-sen en oéled.	under this corner of the hearth.
Ne hellé dén logein ér gampr	No one can sleep in that room
gued er 'hri en tri inosant	for the crying of the three innocents
Gued er 'hri en tri inosant	For the crying of the three innocents
houlenné oléù er vadiant	asking for baptismal oil,
'Houlen oléù er vadiant	Asking for baptismal oil and the
an mammic peur er zacremant.	sacrament for their poor mothers.
Sant Yann hag e laré	Sant Yann said then
d'é hoér Mari un noz e oé:	to his sister Mari one night:
– Zaù ahanesé d'alum golaou	– Get up from there and fetch a light
ma hreemb-ni hor paquadaou	so we may pack up our belongings,

Ma hreemb-ni hor paquadaou eit mont te valé dré er vrou	So we may pack up our belongings to go and journey through the land;
Eit mont te valé dré er vro de glah' bélec d'hon euredo	To go and journey through the land and find a priest who will marry us.
– N'é chet béleg é Breih-Izél euredché 'r breur hag er hoér	– There is no priest in Breiz-Izel who would marry brother and sister.
Zant Iañn hag e laré tréh Porh Louis un dé e oé:	Sant Yann said one day on the beach at Port-Louis:
– Pas chet guéled [aveid] an dé tér famélen 'passein anzé?	– Have you not seen today three women passing this way?
Tér famelen bizajaou moén ha int gùisqued ér sei melén	Three women with thin faces all dressed in yellow silk
Na int gùisqued ér sei melén gueté beb a varh' du poulén	They are dressed in yellow silk, each with a black foal.
Sant Iañn hag a laré 'tréah Porh Loius un dé e oé:	Sant Yann said one day on the beach at Port-Louis:
– Er mor e zu [doh] men gùélet hag en douar bras n'em andur quet	The sea blackens at the sight of me and the earth does not endure me.
Nag en douar bras n'em andur quet er vein didan d'ein zo faontet	The earth does not endure me: the rocks split beneath me.
Me guermérei rezolusion monet bamdé d'en overen	I make a resolution to go to mass every day;
Monet bamdé d'en overen beb en eil dé d'en absolven.	To go to mass every day, and every other day to absolution.

  In his unpublished notes to this song, which he calls 'mutilé', Yves le Diberder comments: 'Visiblement il manque le récit des épreuves que durent subir les pauvres errants' (Clearly this lacks an account of the trials the poor wanderers had to undergo).[22] Though no other fragments or versions of the story were known to him at the time, that perception of narrative lack is sound: crimes of this kind are rare in Breton folklore and would normally call for serious and bloody penance. 'Mass every day' is not enough. This is borne out by an analogue which has recently come to light from Bro Dreger, in which the protagonist is a priest who asks to be burned alive for his sins, and over whose ashes a dove and crow fight for his soul; interestingly, in this version he is damned, and there is no question even of salvation, much less sanctity.[23] Because the last two couplets of 'St Yann Bubry' are not strong enough to pull the song convincingly into the pattern of sin-repentance-redemption, one is left with the feeling that this character is somehow sanctified in spite of, or because of, his extreme behaviour.

With its taboo subject-matter and extraordinary imagery, the song deserves closer attention than can be given here, but it does represent an important moment in the 'life' of a local saint. The piece demands a kind of double focus – it is simultaneously a part of, and apart from, the wider moral framework, the invisible pattern. Much of the unsettling nature of the piece must come from the contradiction between part and whole: a saint whose 'life' is a catalogue of horror, and whom creation itself rejects, denied an actual redemption, though not the possibility of one.

Of Yann Bubry himself there is little to tell; there do not seem to be any local legends to add to his enigmatic story, and indeed the chapel at Bubry is not dedicated to Yann but to St Yves. Le Diberder, following work by Joseph Loth, suggests that the popular Yves has replaced an earlier saint; but of him, if he existed, nothing is known.[24]

Two Songs of Sant Yann

Sant Yann Bubry is an exceptionally dark character among the saints of the Breton song tradition, but there are other instances of misbehaviour which, though rather different in kind, have a similarly unsettling effect. Again, I would suggest that the natural processses of orality have a part to play, this time in upsetting the necessary balance in the contract between believer and saint. Especially interesting for the exploration of this are songs about illness, and these bring us back to the kind of anxieties expressed in the rituals like that at Saint-Servais.

In Brittany many disorders and diseases are named after saints: they can be found lined up under *droug* in any Breton dictionary, from *droug Sant Anton* (the infectious skin disease St Antony's Fire) to *droug Sant Maodez* (swollen knees), and from *droug Sant Tujen* (rabies) to *droug Sant Yann* (epilepsy). Two songs (again, both collected in the Bro Wened area) deal directly with *droug Sant Yann*. The first contains a graphic description of an epileptic attack.[25]

Me merh, mar det te sant yehan,	Daughter if you go to St Yann,
Ne hret ket goab ag er ré klan,	do not mock the afflicted.
Ne hret ket goab, hret ket déjan	Do not mock the afflicted,
Ag'ré gouéh é droug sant Yehan.	do not insult those with St Yann's disease.
É Sant Yehan pe arriùas,	When she got to St Yann
Ar varlen er groéz é choukas,	she sat on the base of the calvary.
Ar varlen er groéz é choukas	She sat up on the calvary
Ha d'hobér goab e n'hum lakas;	and began to tease the afflicted.
Ha d'hobér goab, d'hobér déjan	To tease the afflicted,
Ag 'ré gouéh é droug sant Yehan,	those with St Yann's disease,
Ag 'ré gouéh é droug sant Yehan,	those with St Yann's disease.
Ben er fin oé hi er hoèhan.	In the end she was the worst of all.
Trihuéh *serviet* koarh ar goarh	Eighteen linen towels
Hi dès bet ruget get hé nerh.	she tore up in her rage.
Trihuèh pautr iouank hi dès chuéhet	Eighteen young men wore themselves out
D'hi hass d'en ilis beniget.	carrying her to the holy church.
Hoah oé ret kavet hé dantér	They had to use her apron
Eit hi hass bedig en autér.	to get her up to the altar.
– Eutreu person, mar em haret,	– Aotrou priest, if you love me,
Difréet hou s'overen bred,	say your mass quickly.
Difréet hou s'overen bred,	Say your mass quickly,
Ke me halon ne harzou ket:	I cannot last long.
Ke me halon ne harzou ket:	I cannot last long:
Droug sant Yehan zou'n droug kalet,	St Yann's disease is a terrible thing.
Droug sant Yehan zou'n droug kalet,	St Yann's disease is a terrible thing,
Doué revirou n'er gouiehèt.	pray God you may never feel it.
O sant Yehan, me sant Patron,	Oh St Yann, my patron saint,
Lamet en droug a me halon	release me from this affliction.
Lamet en droug a me halon	Release me from this affliction
Ha me hrei d'oh un donézon.	and I will give you an offering.
Ha me hrei d'oh un donézon	And I will give you an offering,
Er gèran vou en én hou pardon:	the fairest of your feast-day:

Ur groéz argand, ur baniél	a silver cross, a banner,
Ur *halice* eur hag ur *ciboér*.	a gold chalice and a goblet.

Ur *halice* eur hag ur *ciboér*	A gold chalice and a goblet,
Ur guskemant de bep autér	and a cloth for every altar;
Hag ur hrouiz koér eit en iliz	And for the church a ring of wax
E hrei open tair zro fornis.	that will go three times around.

É Sant Yehan hés ur boket	At St Yann there is a flower
N'en dé na ru ma violet	that is neither red nor violet,
N'en dé na ru na violet	that is neither red nor violet,
Meit ag el liw get er hlinved.	but the colour of sickness.

É sant Yehan hès ur fetan	At St Yann there is a fountain
Én hi é huellér d'er ré klan.	where the sick find healing.

Here the divine punishment is caused, harshly but with some justice, by the girl's lack of respect for the suffering of others. The saint is frightening, but within his rights (though it is worth noting that he is the *cause* of the disease that bears his name, as well as its healer). It is harder, however, to feel the same about the following encounter, in which the same saint appears, sounding more like an angry Zeus or Apollo than the luminous precursor of Christ:[26]

Disul vitin ha mitin mat	Sunday morning and early too
Me 'mont d'er poul guet men dilhad.	I took my washing to the pool.

Me 'mont d'er poul guet men dilhad	I took my washing to the pool
commancet golhein men dilhad.	And began to wash my clothes.

Commancet golhein men dilhad	As I began to wash my clothes
commans er bic de raguellat.	the magpie started to chatter.

Commans er bic de raguellat	The magpie began to chatter
hag er brindi de grial 'ouac'.	and the crows to cry 'ouac'.

Nag er brindi de grial 'ouac'	And the crows to cry 'ouac';
aoutrou Yann de me scandalat.	Aotrou Yann scolded me:

– Hui e gan gué hag e holh güèn.	– You sing gaily, you wash white!
– N'gannan quet gué, n'holhein quet guèn	– I do not sing gaily, nor wash white,

Ol dud me zy zo chomet clan	All the people in my house are sick
guet clénüèt sant Yann, e gredan.	with St Yann's illness, I believe.
– Querhet d'er guér ahanésé	– Go back home immediately
pe m'hou laquei clanüoh eité.	or I shall make you more ill than they.
– Aotrou sant Yann, me escuzet	– Aotrou Sant Yann, forgive me
oèn quet bet én overèn-bret	I didn't go to high-mass
Oèn quet bed én overèn-bred	I didn't go to high-mass.
n'em oé quet claüet pron erbet	I didn't hear any sermon.
N'em oé quet claüet pron erbet.	I didn't hear any sermon.
na dén ziar dro n'oé d'ein laret	No one here told me
Na dén ziar dro n'oé d'ein laret	No one around here told me,
houien qued oé hou couél miret.	I didn't know it was your reserved feast.
– Na men gouél-mé n'oé quet cuhet	– My feast-day is not hidden
boud e hras ha tan ha moguèt	They make smoke and fire
Boud e hras ha tan ha moguèt	They make smoke and fire
quen couls den dud ha d'er lonnèd.	as much for the people as for the animals.
Étré Monterlez ha Zan-Yann	Between Morlaix and Zant-Yann
é hèo on hènt pras neüé-flam	there is a wide and brand new road.
E hèo on hènt pras neüé-flam	There is a wide and brand-new road
e zo seih lèw tré en daou bèn	seven leagues long from end to end.
E zo seih lèw tré en daou bèn	Seven leagues long from end to end
Doué de gonfort 'nhani 'r pourmén.	God give strength to those that walk it!
Aotrou person, querhet d'ho ovrèn-bred	Aotrou parson, go to your mass
pe'han d'er guér hèmb hé hlaüet	so those at home can hear it;
Aotrou person, laret hou cosperaou	Aotrou parson, say your vespers
pe'han d'er guér hèmb hé chilaou	so those at home may listen to them,
Pe'han d'er guér hèmb hé chelaou	So those at home may listen to them,
ba me sy ma bras er poéniaou.	for in my house there is much pain.

The fire and smoke, 'as much for people as animals', refers to the St John's Eve bonfire, the focus of prophylactic and healing rites across Europe.[27] Ignoring them, or not noticing them, the girl is guilty of insulting the saint and is threatened with punishment; the transgression is hers. This is a 'safe' interpretation of the song, and one that would certainly not run counter to the prevailing acceptance of suffering in the name of religion that can be found throughout the Breton folk tradition.

Again, however, I would like to suggest that this song is quite capable of carrying an alternative (or simultaneous) interpretation – that sympathy for the girl makes the saint look positively cruel. The whole encounter is deeply unsettling, from the opening birds of ill omen to the very setting: the washing place is, after all, the *lieu de rencontre* (meeting place) for young girls and strange men in many songs, and those seductions, not all of them pretty, give an odd edge to this conversation which is intensified by the saint's high-handedness, his threats and the helpless position of the speaker. Most disturbing of all is the houseful of people already suffering and the fact that their pain is the last and lingering note of the song.

There are formal reasons, too, for this effect. One, as in the earlier example, is the lack of narrative resolution. Another is perspective. In the *vita* the saint is the hero: the reader or listener identifies with him or her, or at the very least is carried through the story from that point of view. The summary striking-down of troublemakers may be briefly shocking, but is rarely cause for concern. Here though, with all context sliced away, the conversation between the saint and the sinner is on a more equal footing; even more dangerously, the encounter is related in the voice of the 'sinner'. Dialogue such as this creates the possibility for genuine freedom from the moral framework, by giving voices to the characters who should be no more than 'examples'. It is not hard to imagine that the sympathetic force of the female 'I'-voice in this song would have been further strengthened by the performance of the singer, Perrine Daniel.

Of course, we do not know how she understood this piece, whether what appear to be markers to 'read' the song in a certain way are the accidental scratches of transmission. If she inherited some knowledge of a fuller narrative framework, it may have been quite obvious to her that the girl is in the wrong. But that is not the necessary response. There are many examples in the song tradition where pity and sympathy for sinners overwhelms the actual sin; indeed, it seems that one of the hallmarks of orality, the proliferation of versions, encourages a single narrative to invite an extremely wide range of moral stances.[28] When the song is unique, as this version appears to be, such questions can be allowed to remain open.

Conclusions

Traditional orally transmitted songs about saints are particularly fertile ground for 'misbehaviour', occupying as they do a shifting territory between full narrative, the complete pattern of the *vita*, and the static image or ritual gesture. Because songs adapt, shorten, fragment – and above all because they dramatize in dialogue – they can break loose of the moral context and give voices to those who unsettle the official order of things. This is not to suggest that such pieces somehow reflect the 'true' voice of a people, challenging a pervasive Christian doctrine which largely encourages them to accept poverty and suffering. It is merely to state that such voices do exist among the others. The approach followed here rejects the interpretation of folk-narrative as the univocal expression of some intrinsic social truth, and rejects a methodology which lumps versions together and extracts meaning from their common denominator. If those versions are fanned out and taken separately, the differences between them can be striking; and since, as we have seen, a single text can carry quite contradictory messages, the multiple possibilities of interpretation really should be given their due. *Possibility* is fundamental to oral tradition: it provides the impulse to change, as every ambiguous moment opens the door for another interpretative development. By its very nature, therefore, oral tradition cannot be 'orthodox'; it cannot deny that there is more than one way of reading a story.

The songs about saints and disease in particular confirm what Jean-Claude Schmitt sees as a fundamental aspect of popular religion, its physicality: 'le texte hagiographique dans la culture populaire est d'abord un langage du corps, du corps du fidèle comme celui du saint' (the hagiographical text in popular culture is first and foremost a language of the body, the body of the believer as well as that of the saint).[29] From the cult of relics to the offering of ex-votos, belief is expressed through touch, sometimes gently (at Saint-Hernin, in a nice gesture, people washed the saint's head to relieve their headaches)[30] and sometimes with a violence to splinter statues. Behind both the songs and the rituals is a constant anxiety about preserving health – or, indeed, a constant suffering.

Traditions about saints, like much else in Breton folklore, lend themselves to the quaint, the picturesque. It is hardly surprising that Anatole Le Braz, our chief witness to many of these traditions, is occasionally guilty of exploiting the 'charm' of his country's traditions for his French-speaking public. But he is too good an observer of people to hide the underlying fact that many of these expressions of belief are born of, and feed on, helplessness and frustration. Indeed, one of the abiding images from his *Au pays des pardons* is his description of a blind man staring into the fire on St John's Eve.[31] Le Braz had met him on the way up to the fire, full of energy and hope, determined to try again: 'Si je n'ai pas été guéri l'an dernier, c'est ma faute: j'aurais dû m'avancer plus près de la flamme' (If I wasn't cured last time it was my own fault: I should have got closer to the fire).

The entire passage evoking the fire itself is a masterly and revealing piece of writing: emotionally persuasive, it is nevertheless careful to situate Le Braz as an educated observer. His intense description of the growing flames captures the excitement of the people who, in their passion, appear increasingly 'primal': 'Ainsi les Celtes primitifs glorifiaient l'Esprit de lumière et de vie, autour des feux de la tribu, sur les pentes de l'Himalaya' (Thus did the primitive Celts glorify the Spirit of light and life, around the tribal fires on the slopes of the Himalayas). The entire 'spectacle' is 'd'une indicible beauté barbare' (of an unspeakable, savage beauty), as is the Breton chant to the fire which punctuates the passage: 'An Tân! An Tân!'. Anthropologist and writer are finely balanced here. As the fire reaches its maximum ferocity, the old blind shoemaker reappears:

> Le rayonnement du dieu est devenu si intense qu'on n'en peut plus supporter ni la chaleur ni l'éclat. Les prêtres ont fui. La multitude ellemême se recule. Il n'y a que l'aveugle du Bois-de-la-Nuit qui, le front découvert et le rosaire aux doigts, s'obstine à braver la fournaise, à fixer sur elle, désespérément, le regard immuable et tragique de ses yeux éteints.

(The radiance of the god is now so intense that the heat and brightness are unbearable. The priests have fled. Even the crowd pulls back. Only the blind man from the Bois-de-la-Nuit remains, bare-headed, fingering his rosary, and stubbornly, desperately, confronting the furnace with tragic, unchanging eyes from which all light has gone out.)

Whether or not this figure of pathos is real (Le Braz's characters are often best understood as types) and in spite of the lovely flowing cadences, the juxtaposition of 'fournaise' and 'yeux éteints' is harsh. It takes Le Braz, I think, beyond the sentimental and the picturesque to real pity. As fellow spectators, that should complicate our response.

Notes

[1] This article was written during a two-year Special Research Fellowship funded by the Leverhulme Trust and the University of Wales, Aberystwyth; I would like to thank both institutions for their support.

[2] The concept of the patterned life is borrowed from Henken, *Welsh Saints*.

[3] See for example Axton, 'Interpretations of Judas'.

[4] For the stories see Luzel, *Légendes chrétiennes;* for the plays Le Menn, *Histoire du théâtre*, and for *Buhez ar Sent* see Le Berre and Le Dû, 'Un siècle d'écrits'.

[5] Laurent, *Aux sources du Barzaz-Breiz*, p. 170.

[6] Laurent, 'Enori'; Milin, 'La Légende bretonne de sainte Azénor', Le Menn, *La Femme au sein d'or*. For a synopsis see Constantine, *Breton Ballads*, pp. 70–2.

[7] Giraudon, *Chansons populaires*, pp. 83–5.

[8] A. Tanguy, 'Anatole Le Braz'; on Brittany and Christianity see especially Croix, *La Bretagne;* Lagrée, *Religion et cultures* and Le Gallo, *Clergé, religion et société*.

[9] Hulse, '"Visiting a dry skull": aspects of the cult of relics in post-Reformation Wales', paper delivered at the conference on Celtic Hagiography and Saints' Cults, University of Wales, Lampeter, 8–10 September 2000.

[10] Luzel and Le Braz, *Soniou*, vol. 1, pp. xxii–xxiii.

[11] Le Braz, *Au pays des pardons*, pp. 12–20.

[12] Croix, *La Bretagne*, pp. 939–40.

[13] A. Tanguy, 'Anatole Le Braz', vol. 2, p. 98.

[14] Le Braz, *Au pays des pardons*, pp. xi-xiv; Nassiet, 'Deux cultes'.

[15] Compare the medieval *clamor* and accompanying 'humiliation' of relics and images used as a strike-tactic during disputes by religious communities between the tenth and thirteenth centuries. Patrick Geary's analysis of the symbolism of the rite (which involved prostrating the relics on a hairshirt, or covering them with thorns) suggests that, at one level, the relics (that is, the saints themselves) are being 'punished' for failing to provide protection. Geary, 'Humiliation of saints'.

[16] Herrieu and Duhamel, *Guerzenneu ha Sonñenneu*, p. 160. The singer is Perrine Daniel.

[17] Henken, *Welsh Saints*, p. 38.

[18] F.-M. Cadic, 'Saint Servais': collected from Le Père Meitour, Noyal-Pontivy. On Cadic and his collections see Postic's introduction to *Les Œuvres de François Cadic: contes*, vol. 1.

[19] See Bremond, Le Goff and Schmitt, *L'"exemplum"*.

[20] Laurent, 'La *Gwerz* de Skolan'; synopsis in Constantine, *Breton Ballads*, pp. 66–70.

[21] The text (first couplet missing in the Breton, but with a French translation) and subsequent notes are from a copy by E. Gilliouard, at the Centre Dastum in Rennes: Catalogue Malrieu 00292. On Perrine Daniel and the collector Yves Le Diberder see Oiry, 'Étude d'un corpus de récits', vol. 1, pp. 13–20, and 'L'École vannetaise'. A question not addressed here (but part of my current research) is the extent to which the saints' songs of Bro Wened form a distinctive tradition compared with the other regions.

[22] See n. 21.

[23] The song was collected by Luzel from his chief singer, Marc'harit Fulup, but never published. A transcription is given in Berthou-Becam, 'Enquête', vol. 2, pp. 178–89.

[24] Loth, 'Une cause'.

[25] F.-M. Cadic, 'Le Chant de la Saint Jean', pp. 51–2. Cadic says this piece was sung round the fire on St John's Eve, very slowly (it took at least twenty minutes), with a female soloist leading the rest of the crowd.

[26] Collected by Yves Le Diberder from Perrine Daniel and her daughter Hélène Flécher, Pont Scorff, 1910 (Copy Gilliouard. Catalogue Malrieu: 00122).
[27] For St John's Eve ceremonies in Brittany see Postic, 'La Saint-Jean'; Le Braz, *Au pays des pardons*, pp. 171–255, F.-M. Cadic, 'Le Mal de Saint Jean'.
[28] For an initial exploration of this see Constantine, *Breton Ballads*, chapters 3 and 4 (versions showing different moral perspectives on leprosy or sexual sin and infanticide mothers).
[29] Schmitt, 'Le Texte hagiographique', p. 383.
[30] A. Tanguy, 'Anatole Le Braz', vol. 1, p. 129.
[31] For the relevant episodes see pp. 224–5; 237–8; 251–2.

12
Magpie hagiography in twelfth-century Scotland: the case of Libellus de nativitate Sancti Cuthberti

><

THOMAS OWEN CLANCY

The strange text known as *Libellus de nativitate* (or sometimes *de ortu*) *Sancti Cuthberti*, and often referred to as the 'Irish Life of St Cuthbert' has attracted some brief and quizzical comment from scholars.[1] This work, composed in the late twelfth century, but known only from a series of fourteenth-century manuscripts, mostly of Durham provenance,[2] is neither a Life, nor Irish, nor, for that matter, is any but the smallest proportion of it actually based on material pertaining to St Cuthbert. For this reason it has, perhaps, proved a disappointment to those who, drawn by the title, have come to it seeking either Irish hagiography or new material on St Cuthbert, resulting in the relative neglect of what is, in fact, an extremely important and intriguing text. Only one edition exists (Raine's in 1838), and that was taken from one of the least satisfactory manuscripts; most accounts of the text do not even give a satisfactory list of the manuscript sources. The closest critical treatment of the text to date is by Madeleine Hope Dodds.[3] There, accompanying a partial summary/ translation of the text, she gave a fairly secure discussion of the origins of the anecdotes within it, although she was distracted by then-current notions about the primitive nature of Irish hagiography – as containing pagan survivals – and on the whole seems to have missed the deepest levels on which the text is significant. Awaiting a new edition, the current contribution can only be an interim statement, and I am conscious that there is much closer textual analysis remaining to be done. Nonetheless, the *Libellus* provides us with insight into the connections, motives and methods of hagiography in southern Scotland in the twelfth century, and has a right to claim our attention as a unique witness to these.

The author of the text is unknown, although Richard Sharpe has argued briefly that he was Reginald of Durham, a theory to which I will return at the end of this chapter.[4] The author does, however, give us a good sense of his background and associations through his fairly detailed account of the evolution of the writing of the *Libellus*, especially in his Preface, Explicit and in a chapter taken from the testimony of one of his informants. Indeed, this is one of the prime reasons the text is of interest. In my understanding of the Preface, he tells us that he had wished for a long time to compile an account of Cuthbert's unknown miracles, and had done much research. Having compiled a book, he circulated it to his various friends. He had in the process of compilation come across a little manuscript (*quaterniuncula*) describing Cuthbert's birth and upbringing in Ireland, which he incorporated. Various figures added their own testimony to the narrative, confirmed it or otherwise added to it, and the final result was the very composite patchwork narrative that the author presents to us.[5] In two places, he names some of his informants and, occasionally, in the body of the text he refers to the sources of particular episodes. Chief in importance in his mind, though he seems to have supplied only a minor portion of the narrative, was Bishop Eugenius (Éogan) of Ardmore, whom we know of in Ireland between 1173 and 1177, and as a supply bishop in Lichfield diocese in 1184–5.[6] Eugenius, he tells us, confirmed for him the veracity of the little manuscript describing Cuthbert's Irish birth.

In addition to Eugenius (who appears in the Preface, in the Explicit and also in a short passage in chapter xii), the Preface notes others:

> After his relation and the truthful attestation of others, namely, *Mattheus* the archbishop and Saint *Malachias* and *Gilibertus* and *Alanus*, bishops, and many ancient priests of Ireland, and the monks and disciples of the said Saint *Malachias* the archbishop, we wrote this with a confident hand; and their sayings or testimonies according as it was necessary for the pursuit of history, we inserted in the following work. Other things also are adopted in their proper place, which we learnt from others or found written in Scottish books (*in Scottorum libris*).[7]

Before we review these informants, it is worthwhile quoting from the Explicit of the *Libellus*, in chapter xxix:

> We have written this from the books and writings of the Scots (*de Scottorum paginis et scriptis*), but because sometimes we have been unable to transfer (*transferre*), expounding and interpreting, every word flowingly, we have laboured to explain the sense and translate it into this tongue (*in

linguam istam transtulimus). Because we have heard certain notable things from most important men and especially from the bishops of Ireland preaching about St Cuthbert's birth, it seemed suitable that we should insert them in this book (*in hoc libello*), and we have connected the figure of one body by joining together diverse parts. For what the holy priests read in their own tongue and country concerning such a child ought not to be buried in silence . . . For Saint *Malachias* related this fully to David, king of Scots, and Maurilius [=Matheus?] the archbishop, his successor, confidently added to it afterwards, and *Eugenius*, bishop of Ardmore, expanded it more clearly; but two other bishops, whose names have dropped out, together with their associates, have poured in our ears still more.[8]

All this paints a very complicated, attenuated picture of the evolution of the *Libellus*. Going into the stew are Scottish and Irish writings (for the author seems to distinguish carefully between Irish and Scottish in his terminology), some of them in Gaelic, apparently, which he (with help? – his renditions of Gaelic names are not inspiring) has translated and adapted; a core narrative told by St Malachy (Mael Maedóc) Ua Morgair to David I (this presumably on the occasion of one of his visits to Scotland in 1139, 1142 or 1148); and various supplementary testimonies: from a Bishop Gilibert, presumably Gille-easpaig or Gilbert bishop of Limerick and papal legate (who died as abbot of Bangor in 1145), from a Bishop Alan, whom I would identify as Gille-Aldan, bishop of Whithorn *c*. 1128–54,[9] and from Archbishop Matheus, cited at the finish as Maurilius (Muirgius) Ua hÉnni, archbishop of Cashel, who was appointed papal legate in 1192 (and in that sense was successor to Malachy, who had been legate from 1140 until his death in 1148), topped by the confirming testimony of Eugenius, bishop of Ardmore.

Two important points regarding dating emerge from this list. One is that the work must have been composed, or finished, in the 1190s: Mattheus Ua hÉnni only became papal legate in 1192, and hence succeeded Malachy.[10] Moreover, as Dodds observed, the author refers to Malachy as *Sanctus Malachius*, and he was canonized in 1190.[11] Equally, as we have seen, Eugenius was present in England in the mid-1180s. On the other hand, the work seems to draw on the testimony of several men who belong more properly to the mid-twelfth century: Malachy (d.1148), Gilbert (d.1145) and Gille-Aldan (d.1154). This leads to a suspicion that there may be two distinct stages to the production of the *Libellus*, a view which close examination will support.

Many of these men are linked in one way or another. Gilbert of Limerick was one of the prime movers in Irish reform, and his term as abbot of Bangor overlapped with the residence there of the man to whom he handed over the papal legacy in Ireland, Malachy or Mael Maedóc Ua Morgair. Both, it may be taken, were in some sense involved in the initiative to establish Cistercians in Ireland, at Mellifont. During one of Malachy's sojourns through Galloway, either in 1139–42 or in 1148 when he established a Cistercian house at *Viride Stagnum*, he certainly would have come in contact with the then bishop in Galloway, Gille-Aldan of Whithorn.[12] Matheus Ua hÉnni, as well as being papal legate and hence in the vanguard of reform, was a Cistercian by training. Forming the background of this text, then, is the testimony of some of the chief reformers of Ireland and one of the reforming bishops of Scotland; three papal legates; three bishops and two archbishops. Stunningly, if his account of their testimonies is to be believed, these pillars of the church have sold our poor author a load of old rope.

It is impossible to get an exact fix on who has told the author what, but we may start with the various elements which we can discern making up the text.[13] There are, perhaps, only two items which actually pertain to St Cuthbert, the supposed subject of the piece. One is a quite vague, misogynistic miracle, in chapter xxix, which has Cuthbert disperse a distracting woman in a puff of smoke.[14] In a more specific item in chapter xxiii, our hero, whom, failing other options, we must call Cuthbert, is sent by his uncles, both bishops (Meldanus and Eatanus, the latter presumably loosely based on Eata, the historical tutor of Cuthbert)[15] to be fostered with a man of Lothian (*vir Lodonicus*) in a place later called Childerschirche. This is Channelkirk now, in the valley of the river Leader, which was dedicated to St Cuthbert, and can be connected with the anonymous Life's account of the saint which describes him tending sheep in the Lammermuirs above the Leader.[16]

This item, which does seem to relate to the cult of Cuthbert proper, brings to an end part of the narrative, and seems to mark a juncture in the text, perhaps the end of the section based around the material from the *quaterniuncula* which the author describes coming across in the Preface. It is the culmination of a long sequence, interrupted by the author for extra testimonies, which sees our hero born and raised in Ireland, baptized at Ardbreccan in Co. Meath as *Mulucc* (ch. ix), journeying to Argyll via Galloway (the account gives a confused dovetailing of versions of this in chs xiii–xx), where he is then fostered with Columba, bishop of Dunkeld (ch. xxi), before being sent by his uncles to Lothian (ch. xxiii). As it stands, this seems to be at least partially a narrative concerning St Mo Luóc, or Moluag, founder of Lismore in Argyll, who died in 592.[17] His name, and certain

Table 12.1. Libellus de nativitate Sancti Cuthberti: structure and suggested sources

Preface, etc	Traditions of Moluag	Traditions of Adomnán	Twelfth-century miracle	Traditions of Cuthbert?
Preface sources=bishops, Eugenius, Matheus, Malachy, Gilbert, Alan	**chs i–viii** (conception and birth)			
	ix–x baptism in Ardbreccan as Mulucc/Muluhoc			
	xi–xii ?Eugenius of Ardmore: child born in Kells			
	xiii–xviii flight to Britain; underwater adventure; loss of gospel and recovery			
	xix–xx leaves Galloway for Letherpen in Argyll			**xix** legends of Irish, Scots and Galwegians: stone currach to Rintsnoc in Rhinns of Galloway
		xxi ? sent to Columba, bishop of Dunkeld for fosterage, with Brigit from Ireland; jealous English clerics		
		xxii ? Brigit returns to Ireland; boy and mother go to Iona; uncles (Scottish bishops) wards of boy		**xxii** Cuthbert given by uncles to holy main in Lothian; church called Childerschirche
		xxiv–xxv Cuthbert at Dull and Weem	**xxvi** miracle of 'St Cuthbert' at Dull/Weem: Madet Maccrie Mor	
		xxvii refutes king's daughter at Corruen (nr. Dull?)	**xxviii** tale of hermit Ralf de Nuers, in Moddri, nr. Gedworth (Bedfordshire)	**xxix** Cuthbert disperses a tempting woman

Explicit
methodology; sources –
Malachy to David; Maurilius abp;
Eugenius bp of Ardmore

circumstantial details, such as the saint's arrival in the vicinity of Lismore, make this certain. Indeed, the episodes in Dunkeld could easily be part of the same original narrative, as Lismore was in the twelfth century part of the diocese of Dunkeld, and in 1183 x 1189 – about the time when this *Libellus* appears to have been written – it became the see of the new bishopric of Argyll.[18]

So part of the narrative concerns Moluag, not Cuthbert. It may well be this narrative which we should link to the testimony of Malachy and Gilbert, since Moluag was traditionally and probably correctly linked with Bangor, the home of both these clerics in the 1140s. Indeed, our main source for the link between Bangor and Moluag is Malachy himself, as in St Bernard of Clairvaux's account of the saint he tells us of the early history of Bangor, including 'one of the sons of that holy community, Luanus by name' who is said to have been 'the founder . . . of a hundred monasteries' in both Ireland and Scotland.[19] Bernard certainly knew these traditions largely through Malachy. The idea that the spine of the 'Irish birth' narrative should be an account based on Moluag, and provided by Malachy, sits well with the description of Malachy's role as described in the Explicit.

Interpolated into the narrative of Moluag in the *Libellus* are various pieces of flotsam and jetsam. Archbishop Matheus offers a short miracle story (ch. xi), concerning the breaking of a little bell, 'called a *kelim* in their language', we are told, and hung in Irish fashion about the boy's neck. This is undoubtedly from *ceólán*, attested both as a name and as a common word for a hand-bell.[20] The story finishes with the boy's miraculous assistance of a smith in repairing it. This story is labelled *Assercio Mathiae Archiepiscopi*.

Immediately following this chapter comes Bishop Eugenius' testimony (ch. xii), which has a fine description of the monastery of Kells, in which, supposedly, the boy was born, and where there was a thriving tourism industry related to him. We are told that Eugenius knows this because he himself was born and raised and educated there. He nonetheless intrudes a plug for his own diocese, Ardmore ('And in his [Eugenius'] episcopal see rests St Declanus [*sic leg.* for *Tedanus*] the bishop, the marvellous raiser of nine dead persons and the worker of many miracles, which while he lived illumined the land'), but cannot resist giving the best compliments to his native country ('the province of his fathers was more famous and more remarkable for fertility than all the other regions of Ireland'). The only other information from Eugenius is given in the opening Preface, where he is quoted as affirming the story of Cuthbert's Irish birth, to a king called *Muriadach* (Muiredach) and a mother *Sabina* (Sadb): these names do not reappear in the rest of the narrative. It may be worth noting that the later creators of the Durham window-cycle employing parts of the *Libellus* misunderstood Eugenius' role and cast him as the bishop who baptized the infant Cuthbert.[21]

The saint's journey to Scotland from Ireland is also fraught with interpolations. In chapter xv we are told: 'Some things must now be interpolated, which are found in the Irish histories (*in hystoria Hybernentium*) and must not be omitted, although they seem to be incredible.'[22] In what follows, up to chapter xviii, several sea-journey stories are told, including the loss of a Gospel overboard, which is eventually restored by a seal (this is reminiscent of the tale told in the history of the wanderings of the monks of Cuthbert),[23] and the adventure the boy has when he goes underwater to free the anchor, and meets an underwater resident, a *heros*, who gives him various vases, which are given allegorical interpretations in chapter xvii. This adventure is very close in form to one described in notes added to the Irish *Liber Hymnorum* and the *Martyrology of Oengus*, relating to St Brigit's monks who acquire a marvellous order or rule and a bell from a submerged oratory under the English Channel en route to Rome to get new liturgical services.[24]

Finally, in chapter xix, before the boy gets to Argyll, yet more extra stories are interpolated: 'we will not be silent about vulgar traditions and beliefs. The Irish, the people of Galloway, and the Scots (*Hybernenses, tam Galwienses et Scotti*) all say . . .'. The author here relates a tale concerning a stone currach in which the boy is placed, which sails away to Galloway 'in that district which is called the Rhinns (*Rennii*), at the port which is called Rintsnoc. At which port on the shore the strong *curroc* of St Cuthbert may be seen.'[25] This is material which could best have come from a Galloway source. There are two possibilities for his source of this account. One is that his Bishop Alan, for whom I believe the only sensible candidate is Gille-Aldan, bishop of Whithorn, had informed him of this. If we are to take the author at his word and imagine that the named authorities all did contribute something, then this intervention suits Gille-Aldan best. The other possibility is that the 'priests and disciples of St Malachy' included the community he established at *Viride Stagnum*, which was perhaps, though it is not certain, the same site as later housed the Premonstratensian abbey of Soulseat. Malachy's community may not have lasted much longer than a few years, and Dodds makes the plausible suggestion that the members of the community may have been incorporated in its sister monastery at Melrose, or perhaps Dundrennan, after it foundered. Soulseat is not very far from the site, which cannot be pinpointed, of the port of Rintsnoc, in the Rhinns of Galloway.[26]

However, the author then has our hero take another ship to Argyll, and he gives quite specific coordinates for where he lands: 'another port called *Letherpen* in *Erregaithle*, which is the land of Gaels (*terra Scottorum*)'. That port is between *Erregaithle* (Argyll) and *Incegal* (Innse Gall: the Hebrides), near a loch which is called *Loicafan*. It cannot be certain, but aside from Lismore itself, which does not really suit the description, the nearby port of Oban seems the most likely site: the modern Gaelic name *an t-òban*, derived from a Norse loanword, merely means 'the port', and it is, indeed, situated in Argyll, but looks out to the Hebrides, and is near to Loch Awe, which must be intended by *Loicafan*.[27]

This part, then, would appear to come from a narrative originally concerning Moluag. I have suggested that the subsequent two chapters, which are chronologically the most hair-raising, may also come from such a narrative. Here Cuthbert is sent to Dunkeld, to be educated by 'St Columba, the first bishop of Dunkeld', and extraordinarily he studies alongside 'a little girl from Ireland called Brigit'.[28] Some brief adventures occur here, and then Brigit returns to Ireland, and Cuthbert's mother goes to Iona, and then to Rome, leaving him in the care of his uncles, who send him to Lothian. This ends the first section of the text.

Abruptly, after the rubric at the end of chapter xxiii 'Here ends the Little Book of the Birth of St Cuthbert taken and translated from Irish histories', chapters xxiv–xxvii shift to a new setting, and once again to a fairly identifiable source. Here, Cuthbert sets out for Scotia (*terra Scotica*), and becomes a hermit at Dull, in Perthshire. He further withdraws to a nearby location called Doilweme – this is Weem, some two miles from Dull, and within its parish originally. Certainly Weem Hill, the location of the stories, is still within the parish of Dull. The miracles stories here involve Cuthbert making his mark on the landscape: a spring and footprints are credited as still being visible and associated with the saint. However, we know the saint who really was the patron of Dull, and whose footprints, well and other landscape features were to be seen there. He is the patron of many of the local places in this part of Atholl: Adomnán, ninth abbot of Iona, for whom there is enough circumstantial evidence to suggest he has an actual historical association with Glen Lyon and the area around Dull.[29] As with Moluag, for whatever reason, the author has here appropriated miracles associated with another saint in order to build up a quite different profile of St Cuthbert. It should be noted here that the chapters relating to Cuthbert's time in Dunkeld could also plausibly be derived from a stratum of Atholl-oriented traditions about Adomnán.

This extends to two further miracles. Both of these belong to a misogynist strain in this latter section of the *Libellus* which matches other texts of the eleventh and twelfth centuries. In the second of these miracles at Dull, the saint makes the earth swallow up a king's daughter who had falsely accused him of fathering her child, at an unidentified place called *Corruen*. The more interesting miracle is one of two more clearly contemporary ones. It involves a man called *Madet Maccrie Mor* in the text, and described as a *comes Scotiae*, in the reign of David I. This is very clearly Matad mac Mael Muire, although the text mangles his name, the mormaer of Atholl, and thus the local authority. Matad was also the father of Harold Maddadson, earl of Orkney.[30] Dull is described here as a sanctuary, but also as forbidden to women, and the miracle involves the punishment of Matad for bringing his wife and daughters there.

Finally, one last source adds another twelfth-century miracle. This relates to a hermit called Ralf de Nuers, in the forest of Moddri near Bedford. We hear of this hermit from local Bedfordshire land grants, which would seem to confirm that it is Bedford the Life refers to, and we should reject the reading *Gedworth* (that is, Jedburgh) in one of the manuscripts.[31] He has an experience of the protection of St Cuthbert in his hermitage, which we are told used to be St Cuthbert's. This is somewhat unlikely in Bedfordshire but, as we have seen, the text is a mass of borrowings from miracles of other saints, and it may be that a miracle relating to this hermit and another saint has been appropriated here.

And that is the end, more or less, of the very disjointed *Libellus*. It remains to provide some general assessment of it. First, its importance. What this text does is show us a very journalistic hagiographer at work, one who has been unable or unwilling to cover over the cracks in his narrative. As a result, we have a startling and discomfiting insight into one hagiographer's methodology. It is a pretty undiscerning one, and admits all sorts of legends and accounts which do not square at all with the historical sources concerning Cuthbert, and which must have been abundantly available to the author. He does not even make an attempt to dovetail his narrative into those other, better-known accounts of St Cuthbert.

His methods and sources have two important ramifications for the history of this period. First, they demonstrate the nature of the relationships between the various strands of the reforming churchmen of Scotland and Ireland.[32] Although St Bernard of Clairvaux's Life of St Malachy provides some sense of intercommunication between Ireland and Scotland in the 1140s (Malachy meets Waltheof, later abbot of Melrose, and David I, the reforming king), the *Libellus* is testimony to a larger range of more informal contacts. As such, it shows one of the real pivotal features of the period of ecclesiastical change in Scotland between 1000 and 1300: increased communication and interaction with churchmen from all parts of Europe as well as Ireland.

Second, his methods show a feature which we can meet elsewhere, the outside hagiographer doing his best with the poor materials with which he was confronted in providing a hagiography for the Scottish churches. However, since our author shows us the seams in his patchwork, he provides for us an excellent overview of a type of magpie hagiography which may have been more common than the more expert seamsmanship of other hagiographers, such as Jocelyn of Furness, allows us to see. Our author did not trouble to conceal his sources or smooth his narrative into a relatively consistent story. Instead, it is plain to us how and whence he has put his elements together. As such, the *Libellus* is instructive: it cautions us, and scholars still seem to need cautioning, against reading Lives such as Jocelyn of Furness's Life of St Kentigern as if they are likely to be history. Equally, it cautions against the 'alchemical' approach taken by some scholars towards hagiographical sources, in which individual elements are precipitated out of the leaden solution, and attempts are made to turn these into nuggets of historical gold. In the case of Cuthbert, we can easily demonstrate that our author's individual elements are just as leaden as the overall amalgam, since we have much better hagiographical and historical *comparanda*. With Scottish saints like Kentigern or Serf or even Moluag, for whom we have scarcely any other stabilizing sources, we construct ecclesiastical history from such elements at our peril.

That does not mean that the individual elements of the *Libellus* are worthless. As has been shown, at least two major sections of the *Libellus* are drawn from the legends of other saints, and drawn so obviously that we are forced to confront this manifest larceny. But this pinching of other saints' legends is valuable to us here, because they preserve traditions of those saints nowhere else preserved. We have no Life of Moluag, who was certainly one of the most important Scottish saints in terms of early medieval cults, both in the north-west and also in the north-east, where Gaelic immigration in the ninth or tenth century may have brought with it local western saints' cults such as that of Moluag.[33]

We have only one other source of any length concerning Moluag: the readings for the feast of the saint in the Aberdeen Breviary.[34] Strikingly, although these differ in a number of instances from the account in the *Libellus*, there is some overlap, suggestive of the possibility that the Breviary readings are based either on the *Libellus* or on a source very like it. In the Breviary, Moluag (*Molocus*) is said to have been trained by St

Brendan (this perhaps derived from overlapping cults in the west); a description of Moluag building churches while his fellow students built secular houses seems to match the incident in chapter xxiii, where, while being trained at *Childerschirche* (Channelkirk), Cuthbert builds toy churches while his classmates build houses.[35] Then follows a story concerning his miraculous helping of a smith to forge a bell for him, plainly modelled on chapter xi, the testimony of Archbishop Matheus. Then we are told of his wishing to travel from Ireland to Scotland, but having been denied a ship, he takes himself off on a stone to Lismore in Argyll. This is close to our chapter xix, but leaves out the journey to Galloway. He cannot convert the locals, so he leaves for Melrose, returning later to Lismore, and thence to Ross, where he died and was buried.

The Breviary appears to have adapted the *Libellus* acount to what was known about the cult of St Moluag, as witness the final journey to Ross. More mysterious is the inclusion of a journey to Melrose – I will return to this in a moment. But all in all, this makes what is preserved in the *Libellus* an early account of the legends of St Moluag, however compromised they may be. I am not suggesting for a moment that they provide us with a historical account of Moluag; rather, they add to a fairly poor stock of twelfth-century or earlier hagiography from Scotland, by which we could potentially deepen our understanding of the development of saints' cults.

Likewise with the stories relating to St Adomnán: as is well known, we have a tenth-century Irish Life of Adomnán,[36] which draws partly on Iona material for some of its stories; we also have a mass of fairly late legend relating to the activities of Adomnán in Glen Lyon. But the *Libellus*, uniquely, provides a narrative to connect with Adomnán's patronage of the parishes of Dull and Weem, and sites within them. As such it is a valuable testimony to the sorts of stories people were telling about Adomnán in the twelfth century or earlier. Notable among them is the miracle relating to the historical figure of Matad, earl of Atholl, a person we know well from charters and other twelfth-century documents. So despite his adaptation of all these sources to the character of St Cuthbert, our author's method has left us with some additional sources for the hagiographical traditions of Argyll and Atholl in the twelfth century and before.

As a final incidental note, the author's sense of Scottish geography is worthy of some attention. He carefully differentiates between Irish, Scots and Galwegians (ch. xix: *Hybernenses; Scotti; Galwienses);* between Argyll and the Hebrides (ch. xix: *Erregaithle; Incegal)*; between Argyll and Scotia (chs xix–xx: *Erregaithle, terra Scottorum; Scotia*), between Lothian and Scotia (cf. ch. xxiii: *vir Lodonicus;* ch. xxiv: *terra Scotica*). This is a fairly nuanced geography, and one, I would suggest, which contributes to a sense of a Scottish place of composition for the work. On the other hand, some separate strands of the *Libellus* show a penchant for idiosyncratic terminology. So, in the sections based in Atholl, there are several references to *fines Pictorum* and *patria Pictorum* (chs xxvi and xxvii), and close attention to these might help to separate these strands out further.

It remains to consider, briefly, whether we can say anything useful about who the author was, and where he was writing. Two arguments have been offered in the past: neither seems precisely to answer the questions posed by the text's structure. Richard Sharpe has recently argued that the author was a Durham man (on account of the manuscript tradition), and indeed that he was Reginald of Durham, who earlier in the century composed a fine book on the miracles of St Cuthbert. As noted above, this point had been made in the previous century by Healy, who noted moreover that one of the main manuscripts of the *Libellus* also contains Reginald's own *Libellus de . . . Cuthberti virtutibus.*[37] Sharpe takes the Preface to describe two *Libelli*, one which the author had prepared previously; the other comprised of the *Libellus de nativitate* itself. As far as I can determine, this is not what the Preface says; rather it is an account of the germination of one *Libellus*, based partly on the author's collecting of miracles, and partly on the *quaterniuncula* he came across, with further, later testimonies added in.

More to the point, the structure and style of our *Libellus* is much inferior to the work of Reginald elsewhere: if it was he, we must take it either that he was extremely old when he wrote the work, or that his doubts about the veracity of the subject made him engage in a sort of damning by faint rhetoric. Certainly there is no sign of the distinctive moralizing so prominent in Reginald's own work. Most problematic, however, is that nowhere in the *Libellus* does Cuthbert come in contact with Durham, Lindisfarne or any other Northumbrian locale outside those which would have been within the hegemony of the kings of Scots in the twelfth century. The farthest south he gets is Lothian, excepting the miracle of Ralf de Nuers, in Bedfordshire, which is hardly germane to a case for Durham authorship either. There is nothing within the *Libellus* to connect Cuthbert the character with Cuthbert the saint of Durham. We may contrast this with the later work of window-cycle makers in Durham and York, who used the *Libellus*, dovetailing it with the more conventional material about Cuthbert's youth and manhood.[38] So the internal evidence suggests that Durham is not the place of composition; the fact that many manuscripts of the Life are found there is easily explained by other means. All the manuscripts are of the fourteenth century, and their inclusion of the *Libellus* was provoked merely by the voracious interest in things relating to Cuthbert there. The material from the *Libellus*, acquired by Durham scribes, bedded thoroughly into local tradition, as witnessed by the window-cycle in the cloister, and the repetition of the miracle which took place at Corruen (probably in Atholl), in the late sixteenth-century collection of Durham folklore.[39] There must also have been manuscripts of the *Libellus* available in Scotland, however: the Aberdeen Breviary, and John of Fordoun and Walter Bower all seem to have known of its traditions. All this suggests that the dominance of the Durham manuscript tradition is not a clear pointer to the *Libellus* having been composed there.

Madeleine Dodds suggested, on the other hand, that the author was a monk of Melrose.[40] Melrose in the twelfth century was a recently founded Cistercian monastery in the south-east of Scotland, and had historical connections to St Cuthbert, but was linked fairly firmly to Scottish interests. Composition at Melrose would explain the Cistercian connections in the personnel of its sources; a good figure to examine is Waltheof, abbot of Melrose from 1148–59. He had met Malachy in York in 1140 and he had been for a time in an abbey in Bedfordshire, which could be the source of the miracle of Ralf de Nuers.[41] (Though equally, since the *Libellus* provides the detail that Ralf de Nuers was professed in the diocese of Lichfield, the miracle could have come through Bishop Eugenius, who had been a suffragan there in the 1180s.[42]) The Cistercian house in Galloway founded by Malachy seems to have been short-lived. The suggestion that some of its Cistercians moved to Melrose seems very plausible: this might account for the 'priests and monks of St Malachy' who are mentioned as sources. One other detail adds to the plausibility of a Melrose connection, either for the *Libellus* as a whole or for the *quaterniuncula*, with its recycling of traditions of Moluag. This is the Aberdeen Breviary version of these Moluag traditions, in which he goes to Melrose and takes vows there. This does not, admittedly, appear in the *Libellus*, but it suggests that the Breviary's source of this material was Melrose.

This line of reasoning could certainly suggest a Melrose provenance for the original *quaterniuncula* which the author says he found, which was based, as he implies, on the testimony of Malachy and, we might infer, Gille-Aldan, Gilbert and others whose floruit was between 1140 and 1154. The story was, we are told, expounded by Malachy to king

David. But there is clearly a second strand to the material: the added testimony of the two Irishmen, Eugenius, bishop of Ardmore, and Matheus, archbishop of Cashel. These must have contributed to the work in the late 1180s and 1190s, judging by their floruits: indeed, Matheus was not archbishop of Cashel until 1186, and not papal legate until 1192. Likewise, as noted above, the author consistently refers to Malachy as *Sanctus Malachias*, suggesting, as Dodds noted, that the text post-dates his canonization in 1190. Our author has also added a fair amount of material from traditions concerning Adomnán: these have been culled from elsewhere, perhaps from the 'Scottish books' he mentions.

By this analysis, then, we are dealing with an ecclesiastic, working in the 1190s, who based his work on a text originally composed in the 1140s or 1150s, perhaps in Melrose. Our author had a devotion to St Cuthbert, suggesting that he too belonged to a monastery with some connection to the saint, which might include many in the southern borders. He had access to two high-status Irish churchmen, though Eugenius had been for a time in England. And he had access to and an interest in northern legends, from Atholl. He also had access to traditions from Galloway. What this suggests is that we are dealing here with an essentially Scottish text, not a Durham one. Written perhaps in Melrose, but certainly somewhere in the area with a devotion to St Cuthbert (the south-west is also possible), the material gives us a broad sense of hagiographical research, of the connections between Ireland and Scotland, and of the development of saints' cults in the twelfth century.

Whatever its authorship, this text's most important implications are in the form of warnings. Hagiographers of the twelfth century could be sober historians, but they could also be magpies. The sources of their anecdotes could be recycled more than once, through several different forms of discourse and testimony. Not even the most venerable of the twelfth-century reformers was trustworthy when it came to a good anecdote or to promoting the importance of his own home patch.

Notes

[1] The only edition is Raine (ed.), 'Libellus'; a summary translation and commentary is in Dodds, 'The Little Book'. On the veracity of its account see Skene, *Celtic Scotland*, vol. 2, pp. 203–7; Healy, 'St Cuthbert'; Grosjean, 'Alleged Irish origin'. Modern accounts are in Sharpe, 'Irish annals'; Bartlett, 'Cults'. Sharpe is at work on a new edition.

[2] For the manuscripts see Raine (ed.), *Miscellanea Biographica*, pp. viii–xi; Craster, 'Red Book of Durham', p. 507.

³ Dodds, 'The Little Book'.

⁴ Sharpe, 'Irish annals', pp. 138–9. The idea was first mooted, I believe, by Healy, 'St Cuthbert', p. 9. Dáibhí Ó Cróinín, following Dennis Bethell, says the author was Laurence of Durham, but neither explains this (chronologically impossible) attribution: 'Augsburg Gospel Codex', p. 190, n. 4; cf. Bethell 'English monks', p. 123, n. 79.

⁵ Sharpe and Healy understand the *libellus* which the author mentions completing and circulating to his friends as an entirely different text, i.e., Reginald of Durham's *Libellus de admirandis beati Cuthberti virtutibus*: see Raine (ed.), *Reginaldi*.

⁶ Bartlett, 'Cults', p. 73; Sharpe, 'Irish annals', pp. 138–9.

⁷ Raine (ed.), 'Libellus', p. 64; trans. based on Dodds, 'Little Book', pp. 65–6.

⁸ Raine (ed.), 'Libellus', pp. 86–7; trans. closely follows Dodds, 'Little Book', p. 93. I suspect that the reference to two names 'dropping out' (presumably those of *Gilibertus* and *Alanus*), represents a flaw in the textual transmission, which may be resolved by recourse to a wider variety of MSS.

⁹ It has been suggested in the past that this was the Cistercian Albinus (Ailbe Ua Mael Muad), bishop of Ferns from 1192 to 1223: see Dodds, 'Little Book', p. 56; Healy, 'St Cuthbert', p. 11; for Albinus' hagiographical activities see Ó Riain, 'St Abbán'; Bartlett, 'Cults', p. 77. However, Gille-Aldan sits better in the nexus of relationships outlined below.

¹⁰ On Matheus, see Gwynn, *Irish Church*, pp. 143–54. He discusses the variant names of the archbishop, Matheus and Mauricius (*sic leg.*?), in contemporary documents, and his Gaelic name, Muirgius, p. 143.

¹¹ Dodds, 'Little Book', p. 55.

¹² Gwynn, *Irish Church*, pp. 125–43; Watt, *Church*, pp. 1–27; Lawlor (ed.), *Life of St Malachy*, §§35, 40, 68. For the problems regarding the location of *Viride Stagnum*, usually identified with Soulseat in Galloway, see Cowan and Easson, *Medieval Religious Houses: Scotland*, pp. 78–9.

¹³ See Table 12.1 for a breakdown of elements and origins.

¹⁴ On this element in the Cuthbert dossier see Tudor, 'Misogyny'; *idem*, 'Cult of St Cuthbert', pp. 456–7.

¹⁵ Though see the interesting comment of Healy, who links them with Mellán and Aedán of Inis Moccu Chéin, in Co. Galway: Healy, 'St Cuthbert', p. 15.

¹⁶ MacKinlay, *Ancient Church Dedications*, p. 248; Colgrave (ed.), *Two Lives*, pp. 68–9.

¹⁷ *AU*, s.a. 592. On the cult of Moluag in eastern Scotland see Penelope Dransart's chapter below.

¹⁸ Cowan and Easson, *Medieval Religious Houses: Scotland*, p. 210.

¹⁹ Lawlor (ed.), *Life of St Malachy*, p. 28.

²⁰ *DIL*, s.v. ceólán.

²¹ Fowler, (ed.) *Rites of Durham*, pp. 75–7: 76.

²² Raine (ed.), 'Libellus', p. 74.

²³ Arnold (ed.), *Historia Ecclesiae*, p. 67.

²⁴ Stokes and Strachan (eds), *Thesaurus*, vol. 2, p. 329; Stokes (ed.), *Félire Óengusso*, pp. 64–7.

²⁵ On *Rintsnoc* see Watson, *History*, pp. 157, 515.

²⁶ Cowan and Easson, *Medieval Religious Houses: Scotland*, pp. 78–9; Dodds, 'Little Book', p. 59.

²⁷ Skene thought that the port was either at Lochmelfort, near Loch Avich; or at Crinan: *Celtic Scotland*, vol. 2, pp. 203–4.

²⁸ On the intrusion of Brigit into the narrative see Bartlett, 'Cults', p. 75.

[29] Taylor, 'Iona abbots', pp. 57–60, 68–9; Watson, *History*, p. 415.

[30] Anderson, *Early Sources*, vol. 2, pp. 139–40.

[31] Doubleday and Page (eds), *Bedfordshire*, vol. 1, pp. 350–1. The evidence of the foundation charter of Beaulieu Priory shows that it 'was founded between 1140 and 1146 upon the site of a hermitage at Moddry in the parish of Clophill, granted to Ralf the hermit by Henry d'Albini', p. 351. For the Gedworth (*Gedewortha*) reading see Craster, 'Red Book', p. 507, n. 4.

[32] This aspect of the hagiography of the period is expertly explored by Bartlett, 'Cults'.

[33] For Moluag and his cult see Forbes, *Kalendars*, pp. 409–11; Watson, *History*, pp. 292–3; MacKinlay, *Ancient Church Dedications*, pp. 157–60; and see Penelope Dransart's chapter below.

[34] Blew (ed.), *Breviarium Aberdonense, pars estiv.*, fol. v.a–viii; summarized in Forbes, *Kalendars*, p. 410.

[35] However, see also the related story in the anonymous Life of Cuthbert, Colgrave (ed.), *Two Lives*, pp. 64–5.

[36] Herbert and Ó Riain (eds), *Betha Adamnáin*.

[37] See above, n. 4.

[38] Fowler (ed.), *Rites of Durham*, pp. 75–7; *idem*, 'St Cuthbert window'; *idem*, 'St Cuthbert window (additional notes)'.

[39] Fowler (ed.), *Rites of Durham*, pp. 35–6, 75–7.

[40] For her arguments, which she admits are circumstantial, see Dodds, 'Little Book', pp. 56–60.

[41] Ibid., p. 92.

[42] We might even speculate that the author of the *Libellus* had himself been in Lichfield diocese for a time, where he both met Eugenius and came across the miracle of Ralf de Nuers.

13
Saints, stones and shrines: the cults of Sts Moluag and Gerardine in Pictland

><

PENELOPE DRANSART

The material culture connected with the cult of saints that I consider here dates largely from the eighth to tenth centuries. Of this material, the shrine fragments are more certainly connected with saints' cults than the symbol stones. Chronologically it is separated from the surviving literary evidence that connects the find-spots with the names of specific saints. I note with interest Mary-Ann Constantine's comment that it does not take much for a functional cult to survive – name and place are sufficient.[1] Here I wish to examine the conjunction of saint's name, place and the presence of antiquities in the locality. My research focuses on the medieval dioceses of Aberdeen and Moray, concentrating in the former on St Moluag (Mo Luóc) and his associations with Mortlach, Clatt and Clova, and in the latter on St Gerardine (Gervadius) at Kinneddar. Instead of dealing with hagiographies in the strict sense of the word, I prefer to discuss what I call hagiographic traditions. This will allow me to stress the importance of material culture (such as shrines for saints' relics) and place-names in the reworking of saints' Lives where the hagiography has apparently been lost. I think it is important to recognize that the process of constructing hagiographical traditions has been at work until the present, since it has implications for the way we understand the past.

A sparse number of written records concerning the Lives of the saints have survived from eastern Scotland. They are all late medieval in date. The earliest consists of the Lives of saints written in metrical verse in a vernacular dialect dating from about 1400. It has been suggested that the dialect was that of Aberdeen, but the editor of the Scottish Text Society version found in it evidence for forms of 'pronunciation other than that of Aberdeen'.² The chief source for the Lives is the *Legenda Aurea*, but other sources were also used. Material for the two Scottish saints included in the book of metrical verse, St Ninian and St Machar, was shared between the two men. Metcalfe noted that there are two 'almost identical' passages in their respective Lives.³ Evidently the compiler relied on a now lost copy of a Latin Life of St Machar, remnants of which have survived in the Aberdeen Breviary.⁴ St Machar was an Irish saint and a follower of St Columba. His cult developed in what was to become the burgh of Old Aberdeen, to where the cathedral was transferred from Mortlach.

Short notices of the lives of saints and a calendar of their feasts as celebrated in Scotland were listed in the Martyrology of Aberdeen.⁵ This compilation was perhaps assembled shortly before the production of the Aberdeen Breviary (*Breviarium Aberdonense*). From at least the seventeenth century, the Aberdeen Breviary has been acknowledged to be the most important source for the Lives of Scottish saints. Historians remind us that it was Scotland's first published book,⁶ and the first national breviary to be produced in Europe.⁷ Bishop William Elphinstone, the founder of the University of Aberdeen, oversaw the collection of the material for it in 1509–10, after the issuing of a licence dated 1508 under the Privy Seal to Walter Chepman and Andrew Miller for printing religious books designed for Scottish usage.⁸

We learn from Kelly and Rogers's compilation entitled *Saints Preserve Us!* that we can invoke St Moluag in cases of insanity and headaches.⁹ St Gerardine is not listed. While St Moluag was a saint of national importance throughout much of Scotland, the cult of St Gerardine acquired local importance in Kinneddar, Moray. I know of no other dedications to the saint. The Aberdeen Breviary is the main source for our documentary knowledge about St Gerardine. In contrast, the information the Breviary gave for St Moluag is contested by conflicting versions of his Life that have arisen from memories of the saint in many different local communities.

Commentators tend to assume that the Latin versions of a saint's Life were written before people devised vernacular versions. It is impossible to trace the origins of the oral traditions, yet there must have been a process of interaction between the verbal and written forms. The maintenance of a saint's cult had to do with ritual practices, such as visits to healing wells or making ex-voto offerings to the saint in question. Saints were remembered through the shrines that held the remnants of their bones, hair, clothing or other objects with which they were associated. The ritualized but very physical contact that people had with the relics of their community's saints ensured that the lives of the saints continued to have meaning for them. These practices would have exerted an influence over how people spoke about the saints and, in turn, over the vernacular versions of a saint's Life that emerged through time. Formal hagiographies undoubtedly presented fuller and more detailed versions of the Life and served periodically to fix the verbal forms. We lack completely the detailed textual evidence for written and rewritten hagiographies that has survived in Brittany.[10] Yet the multiplicity of vernacular versions must also have made their mark, with the commissioning of new hagiographies written to replace lost ones, or to spread the cult of the saint further afield.

Adomnan's Life of St Columba is an exceptional document in Scotland, as so very few hagiographies have survived. Yet despite the loss of most of the written texts, people in local communities still remember some of their local saints up to the present, even if only in a vestigial manner. Material culture has contributed towards the maintenance of such hagiographical traditions, in the form of fragments of carved stones and archaeological sites. The very existence of such classes of material presents its own problems, because people can transfer their memories to convenient physical props that they perceive to have been associated with a local saint.

Place-name studies also constitute another form of evidence indicating that an area has a particular focus on a saint. Such evidence may have a surprisingly long-lasting character.[11] In his study of Scottish hagiology, Alexander Boyle commends Watson, author of *The History of the Celtic Place-Names of Scotland*, for the importance of his contribution.[12] Placenames, as Watson explained, often retain the names of saints. The conjunction of archaeological evidence with the names of saints at specific localities provides the basis for cults that have survived into the present, as is the case with Sts Moluag and Gerardine, discussed here.

Moluag / Mo Luóc / Molocus[13]

The name of the saint is derived from *Lugaid, Lughaidh* (Ogam *Lugudeccas*), pronounced Lua, with the endearing suffix *-óc* at the end and the honorific *mo-* as a prefix.[14] He appears in the Irish metrical *félire* or martyrology attributed to Oengus the Céle Dé as 'Moluóc the pure, fair, sun of Lismore of Alba'.[15] Mo Luóc's day is 25 June and he is listed as Bishop and Confessor in the following calendars:

Kalendarium Drummondiense
Junii (25) VII Kalend. In Britannia Sancti Confessoris Moluoc.[16]

Kalendarium de Nova Farina [Ferne]
Junius A vii kl Moloci episcopi.[17]

Kalendarium de Arbuthnott
Junius A vii kl S. Moloci epi & cof. dup fm.[18]

Kalendarium Breviarii Aberdonensis
A vii kl Moloci epi.[19]

Adam King's Kalendar
Ivnii 25 S. Molonache bischop and confess. In Scotland disciple to S. Brandan vnder king Eugenius 4. 629.[20]

Menologium Scoticum (Dempster)
Junius. In Scotia Molonathi episcopi S. Brandani discipuli.[21]

Kalendar of David Camerarius
Junius. 25 die. Sanctus Molonachus sive Moluchus Episcopus & Confessor qui pro viribus in Marria Scotiae prouinciâ proximorum saluti studuit.[22]

In the *Breviarium Aberdonense*,[23] St Molocus is described as a Scot who followed St Brendan. One of his miracles concerned an iron bell, which the saint commissioned, but which the smith said he could not make as he lacked coal (presumably charcoal). Mo Luóc immediately collected a bundle of rushes or reeds to serve as fuel. These were miraculously sufficient to make the bell, which at the time of writing was claimed still to exist in the cathedral church of Lismore. The reference to an iron bell is significant. In Scotland, at least fourteen quadrangular hand-bells have survived, each constructed from a single sheet of iron and coated in bronze. In Ireland, iron bells are thought to date from the seventh to the tenth centuries. Cast bronze hand-bells have a more limited temporal and geographical distribution. Cormac Bourke has suggested that iron bells were associated with monastic churches in Ireland and with the Columban church in Scotland, while the bronze bells might have been employed by churches controlled by Armagh.[24] Some of the hagiographical traditions concerning Mo Luóc indicate that he had a competitive relationship with Columba. If one accepts these traditions, as well as Bourke's suggestion that churches of the so-called 'Columban federation' used iron bells, one would have to accept that the two saints were contemporaries.

Another version of Mo Luóc's origins was given in the Life of St Malachy, where the author, St Bernard, lists him as a follower of St Comgall at Bangor.[25] Although the sources disagree as to whether he was trained by Brendan or Comgall, it seems as though his origin was in Ireland rather than Scotland, as his association with an iron handbell suggests. Macquarrie has pointed out that the Aberdeen Breviary sometimes made claims for Scottishness for saints who were more likely to have been Irish.[26]

The Aberdeen Breviary relates how Mo Luóc sailed from Ireland in the company of a group of men. When they refused to go further to more distant places, the stone on which he stood floated to sea and took him to the island of Lismore. At first the people of Lismore would not listen to his Christian message, and so he went to the abbey of 'Meloros' (*sic*), whose abbot sent him back to Lismore where his mission was successful. If this is a reference to Melrose in the Borders, rather than to another place of the same name such as the Melrose near Macduff, then it is anachronistic. The *Origenes Parochiales Scotiae* reported some sources saying that Mo Luóc was buried at Lismore, while according to other sources his relics were retained there.[27] One of the most important of these is the *bachall mór*, which still exists. It is a plain staff formerly covered with copper. Archibald Campbell, son of the earl of Argyll, granted land on Lismore and the custody of the crosier to John McMolmore Vic Kevir and his male heirs in 1544, in honour of the Blessed Virgin and Mo Luóc.[28] For centuries the Livingstone family, known locally as the barons of Bachall, has held the freehold.

Mo Luóc's associations with Lismore and Rosemarkie have been given more attention in published literature than his links with communities in north-eastern Scotland. Archibald Scott mentioned dedications to the saint in north-eastern Scotland and referred to 'the old tradition [that] he died while visiting his churches in the Garioch'.[29] A modern painting by Amanda Potts depicting Mo Luóc as the bringer of Christianity to the Garioch hangs in the parish church of Chapel of Garioch, Aberdeenshire (Figure 13.1). It makes a visual point that emphasizes beliefs still current in the parish concerning the saint's mission to the area. However, rather than attempting to list all the known associations, my aim here is to examine his associations with Mortlach, Clatt and Clova.

Mortlach
The centre of the diocese that was to be named after Aberdeen was originally at Mortlach, which in more recent times was incorporated into Banffshire. According to tradition, St Moluag of Lismore established a

monasterium at Mortlach in the sixth century. Because some of the Irish annals listed his obit *c*.592,[30] the community of Mortlach has him founding their church about 566.[31]

Evidence of Pictish settlement in Mortlach is attested by a Class I Pictish stone,[32] now inside the church, and a Class II stone known as the Battle stone, which is located in the burial ground by the Dullan Water (Figure 13.3). John Stuart discounted the supposition that the latter 'was erected to commemorate a victory which our second Malcolm is said to have achieved over the Northmen at this place in the year 1010'.[33] The cross-bearing face contains the image of a cross surmounted by fish monsters and forms part of a particularly Pictish visual treatment of the Resurrection.[34] Nearby is Pettyvaich, with the place-name dative-locative of pit + *bàitheach* 'cow-house, byre'.[35] Pit- is a Pictish place-name term for a portion or share of land (from the Low Latin *petia*, 'a piece').[36] As Macdonald and Laing comment, there is 'cumulative evidence' for an early monastic foundation at Mortlach.[37]

In 1063, King Malcolm II reputedly granted the church of Mortlach to Bean, the first of the Aberdeen bishops whose name has survived, for building the episcopal seat.[38] In addition to lands at 'Murtlach' the king granted him the churches of 'Cloveth' (Clova, now in Kildrummy parish) and 'Dulmeth' (Dunmeth, now in Glass). Bean, Denortius and Cormac were the earliest bishops of the diocese to be recorded at the *monasterium*, which is listed as having five associated churches in a papal bull of 1157, including 'Cloveth'.[39] Nechtan, the fourth recorded bishop, transferred the cathedral to Old Aberdeen.[40] According to Ian Cowan, Nechtan (bishop 1131 x 1132) probably moved the site of the see from Mortlach to Old Aberdeen under pressure from Rome as part of the diocesan reorganization instigated by David I.[41]

From the perspective of historians working on the early church before the reforms of David I, Mortlach as an episcopal centre is 'fairly insubstantial'.[42] Academic authors tend to be far more cautious than the confident-sounding notice outside the church implies. Yet Mortlach seems to have retained its importance until at least the fourteenth century, to judge from two unrelated pieces of information. Despite its apparently distant location in the hills, Mortlach was one of the most heavily taxed churches in the deanery of Mar. In the 1275–6 taxation of the churches and benefices in Scottish dioceses known as Bagimond's Roll, Mortlach was taxed at 'lxvjs. viijd'.[43] Within a century its rental was set at 30 merks.[44] This later taxation was the highest to be applied in the whole of the deanery of Mar and it was equalled only by the charges applied to two other churches: Munymusk, and the church and vicarius of Obeyn and Tylynathtlayk. At the other end of the scale, the parish churches at Fetternear, Cloveth and Kyndrochet (now Braemar) were taxed only 3½ merks apiece.[45]

Secondly, in the 1330s, Bishop Alexander de Kininmund constructed an episcopal manor at Mortlach, as part of his grand building programme, which included constructing another manor at Old Rayne, a palace at Old Aberdeen and reconstructing on a larger scale the summer palace at Fetternear.[46] Boece recorded that Kininmund spent Christmas at Mortlach, Easter at Aberdeen, summer at Fetternear and autumn at Old Rayne.[47]

Let us return to Mortlach kirk and the claim by its contemporary parishioners that it was founded in 566. The church's leaflet contains a brief Life of Mo Luóc.[48] It enlarges on the saint's miraculous voyage to Lismore: in his race to reach the holy island before Columba, Mo Luóc cut off his little finger and cast it on to the island so as to claim Lismore as his territory, which he blessed in the name of the Trinity. Columba was forced to go on and as a result he discovered Iona. Now this story is scarcely mentioned in the nineteenth-century scholarly works that deal with Mo Luóc. It is found neither in *OPS* nor in Bishop Forbes's *Kalendars of Scottish Saints*, as though it were beneath their dignity to include it. Needless to say, it was the first aspect of the Mo Luóc story that I heard in my own childhood in Aberdeenshire. The value of the story, I now realize, is that it is a reminder of the relic cult, as though a finger of the saint had been kept and the story sought to explain the existence of the relic. Significantly, Ian Carmichael reported that in Lismore some people thought that the saint's name derived from *mo ludag*, 'my little finger'.[49]

Some early medieval descriptions emphasized the wholeness and incorruptibility of saints' bodies (for instance that of St Cuthbert). Despite the strict Roman municipal laws which forbade the disturbance of coffins, historians such as Jonathan Sumption and Barbara Abou-El-Haj point out that an alternative attitude to bodily relics arose gradually, from at least the second century and especially after the seventh century.[50] Clergy, rulers and pilgrims eagerly sought to obtain parts of saints' bodies. By 1215 the Lateran Council was forced to stipulate that relics be contained in reliquaries. The lack of respect that medieval believers had for the integrity of saints' bodies reminds us that a deceased person who was perceived as a miracle worker and who had been recognized as a saint was no longer treated as an individual. He or she became a *dividual*, whose body might be shared by many different communities of believers. Once those communities had access to saints' relics, they were able to develop their own local histories concerning their saint.[51]

Clatt

The church of Clatt was dedicated to Mo Luóc. It constitutes another instance of an ancient church site originally contained by an elliptical boundary, from within which some Pictish Class I stones have been recovered (Figure 13.2).[52] However, documentary references to the community survive only from much later. According to John Stuart, '[t]he church of Clatt was dedicated to St Moloch, and under the name of the Schira de Clat, the parish formed part of the first possessions of the See of Aberdeen on its translation by King David I'.[53]

James IV made the settlement a burgh of barony in 1501 with a weekly 'mercat' (market) and a yearly St Molloch's fair, which lasted for eight days.[54] In the closing years of the fifteenth century, Clatt probably had a role in the compilation of the Aberdeen Breviary, in the person of the rector of the church, Duncan Scherer. Leslie Macfarlane, the biographer of Bishop Elphinstone, argued that Scherer contributed to compiling or copying the office of St Moluag for Bishop Elphinstone. He observed that in his will Scherer left an annual rent of 13s 4d for the vicars' choral to say mass for his soul on 25 June each year, and that Scherer owned Torquemada's 1485 'Gloss on the Psalter', indicating that he was actively interested in liturgical reform, for which purpose the compilation of the Breviary was intended.[55] After Scherer's death in 1503, one of the bishop's relatives, William Elphinstone, received the rectorship. The new rector might have finished the office of St Moluag if it had been left incomplete.[56]

Therefore, Clatt is another instance of an early church foundation, to judge from the archaeological evidence, with documentary evidence for a late fifteenth- and early sixteenth-century cult of Mo Luóc.

Clova

Clova was styled as the monastery of Cloveth dependent on Mortlach in 1157.[57] In 1869, John Stuart accepted that the ruins of a church and the nearby well, with its local name of Simmerluak's well, preserved 'the connection of Cloveth with the mother church of Mortlach'.[58] W. Douglas Simpson accepted the antiquity of the site, but pointed out that the surviving remains were of the parish church which 'in the Roman fashion was dedicated to St Luke' because of the similarity between the names Luke and Luóc.[59] The presence of antiquities of a medieval date from the site helps to provide cumulative, albeit circumstantial, evidence for the chains of associations that occur between the names of saints and specific locations in the minds of local people (Figure 13.4). Simpson argued that the medieval church replaced the early Christian monastery and the name of the Celtic founder outlived the medieval dedication in the local name Sommiluak or Simmerluak for both the chapel and the well. He pointed out that there was much archaeological evidence from the immediate area, showing evidence for continuity in settlement from the Iron Age and earlier. If he had been writing today, he might have drawn attention to the pit place-name that has survived as the name of a burn (Pitenteach). More recently, doubt has been cast on the existence of an early Christian foundation dedicated to Mo Luóc at Clova. Easson placed the monastery in his 'rejected or doubtful' category.[60] However, locally the archaeological site is still regarded as a 'monastery' and the belief that Pope Boniface IV visited the well is also current.

The reference to Boniface leads to another complication in Mo Luóc's story. Boniface is usually combined with Bishop Curetán, apparently one of the guarantors of the Cáin Adomnáin in 697.[61] This composite figure is sometimes associated with King Nechtan at Restenneth. The Aberdeen Breviary, Hector Boece's *Chronicles of Scotland* (translated into Scots in 1531) and Jhone Leslie's *Historie of Scotland* (translated into Scots in 1596) all report that Mo Luóc joined Boniface in his travels and that both saints were buried in Rosemarkie. Aidan MacDonald pointed out that Roger of Hovenden, who died *c*.1201, wrote: 'It is said, moreover, that in the cathedral church of the bishopric of Ross, which is called Rosemarkie (*Rosmarcin*), Blessed Boniface, the pope, was buried, who was fourth after Blessed Gregory.'[62] To MacDonald this means that St Boniface and Pope Boniface had already been identified with Rosemarkie by the end of the twelfth century.[63]

From an entry in the Martyrology of Aberdeen, it is evident that Rosemarkie had some important relics of Mo Luóc.[64] The Breviary of Aberdeen evidently picked up on Rosemarkie's claim for a pre-eminent position concerning the cult of the saint. Although William Elphinstone was bishop of Aberdeen, the Breviary did not mention Mortlach and other communities in the diocese that associated themselves closely with Mo Luóc. However, Aidan MacDonald observed that Elphinstone had been bishop of Ross (the diocese in which Rosemarkie is situated) from 1481, although he was never formally consecrated.[65] In 1483 he was made bishop of Aberdeen. Leslie Macfarlane thought that Bishop Elphinstone might never have gone to Rosemarkie and that he was probably in Edinburgh during those years. It is perhaps significant that Elphinstone had also previously been archdeacon of Lismore in 1478 and 1479, hence it is likely that he was aware of the importance of Mo Luóc at these different places.[66] Mo Luóc was a saint who was claimed by many different communities whose local versions of the cult probably competed with each other.

St Gerardine / Gervadius[67]

In contrast with Mo Luóc's associations with many different communities, St Gerardine is connected with Kinneddar in the diocese of Moray. He appears as a Confessor in the lists compiled by Bishop Forbes, and his day is 8 November:

Kalendarium Breviari Aberdonensis
Noũeber vii d vi id Geruadii cfes. ix.lc.[68]

Adam King's Kalendar
November 8 S. Geruade confess. and bischope of Murray vnder king Achaius. 812.[69]

Menologium Scoticum (Dempster)
November IIX Elgini Gervadii Moraviensis episcopi, qui sub Achaio rege fœderis cum Gallia perpetuum feriendi autor fuit, & sanctis Alcuino, Clemente, Rabano, & Joanne ad S. Carolam Magnum a mandatis ipse in Scotia substitit, ut populum verbo a exemplo instrueret. [70]

Kalendar of David Camerarius
November 9 [sic] Die. Sanctus Gernadius Episcopus Morauiensis.[71]

Kinneddar was the place where an Irish saint and miracle worker, known locally as St Gerardine, and as the Confessor Gervadius in the Aberdeen Breviary, 'had a stone bed'.[72] He had wolves for helpers, one of them being yoked for ploughing. Bishop Forbes suggested that he died in 934, because the events contained in the Breviary concerned a battle with the English that seemed to indicate the invasion of the north by Æthelstan.[73] However, the evidence is circumstantial, and if he lived earlier, as suggested by Adam King in the above list, his relics might have been placed in one of the shrines that have been recovered from the site. John Stuart named the saint Gernadius (using the spelling of the David Camerarius entry) and mentioned that he had an 'oratory or penance cell in the neighbourhood'.[74]

A Class I Pictish stone was recovered from the demolition of the Kinneddar manse in 1855, and other fragments of Class III stones came from walls surrounding the manse as well as from the old churchyard.[75] A study of these fragments shows that there were at least two, and possibly three, carved stone shrines at Kinneddar. The conventional use of the term 'sarcophagus' is misleading when applied to these Pictish stone structures. They were not long enough to contain the body of a deceased person in a supine position with the legs extended. Charles Thomas preferred the term 'shrine' in his discussions of the sculptured stones from St Ninian's Isle and Papil.[76] Pictish shrines often consist of four corner posts or blocks, which were dug into the ground and supported the four side panels. The earliest Kinneddar shrine is fragmentary. Its iconography is similar to the more complete St Andrews shrine and it perhaps contains a visual reference to the Harrowing of Hell.[77]

The most complete shrine panel from Kinneddar is of an unusual type in which the 'corner blocks' and 'side panel' were carved in one piece (Figure 13.5).[78] In Thomas's typology, it is of a hybrid form.[79] The panel is grooved, like Thomas's Jedburgh type, but it was carved to resemble the separate end panel and corner blocks of a shrine such as St Andrews. Another fragmentary stone from Kinneddar, perhaps originally forming part of the same shrine, is stylistically comparable with a carved stone from Lemanaghan, Ireland,[80] a site that was associated with the cult of St Manchán.

Michael Herity has proposed that three main elements formed the focus of western ecclesiastical foundations: cross-slab, saint's tomb or bed (*leaba*), and rectangular oratory.[81] If the third element existed at Kinneddar, then the oratory probably lies beneath the cruciform church detected in a resistivity survey in the churchyard.[82]

It would seem that Kinneddar had the relics of at least one very important saint for whom the shrine with the David imagery was designed, perhaps in the eighth century, possibly for a royal patron. The stylistically later shrine with its non-figurative imagery and its unusual construction may have replaced this shrine, perhaps in the late ninth or tenth century. Alternatively, the second shrine may have been erected to house the relics of another saint or saints.

St Gerardine is the only saint whose name has been remembered in recent hagiographical traditions in the locality – perhaps the existence of the important stone shrines helped people to keep his cult active, whether or not his relics were housed in them. This made the cult worthy of inclusion in the Aberdeen Breviary. In the nineteenth century, when the burgh of Lossiemouth was established, St Gerardine appeared in the burgh seal and the Church of Scotland dedicated its church there to him.[83]

Concluding comments

Various authors have stressed that hagiographies are not biographies as we understand them, and they are certainly not historical accounts.

Alexander Boyle commented that they were written to 'edify the faithful' or to enhance 'the community of followers who grew up . . . in and around the areas where the saint carried out his [or her] work of evangelisation'.[84] For Aidan MacDonald, hagiography is a special form of literature, one that is likely to have been paralleled by an oral tradition. He urged caution in using hagiographies: 'Whatever use historians and archaeologists may put hagiography to as a quarry of raw material, it must still be treated with consideration, not as failed history or archaeology, but as hagiography.'[85]

Some of the information I have used comes from Hector Boece, the first Principal of the University of Aberdeen, author of *Murthlacensium et aberdonensium espicoporum vitæ*[86] and *Scotorum historiæ a prima gentis origine*. As a historian, he has been accused of peddling 'spurious' or 'unreliable' information. However, Aidan MacDonald has pointed out that he was probably one of the compilers who worked on Bishop Elphinstone's Breviary. In the *Chronicles* he made some attempt to separate the St Boniface–Queritinus figure from Pope Boniface IV, but he still kept them as contemporaries.[87] Instead of regarding him as a failed historian, I prefer to see him as a precursor of Sir James Frazer and *The Golden Bough* in that he assembled a vast array of disparate pieces of information which it was impossible to verify.

As a consequence I find it unsatisfactory to characterize medieval hagiographers as indiscriminate collectors. To regard the learned church leaders who compiled the Latin versions of saints' Lives as being distanced from the mass of common people among whom the anecdotal information circulated is to present medieval culture through the lens of an elite versus popular dichotomy. Church leaders and powerful patrons were precisely the people who provided the material culture, such as the Kinneddar shrines, for housing the relics of saints and promoting the cult of saints. The basis of my chapter has been the material and oral culture, place-names and the documentary sources – these elements form configurations that shift through time, but paradoxically also ensure that certain saints have a cult that still survives in the present. The hagiographies are nourished by memories of the material remains and place-names.

Barbara Abou-El-Haj observed that the medieval cult of saints did not 'unfold as a continuous history'.[88] She examined a class of pictorial hagiographies dating from the eleventh to the thirteenth centuries produced in western European countries, pointing out that there were periods of up to 500 years between the first Lives of the saints and the later versions. This is very much the case in north-eastern Scotland, where we have evidence for Pictish remains and early church sites, but written sources survived in late medieval and Renaissance documents. The carved stones from Mortlach, Clatt and Kinneddar share characteristics with Insular art of the second half of the first millennium as well as displaying particular Pictish designs not found elsewhere in Insular art.

The later Lives were written in Latin or in vernacular Scots dialect. The Aberdeen Breviary resulted from liturgical reforms that Bishop Elphinstone began to instigate in the diocese of Aberdeen in the late fifteenth century. It was designed for Scotland, to replace the Sarum rite that dated back to the thirteenth century.[89] In 1855, David Laing cited evidence for a belief current in the second half of the fifteenth century that Edward I had forcibly imposed the Sarum rite, which excluded most of the Celtic saints people venerated in Scotland, and had ordered the burning of Roman service books.[90] Laing commented that, in reality, Scottish bishops introduced the Sarum rite, not Edward I. Nevertheless, the Aberdeen Breviary was intended to meet the need for providing a liturgy that respected the practices of people in local communities where those saints were (and are) still remembered.

Late fifteenth-century written accounts of saints' Lives purporting to date back to Pictish times do not cast light on the carving of the Pictish monuments. Yet the continued existence of those monuments at places where there was evidently continuity in the veneration of certain saints tends to support the antiquity of the dedications to the saints recorded in the Aberdeen Breviary. People incorporate the presence of antiquities into their understandings of the saints of their locality.[91]

Notes

[1] Discussion at the conference on Celtic Hagiography and Saints' Cults, University of Wales, Lampeter, 8–10 September, 2000.

[2] Metcalfe (ed.), vol. 1, *Legends*, p. xxii.

[3] Ibid., pp. xx–xxi.

[4] Ibid., pp. xix.

[5] Forbes, *Kalendars*, pp. 125–37.

[6] Galbraith, *St Machar's Cathedral*, p. 5; Macquarrie, *Saints of Scotland*, p. 7.

[7] Macfarlane, 'Divine Office', p. 12.

[8] Boyle, 'Some saints' lives', p. 95.

[9] The invocation against insanity comes from the Teampull Mor, dedicated to Mo Luóc, near the Butt of Lewis, where it was recorded in the nineteenth century that 'lunatics' were taken to be cured – they had to walk seven times round the chapel, then they were sprinkled with water from St Ronan's well, after which they were bound and taken to spend the night next to the altar in the chapel (Mitchell, 'Various superstitions', pp. 267–8). Mo Luóc was also invoked for rheumatism. People sat in his 'chair' (a natural rock formation) on Lismore to seek a cure (Carmichael, *Lismore in Alba*, pp. 46 and 61).

[10] Bernard Merdrignac, this volume.
[11] Padel, 'Local saints and place-names'.
[12] Boyle, 'Notes', p. 61. For Watson's discussion of the place-names associated with St Moluag in Aberdeenshire, see his *History*, p. 293.
[13] Moluag is the version of the name that is recognized locally in north-eastern Scotland; Mo Luóc is the spelling, favoured in some academic texts, that makes clearer the etymology of the name, while Molocus is a Latin variant. Moloch and Molloch are other forms that have been used. Bearing in mind that different sources of information are used in this article, including orally collected information and documentary sources, my choice of spelling is sometimes arbitrary, but I always respect the forms used by a particular author when citing directly from his or her text.
[14] Forbes, *Kalendars*, p. 409; Stokes, 'Calendar of Oengus', p. ccxciii; Watson, *History*, p. 292.
[15] 'Iamluoc glangelda/ grian liis [*recte* liss] mor de alba' (Bodleian Rawlinson 505, fol. 215); 'Iamluoc anorba/ grian lismoir de alba' (Bodleian Laud 610, fol. 65); 'Iamluoc glan geldai/ grian liss moir dealbai' (Lebar Brecc, p 90) in Stokes, 'Calendar of Oengus', p. xcv.
[16] Forbes, *Kalendars*, p. 16. 'Calendar of Drummond: June 25 [seventh before Kalends of July]/ In Britain [Feast] of S. Moluoc, Confessor.'
[17] Ibid., p. 72. 'Calendar of New Ferne/ June 25 [seventh before Kalends of July]: [Feast] of [S.] Moloc, Bishop.'
[18] Ibid., p. 101. 'Calendar of Arbuthnott/ June 25 [seventh before Kalends of July]: [Feast] of S. Moloc, Bishop and Confessor; greater double feast.'
[19] Ibid., p. 117. 'Calendar of the Aberdeen Breviary/ June 25 [seventh before Kalends of July]: [Feast] of [S.] Moloc, Bishop.'
[20] Ibid., p. 155.
[21] Ibid., p. 203. 'Scottish (Monthly) Calendar (Dempster)/ June. In Scotland [Feast of] S. Molonathus Bishop, disciple of S. Brandan.'
[22] Ibid., p. 238. 'June, 25th day: S. Molonach or Moluch, Bishop & Confessor, who in the Murray district of Scotland worked with all his might for the salvation of all about him [all in the neighbourhood].'
[23] *Breviarium Aberdonense*, Pars Estiva, fol. v.
[24] Bourke, 'Hand-bells', pp. 465–6.
[25] A seventeenth-century version of the Life of St Malachi records: 'Nempè nobilissimum extiterat ante sub primo patre *Congello* multa millia monachorũ generans, multorum monasteriorum caput . . . ita vt vnus ex filijs sanctæ illius congregationis nomine Luanus, centum solus monasteriorum fundator extitisse feratur' (There is no doubt that it had previously become very notable under its first head, Congellus, producing many thousands of monks, and being the chief among many monasteries . . . so that one of the sons of that holy congregation, named Luan, is said to have been the sole founder of one hundred monasteries), Messingham, *Florilegium*, p. 356. It suits my purpose here to cite this version rather than Bernard's twelfth-century Life, which Messingham presumably used, because I am interested in the reworking of saints' Lives rather than seeking versions claimed to be 'original'.
[26] Macquarrie, *Saints*, p. 8.
[27] Innes (ed.), p. 159, n. 9, hereafter *OPS*.
[28] *OPS*, p. 163. The lands were named as Peynabachalla, or 'pennyland of the bachall' and Peynchallen. See Watson, *History*, p. 266.
[29] A. B. Scott, *Pictish Nation*, pp. 237–8. In his list of north-eastern dedications he gave New Machar, Clatt, Migvie and Tarland, of which only Clatt is in the Garioch. He did not cite any authority to support his reference to 'the old tradition'. The parish

church in Rhynie is also dedicated to Mo Luóc (Macdonald and Laing, 'Early ecclesiastical sites', p. 142).

[30] Stokes (trans.), *Annals of Tigernach*, vol. 1, p. 119.

[31] Mortlach church produced an undated leaflet giving an outline of its history. Moray District Council's Department of Recreation later took over the publication of the same leaflet. It is also undated.

[32] Simpson, 'Notes', pp. 274–5.

[33] Stuart, *Sculptured Stones*, p. 7.

[34] Illustrated in Stuart, *Sculptured Stones*, Plate 14. For a discussion of the treatment of the Resurrection in Pictish art, see Dransart, 'Maiden stone', pp. 16–18, and Dransart, 'Images of bodily resurrection in Pictish art', precirculated paper, *Thinking Through the Body*, University of Wales, Lampeter, 20–2 June 1998. Early Christian understandings of the Resurrection were intimately connected with the cult of saints.

[35] Watson, *History*, p. 411.

[36] Ibid., p. 408.

[37] Macdonald and Laing, 'Early ecclesiastical sites', p. 143.

[38] 'Malcolmus Rex Scotorum . . . hac presenti carta mea confirmasse Deo et Beate Marie et omnibus Sanctis et episcopo Beyne de Murtlach ecclesiam de Murthlach vt ibidem construatur sedes episcopalis' (I, Malcolm, King of Scots [declare that I] have confirmed by this my present charter before God and Blessed Mary and all the Saints, and to Bishop Beyne of Murtlach, the church of Murthlach, so that the episcopal seat may be built there), Robertson, *Collections*, p. 141. The charter is regarded as spurious; see Anderson, *Early Sources*, vol. 1, pp. 433 and 525.

[39] Cowan, 'Medieval church', p. 21.

[40] As recorded by Keith, 1732, in Robertson, *Collections*, p. 141; see also Forbes, *Kalendars*, p. 239.

[41] Cowan, 'Medieval church', p. 23.

[42] Macquarrie, 'Early Christian religious houses', p. 133.

[43] Dunlop, 'Bagimond's Roll', p. 66.

[44] Innes (ed.), *Registrum Episcopatus Aberdonensis*, vol. 2, p. 52; Dunlop, 'Bagimond's Roll', p. 13.

[45] A greater distinction is evident in Pope Nicholas's Taxation of 1290 between richer and poorer parishes in the deaneries of Linlithgow and Fife. St Michael's, Linlithgow, was taxed 110 merks, the Haly Rude, Stirling, 50 merks and Auldcathie and Slamannan 4 merks apiece. See G. Barrow, *Kingship*, p. 74.

[46] Dransart and Bogdan, *Fetternear 1995*, p. 13.

[47] Moir, *Boece's Bishops*, pp. 19–20.

[48] See n. 31, above.

[49] Carmichael, *Lismore in Alba*, p. 35.

[50] Sumption, *Pilgrimage*, pp. 24–31; Abou-El-Haj, *Medieval Cult*, p. 230, nn. 174 and 175.

[51] Saints' relics were often revealed in dreams, which could lead to an unnatural multiplicity of body parts when people in different places dreamt of the same body part. Church councils sought to control such dreams and visions from at least the early fifth century; Sumption, *Pilgrimage*, pp. 26–7.

[52] Allen and Anderson, *Early Christian Monuments*, Part 3, pp. 157–8; Ritchie, 'Sculptured stones of Clatt', pp. 203–4. For the layout of Clatt, see the 25-in. 1866 Ordnance Survey map (Aberdeenshire XLIII.10).

[53] Stuart, *Sculptured Stones*, p. 4. He did not give his sources for this information.

[54] Robertson, *Collections*, pp. 620–1.

[55] Macfarlane, *William Elphinstone*, p. 241.

⁵⁶ Ibid., p. 241.
⁵⁷ Cowan, 'Medieval church', p. 21.
⁵⁸ Stuart, *Book of Deer*, p. ix. He gave as his sources *Breviarium Aberdonense*, Pars Estiva, fol. vi, and Boece, *Scotorum Historiæ*, fol. clxxviii.
⁵⁹ Simpson, *Origins*, p. 21.
⁶⁰ Easson, *Medieval Religious Houses*, p. 194.
⁶¹ Ní Dhonnchadha, 'The guarantor list', p. 191.
⁶² MacDonald, *Curadán*, pp. 29–30.
⁶³ MacDonald has Boniface IV as the third pope after Gregory. The *Acta Sanctorum* lists four names after Gregorius I: 'Savinianus sedit annum I. menses V. dies X. Bonifacius III, sedit mens. VIII. dies XXVIII. Deusdedit sedit annos V. dies XIII. Bonifacius IV. sedit annos XII. mens XI. dies XVII' (Savianus reigned for 1 year, 5 months and 10 days; Boniface III for 8 months and 28 days; Deusdedit for 5 years and 13 days; Boniface IV for 12 years, 11 months and 17 days), Janningus (ed.), *Acta Sanctorum*, vol. 6, Part II, p. 55.
⁶⁴ The entry in the Martyrology of Aberdeen is as follows: 'vij. Kl. Julij [sic] In Scocia Sancti Moloci episcopi cuius reliquie gloriose apud Rosmarky: varie de eo dedicantur ecclesie' (On the seventh day before the Kalends in July in Scotland [is kept the Feast] of S. Moloc, Bishop, whose glorious relics/remains rest at Rosemarkie; various churches are dedicated in his name), Forbes, *Kalendars*, p. 132.
⁶⁵ MacDonald, *Curadán*, p. 27.
⁶⁶ Innes (ed.), *Registrum Episcopatus Glasguensis*, vol. 2, p. 439; Macfarlane, *William Elphinstone*, pp. 79–85.
⁶⁷ Gerardine is the current version of the saint's name that has been known locally since at least the eighteenth century, as reported by Grant and Leslie, *A Survey of the Province of Moray*, p. 122. Gervadius is a version used in documents written in Latin. Bishop Forbes, *Kalendars*, p. 355, suggested that the name might originally have been Garnard or Gartnat. This only remains a suggestion.
⁶⁸ Forbes, *Kalendars*, p. 122. 'Calendar of the Aberdeen Breviary/ November 7 [seventh day before Ides of November]; [Feast] of S. Gervadius, Confessor, nine lessons [i.e. an office of nine lessons – *novem lectionum* is celebrated on his day]'.
⁶⁹ Ibid., p. 167.
⁷⁰ Ibid., p. 218. 'Scottish (Monthly) Calendar (Dempster)/ November 8th at Elgin: [Feast of] Gervadius bishop of Moray, who in the time of king Achaius was author/instigator of a permanent treaty with Gaul/France; & when the blessed Alcuin, Clement, Rabanus & John had been dispatched to the Holy [Roman Emperor] Charlemagne, he himself remained in Scotland to instruct the people by word & example.'
⁷¹ Ibid., p. 242. 'November ninth day. Saint Gernadius Bishop of Moray.'
⁷² Ibid., p. 354; see also Cooper, 'St Gerardine', p. 111.
⁷³ Forbes, *Kalendars*, p. 354–5.
⁷⁴ Stuart, *Sculptured Stones*, p. 40. He gave as his source the *Quarterly Review*, June 1849, p. 113. He thought it the same as the cave referred to in the following terms:
'Another [cavern] behind the village of Lossiemouth had, in ancient times, been formed into a small hermitage not exceeding 12 feet square; it was completed by a handsome Gothic door and window, and commanded a long but solitary view along the eastern shore. These artificial decorations were torn down about 30 years ago by a rude shipmaster, and, in the course of working the quarries, the whole cave has been destroyed. There was a fount in the rock above the hermitage, called St. Gerardine's Well.' For this information he cited Grant and Leslie, *A Survey of the Province of Moray*, p. 122.

[75] Stuart, *Sculptured Stones*, p. 40; Allen and Anderson, *Early Christian Monuments*, Part 3, pp. 142–9 and 507–8.

[76] C. Thomas 'Sculptured stones and crosses', p. 20; *idem*, 'The double shrine "A"', p. 286.

[77] Dransart, 'Two shrine fragments', p. 236.

[78] Ibid, pp. 236–8.

[79] C. Thomas, 'Form and function', pp. 84–5.

[80] Crawford, 'The early slabs at Lemanaghan', p. 156.

[81] Herity 'The layout of Irish early Christian monasteries', p. 105.

[82] Aspinall, Bogdan and Dransart, 'Kinneddar', p. 35. The coastal cave on Holyman Head noted by Stuart has been removed by quarrying. See n. 74 above.

[83] Cooper, 'St Gerardine', p. 105.

[84] Boyle, 'Notes', p. 59.

[85] MacDonald, *Curadán*, p. 4.

[86] Moir (ed. and trans.), *Boece's Bishops of Aberdeen*.

[87] MacDonald, *Curadán*, p. 27.

[88] Abou-El-Haj, *Medieval Cult*, p. 1.

[89] Macfarlane, 'Divine Office', pp. 9–15.

[90] Laing, *Preface*, pp. ix–xi. Laing cited a letter written by Mr Edgar of Rome, secretary to the Old Pretender, which named Hector Boece as one of the authors who implied that Edward I was responsible for the imposition of the Sarum rite, an implication that became more pointed in Bellenden's translation. In *Scotorum historiæ* (fol. cccix, 1527 edition, fol. 298, 1576 edition), Boece said: 'Itaque historias omnes Scotorum, omnia sacrarum juxta atque prophanarum rerum volumina concremari ubique praecipit, magna decreta poena qui præceptum contempsisset Libros Sacros Anglico ritu conscribi jussit, utque eos solos haberent, edixit' (And so issued instructions that all the histories of the Scots and all their books, sacred (or liturgical) and secular alike, should be everywhere burned, prescribing a heavy penalty for any who ignored his command. He gave orders that sacred (or liturgical) books should be compiled according to the English rite, and that these alone should be in use). In his translation of Boece's work, *Heir beginnis the history and croniklis of Scotland*, Bellenden translated the last part thus: 'He gart the Scottis wryte bukis efter the Use of Sarum, and constrainit thaym to say efter that Use' (fol. ccix).

[91] I am grateful to the Moray Society and Susan Bennett, curator of the Elgin Museum, for making it possible for me to examine the Kinneddar stones, and to the British Academy for financial support towards my research. I wish to thank Morton Gauld for the Latin translations.

14
Pre-Reformation saints' cults in Cornwall, with particular reference to the St Neot windows

>≺

JOANNA MATTINGLY

Introduction

The survival of a largely complete pre-Reformation glazing scheme at St Neot church in Cornwall offers a rare opportunity to consider religious belief in a parochial context.[1] The glass mainly dates from the 1480s to the 1530s and donors span all social classes, from local labourers to the earl of Devon, and both sexes. This allows comparisons to be made between elite and popular beliefs. The identification of the St Neot north aisle as a place where local saints' cults were accommodated, in contrast to the international saints and didactic subjects of the south aisle, provides the starting point for this present study.[2] Owing to past restorations, most notably that by Hedgeland in 1825–9, some windows are no longer *in situ* and it has been necessary to use a reconstruction as the basis for what follows.[3]

St Neot was one of Cornwall's early monastic sites and was a minster church of priests and clerks in 1086, but thereafter declined to become an ordinary parish church.[4] Nevertheless, as will be argued here, St Neot remained important as a Cornish cult centre down to and beyond the Reformation, and nearby cult sites are commemorated in its north-aisle windows. As far as is known, Cornish had ceased to be spoken in this area a good two centuries before the windows were installed, and east Cornwall is generally considered to have been the most anglicized part of the county. The present study will consider how the visual evidence of the St Neot windows relates to the large quantity of saints to be found in 'Celtic' areas.[5]

The St Neot glazing scheme and the donors

St Neot is one of Cornwall's largest parishes and comprises over 12,500 acres. It lies in east Cornwall near Liskeard and includes a large part of Bodmin Moor. Domesday manors cluster in the fertile southern part of the parish, bounded on the south by the river Fowey, and the parish was divided into east and west parts by the St Neot river.[6] By the late fifteenth century tin mining was important and a process of gentrification produced many sub-manors. Indeed, St Neot church was largely rebuilt and glazed with tin-generated wealth from the late 1470s to the early 1530s.[7]

Four distinct phases of pre-Reformation glazing can still be identified at St Neot: early fifteenth century, *c*.1480–90, *c*.1500–10 and *c*.1520–30. The west window in the tower could have been part of a still earlier fourteenth-century scheme but is no longer extant, and three dated windows of 1528–30 are part of the final glazing scheme. In view of St Neot's phased enlargement over forty or more years, it is perhaps not surprising that there was no single concerted scheme like that found at Fairford in Gloucestershire or King's College in Cambridge – the only places in England where complete glazing schemes of similar date have survived. Unlike these two Renaissance schemes, the St Neot glass comes from an older, late-medieval tradition.[8]

Individual saints in groups of four predominate at St Neot, with four of the more expensive multi-panelled narrative windows appearing in phases 2–4. Some duplication of themes and subjects does occur, but rarely within a phase. Narrative windows comprise two windows which may once have covered Old Testament scenes from the Creation to the Sacrifice of Isaac, and two of Lives of individual saints – St George and St Neot. At Great Malvern the Life of that church's founder, St Werstan, and Old Testament scenes were similarly depicted in multi-panel form and it is notable that the founder's Life, like that at St Neot, appears on the north side.[9]

The donors of the St Neot windows were mainly laymen and laywomen. Clerical influence can be suggested in only one or two cases. For instance, Robert Tubb, vicar of St Neot from 1508 to 1544, is among the family donors, while the Old Testament windows at St Neot have been tentatively linked to the themes of the *Cornish Ordinalia*.[10] Internal evidence suggests that the *Ordinalia*, a three-day cycle of miracle plays in the Cornish language, was written at Glasney College, Penryn, some forty miles from St Neot, *c*.1400; but it would not have been performed in a non-Cornish-speaking area like St Neot. Bodmin's Corpus Christi plays could have provided inspiration, being more accessible in terms of language and location, but a Glasney link is still possible.[11] From *c.* 1467–79, a James Calway was sacristan of Glasney and became a canon there in 1479–80. Although Calway or Callaway is not an uncommon surname within the region, only the Callaways of St Neot appear to have had the right social standing to produce a canon of Glasney.[12] The dating of the Creation and Noah windows to the 1480s or 1490s, just after James Calway's period of office, and the fact that the Callaways also paid for a north-aisle window at St Neot in about 1525, may make this a subject worth further exploration.

Most south-aisle windows at St Neot were donated by gentry or freeholders, often with interests in local tin-works, with the lost west window being given by the Courtenay earls of Devon. As might be expected, the saints chosen for this aisle were, with the exception of St Neot, international in provenance. Didactic subjects like the Four Evangelists and the 'Warning to Sabbath-breakers' were also chosen and presumably reflect the religious preferences of the parish elite.[13]

The north-aisle donors are more varied and comprise the maritally linked Callaway and Tubb tin-entrepreneurs and gentry, the Tiverton-based glaziers of the north aisle and, most significantly, three single-sex groups. These groups are the wives of the western part of the parish, the 'sisters' (probably young unmarried women) and the young men, with windows dated 1528, 1529 and 1530 respectively (see Figures 14.1–14.3). Parallels for these windows once existed in the north aisle of South Mimms church in Hertfordshire where, in 1526, the young men and maids donated one window and the 'good women' (wives) another, but the subjects chosen were unfortunately not recorded.[14]

Single-sex groups were to be found in most West Country and English parishes and tended to comprise those too young, or of the wrong gender to be involved or to gain prominence in guilds. They were distinguished by their parish-wide membership and, like the more elitist and mostly mixed-gender guilds, appointed wardens and kept accounts. The wives of the western part of St Neot would have had at least forty members and probably considerably more, although only twenty are shown as donors in the window (Figure 14.1).[15] Contributions for these parochial-group windows would have come in the form of pennies and halfpennies and the remainder raised by fund-raising: additional church ales, dancing, plays and the like. The actual cost of a glass window is likely to have been in the region of £2–£3, and narrative windows were more expensive than windows of individual saints.[16]

Cornish saints' cults commemorated at St Neot

No fewer than six Cornish saints formerly appeared in the St Neot north-aisle windows and there may once have been one or two more in the lost north-west window (Figures 14.1–14.4).[17] More significantly, all but one of the north-aisle Cornish saints appear in the single-sex group windows and, thus, may be representative of belief at the popular rather than elite level. St Mabyn or Mabena of St Mabyn and St Meubred or Meberede of Cardinham occur in the 1528 window from the wives of the western part of the parish (Figure 14.1). St Patric or Petroc of Bodmin and St Manac or Manc of Lanreath are shown in the sisters' window of 1529 (Figure 14.2), while St Lallu of Menheniot or an otherwise unidentified 'Celtic' saint was once in the slightly earlier Callaway window further east in the same aisle (Figure 14.4).[18] The most important window in this aisle was the narrative Life of St Neot, a Cornish saint appropriated by the Anglo-Saxons and patron saint of this parish (Figure 14.3). This window was given by the young men of the parish in 1530 and will be described separately below.

None of the other five Cornish saints was the patron of an adjoining parish to St Neot. All were patrons of parishes at one remove, with Bodmin and St Mabyn at two removes. The geographical location is interesting with Bodmin, Cardinham and St Mabyn to the west, Lanreath to the south, and Menheniot to the south-east. The absence of any Cornish saint whose cult is located to the north or east is striking, though such saints are rarer in the east, and also one or two could have appeared in the north-west window formerly.[19]

The Cornish saints actually shown in the windows fall into a number of distinct types. St Petroc was of regional importance and has two surviving Lives and a reasonably full hagiographical dossier.[20] Lallu seems to be named in a tenth-century list of Cornish saints, while the twelfth-century list of the children of Brychan is represented by St Mabyn.[21] The other two Cornish saints – Meubred and Manac – were part of a saintly trio with St Wyllow of Lanteglos-by-Fowey in mid- and south Cornwall.[22] Welsh origins were claimed for St Petroc and St Mabyn and Irish for St Meubred yet all three may have been Cornish cults originally, like the otherwise unknown Lallu and Manac. Indeed, in the case of Meubred, Worcestre recounts an alternative tradition, current in 1478, that the saint was born in Cardinham parish.[23] Royal origins were attributed to three of these Cornish saints: Meubred and Petroc being kings' sons and Mabyn a king's daughter.[24] Unfortunately, with one notable exception, the depictions of these Cornish saints differ little from their international counterparts in St Neot church.

St Meubred is the only one of the Cornish saints to be depicted in an individual way. He is shown as a bearded hermit-confessor with a fourteenth-century-style lawyer's cap on his head, a staff in his hand and a second head under his arm (Figure 14.1). According to Roscarrock, there was a window of this saint in the church at Cardinham, and this may have served as a model for the St Neot one.[25] In the St Neot windows two other Cornish saints, St Petroc and St Manac, are shown as bishops, although both were better known as hermits (Figure 14.2). The former is shown wearing a green chasuble with mitre and crosier, the latter with a mitre, crosier and red cope or cloak of martyrdom. St Mabyn in Figure 14.1 has a crown and holds a palm leaf which also signifies her status as a martyr, while St Lallu appears as a hermit (Figure 14.4).[26]

All of the Cornish saints depicted in the north aisle at St Neot had active, late-medieval cults, and those of St Petroc and St Neot are especially well documented. St Petroc, hermit, abbot, bishop and confessor was the 'best-known saint of Cornwall' in the medieval period.[27] Bodmin was the centre of his cult, and four other Cornish parish churches, including the original cult site at Padstow, and some chapels had the dedication St Petroc. Other dedications occur in Devon, Somerset, Wales and Brittany. Petroc's earliest Life dates from the mid-eleventh century and a second from the late twelfth century, and both appear to have been written at Bodmin.[28] All other Cornish saints depicted in the St Neot windows are associated with a single parish church dedication.

A common feature of saints' cults in Cornwall (and no doubt elsewhere) is the presence of a second cult site comprising a holy well and associated chapel. Usually dedicated to the same patronal saint, these generally lay within a mile of the parish church. Possible late medieval well-house structures survive at Cardinham, where the chapel appears to have been built above the well, and at St Petroc's well in Bodmin, with further sites at St Mabyn, Menheniot and probably Lanreath.[29] Petroc, Meubred and even Lallowe were in use as Christian names pre- and post-Reformation, although only the first was common. At Menheniot, as late as 1562, a St Cleer man gave 12d to the store of St 'Lallo' confirming that the cult was not restricted to Menheniot parish.[30]

The cult of St Neot

The patronal saint's cult at St Neot is one of the best documented and most important in Cornwall. Like St Petroc and St Piran, the hybrid St Neot was a saint of regional, if not national, importance. First mentioned as a secondary saint to St Gueriir in the Life of King Alfred compiled by Asser before 909, Neot may also appear in a tenth-century list of Cornish saints as Nioth.[31] By the mid-eleventh century, when the saint's body had been removed to England, Neot had acquired an Anglo-Saxon royal pedigree. Two Lives and a homily of mid-eleventh- to twelfth- or thirteenth-century date follow the Anglo-Saxon lineage, although a Cornish origin is more likely.[32]

Neot appears as a hermit in the St Neot windows which follow the story of the Anglo-Saxon tradition (Figure 14.3). In the Borlase window of c.1505 in the south aisle, Neot was dressed 'in blue drapery, his head with the tonsure, a cross in his right hand' (Figure 14.5).[33] The first two scenes of the young men's window (Figure 14.3) show Neot giving up his throne to a younger brother in order to become a monk at Glastonbury. The saving of the stag by St Neot, while reading the psalter and bathing his feet in his well, is the subject of panel 3 which also shows the huntsman presenting his horn to St Neot.[34] In the fourth panel an angel gives St Neot three fish – a never-ending supply if only one was caught from the well and consumed each day.

Panels 5 to 8 concern the trials and tribulations of Barrius or Barry, the servant of St Neot. In the first of these panels Barrius is shown at St Neot's bedside. In the next, Barrius grills a fish on a gridiron and then offers it with another, differently prepared, to tempt his sick master to eat. The eighth panel shows Barrius being made to tip both fish back into the well where they are miraculously restored to life. Although Leland was told in c.1538 when he visited St Neots in Huntingdonshire that Barrius was buried there, William Worcestre found in 1478 that a St Barnic bishop, called in English St Barre, was buried at Fowey and, as late as 1878, Fowey feast-day was held on 31 July, St Neot's Day. However, the Fowey saint is generally identified with St Finbarrus of Cork. The possibility remains that, at both Fowey and St Neot, Barrius had acquired a separate 'local' identity by the late medieval period.[35]

The young men's window (Figure 14.3) concludes with the theft of St Neot's oxen, the substitution of stags to pull Neot's plough, the return of the oxen by a penitent robber, and finally St Neot kneeling to receive the Pope's blessing. By ending with Neot's visit to Rome in panel 12, the question of St Neot's burial place is not even raised and the patronal saint's international importance is demonstrated.

The position of the young men's window, immediately opposite the south door where pilgrims and others would have entered St Neot church, seems to have been deliberately selected for maximum impact. The late-medieval cult of St Neot in Cornwall centred on the church. According to the eleventh-century Life of St Neot, seven years after the saint's death his body was translated to a more fitting site on the north side of the high altar and reburied prior to its translation to Eynesbury in Huntingdonshire. This translation took place c.970–80 and Eynesbury was then renamed St Neots. An eleventh-century enquiry stated that only one arm was left behind at St Neot in Cornwall.[36]

The saint's supposed tomb remains on the north side of the chancel and is part of an elaborate fourteenth- or fifteenth-century structure which may have doubled as an Easter sepulchre (Figure 14.9). This could have been built over the site of St Neot's second, late ninth-century, tomb which is mentioned in the mid-eleventh-century Life.[37] In 1786 a stone casket of only 18 by 14 inches, which might have originally contained St Neot's arm-bone, was noted by Forster, then rector of Boconnoc. It protruded from the back of St Neot's tomb and must have been located in the small strip of wall on the south side of the north chapel. Lysons later referred to 'a stopt up piscina' as the shrine site but, if correct, this would have been a tertiary site.[38]

Revd John Whitaker visited St Neot in October 1795 and noted that, a few days after his visit, inebriated workmen 'broke up the whole repository':

> [The stone casket] appeared to be no casket at all . . . so contracted in its dimensions, as to be within the facing wall only ten inches and a half by nine. It thus reached nearly up to the original wall, ending only two inches and a half from it. In this wall was found the real repository of St Neot's remains; a large cavity, apparently not made with the wall, but dug into it after its construction, being perfectly rude and formless. To guard the remains in it more securely, the mouth was closed with a stone; while the seeming casket was made to extend from it into sight, and was therefore formed neatly of four wrought stones. This was found to contain nothing . . . But in the cavity was found a mould-earth, very fine in itself, yet adhering in clots, and dark in colour . . . the very last and evanescent relics . . . of that body . . . once actuated by the high-set soul of a St Neot.[39]

The association of St Neot church in Cornwall with healing goes back to the time of King Alfred and Neot's predecessor, St Gueriir, while the healing properties of St Neot's dust were recorded from the fourteenth century.[40] A chapel of St Neot is first mentioned in 1380 as an additional cult-site and was, no doubt, associated with the surviving holy well which lies a quarter of a mile from the church. By the early nineteenth century, the well specialized in the cure of weakly children who were brought from as far away as Exeter to be bathed there on the first three mornings in May.[41] This well was also the source of baptismal water for the church and Neot is found as a Christian name both before and after the Reformation. For instance, a Nyott Isack was buried at St Neot in 1552 and boys there were still being baptized with this name in 1563, 1565 and 1593. A Niotte Woodward, rector of Boconnoc, who died in 1574 and a Niett Doubt who was married at Padstow in 1603 may also have been born at St Neot.[42] A guild of St Neot was based in the parish church and was wealthy enough to be taxed in 1544; its members may have included Nicholas and Katherine Burlas who chose to include Neot in their southaisle window (Figure 14.5).[43]

The St Neot windows (Figures 14.3 and 14.5) fail to portray the saint's small size, a notable feature of the version of the second Life seen by Leland in the Huntingdonshire church in c.1538, but later Cornish folklore made the saint a dwarf.[44] That the cult continued to flourish, or was reintroduced after the Civil War, is also clear from a reference in the churchwardens' accounts of 1681 to 6s for 'making the frame for St Neott verses', continuing visits to the holy well and local legends involving a cross base and Crow Pound.[45] The verses – which reinforce the claim of St Neot in Cornwall to have the original bones of its saint – once hung over the tomb but are now removed to the north wall at the back of the church. The first and last verses are as follows:[46]

> Consuming time Neotus flesh & bones to dust translated
> A sacred tomb this dust inclos'd which now is ruinated
> Though flesh, and bones, and dust, and tomb, thro tract of time be rotten
> Yet Neot's fame remain with us, which nere shall be forgotten ...
>
> For why? a college here of clarks he had, whose fame encreased,
> When as his corps were clad in clay, and he from hence deceased,
> Some say his bones were carry'd hence, St Needs will have it so,
> Which claims the Grace of Neot's tomb, but hereto we say No.

St Neot's cult was also well known in England and Normandy due to the translation, termed theft in some accounts, of most of St Neot's corporeal remains to Eynesbury, thereafter St Neots, in Huntingdonshire in the late tenth century. By the eleventh century, Crowland abbey in Lincolnshire claimed to hold St Neot's bones too and, as late as 1680, the saint's jawbone was among the possessions of the abbey of Bec, the connection in the latter case being that the abbey of Bec in Normandy owned the Huntingdonshire priory by 1081. Numerous other relics of St Neot existed formerly, and c.1540 included a hair shirt and a comb made from a bone and fish teeth at St Neots in Huntingdonshire. The saint was also included in calendars and litanies from the eleventh century or later at Exeter, Sherborne and elsewhere and was even credited, curiously, with the foundation of New College, Oxford.[47]

Other saints in the St Neot north-aisle windows who may have been honoured locally

The inclusion of two other international patrons of local churches, St German in the Callaway window (Figure 14.4), and St Clair or Clere in the sisters' window (Figure 14.2), could be further evidence that the north-aisle windows commemorate active, late-medieval saints' cults. St German, bishop of Auxerre, is depicted as such in the Callaway window (Figure 14.4). He was venerated at St Germans by the mid-tenth century and relics of his were said to be kept there. Further relics were acquired from Auxerre in 1358: a small arm-bone and part of the relic cloth.[48] These may have been housed in the bishop's tomb noted by Leland in c.1540; other relics being at Exeter, Auxerre and elsewhere. As Leland wrote:

> Beside the hye altare of the same priory on the right hand ys a tumbe yn the walle with an image of a bisshop, and over the tumbe a{n} xi. bisshops paynted with their names and verses as token of so many bisshops biried theere, or that ther had beene so many Bisshoppes of Cornwalle that had theyr seete theer.[49]

This tomb seems to have lain on the south side of the high altar adjoining the south aisle, which was originally the only parochial part of the church.

A church at Rame was also dedicated to this saint, as was a chapel in Padstow parish and, given that the site at St Germans had served as the Cornish bishopric from the 930s to 1050, a distinctive Cornish saint is possible. In any case, a local dimension had been added to the official legend by the medieval period and it was claimed that St German of Auxerre had worked as both a bishop and confessor in Cornwall. He is often depicted with Petroc as founder of the Cornish see and shared a feast-day with St Neot (see Table 14.1, p. 263).[50]

St Clair of St Cleer is shown as one of the three bishops in the sisters' window at St Neot (Figure 14.2). The chantry returns of 1555–6 unusually record a shrine at St Cleer church which could have contained a relic of the French bishop-saint; the only other shrine being noted at Liskeard.[51] The shrine was almost certainly connected with, and indeed may have resembled, the exceptionally elaborate, though much rebuilt, well-chapel (Figure 14.6) which lies a quarter of a mile down the road from St Cleer church. Constructed of granite, with a corbelled roof ornamented with pinnacles, open arcades on three sides to allow maximum access to the water, and pillars with carved capitals, the well-chapel once had a large bathing pool behind. This suggests an active pre-Reformation healing cult specializing in curing the insane, although the name 'Cleer' is also associated with eye-wells.[52] Clere occurs as a Christian name in the parish by 1535.[53]

Other north-aisle saints with a possible local relevance include St Mary, Christ and All Saints (Figures 14.1–14.2).[54] St George can probably be disregarded, although there may have been a guild dedicated to this saint in St Neot church.[55] The *pietà* which appears in the window of the wives of the western part of the parish (Figure 14.1) could relate to the cult of the Virgin Mary, although recent research shows that nationally this cult appealed more to men. Alternatively, it may be part of Christocentric devotions and have been chosen by the wives because it emphasizes Mary the grieving mother, rather than the young virgin.[56] The chapel of Our Lady of Park (in the old Duchy Park), with its associated holy well in the neighbouring parish of Liskeard, was the major centre of Marian devotion in the locality and renowned in the pre-Reformation period as a pilgrimage centre.[57]

One of the two Jesuses depicted in the north aisle of the church might refer to an active late-medieval devotion – a crucified Christ appearing in the Callaway window, while Jesus once showed his wounds in the wives' window. Figure 14.1 shows a 'resurrected' Christ in place of the latter. The cult of Jesus was extremely popular in the late medieval period, in England from the 1450s centring on a chapel in the crypt of St Paul's cathedral, London.[58] The Marke family, with one or two other Liskeard residents, acted as pardoners for the London guild from 1506 to 1533, collecting all donations made in the diocese of Exeter. There was a Jesus chapel in Liskeard parish church, a silver shrine which may have contained his relics, and presumably a guild. Friday masses were said there until 1548 and the devotion here, and elsewhere, attracted the wealthy as well as the middling sort.[59] The shrine of St Neot in St Neots, Huntingdon, coincidentally, stood in the Jesus chapel there.[60]

All Saints, depicted as God holding a number of naked souls in a napkin, is the last panel of the sisters' window (Figure 14.2) and might be an indirect reference to a chapel in the neighbouring parish of St Pinnock. The chapel of All Saints, probably located at South Bosent, was licensed in 1437 and masses were to be said on All Saints Day, St Keyne's Day, the third Rogation Day and on 11 May.[61] Like the chapel of Our Lady of Park this was probably dissolved in 1548. The possibility that some of these other saints in the women's windows at St Neot might relate to local chapels is certainly worthy of further consideration and provides a contrast with the Cornish saints depicted, who were patrons of parish churches rather than chapels.

Saints' tombs, relics and pilgrimage in Cornwall

The claim to possess corporeal relics of one's patron saint appears to link most of the Cornish cults, St Neot's own cult and some of the other cults and devotions depicted in the north-aisle windows at St Neot. In addition to St Neot (Figure 14.9), specific references to tombs of saints have been found for Cardinham, Lanreath, Bodmin and possibly St Germans, and to shrines at St Cleer and Liskeard. At St Mabyn and Menheniot a former tomb could be implied because the saint was presumed to have lived and died there and has no other known dedication.[62] These documentary sources can be supplemented by other evidence, such as the ivory reliquary casket of mid- to late twelfth-century date (Figure 14.7) which survives at Bodmin together with a detailed account of the theft and return of the saint's bones in 1177.[63] At Cardinham, the thirteenth- or early fourteenth-century Easter sepulchre (Figure 14.8), with trefoilheaded statue niche above, on the north side of the chancel, may have been designed to cover the saint's tomb, as at St Neot, while parts of the shrines of two of St Mabyn's sisters have been identified at St Endellion and St Issey (Figures 14.10 and 14.11) and a fragment at St Mabyn.[64]

St Petroc's ivory relic casket or feretory at Bodmin (Figure 14.7) which dates from the mid- to late twelfth century measures 18.5 inches long by 11.5 inches wide by 9.25 inches high and could have held the saint's thigh bones.[65] The casket may have been displayed originally on the saint's 'tomb'.[66] William Worcestre noted in 1478 that St Petroc lay in a beautiful shrine facing the Lady chapel, while John Leland writing after the dissolution of the priory stated in 1542–3 that 'the shrine and tumbe of S. Petrock yet standith in th'est part of the chirche'.[67] This suggests a similar location to the tomb of St Erkenwald at St Paul's in London which was built against the back of the reredos of the high altar, but it is unclear if the priory or parish church is meant.[68] Evidence in favour of a church location, apart from greater accessibility for pilgrims, is that a chapel was attached to the east end of Bodmin church until 1776.[69] This Lady chapel appears to have been the location of an altar of St Petroc by 1469, if not 1453, and had its own chalice. It was maintained by the skinners and glovers, the most important of the town's five trade guilds, who took St Petroc as their patron until at least the 1560s.[70]

A panel of a possible tomb of Mabyn survives in the form of a credence table at St Mabyn. The panel with cusped tracery head appears to be of limestone. At least six of the children of Brychan in the twelfth-century Hartland list had tombs and it is possible that all were once so honoured. Tombs or shrine bases survive at St Endellion and St Issey (Figures 14.10 and 14.11) and fragments of another at Hartland in Devon.[71] The former two shrines are carved from catacleuse, an almost black greenstone quarried near Padstow, which was also used for the west doorway at St Mabyn.[72]

Both the St Endellion and St Issey shrines (Figures 14.10 and 14.11) have eight-inch- deep, ogee-headed, kneeling niches around the base so that pilgrims could get closer to the bones encased within, or under, the tomb. While St Endelient's shrine has eight such niches, St Issey's shrine only has five, although a sixth can be reconstructed. The reason for this discrepancy seems to be the respective locations of these shrines; the former may have been under the arch to the north of the high altar as it is four sided, while St Issey's could have butted against the north and east walls of the chancel and thus required only two sides.[73]

Sculpted figures were a feature of the Hartland and St Issey shrines and in the latter case filled the spandrels over the kneeling niches. Twenty figures out of a possible twenty-four survive at St Issey (Figure 14.11) and now comprise twelve men and eight women. All the men are depicted in clerical garb and include a hermit-confessor with a crutch and rosary, at least three bishops and a priest holding a cruet or vase. The women have longer faces, wear tighter-waisted long gowns and sometimes head-dresses; attributes are restricted to rosary beads in one case and a cross in another.[74] The best explanation for these figures, in view of the lack of saintly attributes and the numerical probability, is that they may represent the twenty-four children of Brychan, who all became missionaries and saints. In this context it could be significant that, at St Mabyn, in about 1500, there was 'a Song or Hymn sung of her signifieing that she had twentie thre[e] brothers and sisters' indicating that holy siblingship was still one of her most remembered features.[75]

According to Padel, more than one in ten Cornish parish churches claimed to have a saint's tomb in the late Middle Ages and there may have been even more at an earlier date.[76] These tombs are recorded from the eleventh century onwards, though, in contrast to Anglo-Saxon sites, they were never restricted to larger churches.[77] Early monastic sites in Cornwall are reasonably well represented among places claiming corporeal relics but not exclusively so. In addition to documentary references, multiple skulls have been found in suggestive locations at the early monastic site of Probus and in St Piran's oratory in Perranzabuloe.[78] St Piran's corporeal relics had been dispersed by 1281, though most were still kept in a portable shrine. The relics were regularly peregrinated around the Hundred of Pydar until the 1550s.[79] A refinement in the early fifteenth century was the encasing of St Piran's head in its own shrine, continental-style, rather than in 'one box or reliquary bound with iron and locked . . . with other relics' as was the case earlier. Similar treatment may have been accorded to a foot of this saint and also to single feet of St Agnes, and of St Ia in Camborne parish, by the sixteenth century.[80]

A few other shrines, in addition to those already discussed, have been found at Cornish sites but very few are of early date. The earliest may be the massive lid of St Materiana's shrine at Minster, a pre-Conquest church. St Materiana was still performing miracles in person, presumably at her tomb, on St James's Day in 1477 when three people, including a lunatic, were cured.[81] Also of possible pre-Conquest date may be the relic niche in the oratory of St Helen or Elide in the Isles of Scilly. According to Charles Thomas: 'the relic-cavity in the oratory might have held only representative relics; but in the later church a separate little aisle, possibly an original grave, and a Purbeck marble shrine-cover assure us that Leland's *gret superstition* was centred on the all-important possession and display of the founder's bones.'[82]

A further small fragment of late medieval date at Lanteglos-by-Fowey could have come from the shrine of St Wyllow recorded in 1478, or from a tomb canopy, while other suggestive pieces of possible shrines or stone canopies have been noted at St Keverne and Davidstow. Relic crosses of triangular form are known at St Allen, Breage, Bodmin, St Keverne and possibly St Neot, and may have contained secondary relics like St Petroc's bell.[83]

Pilgrimages provide a linking theme and economic rationale for the elaboration of many Cornish shrines in the late medieval period and also, perhaps, for some of the Perpendicular enlargement of churches. St Neot, Bodmin, Cardinham, St Mabyn, Menheniot and St Cleer all acquired processional-height north and south aisles in this period, as did many others, and Lanreath a south aisle at least. As Duffy has indicated, traditional shrines were being neglected on the eve of the Reformation as 'new and more powerful helpers' were sought and this may provide the religious context for the stained-glass depiction of neighbouring local cult-sites that were visitable.[84] West Country pilgrims were still going on pilgrimage along the Fosse Way in the 1530s and to Henry

VI's shrine at Windsor as late as 1543 in 'flocks' and 'plumps'. Other relics of Henry VI, ultimately an unsuccessful candidate for sanctity, could be found at St Michael's Mount, but not the headache-curing hat.[85]

Both Henry VI and St Thomas Becket, two of the most popular 'pilgrimage' saints, representing new and old devotions, appear in surviving wall-paintings in the south aisle of Breage church with St Giles, whose shrine en route to Compostela and Jerusalem became an important pilgrimage centre.[86] It may also be significant that Henry VI appears on the painted screen at Lanreath where the corporeal remains of St Manac were to be found and that Breage, too, claimed to hold the body of its patron saint.[87] As at St Neot, the north aisle of Breage church appears to have been reserved for local dedications: the patronal saints of nearby churches and chapels. These included the Brittonic St Corentin of Cury, and international saints like St Hilary, St Michael (Helston or the Mount) and possibly St Augustine, the dedication of an important chapel at Binnerton in the neighbouring parish of Crowan.[88] At Lanivet, wall paintings of didactic subjects like the 'Warning to Sabbath-breakers', 'Christ showing his wounds' and 'Maria Misericordia' all once occurred in the south aisle, with St Crede, a possible Cornish saint and patroness of the church of Creed and of a chapel in Padstow parish, in the north aisle.[89] The real message of the St Neot windows may be that the needs of poorer or older people, especially women, for pilgrimages could be catered for by cult and other devotional sites closer to home. Table 14.1 is an attempt to collate all the dates that could relate to the cult figures in the St Neot windows. Perhaps, not surprisingly, this shows a good all-year-round spread of feasts with a concentration in the warmer months from just after Easter to November.[90]

Conclusion

The cults and devotions depicted in the St Neot north aisle were predominantly local, often 'Celtic', usually based on corporeal relics, and very active on the eve of the Reformation. At least four, including St Neot, were of pre-Conquest origin.[91] The cult of St Neot has been one of the most enduring of local cults, with a strong folkloric tradition to set against a 1,100-year-old hagiographical one. It is certainly possible that the inclusion of other east Cornwall cults, based on the possession and display of a patron saint's corporeal relics, was intended to bolster St Neot's claims in the run-up to the Reformation (Figure 14.9). A related, though less clear element, is how far cults or devotions were selected for the north-aisle windows at St Neot because of their healing reputations. Proximity to a saint's bones was clearly considered efficacious as shown

Table 14.1. Calendar of feast-days possibly associated with local cult-sites depicted in north-aisle windows at St Neot

1 January:	Circumcision (Jesus chapel at Liskeard?)
6 January:	Epiphany (Jesus chapel at Liskeard?)
2 February:	Purification/Candlemas (chapel of Our Lady of Park near Liskeard?)
15 March–18 April:	Palm Sunday (Jesus chapel at Liskeard?)
22 March–5 April:	Easter Sunday (Our Lady of Park/Liskeard)
25 March:	Annunciation/Lady Day (chapel of Our Lady of Park near Liskeard?)
27 March:	Resurrection (Jesus chapel at Liskeard?)
23 April:	St George (possible guild at St Neot or Lostwithiel?)
29 April–2 June:	3rd Rogation Day (All Saints Chapel, St Pinnock)
7 May–10 June:	Thursday before Whitsun/Pentecost (Cardinham, Lanreath)
10 May–3 June:	Pentecost (Jesus chapel at Liskeard?)
11 May:	Saturday after the Ascension (All Saints Chapel in St Pinnock parish in 1437)
21 May–24 May:	Corpus Christi (Jesus chapel at Liskeard?)
27 May:	St German, bishop and confessor (St Germans)
4 June:	St Petroc (Bodmin)
25 June:	Salutation (chapel of Our Lady of Park near Liskeard?)
2 July:	Visitation (chapel of Our Lady of Park near Liskeard?)
31 July:	St Neot (St Neot) and parish feast at Fowey (St Barry) and St Germans (St Germans)
7 August:	Name of Jesus (Jesus chapel at Liskeard?)
15 August:	Assumption/Crowning of Virgin (chapel of Our Lady of Park near Liskeard?)
8 August:	Nativity of Virgin Mary (chapel of Our Lady of Park near Liskeard?)
14 August:	Exaltation of St Petroc (Bodmin)
25 August:	St Barry (companion of St Neot at Fowey)
8 October:	St Keyne (All Saints Chapel in St Pinnock parish) and translation of St Petroc (Bodmin)
10 October:	St Clair, bishop of Nantes (St Cleer)
1 November:	All Saints (All Saints Chapel in St Pinnock parish)
18 November:	St Mabena (St Mabyn)
21 November:	Presentation of Virgin (chapel of Our Lady of Park near Liskeard?)
25 December:	Nativity of Jesus (Jesus chapel at Liskeard?)

Note the concentration of Cornish dedication feasts around Whitsun week – the annual week's holiday and usually the start of better weather.

Sources: Worcestre, *Itineraries*; Toulmin-Smith (ed.), *Leland*; Orme, *Roscarrock*. (Spellings of saints' names taken from Orme, *Saints of Cornwall*).

by the kneeling niches of the shrines at St Endellion and St Issey (Figures 14.10 and 14.11), or by the miracle cures at Minster in 1477.[92] Additional cult sites comprising holy wells and chapels have been found for most of the local saints depicted at St Neot and in many other Cornish parishes. At St Neot, both before and after the Reformation, saintly dust and holy water combined to cure sick animals and/or weak children, and Neot's holy well appears in no fewer than four of the twelve panels of the young men's window. Of the other saints honoured locally and depicted in the north-aisle windows, only St Cleer was renowned for healing; post-Reformation, the well there (Figure 14.6) had a reputation for curing the lame and the blind.[93]

Most of the locally revered saints were chosen by women of middling social status in contrast to the international saints and didactic subjects selected by their social superiors – the gentry and freeholders – for the south-aisle windows at St Neot. The patron saint of St Neot having been appropriated by the young men (Figure 14.3), the women of the parish had to look further afield for inspiration. Only two female role models, St Mary and St Mabyn, were included and both appear in the wives' window (Figure 14.1). 'An enthusiasm for corporeal remains' seems to have affected choices and the women's windows may have acted as signposts for the faithful, as it were, pointing out other local places, besides St Neot, where saints' bodies or relic shrines could be seen and to which a pilgrimage might be worthwhile.[94] The St Neot windows thus provide a glimpse into the beliefs and religious interests of the whole parish rather than just its elite, something that can rarely be recovered from official records like churchwardens' and guild accounts alone.

The fifteenth and early sixteenth centuries can be perceived as a period when a real interest in the 'local' past first manifested itself, along with a confident sense of county community.[95] This was the case in England, too, where the burial places of Anglo-Saxon saints were also being revered. The Cornish experience was different, with lesser churches making the same claims to hold their patron saints' bodies as larger ones. At the same time, commonplaces of Cornish hagiographical tradition, such as foreign origins and royal blood, were beginning to be challenged at a popular level as people sought more local and paradoxically, in some cases, more authentic explanations for their saints. Mostly, however, the St Neot windows show saints that were honoured locally, not saints that had become or were becoming localized. According to Padel, 'what matters is not so much the origin of a particular cult, or whether its saint was "the same" as another, but the expectation in Celtic areas that a saint *should* be local'.[96] At St Neot, on the eve of the Reformation, this expectation, in some form, seems to have survived the loss of the Cornish language by at least 200 years, and the loss of the saint's body by six centuries.[97]

Notes

[1] Registrars of the archdeaconry of Cornwall resided at St Neot, and held court there from 1600 to 1750. Their presence may have helped to protect the church glass from iconoclasts in 1651. Only the subjects of the three west windows are unrecorded, probably because they were destroyed in the great storm of 1703. See Polsue, *History of Cornwall*, vol. 3, p. 408 and Mattingly, 'Stories', pp. 9–10, 53, n. 54.

[2] Whitaker, *Life of St Neot*, pp. 214–15. South-aisle didactic subjects include a 'Warning to Sabbath-breakers', the Evangelists and the Three Marys.

[3] Mattingly, 'Stories', pp. 24–49.

[4] Olson, *Early Monasteries*, pp. xiv, 51, 89; see also Orme, *Saints of Cornwall*, p. 202.

[5] Padel, 'Local saints and place-names', sets out many of the most up-to-date arguments for Cornwall being different from England in its density of local cults. The term Cornish saints will be used, throughout this article, for all 'Celtic' saints honoured in Cornwall regardless of whether they are honoured elsewhere. Orme, *Saints of Cornwall*, p. 22, identifies no fewer than 142 distinct 'Celtic' saints venerated in Cornwall.

[6] Austin, Gerrard and Greeves, 'Tin and agriculture', pp. 23–7.

[7] Ibid., pp. 31–3 and see also Mattingly, 'Tin miner'.

[8] Mattingly, 'Stories', pp. 10–12, for dating glazing. See also Brown and MacDonald, *Life, Death and Art* and Wayment, *King's College Chapel*.

[9] Hamand, *Ancient Windows*, pp. 13–27. Old Testament windows were in the south clerestory originally.

[10] Mattingly, 'Stories', p. 41; Nance, 'Painted windows', pp. 244–8; Newlyn, 'Unconventional evidence', pp. 1–7.

[11] Newlyn, Joyce, Hays and McGee, *Dorset. Cornwall*, pp. 398, 408–9, 469–73.

[12] Peter, *Glasney Collegiate Church*, pp. 91, 164; Whetter, *History of Glasney College*, pp. 51–2. The latter is probably right in equating James Calway with the Thomas Keyleway appointed sacristan in 1467.

[13] Guild dedications follow a similar pattern, Mattingly, 'Medieval parish guilds', pp. 305–17. For St Neot window-donors see Mattingly, 'Stories', p. 20.

[14] There was probably also a wives' organization for the eastern part of the parish including the village of St Neot. The lost north-west window could have been glazed by them in about 1531. Cass, *South Mimms*, p. 49. The wives' group of Walberswick in Suffolk also contributed 9s for a new window *c*.1495 (French, 'Maidens' lights', p. 402).

[15] Mattingly, 'Medieval parish guilds', pp. 291, 321–2. Parish groups do not appear to have charged an entry fee, in contrast to guilds, and seem to have attracted the middling sort: yeoman, husbandmen and some labourers and craftsmen. French, 'Maidens' lights', pp. 415–17 confirms that the parish's wealthiest women did not serve as guild or single-sex group wardens and the husbands of perhaps as many as a third of the female wardens could not be traced in tax lists. Had she distinguished guilds from parochial groups, the proportion of taxpaying husbands might have been even less. Stoate, *Cornwall Subsidies*, p. 105, lists eighty male taxpayers suggesting a St Neot population of almost 500 in 1525.

[16] Peter and Peter, *Histories of Launceston*, p. 313, notes a payment of £3 for an east window in St Mary Magdalene, Launceston, 1543–4, but most glazing would have been a little cheaper than this. See Brown and O'Connor, *Glass-Painters*, p. 41, for comparative rates.

[17] See n. 5 above for definition of Cornish saints.

[18] The identification of St Patric with Petroc is made more likely because the form Patryk appears at Bodmin in 1543 but Lallu is more problematic. The latter inscription was already in poor condition when antiquarians first visited and only the final four letters were decipherable. A plausible reconstruction of the name is Lallavy, close to the genitive form of Lallu, but elsewhere in St Neot church saints' names always appear in the nominative case. The best explanation appears to be that the donor family of Callaways (also rendered Callavy in this window) were trying to make a claim to a saintly lineage by distorting the rules of grammar (Orme, *Saints of Cornwall*, pp. 214, 165). The Callaways and Tubbs held land in Menheniot.

[19] St Neot parish is bounded clockwise from the north by Blisland (and Temple), Altarnun, St Cleer, Liskeard, St Pinnock, Braddock and Warleggan parishes, but only the patron of St Cleer, who is not a Cornish saint, is definitely included in the St Neot windows. If the west window in the north aisle included local saints from the north or east, possible candidates might have been St Non of Altarnun, St Breward, St Cleder of St Clether, St Keri of Egloskerry, St Keyne or St Melor of Linkinhorne. See Orme, *Saints of Cornwall*, pp. 74, 89, 158–9, 162–3, 186–7, 205–6.

[20] Jankulak, *St Petroc*, p. 1.

[21] Olson and Padel, A tenth-century list', p. 56; Orme, *Roscarrock*, pp. 45–50.

[22] Worcester, *Itineraries*, pp. 97–9, 107 (NB: burial places are muddled up in the first of these entries).

[23] Farmer, *Oxford Dictionary of Saints*, pp. 272, 300, 351. Worcester, *Itineraries*, p. 97 records that 'according to the statement of the wife of?? of the church "Meubred" was born in the parish'.

[24] Ibid., p. 97; Orme, *Saints of Cornwall*, p. 214; idem, *Roscarrock*, p. 45.

[25] Ibid., pp. 91, 155. Standard depictions may have been cheaper than more individual ones, John Blair (personal communication).

[26] These panels are much restored with the exception of St Meubred and St Petroc.

[27] Jankulak, *St Petroc*, p. ix.

[28] Ibid., p. 1 map 2, pp. 10–16, 73–114, 141–6.

[29] For Cardinham see Quiller-Couch, *Ancient and Holy Wells*, pp. 22–4. For Bodmin, St Mabyn and Menheniot see Lane-Davies, *Holy Wells*, pp. 7, 22–3, 33, and see also Mattingly, 'Pre-Reformation holy wells', pp. 8–11, especially p. 10. No site is recorded for Lanreath but a distinct chapel and well are likely as c.1269 chapels of St Dunstan and St Manac, and Holy Trinity were noted. Trefraul chapel, in the south, may have had the latter dedication while a possibility for the former, according to Carole Vivian, is about a mile from the church at Brazemoor – an area of detached glebe with a notable spring. There is also a well in the village but no tradition that this was ever holy.

[30] Such names are rare before parish registers begin suggesting that they appealed more to those of lower social status, Orme, *Saints of Cornwall*, pp. 191, 217, for Meubred and Petroc. A Lallowe Jolle, or Yelle, who was married at St Columb in 1551, and died there in 1596, could have been born in Menheniot parish, while a Lallowe Nicholas occurs from 1595 and died in 1648 at St Columb. See transcript of St Columb Major parish registers in RIC; CRO, P144/5/1, fol. 12^v.

[31] Orme, *Saints of Cornwall*, p. 200, seems to follow Keynes and Lapidge, *Alfred the Great* in regarding the reference 'and now *Sanctus Niot* lies there as well' as dating

from Asser's time rather than being a later interpolation; Olson and Padel, 'A tenthcentury list', pp. 49–51.

[32] Dumville and Lapidge (eds), *Vita Prima*, pp. lxxv-cxxiv, 111–142. For a discussion of origins see Olson, *Early Monasteries in Cornwall*, pp. 85–6; Doble, *St Neot*, pp. 2, 30–1; and Orme, *Saints of Cornwall*, pp. 200–2, especially p. 202. For earlier spellings of the place-name see Padel, *Cornish Place-Names*, p. 128.

[33] Samuel Lysons's pre-1814 account of the windows, BL, Add. MSS 9462, fol. 48. I am grateful to Paul Cockerham for drawing my attention to this.

[34] An abridged Life on the lines of John of Tynemouth's fourteenth-century *Nova Legenda Anglie* or the Capgrave version published in 1516 (which only omits the first panel detail) may have been the model here rather than *Vita I* or *Vita II* according to Gilbert, *Historical Survey of Cornwall*, p. 942. The hunting horn was reputedly preserved in St Petroc's church (Bodmin), Orme, *Saints of Cornwall*, p. 201, and Rushforth, 'Windows of St Neot', p. 178.

[35] For St Finbarr see Ó Riain, 'The Irish element'. Barrius is named in the St Neot windows and also in the second Life of St Neot. Orme, *Saints of Cornwall*, p. 202; *idem*, *Church Dedications*, p. 82. Worcestre, *Itineraries*, p. 107; Doble, *St Neot*, pp. 31–2. The fish also appear on four roof bosses in this aisle.

[36] Orme, *Saints of Cornwall*, pp. 201–2. The second Life depicts the second translation as a theft like that of St Petroc's relics in 1177 (Doble, *St Neot*, pp. 18–19). The north chapel may originally have extended further east.

[37] Doble, *St Neot*, pp. 26–7. *Vita I* dates Neot's death to 871 x 878; Orme, *Saints of Cornwall*, p. 201.

[38] Forster, *Some Account*, p. 7 and BL, Add. MSS 9462, fol. 49.

[39] Whitaker, *Life of St Neot*, pp. 209–11.

[40] Orme, *Saints of Cornwall*, pp. 133–4; Whitaker, *Life of St Neot*, p. 204 and n. 3.

[41] Orme, *Saints of Cornwall*, p. 203; Polsue, *History of Cornwall*, vol. 3, p. 408. The well is mostly of 1852 and was restored in 1997.

[42] Orme, *Saints of Cornwall*, p. 203, and supplemented from 'St Neot Parish Register typescript' at CRO; Rolfe, 'Cornwall Incumbents' at RIC; Phillimore, Taylor and Glencross (eds), *Marriages*, vol. 6, p. 76.

[43] Stoate, *Cornwall Subsidies*, p. 106.

[44] Doble, *St Neot*, pp. 20–1. This Life includes the stories of the three fish and theft of the oxen which are depicted in the window; Whitaker, *Life of St Neot*, p. 205, and Forster, *Some Account*, pp. 7 and 15 n. 14, refer to the stone casket as the saint's coffin.

[45] CRO, P162/5/1, p. 423 and Doble, *St Neot*, pp. 21, 30, for two Cornish legends recorded in the eighteenth century. The first, involving the cross base opposite the south porch, is a variant of the Life Leland noted in *c*.1538 and concerns the diminutive saint's efforts to open his church door, while the second, otherwise unrecorded, story credited St Neot with banishing all the crows in St Neot parish to Crow Pound.

[46] Borlase recorded the verses in about 1753 (Morrab Library, Borlase, vol. T, p. 51), but they are noted in most subsequent antiquarian sources and are still extant. The verses cannot be much earlier than 1681 and one wonders if John Anstis (aged 11 in 1681) or his father, registrar of the St Neot-based archdeaconry of Cornwall, were responsible (see Wagner and Rowse, *John Anstis*, p. 1).

[47] Presumably St Neot's supposed relationship to King Alfred had added to Neot's 'collectability'. Orme, *Saints of Cornwall*, pp. 200–3.

[48] For the Life of this saint see Doble, *S. German of Auxerre* and Orme, *Saints of Cornwall*, p. 128.

[49] Toulmin-Smith (ed.), *Leland*, vol. 1, p. 324.

[50] Orme, *Saints of Cornwall*, pp. 127–9; Rutt, *'Missa Propria';* Picken, 'St German'; Jankulak, *St Petroc*.

51 Snell, *Chantry Certificates*, p. 56. Another example of such localization seems to have occurred at St Agnes, see Mattingly, 'A well without water?', pp. 6, 8–9.

52 Quiller-Couch, *Ancient and Holy Wells*, pp. 36–41; Leggatt and Leggatt, *Healing Wells*, p. 28. The former records its use by lame and blind people in the nineteenth century.

53 Stoate, *Cornwall Military Survey*, p. 168.

54 The Harys and Tubb windows have been excluded, although the former may include east-Devon dedications e.g. Halberton and Sampford Peverell, see Orme, *Church Dedications*, pp. 166, 197 and Mattingly, 'Stories', pp. 20–1, 41–3. Whitaker, *Life of St Neot*, p. 215 suggests that St Leonard in the Harys window may be the patron saint of a Bodmin chapel.

55 Mattingly, 'Medieval parish guilds', pp. 302, 305–6, 311.

56 Christine Peters (personal communication) via John Blair. St Mary was also the most popular guild dedication, Mattingly, 'Medieval parish guilds', p. 305.

57 Christocentric figures are not normally associated with local cults, as Blair has pointed out, but the Cornish experience may have differed from the rest of England in this respect. For Our Lady of Park see Henderson, *Cornish Church Guide*, p. 148, and note that there was also a chapel of Our Lady of Lamellion in the same parish. As two of the other saints depicted in the window paid for by the wives of the western part of the parish are patrons of churches to the west of St Neot, the *pietà* could refer to a chapel of Our Lady in Bodmin or Braddock church which was also dedicated to St Mary.

58 New, 'Fraternity'.

59 Ibid.; CRO, B/Lisk/99, m. 2; /171; Snell, *Chantry Certificates*, pp. 32–3, 56. This shared interest, representing both elite and popular beliefs, could account for Jesus depictions in the windows of the gentry family of Callaway and the wives' group in addition to two full crucifixions elsewhere in the church. However, in a Cornish context the available evidence suggests that Liskeard was the major cult-centre in Cornwall, and possibly Devon, for the Holy Name of Jesus, which is the point at issue here.

60 Forster, *Some Account*, pp. 25–6.

61 Dunstan, *Register*, vol. 2, p. 46. Padel (personal communication) suggests that this is another example of respect for the saint of a neighbouring parish, as St Keyne almost adjoined St Pinnock.

62 Worcestre, *Itineraries*, pp. 87, 97, 107; Toulmin-Smith (ed.), *Leland*, vol. 1, pp. 180, 324; Snell, *Chantry Certificates*, p. 56; *idem*, *Edwardian Inventories*, pp. xv, 3; Orme, *Roscarrock*, p. 86; *idem*, *Saints of Cornwall*, p. 165.

63 Pinder-Wilson and Brooke, 'The reliquary of St Petroc'; Jankulak, *St Petroc*.

64 Pevsner, *Cornwall*, pp. 51, 178–9, does not identify these as shrines, for which see Orme, *Roscarrock*, p. 130 and Chudleigh, 'History of St Issey'.

65 Pinder-Wilson and Brooke, 'The reliquary of St Petroc', pp. 267–8. See also Doble, 'The relics of Saint Petroc', p. 415, which includes slightly larger measurements.

66 An annotated copy of Maclean's *History of Trigg Minor*, vol. 1, at the RIC includes a sketch and note on p. 170 that a 'top stone of a high tomb or altar' was recycled as a tomb in 1548.

67 Worcestre, *Itineraries*, p. 87; Toulmin-Smith (ed.), *Leland*, vol. 1, p. 180.

68 Wall, *Shrines*, pp. 106–7.

69 Pinder-Wilson and Brooke, 'The reliquary of St Petroc', p. 262, n. 2.

70 Mattingly, 'Medieval parish guilds', p. 312; CRO, PB 4/7; Snell, *Edwardian Inventories*, p. 31; CRO, B/Bod 280.

71 I am grateful to my husband, Alex Hooper, for pointing out the St Mabyn panel to me. For Nectan at Hartland and John at Instow in Devon, Morwenna at

Morwenstow and Endelient at St Endellion see Padel, 'Local saints and place-names' and Blair, 'A saint for every Minster?'. A shrine at St Enoder is mentioned in a will of 1528 (Orme, *Saints of Cornwall*, p. 114), and the St Issey shrine is now a reredos.

[72] Paul Cockerham (personal communication) believes that this workshop was Padstow-based and operating in the last quarter of the fifteenth century rather than in 1400 as sometimes stated.

[73] St Endelient's shrine was removed to the south aisle after being 'defaced in king Henrie the 8 time' while St Issey's shrine was taken from the chancel and reused as the tower step by 1753, Orme, *Roscarrock*, p. 73; Chudleigh, 'History of St Issey'.

[74] The figures are arranged as follows: three male and one female, one male and three female, two male and two female, four male, two male and two female, a pattern which suggests that the proposed missing panel may have depicted four females.

[75] Orme, *Roscarrock*, p. 86.

[76] Padel, 'Local saints and place-names', appendix. An increasing number of claims may have been made in the late-medieval period too, but the sites are now lost.

[77] Ibid.; Blair, 'A saint for every Minster?'.

[78] In the former case the church guide states that two skulls were found in 1851 'walled up in a reliquary in a wall on the north side of the altar', and for three skulls at the latter site see Wall, *Shrines*, pp. 88–9.

[79] Orme, *Saints of Cornwall*, pp. 221–2; Olson, 'Religious processions', p. 25.

[80] Sir John Arundell left money in his will for the head reliquary in 1433, Orme, *Saints of Cornwall*, p. 221; RIC, Henderson MS. 66, pp. 162–3; CRO, PD/322, fol. 49.

[81] Worcestre, *Itineraries*, pp. 29, 31; C. Thomas, *Drowned Landscape*, p. 192. For comparative Welsh material see N. Edwards, 'Celtic saints', and for early English shrines see Rollason, 'Lists of saints', pp. 87–93 and Blair, 'A saint for every Minster?'.

[82] C. Thomas, *Drowned Landscape*, p. 192.

[83] For a reference to St Wyllow's tomb see Worcestre, *Itineraries*, pp. 106–7. I am grateful to Andrew Langdon for these references. For St Petroc's bell and its use in freeing slaves in the eleventh century see Doble, *St Petroc*, p. 36.

[84] E. Duffy, *Stripping of the Altars*, p. 195.

[85] Ibid., p. 193; Foxe, *Acts and Monuments*, vol. 5, p 469; Snell, *Edwardian Inventories*, p. 27. Other evidence of a strong interest in pilgrimage in the St Neot area includes a guild of St Mary of Walsingham at Bodmin in 1469–71 and an image of St Whyte (probably the patron saint of Whitchurch Canonicorum in Dorset where a pre-Reformation shrine survives) at the Bery chapel of the Holy Rood at Bodmin. The latter was repaired at a cost of 8d in 1505–6: see Mattingly, 'Medieval parish guilds', p. 311 and CRO, B/Bod 314/1.

[86] Enys, Peter and Michell Whitley, 'Mural paintings', pp. 141–2, Plates 7–9; Farmer, *Oxford Dictionary of Saints*, p. 184.

[87] Worcestre, *Itineraries*, pp. 107 and 29.

[88] At Breage, a didactic 'Warning to Sabbath-breakers' and St Christopher also appear in the north aisle: see Enys, Peter and Michell Whitley, 'Mural paintings', pp. 141–2, Plates 1–9. For Binnerton chapel see Henderson, *Cornish Church Guide*, p. 81.

[89] For Lanivet see Enys, Peter and Michell Whitley, 'Mural paintings', p. 144 and Couch 'Parochialia', pp. 76–80 and Plate 3. Crede may appear as Crite in the tenthcentury list of Cornish saints, but this refers to the patron saint of Creed parish, see Olson and Padel, 'A tenth-century list', p. 60.

[90] Phythian-Adams, *Local History and Folklore*, p. 22, divided the year into ritual and secular halves at Christmas and midsummer, respectively, but this is probably too simplistic.

[91] The others being St Petroc, St German and, probably, St Lallu.

[92] Worcestre, *Itineraries*, pp. 29, 31.
[93] Quiller-Couch, *Ancient and Holy Wells*, pp. 37, 169.
[94] For a list of such sites see Padel, 'Local saints and place-names', appendix.
[95] I am grateful to Isobel Harvey for suggesting this to me.
[96] Padel, 'Local saints and place-names', n. 51.
[97] I would especially like to thank Oliver Padel, Isobel Harvey, Nicholas Orme, John Blair and Christine Peters for commenting on previous drafts of this article and suggesting several significant improvements. Oliver, John and Nancy Edwards also generously sent me copies of unpublished material. I would also like to thank Carole Vivian for discussions about Lanreath, Bob Osborne for access to Marion Chudleigh's manuscript history of St Issey, and Angela Broome and Rob Cooke of the Courtney Library, Royal Institution of Cornwall, for their help with research and illustrations.

15
Alba Longa in the Celtic regions? Swine, saints and Celtic hagiography

><

KAREN JANKULAK

This chapter will examine a rich and varied body of material from saints' Lives concerning (for the most part) the situating of a saint's church with respect to the activities of swine, either wild or domestic. Although such episodes might seem frivolous, their investigation can be, in fact, profoundly illuminating in two main ways: first, the geographical distribution of the motif is unarguably 'Celtic', occurring in Ireland, Scotland, Wales, Somerset, Cornwall and Brittany; the few non-Celtic episodes, found in the west of England, occur in an arguably Celtic context. While such a study will not provide a final decision on whether or not 'Celtic' is an accurate term with regard to hagiography, it certainly shows the pertinence of such a term in individual cases, something that is too often overlooked. The second question posed by this material one might see as somewhat less controversial: that is, the material strongly suggests ultimate, if indirect, reliance for this motif on the foundation myth of Alba Longa, found in its earliest, and probably most accessible, state in Virgil's *Aeneid*. Here we have a case of a motif which might at first glance be seen as 'native' in origin, but which harks back, at least in part, to a classical legend.

The study of these episodes transcends, I would argue, the somewhat dry categorizing which forms the compilation and study of groups of motifs. Most motif indices or studies depending on them either treat their subjects on a purely literary level, or take either the common occurrence, or rarity, of certain motifs as significant in a historical sense.[1] This latter habit especially afflicts the study of the Lives of saints: certain common motifs are identified as depicting social reality, or, in contrast, any digression from features thought of as generically determined is examined as being at least potentially historically descriptive, due to its perceived unusual and therefore incidental nature.[2] For the most part, however, the information gathered into motif indices is of uncertain significance for the historian.[3] This study shares, for the most part, the achronological context of the motif indices – its material spans a considerable amount of time. Yet these stories of foundation[4] (including but not limited to those of an onomastic import) belong to a particular category, that of synthetic pseudo-history, a genre which has been increasingly explored as a source for the study of *mentalités*.[5]

It is worth outlining a typical example of this type of tale: a saint who has been granted a tract of land seeks to find his own particular site on which to found his church. An angel comes in a vision to describe how this is to be done, with reference to the activities of one or more domestic pigs or wild swine. Events occur as described in the vision, with the pig usually *in situ* marking the intended spot. There the saint builds his church.

The geographical distribution of the motif, as noted above, is notably 'Celtic'. It appears, albeit with variations, in Lives from almost all the Celtic regions. It appears in a Life from Scotland: that of Jocelyn of Furness's twelfth-century Life of St Kentigern.[6] Lives from Wales form a visible cluster: these include the eleventh-century Life of St Cadog by Lifris of Llancarfan (a version of the episode is also found in its twelfthcentury revision by Caradog of Llancarfan);[7] a twelfth-century Life of St Brynach;[8] the twelfth-century 'Life' of St Dyfrig found in the Book of Llandaf;[9] as well as the twelfth-century Life of St Illtud.[10] Lives from Ireland are the most numerous, probably due to the overwhelming number of existing medieval Lives of saints from Ireland: there are the Lives (two Latin and one Irish) of St Rúadán;[11] a Latin Life of St Mochoemóc;[12] the Lives (two Latin and one Irish) of St Fínán;[13] and the Lives (one of the two Latin Lives and both of the Irish Lives) of St Ciarán of Saigir.[14] There is also a similar episode concerning St Patrick's disciple Fíacc found in the *Vita Tripartita* and related versions;[15] one might cite as well one version of the Life of St Finnian of Clonard,[16] although with reservations (for which see below). Lives from Brittany belong to this group in a slightly more tangential fashion: these include the Life of St Paul Aurélien, composed in 884;[17] as well as the ninth-century Life of St Malo by Bili – the episode in this latter Life, however, does not conform exactly to type: in it, the saint resurrects a sow with living motherless piglets for the local lord, and obtains a grant of land thereby.[18] There are Lives from Devon and Cornwall, although again these digress considerably from the pattern: in the eleventh- or twelfth-century Life of St

Nectan the saint finds a sow and piglets on behalf of a swineherd, which leads to a donation of land to the saint;[19] and the Life of St Piran can be included only inasmuch as it is at this point a copy of the Life of St Ciarán of Saigir.[20] Somerset also features as the probable place of composition of the eleventh- or twelfth-century Life of St Cyngar, which includes an episode conforming more to type.[21] Finally, although it is not the Life of a saint, there is the twelfth-century *De antiquitate Glastonie ecclesie* by William of Malmesbury in which there is an account relating the chase of a sow which results in the name Glastonbury[22] – it is not entirely clear whether this should be ascribed to William or to his interpolator.[23]

In addition, there are two apparent examples of the motif occurring in an Anglo-Latin context. The first is found in the early eleventh-century Life of St Ecgwin by Byrhtferth.[24] The second, perhaps less directly related to the motif under discussion, is an episode found in the two fourteenth-century versions of the Life of St Fremund.[25] These will be discussed further below.

The earliest example of this type of motif is arguably that found in Wrmonoc's Life of St Paul Aurélien, composed, as the author tells us in his Preface, in 884. St Paul comes to a city (*oppidum*) and finds a spring, which he blesses in the name of the Holy Trinity. On entering the *castellum* he finds a wild sow (*sus*) suckling piglets; immediately the swine are tamed and henceforth form the basis of the king's domestic herd. Other beasts and insects are similarly tamed. The episode does not entirely correspond to the type described above: the sow partly marks a spot for the saint at what is to be his chief cult-site, but this is on a preexisting site rather than the blank slate of a wilderness. More importantly, the function of the sow and piglets is as domestic provision. It has been argued (mainly by Louis Pape) that this episode is more or less directly related to that of the *Aeneid*,[26] and indeed it is tempting to ascribe its digressions from what we might label the 'Celtic' type to a more faithful rendering of the classical motif. Nevertheless, it will be argued here, this is not entirely accurate.

The earliest example of an episode conforming more to our type is found in Lifris of Llancarfan's Life of St Cadog, dated to the late eleventh century.[27] St Cadog prays for a sign showing where he should situate his church on the tract of land newly granted to him (partly through the agency of a swineherd). An angel appears to him saying that he will find a place for building an *oratorium*, and that he will see a white boar (*aper candidus*), bristly and of great age, leap out and land upon the spot where he should build his *templum* in the name of the Holy Trinity.

Where the boar stops a second time, the saint is to build a *dormitorium*, and where it makes a third stop he is to build a *refectorium*. This happens as foretold, the saint marking each position with twigs. Note that the *vita*, however, contains a separate onomastic episode that explains the name of the site, with regard to a stag (*carfan*).[28]

Various links can be seen within the Lives in question. The dedication of the church to the Holy Trinity is a feature of several of the Welsh episodes: it appears in the Lives of Dyfrig, Illtud and Cyngar, as well as those of St Cadog. Doble viewed it as a sign of Norman influence,[29] but it is worth keeping in mind that it also figures in the ninth-century Life of St Paul Aurélien. The Life of St Paul Aurélien also, as Doble commented (ignoring however the similarity of dedication), uses the terms *habitacula* and *oratorium* for one of the monasteries built by the saint,[30] although not at his main church, which occupied the place indicated by the swine. The Lives of Dyfrig, Cyngar and Illtud all use similar terms for the buildings resulting from the swine foundation-episode: *oratorium et habitaculum* in the case of the first two saints, and *oratorium* in the case of the third. While these terms, and the dedication to the Holy Trinity, might suggest the influence of the Life of St Paul Aurélien, the Life has left no sign of its otherwise unique version of these events. Very probably the similarities between the Lives of Sts Cadog, Dyfrig and Illtud show interdependence between these four Lives rather than dependence on the Life of St Paul Aurélien. The episode in the Life of Illtud is essentially a marginal addition, not fully integrated into the story (note that Dyfrig appears in the episode). This is also true of the episode which is found in only one version of the Life of Finnian of Clonard: an angel tells the saint that he must seek his place or proper resurrection, with no mention of swine. The saint goes to Clonard and decides to stay there. A marginal gloss notes that 'et, cum locum intraret, aper mire magnitudinis, qui ibi habitatat, aufugit' (when he came to the place, he saw fleeing a marvellous great boar which lived there).[31] The gloss, one suspects, has resulted from a familiarity with the motif, as has, probably, the episode in the Life of St Cyngar (as Doble noted), a Life which shows little local knowledge of the saint.[32] The Life of St Kentigern relates the episode immediately after the saint has been granted Llancarfan, the home of St Cadog (the colour of the pig, *candidus*, is also the same in the Lives of Cadog and Kentigern – elsewhere they are mostly *alba*). Finally, it is worth restating, the appearance of the motif in the Life of St Piran is entirely circumstantial, resulting simply from the wholesale plagiarism of the Life of the Irish St Ciarán. It might be argued that these links show that the motif is in fact of fairly limited distribution initially, and should not be characterized as 'pan-Celtic'. Nevertheless, the spread of the motif, even into less than obvious narrative contexts, surely shows the notable interconnectedness of these Celtic Lives.

Byrhtferth's Life of St Ecgwin is one of two non-Celtic Lives in which this motif appears (see below for the Life of St Fremund); with the exception of the Life of St Paul Aurélien, it pre-dates all the datable Lives, having been composed in the early eleventh century.[33] This somewhat bizarre Life, self-consciously composed in so-called 'hermeneutic Latin'[34] relates how the saint places four swineherds in authority over the land he has received from King Æthelred and over his pigs. A constantly absconding sow, described as a *thesaurum*, panics the pre-eminent swineherd, Eoves, from whom will come the name of the place, Evesham.[35] She goes away and returns with seven piglets. A second escape produces an unspecified number of piglets which are completely white *(albus)* except for their ears and feet. A third escape produces nine piglets. The swineherd locates the sow at the site of a marvellous vision of three virgins *(virgines)*.[36] A report of the vision comes to St Ecgwin, who goes to the site and sees the virgins, the chief of whom he correctly understands to be the Mother of God. She blesses Ecgwin and vanishes, and he promises to erect an *oratorium* there. The Life follows with a series of charter-like narrations, most told in the first person from the saint's point of view.

There is a particular connection between the cult of Ecgwin and Wales, in particular with St Cadog. The manuscript of what is perhaps best viewed as a somewhat haphazard collection of Insular Norman *Celtica*, London, BL, MS Cotton Vespasian A.xiv, 'Vitae Sanctorum Wallensium' ('a peculiar collection both for what it brings in and for what it leaves out', as Kathleen Hughes described it),[37] seems to have included St Ecgwin in its calendar and also contains a genealogy connecting Ecgwin to the family of St Cadog (by making Ecgwin a brother of Cadog). As far as I know, this connection is made nowhere else, neither in any text referring to St Cadog nor in any text referring to St Ecgwin, although a fourteenth-century homily does state that Ecgwin was born in Wales.[38] While it is not surprising that Ecgwin might have been linked to Cadog as opposed to another saint (Cadog, as Hughes points out, dominates the manuscript),[39] Ecgwin's presence there at all, among otherwise standard Roman and more or less obscure Celtic saints, is puzzling.

Most of these episodes represent fairly straightforward tales of a saint finding, through the agency of the pig, a particular location designated by God for his church. The Life of St Brynach, for example, presents an uncomplicated account of pigs used as signs of God's will as regards the placing of the saint's church. It is notable that the tale has permeated local lore: the nearby mountain on which the saint is said to have had his vision has been known as *Carn Ingli* from the thirteenth century.[40] The Life of St Fínán deviates from the usual pattern only inasmuch as it replaces the angel with St Brendan. The Life of St Rúadán also presents minor variations on the pattern, using the pig's presence as a signal that the proper spot has been chosen: when the saint arrives at the designated spot he sees a boar. Yet, as there is no mention of a pig by the prophesying angel, it seems probable that the episode represents the same poorly integrated marginal addition found in various states in the Lives of Finnian and Illtud (as described above). While the Life of St Cadog also essentially conforms to the established pattern, it does present what may be significant differences as well: while on the one hand the fact of the boar marking the site is presented as a self-conscious and complicated ritual, on the other hand it includes at least one element, a swan who makes its nest where the boar lives and who also flies out when startled by the saint, who nevertheless is not mentioned either in the angelic instructions or in their subsequent fulfilment. This leaves an unsatisfying gap in an otherwise relatively careful and detailed portrait (why mention the swan at all?), one which is rectified in the Life as rewritten by Caradog of Llancarfan, in which the swan appears, equal to the boar, in the list of signifiers of location, and in which both boar and swan are given an explicit allegorical explanation (the former represents 'defenders of the realm', *patrie defensores*, the latter 'scholars and disciples', *doctores et discipulos*).[41]

The Life of St Ciarán (and thus the Life of St Piran) should perhaps be put to one side: in it the saint tames a wild boar, who helps the saint collect the materials with which to build his church (or prepare his cemetery). The Life somewhat enigmatically notes: 'Ille aper primus discipulum quasi monachus sancti Kyrani in illo loco fuit' (That boar was the first disciple, as it were a monk, of St Ciarán, in that place).[42] Both vernacular versions of the Life of St Ciarán include a similar statement.

There are only two examples of the onomastic possibilities of the motif being exploited, although it should be kept in mind that the Glastonbury Chronicle and the Life of St Ecgwin explain place-names with reference to the names of swineherds. The Life of St Dyfrig presents a brief and unadorned narration explaining the significance of the name of the place at which his church is situated, *Mochros* (that is Moccas on the Wye), which it etymologizes as the words for 'pigs' *(moch)* and 'place' *(ros* – heath). Although the whiteness of the pig is mentioned, the placename *Mochros* is due only to the existence of the pig. The Life of St

Mochoemóc, on the other hand, explains *Liath* (Líath Mór, or Líath-Mo-Choem-óc, in Co. Tipperary, according to Kenney, now Borrisoleigh),[43] the place-name resulting from the encounter with the swine, with reference to the colour of the animal: it is a large boar, white with age *(canus)*, whose equivalent in Irish, the Life states, is *liath*. The lack of onomastic material associated with swine in the other Lives under discussion is surprising when one considers the extravagant onomastic tales and asides inspired by swine in Celtic vernacular literature, in particular those found in the Welsh tales *Math uab Mathonwy, Culhwch ac Olwen*, and the material found in the versions of the 'Three Powerful Swineherds' triad,[44] as well as in the Irish *fianaigecht*.

The colour of the swine is not always mentioned: it does not figure in the Lives of Illtud, Cyngar, Paul Aurélien, Rúadán, Fínán, Finnian and Ciarán. When it is mentioned it is always some variation on white: the Lives of Kentigern and Cadog describe the pigs as *candidus*, those of Brynach and Dyfrig as *alba*, that of Mochoemóc as *canus* and *liath*. Although the whiteness of the pig has been taken as a sign of its otherworld, Celtic (that is, pagan) nature, it is worth noting that the pigs never have red ears or extremities (with perhaps the notable exception of the Life of St Ecgwin, in which the sow is white except for her ears and feet – they being of unspecified colour) as do other otherworld animals. Moreover, the whiteness of the pig can be better explained with reference to what is arguably one important archetype of the episodes in these Lives, the tale concerning the name of Alba Longa as found, among other places, in the *Aeneid*.

In Book III of the *Aeneid*, Aeneas is told by Helenus that he will, at a certain point, find a sow with a litter of thirty piglets lying on the ground; this shall be the site of the unnamed city his descendants are to found. This is to be a sign to Aeneas that he should rest from his travelling.[45] Later, in Book VIII, Aeneas arrives at the stated location. There, the god of the river Tiber comes to Aeneas in a dream, speaks prophetically about Aeneas' ultimate destination and, as a sign that this is no mere dream, indicates that Aeneas will find a white sow and thirty white piglets on the shore of the river. The number of piglets represents the number of years after which Aeneas' son, Ascanius, will found a city, 'Alba of glorious name'. Aeneas duly finds the sow, and sacrifices her and the piglets.[46] Alba Longa, chief among the Latin-league cities and allegedly destroyed by Rome in the seventh century BC, figures in origin legends as a precursor of Rome, founded by Aeneas' son Ascanius, who in turn is taken to be an ancestor of Romulus and Remus.[47] The tale, as told in Book VIII, has a clearly onomastic aspect: the sow's white colour, *alba*, is explicitly connected with the name of the city, as is the number of piglets with its founding – neither aspect especially figures in Book III. Indeed, by Book VIII the role of the sow has undergone a subtle shift, its precise significance obscured by a textual problem: in Book III the spot on which the sow is found has deliberate significance: 'is locus urbis erit' (that will be the site of the city) (line 393). In the context this must mean that the site marked by the swine is that upon which Aeneas is to found a city, presumably Lavinium as R. D. Williams remarks; its settlement then is to be moved to Alba Longa after thirty years by Aeneas' son.[48] The line, however, is repeated in Book VIII ('hic locus urbis erit' (here will be the site of the city), line 46), although only in some (and not in the main) manuscripts – there is general agreement that it makes no sense in the context there, that the location of Alba Longa cannot be reconciled with the location as described in Book VIII.[49]

The legend is referred to by Varro in terms more or less corresponding to Virgil's (Varro, however, makes the distinction between the founding of Alba Longa and Lavinium far more clearly), with the added detail that the sow had escaped from Aeneas' ship. This detail is also present in earlier variants of the legend (some of which concern a black sow) in which a sow is followed to the site rather than found at it.[50] The legend seems to be datable to at least the third century BC, with Virgil's version of it, although somewhat confused, as its fullest explication. Knowledge of the episode in the Middle Ages, however, is unclear. Augustine, for example, mentions Alba Longa but not pigs. Michael Herren has argued that direct knowledge among the Irish of classical works, including Virgil, was limited before the ninth century, although indirect access via commentaries was impressive.[51] Irish scholars knew various classical tales in the later Middle Ages,[52] and by the fourteenth century a version of the *Aeneid*, complete with the two swine episodes, had been translated into Irish.[53] Breton hagiographers seem to have been familiar with several classical poets, most often Virgil (in particular, the first books of the *Aeneid*),[54] but, as Neil Wright has argued, used these 'primarily as a source of elevated or emotive vocabulary'.[55]

As noted above, the Life of St Paul Aurélien (which also contains borrowings and echoes of Virgilian vocabulary) is often viewed as a close relative of the *Aeneid*, and in some ways this is true: the pig of the *Aeneid* episode is sacrificed by Aeneas, thus achieving a functional significance which is not entirely unlike that of the pig in the Life of St Paul Aurélien. Nevertheless the episode in the Life of St Paul Aurélien omits, needlessly, one might point out, what is arguably the main point of the *Aeneid*'s tale: the pig in the Life is not said to be white. This perhaps highlights the main difference between the episode in the *Aeneid* and those in the Lives here under discussion: the latter's notable lack of onomastic import, whether or not connected to the colour of the pig (as opposed to its existence). In this respect, the Life of St Mochoemóc is the only one to relate closely to the *Aeneid*.

In this context it is interesting to see how piglets are mentioned (or not) in these Lives. The number of piglets, thirty, is of primary importance to the classical legend, perhaps as much as the whiteness of the pigs. Piglets are mentioned in several of the Lives: those of Brynach, Dyfrig, Paul Aurélien and Nectan; they are numbered in the Lives of Illtud (where they are six), Malo (eight), and Ecgwin (seven and nine). Only in one comparable group of texts are they given as thirty – this is in the two versions of the Anglo-Latin Life of St Fremund. In this Life, a pilgrim at the tomb of the Lord in Jerusalem hears a voice ordering him to go home and giving him directions to a buried treasure *(thesaurus,* the same word as used to describe the sow in the Life of St Ecgwin), that is, the relics of St Fremund. These are to be marked by a sow (of no particular colour) and thirty piglets, which are to lead the pilgrim to the site, rather than being *in situ* as a sign. All happens as foretold. This Life, like the Life of St Paul Aurélien, is visibly different from the group of 'Celtic' Lives and, as in the Life of St Paul Aurélien, these very differences suggest a similarity to the episode in the *Aeneid*.[56]

This is not the only hagiographical example of the pigs being chased rather than acting as markers *in situ:* the Lives of Kentigern, Nectan and Ecgwin also feature pigs leading rather than marking. This is most often the case as well in non-hagiographical literature: when pigs have something to signify they usually lead a chase to the spot (as in, for example, *Math uab Mathonwy).* Patrick Sims-Williams has argued against the 'exaggerated' Celticity of this latter motif (that is, pigs acting as guides to a burial site), noting that the Life of St Kenelm of Gloucestershire contains an analogous episode with a cow as a guide.[57] One might argue that one analogue (involving a cow, which is of course entirely different) does not neccessarily make the case. Certainly animals often act as helpers to saints as well as to non-saintly protagonists. Other animals, in particular oxen pulling a cart, mark out a saint's territory or, in the case of Muirchú's Life of St Patrick, take his relics to their proper resting place (thus avoiding a bitter dispute).[58] Animal helpers form a broad category indeed. Pigs in particular inhabit wastelands and can therefore logically lead a person to something hidden in such places.[59] In this connection one might cite the Irish Life of St Patrick, known as the *Vita Tripartita,* in which a pig digs up gold with which St Patrick pays his ransom.[60]

It is important to recognize the difference between a narrative motif, which may follow certain patterns and have certain consequences in the *telling* of a tale, and those episodes under investigation here. The stories of swine marking the site of a saint's first church, almost always his most important church and often explicitly, through angelic prophecy, described as the site of his resurrection, clearly must carry authority beyond mere narrative convenience, despite their apparent whimsy. They form a large and coherent group. This of course immediately raises questions regarding the intended audience for such Lives, questions already raised, for example, in another context with respect to Lifris of Llancarfan's Life of St Cadog: while some have seen in the Life a warning to Norman encroachers, Wendy Davies has compellingly argued that the Life makes most sense if taken to be aimed at a local, Welsh audience, which might itself encroach upon the church's estates and privileges.[61] The Life of St Cadog is a very good illustration, both in its swine episode and in other episodes, of the clear trend among Lives of Celtic saints to partake of narrative devices more commonly associated with vernacular and 'secular' tales.

These foundation tales including swine cannot be dismissed as mere onomastic fancy rather than sternly authoritative foundation tales as such. While the Celtic vernacular tradition shows great interest in onomastic material and, in particular, events involving swine seem to inspire long flights of onomastic fancy, the onomastic possibilities of the swine material is surprisingly unused among the Lives under investigation. Only two Lives, those of Dyfrig and Mochoemóc, give onomastic explanations. This surely indicates a particular and, arguably, a coherent idea on the part of the hagiographers as regards the uses to which such episodes might properly be put.

In conclusion, several points can be argued. First, that the material discussed here is notably 'Celtic' in its distribution, and that this is probably not coincidental. Although this can and probably, for the most part, should be ascribed to borrowing between the various Lives rather than to some sort of inherent 'Celticity' of the motif, it does not lessen the significance of its distribution. Clearly, these Lives form a distinct-ive group. That the Lives also show distinct affinities with non-hagiographical Celtic literature (in particular with the discovery of Lleu in *Math uab Mathonwy*, itself a notoriously peculiar tale) is a separate, although undeniable, issue.

Second, while the main lines of the debate over influences in Celtic literature have focused (especially as concerns the Irish material) on a polarity between biblical versus 'native' tradition, the classical material has been perhaps overlooked. Although the relationship between the Lives discussed here and the tale found in the *Aeneid* is not uncomplicated, there is, clearly, some relationship. No doubt it is to this relationship that the Lives in question owe their consistency as a group, their frequent invocation of the colour of the swine in question, and their deployment of an origin legend without the onomastic flourish one might otherwise expect as giving such episodes their real significance. Wrmonoc's Life of St Paul Aurélien and the Life of St Fremund stand apart from the rest of the Lives discussed here precisely inasmuch as they include details conforming to details of the *Aeneid* episode (the function of the swine as provision in the former, the number of piglets in the latter), rather than broadly conforming, as do the other Lives, to the overall thrust of the *Aeneid's* episode.

Third, a minor debate about the servile and therefore originally pagan significance of swine and swineherds in other Celtic texts, most notably the accounts of the foundation of Cashel by Conall Corc,[62] has perhaps glossed over the practicalities of being a swineherd. Swine inhabit wastelands and roam in search of mast – this makes them ideal for the sort of marking out of unclaimed territory we often find in such accounts. It might also be noted that while some texts seem to cite specifically the servility of swineherds (the *Vita Tripartita*, for example, notes that it would have been more fitting for St Patrick to have been a shepherd than a swineherd),[63] the earliest vernacular Life of St Brigit (ninth-century) contains an episode similar to one in the earlier Latin Life by Cogitosus (but not found in the *Vita Prima*, which is otherwise much closer to the vernacular Life), presumably based on the same source. The miracle in the Latin Life concerns the sheep under the saint's care;[64] in the vernacular Life these have been turned into pigs (*mucc*).[65] Food for thought.

Notes

[1] Bray, 'The study', pp. 268–9.

[2] See especially Wooding, 'St Brendan's boat'.

[3] Indeed, Bray concludes her discussion of the purpose of motif indices by arguing, reasonably enough in the circumstances, that 'A motif index is thus a useful reference point, a foundation for the interpretation of the Lives as hagiographical literature, rather than as strictly historical or philological sources' ('The study', p. 276).

[4] A comprehensive study of the historiography and genre of monastic-foundation history, with reference principally to Bavarian cases studies, can be found in Kastner, *Historiae fundationum monasteriorum*, especially pp. 71–130.

[5] See, for example, Dumville, *Histories and Pseudo-Histories*, especially ch. VII, '

The historical value of the *Historia Brittonum*; Carey, *The Irish National Origin Legend*; idem, 'Native elements'; Sims-Williams, 'Some functions'.

[6] Lapidge and Sharpe, *Bibliography*, no. 1018; Forbes (ed. and trans.), *Lives*, pp. 75–8 and pp. 201–4.

[7] Lapidge and Sharpe, *Bibliography*, nos 34 and 38; *VSBG*, pp. 40–5; Grosjean (ed.), 'Vie de S. Cadog', pp. 50–2.

[8] Lapidge and Sharpe, *Bibliography*, no. 102: *VSBG*, pp. 6–9.

[9] Lapidge and Sharpe, *Bibliography*, no. 92; J. G. Evans and Rhys (eds), *The Text*, pp. 80–1.

[10] Lapidge and Sharpe, *Bibliography*, no. 97; *VSBG*, pp. 202–3.

[11] Lapidge and Sharpe, *Bibliography*, nos 483 and 397; Kenney, *Sources*, no. 184.iv; Plummer (ed.), *Vitae*, vol. 2, p. 241; Heist (ed.), *Vitae*, p. 161; *BNE*, vol. 1, p. 317, vol. 2, p. 309.

[12] Lapidge and Sharpe, *Bibliography*, no. 481; Plummer (ed.), *Vitae*, vol. 2, p. 170.

[13] Lapidge and Sharpe, *Bibliography*, nos 482 and 396; Kenney, *Sources*, no. 211.iii; Plummer (ed.), *Vitae*, vol. 1, pp. 88–9; Heist (ed.), *Vitae*, p. 154; Macalister, 'The Life', pp. 552–3.

[14] Lapidge and Sharpe, *Bibliography*, no. 488; Kenney, *Sources*, nos 124.i and 124.ii; Plummer (ed.), *Vitae*, vol. 1, p. 219; *BNE*, vol. 1, pp. 104, 111; vol. 2, pp. 100, 109. The episode is not found in the Salmanticensis *Vita* (Heist (ed.), *Vitae*, pp. 346–53).

[15] Kenney, *Sources*, no. 135; Stokes (ed.), *Tripartite Life*, vol. 1, pp. 190–3; also the same story (with variations in orthography), *idem*, vol. 2, pp. 346–7; and again the same story, Stokes and Strachan (eds), *Thesaurus*, vol. 2, pp. 242–3. St Patrick, the subject of the various texts, acts as a mediator between Fíacc and the angelic command in the founding of Fiacc's church of Slébte.

[16] Lapidge and Sharpe, *Bibliography*, no. 389; Heist (ed.), *Vitae*, p. 101.

[17] Lapidge and Sharpe, *Bibliography*, no. 828; Cuissard (ed.), 'Vie', pp. 442–3; D. Plaine (ed.), 'Vita', pp. 240–1.

[18] Lapidge and Sharpe, *Bibliography*, no. 825: Le Duc, *Vie*, pp. 110–15. The episode also appears in the Old English Life of the saint, as well as with variations in the anonymous Lives.

[19] Grosjean (ed.), 'Vie de S. Rumon', p. 400.

[20] Lapidge and Sharpe, *Bibliography*, no. 112; Grosjean (ed.), 'Vita S. Ciarani', pp. 229–30.

[21] Lapidge and Sharpe, *Bibliography*, no. 116; Robinson (ed.), 'A fragment', p. 101.

[22] J. Scott, *The Early History*, pp. 52–3 and 188; see also John of Glastonbury's *Chronicle of Glastonbury Abbey*: Carley (ed.) and Townsend (trans.), pp. 10–13; cf. also Meyer (ed.), *Sanas Cormaic*, p. 75.

[23] See most recently Thornton, 'Glastonbury', especially pp. 199–200.

[24] Giles (ed.), *Vita*, pp. 363–76.

[25] Horstman (ed.), *Nova Legenda Anglie*, vol. 1, pp. 455–6; see also ibid., vol. 2, pp. 696–7. The two Lives differ in only minor details.

[26] Merdrignac, 'Truies et verrats', pp. 144–7 and references there. I wish to thank Bernard Merdrignac for giving me a copy of this valuable article, which I would not have seen otherwise.

[27] W. Davies, 'Property rights', p. 519.

[28] The pig episode of Lifris' Life of St Cadog, its relation to the onomastic tale found in the Life, and its revision by Caradog of Llancarfan form the subject of research in progress, which I hope to publish soon.

[29] Doble, *Lives*, pp. 74–5, n. 46, and p. 107, n. 53; see also Brooke, *The Church*, pp. 39, n. 93, and p. 40, n. 96.

[30] Cuissard (ed.), 'Vie', p. 439.
[31] Heist (ed.), *Vitae*, p. 101.
[32] Doble, 'Saint Congar', p. 90 and n. 83.
[33] Lapidge, 'The medieval hagiography', pp. 77–8; see also Townsend, 'Anglo-Latin hagiography', pp. 412–21. I would like to thank David Townsend for pointing me (many years ago!) towards the subject of swine in the Ecgwin and Celtic hagiography.
[34] See Lapidge, 'The hermeneutic style'.
[35] *Idem*, 'Byrhtferth', pp. 346–7.
[36] Cf. the three *virgines* who wash the Virgin Mary's body in the Pseudo-Melito *Transitus Mariae*. For the Latin and Welsh versions, see Elliott, *The Apocryphal New Testament*, p. 711; J. E. C. Williams (ed.), '*Transitus Beatae Mariae*', pp. 133 and 135.
[37] Hughes, 'British Museum MS. Cotton Vespasian A.xiv', pp. 188, 199–200.
[38] Harris, 'The kalendar', pp. 42–4.
[39] Hughes, 'British Museum MS. Cotton Vespasian A.xiv', p. 191.
[40] The form *Mons Angelorum* appears in the Life itself *(VSBG*, p. 10) but the form *Carn Ingli* is attested in several early seventeenth-century copies of thirteenth-century texts (Charles, *The Place-Names*, vol. 1, p. 163).
[41] Grosjean, 'Vie de S. Cadog', p. 52.
[42] Plummer (ed.), *Vitae*, vol. 1, p. 219.
[43] Kenney, *Sources*, p. 455.
[44] Bromwich (ed.), *Trioedd*, nos 26 and 26W, pp. 44–54.
[45] Virgil, *Aeneid*, III.389–93, in Fairclough (ed. and trans.), *Virgil*, vol. 1, pp. 398–9.
[46] Virgil, *Aeneid*, VIII.42–8, 80–5, in Fairclough (ed. and trans.), *Virgil*, vol. 2, pp. 62–7.
[47] Hornblower and Spawforth, *Oxford Classical Dictionary*, p. 50.
[48] Virgil, *Aeneid, Bk III*, R. D. Williams (ed.) *P. Vergili*, pp. 138–9.
[49] Conington and Nettleship (eds), *The Works of Virgil*, vol. 3, p. 91, n. 42. The location of Lavinium, as well, cannot be reconciled with that described in Book VIII, but that is a separate problem.
[50] Varro, *De Lingua Latina*, V.144, Kent (trans.), *Varro*, vol. 1, pp. 134–7; Varro, *De Re Rustica*, II.18, Guiraud (ed. and trans.), *Varron*, vol. 2, pp. 41, 126–7. See, for the legend in general, *Aeneid, Bk II*, R. D. Williams (ed.), *P. Vergili*, pp. 137–9.
[51] Herren, 'Classical and secular learning', pp. 124–5; see also *idem*, 'The transmission'.
[52] See Carney, *Studies; idem*, 'Early Irish literature', pp. 128–30; Freeman, 'A Middle Irish version'.
[53] Calder (ed. and trans.), *Imtheachta Aeniasa*, pp. 10–11, 114–15.
[54] Riché, 'Les Hagiographes bretons', p. 655.
[55] N. Wright, 'Vergilian borrowings', p. 174. See also Kerlouégan, 'Les Citations d'auteurs latins profanes'; Merdrignac, 'L'Eneide'.
[56] The tradition of St Guthlac appears to have included something similar: a sculpture is said to have existed over the west doorway of Croyland abbey depicting Guthlac with a sow and piglets, apparently relating to a local tale of Guthlac finding, as prophesied, the sow and the piglets (thirty in number) under a willow tree, where he was to build his church (Graham Jones, personal communication). The medieval accounts of Guthlac, however, show no sign of this story.
[57] Sims-Williams, 'The evidence', p. 238 and n. 10.
[58] Bieler (ed. and trans.), *The Patrician Texts*, pp. 121–2.
[59] See also Henken, *Welsh Saints*, pp. 88–90.
[60] Stokes (ed.), *Tripartite Life*, vol. 1, pp. 94–5; the same story appears in the later Lismore version of Patrick's Life: Stokes (ed. and trans.), *Lives of Saints*, pp. 6 and

154; it is also found in the *Annals of Clonmacnoise:* Murphy (ed. and trans.), *The Annals*, p. 63.

[61] W. Davies, 'Property rights' *pace* Borst, 'A reconsideration'.

[62] Sproule, 'Politics'; Ní Chatháin, 'Swineherds'; Ford, 'A highly important pig'.

[63] Stokes (ed.), *Tripartite Life*, vol. 1, pp. 16–17.

[64] Lapidge and Sharpe, *Bibliography*, nos 302 and 372: Bollandus *et al.* (eds), *Acta Sanctorum*, February, vol. 1, p. 136 (ch. 7).

[65] Kenney, *Sources*, no. 152.ii; Ó hAodha (ed.), *Bethu Brigte*, p. 2; the episode also occurs in a later Irish Life of Brigit: Kenney, *Sources*, no. 152.i; Stokes (ed. and trans.), *Lives of the Saints*, pp. 37 and 185.

Works Cited

Abou-El-Haj, B., *The Medieval Cult of Saints: Formations and Transformations*, Cambridge, 1994.
Abrams, M. H., *A Glossary of Literary Terms*, 6th edn, New York, 1993.
Adomnán, *Vita Sancti Columbae*, A. O. Anderson and M. O. Anderson (eds), *Adomnan's Life of Columba*, London, 1961; rev. edn, Oxford Medieval Texts, 1991.
Allen, J. R. and Anderson, J., *The Early Christian Monuments of Scotland*, Edinburgh, 1903.
Anderson, A. O., *Early Sources of Scottish History A.D. 500 to 1286*, Stamford, 1990.
Angell, L. H., '*Gwyrthyeu e Wynvydedic Veir:* astudiaeth gymharol ohonynt fel y'u ceir hwynt yn llawysgrifau Peniarth 14, Peniarth 5 a Llanstephan 27', MA thesis, University of Wales, Cardiff, 1938.
an Irien, J., 'Saints du Cornwall et saints bretons du Ve au Xe siècle' in M. Simone (ed.), *Landévennec et le monachisme Breton dans le haut Moyen Âge*, Banalec, 1986, pp. 169–88.
Arnold, T. (ed.), *Symeonis Monachi Opera Omnia, I. Historia Ecclesiae Dunhelmensis*, Rolls Series 75 (2), London, 1882.
Arnold, C. J and Hugget, J. W., 'Mathrafal, Powys: a re-assessment', *BBCS 33* (1986), 436–51.
—, 'Excavations at Mathrafal, Powys, 1989', with a contribution by Huw Pryce, *Montgomeryshire Collections* 83 (1995), 59–74.
Aspinall, A., Bogdan, N. Q. and Dransart, P. Z., 'Kinneddar', *Discovery and Excavation in Scotland*, New Series 2 (1995), 35–6.
Austin,. D., Gerrard, G. A. M., and Greeves, T. A. P., 'Tin and agriculture in the Middle Ages and beyond: landscape archaeology in St Neot parish, Cornwall', *Cornish Archaeology* 28 (1989), 5–251.
Axton, R., 'Interpretations of Judas in Middle English Literature', in Boitani and Torti (eds), *Religion in the Poetry*, pp. 179–97.

Balcou, J. and Le Gallou, Y., *Histoire littéraire et culturelle de la Bretagne*, 3 vols, Paris/Geneve, 1987.
Bammesberger, A., and Wollmann, A. (eds), *Britain 400–600: Language and History*, Heidelberg, 1990.
Baring-Gould, S. and Fisher, J., *The Lives of the British Saints*, 4 vols, London, 1907–13.
Barrow, G. W. S., *Kingship and Unity Scotland 1000–1306*, Edinburgh, 1996.
—, *The Kingdom of the Scots*, London, 1973.
Bartlett, R. 'Rewriting saints' Lives: the case of Gerald of Wales', *Speculum* 58 (1983), 598–613.
—, 'Cults of Irish, Scottish and Welsh saints in twelfth-century England', in B. Smith (ed.), *Britain and Ireland 900–1300: Insular Responses to Medieval European Change*, Cambridge, 1999, pp. 67–86.
Bartrum, P. C. (ed.), 'Pedigrees of the Welsh tribal patriarchs', *NLWJ* 13 (1963), 93–146.
— (ed.), *Early Welsh Genealogical Tracts*, Cardiff, 1966.
Bell, H. I. (ed.), *Vita Sancti Tathei and Buched Seint y Katrin*, Bangor, 1909.
Bentley, J., *The Way of Saint James*, London, 1992.
Berthou-Becam, L., 'Enquête officielle sur les poésies populaires de la France 1852–1876: collectes de langue bretonne', Doctoral dissertation, Université de Rennes II, 1998.
Best, R. I. and Lawlor, H. J. (eds), *The Martyrology of Tallaght from the Book of Leinster and MS. 5100–4 in the Royal Library, Brussels*, Henry Bradshaw Society 68, London, 1931.
Bethell, D., 'English monks and Irish reform in the eleventh and twelfth centuries', in T. D. Williams (ed.), *Historical Studies: Papers read before the Irish Conference of Historians* 8, Dublin, 1971, pp. 111–35.
Bevan, W. L. (ed.), *Diocesan Histories, St Davids*, London, 1888.
Bhreathnach, E., 'Temoria: Caput Scotorum?', *Ériu* 47 (1996), 67–88.
Bieler, L., 'The "Creeds" of St Victorinus and St Patrick', *Theological Studies* 9(1949) 121–4.
— (ed.), 'Libri epistolarum sancti Patricii episcopi', *Classica et Mediaevalia* 11 (1950), 1–150 and 12 (1951), 79–214; rpr. as *Royal Irish Academy Dictionary of Medieval Latin from Celtic Sources*, Ancillary Publications 4, Dublin, 1993.
—, 'The Celtic hagiographer', *Studia Patristica* 5 (1962), 243–65.
— (ed.), *Four Latin Lives of St. Patrick*, Scriptores Latini Hiberniae 8, Dublin, 1971.
—, 'Hagiography and romance in Medieval Ireland', *Medievalia et Humanistica* 6 (1975), 13–24.
— (ed.), *The Irish Penitentials*, Dublin, 1975.
— (ed. and trans.), *The Patrician Texts in the Book of Armagh*, Scriptores Latini Hiberniae 10, Dublin, 1979.
Binchy, D. A., 'Patrick and his biographers ancient and modern', *Studia Hibernica* 2 (1962), 7–173.

Blair, J., 'A saint for every minster? Local cults in Anglo-Saxon England', in Sharpe and Thacker (eds), *Local Saints and Local Churches*.

Blew, W. (ed.), *Breviarium Aberdonense*, Bannatyne, Maitland and Spalding Clubs, 1854.

Blockley, R. C., 'The date of the "Barbarian Conspiracy"', *Britannia* 11 (1980) 223–6.

Boece, H., *Scotorum historiæ a prima gentis origine* . . ., Paris, 1526–7.

—, *Heir beginnis the history and croniklis of Scotland*, J. Bellenden (trans.), Edinburgh, 1540.

Boitani, P. and Torti, A. (eds), *Religion in the Poetry and Drama of the Late Middle Ages in England*, Cambridge, 1990.

Bokenham, O., *Legendys of Hooly Wumman*, M. S. Serjeantson (ed.), London, 1938.

Bollandus, J. et al. (eds), *Acta Sanctorum quotquot in toto orbe Coluntur*, Brussels, 1643–1910; 3rd edn, Paris and Brussels, 1863–1940.

Bonner, G., Rollason, D., Stancliffe, C. (eds), *St Cuthbert, His Cult and His Community*, Woodbridge, 1989.

Bonnerue, P. (ed.), *Benedicti Anianensis Concordia regularum*, 2 vols, Turnhout, 1999.

Borst, K. G., 'A reconsideration of the *Vita Sancti Cadoci*', in P. K. Ford (ed.), *Celtic Folklore and Christianity: Studies in Memory of William W. Heist*, Santa Barbara, California, 1983, pp. 1–15.

Bouet, P. and Kerlouégan, F., 'La Réécriture dans le latin du haut Moyen Age', *Lalies. Actes des sessions de linguistique et de littérature* 8 (Aussois 26–31 août 1986), pp. 153–68.

Bourgealt, C., 'The monastic archetype in the Navigatio of St Brendan', *Monastic Studies* 14 (1983), 109–21.

Bourgès, A.-Y., 'De la vita de saint Cunual à celles des saints Tugdual, Maudez, et Efflam', *Trégor vivant. Mélanges offerts à la mémoire de Nicole Chouteau*, [Perros-Guirec], 1997, pp. 141–51.

Bourke, C., 'The hand-bells of the early Scottish church', *Proc. Soc. Antiq. Scotl.* 113 (1983), 464–8.

Bowen, E. G., 'The cult of Dewi Sant at Llanddewibrefi', *Ceredigion* 2 (1952–5), 61–5.

—, *The Settlements of the Celtic Saints in Wales*, Cardiff, 1954.

—, *The Saint David of History, Dewi Sant: Our Founder Saint*, Aberystwyth, 1982.

—, *Dewi Sant/Saint David*, Cardiff, 1983.

Boyer, R., 'An attempt to define the typology of medieval hagiography,' in H. Bekker-Nielsen (ed.), *Hagiography and Medieval Literature*, Odense, 1981, pp. 27–36

Boyle, A., 'Some saints' lives in the Breviary of Aberdeen', *AB* 94 (1976), 95–106.

—, 'Notes on Scottish saints', *The Innes Review* 32 (2) (1981), 59–82.

Bozon, N., *Three Saints' Lives by Nicholas Bozon*, M. A. Klenke (ed.), New York, 1947.

Bradley, I., *The Celtic Way*, London, 1993.

—, *Celtic Christianity: Making Myths and Chasing Dreams*, Edinburgh, 1999.

Bradshaw, P. F., *The Search for the Origins of Christian Worship*, London, 2002.

Bramley, K. A. et al. (eds), *Gwaith Llywelyn Fardd I ac Eraill o Feirdd y Ddeuddegfed Ganrif*, Cardiff, 1994.

Bray, D. A., *A List of Motifs in the Lives of the Early Irish Saints*, Helsinki, 1992.

—, 'Allegory in the *Navigatio Sancti Brendani*', *Viator* 26 (1995), 7; rpr. Wooding (ed.), *The Otherworld Voyage*, p. 181.

—, 'The study of folk-motifs in early Irish hagiography: problems of approach and rewards at hand', in Carey, Herbert and Ó Riain (eds), *Studies in Irish Hagiography*, pp. 268–77.

Breeze, A, 'The Battle of Brunanburgh and Welsh Tradition', *Neophilologus* 83 (1999), 479–82.

Bremond, C., Le Goff, J. and Schmitt, J.-C., *L' "exemplum"*, Typologie des sources du moyen âge occidental 40, Turnhout, 1982.

Brett, C., 'L'Hagiographie de saint Guénolé de Landévennec: le témoignage du manuscrit de Cardiff', in M. Simon (ed.), *Landévennec et le monachisme breton*, pp. 253–67.

Breviarium Aberdonense, Edinburgh 1510; rpr. London, 1854.

Bromwich, R. (ed.), *Trioedd Ynys Prydein*, 2nd edn, Cardiff, 1961.

— (ed.), *The Beginnings of Welsh Poetry: Studies by Sir Ifor Williams*, 2nd edn, Cardiff, 1982.

Brooke, C. N. L., 'St Peter of Gloucester and St Cadog of Llancarfan', in N. K. Chadwick and K. H. Jackson (eds), *Celt and Saxon*, Cambridge, 1963, pp. 258–322.

—, *The Church and the Welsh Border in the Central Middle Ages*, Woodbridge, 1986.

Brown, S. and O'Connor, D., *Glass-Painters (Medieval Craftsmen)*, London, 1991; rpr. 1993.

Brown, S. and MacDonald, L. (eds), *Life, Death and Art – The Medieval Stained Glass of Fairford Parish Church*, Stroud, 1997.

Bullock-Davies, C., *Professional Interpreters and the Matter of Britain*, Cardiff, 1966.

Burdett-Jones, M., 'Gweddi anarferol', *Y Cylchgrawn Catholig 3* (1994), 35–6.

Burgess, G. and Strijbosch, C., *The Legend of St Brendan – A Critical Bibliography*, Dublin, 2000.

Burgess, G. and Wogan-Browne, J. (ed. and trans.), *Virgin Lives and Holy Deaths*, London, 1996.

Byfield, C. E., 'A new edition of *Buched Seint y Katrin*', M.Phil. thesis, to be submitted to the University of Wales, Cardiff.
Cadic, F.-M., 'Le Chant de la Saint Jean', *Revue de Bretagne, de Vendée et d'Anjou* 18 (1897), 47–54.
—, 'Le Mal de Saint Jean', *Paroisse Bretonne de Paris*, 1908 (8).
—, 'Saint Servais', *Paroisse Bretonne de Paris*, 1909 (2).
Calder, G. (ed. and trans.), *Imtheachta Aeniasa. The Irish Aeneid*, London, 1907.
Campbell, J., 'Some twelfth-century views of the Anglo-Saxon past', *Peritia* 3 (1984), 131–5.
Carey, J., *The Irish National Origin-Legend: Synthetic Pseudohistory*, Cambridge, 1994.
—, 'Native elements in Irish pseudohistory', in Doris Edel (ed.), *Cultural Identity and Cultural Integration*, Dublin, 1995, pp. 45–60.
Carey, J., Herbert, M. and Ó Riain, P. (eds), *Studies in Irish Hagiography. Saints and Scholars*, Dublin, 2001.
Carley, J. P. (ed.) and Townsend, D. (trans.), *The Chronicle of Glastonbury Abbey*, Suffolk, 1985.
Carmichael, I., *Lismore in Alba*, published privately, n.d. [*c*.1848].
Carney, J., *Studies in Irish Literature and History*, Dublin, 1955.
—, 'Early Irish literature: the state of research', in G. Mac Eoin, A. Ahlqvist and D. Ó hAodha (eds), *Proceedings of the Sixth International Congress of Celtic Studies held in University College, Galway, 6–13 July 1979*, Dublin, 1983, pp. 113–30.
Carrée, A., and Merdrignac, B. (eds), *La Vie latine de saint Lunaire. Textes, traduction, commentaires*, Landévennec, 1991.
Cartwright, J., 'The desire to corrupt: convent and community in medieval Wales', in D. Watt (ed.), *Medieval Women in their Communities*, Cardiff, 1997, pp. 20–48.
—, Y *Forwyn Fair, Santesau a Lleianod: Agweddau ar Wyryfdod a Diweirdeb yng Nghymru'r Oesoedd Canol*, Cardiff, 1999.
—, 'Dead virgins: feminine sanctity in medieval Wales', *Medium Ævum* 71 (1) (2002), 1–28.
—, '*Buchedd Catrin:* a preliminary study of the Middle Welsh Life of St Katherine of Alexandria and her cult in medieval Wales', in K. J. Lewis and J. Jenkins (eds), *St Katherine of Alexandria: Texts and Contexts in Medieval Europe*, Brussels, forthcoming.
Casel, O., *The Mystery of Christian Worship*, London, 1962.
Cass, F. C., *South Mimms*, Westminster, 1877.
Cassard, J.-C., 'La Mise en texte du passé par les hagiographes de Landévennec', *BSAF* 122 (1993), 361–86.
Chadwick, H., *Priscillian of Ávila: The Occult and the Charismatic in the Early Church*, Oxford, 1976.
Chadwick, N. K., 'Intellectual life in west Wales in the last days of the Celtic

Church', in N. K. Chadwick, Hughes, Brooke and Jackson (eds), *Studies in the Early British Church*, pp. 121–82
—, *Early Brittany*, Cardiff, 1969.
Chadwick, N. K., Hughes, K., Brooke, C. and Jackson, K. (eds), *Studies in the Early British Church*, Cambridge, 1958.
Charles, B. G. *The Place-Names of Pembrokeshire*, 2 vols, Aberystwyth, 1992.
Charles-Edwards, G., 'The scribes of the Red Book of Hergest', *NLWJ* 21 (1979–80), 245–56.
Charles-Edwards, T. M., 'The seven bishop-houses of Dyfed', *BBCS* 24 (1971), 247–62.
—, 'The social background to Irish *peregrinatio*', *Celtica* 11 (1976), 43–59; rpr. Wooding (ed.), *The Otherworld Voyage*, pp. 94–108.
—, 'Bede, the Irish and the Britons', *Celtica* 15 (1983), 42–52.
—, *Early Christian Ireland*, Cambridge, 2000.
—, '*Erlam*' in Sharpe and Thacker (eds), *Local Saints and Local Churches*.
Charles-Edwards, T. M. and Jones, N. A., '*Breintiau Gwŷr Powys*: the liberties of the men of Powys', in T. M. Charles-Edwards, Owen and Russell (eds), *The Welsh King*, pp. 191–223.
Charles-Edwards, T. M, Owen, M. E. and Russell, P. (eds), *The Welsh King and his Court*, Cardiff, 2000.
Chédeville, A. and Guillotel, H., *La Bretagne des saints et des rois V^e–Xe siècle*, Rennes, 1984.
Chudleigh, M., 'History of St Issey', unpublished manuscript, 1920s – copy to be lodged at the Courtney Library, RIC.
Cicero, *De diuinatione*, O. Plasberg and W. Ax (eds), Stuttgart, 1938.
Colgrave, B. (ed.), *Two Lives of Saint Cuthbert*, Cambridge, 1940.
Conington, J., and Nettleship, H. (eds), *The Works of Virgil*, 4th edn, 3 vols, London, 1883–98; rpr. Hildesheim, 1963.
Conneely, D., *St Patrick's Letters: A Study of their Theological Dimension*, P. Bastable et al. (eds), Maynooth, 1993.
Connolly, S., 'Vita prima Sanctae Brigitae: background and historical value', *JRSAI* 119 (1989) 5–49.
Connolly, S., and Picard, J.-M. (trans.), 'Cogitosus: Life of Saint Brigit', *JRSAI* 117 (1987) 11–27.
Constantine, M.-A., *Breton Ballads*, Aberystwyth, 1996.
—, 'A Breton Mary Magdalene: the *gwerz* of Mari Kelenn', in E. Andreassen (ed.), *Vision and Identities*, Tórshavn, 1996, pp. 73–92.
Cooper, J., 'St Gerardine: a chapter in the ecclesiastical history of Moray', *Transactions of the Aberdeen Ecclesiastical Society* 8 (1893), 105–16.
Couch, T. C., 'Parochialia – Lanivet', *JRIC* 1 (1864–5), 71–81.
Cowan, I. B., 'The medieval church in the diocese of Aberdeen', *Northern Scotland* 1(1) (1972), 19–48.
Cowan, I. B. and Easson, D. E., *Medieval Religious Houses: Scotland*, 2nd edn, London, 1976.

Cowley, F. G., 'A note on the discovery of St David's body', *BBCS* 19, (1960), 47–8.
—, 'The church in Glamorgan from the Norman Conquest to the beginning of the fourteenth century' in T. B. Pugh (ed.), *Glamorgan County History*, vol. 3, Cardiff, 1971, pp. 87–134.
Craster, H. H. E., 'The Red Book of Durham', *English Historical Review* 40 (1925), 504–32.
Crawford, H. S., 'The early slabs at Lemanaghan, King's County', *JRSAI* 41 (2) (1911), 151–6.
Croix, A., *La Bretagne aux 16e et 17e siècles: la vie – la mort – la foi*, 2 vols, Paris, 1981.
Crouch, D., 'Urban, first bishop of Llandaff', *JWEH* 6 (1989), 1–15.
—, *William Marshal, Court, Career and Chivalry in the Angevin Empire 1147–1219*, Longman, Harlow, 1990.
Cuissard, M. Ch. (ed.), 'Vie de saint Paul de Léon en Bretagne', *RC* 5 (1881–3), 413–60.
Cule, J., 'Some early hospitals in Wales and the border', *NLWJ* 20 (1977–8), 97–130.
Curran, M., *The Antiphonary of Bangor*, Dublin, 1984.
Cusack, P., *An Interpretation of the Second Dialogue of Gregory the Great: Hagiography and St. Benedict*, Lewiston/Queenston/Lampeter, 1993.
Daniel, R. I., 'Y ffynhonnau yng nghanu'r Cywyddwyr', *Dwned* 7 (2001), 65–81.
Davies, C. T. B., 'Cerddi'r tai crefydd', MA thesis, University of Wales, Bangor, 1973.
Davies, J., *A History of Wales*, London, 1993.
Davies, J. C. (ed.), *Episcopal Acts and Cognate Documents Relating to Welsh Dioceses 1066–1272*, 2 vols, Cardiff, 1946–8.
—'The Strata Marcella charters', *Montgomeryshire Collections* 51 (1949–50), 164–81.
Davies, J. L., 'The Roman period' in J. L. Davies, and D. P. Kirby (eds), *Cardiganshire County History*, vol. 1, Cardiff, 1994, pp. 275–317.
Davies, O., *Celtic Christianity in Early Medieval Wales*, Cardiff, 1996.
—, (trans.) with collaboration of O'Loughlin, T., *Celtic Spirituality*, Mahwah NY, 1999.
Davies, R. R., *Conquest, Coexistence and Change: Wales 1063–1415*, Oxford and Cardiff, 1987.
—, *Domination and Conquest: The Experience of Ireland, Scotland and Wales 1100–1300*, Cambridge, 1990.
—, '"Keeping the natives in order", the English king and "Celtic" rulers 1066–1216', *Peritia* 10 (1996), 225–36.
—, *The First English Empire*, Oxford, 2000.
Davies, W., '*Braint Teilo*', *BBCS* 27 (1974–6), 123–37.
—, *The Llandaff Charters*, Aberystwyth, 1979.

—, 'Property rights and property claims in Welsh "Vitae" of the eleventh century', in E. Patlegan and P. Riché (eds), *Hagiographie, cultures et societés IVe–XIIe siècles*, Paris, 1981, pp. 515–33.

—, *Wales in the Early Middle Ages*, Leicester, 1982.

—, 'The myth of the Celtic Church', in N. Edwards and A. Lane (eds), *The Early Church in Wales and the West*, Oxbow Monograph 16, 1992, pp. 12–21. de La Borderie, A., 'Saint Tudval: texte des trois vies anciennes de S. Tudval', *Mémoires de la Société archéologique des Côtes-du-Nord* New Series 2 (1886–7), 77–122 and 284–365.

de Paor, Liam, *Saint Patrick's World: The Christian Culture of Ireland's Apostolic Age*, Dublin, 1993.

De Smedt, C. (ed.), 'Vita S. Winwaloei primi abbatis Landevencensis auctore Wurdestino', *AB* 7 (1888), 167–264.

de Voragine, J., *Legenda Aurea*, T. Graesse (ed.), Dresden, 1846.

—, *The Golden Legend: Readings on the Saints*, W. Granger Ryan (trans.), 2 vols, Princeton, 1993.

Delehaye, H., *L'Œuvre des Bollandistes à travers trois siècles – 1615–1915*, 2nd edn, Brussels, 1959.

d'Evelyn, C. and Mill, A. J. (eds), *The South English Legendary*, 3 vols, EETS O.S. 235, 236, 244, London, 1956–9.

Doble, G. H., *S. German of Auxerre, Patron of S. Germans, Cornwall*, Shipton-on-Stour, 2nd edn, 1928.

—, *St Neot, Abbot and Confessor*, Exeter, 1930.

—, *Saint Suliau and Saint Tysilio*, Guildford and Esher, 1936.

—, *St Petroc*, Shipston-on-Stour, 3rd edn, 1938.

—, 'The relics of Saint Petroc', *Antiquity* 13 (1939), 403–15.

—, 'Saint Congar', *Antiquity* 19 (1945), 32–43, 85–95.

—, *Lives of the Welsh Saints*, D. S. Evans (ed.), Cardiff, 1971.

Dodds, M. H., 'The Little Book of the Birth of St Cuthbert', *Archaeologia Aeliana* 4th Series 6 (1929), 52–94.

Doherty, C. 'The cult of St Patrick and the growth of the political power of Armagh in the seventh and eighth century', in J. M. Picard (ed.), *Ireland and Northern France 600–850*, Dublin, 1991, pp. 53–94.

Dolbeau, F., 'Les Hagiographes au travail: collecte et traitement des documents écrits (IXe-XIIe siécle)', in Heinzelmann (ed.), *Manuscrits hagiographiques*, pp. 49–76.

—, 'Les Travaux français sur l'hagiographie médiolatine (1968–1998)', *Hagiographica* 6 (1999), 23–68.

Doubleday, H. A. and Page, W. (eds), *History of Bedfordshire*, 4 vols, Victoria History of the Counties of England, London, 1904–20; rpr. 1972.

Dransart, P., 'The Maiden Stone of Bennachie', *Bennachie Notes* (November 1988), 10–22.

—, 'Two shrine fragments from Kinneddar, Moray', in M. Redknap et al. (eds), *Pattern and Purpose in Insular Art: Transactions of the Fourth International Conference on Insular Art*, Oxford, 2001, pp. 233–40.

Dransart, P. and Bogdan, N. Q., *The Scottish Episcopal Palaces Project: Fetternear 1995*, Lampeter, 1996.
Duchesne, L., 'Les Trois vies anciennes de S. Tudval', *RC* 10 (1889), 253–5. —, 'La Légende de sainte Marie-Madeleine', in L. Duchesne, *Fastes Episcopaux de l'Ancienne Gaule*, 3 vols, Paris, 1907–15, pp. 321–60.
Duffy, E., *The Stripping of the Altars – Traditional Religion in England 1400–1580*, New Haven and London, 1992.
Duffy, S., 'The 1169 invasion as a turning-point in Irish-Welsh relations', in B. Smith (ed.), *Britain and Ireland 900–1300*, Cambridge, 1999, pp. 98–113. Duine, F., *Sources hagiographiques de l'histoire de Bretagne*, Rennes, 1918. —, *Memento des sources hagiographiques de l'histoire de Bretagne*, Rennes, 1918.
Dumville, D. N., *Saint David of Wales*, Kathleen Hughes Memorial Lecture on Medieval Welsh History, Department of Anglo-Saxon, Norse and Celtic, University of Cambridge, 2001.
—, 'Brittany and "Armes Prydein Vawr"', *EC* 20 (1983), 145–59.
—, 'Two approaches to the dating of *Nauigatio Sancti Brendani*' *Studi Medievali* 29 (1988), 87–102; rpr. in Wooding (ed.), *The Otherworld Voyage*, pp. 120–32.
—, *Histories and Pseudo-Histories of the Insular Middle Ages*, Aldershot, 1990.
Dumville, D. N. et al., *Saint Patrick, AD 493–1993*, Studies in Celtic History 13, Woodbridge, 1993.
Dumville, D. N., and Lapidge, M. (eds), *The Anglo-Saxon Chronicle*, vol. 17, *The Annals of St Neots with Vita Prima Sancti Neoti*, Cambridge, 1984.
Dunlop, A. I., 'Bagimond's Roll. Statement of the tenths of the Kingdom of Scotland', *Miscellany of the Scottish History Society* 6 (1939), 1–77.
Dunn, M., 'Gregory the Great, the vision of Fursey and the origins of purgatory', *Peritia* 14 (2000), 24–89.
Dunstan, G. R. (ed.), *The Register of Edmund Lacy, Bishop of Exeter, 1420–1455*, 5 vols, Devon and Cornwall Record Society, Torquay, 1963–72.
Dwnn, L., *Heraldic Visitations of Wales*, 2 vols, Llandovery, 1846.
Easson, D. E., *Medieval Religious Houses in Scotland: With an Appendix on the Houses in the Isle of Man*, London, 1957.
Edwards, N., 'Celtic saints and early medieval archaeology', in Sharpe and Thacker (eds), *Local Saints and Local Churches*.
—, *The Archaeology of Early Medieval Ireland*, London, 1990.
Edwards, N. and Lane, A. (eds), *The Early Church in Wales and the West*, Oxbow Monograph 16, 1992.
Edwards, O. T., *Matins, Lauds and Vespers for St David's Day*, Cambridge, 1990.
Eggert, C. E. (ed.), *The Middle Low German Version of the Legend of Mary Magdalen*, Bloomington, 1902.
Elliott, J. K. (trans.), *The Apocryphal New Testament*, rev. rpr. Oxford, 1999.

Emanuel, H. D., 'An analysis of the composition of the *Vita Cadoci*', *NLWJ* 7 (1951–2), 217–27.
Enright, M. J., *Iona, Tara and Soissons: The Origins of the Royal Anointing Ritual*, Berlin, 1985.
Enys, J. D., Peter, T. C. and Michell Whitley, H., 'Mural paintings in Cornish churches', *JRIC* 15 (1901–2), pp 136–60.
Esposito, M., 'On the earliest Latin Life of St Brigid of Kildare', *PRIA* 30 (1912), 307–26.
—, 'Notes on Latin learning and literature in mediaeval Ireland, IV. On the early Latin Lives of St Brigid of Kildare', *Hermathena* 24 (1935), 120–65.
—, 'The Patrician problem and a possible solution', *Irish Historical Studies* 10 (1956) 38, 131–55.
Etchingham, C., *Church Organisation in Ireland AD 650–1000*, Naas, 1999. Evans, D. S. (ed.), *Buchedd Dewi*, Cardiff, 1959.
—, *Medieval Religious Literature*, Cardiff, 1986.
— (ed.), *Historia Gruffud vab Kenan*, Cardiff, 1977.
— (ed.), *The Welsh Life of St David*, Cardiff, 1988.
Evans, G., *Land of My Fathers: 2000 Years of Welsh History*, Talybont, 1992. Evans, H., *Tŵr y Felin History and Guide to St Davids*, 2nd edn, St Davids, 1923.
Evans, J. G., *Report on Manuscripts in the Welsh Language*, 2 vols, London, 1899–1903.
Evans, J. G. and Rhys, J. (eds), *The Text of the Book of Llan Dav*, Oxford, 1893; rpr. Aberystwyth, 1979.
Evans, J. W, 'The survival of the *clas* as an institution in medieval Wales', in N. Edwards and Lane (eds), *The Early Church in Wales and the West*, pp. 33–40.
—, 'The Reformation and St Davids Cathedral', *JWEH* 7 (1990), 1–16. –, 'From Bernard to Bec', *Pembrokeshire County History*, vol. 2 (forthcoming).
Everard, J., *Brittany and the Angevins 1158–1203*, Cambridge, 2000. Fairclough, H. R. (ed. and trans.), *Virgil*, rev. edn, 2 vols, Cambridge, MA, 1999.
Farmer, D. H., *The Oxford Dictionary of Saints*, 4th edn, Oxford, 1996. Farnhill, K. (ed.), *English Parish Guilds*, Exeter, forthcoming.
Fawtier, R., 'Une Rédaction inédite de la Vie de saint Guénolé', *Mélanges d'archéologie et d'histoire de l'Ecole Française de Rome* 22 (1912), 2–44.
— (ed.), *La Vie de saint Samson*, Paris, 1912.
Fenton, R., *A Historical Tour through Pembrokeshire*, Haverfordwest, 1994. Flanagan, M.-Th. *Irish Society, Anglo-Norman Settlers, Angevin Kingship*, Oxford, 1989.
Fleuriot, L., *Les Origines de la Bretagne*, Paris, 1980.
Flint, V. J., *The Rise of Magic in Early Medieval Europe*, Princeton, 1991.
Flobert, P. (ed.), *La Vie ancienne de saint Samson de Dol*, Paris, 1997.
Forbes, A. P., *Kalendars of Scottish Saints*, Edinburgh, 1872.

— (ed. and trans.), *Lives of S. Ninian and S. Kentigern Compiled in the Twelfth Century*, Edinburgh, 1874.
Ford, P. K. (ed.), *Celtic Folklore and Christianity*, Santa Barbara, 1983.
—, 'A highly important pig', in A. T. E. Matonis, D. F. Melia and E. P. Hamp (eds), *Celtic Language, Celtic Culture: A Festschrift for Eric P. Hamp*, Van Nuys, California, 1990, pp. 292–304.
Forster, B., *Some Account of the Church and Windows of St. Neot's, in Cornwall*, London, 1786.
Foster Evans, D. (ed.), *Gwaith Hywel Swrdwal a'i Deulu*, Aberystwyth, 2000.
Fowler, J. T., 'On the St Cuthbert window in York Minster', *Yorkshire Archaeological and Topographical Journal* 4 (1877), 249–376.
—, 'On the St Cuthbert window in York Minster (additional notes)', *Yorkshire Archaeological and Topographical Journal* 11 (1891), 486–501.
— (ed.), *The Rites of Durham, being a Description or Brief Declaration of all the Ancient Monuments, Rites, and Customs belonging or being within the Monastical Church of Durham before the Suppression written 1593*, Surtees Society 107 [1902:2], Durham, 1903.
Foxe, J., *Acts and Monuments*, J. Pratt (ed.), 5 vols, London, 1877.
Freeman, P. M., 'A Middle Irish version of the Romulus and Remus story', *Proceedings of the Harvard Celtic Colloquium* 11 (1991), 1–13.
French, K. L., 'Maidens' lights and wives' stores: women's parish guilds in late medieval England', *Sixteenth Century Journal*, 29 (2) (1998), 399–425.
Frere, S. S., *Britannia: A History of Roman Britain*, 3rd edn, London, 1987. Fulton, H., 'Medieval Welsh poems to nuns', *CMCS* 21 (1991), 87–112. Galbraith, J. D., *St Machar's Cathedral: The Celtic Antecedents*, Friends of St Machar's Cathedral Occasional Papers 8, Aberdeen, 1982.
Galletier, E. (ed.), *Panegyricus Theodosio Augusto*, Paris, 1955.
Geary, P., 'Humiliation of saints', in S. Wilson (ed.), *Saints and their Cults: Studies in Religious Sociology, Folklore and History*, Cambridge, 1984, pp. 123–40.
Geiriadur Prifysgol Cymru, Cardiff, 1950.
Geoffrey of Monmouth, *The History of the Kings of Britain*, L. Thorpe (trans.), London, 1966.
Gerald of Wales (=Giraldus Cambrensis), *Giraldi Cambrensis Opera*, J. S. Brewer, J. F. Dimock and G. F. Warner (eds), 8 vols, Rolls Series, London 1861–91.
—, *De Invectionibus: The Book of Invectives of Giraldus Cambrensis*, W. S. Davies (ed.), Y *Cymmrodor* 30 (1920).
—, *Speculum Duorum: A Mirror of Two Men*, Y. Lefèvre and R. B. C. Huygens (eds), B. Dawson (trans.), Cardiff, 1974.
—, *Expugnatio Hibernica: The Conquest of Ireland*, A. B. Scott and F. X. Martin (eds and trans.), Dublin, 1978.
—, *The Journey through Wales/The Description of Wales*, L. Thorpe (trans.), Harmondsworth, 1978.
Gilbert, C. S., *An Historical Survey of Cornwall*, 2 vols, London, 1817–20.

Giles, J. A. (ed.), *Vita quorundum Anglo-Saxonum: Original Lives of Anglo-Saxons and Others who Lived Before the Conquest*, Caxton Society 16, 1854; rpr. New York, 1967.
Gillingham, J., 'Henry II, Richard I and the Lord Rhys', *Peritia* 10 (1996), 225–36.
Giraldus Cambrensis *see* Gerald of Wales.
Giraudon, D., *Chansons populaires de Basse-Bretagne sur feuilles volantes*, Morlaix, 1985.
Goodich, M. E., *Violence and Miracle in the Fourteenth Century*, Chicago, 1995.
Goodburn, R., and H. Waugh (compilers), *Epigraphic Indexes* of *Roman Inscriptions of Britain* I, Gloucester, 1983.
Grant, J. and Leslie, W., *A Survey of the Province of Moray: Historical, Geographical and Political*, Aberdeen, 1798.
Graves, E. Van Tassel, *The Old Cornish Vocabulary*, University microfilms, Ann Arbor, 1962.
Gray, M., *Images of Piety: The Iconography of Traditional Religion in Late Medieval Wales*, Oxford, 2000.
Gregory of Tours, *Historia Francorum*, H. Omont and G. Collon (eds), *Grégoire de Tours. Histoire des Francs*, Paris, 1886–93.
Gresham, C. A., 'The Cymer Abbey charter', *BBCS* 31 (1984), 142–57.
Griffith, W. P. (ed.), *Ysbryd Dealltwrus ac Enaid Anfarwol: Ysgrifau ar Hanes Crefydd yng Ngwynedd*, Bangor, 1999.
Grimm, V., *From Feasting to Fasting: The Evolution of a Sin*, London, 1996.
Grosjean, P. (ed.), 'Vita S. Ciarani episcopi de Saigir ex codice hagiographico Gothano', *AB* 59 (1941), 217–71.
— (ed.), 'Vie de S. Cadoc par Caradoc de Llancarfan', *AB* 60 (1942), 35–67.
— (ed.), 'Vie de S. Rumon. Vie, invention et miracles de S. Nectan', *AB* 71 (1953), 359–414.
—, 'The alleged Irish origin of St Cuthbert', in C. F. Battiscombe (ed.), *The Relics of St Cuthbert*, Oxford, 1956, pp. 144–54.
Gruffydd, R. G. and Owen, H. P., 'The earliest mention of St David?', *BBCS* 17 (1956–8), 185–93.
—, 'The earliest mention of St David? An addendum', *BBCS* 19, (1961), 231–32.
Guillotel, H., 'Les Vicomtes de Léon aux XIe-XIIe siècles', *Mémoires de la Société d'histoire et d'archéologie de Bretagne* 51 (1971), 29–51.
—, 'Recherches sur l'activité des *scriptoria* bretons du IXe siècle', *Mémoires de la Société d'histoire et d'archéologie de Bretagne* 62 (1985), 9–36.
—, 'Le Dossier hagiographique de l'érection du siège de Tréguier', in G. Le Menn, J.-Y. Le Moing, *Bretagne et pays celtiques. Langues, histoire, civilisation. Mélanges offerts à la mémoire de Léon Fleuriot*, Saint-Brieuc/ Rennes, 1992, pp. 213–26.

Guiraud, C. (ed. and trans.), *Varron. Économie rurale*, 3 vols, Paris, 1978–97.
Gwyndaf, R., 'The Welsh folk narrative tradition: continuity and adaptation', *Folk Life 26* (1987–8), 78–100.
Gwynn, A., *The Irish Church in the Eleventh and Twelfth Centuries*, G. O'Brien (ed.), Dublin, 1992.
Gwynn, E. (ed.), *The Rule of Tallaght*, Dublin and London, 1927.
Haddan, A. W. and Stubbs, W. (eds), *Councils and Ecclesiastical Documents relating to Great Britain and Ireland*, Oxford, 1869.
Hamand, L. A., *The Ancient Windows of Great Malvern Parish Church*, St Albans, 1947; rpr. 1978.
Hamon, M., *Vies de saints bretons et Règles monastiques*, Hagiographie bretonnne – *Sent kozh hor bro*, Rennes, 1998.
Hanson, R. P. C., 'The rule of faith of Victorinus and of Patrick', in J. J. O'Meara, B. Naumann (eds), *Latin Script and Letters AD 400–900*, Leiden, 1976, pp. 25–36.
—, *The Search for the Christian Doctrine of God: The Arian Controversy 318–381*, Edinburgh, 1988.
Hanson, R. P. C. and C. Blanc (eds), *Saint Patrick, Confession et Lettre à Coroticus*, Paris, 1978.
Harris, S. M., *Saint David in the Liturgy*, Cardiff, 1940.
—, 'The kalendar of the *Vitae Sanctorum Wallensium*', *Journal of the Historical Society of the Church in Wales 3* (1953), 3–53.
Harvey, A., 'The significance of *Cothraige*', *Ériu 36* (1985), 1–9.
Haskins, S., *Mary Magdalen Myth and Metaphor*, New York, 1993.
Healy, J., 'Was St Cuthbert an Irishman?', *Irish Ecclesiastical Record* 2nd Series 9 (1888), 1–16.
Heinzelmann, M. (ed.), *Manuscrits hagiographiques et travail des hagiographes*, Sigmaringen, 1992.
—, 'Manuscrits hagiographiques et travail des hagiographes: l'exemple de la tradition manuscrite des Vies anciennes de sainte Geneviève de Paris', in Heinzelmann (ed.), *Manuscrits*, pp. 9–16.
Heist, W. W., 'Dermot O'Donohue and the Codex Salmanticensis', *Celtica* 5 (1960), 52–63.
— (ed.), *Vitae Sanctorum Hiberniae ex codice olim Salmanticensi nunc Bruxellensi*, Société des Bollandistes, Subsidia Hagiographica 28, Brussels, 1965.
—, 'Myth and folklore in the Lives of Irish Saints', *Centennial Review* 12 (1968), 181–93.
Henderson, C., *The Cornish Church Guide*, Truro, 1928.
Henken, E. R., *Traditions of the Welsh Saints*, Cambridge, 1987.
—, *The Welsh Saints: A Study in Patterned Lives*, Cambridge, 1991.
—, *National Redeemer: Owain Glyndŵr in Welsh Tradition*, Cardiff/Ithaca, 1996.
Hennessy, W. M. (ed.), *Chronicon Scotorum: A Chronicle of Irish Affairs from the Earliest Times to AD 1135*, London, 1866.

Herbert, M., *Iona, Kells, and Derry: The History and Hagiography of the Monastic Familia of Columba*, Oxford, 1988; rpr. Dublin, 1996.
—, 'Hagiography', in K. McCone and K. Simms (eds), *Progress in Medieval Irish Studies*, Maynooth, 1996, pp. 79–90.
—, 'Literary sea-voyages and early Munster hagiography', in R. Black, W. Gillies and R. Ó Maolalaigh (eds), *Celtic Connections: Proceedings of the 10th International Congress of Celtic Studies: Language, Literature, History, Culture*, East Linton, 1999, pp. 182–9.
—, 'The *Vita Columbae* and Irish hagiography: a study of *Vita Cainnechi*', in Carey, Herbert and Ó Riain (eds), *Studies in Irish Hagiography*, pp. 31–40.
Herbert, M. and Ó Riain, P. (eds), *Betha Adamnáin: The Irish Life of Adamnán*, Irish Texts Society 54, London, 1988.
Herity, M. 'The layout of Irish early Christian monasteries', in P. Ni Chatáin and M. Richter (eds), *Ireland and Europe: The Early Church*, Stuttgart, 1984, pp. 105–16.
Herren, M., 'Classical and secular learning among the Irish before the Carolingian renaissance', *Florilegium* 3 (1981), 118–57.
—, 'The transmission and reception of Graeco-Roman mythology in Anglo-Saxon England, 670–800', *Anglo-Saxon England* 27 (1998), 87–103.
Herrieu, L. and Duhamel, M., *Guerzenneu ha Sonnenneu Bro-Guéned*, 1930; rpr. Paris, 1997.
Herzfeld, G. (ed.), *An Old English Martyrology*, London, 1900.
Hood, A. B. E. (ed. and trans.), *St. Patrick: His Writings and Muirchú's Life*, London, 1978.
Hornblower, S., and Spawforth, A. (eds), *Oxford Classical Dictionary*, 3rd edn, Oxford, 1996.
Horstmann, C. (ed.), *Sammlung Altenenglische Legenden*, Heilbronn, 1878.
— (ed.), *Altenglische Legenden*, Heilbronn, 1881.
— (ed.), *The Early South English Legedendary or Lives of Saints*, EETS O.S. 86, London, 1888.
— (ed.), *Nova Legenda Anglie*, 2 vols, Oxford, 1901.
Howlett, P. R. (ed. and trans.), *The Book of Letters of Saint Patrick the Bishop*, Dublin, 1994.
Hufstader, A., 'Lefèvre d'Etaples and the Magdalen', *Studies in the Renaissance* 16 (1969), 31–60.
Hughes, K., *Early Christian Ireland*, Ithaca, 1972.
—, *Celtic Britain in the Early Middle Ages. Studies in Scottish and Welsh Sources*, D. Dumville (ed.), Woodbridge, 1980.
—, 'The Celtic Church: is this a valid concept?', *CMCS* 1 (1981), 1–20.
—, 'British Museum MS Cotton Vespasian A xiv *(Vitae Sanctorum Wallensium)* its purpose and provenance', in N. K. Chadwick, Hughes, Brooke and Jackson (eds), *Studies in the Early British Church*, pp. 183–200.
—, *The Welsh Latin Chronicles, Annales Cambriae and Related Texts*, Oxford, 1974.

Hurter, H. (ed.), '*Sancti Hieronymi Vita S. Pauli Primi Eremitae*', in W. Oldfather (ed.), *Studies in the Text Tradition of St Jerome's* 'Vitae Patrum', Urbana IL, 1943, pp. 36–42.

Huws, D., *Medieval Welsh Manuscripts*, Cardiff, 2000.

Innes, C. N. (ed.), *Registrum Episcopatus Glasguensis: munimenta ecclesie Metropolitane Glasguensis a sede restaurata secuto ineunte XII ad Reformatum religionem*, 2 vols, Edinburgh, 1843.

—, *Registrum Episcopatus Aberdonensis: ecclesiæ cathedralis Aberdonensis regesta que extant in unum collecta*, 2 vols, Edinburgh, 1845.

—, *Origines Parochiales Scotiae. The Antiquities Ecclesiastical and Territorial of the Parishes of Scotland*, vol. 2 (1), Edinburgh, 1854.

Jackson, K. H., 'The Colloquy of Llywelyn and Gwrnerth', *ZCP* 21 (1938), 21–32.

—, *Language and History in Early Britain*, Edinburgh, 1953.

—, 'The Idnert inscription: date and significance of Id-', *BBCS* 19 (1960-2), 232–4.

—, *A Historical Philology of Breton*, Dublin, 1967.

—, 'Romano-British names in the Antonine Itinerary', *Britannia* 1 (1970), 68–82.

James, C., 'Llwyr wybodau, llên a llyfrau: Hopcyn ap Thomas a'r traddodiad llenyddol', in H. T. Edwards (ed.), *Cwm Tawe*, Llandysul, 1993, pp. 4–44.

James, H., 'The cult of St David in the Middle Ages' in M. Carver (ed.), *In Search of Cult: Archaeological Investigations in Honour of Philip Rahtz*, Woodbridge, 1993, pp. 105–11.

—, 'The cult of St David', *Journal of the Pembrokeshire Historical Society* 7 (1996-7), 5–25.

James, J. W. (ed.), *Rhigyfarch's Life of St David*, Cardiff, 1967.

—, 'The Welsh versions of Rhigyfarch's Life of St David', *NLWJ* 9 (1955-6), 1–21.

James, L. T. H. and Evans, T. C. (eds), *Hen Gwndidau, Carolau, a Chywyddau*, Bangor, 1910.

Jankulak, K., *The Medieval Cult of St Petroc*, Woodbridge, 2000.

Janningus, C. (ed.), *Acta Sanctorum Junii. Ex Latinis & Græcis aliarumque gentium monumentis, servata primigenia scriptorum phrasi . . .*, vol. 6, Part II, Venice, 1746.

Jenkins, D. (ed.), *The Law of Hywel Dda*, Llandysul, 1986.

Jenkins, D. and M. E. Owen (eds), *The Welsh Law of Women*, Cardiff, 1980.

Johnston, D. R. (ed.), *Gwaith Iolo Goch*, Cardiff, 1988.

— (ed.), *Iolo Goch: Poems*, Llandysul, 1993.

— (ed.), *Gwaith Lewys Glyn Cothi*, Cardiff, 1995.

Jones, A. H. M., Martindale, J. R. and Morris, J. (eds), *Prosopography of the Later Roman Empire I, AD 260–395*, Cambridge, 1971.

Jones, C. W. (ed.), *Bedae Opera de Temporibus*, Cambridge, MA, 1943.

Jones, D. J. (=Gwenallt), 'Cerddi'r saint a'r bucheddau cyfatebol', MA thesis, University of Wales, Aberystwyth, 1929.

—, 'Buchedd Mair Fadlen a'r *Legenda Aurea*', *BBCS* 4 (1929), 325–39.

Jones, E. (ed). *Gwaith Llywarch ap Llywelyn 'Prydydd y Moch'*, Cardiff, 1989.

Jones, G., 'Gwyrthyeu y Wynvydedic Veir', *BBCS* 9 (1937), 14–48, 334–41 and *BBCS* 19 (1939), 21–33.

Jones, G., *Saints of Wales: An Inventory of Religious Devotion*, Aberystwyth, forthcoming.

Jones, G. H., *Celtic Britain and the Pilgrim Movement*, London, 1912.

Jones, H. L. and Rowlands, E. I. (eds), *Gwaith Iorwerth Fynglwyd*, Cardiff, 1975.

Jones, L. E. 'Golygiad newydd o *Fuchedd Gwenfrewy*', M.Phil. thesis, University of Wales, Cardiff, 2000.

Jones, N. A., 'The Mynydd Carn prophecy', *CMCS* 38, (1999), 73–92.

Jones, N. A. and Parry Owen, A. (eds), *Gwaith Cynddelw Brydydd Mawr*, 2 vols, Cardiff, 1991 and 1995.

Jones, N. A and Pryce, H. (eds), *Yr Arglwydd Rhys*, Cardiff, 1996.

Jones, T. (ed.), *Brut y Tywysogyon (Red Book of Hergest Version)*, Cardiff, 1952.

— (ed.), *Brut y Tywysogion, Peniarth MS 20 Version: Translation with Notes*, Cardiff, 1952.

— (ed.), *Brenhinedd y Saesson*, Cardiff, 1971.

Jones, W. B. and Freeman, E. A., *The History and Antiquities of St David's*, London, 1856.

Kastner, J., *Historiae fundationum monasteriorum. Frühformen monasticher Institutionsgeschichtsschreibung im Mittelalter, Münchener Beiträge zur Mediävistik und Renaissance-Forschung* 18, München, 1974.

Kelly, S. and Rogers, R., *Saints Preserve Us!* London, 1995.

Kenney, J. F., *The Sources for the Early History of Ireland: Ecclesiastical: An Introduction and Guide*, New York, 1929, 2nd edn 1966; rpr. Dublin, 1997.

Kent, R. G. (trans.), *Varro. On the Latin Language*, 2 vols, Cambridge, MA and London, 1958.

Kerlouégan, F., 'Les Vies de saints bretons les plus anciennes dans leur rapports avec les Iles Brittaniques', Herren., M. (ed.), *Insular Latin Studies*, Toronto, 1981, pp. 195–213.

—, 'Les Citations d'auteurs latins profanes dans les Vies de saints bretons carolingiennes', *EC* 18 (1981), 181–95.

—, 'Les Citations d'auteurs latins chrétiens dans les vies de saints bretons carolingiennes', *EC* 19 (1982), 215–57.

—, 'Approche stylistique du latin de la *Vita Pauli Aureliani*', in M. Simon (ed.), *Landévennec et le monachisme breton*, pp. 207–17.

—, 'Landévennec à l'école de Saint-Sauveur de Redon?', in M. Sot (ed.), *Haut Moyen-Age. Culture, éducation, et société. Études offerts à Pierre Riché*, Paris, 1990, pp. 315–22.

—, 'La *Vita Pauli Aureliani* témoin de l'émergence des *Institutiones, Grammaticae* de Priscien dans l'enseignement au IXe siècle', in Institut de Recherches et d'Histoire des Textes, *De Tertulien aux Mozarabes, t. 2, Antiquité tardive et christianisme ancien (Vie – IXe siècle). Mélanges offerts à Jacques Fontaine*, Paris, 1992, pp. 183–9.

Keynes, S. and Lapidge, M. (eds), *Alfred the Great: Asser's Life of King Alfred and Other Contemporary Sources*, London, 1983.

Kirby, D., 'A note on Rhigyfarch's *Life of St David*", *WHR* 4 (1969), 292–7.

Koch, J. T., 'When was Welsh literature first written down?', *SC* 20–1 (1985–6), 43–66.

—, '*Cothairche*, Esposito's theory, and Neo-Celtic lenition', in Bammesberger and Wollmann (eds.), *Britain 400–600*, pp. 179–202.

Lagrée, M., *Religion et cultures en Bretagne: 1850–1950*, Paris, 1992.

Laing, D., *A Preface to the Breviarium Aberdonense*, Edinburgh, 1855.

Lane-Davies, A., *Holy Wells of Cornwall*, Redruth, 1970.

Lapidge, M., 'The hermeneutic style in tenth-century Anglo-Latin literature', *Anglo-Saxon England* 4 (1975), 67–111.

—, 'The medieval hagiography of St Ecgwine', *Vale of Evesham Historical Society Research Papers* 6 (1977), 77–93.

—, 'Byrhtferth and the *Vita S. Ecgwini*', *Mediaeval Studies* 41 (1979), 331–53.

Lapidge, M., and Sharpe, R., *A Bibliography of Celtic–Latin Literature 400–1200*, Dublin, 1985.

Laurent, D., 'La *Gwerz* de Skolan et la légende de Merlin', *Ethnologie française* 1 (3–4) (1971), 19–54.

—, 'Enori et le roi de Brest', in *Études sur la Bretagne et les pays celtiques: mélanges offerts à Yves le Gallo*, Cahiers de Bretagne Occidentale 6, Brest, 1987, pp. 207–24.

—, *Aux sources du Barzaz-Breiz: la mémoire d'un peuple*, Douarnenez, 1989.

Lawlor, H. J. (ed.), *St Bernard of Clairvaux's Life of St Malachy of Armagh*, London, 1920.

Le Berre, Y., and Le Dû, J., 'Un Siècle d'écrits en langue bretonne: 1790–1892', in L. Le Guillou and D. Laurent (eds), *Histoire littéraire et culturelle de la Bretagne*, 3 vols, Paris and Geneva, 1989, vol. 2, pp. 251–91.

Le Berre Y., Tanguy, B. and Castel, Y.-P. (eds), *Buez santez Nonn, Mystere Breton, Vie de sainte Nonne*, Minihi-Levenez, 2000.

Le Braz, A., *Au pays des pardons*, 21st edn, Paris, 1927.

—, *Les Saints bretons d'après la tradition populaire* [various articles], *Annales de Bretagne* (1893–7).

Le Duc, G. (ed. and trans), *Vie de Saint-Malo, évêque d'Alet. Version écrite par le diacre Bili*, Rennes, 1979.

Le Gallo, Y., *Clergé, religion et société en Basse-Bretagne de la fin de l'ancien régime à 1840*, 2 vols, Editions Ouvrières [n.p.], 1991.

Le Grand, A., *Les Vies des saints de la Bretagne Armorique par Fr Albert le Grand*, M. D.-L. M de Kerdanet (ed.), St Trouve, 1837; 5th edn, Quimper, 1901.
Le Huërou, A., 'La Réécriture d'un texte hagiographique au XIIe siècle: la *Vita sancti Sansonis* de Baudri de Bourgueil', *Annales de Bretagne et des pays de l'Ouest* 108 (2) (2001), 17, 8–30.
Le Menn, G., *La Femme au sein d'or*, [Saint-Brieuc], 1985.
—, *Histoire du théâtre populaire Breton XVe-XIXe*, [Saint-Brieuc], 1983.
Leclercq, J., 'L'Ecriture sainte dans l'hagiographie', *Settimane di Spolete* 10 (1963), 819–35.
Leggatt, P. O. and Leggatt, M. D., *The Healing Wells: Cornish Cults and Customs*, Redruth, 1987.
Lewis, C. P., 'Gruffudd ap Cynan and the Normans', in K. L. Maund (ed.), *Gruffudd fab Cynan: A Collaborative Biography*, Woodbridge, 1996, pp. 61–78.
Lewis, H. (ed.), *Brut Dingestow*, Cardiff, 1942.
—, *Hen Gerddi Crefyddol*, Cardiff, 1931.
Lewis, H., Roberts, T. and Williams, I. (eds), *Cywyddau Iolo Goch ac Eraill*, Cardiff, 1972.
Lewis, K. J., 'Model girls? Virgin-martyrs and the training of young medieval women in late medieval England', in K. J. Lewis, N. J. Menuge and K. M. Phillips (eds), *Young Medieval Women*, Stroud, 1999, pp. 25–46.
Lewis, M., 'Astudiaeth o orgraff Hen Gymraeg gan ei chymharu ag orgraff Hen Wyddeleg', MA thesis, University of Wales, Aberystwyth, 1961.
Lhuyd, E., *Parochialia*, R. H. Morris (ed.), London, 1909–11.
Light, L., 'Versions et révisions du texte biblique', in Riché and Lobrichon (eds), *Le Moyen Age et la Bible*, pp. 55–93.
Lloyd, J. E., *A History of Wales from the Earliest Times to the Edwardian Conquest*, 3rd edn, 2 vols, London, 1948.
Lloyd-Jones, J., 'emyr, ymer, ymher', *BBCS* 11 (1941–4), 34–6.
—, *Geirfa Barddoniaeth Gynnar Gymraeg*, Cardiff, 1931–63.
Lloyd-Morgan, C., 'More written about than writing? Welsh women and the written word', in H. Pryce (ed.), *Literacy in Medieval Celtic Societies*, Cambridge, 1998, pp. 149–65.
Lobineau, G-A, *Les Vies des saints de Bretagne avec une addition à l'histoire de Bretagne*, Rennes, 1725.
Loomis, C. G., *White Magic: An Introduction to the Folklore of Christian Legend*, Cambridge, MA, 1948.
Lot, F., *Mélanges d'histoire bretonne*, Paris, 1907.
— (ed.), 'Vita Sancti Machutis par Bili', in Lot, *Mélanges*, pp. 340–430.
Loth, J., 'Une cause de la popularité de Saint Yves', *Annales de Bretagne* 4 (1889), 632–3.
—, *Les Noms des saints bretons*, Paris, 1910.
Lovegrove, E. W., 'St David's Cathedral', *Arch. Camb.* 77 (1922), 360–82.

Luzel, F.-M., *Légendes chrétiennes de la Basse-Bretagne*, 2 vols, Paris, 1881.
Luzel, F.-M., and Le Braz, A., *Soniou Breiz-Izel: chansons populaires de la Basse-Bretagne*, 2 vols, Paris, 1890.
Mac Airt, S. and Mac Niocaill, G. (ed. and trans.), *The Annals of Ulster (to A.D. 1131)*, Part I. Text and Translation, Dublin, 1983.
Macalister, R. A. S. (ed. and trans.), 'The Life of Saint Finan', *ZCP* 2 (1899), 545–65.
McCone, K., 'An introduction to early Irish saints' Lives', *Maynooth Review* 11 (1984), 26–59.
McCone, K. R., 'Brigit in the seventh century: a saint with three Lives?', *Peritia* 1 (1982), 107–45.
MacDonald, A., *Curadán, Boniface and the Early Church of Rosemarkie*, Rosemarkie, 1992.
Macdonald, A. D. S. and Laing, L. R., 'Early ecclesiastical sites in Scotland: a field survey, Part II', *Proc. Soc. Antiq. Scotl.* 102 (1969–70), 129–45.
Macfarlane, L. J., *William Elphinstone and the Kingdom of Scotland 1431–1514. The Struggle for Order*, Aberdeen, 1985.
—, 'The Divine Office and the Mass', in J. Geddes (ed.), *King's College Chapel, Aberdeen, 1500–2000*, Leeds, 2000, pp. 6–27.
McKenna, C. (ed.), 'Canu Cadfan', in Bramley et al. (eds), *Gwaith Llywelyn Fardd I*, pp. 9–32.
—, 'The hagiographic poetics of *Canu Cadfan*', in K. A. Klar, E. E. Sweetser and C. Thomas (eds), *A Celtic Florilegium: Studies in memory of Brendan O Hehir*, Andover, MA, 1996, pp. 121–37.
MacKinlay, J. M., *Ancient Church Dedications in Scotland: Non-Scriptural Dedications*, Edinburgh, 1914.
Maclean, Sir J., *The Parochial and Family History of the Deanery of Trigg Minor*, 3 vols, London and Bodmin, 1873–9.
McLynn, N. B., *Ambrose of Milan: Church and Court in a Christian Capital*, Berkeley and Los Angeles, 1994.
Mac Mathúna, S., 'Contribution to a study of the voyages of St Brendan and St Malo', in C. Laurent and H. Davis (eds), *Irlande et Bretagne. Vingt siècles d'histoire. Actes du colloque de Rennes (29–31 mars 1993)*, Rennes, 1994, pp. 41–55.
—, 'The structure and transmission of early Irish voyage literature', in H. L. C. Tristram (ed.), *Text und Zeittiefe*, Tübingen, 1994, pp. 313–57.
Macquarrie, A., 'Early Christian religious houses in Scotland: foundation and function', in J. Blair and R. Sharpe (eds), *Pastoral Care before the Parish*, Leicester, 1992, pp. 110–33.
—, *The Saints of Scotland*, Edinburgh, 1997.
MacQueen, J., *Numerology – Theory and Outline History of a Literary Mode*, Edinburgh, 1985.
McSparran, F. and Robinson, P. R. (eds), *Cambridge University Library MS Ff.2.38*, London, 1979.

Maître, L., and de Berthou, P. (eds), *Cartulaire de Sainte-Croix de Quimperlé*, Paris-Rennes, 1904.
Martindale, J. R. (ed.), *Prosopography of the Later Roman Empire II, AD 395–527*, Cambridge, 1980.
Matthews, J., *Western Aristocracies and Imperial Court, AD 364–425*, Oxford, 1975.
Mattingly, H., Pearce, J. W. E. and Kendrick, T. D., 'The Coleraine Hoard', *Antiquity* 11 (1937) 39–45.
Mattingly, J., 'The medieval parish guilds of Cornwall', *JRIC* New Series 10 (1989), 290–329. This will be superseded by 'Cornwall' chapter in Farnhill (ed.), *English Parish Guilds*.
—, 'Pre-Reformation holy wells in Cornwall: sites, structures and functions', *The Poly: The Magazine of the Royal Cornwall Polytechnic Society* (1997–8), 8–11.
—, 'A well without water?', *Journal of the St. Agnes Museum Trust* 14 (1998), 4–14.
—, 'Stories in the glass – reconstructing the St Neot pre-Reformation glazing scheme', *JRIC* New Series 2, vol. 3 (3) (2000), 9–55.
—, '"A tin miner and a bal maiden" – further research on the St Neot windows', *JRIC* New Series 2, vol. 3 (4) (2001).
Mauss, M., *The Gift: Forms and Functions of Exchange in Archaic Societies* (trans.), I. Cunnison, New York, 1967.
Meek, D. E., *The Quest for Celtic Christianity*, Edinburgh, 2000.
Meens, R., 'Pollution in the early Middle Ages: the case of food regulations in penitentials', *Early Medieval Europe* 4 (1995), 3–19.
—, 'The uses of Old Testament in early medieval canon law', in Yitzhak Hen and Matthew Innes (eds), *The Uses of the Past in the Middle Ages*, Cambridge, 2000, pp. 73–5.
Merdrignac, B., 'L'Eneide et les tarditions anciennes des bretons', *EC* 20 (1983), 199–205.
—, *Recherches sur l'hagiographie armoricaine du VIIe au XVe siècle. tome 1. Les saints bretons, témoins de Dieu ou témoins des hommes*, Dossiers du Ce. R.A.A., Saint-Malo, 1985.
—, 'La Quadrature du cercle dans la *vita* Sulini', Le Dossiers du Ce. R.A.A., 15, 1987.
—, 'Saint Guénolé et les monachismes insulaire et continental au haut Moyen Age', *Annales de Bretagne* 95 (1988), 15–40.
—, *Les Vies de saints bretons durant le haut Moyen Age*, Rennes, 1993.
—, 'La Désacralisation du mythe celtique de la navigation vers l'autre monde: l'apport du dossier hagiographique de saint Malo', *Ollodagos* 5 (1993), 13–43.
—, '"Grégoire", "Fidèle": des fantômes dans l'hagiographie bretonne', *BSAF* 126 (1997), 265–9.
—, 'Truies et verrats, cochons et sangliers, porcs et porchers dans les *Vitae*

des saints bretons du Moyen Âge', in Ph. Walter (ed.), *Mythologies du Porc*, Grenoble, 1999, pp. 123–53.

—, 'Ut vulgo refertur: tradition orale et littérature hagiographique en Bretagne au Moyen Age', in C. Laurent, B. Merdrignac and D. Pichot (eds), *Mondes de l'Ouest et villes du monde. Regards sur les sociétés médieévales. Mélanges en l'honneur d'André Chédeville*, Rennes, 1998, pp. 105–14.

Messingham, T. *Florilegium Insulæ Sanctorum seu Vitæ et Acta Sanctorum Hiberniæ*, Paris, 1624.

Metcalfe, W. M. (ed.), *Legends of the Saints in the Scottish Dialect of the Fourteenth Century*, 3 vols, Scottish Text Society, Edinburgh and London, 1896.

Meyer, K. (ed.), *Cáin Adamnáin, An Old-Irish Treatise on the Law of Adamnan*, Oxford, 1905.

— (ed.), 'The Laud genealogies and tribal histories', *ZCP* 8 (1912), 291–338.

— (ed.), *Sanas Cormaic: Anecdota from Irish Manuscripts*, vol. 5, Dublin 1913; rpr. and corrected, Felinfach, 1994.

Meyer, P., 'Légendes pieuses en provençal', *Histoire littéraire de la France* 32 (1898), 78–100.

Middleton, G., *The Streets of St Davids*, St Davids, 1977.

Milin, G., 'La Légende bretonne de sainte Azénor et les variantes médiévales du conte de la femme calomniée: éléments pour une archéologie du motif du bateau sans voiles et sans rames', *Mémoires de la Société d'histoire et d'archéologie de Bretagne* 67 (1990), 303–20.

Miller, M., *The Saints of Gwynedd*, Woodbridge, 1979.

Millett, B., 'The audience of the saints' Lives of the Katherine Group', *Reading Medieval Studies* 16 (1990), 247–68.

Millett, B. and Wogan-Browne, J. (eds), *Medieval English Prose for Women: Selections from the Katherine Group and Ancrene Wisse*, Oxford, 1990.

Mirk, J., *Mirk's Festial: A Collection of Homilies by Johannes Mirkus*, T. Erbe (ed.), London, 1905.

Misrahi, J., 'A *vita sanctae Mariae Magdalenae* (B.H.L. 5456) in an eleventh-century manuscript', *Speculum* 18 (1943), 335–9.

Mitchell, A., 'On various superstitions in the north-west highlands and islands of Scotland, especially in relation to lunacy', *Proc. Soc. Antiq. Scotl.* 4 (1862), 251–88.

Mittendorf, I., 'The Middle Welsh Mary of Egypt and the Latin source of the *Miracles of the Virgin Mary*', in E. Poppe and B. Ross (eds), *The Legend of Mary of Egypt in Medieval Insular Hagiography*, Dublin, 1996, pp. 205–36.

Mohrmann, C., *The Latin of Saint Patrick*, Dublin, 1961.

Moir, J. (ed. and trans.), *Boece's Bishops of Aberdeen*, Aberdeen, 1894.

Mommsen, Th. (ed.), *Chronica Minora saec. IV. V. VI. VII*, 3 vols, Berlin, 1891–8.

Moore, C. A., *Daniel, Esther and Jeremiah: The Additions*, New York, 1977.
Murphy, D. (ed. and trans.), *The Annals of Clonmacnoise*, Dublin, 1896.
Mycoff, D. A., *A Critical Edition of the Legend of Mary Magdalene from Caxton's Golden Legend of 1487*, Salzburg, 1985.
—, *The Life of Saint Mary Magdalene and of Her Sister Martha*, Kalamazoo, 1989.
Mytum, H., *The Origins of Early Christian Ireland*, London, 1992.
Nagy, J., *Conversing with Angels and Ancients*, Ithaca, 1997.
Nance, R. M., 'Painted windows and miracle plays', *Old Cornwall* 5 (1955), 244–8.
Nash-Williams, V. E., *The Early Christian Monuments of Wales*, Cardiff, 1950.
Nassiet, M., 'Deux cultes de fertilité, un invariant (1770–1855)', *Annales de Bretagne* 100 (1993), 499–508.
New, E., 'The fraternity of the holy name of Jesus in St Paul's Cathedral, *c.* 1450–*c.*1560', in Farnhill (ed.), *English Parish Guilds*.
Newlyn, E., 'Unconventional evidence of early drama: the stained and painted glass of St Neot's Church, Cornwall', *Records of Early English Drama Newsletter* 16 (2) (1991), 1–7.
Newlyn, E. S., Joyce, S. L., Hays, R. C., and McGee, C. E. (eds), *Dorset. Cornwall*, Toronto, 1999.
Ní Chatháin, P., 'Swineherds, seers, and druids', *SC* 14–15 (1979–80), 200–11.
Ní Dhonnchadha, M., 'The guarantor list of *Cáin Adomnáin*, 697', *Peritia* 1 (1982), 178–215.
Ní Mhaonaigh, M., '*Nósa Ua Maine*: fact or fiction', in T. M. Charles-Edwards, Owen and Russell (eds), *The Welsh King*, pp. 362–81.
Nilson, B., *Cathedral Shrines of Mediaeval England*, Woodbridge, 1998.
Norberg, D., *Introduction à l'étude de la versification latine médiévale*, Stockholm, 1958.
O' Brien, M. A. (ed.), *Corpus Genealogiarum Hiberniae*, 5 vols, Dublin, 1962.
Ó Caoimh, T., 'St Brendan sources: St Brendan and early Irish hagiography', in J. de Courcy Ireland and D. C. Sheehy (eds), *Atlantic Visions*, Dún Laoghaire, 1989, pp. 17–24.
Ó Carragáin, E., 'The meeting of Saint Paul and Saint Antony: visual and literary uses of a Eucharistic motif', in G. MacNiocaill (ed.), *Keimelia: Studies in Medieval Archaeology and History in Memory of Tom Delaney*, Galway, 1988, pp. 1–58.
Ó Cróinin, D., 'Early Irish annals from Easter tables: a case reinstated', *Peritia* 2 (1983), 74–86.
—, 'New Light on Palladius', *Peritia* 5 (1986) 276–83.
—, 'Is the Augburg Gospel codex a Northumbrian manuscript?', in Bonner, Rollason and Stancliffe (eds), *St Cuthbert*, pp. 189–201.
—, *Early Medieval Ireland 400–1200*, London, 1995.

O'Dwyer, P., *Céli Dé: Spiritual Reform in Ireland 750–900*, Dublin, 1981.
Ó hAodha, D., (ed.), *Bethu Brigte*, Dublin, 1978.
Oiry, M., 'Étude d'un corpus de récits d'êtres fantastiques recueillis sur la côte morbihannaise au début du siècle', Doctoral dissertation, Ecole des Hautes-Etudes en Sciences Sociales, Paris/CRBC, Brest, 4 vols, 1985.
—, 'L'Ecole vannetaise (1825–1916) et les collectes d'Yves le Diberder (1910–1916)', in Postic (ed.), *La Bretagne*, pp. 177–89.
O'Loughlin, T., 'Distant islands: the topography of holiness in the *Nauigatio sancti Brendani*', in M. Glasscoe (ed.), *The Medieval Mystical Tradition – England, Ireland and Wales*, Woodbridge, 1999, pp. 1–20.
—, *Celtic Theology: Humanity, World and God in Early Irish Writings*, London, 2000.
—, *Journeys on the Edges: The Celtic Tradition*, London, 2000.
—, 'The tombs of the saints: their significance for Adomnán', in Carey, Herbert and Ó Riain (eds), *Saints and Scholars*, pp. 1–14.
—, 'The monastic liturgy of the Hours in the *Nauigatio sancti Brendani*: a preliminary investigation', in J. Higgins and C. Cunniffe (eds), *Aspects of Clonfert and its Vicinity*, Galway, forthcoming.
Olson, L., *Early Monasteries in Cornwall*, Woodbridge, 1989.
—, 'Cornish rural religious processions', *Australian Celtic Journal* 1 (1988), 22–9.
Olson, L. and Padel, O. J., 'A tenth-century list of Cornish parochial saints', *CMCS* 12 (1986), 33–71.
O'Meara, J. J. (trans), *The Voyage of St Brendan*, Gerrard's Cross, 1979.
O'Rahilly, T. F., *The Two Patricks: A Lecture on the History of Christianity in Fifth-century Ireland*, Dublin, 1942.
Ó Riain, P., 'The Irish element in Welsh hagiographical tradition', in D. Ó Corráin (ed.), *Irish Antiquity*, Cork, 1981, pp. 291–303.
—, 'Towards a methodology in early Irish hagiography', *Peritia* 1 (1982), 146–59.
—, 'St Abbán: the genesis of an Irish saint's Life', in D. E. Evans, J. G. Griffiths and E. M. Jope (eds), *Proceedings of the Seventh International Congress of Celtic Studies, 1983*, Oxford, 1986, pp. 159–70.
— (ed.), *Corpus Genealogiarum Sanctorum Hiberniae*, Dublin, 1985.
—, 'The saints and their *amanuenses*: early models and later issues', in S. N. Tranter and H. L. C. Tristram (eds), *Early Irish Literature – Media and Communication – Mündlichkeit und Schriftlichkeit in der frühen irischen Literatur*, Tübingen, 1989, pp. 267–80.
— (ed.), *Beatha Bharra: Saint Finbarr of Cork*, London, 1994.
—, *Anglo-Saxon Ireland: The Evidence of the Martyrology of Tallaght*, H. M. Chadwick Memorial Lectures 3, Cambridge, 1993.
—, 'Codex Salmanticensis: a provenance *inter Anglos* or *inter Hibernos*?', in T. Barnard, D. Ó Cróinín and K. Simms (eds), *'A Miracle of Learning': Studies in Manuscripts and Irish Learning. Essays in Honour of William O'Sullivan*, Aldershot, 1998, pp. 91–100.

—, 'When and why was *Cothraige* first equated with Patricius?', *ZCP* 49–50 (1997), 698–709.
Orlandi, G., *Navigatio S. Brendani: 1 Introduzione*, Milan, 1968.
Orme, N. (ed.), *Nicholas Roscarrock's Lives of the Saints: Cornwall and Devon*, Exeter, 1992.
—, *English Church Dedications – with a Survey of Cornwall and Devon*, Exeter, 1996.
—, *The Saints of Cornwall*, Oxford, 2000.
O'Sullivan, W., 'A Waterford origin for the *Codex Salmanticensis*', *Decies* 54 (1998), 17–24.
Oulton, J. E. L., *The Credal Statements of St Patrick*, Dublin, 1940.
Owen, M. E., 'Prolegomena to a study of the historical context of Gwynfardd Brycheiniog's poem to Dewi', *SC* 26–7 (1991–2), pp. 51–79.
—, 'Trois poèmes en gallois sur des saints gallois liés à la Bretagne', *Journées d'études sur la Bretagne et les Pays Celtiques*, Brest, 1991–2.
— (ed.), 'Canu i Ddewi', in Bramley et al. (eds), *Gwaith Llywelyn Fardd I*, pp. 435–78.
Padel, O. J., *A Popular Dictionary of Cornish Place-Names*, Penzance, 1988.
—, 'Local saints and place-names in Cornwall' in Sharpe and Thacker (eds), *Local Saints and Local Churches*.
Painter, K. S., 'A Roman silver hoard from Canterbury', *Journal of the British Archaeological Association* 28 (1965), 1–15.
—, 'A late-Roman silver ingot from Kent', *Antiquaries Journal* 52 (1972), 84–92.
Parry, T. (ed.), *Gwaith Dafydd ap Gwilym*, Cardiff, 1952.
Parry Owen, A., 'Canu Cynddelw Brydydd Mawr i Dysilio Sant', *Ysgrifau Beirniadol* 19 (1992), 73–99.
Parry Owen A. (ed.), 'Canu Tysilio', in N. A. Jones and Parry Owen (eds), *Gwaith Cynddelw Brydydd Mawr*, vol. 1, pp. 15–50.
Parry-Williams, T. H. (ed.), *Canu Rhydd Cynnar*, Cardiff, 1932.
Périn, P., and Feffer, L.-C., *Les Francs, Tome 1: à la conquête de la Gaule*, Paris, 1987.
Peter, R. and Peter, O. B., *The Histories of Launceston and Dunheved in the County of Cornwall*, Plymouth, 1885.
Peter, T., *Glasney Collegiate Church*, Camborne, 1903.
Pevsner, N., *Cornwall*, Harmondsworth, 1951.
Pharr, C. (trans.), *The Theodosian Code and Novels and the Sirmondian Constitution*, Princeton, 1952.
Philippart, G., 'Jean, évêque d'Arezzo, auteur de *De Assumptione* de Reichenau', *AB* 92 (1974), 345–6.
—, 'Le Manuscrit hagiographique latin comme gisement documentaire. Un parcours dans les *Analecta Bollandiana* de 1960 à 1989', in Heinzelmann (ed.), *Manuscrits hagiographiques*, pp. 17–48.
—, 'Pour une histoire générale, problématique et sérielle de la littérature et

de l'édition hagiographiques latines de l'Antiquité et du Moyen Age', *Cassiodorus* 2 (1996), 197–213.

Phillimore, W. P. W., Taylor, T. and Glencross, J. H. (eds), *Cornwall Parish Registers Marriages*, 6 vols, London, 1900.

Phythian-Adams, C., *Local History and Folklore: A New Framework*, London, 1975.

Picard, J. M., 'The marvellous in Irish and continental saints' Lives of the Merovingian period,' in H. B. Clarke and M. Brennan (eds), *Columbanus and Merovingian Monasticism*, Oxford, 1981, pp. 91–103.

Picken, W. M. M., 'St German of Cornwall's Day', rpr. in O. J. Padel (ed.), *A Medieval Cornish Miscellany*, Chichester, 2000, pp. 115–20.

Pinder-Wilson, R. H. and Brooke, C. N. L., 'The reliquary of St Petroc and the ivories of Norman Sicily', *Archaeologia* 104 (1973), 261–305.

Plaine, D. (ed.), 'Vita Sancti Pauli episcopi Leonensis in Britannia Minori auctore Wormonoco', *AB* 1 (1882), 208–58.

Plaine, F. B. (ed.), 'Vita antiqua S. Samsonis Dolensis episcopi', *AB* 6 (1997), 77–150.

Plummer, C., (ed.), *Vitae Sanctorum Hiberniae*, 2 vols, Oxford, 1890; rpr. 1968.

—, 'Some new light on the Brendan legend', *ZCP* 5 (1905), 124–41; rpr. Wooding, *The Otherworld Voyage*, pp. 1–14.

— (ed. and trans.), *Bethada náem nÉrenn: Lives of Irish saints*, 2 vols, Oxford, 1922; rpr. 1968.

—, *Miscellanea Hagiographica Hibernica*, Société des Bollandistes, Subsidia Hagiographica 15, Brussels, 1925.

Polsue, J., *History of Cornwall*, 4 vols, London, 1867–72.

Poole, A. L., *From Domesday Book to Magna Carta*, Oxford, 1951.

Postic, F., 'La Saint-Jean en Finistère: richesse et gravité d'un rituel', *Ar Men* 8 (1987), 44–61.

— (ed.), *Les Œuvres de François Cadic: contes et légendes de Bretagne*, vol. 1, Rennes, 1997.

— (ed.), *La Bretagne et la littérature orale en Europe*, Brest, 1999.

— (ed.), *Les Œuvres de François Cadic: les récits légendaires*, Rennes, 2000.

Poulin, J.-C., 'Hagiographie et politique. La première Vie de saint Samson de Dol', *Francia* 5 (1977), 1–26.

—, 'Le Dossier de saint Samson de Dol', *Francia* 15 (1987), 701–31.

—, 'Les Dossiers de S. Magloire de Dol et de saint Malo d'Alet', *Francia* 17 (1990), 159–210.

—, 'Le Dossier de saint Guénolé de Landévennec', *Francia* 23 (1996), 167–205.

—, '*Liber iste vocatur Vita Samsonis*. Un légendier factice du XIIe siècle constitué de livres hagiographiques', *AB* 117 (1999), 133–50.

—, 'Les Dossiers des saints Lunaire et Paul Aurélien', in M. Heinzelmann (ed.), *L'Hagiographie du haut Moyen-Âge en Gaule du Nord. Manuscrits,*

textes, et centres de production, Beihefte der Francia 52, Stuttgart, 2001, pp. 193–248.
Pryce, H., *Native Law and the Church in Medieval Wales*, Oxford, 1993.
—, 'Gerald's Journey through Wales', *JWEH* 6 (1989), 17–34.
—, 'A new edition of the *Historia divae Monacellae*', *Montgomeryshire Collections* 82 (1994), 23–40.
—, 'Owain Gwynedd and Louis VII. The Franco-Welsh diplomacy of the first Prince of Wales', *WHR* 19 (1998), 1–28.
—, 'Yr eglwys yn oes yr Arglwydd Rhys', in N. A. Jones and Pryce (eds), *Yr Arglwydd Rhys*, pp. 145–77.
Quiller-Couch, M. and L., *Ancient and Holy Wells of Cornwall*, London, 1894; rpr. 1994.
Raftery, B., *Pagan Celtic Ireland: The Enigma of the Irish Iron Age*, London, 1994.
Raine, J. (ed.), *Reginaldi monachi Dunelmensis Libellus de admirandis beati Cuthberti virtutibus quae novellis patratae sunt temporibus*, Surtees Society 1, Durham, 1835.
— (ed.), 'Libellus de nativitate Sancti Cuthberti', in Raine (ed.), *Miscellanea Biographica*, pp. 63–87.
— (ed.), *Miscellanea Biographica*, Surtees Society 8, London/Edinburgh, 1838.
Raison du Cleuziou, J., 'La Navigation du moine saint Malo', *Bulletin et Mémoires. Société d'emulation des Côtes-du-Nord* 86 (1957), 45–60.
Rees, A. and Rees, B., *Celtic Heritage*, Llandybïe, 1973.
Rees, E., *Celtic Saints: Passionate Wanderers*, London, 2000.
Rees, N., *St David of Dewisland*, Llandysul, 1997.
Rees, W. J. (ed.), *The Liber Landavensis*, Llandovery, 1840.
— (ed. and trans.), *Lives of the Cambro-British Saints*, Llandovery, 1853.
Remfry, P. M., 'Cadwallon ap Madog Rex de Delvain and the re-establishment of local autonomy in Cynllibiwg', *Transactions of the Radnorshire Society* 65 (1995), 11–26.
Rhŷs, J., *Celtic Folklore: Welsh and Manx*, Oxford, 1891.
Richards G. M., *Welsh Administrative and Territorial Units*, Cardiff, 1969.
Richards, M., 'Buchedd Mair o'r Aifft', *EC* 2 (1937), 45–9.
—, 'Buchedd Fargred', *BBCS* 11 (1939), 324–34, and *BBCS* 13 (1949), 65–71.
Richards, W. L. (ed.), *Gwaith Dafydd Llwyd o Fathafarn*, Cardiff, 1964.
Riché, P., 'Les Hagiographes bretons et la renaissance carolingienne', *Bulletin philologique et historique* (1966), 651–9.
—, 'Instruments de travail et méthodes de l'exégète à l'époque carolingienne', in Riché and Lobrichon (eds), *Le Moyen Age et la Bible*, pp. 147–161.
Riché, P. and Lobrichon, G. (eds), *Le Moyen Age et la Bible*, Paris, 1984.

Richter, M., 'The Life of St David by Giraldus Cambrensis', *WHR* 4 (1968–9), 381–6.
—, *Medieval Ireland: The Enduring Tradition*, Dublin, 1988.
—, *The Oral Tradition in the Early Middle Ages*, Turnhout, 1994.
Ritchie, J. 'The sculptured stones of Clatt, Aberdeeshire', *Proc. Soc. Antiq. Scotl.* 44 (1909–10), 203–15.
Rivet, A. L. F., and Smith C. C., *The Place-names of Roman Britain*, London, 1979, pp. 276–7.
Roberts, B. F., 'Un o lawysgrifau Hopcyn ap Thomas o Ynys Dawe', *BBCS* 22 (1967), 223–8.
—, 'Geoffrey of Monmouth's *Historia* and *Brut y Brenhinedd*', in R. Bromwich, A. O. H. Jarman and B. F. Roberts (eds), *The Arthur of the Welsh*, Cardiff, 1991, pp. 97–116.
—, 'Enlli'r Oesoedd Canol', in R. G. Jones and C. J. Arnold (eds), *Enlli*, Cardiff, 1997, pp. 21–48.
Roberts, T. (ed.), *Gwaith Tudur Penllyn ac Ieuan ap Tudur Penllyn*, Cardiff, 1958.
Roberts, T. and Williams, I. (eds), *The Poetical Works of Dafydd Nanmor*, Cardiff, 1923.
Robertson, J. (ed.), *Collections for a History of the Shires of Aberdeen and Banff*, Aberdeen, 1843.
Robinson, J. A. (ed.), 'A fragment of the Life of St Cyngar', *Journal of Theological Studies* 20 (1918–19), 97–108.
Robson, P. A., *The Cathedral Church of Saint David's: A Short History and Description of the Fabric and Episcopal Buildings*, Bell's Cathedral Series, London, 1901; rpr. 1907.
Rolfe, J. S., 'Cornwall incumbents and patrons transcribed from Hennessy's institutions', unpublished manuscript notebook at RIC, 1903–13.
Rollason, D. W., 'Lists of saints' resting-places in Anglo-Saxon England', *Anglo-Saxon England* 7 (1978), 61–93.
Rowland, J. (ed. and trans.), *Early Welsh Saga Poetry*, Cambridge, 1990.
Rowlands, M. J., 'Kinship, alliance, and exchange in the European Bronze Age', in J. Barrett and R. Bradley (eds), *Settlement and Society in the British Later Bronze Age*, B.A.R. British Series 83 (1), Oxford, 1980, pp. 15–56.
Rushforth, G. McN., 'The windows of the church of St Neot, Cornwall', *Exeter Diocesan Architectural and Archaeological Transactions*, 3rd Series 4 (1937), 150–90.
Russell, P., Review of Bammesberger and Wollmann (eds), *Britain 400–600*, in *SC* 26–7 (1991–2), 265–70.
Rutt, R., '*Missa Propria Germani Episcopi* and the eponym of St Germans', *JRIC*, New Series 7 (1977), 305–9.
Saxer, V., *Le Culte de Marie Madeleine en Occident des origines à la fin du Moyen Age*, Auxerre-Paris, 1959.

Sayce, R. U., 'The one-night house and its distribution', *Folklore* 53 (1942), 161–3.

Schmitt, J.-C., 'Le Texte hagiographique dans la culture populaire', *Ethnologie française* 10 (4) (1980), 380–4.

Scott, A. B., *The Pictish Nation its People and its Church*, Edinburgh and London, 1918.

Scott, J. (ed. and trans.), *The Early History of Glastonbury. An Edition, Translation, and Study of William of Malmesbury's De Antiquitate Glastonie Ecclesie*, Woodbridge, 1981.

Selmer, C. (ed.), *Navigatio Sancti Brendani Abbatis*, Notre Dame Publications in Medieval Studies 16, South Bend IA, 1959; rpr. Dublin, 1989.

Severin, T., *The Brendan Voyage*, London, 1976.

Sharpe, R., '*Vitae S Brigitae*: the oldest texts', *Peritia* 1 (1982), 81–106.

—, 'Were the Irish annals known to a Northumbrian writer?', *Peritia* 2 (1983), 137–9.

—, 'Gildas as a Father of the Church', in M. Lapidge and D. Dumville (eds), *Gildas, New Approaches*, Woodbridge, 1984, pp. 193–205.

—, 'Saint Mauchteus, *discipulus Patricii*', in Bammesberger and Wollmann (eds), *Britain 400–600*, pp. 85–93.

—, *Medieval Irish Saints' Lives: An Introduction to Vitae Sanctorum Hiberniae*, Oxford, 1991.

—, (trans.), *Adomnán of Iona: Life of St Columba*, Harmondsworth, 1995.

Sharpe, R. and Thacker, A. (eds), *Local Saints and Local Churches in the Early Medieval West*, Oxford, forthcoming.

Sheldrake, P., *Spirituality and History: Questions of Interpretation and Method*, London, 1991.

Short, I. and Merrillees, B. (eds), *The Anglo-Norman Voyage of St Brendan*, Manchester, 1979.

Simon, M., *L'Abbaye de Landévennec de saint Guénolé à nos jours*, Rennes, 1985.

— (ed.), *Landévennec et le monachisme breton dans le haut Moyen Age. Actes du colloque du 15ème centenaire de l'abbaye de Landévennec (25–27 avril 1985)*, Landévennec, 1986.

Simpson, W. D., *The Origins of Christianity in Aberdeenshire (illustrated)*, Aberdeen, 2nd edn, 1925.

—, 'Notes on Lulach's stone, Kildrummy, Aberdeenshire; a symbol stone recently found in Mortlach churchyard, Banffshire; and other antiquities', *Proc. Soc. Antiq. Scotl.* 12 (1925–6), 273–80.

Sims-Williams, P., 'The evidence for vernacular Irish literary influence on early mediaeval Welsh literature', in D. Whitelock, R. McKitterich and D. Dumville (eds), *Ireland in Early Mediaeval Europe*, Cambridge, 1982, pp. 235–57.

—, 'Some functions of origin stories in early medieval Wales', in T.

Nyberg, I. Piø, P. M. Sørensen and A Trommer (eds), *History and Heroic Tale: A Symposium*, Odense, 1985, pp. 97–131.

—, 'Dating the transition to Neo-Brittonic: phonology and history, 400–600', in Bammesberger and Wollmann (eds.), *Britain 400–600*, pp. 217–62.

Skene, W. F., *Celtic Scotland: A History of Ancient Alban*, 3 vols; *Church and Culture*, vol. 2, Edinburgh, 1877.

Smith, J., 'Oral and written: saints, miracles, and relics in Brittany *c.*850–1250, *Speculum* 65 (1990), 309–4,

Smith, J. B., 'Treftadaeth Deheubarth' in N. A. Jones and Pryce (eds), *Yr Arglwydd Rhys*, pp. 18–52.

—, 'Cymer abbey and the Welsh princes', *Journal of the Merioneth Historical and Record Society* 13 (1999), 101–18.

Smith, J. R. (ed.), *The Lives of St Mary Magdalene and St Martha*, Exeter, 1989.

Smith, L. and Taylor, J. H. M. (eds), *Women, the Book and the Godly: Selected Proceedings of the St Hilda's Conference, 1993*, Cambridge, 1995.

Smyth, A. P., 'The earliest Irish annals: their first contemporary entries, and the earliest centres of recording', *PRIA* 72 (1972), 1–48.

Snell, L. S., *The Chantry Certificates for Cornwall*, Exeter, 1953.

—, *The Edwardian Inventories of Church Goods in Cornwall*, Exeter, 1955.

Sproule, D., 'Politics and pure narrative in the stories about Corc of Cashel', *Ériu* 36 (1985), 11–28.

Stancliffe, C., *St. Martin and his Hagiographer: History and Miracle in Sulpicius Severus*, Oxford, 1983.

—, 'The miracle stories in seventh-century Irish saints' Lives', in J. Fontaine and J. N. Hillgarth (eds), *The Seventh Century: Change and Continuity*, London, 1992, pp. 87–115.

Stevenson, J., 'The monastic rules of Columbanus', in M. Lapidge (ed.), *Columbanus, Studies on the Latin Writings*, Woodbridge, 1998, pp. 203–16.

Stevenson, W. H. (ed.), *Asser's Life of Alfred*, Oxford, 1959.

Stoate, T. L. (ed.), *Cornwall Subsidies in the Reign of Henry VIII – 1524 and 1543 and the Benevolence of 1545*, Bristol, 1985.

—, *The Cornwall Military Survey 1522 with the Loan Books and a Tinner's Muster Roll c.1535*, Bristol, 1987.

Stokes, W. (ed.), *Three Irish Glossaries*, London, 1862.

— (ed. and trans.), *The Tripartite Life of Patrick with Other Documents Relating to that Saint*, 2 vols, London, 1887; rpr. 1965.

—, 'On the Calendar of Oengus', *Transactions of the Royal Irish Academy*, Irish Manuscript Series 1, Dublin, 1880.

— (ed. and trans.), *Lives of Saints from the Book of Lismore*, Oxford, 1890.

— (trans.), *The Annals of Tigernach*, 2 vols, Felinfach, 1993; rpr. from *RC* (1895–6).
— (ed.), *Félire Óengusso Céli Dé: The Martyrology of Oengus the Culdee*, Henry Bradshaw Society 29, London, 1905; rpr. Dublin 1984.
Stokes, W., and Strachan, J. (eds), *Thesaurus Paleohibernicus*, 2 vols, Cambridge, 1901–3.
Strickland, M., *War and Chivalry*, Cambridge, 1996.
Stuart, J., *Sculptured Stones of Scotland*, Aberdeen, 1854.
—, *The Book of Deer*, Aberdeen, 1869.
Sulpicius Severus, *Chronicle*, G. de Senneville-Grave (ed.), *Chroniques*, Paris, 1999.
Sumption, J., *Pilgrimage. An Image of Mediaeval Religion*, London, 1975.
Tanguy, A., 'Anatole Le Braz [1859–1926] et la tradition populaire en Bretagne: analyse de quatre carnets d'enqûetes', Doctoral dissertation, 5 vols, Université de Bretagne Occidentale, Brest, CRBC, 1997.
Tanguy, B., 'De la Vie de saint Cadoc à celle de saint Gurthiern', *EC* 26 (1989), 159–85.
—, *Saint Hervé, Vie et Culte*, Minihi-Levenez, 1990.
Tasker, E. G., *Encyclopaedia of Medieval Church Art*, London, 1993.
Taylor, S., 'Seventh-century Iona abbots in Scottish place-names', in D. Broun and T. O. Clancy (eds), *Spes Scotorum, Hope of Scots: Saint Columba, Iona and Scotland*, Edinburgh, 1999, pp. 35–70.
Taylor Scott, J., 'Plan and elevation of the cathedral', *The Builder* 63, no. 2, (1892).
Thomas, C., 'Sculptured stones and crosses from St Ninian's Isle and Papil', in A. Small, C. Thomas and D. M. Wilson, *St Ninian's Isle and its Treasure*, London, 1973, pp. 8–44.
—, *Christianity in Roman Britain to AD 500*, Berkeley and Los Angeles, 1981.
—, 'The double shrine "A" from St Ninian's Isle, Shetland', in A. O'Connor, and D. V. Clarke (eds), *From the Stone Age to the 'Forty-Five'*, Edinburgh, 1983, pp. 285–92.
—, *Exploration of a Drowned Landscape – Archaeology and History of the Isles of Scilly*, London, 1985.
—, *And Shall these Mute Stones Speak?* Cardiff, 1994.
—, 'The Llanddewi-brefi "Idnert" Stone', *Peritia* 10 (1996), 136–83.
—, 'Form and function', in S. M. Foster (ed.), *The St Andrews Sarcophagus: A Pictish Masterpiece and its International Connections*, Dublin, 1998, pp. 84–96.
Thomas, G. C. G., *The Charters of the Abbey of Ystrad Marchell*, Aberystwyth, 1997.
Thomas, S., 'Land occupation, ownership and utilisation in the parish of Llansantffraid', *Ceredigion* 3 (1956–9), 124–55.
Thompson, E. A., *Who was St. Patrick?*, Woodbridge, 1985.
Thornton, D. E., 'Glastonbury and the Glastening', in L. Abrams and

J. Carley (eds), *The Archaeology and History of Glastonbury Abbey*, Woodbridge, 1991, pp. 191–203.

—, 'Early medieval Louth: the kingdom of Conaille Muirtheimne', *County Louth Archaeological and Historical Journal* 24 (1) (1997), 139–50.

Thurston, H., and Attwater, D. (ed., rev. and supplemented), *Butler's Lives of the Saints*, vol. 3, New York, 1956.

Tomlin, R., 'The date of the "Barbarian Conspiracy"', *Britannia* 5 (1974), 303–9.

Toulmin-Smith, L. (ed.), *Leland's Itinerary in England and Wales*, 5 vols, London, 1964.

Townsend, D., 'Anglo-Latin hagiography and the Norman transition', *Exemplaria* 3 (1991), 385–433.

Trier, J., 'Holy wells in Pembrokeshire (including those of St David and St Mary) and their possible association with pilgrim routes', M.Phil. thesis, to be submitted to the University of Wales, Lampeter.

Tudor, V., 'The misogyny of Saint Cuthbert', *Archaeologia Aeliana* 5th series 12 (1984), 157–67.

—, 'The cult of St Cuthbert in the twelfth century: the evidence of Reginald of Durham', in Bonner, Rollason and Stancliffe (eds), *St Cuthbert*, Woodbridge, 1989, pp. 447–67.

Tyndale, A. I., 'A study of the names in Chrétien de Troyes', Ph.D. thesis, University of Wales, Aberystwyth, 1999.

Van der Straeten, J., *Les Manuscrits hagiographiques d'Orléans, Tours, et Angers*, Brussels, 1982.

Van Hamel, A. G. (ed.), *Compert Con Culainn and Other Stories*, Dublin, 1933.

Van 'T. Spijker, L., 'Province ecclésiastique de Tours', in G. Philipart, *Hagiographies. Histoire internationale de la littérature hagiographique latine et vernaculaire en Occident des origines à 1550*, vol. 2, Turnhout, 1996, pp. 248–58.

Vauchez, A., 'Le Saint' in J. Le Goff (ed.), *L'Homme médiéval*, Paris, 1989, pp. 345–80.

Vendryes, J., 'Saint David et le roi Boia', *RC* 45 (1928), 159–64.

Wade-Evans, A. W., 'Parochiale Wallicum', *Y Cymmrodor* 22 (1910), 22–124.

—, 'Rhigyfarch's Life of St David', *Y Cymmrodor* (1913), 1–73.

— (ed.), *Life of St David*, London, 1923.

— (ed. and trans.), *Vitae Sanctorum Britanniae et Genealogiae*, Cardiff, 1944.

Wagner, A. and Rowse, A. L., *John Anstis, Garter King of Arms*, London, 1992.

Walker, G. S. M. (ed.), *Sancti Columbani Opera*, Scriptores Latini Hiberniae 2, Dublin, 1970.

Wall, C., *Shrines of British Saints*, London, 1905.

Walsh, J. T., and Begg, C. T., '1 and 2 Kings', in R. E. Brown, J. A. Fitzmyer and R. E. Murphy (eds), *The New Jerome Biblical Commentary*, London 1990.

Walsh, M., and Ó Cróinín, D. (ed. and trans.), *Cummian's Letter 'De controversia Paschali' and the 'De ratione Computandi'*, Toronto, 1988.

Ward, B., *Miracles and the Medieval Mind*, Philadelphia, 1982; rev. edn 1987. Warren, W. L., *Henry II*, London, 1973.

Watson, W. J., *The History of the Celtic Place-Names of Scotland*, Edinburgh and London, 1926

Watt, J., *The Church in Medieval Ireland*, 2nd edn, Dublin, 1998.

Wayment, H., *King's College Chapel Cambridge: The Great Windows Introduction and Guide*, Cambridge, 1992.

Weatherly, E. H. (ed.), *Speculum Sacerdotale*, London, 1936.

Weber, R., *Biblia Sacra Vulgata*, 2nd rev. edn, Stuttgart, 1975.

Welsh Department, Board of Education, *Dydd Gŵyl Dewi Sant*, Cardiff, 1915.

Whetter, J., *The History of Glasney College*, Padstow, 1988.

Whitaker, J., *The Life of St Neot the Oldest of the Brothers to King Alfred*, London, 1809.

Wightman, E. M., *Gallia Belgica*, Berkeley and Los Angeles, 1985.

William of Malmesbury, *Gesta Regum Anglorum/History of the English Kings*, R. A. B. Mynors, R. M. Thomson and M. Winterbottom (ed. and trans.), 2 vols, Oxford, 1999 and 2000.

Williams, A. G., "Norman lordship in south-east Wales during the Reign of William I', *WHR* 16 (1992–3), 445–66.

Williams, B. H., *Ambrose of Milan and the End of the Nicene-Arian Conflicts*, Oxford, 1995.

Williams, D. H., 'Cistercian nunneries in medieval Wales', *Cîteaux* 26 (1975), 155–74.

—, 'Usk nunnery', *Monmouthshire Antiquary* 4 (1980), 44–5.

—, *The Welsh Cistercians*, Caldey Island, 1983.

Williams, G., *The Welsh Church from Conquest to Reformation*, Cardiff, 1962.

—, *Religion, Language and Nationality in Wales*, Cardiff, 1979.

Williams, H. (ed.), *Gildas*, Cymmrodorion Record Series 3, London, 1901.

Williams, I. (ed.), *Pedeir Keinc y Mabinogi*, Cardiff, 1930.

— (ed.), *Gwyneddon 3*, Cardiff, 1931.

— (ed.), *Canu Llywarch Hen*, Cardiff, 1935.

—, 'Protestaniaeth Wiliam Middleton', *BBCS* 8 (1936), 242–7.

— (ed.), *Armes Prydein o Lyfr Taliesin*, Cardiff, 1955; rpr. 1999.

— (ed.) *Armes Prydein: The Prophecy of Britain from the Book of Taliesin*, English version by R. Bromwich, Dublin, 1972.

—, *Beginnings of Welsh Poetry*, Rachel Bromwich (ed.), 2nd edn, Cardiff, 1980.

Williams, I. and Williams, J. L. (eds), *Gwaith Guto'r Glyn*, Cardiff, 1961.

Williams, J. ab I. (ed.), *Annales Cambriae*, Kraus Reprints, Wiesbaden, 1965.
Williams, J. E. C., 'Bucheddau'r saint', *BBCS* 11 (1941–4), 149–57.
—, 'Buchedd Dewi', *Llên Cymru* 5 (1958–90), 105–8.
— (ed.), '*Transitus Beatae Mariae* a thestunau cyffelyb', *BBCS* 18 (1959), 131–57.
—, 'Buchedd Catrin Sant', *BBCS* 25 (1973), 247–68.
—, 'Rhyddiaith grefyddol Cymraeg Canol (1)', in G. Bowen (ed.), *Y Traddodiad Rhyddiaith yn yr Oesau Canol*, Llandysul, 1974, pp. 312–59.
—, *The Poets of the Welsh Princes*, Cardiff, 1994.
Williams, P. L., '"Ar ganghennau'r gynghanedd": agweddau ar y goedwig yn llenyddiaeth yr Oesoedd Canol', *Dwned* 6 (2000), 55–76.
Williams, R. (ed.), 'The Life of Griffith ap Cynan', *Arch. Camb.*, 3rd Series 12 (1866), 30–45, 112–31.
Williams, R. D. (ed.), *P. Vergili Maronis. Aeneidos. Liber Tertius*, Oxford, 1962.
Williams-Jones, K., 'Llywelyn's charter to Cymer Abbey in 1209', *Journal of the Meirioneth Historical and Record Society* 3 (1957–60), 45–78.
Willis, B., *A Survey of the Cathedral Church of St David's*, London, 1717.
Willis-Bund, J. W. (ed.), *An Extent of All the Lands and Rents of the Lord Bishop of St Davids Usually Called The Black Book of St David's*, London, 1902.
Wogan-Browne, J., '"Clerc u lai, muïne u dame"; women and Anglo-Norman hagiography in the twelfth- and thirteenth-centuries', in C. M. Meale (ed.), *Women and Literature in Britain, 1150–1500*, Cambridge, 1993, pp. 61–85.
Wooding, J. M., 'Monastic voyaging and the *Nauigatio*', in Wooding (ed.), *The Otherworld Voyage*, pp. 226–45.
— (ed.), *The Otherworld Voyage in Early Irish Literature: An Anthology of Criticism*, Dublin, 2000.
—, 'St Brendan's boat: dead hides and the living sea in Columban and related hagiography', in Carey, Herbert and Ó Riain (eds), *Studies in Irish Hagiography*, pp. 77–92.
—, 'The Latin version', in G. Burgess and W. R. J. Barron (eds), *The Voyage of St Brendan Theme and Variation*, Exeter, 2001, pp. 14–25.
—, 'St Brendan, Clonfert and the ocean: charting the voyages of a cult', in J. Higgins and C. Cunniffe (eds), *Aspects of Clonfert and its Vicinity*, Galway, forthcoming.
—, 'Les Saints et le bétail dans *Nauigatio sancti Brendani abbatis*', *Britannica Monastica*, forthcoming.
Worcestre, W., *Itineraries*, J. H. Harvey (ed.), Oxford, 1969.
Wright, N., 'Some further Vergilian borrowings in Breton hagiography of the Carolingian period', *EC* 20 (1983), 161–75.
Wright, T. (ed.), *Three Chapters of Letters Relating to the Suppression of the Monasteries*, London, 1843; rpr. New York, 1968.
Yardley, E., *Menevia Sacra*, F. Green (ed.), London, 1927.

Zupita, J. (ed.), 'Das Leben der heiligen Maria Magdalena', *Archiv für das Studium der neuren Sprachen und Litteraturen* 47 (1893), 207–24.

Index

Abbán, saint, Life of 150
Abdego 126
Aberconwy, abbey of 73 n.106
Aberdeen, dialect of 232–3
  diocese of 232, 236, 237, 239, 244
  University of 233
Aberdeen Breviary *(Breviarium Aberdonense)* 225, 228, 233, 235, 239–40
  Calendar of 241, 247 n.68
Aberdeenshire 236, 238, 245 n.12, Fig. 13.1
Abergwili 53
Abraham, bishop of St Davids 15
Achaius, king 247 n.70
Acta Sanctorum 50, 195 nn.5, 15, 247 n.63
Adam 124
Adomnán, saint and abbot of Iona 7, 102, 121 n.70, 133, 157, 163–4, 223, 226, 229, 234
Áed Allán, king of Tara 155
Áed mac Bricc, saint, Life of 150
Áed mac Néill, king of Tara 155
Áedán, king 133
Aedán of Inis Moccu Chéin 230 n.15
Aeneas 277
Aeneas, father of St Cadfan 47
Aeneid 271, 273, 277–9, 281
  Irish translations of 278
  influence on Breton hagiographers 278
Age of the Saints 104
Aeron, river 53–4
Æthelred, king 275
Æthelstan, king of England 33, 241
aetiology 29
Aghaboe, church of 150
Agnes, saint 261
Aífe, daughter of Diarmait mac Murchada 65
Ailbe (Elfyw), saint 16, 163, 166, 169, 172
  Life of 148, 150, 159 n.5, 162–3, 174 n.18, 176 n.51
  monastery of 172
Ailbe Ua Mael Muad, bishop of Ferns 230 n.9
Ailego, river 71 n.61
Airgíalla 150, 151, 159 n.19
Aix-en-Provence 85, 89, 91
Alan (Alanus, Gille-Aldan), bishop of Whithorn 217, 220, 222, 230 n.8
Alba Longa 271, 277–8
Alcuin 178–9, 186
Alcuin, saint 247 n.70
Alet 181–2
Alexander de Kininmund, bishop of Aberdeen 238
Alfred, king 255, 267 n.47
  Life by Asser 14, 33, 253–4
All Saints 246 n.38, 258
  image in stained glass 258, Fig. 14.2
Altarnun 9 n.7, 266 n.19
Alun, river 19
  valley 17
Amator, bishop of Auxerre 103, 118 n.5
Ambrose of Milan, saint 86, 110, 116–17, 121 n.79
Ammanford 23 n.25
Anatolius, bishop of Laodicea 121, n.75
anchorites 37, 78, 166, 170
Ancrene Wisse 77–8, 98 n.2
Andrew, saint 4, 20–1
angels 26, 32, 72 n.83, 89, 93, 138, 139, 142, 254, 272, 273, 274, 276, 280
Anglesey 41, 50, 59, 61, 63–4, 74 n.121
Anglo-Norman, influence on Wales 30
Anglo-Saxons 3, 30, 42, 66, 105, 252, 254, 260
Anjou 61
  count and countess of 190
Anna, saint, Welsh Life of 44 n.48

Annales Cambriae 13, 16–17, 23 n.26
Annes wraig Rhydderch 101 n.86
Anstis, John 265 n.46
Antiphony of Bangor 196 n.36
Antony, saint 170, 176 nn.48–9, 207
apocrypha 7, 136
  medieval 198
Apollo 209
Apollonia, saint 96
Aran 171
Arbogastes 109
Archenfield 51
Ardstraw, church of 151, 157
Ardbreccan 219, 220
Ardmore, diocese of 220, 221
aretalogy 139–40, 142
Arfon 76 n.158
Argyll 219, 220, 221, 222, 223, 226
  earl of 236
Arianism 111, 117, 120 nn.42–3
Armagh 52, 115–16, 121 n.74, 157, 159 n.16, 235
  Book of 157
Armes Prydein 14, 33–4, 38, 52, 63, 68, 71 n.61, 73 n.95
Arras 184
Arthur, king 31, 36
Arundell, John, Sir 269 n.80
Ascanius 277–8
Asherah 127, 134 n.22
Asia 90
Asser 14, 33, 254, 266–7 n.31
Áth dá Ferta 155
Atholl 223–4, 226, 227, 228–9
Aubin of Angers 190
Auchinleck Manuscript 85
Augustine of Hippo, saint 51, 120 n.45, 140, 166, 169, 262, 278
  Confessiones of 120 n.45
Auxentius, bishop of Milan 111
Auxerre (Alsiodorum) 103, 118 n.5, 257
Azarian, Prayer of 134 n.14

Baal 127
Babylon 5, 126–7
Babylonia 134 n.7
Báetán Ua Nia Taloirc 163
Bagimond's Roll 237
Bairre, saint, Life of 143–4
Baíthéne, saint, Life of 149, 151, 153
Bala 37
Ballinrees 106, 108
  ingot of 106–8, 112
Banffshire 236

Bangor, Ireland 218, 236
  abbot of 218
  church of 150
Bangor, Wales 35, 38, 53, 66–7, 76 n.158
Bangu, reliquary bell of St David 13–14, 54, 72 n.82
Bannaventa 118 n.2
Bardsey Island *see* Enlli
Barlow, bishop of St Davids 12–13, 16
Barnic (Barre), saint 254
Barrind 168, 171
Barrius (Barry) 254, 267 n.35
Barry Island, Pembrokeshire 23 n.37
Baschurch, churches of 73 n.95
Bath 11
Baudri de Bourgueil, archbishop of Dol 193–4, 197 nn.71, 75
Bauto 108–9
Bavaria 281 n.4
Bean (Beyne), bishop of Aberdeen 237
Beaulieu, priory of 231 n.31
Beaumont-sur-Oise 182
Bec, abbey of 256
Bede 121 n.70
  Historia ecclesiastica gentis Anglorum 174 n.16
Bedford 224
Bedfordshire 220, 224, 227, 228
Benedeit 169
Benedict of Aniane 188–9
  Concordia Regularum 189
Benedict, saint 189
  Rule of 183–5, 188–9
Benedictines 183
Benineus 131
Berach, saint 144
  Irish Life of 144
Bernard, bishop of St Davids 12–13, 17–18, 22 n.17, 36, 52, 64, 66
Bernard of Clairvaux, saint 221, 224, 236, 245 n.25
Bethany 84, 95
Betws 23 n.25
Beuno, saint 4, 26, 29, 31, 37–8
  Welsh Life of 26, 29, 37
Bevis of Hampton 97, 101 n.85
Bible 84, 109, 136, 177, 178, 179
biblical characters 5, 11, 83–5, 87–9, 93, 125–6, 129, 132–3, 134 n.20, 140, 168–9, 207–11, 239, 242, 250–1, 268 n.71
  see also hagiography, influence of scriptural sources on
Bili, deacon of Alet 181–2, 191–2, 272

Index

Binnerton, chapel of 262
Bleddfa, church of 93
Blisland 266 n.19
Boconnoc 255–6
Bodmin 253, 268 n.57, 269 n.85, Fig. 14.7
   church of 252–3, 259, 261, 263, 267 n.34
   holy well of 266 n.29
Bodmin Moor 250
Boece, Hector 240, 243, 248 n.90
Boia 32, 52, 64, 71 n.71, 72 n.84
Bois-de-la-Nuit 213
Bollandists 50, 179, 184
Bonedd y Saint 47
Boniface III, pope 240, 243, 247 n.63
Bonport Legendary 183
Borlase 267 n.46, Fig. 14.5
Bower, Walter 228
Bozon, Nicholas 85, 88, 99 n.54
Braddock 266 n.19, 268 n.57
Braemar (Kyndrochet), church of 238
Braspartz 48
   chapel of 48
Brazemoor, church of 266 n.29
Breage, church of 262, 269 n.88
Brega 126–7, 153, 156–7
Brecknock 51
Brecon, church of 62
Brendan, saint 1, 6, 161–73, 226, 235, 245 n.21, 276
   Anglo-Norman Life of 3, 169, 175 n.44
   Betha Brénnain 161, 175 n.30
   later Irish versions of the Life of 166
   Nauigatio sancti Brendani abbatis 6, 161–73, 173–4 n.3, 174 n.6, 175 n.41, 192–3
   Second Life of 149–50
   Vita Brendani 161–6, 173–4 n.3, 174 n.6, 175 n.41
Breton language 67, 200
Breward, saint 266 n.19
Brigit, saint 1, 27–8, 136, 138, 154, 157, 220, 222–3, 230 n.28
   Bethu Brigte 121 n.74, 281, 284 n.65
   Vita Brigitae by Cogitosus 116, 121 n.74, 143, 281
   Vita Prima 121 n.74, 142–3, 145, 281
Britain 33, 36, 48, 105–7, 110, 151, 120
Brittany 1–2, 6–7, 33, 45, 47, 48, 50, 51, 61, 74 n.126, 184, 185, 189, 190, 199, 200–1, 207, 214 n.8, 215 n.27, 234, 253
Bro Dreger 207
Bro Gerne 201
Bro Wened 201
Brochfael Ysgithrog 48–9, 50, 100 n.58

Brook of Kishon 127
Brunanburh, battle of 63, 75 n.134
Brut y Tywysogion 57, 67
Brychan Brycheiniog, eponymous ruler of Brycheiniog 69 n.15, 260
   genealogy of 252
Brycheiniog, kingdom of 69 n.15
Brynach, saint 29
   Life of 272, 275, 277, 278
Bubry 204
   chapel of 207
Budoc, saint 200
   Life of 200
Buellt 49
Buhez ar Sent 199, 214 n.4
Builth Wells 50
Burlas, Katherine 256
Burlas, Nicholas 256
Butt of Lewis 244 n.9
Byrhtferth 273

Cadfan, saint 5, 45–8, 56–9, 67–8, 74 n.110
   'Canu Cadfan' by Llywelyn Fardd 28, 45–8, 55–9, 68, 68 n.1, 69 n.9
   crosier of 58
   Gospel Book of 58
   Lives of 181
   parentage of 46–7
   see also Tywyn
Cadfan ap Cadwaladr 57
Cado, saint 181
Cadog, saint 23 n.29, 29, 35, 273, 274
   founds church 29, 273–4
   Life by Caradog of Llancarfan 272, 276
   Life by Lifris of Llancarfan 28, 34–5, 272–3, 276–7, 280, 282 n.28
Cadwaladr 33
Cadwaladr ap Gruffudd ap Cynan, lord of Meirionnydd 57
Cadwallon ap Madog ab Idnerth, lord of Maelienydd 62
Cadwgan 56
Caerbwdi 18
Caereinion 60
Caerleon 36
Cainnech, saint, Life of 150, 159 n.5
Cáin Adomnáin 240
Cáin Phátraic, 159 n.24
Calendar of Arbuthnott 245 n.18
Calendar of Drummond 245 n.16
Calendar of New Ferne 245 n.17
Calixtus II, pope 13, 17, 22 n.18, 24 n.51, 52
Callaways of St Neot 251, 266 n.18

Calway, James 251, 265 n.12
Camarch, church of 49–50
Cambourne 261
Cambridge 250
Campbell, Archibald 236
Canterbury 13, 30, 34, 42, 52, 63
  archbishops of 12, 36
  Chapter of 66
Canticum Trium Puerorum 134 n.14
'Canu Heledd' 73 n.95
Capel y Pistyll 21
Caradog, saint 23 n.37
  Life of 15
Caradog of Llancarfan 272, 276
Carannog, saint 29
  crosier of 29
Cardinham 252–3, 259, 261, 263, 266 n.29, Fig. 14.9
Carmarthen, Greyfriars of 19, 24 n.52
Carn Ingli 276, 283 n.40
Carolingian period 6, 180–1, 184, 185–6, 193
Caron 56
Cartulary of Quimperlé 181–2
Cashel 281
Cassian, John 166
Cassiodorus 177
Catalogue of the Saints of Ireland 33
Catholicism 84, 200–1
Caxton, William 85
  Golden Legend 85
Cedifor ap Daniel, archdeacon of Cardigan 23 n.27
Cedonius (Acedemus) 87–8
Celestine, pope 115
Céli Dé 6, 161, 167, 171
'Celtic' Christianity 3–4, 8 n.2
'Celtic' Church 3–4
Celtic otherworld 29, 100 n.58, 277
Cenél Conaill 157
Cenél nÉogain 155–8
Ceredig ap Cunedda Wledig, eponymous ruler of Ceredigion 52
Ceredigion 52, 57, 92
Ceri, churches of 161
Cerrigydrudion 93
  church of 93
Châlon-sur-Saône, council of 190
Channelkirk (Childerschirche) 219, 226
Chapel of Garioch, church of 236, Fig. 13.1
Charlemagne, king of the Franks and emperor 178–9, 186, 247 n.70
Admonito generalis 178
Epistola generalis 178
Charles I (the Bald), king of France and emperor 188

Chepman, Walter 233
Cheshire 100–1 n.7
Chester le Street 15
Chichele, bishop of St Davids and archbishop of Canterbury 12
Childebert, king 190
Childerschire 220
Chrétien de Troyes 61
  Erec 61
  Perceval 61
Christianity 15, 88, 91, 105, 114, 124, 127, 130, 214 n.8
Christmas 204–5, 238
Christopher, saint, painting of 269 n.88
Chronicles of Scotland 240, 243
Church eastern 84
  French 186
  in Britain 112, 116
  Irish 103, 114
  of Scotland 242
  Welsh 4, 24 n.39, 30, 34–7, 63, 66
  see also under individual churches
Ciannacht Bregg, people of 156
Ciarán of Clonmacnois 156
  Life of 154
Ciarán of Saigir, saint, Latin and Irish Lives of 145, 272, 273, 274, 276, 277
  Life in Codex Salmanticensis 150
Cilgerran 64
Cistercians 66, 68, 69 n.9, 73 n.106, 182, 219, 228, 230 n.9
Civil War, English 256
Clair (Clere), saint 257–8, 264
  image in stained glass 257, 266 n.19, Fig. 14.2
  holy well of Fig. 14.6
Cland Cholmáin 155, 157
clasau 14, 15, 23 n.25, 30, 37, 46, 55, 65, 66–8, 69 n.15
classical legend 2, 8, 271, 273, 277–9
Clatt 8, 232, 236, 239, 245 n.29
  church of 239
Class I stone 239, 244, Fig. 13.2
Cleder, saint 266 n.19
Clement, saint 247 n.70
Clogher, church of 150
Clonard 274
Clonenagh, church of 150
Clones 159 n.10
Clonfert, church of 150, 171
Clonfertmulloe 148
  church of 6, 150, 151–3
Clonmacnoise (Clonmacnois) 156, 160 nn.33–4

Index

abbot of 160 n.34
church/monastery of 21
Clophill
  parish of 231 n.31
Clova (Cloveth) 8, 232, 236, 239–40
  carved stone cross 239, Fig. 13.4
  church of 238, 239
  holy well of 240
  monastery of 239–40
Cluniacs 182
Clynnog Fawr 29
  church of 23 n.27, 37–8
Codex Salmanticensis 6, 14–58, 158 n.4, 159 n.7, 282 n.14
Cóemgen, saint 144
  Life of 144, 150
Coetleu, synod of 194
Cogitosus 116, 121 n.74, 143
Coleraine, 106
Colmán of Lynally, saint, Life of 150
Colmán of Dromore, saint, Life of 150, 153
Colmán of Inishboffin, saint 153
Cologne 109
Columba, bishop of Dunkeld 219, 220, 223
Columba of Iona, saint 69 n.15, 71 n.59, 138, 238
  church of 235
  Life in Codex Salmanticensis 149, 151, 154
  Vita Columbae by Adomnán 133, 136, 157, 162–4, 234
Columbanus 116, 121 n.75, 165
  Life of 196 n.36
Comgall of Bangor, saint 156, 236
  Life of 150
Commentary on the Apocalypse 111
Compert Con Culainn 115
Conailli Muirthemne 153, 154–6, 160 n.32
Conaire Mór 124
Conall Corc 281
Connaught 150, 156
Connor, church of 151
Constantine III, usurper/pretended emperor 106
Continent 15, 67, 113, 136
Corca Dhuibhne 171
Corcu Óche 152, 159 n.13
Corentin of Cury, saint 262
Cormac, bishop of Aberdeen 237
Cormac Ua Liatháin 163–4, 174 n.16
Cornish language 67, 249–50, 265
Cornish Ordinalia 250
Cornouaille 51
Cornwall 1, 8, 9 n.7, 15, 33, 36, 51, 249–65, 265 n.5, 272
  archdeaconry of 265 n.1
Coroticus 104, 108
Corruen 220, 228
Courteney, earls of Devon 251
Creation 250–1
Crede, saint 262, 269 n.89
Creed, church of 262
Creed of Athanasius 80
Cregrina 53–4
Críth Gablach 174 n.11
Cromwell, Thomas 12
Crónán, saint, Life of 150
Cross Square, St Davids 20
Crowan, parish of 262
Crowland 11
  abbey of 256
Crow Pound 256, 267 n.45
Croyland, abbey of 283 n.56
Cuanna, saint, Life of 149
Culhwch ac Olwen 277
Cummian 115, 117
Cunual, saint, Life of 189
Cunedda Wledig 52
Curig, saint 31
Cuthbert, saint 2, 15, 216–29
  and the landscape at Dull 223
  anonymous Life of 231 n.35
  baptism of 222
  birth and upbringing of 217–18, 220, 221
  education of 223
  Libellus de admirandis beati Cuthberti virtutibus 227, 230 n.5
  Libellus de nativitate Sancti Cuthberti 2, 7, 216–31: and traditions of Adomnán 7, 220, 223, 229; and traditions of Moluag 219–23, 225–6; as testimony to intercommunication between Ireland and Scotland 7, 224–9; authorship of 217, 227–9, 230 n.4; dating of 218, 228–9; Galloway influence on 220, 222, 228–9; structure and style of 220, 227
  pictorial Life of 222, 227
  sea journey of 222–3
Cyfeiliog 60
Cymer, abbey of 66, 73 n.106
Cynan 33
Cynan ab Owain Gwynedd 57–8
Cynan Garwyn 49
Cynddelw Brydydd Mawr, poet 5, 28, 45, 46, 48–51, 59
Cynddylan, ruler of Powys 73 n.95

Cynfan ap Hefan 73 n.106
Cynfig, saint 93
Cyngar, saint, Lives of 273, 274, 276, 277
Cynllaith, commote of 60

d'Arbrissel, Robert, Life by Baudri de Bourgueil 194
d'Etaples, Jacques Lefèvre 85
Dafydd ap Gwilym, poet 12, 31
Dafydd Llwyd o Fathafarn, poet 38–9
Dafydd Nanmor, poet 31
Daig, saint, Life of 6, 151, 154–7, 159 n.19
Dálach mac Muirchertaig 158
Daniel ap Sulien 23 n.27
Daniel, Book of 5, 125–8
Daniel, Perrine, singer 204, 211, 215 n.26
David (Dewi), saint 1, 2, 4–5, 10–21, 26, 32–42, 45–6, 51–4, 61–8, 74 n.122, 85
  altar of 13–14
  and nationalism 4, 32–42
  and oral tradition 52, 71 n.72
  and the Angevin Empire 61, 74 n.126
  and Welsh Nonconformism 5, 40
  as *aquaticus* 71 n.58, 76, n.76
  as archbishop 17, 34–6
  as symbol of Welshness 4–5, 38–42
  canonization of 13, 17, 22 n.18, 24 n.51, 52
  'Canu Dewi' by Gwnfardd Brycheiniog 5, 22 n.22, 32–3, 45–6, 51–7, 61–5, 68, 68 n.1, 69 n.9
  dedications to 44 n.50, 51–3
  genealogy of 52, 71 nn.73–4
  Latin Life by Gerald of Wales 11, 36–7, 44 n.38, 52, 71 n.70
  office of 38, 52
  other Latin Lives of 43 nn.25, 28, 44 n.38, 52, 67
  shrine of 12–21, 24 nn.55–6, Fig. 1.3
  superiority over other saints 2, 4, 14, 32, 52, 54, 61, 71 n.68
  Vita Dauidis by Rhigyfarch 2, 4, 11–12, 16, 32, 34–5, 43 nn.25, 28, 44 nn.38, 59, 45, 52, 54, 62, 66–7, 71 n.62, 163, 174 n.13
  Welsh Life of 32, 37, 42, 43 nn.25, 28, 44 nn.38, 59, 71 n.69
  see also relics *and* St Davids
David (Old Testament), king 11, 242
David I, king of Scots 218, 224, 229, 237, 239
David Fitzgerald, bishop of St Davids 62

Davidstow 261
De antiquitate Glastonie ecclesie 273, 276
De littera colendis 186
Déclan of Ardmore, saint 153
Declanus, saint 221
Deheubarth 14, 22 n.22, 46, 56, 64, 67, 74 n.122, 75 n.152
  lord of 56
  see also Rhys ap Gruffudd
Deiniol, saint 35
Denortius, bishop of Aberdeen 237
Derry, county 106
Deusdedit, pope 247 n.63
Devenish 156
Devil (Satan) 132–3, 138, 139, 175 n.30
Devon 253, 260, 268 nn.59, 71, 272
  earl of 249, 251
Dewi Sant *see* David
Diarmait mac Murchada, king of Leinster 64–5
Dicuil 175 n.41
Dinorben 49–50
Dirinon 2
Dobarchú 175 n.30
Doged, saint, holy well of 31
Dol, abbey and abbot of 194
Dominicans 96
Domnall, king of Tara 155
Domnonée 51
Donat 196 n.36
Dorset 269 n.85
Doubt, Niette 256
Dromore, church of 150
druids 6, 124, 137, 142, 157
Druim Inasclaind (Dromiskin), church of 155
Druim Snechta (Drumsnat), church of 6, 151–3, 159 n.10
du Chesne, André 194
Duault 201–2
Dublin 33, 178
'Dublin collection' 149
Dubthach 130
Dull 220, 223–4, 226
  holy well of 223
Dullan Water, river 237
Dundalk 155
Dundrennan, monastery of 222
Dunkeld 221
  diocese of 221
Dunmeth 237
Dunod, saint 99 n.27
Dunstan, saint 266 n.29
Durham, cathedral church of 15, 216, 223, 227–8
  stained glass at 222, 227–8

Dwynwen, saint 31
Dyfed 51, 65
Dyfrig (Dubricius), saint 29, 35–6
   Life of 30, 45, 272, 274, 276, 277, 279, 280

Eadmer 66
Easter 115–18, 174 n.7, 175 n.39, 238, 262
   Bunny 103
   celebration in the Nauigatio sancti Brendani abbatis 166–7, 172
   cycles 115–18, 121 nn.70, 75
   first Easter Day 130
   liturgy 124, 134 n.15
   Monday 65
   sepulchre 100–1 n.76, 259, Figs 14.8–14.9
   Vigil at Tara 123–33
   Vigil in the Life of St Malo 192
Eatanus, bishop 219
Ecgwin, saint
   genealogy connects him with St Cadog 275
   Life by Byrhtferth 273, 275, 276, 277, 279, 283 n.33
   supposed to have been born in Wales 275
Edinburgh 240
Edmund Tudor 19, 24 n.52
Ednyfed Meirionnydd 73 n.109
Ednywain ap Bradwen of Meirionnydd 73 n.106
Edudful ferch Gadwgan 12, 22 n.12
Edward I, king of England 24 n.56, 244, 248 n.90
Edwardian Conquest 45
Efa ferch Maredudd ab Owain 80
Efflam, saint 199
   Breton ballad of 199
   Life of 189
Eifionydd 50, 59
Egloskerry 266 n.19
Éicnechán son of Dálach 158
Eleanor, queen of England 24 n.56
Elen wraig Hywel of Moelyrch 95
Elfael 13, 72 n.82
Elfan of Powys 73 n.95
Elgin 241, 247 n.70
Elgin Museum 248 n.91, Fig. 13.5
Elijah 126–7, 131
Elliw ferch Henri 96
el Mejdel 84
Elphinstone, William, bishop of Aberdeen, 233, 239, 240, 243, 244
Emly 150
Emyr Llydaw 48, 70 n.27

Enda 170
Endelienta, saint 259–60, 268–9 n.71
   shrine of 259–60, 264, 268–9 nn.71, 73, Fig. 14.10
England 11, 12, 41, 52, 66, 185, 218, 229, 250, 251, 254–7, 258, 264, 265 n.5
English, language 222
English, people 26, 29, 33, 38, 52
English Channel 222
Enlli (Bardsey Island) 47
Enori, saint 199
   Breton ballad of 199–200
Éogan of Ardstraw, saint, Life of 6, 151, 157–8, 159 n.19
Éogan mac Néill 156
Éoganachte 159 n.13
Eoves 275
Ephesus 85
Epiphany 172, 263
Erkenwald, saint 259
érlam 156
Errc, saint 127
Eucharist 172
Euddogwy (Oudoceus), Life of 30, 45
Eugenius (Eogan) of Ardmore, bishop 217–18, 220, 221, 228–9, 231 n.42
Europe 2, 138, 141, 200, 204, 225
Evans, Gwynfor, MP 42
Evans, Thomas 79
Evesham 275
excommunication 85
exempla 204
Exeter 255, 257, 258
exorcism 138–9
Eynesbury *see* St Neots, Huntingdonshire

Fairford 250
Farney 159 n.10
Faroe Islands 162, 175 n.41
feast-days 96, 149, 169
   All Saints 258, 263
   and north-aisle windows at St Neots 263
   and the Lives in the *Codex Salmanticensis* 6, 149–53
   Corpus Christi 251, 263
   Pentecost 172
   St Baíthene 149
   St Clair 263
   St Columba 149
   St Colmán of Inishboffin 153
   St David 9 n.6, 33, 35, 39–42
   St Declán of Ardmore 153
   St Dwynwen 41
   St Ecgwin 275

St Gerardine 241, 247 nn.68–71
St German 257, 263
St Guénolé 187
St James 10, 261
St Keyne 258, 263
St Mabena 263
St Martha 92
St Mary Magdalene 83, 92, 99 n.26
St Mary of Egypt 83
St Moluag 234–5, 239, 245 nn.16–22
St Neot 254, 257, 263
St Petroc 263
St Senán of Láthrach Brúin 153
St Suliau 51
St Tysilio 51
St Ultán of Ard Breccáin 153
St Valentine 41
St Yann (St John's Eve) 208, 211, 213, 214 n.25, 215 n.27
third Rogation Day 258, 263
see also pardon
Fernmag, kingdom of 151–2, 159 n.10
Ferns, church of 150
Fetternear, church of 238
episcopal palace of 238
Fíac 272
Fiachna mac Lugaid 157
fianaigecht 277
Fínán, saint, Latin and Irish Lives of 150, 272, 276–7
Finbarr of Cork, saint 254, 267 n.35
Finistère 48
Finnian of Clonard, saint, Life of 165, 272, 274, 276, 277
Fintan, saint 144
Life of 143–4, 150
Fishguard 24 n.42
Fitzalans of Oswestry, marcher lords 67
Flannán, saint, Life of 150
Flécher, Hélène 215 n.26
Fleury-sur-Loire, monastery of 179
Fochart 155
Forbes, bishop of Brechin 241, 247 n.67, 255
Forster, rector of Boconnoc 255
Fosse Way 261
Fowey 254, 263
river 250
France 67, 84, 185, 247 n.70
Frankfurt, council of 186
Franks 108
Fremund, saint, Lives of 273, 275, 279, 281
French language 200, 213
Fronto, bishop 90–2

Galatia 90
Galilee, river 84
Galloway 219, 220, 222, 229
monastery of 228
Galway, county 230
Galwegians 220, 226
Garddun 48–9
Garioch, the 236, 245 n.29, Fig. 13.1
Garthbrengi 53–4
Gaul 85, 105, 107–9, 114, 118, 247 n.70
Gedworth 220
Geoffrey of Monmouth 36, 48, 67
Historia Regum Brittanniae 36, 48, 67
George, saint 250, 258
image in stained glass 250
Gerald of Wales (Giraldus Cambrensis) 11, 13, 20, 21 n.6, 22 n.17, 23 n.25, 36–7, 44 n.38, 52, 56, 62, 64, 67, 72 nn.77, 82, 73 n.105, 74 nn.124, 131
Gerardine (Gervadius), saint 232–3, 241–2
associations with Kinneddar 8, 241–2
church dedications 242
different versions of the saint's name 247 n.67
German of Auxerre, saint 3, 257, 269 n.91
image in stained glass 257, Fig. 14.4
Germany 84
Gilbert (Gilibertus), bishop of Limerick 217–19, 220, 228, 230 n.8
Gildas, saint 31–2, 43 n.28, 102–3, 105, 108, 165, 201
De excidio Britanniae 103, 104
Giles, saint 262
Gilte Legende 85
Glasgwm, church of 13–14, 53–4, 72 n.82
Glasney College 250–1
Glass 237
Glastonbury 11, 22 n.16, 254, 273
Glendalough, church of 150
Glen Lyon 223, 226
'Gloss on the Psalter' 239
Gloucestershire 250, 279
Glyn Rhosyn (Vallis Rosina) 10, 16–17, 32, 43 n.25, 72 n.83
God 45, 58, 60, 125, 126, 127, 129, 130, 132–3, 178, 246 n.38
Gogynfeirdd (court poets) 5, 45–6, 52, 55, 57, 68, 68 nn.8–9, 89, 101 n.79, 136, 137, 140, 141, 143, 144, 164–5, 169, 171, 203, 258
Goldcliff, church of 92
Gower, church of 23 n.25
Grappenhall, church of 100–1 n.7
Gratian, Roman emperor 108

Great Malvern 250
Greek, language 84, 188
Gregory I (the Great), pope 85, 127, 240, 247 n.63
  homilies of 85
Gregory VII (Hildebrand) 190
Gregory of Tours, saint 109
  Historia Francorum 109
Gresford, church of 95–6
Gruffudd ap Cynan 15
Gruffudd ap Maredudd ab Owain 80
Gruffudd Bola, translator 80
Guénolé, saint 47–8, 188, 196 n.60
  alphabetical hymn by Clement 185
  brief Life by Wrdisten or Clement 185, 193
  Lives by Wrdisten 6, 177, 181, 185–9, 193
Gueriir, saint 253, 255
guilds 113, 251, 256, 258, 259, 264, 265 nn.13, 15, 268 n.56
Guillaume, Norman clerk 99 n.45
Guthlac, saint 283 n.56
  image of 283 n.56
Guto'r Glyn, poet 95
Gutun Ceiriog, poet 93
Gutun Owain, poet and scribe 79
Gwen Teirbron, mother of St Cadfan 47–8, 68, 70 n.27
Gwenallt (David James Jones), poet 81–2
Gwened 202
Gwenfrewy (Winifred), saint, Latin Life by Robert of Shrewsbury 78
  Welsh Life of 44 n.48, 78–9, 98 n.7, 99 n.27
Gwenhwyfar (Guinevere), queen 31
Gwent 51
Gwyddfarch, saint 49, 59, 74 n.116
Gwynedd 38, 49–50, 57, 59, 60, 64, 74 n.119
Gwynfardd Brycheiniog, poet 5, 13–14, 23 n.27, 32, 45, 46, 52, 54, 56, 61–5, 69 n.10, 74 n.121
Gwynllyw, saint 28–9
  Life of 28, 68 n.8
  poetry no longer extant to 68 n.8
Gwynllwg, kingdom of 69 n.15
Gyffin, church of 95

Haearnmed, St Sulien's sister-in-law 50
Hafgan 100 n.58
hagiography
  and onomastic tales 53, 72 n.77, 272–7, 280–1
  as ballads/songs 7, 198–213
  as folk narrative 7, 22 n.9, 138–9, 199–201, 204, 212
  as framework for monastic life 161
  as holy relic 97
  as literature 139, 225, 243
  as liturgical narrative 6, 162
  as performance 133
  as political tool 1, 3, 5, 12, 27–42, 45–6, 51, 54–68, 68 n.1, 123, 138, 145, 157–8, 162, 185, 189
  as sacred writings 3, 124, 177
  as spiritual edification 78, 97, 137–8, 146, 177, 193, 243
  as unorthodox interpretations of sanctity 7, 198–213
  audiences of 5, 46, 57–8, 60, 62, 77–8, 80–1, 89, 93, 94–5, 96–7, 188, 204, 249
  borrowings of hagiographical elements 2, 7, 177–95, 201, 216–29, 280
  Celtic 162, 271, 275, 279, 280, 283 n.33
  for recitation on feast-days 96, 149, 151, 187
  influence of scriptural sources on 3, 124–33, 186
  influence of secular vernacular literature on 8, 115, 136–7, 277, 280
  Insular 123
  Norman influence on 274, 280
  oral 3, 7, 8, 50, 52, 71 n.72, 116, 146, 198–213, 233, 243
  patterns within 82–3, 99 n.27, 141–2, 198, 214 n.2
  pictorial 3, 8, 95–6, 100–1 n.7, 199, 222, 227, 243, 249–65
  poetic 1, 5, 10–14, 27–8, 31, 38–9, 45–68, 92–5, 256
  production of 3, 85, 137, 139, 177–95, 216, 224–5, 243–4
  purpose of 3–5, 12, 65, 77–8, 97–8, 139, 171, 183, 185, 187, 198–9, 216
  rewriting 7, 85, 177–95, 234, 276
  vernacular 1, 2–3, 37, 44 n.48, 45, 66, 77–83, 98, 144, 166, 193, 197 n.65, 198–213, 232, 234, 244, 276, 280
  voyage tales 6, 161–73, 174 n.6, 192–3, 222–3, 238
Hali Meiðhad 78
Harlech 93
Harrowing of Hell 242
Hartland 260, 268 n.71
Hebrew 125
Hebrides 223, 226
Helen, saint, Invention of Cross by 80
Helen (Elide), saint 261
Helenus 277
Helston 262

Hen Fynyw 11, 15–16
   church of 53
Hendregadredd Manuscript 68 n.9
Henllan, church of 53
Henoc, cousin of St Samson 181
Henry I, king of England 64, 66
Henry II, king of England 52, 61, 64–6, 72 n.77, 74 nn.123–4, 75 n.142
Henry VI, king of England, shrine of 261–2
Henry VII, king of England 31, 40
Henry ab Arthen ab Sulien 23 n.27
Henry d'Albini 231 n.31
Hereford, bishop of 13
heresy 110, 113
hermits 26, 100 n.59, 166, 169–70, 194, 220, 223, 231 n.31, 247 n.74, 253–4
Hernin, saint, statue of 212
Herod, king 5, 125, 126, 129, 133, 134 n.20
Hertfordshire 251
Hervé, chaplain to William Rufus 66–7
Hervé, saint 66
Heywood Hill 95
Hilary, saint 262
Himalayas 213
Hinworet, bishop of Léon 179
Hisperica Famina 186
Historie of Scotland 240
Hoddnant 32, 43 n.25, 71 n.71
Holy Rood 269 n.85
Holy Scripture 3, 132, 177–9, 186
Holy Spirit 132, 175 n.44, 177, 203
Holy Trinity 3, 16, 18, 238, 266 n.29, 273, 274
Holyman Head 248 n.82
Holywell 78
holy wells 1, 92, 100 n.69, 199, 223, 233, 244 n.9, 253, 258, 264, 266 n.29, 268 n.52
   in St David's area 22 n.9, 25 n.62
   of St Cleer 258, 264, Fig. 14.6
   of St David 44 n.50
   of St Doged 31
   of St Gerardine 247 n.74
   of St Lallu 253
   of St Mabyn 253
   of St Manc 253, 266 n.29
   of St Mary Magdalene 93, 100 n.69
   of St Neot 254–6, 264
   of St Petroc 253
   of St Ronan 244 n.9
   of St Yann 209
   Simmerluak's 239–40
Honorius, Western Roman emperor 106
Honourable Society of Cymmrodorion 40

Hopcyn ap Tomas 81
Huinél, saint 203
Huntingdonshire 3, 256
Hyfaidd, king of Dyfed 23 n.31
Hywel ab Emyr Llydaw 48
Hywel ab Owain Gwynedd 57, 64
Hywel Dda 33
Hywel Fychan 79, 82
Hywel of Moelyrch 95

Ia, saint 261
Iago, St Sulien's brother 50
Iasconius 167, 172–3
iconoclasts 265 n.1
iconography 199, 242, 253–4
Idunet, saint, statue of 201
Ieuan ap Rhydderch, poet 10–13, 101 n.86
Ieuan ap William ap Dafydd 79, 82, 97
Ieuan Gwas Padrig, saint 93
   image in stained glass 93
   Welsh Life of 93
Ieuan Llwyd Brydydd, poet 31
Illtud, saint 27, 30
   Life of 30, 272, 274, 276, 277, 279
Immram Maíle Dúin 173–4 n.3
Inishowen 155
Iniskeen, church/monastery of 155–6, 159 n.22
Instantius 110
Instow 268–9 n.71
Insular, art 244
Iolo Goch, poet 10–12
Iona 151, 220, 223, 238
Ireland 1, 5–6, 8 n.2, 15, 32, 52, 53, 64–5, 69 n.15, 105, 107, 123–4, 139, 146, 148, 153, 166, 167, 217, 220, 235
Irish language 105, 112
Iron Age 240
Isack, Nyott 256
Island of Imma 192
Island of Sheep 165, 166, 168, 172–3
Isles of Scilly 110, 261
Isidore of Seville 177
Israel 126, 127, 129, 132
Issey, saint 259–60
   shrine of 259–60, 264, Fig. 14.11
Itala 178
Italy 84, 117
Íte, saint 152, 164
   Life of 159 n.13
Ithel ap Cadwgan 56

Jacobus de Voragine 85–7, 90
   Legenda Aurea 85–91, 96, 233

Jael 132
James, saint 261
James IV, king of Scots 239
Jehan de Vignay 85
Legende Dorée 85
Jerome, saint 125–6, 134 n.17, 166, 176 n.48, 177
Jerusalem 10, 11, 14, 34, 38, 44 n.38, 262, 279
Jesus Christ 11, 31, 84, 87, 91, 93–5, 111, 124, 125, 130, 132, 138, 140, 169, 209, 258, 262, 268 nn.57, 59, 279
  Ascension of 85
  Crucifixion of 10
  image in stained glass Fig. 14.1
  Resurrection of 84, 167, 237, 246 n.34, 263
Jocelyn of Furness 225, 272
John, bishop of Arezzo 188
John, saint and Evangelist 85, 87, 93, 268 n.71
  Welsh Life of 80
John of Fourdoun 228
John of Tynemouth 267 n.34
  Nova Legenda Anglie 267 n.34
John the Baptist 125, 132
Jonah 125, 132
Jonas of Bobbio 196 n.36
Jones, John, of Gellilyfdy 79, 82
Joyce, James 178
  Ulysses 178
Judgement Day 49, 72 n.83, 94
Justinian, saint 4, 11, 15

Kalendar of Adam King 241
Kalendar of David Camerarius 241
Kalendars of Scottish Saints 238
kantikou 200
Katherine of Alexandria, saint, Welsh Life of 44 n.48, 77, 78–81, 91, 99 n.27, 100 n.62
  fifteenth-century English verse Life of 100 n.62, 101 n.85
Katherine Group, Lives of 77
Kells 220
  monastery of 221
Kenelm, saint, Life of 279
Kenfig, church of 92
Kent 106, 107
Kentigern, saint 272
  Life by Jocelyn of Furness 225, 272, 274, 277, 279
Keri, saint 266 n.19
Kerne 202

Kevin of Glendalough, saint 153
Keyne, saint 266 n.19
Kildare 121 n.74
Kildrummy, parish of 237
Killabban, church of 150
Killaloe, church of 150
Killeedy 152
King's College, Cambridge 250
Kinneddar 8, 232, 233, 241
  church of 241–2
  Class I stone 241, 244
  Class III stones 241
  shrine panel 243–4, Fig. 13.5
Kinnitty, church of 150
Knights Hospitallers 93
Knockespoch House Fig. 13.2

Laisrén, saint, Life of 150
Lallu (Lallo), saint 252–3, 266 n.18, 269 n.91
  image in stained glass 252, Fig. 14.4
Lammermuirs 219
Landévennec, abbey of 2, 177, 179, 181, 185–8, 193
Lanivet, church of 262
  wall paintings 262, 269 n.89
Lanreath 252, 259, 262, 263
Lanteglos-by-Fowey 252, 261
Latin, language 12, 45, 48, 80, 90, 105, 109, 185, 190
Launceston 266 n.16
Laurence of Dublin 150
Laurence of Durham 230 n.4
Lavinium 277, 283 n.49
Lazarus 84, 88, 89
Le Braz, Anatole 200–1, 212–13
Le Diberder, Yves 206–7
Le Folgoet, collegiate church of 50
Leader, river 219
Léhon 181
Leinster 148, 150–1, 153
  kingdom of 64–5, 155
Leinstermen 155
Leland, John 256, 257, 261, 263, 267 n.45
Lemanaghan 242
  carved stone of 242
Lent 187
Leominster 11
Léon 7, 201
  bishop of 204
  Breviary of 50–1
  cathedral church of 50
  diocese of 190
Leonard, saint 268 n.54

Leslie, Jhone 240
Letherpen 220
Leviathan 90
Lewys Glyn Cothi, poet 22 n.12, 31, 96
Lhuyd, Edward 93
Líath Mór (Líath-Mo-Choem-óc, now Borrisoleigh) 277
Libellus de nativitate Sancti Cuthberti see Cuthbert *Liber Hymnorum* 222
Liber Landavensis 23 n.25, 30, 45, 272
Lichfield, diocese of 217, 228, 231 n.42
Liffey, river 156
Lifris of Llancarfan 23 n.27, 34, 272, 272, 280, 282 n.28
Limerick, county 152
Lincolnshire 256
Lind Duachaill (Annagassan), 155
Lindisfarne 15, 227
Linkinhorne 266 n.19
Lisieux (Lieuvin) 190
Liskeard 250, 257, 259, 263, 266 n.19, 268 n.59
Lismore 221, 223, 226, 234, 238, 236, 244 n.9
   cathedral church of 150, 235, 240
Litany of the Pilgrim Saints 173–4 n.3
liturgy 6, 52, 124, 125–6, 128, 134 n.15, 162, 171, 174 n.8, 183
Livingstone, family of 236
Livy 186
Llanarth, church of 53–4
Llanbadarn Fawr, abbots of 73 n.105
   church/monastery of 14, 30, 36
Llancarfan 23 n.27, 274
Llandaf, bishops of 13
   cathedral church/monastery of 38, 56
   diocese of 30, 32, 69 n.12
Llanddewi y Crwys, monastery of 14, 53–4
Llanddewibrefi 11, 14, 61, 67, 69 n.14, 71 n.72, 72 nn.77, 85
   anchorite of 37
   church of 14, 23 n.29, 35, 46, 53–6, 62, 65, 68, 75 n.146, 76 n.159
   early Christian stones 22 n.24
   'Idnerth' stone 72 n.85
   priests of 23 n.28
   Synod of 34–5, 54, 62–3, 75 n.146
Llandeilo Fawr, church of 14, 36
Llanfaes, church of 53–4
Llanfair Nant-y-gof, chapel of 93
   holy well of 93, 100 n.68
Llangadog, church of 53–4
Llangeitho 80

Llangyfelach, church of 13–14, 23 n.25
Llan-non, Ceredigion 92
Llanstinian 24 n.42
Llantwit Major, church of 30, 95, 100–1 n.7
Llech Lafar 19, 72 n.77, 74 n.124
Lleu Llaw Gyffes 280
Lleuddad (Llawddog), saint 27, 47, 57–9, 70 n.25, 74 n.110
Llyfr Coch Hergest *see* Red Book of Hergest
Llyfr Coch Talgarth *see* Red Book of Talgarth
Llyfr Gwyn Rhydderch *see* White Book of Rhydderch Llyndu 56
Llywarch Brydydd y Moch, poet 73 n.106
Llywelyn ap Gruffudd, prince of Wales 37, 41
Llywelyn ap Iorwerth (Llywelyn Fawr), prince of Gwynedd 37
Llywelyn ap Madog 60
Llywelyn Fardd, poet 5, 28, 45, 46–8, 55, 57–9
Lochru 127
Loégaire mac Néill, king of Tara 5, 104, 124, 126–7, 133
Loígsi 148, 151
London 40, 258, 259
Lorrha, church of 150
Lossiemouth 247 n.74
   burgh of 242
Lothian 219, 220, 223, 227
Louénan, disciple of St Tudual 189–90
Louis the Pious 188
Louth 155
   church/monastery of 151, 157, 159 n.22
   county 153–4
Low Countries 201
Lucet Máel 130
Lugaid mac Sétnai 157–8
Luke, saint 239
Lunaire (Léonor, Liénoire), saint 184
Life of 182–4, 193
Lynally, church of 150

Mabinogion 81
Mabyn (Mabena), saint 8, 252–3, 259–60
   image in stained glass 252–3, Fig. 14.1
Mac Caírthinn, saint, Life of 150
Machar, saint, Latin Life of 233
   Scottish Life of 233
Maches, saint 99 n.27
McMolmore Vic Kevir, John 236
Mac Nisse, saint, Life of 6, 151, 159 n.19

Index

Mac Tighearnán, John 159 n.19
Maddadson, Harold, earl of Orkney 224
Madet Maccrie Mor 220
Madog ap Maredudd, prince of Powys 59–61, 66–7
Madog ap Selyf, translator 80
Maédóc of Ferns, saint 149–50
Máel Dúin 173–4 n.3
Maelgwn, king of Gwynedd 28
Maelgwn ab Owain Gwynedd 64
Maelienydd 61–2
Maelrhys, saint 48
Máelruain of Tallaght 167, 175 n.33
Maenordeifi 53
Maes Cogwy (Maserfelth), battle of 49, 55, 60
magic 140–1
   black 110, 130, 140
   white 137, 140
Mag Muirthemne 155
Mag nArnaide, church of 150
Magloire, saint, Life of 177
Magnus Maximus, Roman emperor 106, 110, 111, 112, 113
Malachy (Malacius, Malachi, Mael Maedóc Ua Morgair), saint 217–19, 220, 221, 222, 228
   canonization of 229
   Lives of 236, 245 n.25
   Life by Bernard of Clairvaux 221, 224
Malcolm II, king of Scots 237
Mallobaudes, king of the Franks 108
Mallt ferch Hywel Selau 12, 22 n.14
Malo, saint 6
   anonymous Lives of 191–3, 282 n.18
   Legendary of 47
   Life by Baudri de Bourgueil 193, 197 nn.71, 75
   Life by Bili 181–2, 191–3, 272, 279
   Life by Sigebert de Gembloux 192–3
   Old English Life of 282 n.18
Manc (Manac), saint 8, 252, 262
   image in stained glass 252, Fig. 14.2
Manchán, saint 242
Maodez, saint 207
Mar, deanery of 237
Marc' harit Fulup, singer 214 n.23
Maredudd ab Owain 80
Maredudd ap Cynan 73 n.106
Mareschal, Gilbert 95
Margaret of Antioch, saint, Welsh Life of 44 n.48, 77–81, 87, 90–1, 99 n.27
Margred ferch Gruffudd Gryg 97
Marke, family 258

Marseilles 85, 88–91, 93
Martel, Geoffrey, count of Anjou 190
Martha, saint 77–98
   as Christ's hostess 91, 94–5
   as representative of the active life 94
   death and burial of 90–2
   encounter with the dragon 90, 92
   intercessory powers of 92, 94
   Lives in various hagiographical collections 85
   Welsh Life of 3, 44 n.48, 77–98
Mathrafal 69 n.14
Martin, bishop of Tréguier 189–90, 193
Martin, saint 110, 120 n.42
   Life by Sulpicius Severus 136
   Welsh Life of 44 n.48, 80
martyrologies 234
   Anglo-Saxon 83
   Roman 83
Martyrology of Aberdeen 33, 240, 247 n.64
Martyrology of Oengus the Culdee 33, 222, 234
Martyrology of Tallaght 33, 83
Mary Magdalene, saint 77–98, 266 n.16
   Anglo-Norman Life of 85, 88, 99 nn.54, 56
   as Christ's physician 95
   as myrrophore 84, 94–5
   as representative of the contemplative life 94
   association with prostitutes 83–4, 87
   Buchedd Mair Fadlen (Welsh Life of) 3, 5, 44 n.48, 77–98
   composite Magdalene 5, 83–5
   in Legenda Aurea 85–91, 96
   intercessory powers of 94, 97–8
   Lives in various hagiographical collections 85, 99 n.45
   Mari Kelenn 99 n.46
   Order of the Penitents of 84
   pre-Ascension life of 85–7, 99 n.45
   relationship with John the Evangelist 85, 87
   sojourn in the desert 83, 89, 93, 99 n.45
   visual depictions of 95–6, 100–1 n.76, 265 n.2
   vita apostolica of 85
   Welsh poetry to 92–5, 100 n.69
Mary of Bethany 84
Mary of Egypt 85
Welsh Life of 44 n.48, 77–81, 83
Matad mac Mael Muire 224, 226
Materiana, saint 261
   shrine of 261
Math uab Mathonwy 277, 279, 280

Matheus (Muirgius) Ua hÉnni, archbishop of Cashel 217–18, 220, 221, 226, 229, 230 n.10
Mathri 24 n.42
Maudez, saint, Life of 189
Mawd ferch Sir William Clement 97
Maxentius 91
Maximin (Maximinus), saint 87, 89
  church of 90
Maximista (Maximilla) 88
Meath, county 153, 219
Mechain, commote of 60
Meidrum, church of 53
Meifod 49, 69 n.14
  church of 21, 23 n.27, 46, 55, 59–61, 66, 68, 74 n.116, 76 n.159
  prior of 60–1
Meilyr Fitzhenry 64, 75 n.140
Meirionnydd 46, 56–9, 68, 73 n.106
Melangell, saint, Life of 100 n.58
Meldanus, bishop 219
Mellán of Inis Moccu Chéin 230 n.15
Mellifont 219
Melor, saint 266 n.19
Melrose 226
  abbey of 7, 222, 228–9, 236
Melwas, king 31
Menheniot 252–3, 259, 261, 266 nn.18, 29
  parish of 253
Menologium Scoticum 241
Merovingian period 136, 139
Mernoc 171, 176 n.51
Meshach 126
Methodism 27, 41
Meubred, saint 8, 252–3, 266 n.23
  image in stained glass 252–3, 266 n.26, Fig. 14.1
  tomb of Fig. 14.8
Michael, saint and archangel 262
Middleton, Wiliam, poet 100 n.69
Mide 148, 150, 155, 157
Migvie, church of 245 n.29
Milan 111, 120 n.42
Miller, Andrew 233
Minster 261
miracle-plays 2, 250–1
miracles 6, 10, 47, 86, 92, 103, 124, 132, *136–46*, 120, 177, 191, 217, 219, 221, 223, 227, 228, 235–6, 261
  as sign of God's will 88, 95, 127, 140–1, 143, 275–6
  'canon' of 6, 137, 142, 146
  of folklore type 138–9, 145
  involving punishment 141, 144, 157

Mirk, John 85
  Festial of 85, 87, 101 n.85
Moccas on the Wye, church of 276
Mochoemóc, saint, Life of 272, 277, 279, 280
Mochta, saint 156–7
  and letter in Annals of Ulster 157
  Life of 6, 151, 155, 157, 159 n.19
  monastery of 155
Mochuille, saint, Life of 149
Mochutu, saint, Life of 150
Moddry 220, 231 n.31
Mo Laisse 156
Moling of Tech Moling, saint 153
Mo Lua of Clonfertmulloe, saint
  First Life of 150, 151–2, 154
  Second Life of 6, 149, 150, 151–3, 154
Moluag (Mo Luóc/Molocus), saint 7, 219–21, 225–6, 232–40, 245 nn.12–13
  and church dedications 237, 239, 244 n.9, 245 n.29, and the Aberdeen Breviary 225–6, 233–56
  as contemporary of St Columba 235
  associations with Bangor, Ireland, 221
  associations with Clatt 8, 232, 236, 239
  associations with Clova 8, 232, 236, 239–40
  associations with Lismore and Rosemarkie (Ross) 219–20, 226, 236, 240
  associations with Mortlach 8, 232, 236–9
  fair of 239
  office of 239
  painting of 236, Fig. 13.1
  similarities between *Libellus de nativitate Sancti Cuthberti* and traditions of Moluag 219–23, 225–6
  variations on the saint's name 234, 245 n.13, Monaghan, county 151, 154
Monaghan Town 159 n.10
Monastery of the Deposit 32
Moray (Murray) 233, 246 n.31, Fig. 13.3
  diocese of 232, 241
  Society 248 n.91
Morfran, abbot of Tywyn 57–8, 74 n.110
Morgannwg, king of 56
Morlaix 210
Morris, Roger 79, 82
Mortlach 8, 232, 236–8
  church of 237, 239, 240, 246 n.31, Fig. 13.3
  Class I stone 237, 244

Class II stone 237, 244, Fig. 13.3
episcopal manor of 238
monastery of 237
Morwenna, saint 268–9 n.71
Morwenstow 268–9 n.71
Moses 125
motifs 140, 142
　building materials for church move from wrong site to approved site 29
　flesh as image of bodily mortality 161
　maritime wanderings 6, 161–4, 192–3, 222–3
　motif indices 143, 271–2, 281 n.3
　swine lead saint to where he is to found church 8, 29, 271–84
　the mortality of the boat of hide 164
　various animals lead saint to where he is to found church 29, 93
Mount Carmel 127
Muirchertach mac Olchobair 175 n.33
Muirchú 5–6, 115, 116, 123–33, 134 nn.6–7, 279
　contacts with Adomnán 133
Muiredach (Muriadach), king 221
Munnu, saint, First Life of 150
　Second Life of 148, 150
Munster 116, 148, 149, 151
Munymusk, church of 237
Mwrog, saint 31
Mynyw (Menevia) 10–21, 32, 36, 43 n.25, 53–4, 63–5, 71 n.71, 72 n.84
　see also St Davids and Glyn Rhosyn
Myrddin 38

Nanninus 109
National Library of Wales 81
Nebuchadnezzar, king of Babylon 5, 125–6, 133
Nechtan, bishop of Aberdeen 237
Nechtan, king of Picts 240
Nectan, saint 268 n.71
　Life of 273, 279
Neot, saint 3, 8, 252–7, 264–6, 266–7 n.31
　homily of 254
　Lives of 254, 267 nn.34, 36, 37, 45
　pictorial Life of 8, 252–4, 267 nn.35, 44, Fig. 14.3
　single image in stained glass Fig. 14.5
　tomb of Fig. 14.2
　verses of 256
Nessán of Mungret, saint 153, 159 n.18
New College, Oxford 257
New Jerusalem 165, 170

New Machar, church of 245 n.29
New Testament 84, 140, 178
Niall Frossach, king of Tara 155
Nicene 111, 120 n.42
　Council of 117
Nineveh 125
Ninian, saint, Life of 233
Nitria 175 n.42
Noah 251
Non, saint 2, 9 n.6, 32, 92, 266 n.19
　Buez santez Nonn 2, 9 n.6, 68
Nonconformism 40
Normandy 182, 256
Normans 12, 30, 37, 66, 75 n.141
Norse, loanwords 223
North Elham, church of 101 n.81
Northern Homily Collection 85
Northumbrians 49
Notre-Dame de Bonport, abbey of 182–4
nunneries 78, 98 n.3, 156

Oban 223
Obeyn, church of 237
Odo of Cluny 85
O'Donnells, family of 158
O'Donohue Lives 148–9, 151, 153–4
Ó Dúnchadha, Diarmaid 148
Odyssey 178
Oenu, abbot of Clonmacnois 160 n.34
Old Aberdeen, episcopal palace of 238
Old Leighlin, church of 150
Old Rayne, episcopal manor of 238
Old Testament 132, 140, 178, 250, 265 n.9
Olmarch 72 n.77
Onachus 90
Origen 95
Orkneys 15
Orléans 184
Osbern 66
Osbern of Bokenham 85
　Legendys of Hooly Wummen of 85
Osraige 149, 151
Oswestry 67
Oudoceus, saint *see* Euddogwy
Owain Cyfeiliog 60, 66
Owain Fychan 60
Owain Glyndŵr 31–2, 37, 39, 41
　Day of 41
Owain Gwynedd, prince of Gwynedd 60–1, 64, 71 n.68, 74 n.119
Owain Lawgoch 37

Pacatus, poet 110
Padarn, saint 34, 36, 48

Padstow 256–7, 262
paganism 104, 105, 108, 123–4, 132, 133, 136–7, 140, 216, 277
Palladius 114–18
  dossier of 103
Papil 242
  sculptured stones of 242
parables 145, 165
Parcrhydderch 80
Paradise of Birds 166, 172
pardon 200–2
  of Saint-Servais 201–2
  of St-Gildas-en Carnöet 201
  see also feast-days
Patrick, saint 1, 2, 4, 5–6, 11, 15, 31–2, 53, 64, 69 n.15, 71 n.59, 72 n.76, 102–18, 123–33, 136, 138, 142, 154, 157–8, 159 n.16, 170, 272
  and the Ballinrees ingot 106–8, 112
  and the Easter cycles 115–18, 121 nn.70, 75
  as celebrant at Ireland's first Easter Vigil 5, 123–33
  as Cothraige 105, 118 n.8
  as first Bishop of Ireland 112, 114
  as patron of the Uí Néill 123–4
  Confessio of 5, 102–5, 110, 112, 118 nn.2, 4
  Epistola ad milites Corotici of 5, 102–5
  Latin style of 109, 112, 114, 120 n.50
  magical coat of 131
  obit of 5, 114–18
  Palladius 114–18, 103
  Purgatory of 80
  Rule of Faith of 111
  the three Patricii 105–14, 118 n.2, 119 nn.9–10
  Vita Patricii by Muirchú 5–6, 102–3, 118 n.5, 123–33, 136, 279
  Vita Tripartita 136, 272, 279, 281
Paul, saint and apostle 168, 169
  cathedral of, London 258–9
Paul of Thebes (the Hermit), saint 166, 169–70, 173
  Vita Pauli by Jerome 170, 176 n.48
Paul Aurélien (Paul de Léon), saint 33
  Life by Vital 179
  Vita Pauli Aureliani by Wrmonoc 33, 179, 181, 186, 272–5, 277–9, 281
Pebydiog, cantref of 23 n.26, 64
Pecham, Archbishop 24 n.51
Pedeir Keinc y Mabinogi 97, 100 n.58
Pembroke, chapel of 92

Pembrokeshire 16
  Group I early Christian monuments of 16
Pengwern 49–50
penance 83, 84, 89, 96, 145, 157, 167, 176 n.47, 203, 206
penitentials 163, 165, 175 n.28
  Canones Adomnani 166
  Canones Hibernenses 166
  Paenitentiale Cummeani 166
penitential poetry 45
Penmynydd 59
Penryn 250
Pentecost 172–3, 191
Perigueux 91
Perranzabuloe 261
Perthshire 223
Peter, monk of Landévennec 188
Peter, saint and apostle 26, 88
Peter de Leia, bishop of St Davids 17
Petroc of Bodmin, saint 252–3, 257, 266 n.18, 267 n.34, 269 n.91
  church dedications of 253
  holy well of 252
  image in stained glass 252–3, 266 n.26, Fig. 14.2
  Lives of 252–3
  reliquary of Fig. 259, 14.7
Petronilla, saint 101 n.81
Pettyvaich 237
Peynabachalla (Peynchallen) 245 n.28
Pharaoh 125, 126, 129, 134 n.20
Pictland 7–8
Picts 105, 235, 243
  Irish 63
  Pictish art 237, 244, 246 n.34, Figs 13.3–13.5
  Pictish place-names 237, 240
pilgrimage 3, 4, 8, 10–13, 16–21, 22 n.9, 35, 38, 52, 54, 88–9, 93, 96, 202, 258–62, 269 n.85, 279
Piran, saint 253, 261
  Life of 273, 274, 276
  oratory of 261
Pitenteach 240
Plaid Cymru 42
Plestin 199
Plougomené 48
pope, the 254
Porphyrius (Porffir) 91, 100 n.62
Port-Louis 206
Porth Clais 15–16, 19, 21, 25 n.62
Porth Stinian 24 n.42
Potts, Amanda, artist 236, Fig. 13.1

Powys 28, 46, 49–51, 59, 60, 69 n.14, 74 n.119
Premonstratensians 222
Priscillian, bishop of Ávila 110, 111, 120 n.42
Priscillianists 110, 112
Probus 261
prostitution 83–4
Protestantism 84
Provence 5, 84–5, 89, 93
Pydar, saint 261

Quimper, bishop of 202
Quntinius, general of Gaul 109

Rabanus, saint 247 n.70
Rahugh, church of 150
Ralf de Nuers, hermit 220, 224, 227, 228, 231 nn.31, 42
Rame, church of 257
Ramsey Island 24 n.42
Ratvili, bishop of Alet 181, 191
Red Book of Hergest 69 n.9, 81
Red Book of Talgarth 79, 80–1, 82, 96
Redon 181
Reformation, Protestant 8, 27, 40, 200, 249, 250, 256, 258, 262
Reginald of Durham 217, 230 n.5, 227
relics 1, 10, 24 n.39, 55, 56, 66, 75 n.134, 121 n.79, 156, 188, 214 nn.9, 15, 232, 233–4, 238, 243, 246 n.51, 259–62
  of Henry VI 261–2
  of Jesus Christ 258
  of St Agnes 261
  of St Cadfan 47
  of St Clair 257
  of St Cuthbert 15, 238
  of St David 4, 13–19, 22 nn.16, 24, 54, Fig. 1.3
  of St Endelientia 259–60, Fig. 14.10
  of St Ercc 135 n.31
  of St Fremund 279
  of St Gerardine 241–2
  of St German of Auxerre 3, 257
  of St Guénolé 187–8
  of St Helen 261
  of St Ia 261
  of St Issey 259–60, Fig. 14.11
  of St Justinian 16
  of St Mabyn 262
  of St Manac 262
  of St Mary Magdalene 86
  of St Meubred Fig. 14.8
  of St Mochta 156–7
  of St Moluag 236, 238, 240, Fig. 14.9
  of St Neot 3, 254–6, 265, Fig. 14.9
  of St Patrick 279
  of St Petroc 259, Fig. 14.7
  of St Piran 261
Remus 277
Renaissance 250
Rennes 214 n.21
Repton 11
Restenneth 240
Rhigyfarch ap Sulien 4, 16, 34, 43 n.25, 45, 52, 163
Rhine, river 108, 109
Rhinns 220, 222
Rhos 63
Rhydderch ab Ieuan Llwyd 80, 97, 101 n.86
Rhymie, church of 246 n.29
Rhys ap Gruffudd, lord of Deheubarth 22 n.22, 61–5, 74 n.121, 75 nn.142, 152
Rhys ap Tewdwr 14–15, 23 n.26
Rhys ap Tomas 81
Richard of Carew, bishop of St Davids 16
Richard Fitz Gilbert of Clare (Strongbow), earl of Pembroke 64–5
Rintsnoc 220
Robert Fitzstephen 64, 67
Robert of Shrewsbury, prior of Shrewsbury 78
Roger of Hovenden 240
Romans 105
Rome 4, 10–11, 13, 17, 24 n.51, 30, 36, 38, 44 n.38, 49, 88–9, 93, 190, 222, 223, 237, 254, 277, 283 n.53
Romulus 277
Roscrea, church of 150
Rosemarkie (Ross) 226, 236, 240
Rúadán, saint, Lives of 150, 272, 276–7
Rudolf of Worms 84
Rufinus 175 n.42
  Historia Monachorum 175 n.42
Rufus, William 66

Sacrifice of Isaac 250
Sadb (Sabina), St Cuthbert's mother 221
Saint-Benoît-sur-Loire, abbey of 184
Saint-Hernin 212
Saint-Martin-de-Tours 179
Saint-Malo 51
  Breviary of 51, 184
  diocese of 50, 183
Saint Melour-des-Ondes 48
Saint-Samson-sur-Risle 194
Saint-Servais 207
  church of 202
  pardon of 201–2

Sainte Baume 89, 93, 100 n.59
saints and ascetism 53, 71 n.75, 137, 144, 163, 165, 171
  and landscape 10–11, 13, 21 n.6, 22 n.9, 27–9, 142–3, 223
  and nationalism 26–7, 31–42
  and place-names 8, 9 n.3, 11, 48, 51, 69 n.15, 232, 234, 243
  Anglo-Saxon 66, 264
  as guardians of the land 4, 27–31, 55
  as holy magicians 6, 27–8, 137
  as inheritors of the druids 6, 137
  as missionaries 26, 91
  as protectors of the people 4, 28, 31, 47, 49, 72 n.90, 55, 59–60, 199
  as providers of food 27–8, 142
  as punishers 7, 88, 90, 131, 157, 203, 209, 211
  as role models 180
  bells of 13, 14, 28, 54, 72 n.82, 144, 221, 222, 235, 261
  Celtic 1, 9 n.3, 66, 77, 102, 201, 244, 249, 252, 264, 265 n.5
  crosiers of 14, 28, 29, 47, 58, 236, 253
  healing powers of 3, 7, 95, 137, 201, 207–11, 212, 233, 244 n.9, 255, 258, 261–3
  intercessory powers of 3, 31, 46, 69 n.13, 72 n.83, 92, 97–8, 100 n.64, 199
  local 1, 3, 4, 8, 9 n.3, 27, 41, 66, 158, 179, 194, 200, 207, 233–4, 238, 244, 252–4, 265 n.5
  misbehaving 7, 202–7
  statues or images of 7, 10, 12, 92–3, 100–1 n.76, 201, 212, 252–3, 250, 258, 265 n.2, 266 n.26, 269 n.85, 283 n.56
  universal 1, 2, 77–98, 136, 249, 258–9, 262
  violence against 7, 201–2, 214 n.15
  see also under saints' names
Samaria, woman of 84
Samson, saint 33, 194
  Acta of 180
  Life by Baudri de Bourgueil 194–5
  Vita Ia of 2, 45, 180–1, 194
  Vita IIa of 194
Sant ap Ceredig 32–3, 52
Santa Claus 103
Santiago de Compostela 10, 19, 96, 262
Savanius, pope 247 n.63
Scattery Island 149, 150
Scandinavians 33
Scherer, Duncan, rector of Clatt 239
Scotia 223, 227

Scotland 1, 7–8, 8 n.2, 15, 33, 36, 272
Scots 105
  dialect 217, 240, 244
  people 220, 222
Scots Gaelic 218, 200, 223, 225
Scott, Gilbert, Sir 18, 25 n.62
Scottish Legendary 232
scribes 69 n.9, 79, 82
Second World War 184
Ségéne of Iona 115
Seirkieran, church of 150
Seisyll Bryffwrch 74 n.121
Senán of Lathrach Briúin 153
Senán of Scattery Island, saint 149, 150
Serf, saint 225
'Seven bishop-houses of Dyfed, The', legal tractate 15
Seven Deadly Sins 84, 87
Severn, river 29
Servais (Servatus), saint 201–3
  Breton ballad of 203
  pardon of 201–2
  statue of 7, 202
Shadrach 126
Sherborne 257
Siân wraig Siôn Bwrch 95
Sigebert de Gembloux 192
Síl nÁeda Sláne 156
Simon the Leper 84
Simon the Pharisee 84, 87
Siôn Bwrch, sir 95
Sisera 132
Sitha, saint 96, 101 n.81
Sizun 51
Skolan, saint? 204
  Breton ballad of 204
Slebech 93
Slieve Bloom 148, 151
Smithfield 16
Society of Gwyneddigion 40
Somerset 2, 253, 271, 273
Song of the Three Young Men 125
Soulseat, abbey of 222
South Bosent 258
South English Legendary 85
South Mimms, church of 251
Speculum Sacerdotale 85
St Agnes 268 n.51
St Allen 261
St Andrews 15, 23 n.35, 242
St Asaph, diocese of 61
St Clears, Wales 93
St Cleer, Cornwall 253, 264, 266 n.19
  church of 257–9, 261

St Clether 266 n.19
St Davids 10–21, 21 n.6, 22 n.9, 30,
    51, 61–2, 66, 71 n.62
  Black Book of 19, 54
  cathedral church of 4, 10–21, 65,
    71 n.64, 75 n.142, 76 n.178, Figs
    1.1–1.3
  chapels of 12, 22 n.9, Fig. 1.2
  Chapter of 12–13
  diocese of 12–14, 62, 65
  see also Mynyw and Glyn Rhosyn
St Endellion, church of 259–60, 264,
    268–9 n.71, Fig. 14.10
St Enoder 268–9 n.71
St Germans 3, 257, 259
St-Gildas-en-Carnoët, *pardon* of 201
St Issey, church of 59–60, 264, 270
    n.97, Fig. 14.11
St Keverne 261
St Keyne 268 n.61
St Mabyn 252–3, 259–60, 266 n.29,
    268 n.71
St Michael's Mount 262
St Mullin's, church of 150
St Neot, Cornwall 265 n.15
  church of 3, 8, 249–65, 265 n.1, 257
    n.46, Fig. 14.9
  parish of 266 n.19
  stained glass at 249–65, Figs 14.1–14.5
St Neot, river 250
St Neots (formerly Eynesbury),
    Huntingdonshire 3
  church of 254–6
St Ninian's Isle 242
  sculptured stones of 242
St Pinnock, chapel of 263, 266 n.19,
    268 n.61
  parish of 258
St Servais, Germany 202
St Suliac 50–1
St Yves 201
Strata Florida, abbey of 67, 69 n.9
Strata Marcella, abbey of 66
Suffolk 265 n.14
Sulien, bishop of St Davids 14–15, 34
Sulien (Suliau), saint, Lives of 50–1, 67
  see also Tysilio
Sulpicius Alexander 109
Sulpicius Severus 109, 119 n.10, 136

Taghmon, church of 150
Taliesin, poet 38
Tallaght 167, 175 n.39
Tara 5, 123, 126
  kingdom of 104, 123, 155
Tarascon 90–2

Tarland, church of 245 n.29
Tatheus, saint 29
Tawe, valley 69 n.9
Teampull Mor 244 n.9
Tecosc Maíle Ruain 167, 175 n.33
Teilo, saint 14, 23 n.25, 34, 36
  Braint Teilo 56
  Life of 30, 45
Temple 266 n.19
Tenby, hospital of 95
Terryglas 148
  church of 150
  thaumatology 132, 136–7
'The song of Dermot and the earl' 140 n.75
Theodosian Code 113
Theodosius 109–10
Theodotian 134 n.17
Thietmar, abbot of 192
Three Powerful Swineherds 277
Three Tribal Thrones of the Island of
    Britain 36
Thomas, saint and apostle, Welsh Life
    of 80
Thomas Becket, saint 20, 262
Tiber, river 277
Tiberianus 110
Tipperary, county 277
Tírechán 115, 116
Tiverton 251
Togail Bruidne Da Derga 124
tombs and shrines 1, 2, 4, 8, 12–21, 24
    nn.52, 55–6, 135 n.31, 232, 233,
    241–2, 243, 254–6, 257–61,
    268–9 nn.71–4, 279, Figs 1.3,
    13.5, 14.7–14.11
  see also relics
Tongres 201
Tours, abbey of 194
Trallwng Cynfyn 53–4
Trefraul, chapel of 266 n.29
Trégor 191
Tréguier 190–1
  diocese of 189–90
Treuddyn, church of 100–1 n.7
Trier 106, 108, 110, 111, 112, 120
    n.42
Tubb, family 251, 266 n.18
Tubb, Richard 250
Tudful, saint 99 n.27
Tudhuarn, priest 182
Tudual, saint 190–1, 193
  Lives of 189–91, 193
Tudur Penllyn, poet 22 n.13
Tujen, saint 207
Twrch 56
Tydecho, saint 48

Tygwyn 11
Tylynathtlayk, church of 238
Tysilio, saint 5, 28, 45–6, 48–51,
    59–61, 66–8
  and church dedications 49
  as principal saint of Powys 28, 49
  associations with Sulien/Suliau
    50–1
  associations with Anglesey 50
  birth of 51
  burial of 59
  'Canu Tysilio' by Cynddelw Brydydd
    Mawr 5, 45–6, 48–51, 55, 59–61,
    68, 68 n.1, 69 n.9
  death of 50–1
  lost Life of 50–1, 67
  parentage of 48–9
  various versions of his name 50
  see also Meifod
Tywi, river 56
Tywyn 57, 69 n.14
  church of 28, 46–7, 55–6, 68, 73
    n.106, 76 n.159

Uí Fhighente 152, 159 n.13
Uí Néill 69 n.15, 123–4, 155–7
Ulster 106, 116, 150–1, 153, 155
  Annals of 115, 155, 157, 159
    n.29
Ulstermen (Ulaid) 155–6
Ultán, saint 153
United States of America 40
Urban, bishop of Llandaf 14, 30, 66
Usk, priory church of 92–3
Ussher, archbishop 159

Valentinian II, Roman emperor 108,
  110, 120 n.42
van der Straeten, Jacques 184
Vannetais 202, 204
Varro 278
Vetus Latina 178
Vézelay 90
Victor, angel 115
Victor, son of Magnus Maximus 109
Victorian period 18
Victorinus of Petavium, martyr 111
Victricius, bishop of Rouen 121 n.79
Vikings 15, 64, 149, 155, 162, 182
Vilaine, river 182, 195 n.27
Virgil 278
Virgin Mary 44 n.48, 74 n.116, 85,
  86, 93, 100 nn.59, 64, 236, 246
  n.38, 268 n.56, 269 n.85
  Gwyrthyeu e Wynvydedic Veir (miracles
    of the Blessed Virgin Mary) 80

images of 12, 100–1 n.76, 258, 265
  n.2
in Life of St Ecgwin 275
Mair o Fynyw 12
Maria Misericordia 262
Our Lady of Park, chapel of 258–9,
  263, 268 n.57
Our Lady of Lamellion, chapel of 268
  n.57
pietà 258, Fig. 14.1
Transitus Mariae (Assumption of the
  Virgin Mary) 80, 283 n.36
Viride Stagnum 219, 222, 230 n.12
Vitae Sanctorum Hiberniae 136–7, 149
Vital, monk of Fleury-sur-Loire 179

Walberswick 265 n.14
Walbert 196 n.36
Wales 1–5, 8 n.2, 14, 15, 31–2, 36, 38,
  43 n.30, 47, 51, 52, 61, 66, 84,
  121 n.70, 200, 253, 272, 275
Waltheof, abbot of Melrose 224, 228
Warleggan 266 n.19
'Warning to Sabbath-breakers' 251,
  262, 265 n.2, 269 n.88
Waugh, Evelyn 163
  Brideshead Revisited 163
Weem 220, 223, 226
Weem Hill 223
Welsh, language 29, 51, 62, 67, 77, 80, 200
Welsh, people 26
Werstan, saint 250
  pictorial Life of 250
Wessex 33
West Country 251
Wexford, county 148
Whitaker, John 255
Whitchurch Canonicorum, church of
  269 n.85
White Book of Rhydderch 79–83,
  96–7, 98 n.9, 101 n.85
Whitesands Bay 11, 19
Whyte, saint, image of 269 n.85
William of Malmesbury 13, 24 n.51,
  273
Williams, Moses 79, 82
Williams, Robert, of Rhydycroesau 79,
  82, 86
William the Conqueror, duke of Normandy and king of England 15,
  34, 52, 66, 71 n.62
Willis, Browne 12
Windsor 261
Winifred, saint, *see* Gwenfrewy
Wiston, church of 93
Woodward, Niotte 256

Worcester, diocese of 66
Worcestre, William 9 n.7, 11–12, 252, 254, 263
Wrdisten, abbot of Landévennec 185
Wrmonoc, monk of Landévennec 179, 181, 186–93, 195 n.13, 281
Wyllow, saint 252
   shrine of 261

Yann, saint (John the Evangelist) 207–11
   Breton ballads of 207–11, 214 n.25
Yann Bubry, saint 204–7
   Breton ballad of 204–7

Yaudet 190
York 228
   cathedral of 227
   stained glass at 227
Ystorya Bown o Hamtwn 97
Ystrad Nynnid 53–4
Ystwyth, river of 47
Yves, saint 201, 207

Zant-Yann (Saint-Jean-du-droit) 210
Zeus 209